Ireland, Philadelphia and the Re-invention of America

Ireland, Philadelphia
and the Re-invention of America
1760–1800

Maurice J. Bric

FOUR COURTS PRESS

Typeset in 10.5 pt on 12.5 pt Ehrhardt by
Carrigboy Typesetting Services for
FOUR COURTS PRESS LTD
7 Malpas Street, Dublin 8, Ireland
e-mail: info@fourcourtspress.ie
and in North America for
FOUR COURTS PRESS
c/o ISBS, 920 NE 58th Avenue, Suite 300, Portland, OR 97213.

A catalogue record for this title is available
from the British Library.

ISBN 978-1-84682-089-2

Printed in England
by Antony Rowe Ltd, Chippenham, Wilts.

"The national character of America will soon be established, and you must determine whether she shall be ranked among those nations who have been eminent for their probity & virtue; whose equity has made them the models and arbiters of the world; or among those who have perished by their folly and corruption."

New York Packet, 24 August 1787

"Everything is uncertain in this Country."

Charles Nisbet, 19 August 1791[1]

"It is patriotism to write in favor of the government – it is sedition to write against it."

John Ward Fenno, 10 October 1798

"our own country [America] fosters in its bosom multitudes of wretches animated by the same infamous principles, and actuated by that same thirst for blood and plunder, which has reduced France to a vast human slaughter-house. The hordes of United Irishmen in America, are alone sufficient for a most extensive scene of ruin, and little doubt can be entertained that they are preparing for it."

Gazette of the United States, 19 November 1798

---

1 Nisbet is quoted from the *Bulletin of the New York Public Library* i (1897), 183; and Fenno from Manning J. Dauer, *The Adams Federalists* (Baltimore 1968), 165.

Contents

Abbreviations

ACHR	*American Catholic Historical Records*
ADA	(Philadelphia) *American Daily Advertiser*
AHR	*American Historical Review*
Annals of Congress	Joseph Gales, compiler, *The Debates and Proceedings in the Congress of the United States ... March 3, 1789 ... May 27, 1824* 42 vols. (Washington, D.C., 1834–56)
APS	American Philosophical Society (Philadelphia)
AQ	*American Quarterly*
BN	*Belfast News-Letter*
CHC	*Cork Hibernian Chronicle*
CR	(Philadelphia) *Carey's Recorder*
DEP	*Dublin Evening Post*
DESA	(Wilmington) *Delaware and Eastern Shore Advertiser*
DG	(Wilmington) *Delaware Gazette*
DH	*Delaware History*
FDJ	*Faulkner's Dublin Journal*
FJ	(Dublin) *Freeman's Journal*
FLJ	(Kilkenny) *Finn's Leinster Journal*
GA	(Philadelphia) *General Advertiser*, from 8 November 1794, the *Aurora*
GIG	(Philadelphia) *Gale's Independent Gazetteer*
GUS	(Philadelphia) *Gazette of the United States*
HistJ	*Historical Journal*
HJ	(Dublin) *Hibernian Journal*
HSD	Historical Society of Delaware (Wilmington)
HSP	Historical Society of Pennsylvania (Philadelphia)
HSt	*Historical Studies*
IG	(Philadelphia) *Independent Gazetteer*
IHS	*Irish Historical Studies*
JEH	*Journal of Economic History*
JHU St	*Johns Hopkins University Studies*
JIntH	*Journal of Interdisciplinary History*
JMH	*Journal of Modern History*
JPE	*Journal of Political Economy*
JPrH	*Journal of Presbyterian History*
JSH	*Journal of Southern History*
LC	Library of Congress (Washington, D.C.)

LCP	Library Company of Philadelphia
LJ	*Londonderry Journal*
MDA	(Baltimore) *Maryland Daily Advertiser*
MHS	Maryland Historical Society (Baltimore)
MVHR	*Mississippi Valley Historical Review*
NA	National Archives (London)
NCEP	*New Cork Evening Post*
NG	(Philadelphia) *National Gazette*
NLI	National Library of Ireland (Dublin)
NS	(Belfast) *Northern Star*
NYDA	*New York Daily Advertiser*
NYDG	*New York Daily Gazette*
NYGWPB	*New York Gazette and Weekly Post Boy*
NYH	*New York History*
NYHS	New York Historical Society
NYJ	*New York Journal*
NYP	*New York Packet*
NYPL	New York Public Library
PEH	(Philadelphia) *Pennsylvania Evening Herald*
PEP	(Philadelphia) *Pennsylvania Evening Post*
PG	(Philadelphia) *Pennsylvania Gazette*
PH	*Pennsylvania History*
PhilG	*Philadelphia Gazette*
PJ	(Philadelphia) *Pennsylvania Journal*
PMHB	*Pennsylvania Magazine of History and Biography*
PorcG	(Philadelphia) *Porcupine's Gazette*
PP	(Philadelphia) *Pennsylvania Packet*
PRONI	Public Record Office of Northern Ireland (Belfast)
RACHS	*Records of the American Catholic Historical Society*
RIA	Royal Irish Academy (Dublin)
SN	(Dublin) *Saunders News-Letter*
Stats. at Large Pa.	James T. Mitchell and Henry Flanders, compilers, *The Statutes at Large of Pennsylvania from 1682 to 1801* 16 vols. (Harrisburg, 1896–1902)
TCD	Trinity College, Dublin
VEP	(Dublin) *Volunteer Evening Post*
VJ	(Dublin) *Volunteer Journal*
VMHB	*Virginia Magazine of History and Biography*
WMQ	*William and Mary Quarterly*, third series, unless otherwise noted

Introduction

During the eighteenth century, the *anciens régimes* of America and Europe were confronted by a new "age of enlightenment," a central theme of which was the promotion of a more critical public sphere.[1] The mood of speculation made a particular impact on the ways in which America interacted with contemporary Britain, Ireland, and France. While the relevant narratives had been driven by what Jack P. Greene has described as "negotiated authorities" between "peripheries and center," changing circumstances highlighted the ways in which the rhetoric of the metropolis could be challenged by peculiarities of place.[2] Thus, while Bernard Bailyn and others have analysed the impact of the underlying ideas of the ancient English constitution on the unfolding revolution in America, later work recognises the ways in which regional circumstances questioned the relevance of an overarching "British paradigm" as both an informing ideological framework and the basis of a viable political culture. This point has also been made in Stanley Elkins's and Eric McKittrick's distinguished study of *The Age of Federalism*.[3] This book offers a comment on

1   The historiography of the Enlightenment is as immense as it is varied. While many of the classic works, such as those of Peter Gay, focus on the great thinkers of the period, recent interpretations have been more wide-ranging over intellectual, political, social, and cultural life and have highlighted topics such as the "rise" of public opinion, sociability, and the evolution of the public sphere. See, for example, Dorinda Outram, *The Enlightenment* (Cambridge, 1995); and James Van Horn Melton, *The Rise of the Public in Enlightenment Europe* (Cambridge, 2001). The first volume of Peter Gay's *The Enlightenment: An Interpretation. The Rise of Modern Paganism* was published in London in 1967. The second volume, sub-titled *Science and Freedom*, was published in New York two years later.

2   Jack P. Greene, *Peripheries and Center: Constitutional Development in the Extended Politics of the British Empire and the United States, 1607–1788* (Athens, Ga., 1987), *Pursuits of Happiness: The Social Development of Early Modern British Colonies and the Formation of American Culture* (Chapel Hill, 1988), and *Negotiated Authorities: Essays in Colonial Political and Constitutional History* (Charlottesville and London, 1994). The italics in the text are mine. A similar idea has informed Christine Daniels and Michael V. Kennedy, eds., *Negotiated Empires: Centers and Peripheries in the Americas, 1500–1820* (New York, 2002).

3   Bernard Bailyn, *The Ideological Origins of the American Revolution* (New York, 1967); J.G.A. Pocock, "The Limits and Divisions of British History: In Search of the Unknown Subject," *AHR* lxxxvii (1982), 311–36, and "British History: A Plea for a New Subject," *JMH* xlvii (1975), 601–21; Stanley Elkins and Eric McKittrick, *The Age of Federalism* (New York and Oxford, 1993), 13 *et passim*. For a reflection on how the Anglo-American Atlantic world has been presented within this historiography, see Alexander Grant and

this historiography by focussing on the Irish immigrants of later-eighteenth-century Philadelphia and, in particular, on how their community influenced the growth of contemporary "party politics" in that city.

Pennsylvania had long been a magnet for Irish immigrants. Its founder, William Penn (1644–1718), had close family connections with Ireland and his Ulster-born provincial secretary, **James Logan*** (1674–1751), ensured that the attractions of the colony were known to the Quaker communities of his proprietor, as well as among his own Presbyterian co-religionists.[4] In eighteenth-century Philadelphia, an influential community of Irish-born merchants also fostered tangible links between the two sides of the Atlantic, and encouraged a steady stream of immigrants from their old country. While historians do not dispute that the Delaware River was the preferred destination of those who chose to leave Ireland, they have varying views on the nature and extent of the passenger flow. R.J. Dickson's assessments, published in 1966, deal with Ulster. However, they have had an enduring influence on the ways in which the contemporary emigration as a whole has been computed, especially for the ten years before the American Revolution. In Chapter 1, I have drawn on the relevant historiography, and especially, on the work of David Noel Doyle, Patrick Griffin, Kerby Miller, Audrey Lockhart, and Marianne Wokeck before arriving at my own assessment of Irish emigration to pre-Revolutionary Philadelphia.[5] In Chapter 3, I have also proposed figures for the pivotal years

Keith Stringer, eds., *Uniting the Kingdom? The Making of British History* (London, 1995); Jane Ohlmeyer, "Seventeenth-Century Ireland and the New British and Atlantic Histories," *AHR* civ (1999), 446–62; J.G.A. Pocock, "The New British History in Atlantic Perspective: An Antipodean Commentary," *ibid.*, 490–500 ; Elkins and McKittrick, *Age of Federalism*, 4–13; J.C.D. Clark, "The Strange Death of British History? Reflections on Anglo-American Scholarship," *HistJ* xl (1997), 787–809; and Nicholas Canny, "Writing Atlantic History; or, Reconfiguring the History of Colonial British America," *AHR* lxxxvi (1999), 1093–1114. For Patricia Bonomi's focus on the importance of local political interests rather than ideology in pre-revolutionary New York, see *A Factious People: Politics and Society in Colonial New York* (New York, 1971). For a similar approach to contemporary Pennsylvania, see Alan Tully, *Forming American Politics: Ideals, Interests, and Institutions in Colonial New York and Pennsylvania* (Baltimore, 1984).

*   For text represented in bold type, see also "Biographical Notes and Further Information."
4   Richard S. Dunn and Mary Maples Dunn, eds., *The World of William Penn* (Philadelphia, 1986); Sally Schwartz, *'A Mixed Multitude.' The Struggle for Toleration in Colonial Pennsylvania* (New York and London, 1987).
5   R.J. Dickson, *Ulster Emigration to Colonial America, 1718–1785* (London, 1966); David Noel Doyle, *Ireland, Irishmen and Revolutionary America, 1760–1820* (Dublin, 1981); Patrick Griffin, *The People with No Name: Ireland's Ulster Scots, America's Scots Irish, and the Creation of a British Atlantic World, 1689–1764* (Princeton, 2001); Kerby A. Miller, *Emigrants and Exiles: Ireland and the Irish Exodus to North America* (New York, 1985); Audrey Lockhart, *Some Aspects of Emigration from Ireland to the North American Colonies between 1660 and 1775* (New York, 1976); and Marianne Wokeck, *Trade in Strangers: The*

between 1783 and 1800 which suggest that the official recognition of American independence interrupted rather than halted the passenger flow from Ireland.

As discussed in Chapter 3, most of the Irish who left for America, whether before or after 1783, looked forward to a "land of Canaan."[6] However, they never found it easy to forget what they had left behind, even when this had involved hardship. Nonetheless, most of them were content to ease themselves into a new nationality in America rather than create a "new Ireland" on the shores of the western Atlantic. In many ways, this reflected the goals of the early colonists to promote an organic and undifferentiated polity in America. As argued in Chapter 2, the Founding Fathers of the new republic also wanted to preserve this ideal. After 1783 the need for stability suggested an obligation to continue as before, even if – or perhaps, because – America was now free of an imperial connection which had supposedly corrupted its governance for so long.[7] Thus, despite the impact of European immigration, the leaders of the new states still stressed the virtues of a single-interest and harmonious polity, and expected their fellow-citizens, whether native-born or not, to do the same. As the work of John K. Alexander and others has suggested, this was also reflected in the organisational and club life of late-eighteenth-century Philadelphia, where it was believed that the interests of society as a whole should supercede those of any one network or group. Thus, while the various benevolent and charitable societies that were founded in the city during the 1770s and 1780s, would assist the unfortunate, and the distressed, they insisted that by so doing, they would also help to ensure social harmony. **Ethnocultural** societies such as the *Friendly Sons of St. Patrick* (founded in 1771) served a similar, if somewhat paradoxical, function by enveloping the peculiarities of national origin, and the ways in which they were marked and celebrated, within the borders of the community as a whole (Chapter 4).[8]

Beginnings of Mass Migration to North America (University Park, Pa., 1999). This historiography, and its influence in the assessment of emigration from Ireland to eighteenth -century America and, in particular, to the Delaware, is discussed in chapters 1 and 3, and also in Appendix I.

6   For a critical evaluation of how Irish emigrants perceived America, both before and after American independence, see Kerby A. Miller, Arnold Schrier, Bruce D. Boling, and David N. Doyle, eds., *Irish Immigrants in the Land of Canaan. Letters and Memoirs from Colonial and Revolutionary America, 1675–1815* (Oxford, 2003).

7   Jack P. Greene, "Empire and Identity from the Glorious Revolution to the American Revolution" in P.J. Marshall, ed., *The Eighteenth Century* (Oxford, 1998), vol. ii of William Roger Louis, editor-in-chief, *Oxford History of the British Empire* 5 vols. (Oxford, 1998–2001), hereafter cited as *Oxford History*, 208–30, and "The American Revolution," *AHR* cv (2000), 92–102.

8   John K. Alexander, *Render Them Submissive: Responses to Poverty in Philadelphia, 1760–1800* (Amherst, 1980); David Waldstreicher, *In the Midst of Perpetual Fetes: The Making of American Nationalism, 1726–1820* (Chapel Hill, N.C., 1996).

From Philadelphia, Irish immigrants also watched how their native country interpreted "democratic revolution," first in America, and later in France.[9] They saw how the **Reform Movement** in Ireland had been killed by the kindnesses of **"free trade"** (1779), and **"legislative independence"** (1782). During the later 1780s, they welcomed political refugees from these disappointments, and saw many of them join the vanguard of a new radicalism in America.[10] Irish-born newspaper editors such as **Mathew Carey** (1760–1839) were particularly important in this regard, not least because they were also active and influential outside the structures of conventional politics and as such, catalysts for political controversy and change.[11] As discussed in Chapter 3, people like Carey were "new Irish" immigrants, confident and optimistic about what they could achieve in America. They also saw no incompatibility between committing to their new home, and retaining the ethno-cultural baggage of the old. Celebrating St. Patrick's Day on 17 March did not diminish loyalty to America which they also proclaimed with sincerity, enthusiasm, and gratitude every 4 July. Neither did a recognition that Irish immigrants in America should not be ashamed to remember, or to help remedy, what they had left behind in the land of their birth.

The public sphere in which these changes were occurring has been analysed by a number of historians, most notably by Joyce Appleby, John Brooke, and David Waldstreicher. Its character had been greatly influenced by the debates on the federal and state constitutions, as well as by the establishment of the governments to which they led. During the 1790s, a mediating space, where

9 For Irish reaction to the American Revolution, see Vincent Morley, *Irish Opinion and the American Revolution, 1760–1783* (Cambridge, 2002); Maurice J. Bric, "Ireland, America and the Reassessment of a Special Relationship, 1760–1783," *Eighteenth-Century Ireland* xi (1996), 88–119; and Maurice O'Connell, *Irish Politics and Social Conflict in the Age of the American Revolution* (Ithaca, 1979). For Ireland and the French Revolution, see Hugh Gough and David Dickson, eds., *Ireland and the French Revolution* (Dublin, 1990). For general comment, see R.R. Palmer, *The Age of Democratic Revolution* 2 vols. (Princeton, 1959 and 1964).

10 The literature on the evolution of reform and radicalism in Ireland is extensive. See R.B. McDowell, *Ireland in the Age of Imperialism and Revolution, 1760–1801* (Oxford, 1979); Nancy Curtin, *The United Irishmen: Popular Politics in Ulster and Dublin, 1780–1840* (Berkeley and London, 1969); and David Dickson, "Bibliography" in T.W. Moody and W.E. Vaughan, eds. *Eighteenth-Century Ireland, 1691–1800* (Oxford, 1986), vol. iv of *A New History of Ireland* 9 vols. (Oxford, 1975–2005), 713–96.

11 For the role of Irish-born radicals, including newspaper editors, in early national America, see Michael Durey, *Transatlantic Radicals and the Early American Republic* (Lawrence, 1997); and Maurice J. Bric, "The Irish Immigrant and the Broadening of the Polity in Philadelphia, 1790–1800" in Eliga H. Gould and Peter S. Onuf, eds., *Empire and Nation: The American Revolution in the Atlantic World* (Baltimore and London, 2005), 159–77.

differing interpretations of what was best for the polity could be discussed in a myriad of clubs and societies, also became more obvious. Here, removed from the slogans and networks of partisan politics, one could agree or disagree. As a result, "outsiders" and "new leaders" no longer necessarily measured their influence by the level of encouragement which they received to become part of the Establishment. Instead, they believed that they could also enrich the polity both on their own terms, and in their own way.[12]

Among others, the nation's first president (1789–97), **George Washington**, was concerned about the adverse challenges of such developments. However, the icons of independence were not as sacred after 1790 as they had been ten years earlier. Indeed, during 1795 and 1796, the man who had come to symbolise American independence was so fiercely vilified for his opinions on political organisation and policy that he decided not to seek re-election.[13] As discussed in Chapters 4 and 5, the nature of the Revolution itself was also widely questioned, as were the very meaning of republicanism, and the type of polity which it fostered. It was inevitable that some of the Founding Fathers would be drawn into these debates, especially when **John Jay** (1745–1829) and **Alexander Hamilton** (1755–1804) chose to support a connection with their former antagonists, the British, over those who had helped them to victory, the French. By the same token, **Thomas Jefferson** (1743–1826) became the *bête noir* of the Anglophiles, while the memory of **Benjamin Franklin** (1706–90) became less "revered" as it was invoked to promote an unequivocal popular sovereignty over a more elite type of governance which many believed was being planned by Jay, Hamilton, and **John Adams** (1735–1826). The unfolding of the French Revolution as an extension of the American Revolution provided an important rhetorical reference for these debates during the 1790s, as did the annual festivities to mark American

12 Joyce Appleby, *Capitalism and a New Social Order: The Republican Vision of the 1790s* (New York, 1984), and "E Pluribus Unum: The Ideological Imperative in Revolutionary America" in Rebecca Starr, ed., *Articulating America: Fashioning a National Political Culture in Early America: Essays in Honor of J.R. Pole* (Lanham 2000); John L. Brooke, "Ancient Lodges and Self-Created Societies: Voluntary Associations and the Public Sphere in the Early Republic" in Ronald Hoffman and Peter J. Albert, eds., *Launching the "Extended Republic." The Federalist Era* (Charlottesville, 1996), 273–377; and Waldstreicher, *In the Midst of Perpetual Fetes*. See also Van Horn Melton, *The Rise of the Public in Enlightenment Europe*, 1–16.

13 Donald H. Stewart, *The Opposition Press of the Federalist Period* (Albany, 1969), ch.13, *et passim*, gives a good sense of how contemporary views of Washington were portrayed and changed during the 1790s. For more recent analysis, see Barry Schwartz, *George Washington: The Making of an American Symbol* (New York, 1987); Paul K. Longmore, *The Invention of George Washington* (Berkeley, Calif., 1988); and Simon Newman, "Principles or Men? George Washington and the Political Culture of National leadership, 1776–1801," *Journal of the Early Republic* xii (1992), 477–508.

independence, and the collapse of the *ancien régime* in France, on 4 and 14 July, respectively. The celebration of the victories of the French armies, as well as the parades and toasts of the various "patriotic" networks and societies which appeared during the 1790s, completed a picture of a country that was looking to foreign, as much as to domestic events, to define itself.[14]

As Jeffrey L. Pasley and others have pointed out, it is easy to understate the level of what Marshall Smelser has called the "phrenzy" in contemporary America about these developments, and, in particular, about a potential war with France (Chapter 5). There were real fears that the country would disintegrate and fall into the hands of "American Jacobins" who would then propel it into the type of chaos that was evident in contemporary Europe. For the governing **Federalists**, immigrants embodied what was foreign, and thus, symbolised the challenges which faced the new republic. As a result, newcomers became central to the argument that since 1789, America had been too welcoming, the polity too accommodating, and access to citizenship and office too open, for those who had not been born in America. In particular, many "new Irish" immigrants had a strong sense of themselves and were taking an increasingly conspicuous part in Philadelphia's political life, and especially, in **Jeffersonian republicanism**. In these circumstances, Federalists came to regard the city's Irish community as an obnoxious sub-set of the population at large. For writers to the Federalist *Gazette of the United States*, the Irish were said to be so attached to their old country that they could never become "truly American." Over fifty years ago, John Higham argued that it was at periods of "crisis," such as the 1790s, that many Americans developed a "lack of confidence" that they could safely accommodate a diversity of manners. In later-eighteenth-century Philadelphia, it was easy to focus such feelings on the Irish, not only because they were numerous and active in the city, but because Ireland had been so greatly influenced by France as well as by Britain.[15]

14 Gordon S. Wood, *The Americanization of Benjamin Franklin* (New York, 2004); Simon P. Newman, *Parades and the Politics of the Street: Festive Culture in the Early Republic* (Philadelphia, 1997), 120–51; and Edward Handler, *America and Europe in the Political Thought of John Adams* (Cambridge, Mass., 1987). For the increasing importance of foreign affairs in American policy and, in particular, on the ways in which both post-1783 Britain and the French Revolution affected contemporary America, see Elkins and McKittrick, *Age of Federalism*, 303–449; and the cited bibliography which lists the major references of relevance.

15 Jeffrey L. Pasley, "1800 as a Revolution in Political Culture" in James Horn, Ellen Lewis, and Peter Onuf, eds., *Democracy, Race & the New Republic: The Revolution of 1800* (Charlottesville and London, 2002), 121–52; Marshall Smelser, "Jacobin Phrenzy: Federalism and the Menace of Liberty, Equality, and Fraternity," *Review of Politics* xiii (1951), 457–82; John Higham, *Strangers in the Land: Patterns of American Nativism 1860–1925* (New Brunswick, 1955). For a discussion of the sense of threat and danger

During the 1790s, the connection between Ireland and France was underlined by the **United Irishmen**. This society had been founded in Belfast in
1791. After the French republic decided through its Propaganda Decrees of
November 1792 "to export its revolution," it was only a matter of time before
the society was proscribed.[16] However, when this happened in May 1794, some
of its more important leaders emigrated to Philadelphia, including **Theobald
Wolfe Tone** (1764–98), **Archibald Hamilton Rowan** (1735–1834), **James
Napper Tandy** (1740–1803), and **Dr. James Reynolds** (d.1808). There, they
were easily identified with "French principles." They also represented a new
type of ethno-cultural leader who could inspire their fellow Irish immigrants
towards Jeffersonian republicanism.[17] To this extent, they reinforced the perceived
connections between the "new immigrant" and the "new politics" which
became even more apparent in a number of pivotal elections in the city during
the second half of the 1790s. Philadelphia's Irish immigrants thus reflected the
move away from the organic polity of older generations, and towards its cultural
antithesis, ethnicity.[18]

that was felt in the America of the 1790s, including how this was being articulated within
a changing political discourse, see James Roger Sharp, *American Politics in the Early
Republic: The New Nation in Crisis* (New Haven and London, 1993).

16 For the Propaganda Decrees, see T.C.W. Blanning, *The French Revolutionary Wars.
1787–1802* (London and New York, 1996), 92. For the United Irishmen, see David
Dickson, Dáire Keogh, and Kevin Whelan, eds., *The United Irishmen. Republicanism,
Radicalism and Rebellion* (Dublin, 1993); and Thomas Bartlett, David Dickson, Dáire
Keogh, and Kevin Whelan, eds., *1798. A Bicentenary Perspective* (Dublin, 2003). For a
useful bibliography of relevant writings, see Kevin Whelan, "Bibliography," in Bartlett,
Dickson, Keogh, and Whelan, eds., *1798*, 659–724.

17 Maurice J. Bric, "The United Irishmen, International Republicanism and the Definition
of the Polity in the United States of America, 1791–1800" in *Proceedings of the Royal Irish
Academy* civ (2004), 81–106; Durey, *Transatlantic Radicals and the Early American
Republic*; David Wilson, *United Irishmen, United States: Immigrant Radicals in the Early
Republic* (Dublin, 1998).

18 Maurice J. Bric, "The Irish and the Evolution of the 'New' Politics' in America" in P.J.
Drudy, ed., *America: Emigration, Assimilation, and Ethnicity* (Cambridge, 1987), 143–68.
The historiography of the "first party system" is extensive and ranges from the view, as
expressed by Charles and Cunningham, for example, that the 1790s was a harbinger of
party, to that of Chambers and Hofstadter, who do not see it in these terms. See Joseph
Charles, *The Origins of the American Party System* (Williamsburg, 1956); Noble E.
Cunningham, *The Jeffersonian Republicans: The Formation of Party Organization,
1789–1801* (Chapel Hill, 1957); William Chambers, *Political Parties in a New Nation: The
American Experience, 1776–1809* (New York, 1963); and Richard Hofstadter, *The Idea of a
Party System. The Rise of Legitimate Opposition in the United States, 1780–1840* (Berkeley
and London, 1969). For a discussion of views on party in later-eighteenth-century
America, see Chapters 2 and 4 below.

From 1797, when the American Society of United Irishmen appeared in Philadelphia, it was easier to suggest that the radical Irish were the fifth column of the extended French Revolution (Chapter 6). One Federalist editor, **William Cobbett** (1763–1835) of *Porcupine's Gazette*, made this cause his own and, together with **John Ward Fenno** (1751–98) of the *Gazette of the United States*, conducted one of the most bitter paper wars of the early republic with his Jeffersonian rivals, notably Matthew Carey, his brother **James Carey** (1762?–1801), editor of *Carey's United States Recorder*, and the Clonmel-educated **William Duane** (1760–1835), editor of the *Aurora*, then the most influential Jeffersonian newspaper in America. These newspapers have been an important source for this study, as have the various pamphlets and broadsides which were published on the issues involved. The bicentenary of the Irish **rebellion of 1798** encouraged historians to revisit and clarify the complex context in which the United Irishmen evolved and much of this work, most notably that of Thomas Bartlett, Louis Cullen, Nancy Curtin, Marianne Elliott, and Kevin Whelan, has been invaluable to my own understanding of the period.[19] The writings of Michael Durey, Marianne Elliott, and David Wilson underline the fact that the United Irishmen were also part of wider international networks which focussed on universal, as well as domestic rights and reforms. This book builds on the work of these scholars to suggest how a society which was so important to the Ireland of the 1790s, also contributed to the re-invention of America after its own revolution.[20]

19 Thomas Bartlett, "The Burden of the Present: Theobald Wolfe Tone, Republican and Separatist" in Dickson, Keogh, and Whelan, eds., *United Irishmen*, 1–15, and ed., *Life and Times of Theobald Wolfe Tone, Compiled and Arranged by William Theobald Wolfe Tone* (Dublin, 1998); Louis M. Cullen, "The 1798 Rebellion in its Eighteenth-Century Context" in Patrick Corish, ed., *Radicals, Rebels and Establishments* (Belfast, 1985), 91–113, and "The 1798 Rebellion in Wexford: United Irishmen Organisation Membership, Leadership" in Kevin Whelan, ed., *Wexford. History and Society* (Dublin, 1987), 248–95; Curtin, *United Irishmen: Popular Politics in Ulster and Dublin*; Marianne Elliott, *Partners in Revolution: The United Irishmen and France* (London, 1982), and *Wolfe Tone: Prophet of Irish Independence* (New Haven and London, 1989); and Kevin Whelan, *The Tree of Liberty: Radicalism, Catholicism and the Construction of Irish Identity, 1760–1830* (Cork and South Bend, 1996, 1998), and *Fellowship of Freedom: The United Irishmen and 1798* (Cork, 1998).
20 Durey, *Transatlantic Radicals and the Early American Republic;* Elliott, *Partners in Revolution*, and *Wolfe Tone*; and Wilson, *United Irishmen, United States.* My doctoral dissertation, which also discussed many of the relevant aspects of Irish radicalism in late-eighteenth-century Philadelphia was submitted in 1990 as "Ireland, Irishmen, and the Broadening of the Late-Eighteenth-Century Philadelphia Polity" (Ph.D. dissertation, The Johns Hopkins University).

While working on this monograph, I have drawn on the collections of a number of libraries in the United States, Ireland, and England. To the staff of these institutions, which I have listed in the bibliography, I owe thanks for their courtesy, professionalism, and advice and, in particular, to the late Edward Carter II of the American Philosophical Society, and Jim Greene of the Library Company of Philadelphia. Fellowships at the Free University of Berlin and Boston College enabled me to re-cast a dissertation which I originally presented to the Johns Hopkins University. I am grateful to my fellow-students at Hopkins and especially, to Arnd Bohm, Marc Harris, and Thomas Purvis, who made cogent criticisms of earlier drafts of this work. I would also like to thank my friends and former colleagues at the McNeill Institute for Early American Studies at the University of Pennsylvania and, in particular, Roderick McDonald, Richard Alan Ryerson, and Michael Zuckerman. During my stay in Philadelphia, Richard S. Dunn and Mary Maples Dunn were gracious and generous advisors and together with the late Dennis Clark, offered the keenest of criticisms with the best of personal encouragement and support.

I would also like to thank my publishers, Four Courts Press, Dublin. I am grateful to them for exempting me from using their house style. In both personal and academic terms, colleagues in Ireland and Britain have also encouraged my research, especially Thomas Bartlett, Nicholas P. Canny, David Noel Doyle, and Eda Sagarra, each of whom commented on the original draft. Jack P. Greene has encouraged my research since I became his graduate student and has criticised it with a directness and generosity which, for those of us who have worked with him as his students, have always marked him as friend as well as mentor. I would also like to thank the Publications Committee of the National University of Ireland for a grant-in-aid towards publishing this monograph, as well as Ms Helen Litton, who compiled the index. Finally, I am grateful for the support which I have received from other friends and colleagues in the School of History and Archives in University College Dublin, the University of Pennsylvania, Boston College, and the Harvard Seminar in Atlantic History. In particular, I would like to thank Richard Aldous, Alvin Jackson, and James McGuire. I would also like to thank Bernard Bailyn, Edgar and Ramona Brady, Sara Balderston, John Brooke, Josepha Clark, Michael and Jane Collins, Louis M. Cullen, Patricia Cullen, Seamus and Anne Cullimore, David Dickson, Robert and Elborg Foster, Robert Emmet Hernan, Robert Jackson, John McCafferty, Kerby Miller, Phil Morgan, Mícheál Ó Cinnéide, Timothy P. O'Neill, Jane Ohlmeyer, Peter and Kirstin Onuf, William O'Reilly, J.G.A. Pocock, Phyllis Ryan, Robert Savage, Mary Catherine Shea, Jeanne Silverthorne, Gerry and Mary Staunton, Ron Walters, Harry White, and the late Sharon Widomski. I also remember my parents, my brother, sister and their families, and especially Les and Estelle, to whom I dedicate this work.

CHAPTER ONE

Ireland and the Colonial Americas

Even before the age of early modern exploration and cartography, Ireland had a sense of America. The Celtic *immrama* and the Christian *navigationes*, or voyage literatures, suggested that there was a *tír tairngire*, or "land of promise," to the west. During the sixteenth and seventeenth centuries the westward voyages of various types of adventurers and speculators gave this imagination a reality which eventually advanced a new age of "enterprise and empire" in Britain and Ireland. For Ireland and the British Americas, they also promoted a shared relationship with the imperial metropolis in London which was reinforced by a *mélange* of political, commercial, and personal networks. Nonetheless, the outward look was developed in its own ways on either side of the Atlantic. In America, it suggested a culture that was driven less by old world histories than by the challenge to establish viable societies in a new environment.[1]

The Burdens of History

During the early modern period America was part of the emerging world of the first British Empire, the foundations of which were laid in Tudor Ireland.[2] During the sixteenth and early-seventeenth centuries the hallmarks of English expansion in Ireland were the plantations. These were intended to establish "the Englishry" although at times, many planters also saw themselves as something more than the mere exponents of a new imperial system. In the words of the English scholar, Sir Thomas Smith (1513–77), they should emulate "Rome,

---

1 Jonathan Wooding, ed., *The Otherworld Voyage in Early Irish Literature* (Dublin, 2000); Theodore K. Raab, *Enterprise and Empire: Merchant and Gentry Involvement in the Expansion of England, 1575–1630* (Cambridge, Mass., 1967). For the political connections between colonial America and contemporary Ireland, see Bric, "Ireland, America and the Reassessment of a Special Relationship;" and Morley, *Irish Opinion and the American Revolution.*

2 The literature on early modern Ireland is extensive. For a recent analysis, see Nicholas Canny, *Making Ireland British* (Oxford, 2001). See also the articles by Jane Ohlmeyer and T.C. Barnard in Nicholas Canny, ed., *The Origins of Empire* (Oxford, 2001), vol.i of *Oxford History*, 124–47 and 309–27, respectively, as well as J.G. Simms, "Bibliography," and Aidan Clarke, Raymond Gillespie, and James McGuire, "Bibliographical Supplement" in T.W. Moody, F.X. Martin, and F.J. Byrne, eds., *Early Modern Ireland, 1534–1691* (Oxford, 1976), vol. ii of *A New History of Ireland*, 634–95 and 696–748, respectively.

Carthage, and all others whither *any notable beginning* hath been" by promoting "English laws and civility" in Ireland. However, the island became more turbulent with the passing of the century and by 1573 Smith admitted that the "hopes of … reforming the Irish were too lightly grounded," or even a "pretence," as the vice-president of Munster, Sir William Herbert (d.1593), put it in 1588. As a result, the more benevolent aspects of plantation were slowly abandoned as well as the possibility that "a mixed plantation of British and Irish … might grow up together in one nation."[3]

After 1610 this change of direction was most clearly seen in the northern province of Ulster, when revised *Orders and Conditions* were presented for the six counties which had been escheated there three years earlier. In effect, the plantation of Ulster now abandoned a policy of anglicising Ulster's native Irish in favour of settling the region with Lowland Scots and English. The plantation designated three types of participant. The first two, the *undertakers* and *servitors*, were to be of Scottish or English origin although the second also included "deserving" corporations such as Trinity College, Dublin, the City of London, and the Established Church. For these, the "adventure" of the plantation was clearly stated: to nurture "civility" and the "true religion" as well as to ensure that the "flight of the earls" had closed the book on Irish opposition to imperial expansion. These aims had little appeal for the majority of the *native Irish*, especially after Sir John Davies, the Irish attorney general (1606–19), argued that plantation was a strategy to enable the Irish "in tongue and heart, and every way else, [to] become English" and so, to move "from barbarism to civility." At least in cultural terms, the fate of the Ulster Irish thus depended, at best, on the scheme's failure and, at worst, on its modification.[4]

Earlier, in the 1560s, the plantation of Munster had also sought to develop a reformed society whose leaders of "eminence or nobility" might curb the

3   Smith is quoted in Nicholas Canny, "Changing Views on Gaelic Ireland," *Topic: 24* xii (1972), 23, and in "Sir Thomas Smith (1513–1577) and the Beginnings of English Colonial Theory," *Proceedings of the American Philosophical Society* lxxxvii (1945), 553. The italics are mine. Herbert is cited in Karl S. Bottingheimer, *English Money and Irish Land* (Oxford, 1971), 13. The final quotation is from Sir John Davies, as in *ibid.*, 9. The different approaches to plantation in early-seventeenth-century Ireland are discussed in Eugene Flanagan, "The Anatomy of Jacobean Ireland: Captain Barnaby Rich, Sir John Davies and the Failure of Reform" in Hiram Morgan, ed., *Political Ideology in Ireland, 1541–1641* (Dublin, 1999), 158–80.

4   T.W. Moody, ed., "The Revised Articles of the Ulster Plantation, 1610," *Bulletin of the Institute of Historical Research* xii (1934–5), 178–83; and Canny, *Making Ireland British*, 187–242. Davies is quoted in Flanagan, "Anatomy of Jacobean Ireland," 173; and in Bottingheimer, *English Money and Irish Land*, 19. For Davies and the colonisation of seventeenth-century Ireland, see Hans S. Pawlisch, *Sir John Davies and the Conquest of Ireland: A Study in Legal Imperialism* (Cambridge, 1985).

"servile nature" of the native majority there. However, as Louis M. Cullen has observed, the attempts to promote a supposed English Paradise in the province were neither viable nor had they the "capacity simultaneously ... to push off roots further afield." The "continual rebellions" of the "wild Irishry" also posed a military as well as a cultural challenge which by 1580 many saw as intractable. Until the 1640s, this plantation was neither as effective nor as organised as the Ulster scheme although as a matter of expediency, some of the native Irish eventually adapted to the new order. Whether successful or not, however, the generic terms of plantation were regarded by the native Irish as "alien," not in the sense that it was "foreign," but because it did not seek to involve them in a positive way. It represented, as G.A. Hayes McCoy put it, "a war of two civilisations" which was intensified by the ways in which other colonisation schemes were outlined and developed in later years, especially during the Cromwellian period. The native Irish did not consider themselves to be, nor were they perceived to be, part of the "promise" of plantation, at least as promoted from Dublin Castle.[5]

In Ulster, the majority of those who identified with the new agenda were of Scottish origin and formed the nucleus of the province's Presbyterian community. Such was the movement of "reliable" and "elite" Scottish tenants to Ireland that in 1636 the Scottish Privy Council resolved that tenants could emigrate only with their landlords' permission. However, these restrictions had limited effect and prior to 1641, an estimated 30,000 families settled in the province. The plantation of Ulster was upset by the civil wars of the 1640s and 1650s but it was subsequently relaunched. By 1660 all but one of Ireland's sixty eight Presbyterian ministers were located in Ulster. Archbishop Edward Synge of Tuam (1659–1741) estimated that a further 50,000 Scottish families settled in the province between 1690 and 1715. Although there were important differences between the later and earlier Scottish immigrations, both inward flows combined to give much of contemporary Ulster an ethno-cultural

5 Nicholas Canny, "Dominant Minorities: English Settlers in Ireland and Virginia, 1550–1650" in A.C. Hepburn, ed., *Minorities in History* (London, 1978), 53; Louis M. Cullen, "The Irish Diaspora of the Seventeenth and Eighteenth Centuries" in Nicholas Canny, ed., *Europeans on the Move: Studies on European Migration 1500–1800* (Oxford, 1994), 119; and G.A. Hayes-McCoy, "Gaelic Society in the late-Sixteenth Century," *HSt* iv (1963), 61. For the Munster plantation, see Michael MacCarthy-Morrough, *The Plantation of Munster: English Migration to Southern Ireland, 1583–1641* (Oxford, 1986). The ideology and organisation of plantation are also analysed in Ciaran Brady and Raymond Gillespie, eds., *Natives and Newcomers: Essays on the Making of Irish Colonial Society, 1534–1641* (Dublin, 1986). For the attitudes of the native Irish to plantation, see Hiram Morgan, "The End of Gaelic Ulster: a Thematic Interpretation of Events between 1534 and 1634," *IHS* xxvi (1988), 8–32; and Canny, *Making Ireland British*, 432–55, *et passim*.

physiognomy which distinguished it from other areas of the island.[6] This heritage also influenced the ways in which the province interacted with British America during the seventeenth and eighteenth centuries.

The elitism of plantation was also reflected in the Penal Laws. While the earlier laws were passed as part of the sixteenth-century reformation of the relationship between church and state, a more comprehensive code was launched after the Williamite Settlement reconfigured the governance of Ireland under a new regime. Largely passed between 1695 and 1710, these later laws sought to ensure that the political and military energies of the Jacobites that had been over-whelmed at the **battles of the Boyne** (1690) and **Aughrim** (1691) would not be recharged through other channels and threaten the legacy of the "Glorious Revolution." Religious tests were attached to holding the franchise and public office, the ownership and inheritance of land, access to education and the professions, and the organisation and practice of religion. As Synge put it in 1731, "the design of these laws is, so to lessen their [Catholic] number or break their power, that they may be no longer formidable to those whom they are justly suspected to have good inclination to destroy."[7] As such, the passage of the Penal Laws complemented plantation and initiated the "age of the Protestant ascendancy" during which the religious, political, and cultural distinctions of earlier years were now, at the dawn of the eighteenth century, legally reinforced.

In seventeenth-century America, a similar association between "civility" and a restricted polity had been informed by the ideology of plantation in Ireland.[8]

---

6 Raymond Gillespie, *Colonial Ulster: The Settlement of East Ulster, 1600–1641* (Cork, 1985), 30; Toby C. Barnard, "Identities, Ethnicity and Tradition among Irish Dissenters, *c*.1650–1750" in Kevin Herlihy, ed., *The Irish Dissenting Tradition 1650–1750* (Dublin, 1995), 42–4; and Guy S. Klett, *Presbyterians in Colonial Pennsylvania* (Philadelphia, 1937), 12. Synge is quoted in Charles A. Hanna, *The Scotch-Irish, or the Scot in North Britain, North Ireland and North America* 2 vols. (New York, 1902) i, 614. For the demographic make-up of early-seventeenth-century Ulster, see Gillespie, *Colonial Ulster*, 50–63.

7 For the Penal Laws, see S.J. Connolly, *Religion, Law and Power: The Making of Protestant Ireland, 1660–1760* (Oxford, 1992); and Thomas Bartlett, *The Fall and Rise of the Irish Nation: The Catholic Question, 1690–1830* (Dublin, 1992). Synge is quoted in T.W. Moody and W.E. Vaughan, eds., *Eighteenth-Century Ireland, 1691–1800* (Oxford, 1986), vol. iv of *A New History of Ireland*, 106.

8 For the Irish background to the settlement of America, see the writings of David Beers Quinn who in many ways, pioneered this historiography. Of particular relevance here are his "Sir Thomas Smith (1513–1577) and the Beginnings of English Colonial Theory;" *The Elizabethans and the Irish* (Ithaca, 1966), and *Ireland and America: Their Early Associations, 1500–1640* (Liverpool, 1991). See also Cecil H. Clough and P.E.H. Hair, eds., *The European Outthrust and Encounter: The First Phase c.1400–c.1700: Essays in Tribute to David Beers Quinn on his 85th Birthday* (Liverpool, 1994) as well as the following by Nicholas Canny: *The Elizabethan Conquest of Ireland: A Pattern Established, 1565–76* (Hassocks, 1976), *Kingdom and Colony: Ireland in the Atlantic World, 1560–1800*

In 1637 John Winthrop (1588–1649) suggested that if Massachusetts was "bound to keep off whatsoever appears to tend to our ruine or damage, then we may lawfully refuse to receive such whose dispositions suite not with ours and whose society will be hurtful to us." For the General Court in 1654, this meant excluding those who reflected "the cruel and malignant spirit that has from time to time been manifest in the Irish nation against this English nation ... [it] hereby declare[d] their prohibition of bringing any Irish men, women or children, into this jurisdiction."[9] Winthrop's concerns were also echoed in laws "to prevent the Growth of Popery" in America. As in its main Irish equivalent, passed in 1704, such legislation imposed penalties on "any Popish bishop, priest or Jesuit" who exercised sacerdotal functions or who would "endeavour to persuade any of her majesty's liege people to embrace and be reconciled to the Church of Rome."[10] Six years earlier, Maryland had imposed a number of duties on incoming Irish Catholic servants because, without them, in the words of the governor, John Seymour (1703–99), "this Province will by farr have too large a share of them [Irish Catholic servants] who in some years may prove very Dangerous." In a similar vein, South Carolina's programmes of assisted emigration were restricted in 1716 so that "none of the servants be [they] either what is commonly called native Irish ... or Roman Catholics" might benefit to the disadvantage of the more desirable Protestant settlers. Thus, by selecting immigrants "through exclusion," as E.P. Hutchinson has succinctly put it, as well as by enshrining Smith's notions of "English laws and civility" in the polity, colonial legislators neither encouraged the immigration of Irish Catholics nor suggested that in the new world, participation in civil society would be free from the prejudices of the old.[11]

(Baltimore, 1988), "Fashioning a British Atlantic World" in Canny *et al.*, eds., *Empire, Society, and Labor: Essays in Honor of Richard S. Dunn*, special supplement to *PH* lxix (1997), 6–45, and his edited collection (with K.R. Andrews and P.E.H. Hair), *The Westward Enterprise: English Activities in Ireland, the Atlantic and America, 1480–1650* (Liverpool, 1978).

9 The quotations are from R.C. Winthrop, ed., *Life and Letters of John Winthrop*, 2 vols. (Boston, 1869) i, 182; and J.D. Butler, "British Convicts Shipped to American Colonies," *AHR* ii (1896), 20. For context, see Michael Zuckerman, *Peaceable Kingdoms: Massachusetts Towns in the Eighteenth Century* (Cambridge, Mass., 1970); Edmund Morgan, *Visible Saints* (Ithaca, 1963). For Winthrop's interest in the evolution of plantation in Ireland, see Roger Thompson, *Mobility and Migration: East Anglian Founders of New England, 1629–1640* (Amherst, 1994), 37–8, 108–9.

10 The quotations are taken from legislation in Maryland. See William H. Browne *et al.*, compilers, *Archives of Maryland* (hereafter cited as *Arch.Md.*) 68 vols. (Baltimore, 1883–1959) xxvi, 340–1. Some of the colonial acts "to Prevent the Further Growth of Popery" are discussed in Francis X. Curran, *Catholics in Colonial Law* (Chicago, 1963). Ireland's 1704 act "to Prevent the Growth of Popery" is analysed in J.G. Simms, "The Making of a Penal Law, 1703–4," *IHS* xii (1960), 105–18.

11 *Arch. Md.* xxii, 497; E.P. Hutchinson, *Legislative History of American Immigration Policy*

In 1704 Thomas Dongan (1634–1715), the Irish-born Catholic governor of New York under James II, explicitly tested the relationship between old and new when he argued that the laws which prevented Catholics from holding land in England did not apply in the colonies. He did not win the case. Over fifty years later, Cecilius Calvert (1605–75), proprietor of Maryland (1632–75), had identified a more pragmatic way for colonies to interpret such matters when he argued that colonial law should not be "repugnant or contrary, but, as neare as conveniently may bee, agreeable to the laws of England." Reinforcing this after the accession of William and Mary, Governor Seymour of Maryland stated that the "declared Enemys of our Church and State" would not be indulged, wherever they lived. Within weeks of his arrival in Maryland, he closed the imposing St. Mary's church in Annapolis, long the symbol of Catholic power in the colony, because he thought that it was "Scandalous and offensive to the Government" to have such a structure in a city where both "a protestant church" and a county court were located. Thereafter, Maryland's Catholics accepted "that the giving [of] offence in the least Manner either to her Majesty ... or to the Governm^t here Establish'd under her is a thing they ... shall with their utmost industry avoid."[12]

Other governors shared this view which was also reflected in legal schedules, colonial charters, official oaths of office, and instructions to colonial governors to promote "the laws and statutes of their Majestys' Kingdom of England" and "liberty of conscience to all persons (*except Papists*)." There was always a vagueness about how these instruments should be regarded in America if only because, as Jack P. Greene has pointed out, no metropolitan law could be implemented without either "implicit or explicit ratification" by the colonies. However, this was a process which worked both ways. Thus, shortly after he took over as governor of Maryland in 1720, Charles Calvert advised his Catholic

---

1798–1965 (Philadelphia, 1981), 389. Seymour is quoted in Beatriz Betancourt Hardy, "Papists in a Protestant Age: the Catholic Gentry and Community in Colonial Maryland, 1689–1776" (Ph.D. dissertation, University of Maryland, 1993), 123, and the Carolina act in Theo D. Jervey, "The White Indented Servants of South Carolina," *South Carolina Historical and Genealogical Magazine* xii (1911), 166. An earlier South Carolina act of 1698 offered a bounty of £13 for each male servant imported, "Irish only excepted"; *ibid.*, 165. In 1704 Maryland imposed a duty of twenty shillings on each Irish Catholic immigrant. Thirteen years later, this was doubled in order "to prevent the importing [of] too great a Number of Irish Papists into this Province;" see *Arch.Md.* xxvi, 349–50 and xxxiii, 109–10, respectively.

12 Lockhart, *Aspects of Emigration*, 135; *Arch. Md.* xxvi, 591–2, 547. Calvert and Seymour are quoted in David W. Jordan, *Foundations of Representative Government in Maryland, 1632–1715* (Cambridge, Mass., 1987), 4 and 166. For an analysis of the dilemmas which religion created for the polity in Maryland, see John D. Kruger, *English and Catholic: The Lords Baltimore in the Seventeenth Century* (Baltimore, 2004).

friends to "peaceably & Quietly Submitt to the Known Laws ... And rest happy under the Indulgence [which was] p[er]mitted to them" outside the bounds of the formal polity. Such views reflected an enduring commitment to the single-interest polity. Even in Pennsylvania, Quaker leaders supposed that among the increasingly "mixed multitudes" of their colony, there was but one "morally superior" interest group (themselves) which could represent the welfare of the community as a whole. Without a trace of irony, this assumption continued even after the Quakers lost their numerical majority in the colony and, although the Penn family later converted to Anglicanism, the idea that "the interest of one part of society" was "the object of the whole polity" endured as an article of political faith in America until the end of the eighteenth century.[13]

The history of the Penal Laws reflects similar paradoxes. American Catholics greatly resented to be "almost reduced to a Levell with our Negros not having even the privilege of voting." In contemporary Ireland, as John Bowes (1691–1767), the Lord Chancellor, noted in 1759, the Penal Laws "did not presume a Papist to exist in the kingdom." Even Maryland's pioneering Toleration Act was suspended in 1649 during war with France so "that none who profess and exercise the Popish Religion" and thus, France's presumed allies, would "be protected" in law. The following century, both Maryland and Pennsylvania doubled taxed Catholic-owned land during the Seven Years' War (1756–63) while Pennsylvania and Virginia also disarmed "Papists, and reputed Papists."[14] Even apart from such emergencies, as Charles Carroll observed in 1759, even if Catholics remained "quiet and unmolested," these "most tyrannical laws ... would always [be] readily" enforced should Parliament choose to do so. It is true that as the colonial elite struck deeper roots during the course of the eighteenth century, and the traditional condescension and political fear of the Catholic abated, the Penal Laws were, more often than not, as dead as the papers on which they were written. This enabled colonial Catholics to

13 Curran, *Catholics in Colonial Law*, 90 *et passim*; Greene, *Peripheries and Centre*, xi. Calvert's advice of 1720 is cited in "Papists in a Protestant Age," 177; Richard A. Ryerson, "Republican Theory and Partisan Reality in Revolutionary Pennsylvania" in Ronald Hoffman and Peter J. Albert, eds., *Sovereign States in an Age of Uncertainty* (Charlottesville, 1981), 104–5, 114. The description of Pennsylvania is taken from Schwartz, *Mixed Multitude*. For the social and political realities which the colonists faced to establish "coherence" in America, see Jack P. Greene, *The Intellectual Construction of America* (Chapel Hill, 1993), 50–6.

14 "Petition of Sundry Roman Catholics ..." as quoted in Jay P. Dolan, *The Catholic American Experience: A History from Colonial Times to the Present Day* (South Bend, 1992), 85; Richard J. Purcell, "Irish Colonists in Colonial Maryland," *Studies* xxiii (1934), 288; Curran, *Catholics in Colonial Law*, 104–7; Ronald Hoffman, *Princes of Ireland, Planters of Maryland: A Carroll Saga, 1500–1782* (Chapel Hill, 2000), 274–5. Bowes is quoted from W.E.H. Lecky, *A History of Ireland in the Eighteenth Century* 5 vols. (London, 1892) i, 470;

exercise a type of influence, often in connivance with Protestant debtors, friends, clients, business partners, and kin, which had not been foreseen by the framers of the laws. This point was made as follows in the preamble to a Maryland act of 1718 concerning the franchise:

> not only [do] professed Papists still multiply and increase in number, but there are also too great numbers of others that adhere to and espouse their interest, in opposition to the *Protestant Establishment* ... too many persons that are either really Papists, or Popishly inclined, act in disguise, and will not make any public profession of their principles, for the better and more effectually carrying on their wicked and malicious designs, [and] for the undermining and subverting *our present Establishment*.[15]

Carroll appreciated that the broader intent of the Penal Laws had been less to persecute colonial Catholics than to isolate them from conventional political power. Although the proprietor tried to protect the colony's Catholics, the advice was to "cause all Acts of [the] Romane Catholique Religion to be done as privately as may be." Even one of the colony's more anti-Catholic governors, John Hart (1715–20), vehemently denied as a "Notorious untruth" that Catholics were "persecuted for *conscience* sake." Instead, he suggested that the Penal Laws reflected a strategy to neutralise the political influence of the "Popish interest within this Province." As a result, the Carrolls and other leading Catholic families had no formal political power between 1690 and the American Revolution. Moreover, as long as the laws remained on the books, they could always be invoked to ensure a due deference to the constituted Anglican establishment of church and state. Although the situation in Pennsylvania was less restrictive, even Penn experienced the reality of the law during a visit to London in 1708 after a "complaint" had been made that Mass was being celebrated in Philadelphia. As he wrote to Logan, "ill use is [being] made of it against us here," despite the declared toleration of Pennsylvania's *Frame of Government* (1682) and *Charter of Liberties* (1701). In a similar context, Lord Baltimore (1731–71) had to enforce the Penal Laws in Maryland more

15 *Arch.Md.* xxxiii, 288. Carroll is quoted from Hoffman, *Princes of Ireland, Planters of Maryland*, xxiv. For the history of the Carrolls under the Penal Laws, see *ibid.* and "Marylando-Hibernicus: Charles Carroll the Settler, 1660–1720," *WMQ* xvi (1988), 226–36. For another case study, see Barbara Hardy,"A Papist in a Protestant Age: The Case of Richard Bennett, 1667–1749," *JSH* lx (1994), 203–28. See also Joseph J. Casino, "Anti-Popery in Colonial Pennsylvania," *PMHB* cv (1981), 284–92; and Mary Augustina Ray, *American Opinion of Roman Catholicism in the Eighteenth Century* (New York, 1936). For the use of the penal laws to undermine the power of Maryland's upper house, where the Catholic interest had traditionally been strong, see Hardy, "Papists in a Protestant Age," 282–7, *et passim*.

rigorously "as the neglecting so to do, may be deem'd a Fault in the administration of Government within the Province" and reminded his governor, Horatio Sharpe (1753–69), "to enforce Parliament's laws against Catholics." In both cases, a more rigorous application of the "anti-Popery" laws followed. It did not last long in either colony and in 1741 Fr. Henry Neale reported that his communicants in Philadelphia had again "all [the] liberty imaginable in the exercise of our business." However, although the Penal Laws were often relaxed and in some cases, totally ignored, Neale knew that Catholic worship was still not *legally* permitted and that he should not adopt a misplaced status for either himself or his church in contemporary Philadelphia.[16] Moreover, such de facto toleration was seldom such as to encourage Catholic Ireland to identify with the grander designs of the first British empire in Ireland or, with the exceptions of the West Indies and Newfoundland, their extension to the Americas.

Aside from the ideology of plantation and the single-interest polity, the attitudes of seventeenth-century colonists were also influenced by another old world view, namely, that the Americas were nothing more than "an outlet to so many idle, wretched people as they have in England," as the Spanish ambassador to London put it in 1611. Most Americans resented the occasional portrayal of their communities as dumping grounds for "rogues and vagabonds," all the more so because in the words of the Derry-born minister of St. Paul's, Rhode Island (1721–57), the Rev. James MacSparran, "though some of these Felons do reform, ... their Malversation has a bad Effect upon the Morals of the lower Class of Inhabitants." In any event, they did not want convicts and servants from Britain and Ireland to become burdens on their fledgling colonies and they regulated European immigration accordingly.[17] In

---

16 *Arch. Md.* xxvi, 44–6; William Robert Shepherd, "History of Proprietary Government in Pennsylvania," *Studies in History, Economics and Public Law, Columbia University* (hereafter, *Columbia Studies*) vi (New York, 1896), 369; John Tracy Ellis, *Catholics in Colonial America* (Baltimore, 1965), 373–4. Hart is quoted in *Arch. Md.* xxxiii, 368 and Baltimore's letters in Hardy, "Papists in a Protestant Age," 275, 285. For Penn's views on toleration, see Paul Douglas Newman, "'Good Will to all men ... from the King on the throne to the beggar on the dunghill': William Penn, the Roman Catholics, and Religious Toleration," *PH* cxi (1994), 457–79.

17 Marcus Jernegan, *Laboring and Dependent Classes in Colonial America, 1607–1783* (Chicago, 1931), 177, 195; Mildred Campbell, "'Of People either too Few or too Many:' The Conflict of Opinion on Population and its Relation to Emigration" in William Appleton Aiken and Basil Duke Hennington, eds., *Conflict in Stuart England: Essays in Honour of Wallace Notestein* (London, 1980), 188. McSparran is quoted from Miller, Schrier, Boling, and Doyle, eds., *Irish Immigrants in the Land of Canaan*, 62. For official views on transporting convicts to America, see Roger Ekirch, *Bound for America: The Transportation of British Convicts to the Colonies, 1718–1775* (Oxford, 1987); and Kenneth Morgan, "English and American Attitudes towards Convict Transportation, 1718–1775," *History* cxxii (1987), 416–31.

1700, for example, Massachusetts forbade the admission of anybody who was "likely to be a charge to the place" and obliged ship captains, "under penalty of £5 for every name that was omitted," to provide the local custom house with the name, description, and "circumstances so far as he knows," of their passengers. In 1722, a year after 6,000 people had been infected by a fever that many associated with recent arrivals from Ireland, Boston's selectmen also announced that they would take bonds from Irish immigrants "to save the town harmless from all charges" and, if necessary, deport any who were being "maintained *at the cost of the province.*" This they did in 1755, for example, when £14 was spent to return an Irishman who had become a charge on the colony.[18] Such actions reinforced the supposed inhospitality of New England as a whole and helped to ensure that the region would not become a prominent destination for Irish emigrants during the colonial period.

Unlike New England, the southern colonies were more concerned about incoming European convicts than with poor white immigrants. While convicts may not have been unwelcome in the early-seventeenth century, by 1671 Virginia's General Court had become so uneasy with the "great nombres of felons and otheyr dessperate villaines sent hither" that it prohibited any further "landing of any jail birds" within its borders. Thereafter, many of these "wicked villaines" were diverted to the West Indies where, in the words of Massachusetts's agent, "it is well known that they will be willingly entertained." In 1717 the Transportation Act widened the list of transportable crimes to include a number of non-capital offences such as vagrancy and between 1735 and 1743, the only period for which official Irish figures are available, over half the convicts who were shipped from Ireland were vagrants. At times, convicts could also be transported as part of a plea bargain, even for minor transgressions. On 8 September 1769 two boys who had been charged with stealing a large silver cup, the property of the dowager countess of Kildare, were set free when "they consented to indent and go on board a ship in the harbour bound for America." In Virginia, such immigrants were no more welcome than they had been before 1671 and many colonists believed that the broader definition of "transport" would renew a type of immigration that they had spent the previous forty years trying to end. As a result, they drew up a schedule of fines which proved to be so prohibitive that they constituted, in the words of Richard West (*c.*1691–1726), lord chancellor of Ireland "a virtual prohibition of convicts" from Britain and

---

18 *The Acts and Resolves, Public and Private, of the Province of Massachusetts Bay, 1692–1786,* 21 vols. (Boston, 1869–1922) i, 451–2 and ii, 244; Jernegan, *Laboring and Dependent Classes,* 192, 195; Stephen Wiberley, "Four Cities: Public Poor Relief in Urban America, 1700–1775," (Ph.D. dissertation, Yale University, 1975), 49. For a discussion of the relevant legislation, see R.W. Kelso, *History of Public Poor Relief in Massachusetts, 1620–1920* (Boston, 1922).

Ireland to the colony. These duties also affected Ireland's servant trade with Virginia in that some merchants were involved in transporting convicts as well as servants. Thus, after the convict trade was heavily taxed in Virginia, many of these merchants looked to Maryland which had accepted the Transportation Act without protest. One merchant observed in 1746 that "convicts and servants sell better [there] & may be imported without any risque." However, both types of immigrant were often associated in the public mind and as a result, the image of Maryland as a harsh station endured for much of the eighteenth century.[19]

As in New England, the regulation of immigration in the middle colonies was influenced by a view that convicts and other poor Europeans might destabilise the community. After its protests against the Transportation Act went unheeded, Pennsylvania passed a Convict Act in 1722 to ensure that those "villaines" who had been welcomed in Maryland would stay there and not invite themselves further north. This act demanded "a true and just account" of all those who entered the colony but, by imposing a duty of £5 on each convict, as well as a bond of £50 "for the good behaviour of such convict persons for the space of one year," it also sought to circumvent the Transportation Act by *provincial* regulation. Seven years later, the Servant Act imposed similar conditions on servants amid fears that the rising tide of German and Irish immigrants might become "a heavy burden and charge upon the inhabitants of this province." Both pieces of legislation had potentially serious implications for Irish emigration to the Delaware Valley. Yet in some ways, they were self-defeating. For example, there were no provisions for checking the accuracy of passenger lists. This was left to the discretion of the ship captain who was merely required to return his lists to the local customs official and he in turn, was obliged only to collect them. Moreover, the laws could be evaded by landing passengers at the Delaware ports of Newcastle and Wilmington. In any event,

19 J.C. Ballagh, "White Servitude in the Colony of Virginia," *JHU St.* xiii, nos. 6–7 (Baltimore, 1895), 36; Jernegan, *Laboring and Dependent Classes*, 48; Samuel McKee, *Labor in Colonial New York, 1664–1776* (New York, 1935), 92; Patrick Fitzgerald, "A Sentence to Sail: The Transportation of Irish Convicts to Colonial America in the Eighteenth Century" in Patrick Fitzgerald and Steve Ickringill, eds., *Atlantic Crossroads: Historical Connections between Scotland, Ulster and North America* (Newtownards, 2001); Doyle, *Irishmen and Revolutionary America*, 64; *FLJ*, 16 Sept. 1769; LC, Davey & Carson Letterbook (1745–50), letter to Robert Travers, dated Dublin, 5 June 1746. West is quoted in Eugene Irving McCormac, "White Servitude in Maryland, 1634–1820," *JHU St.* xxii, nos.3–4 (Baltimore, 1904), 102. For the official statistics on convicts, see *The Journals of the House of Commons of the Kingdom of Ireland* 17 vols. (Dublin, 1782–1801), (hereafter, *Commons Journals. Ireland*) iv, appendix cciii–ccxlv. From these, Roger Ekirch infers that "more than 16,000" may have been transported from Ireland between 1718 and 1745; Ekirch, "Bound for America: A Profile of British Convicts Shipped to American Colonies, 1718–1775," *WMQ* xlii (1985), 186–7.

the Privy Council found in 1742 that they were incompatible with imperial law and duly revoked them.[20]

In New York, ship captains were asked to furnish lists of passengers within twenty four hours of arrival and to return to their port of origin those who had come without property, "manuall craft or occupaceon," or security "for their well demeanor." The colony's revised "Duke's Laws" (1683) included immigrants within the terms of their poor laws although by 1701 New York had repealed many of these laws as being "inconvenient and burthensome." Moreover, its law of 1721 "to prevent vagrant and idle persons from being a charge and expense" on the colony was not specifically associated with immigrants while the requirement to file passenger lists was largely ignored. One of the city's newspapers, the *Independent Reflector*, later challenged such official apathy on "the importation of mendicant foreigners" and warned that "that which is virtuous in Theory, becomes vicious in Practice." Such protests were half-hearted. In any event, the colony did not consider poverty, however it was explained, to be an acute social problem until well into the eighteenth century. Thus, both New York and Pennsylvania used their respective laws on the poor and the marginal to regulate European immigration in a pragmatic manner as well as in ways which would not discourage Irish emigrants from considering the real opportunities which America offered.[21]

A number of books and pamphlets also encouraged potential emigrants, whatever their background and focus, to look beyond colonial charters and laws. Most of these writings described the flora, fauna, produce, climate, topography, and potential of the American colonies which in the words of one, "sagacious industry and long acquaintance will discover." The tracts which Penn published between 1681 and 1686 offered religious toleration as well as practical information on subjects which ranged from the organisation and management of the Atlantic voyage to the acquisition, seeding, and stocking of land. In 1710 and 1712, respectively, Thomas Nairne and John Norris published what Greene has

20 *Stats. at Large Pa.* iii, 264–8; and iv, 135–40, 164–71; Thomas M. Truxes, *Irish-American Trade, 1660–1783* (New York, 1988), 128. For an analysis of these laws, see Schwartz, *Mixed Multitude*, ch.4 *et passim.*

21 *Colonial Laws of New York from the Year 1664 to the Revolution* 5 vols. (Albany, 1894–6) i, 132; Steven J. Ross, "'Objects of Charity:' Poor Relief, Poverty, and the Rise of the Almshouse in Early-Eighteenth-Century New York City" in William Pencak and Conrad Edick Wright, eds., *Authority and Resistance in Early New York* (New York, 1988), 140–1; Michael Kammen, *Colonial New York: A History* (New York, 1965), 297–8. The 1721 law is quoted in Samuel McKee, "Indentured Servitude in Colonial New York" *NYH* xxxi (1931), 153–4. For a general analysis of the city's attitudes to the poor and poverty, see Robert E. Cray, *Paupers and Poor Relief in New York City and its Rural Environs, 1700–1830* (Philadelphia, 1988).

described as "the two fullest, best informed, and most systematic" of all the promotional pamphlets on South Carolina.[22] As with private letters, such accounts were often complemented by the promotions of colonial agents. In 1669, for example, Carolina's proprietors sent a representative to Ireland to advertise their colony while Charles Carroll, the Irish-born attorney general of Maryland (1689–1715) and clerk of Lord Baltimore's land office (1694–1713), visited Ireland in 1701. While there, Carroll publicised what was on offer in Maryland, including "good" land. Penn also appointed agents in a number of European cities, including Dublin, soon after his patent was confirmed in 1681. However, it was not until the early decades of the eighteenth century that Penn's promise of civil and religious freedom struck a more responsive chord in Ireland. This was a time when the implementation of the Penal Laws was at its most rigorous, New England was fading as an option for Irish settlers, and the Ulster-born Logan was appointed as Penn's provincial secretary. Thus, Logan noted that the Irish immigrants who came to Pennsylvania during the 1720s "say the Proprietor [had] invited People to come & settle his Countrey, [and that] they are come for that end."[23]

Promoters also sought to answer some of the more negative characterisations of life in America. For example, George Alsop's widely-circulated *Character of the Province of Maryland* (London, 1666) denounced those "clappermouth jaws of the vulgar" whose "abusive exclamations" had "stigmatiz'd" Maryland servants "for slaves." In Alsop's view, such critics would thoughtlessly and ignorantly discourage the "poor and industrious" of the old world from coming to America where they might advance and better themselves.[24] While Alsop

22 Andrew White, *A Relation of the Colony of the Lord Baron of Baltimore* (London, 1633) in Richard Walsh, ed., *The Mind and Spirit of Early America: Sources in American History, 1607–1789* (New York, 1969), 28; Abbott E. Smith, *Colonists in Bondage: White Servitude and Convict Labor in America, 1607–1776* (Chapel Hill, 1947), 59: Jack P. Greene, ed., *Selling a New World: Two Colonial South Carolina Promotional Pamphlets. By Thomas Nairne and John Norris* (Columbia, S.C., 1989), 2. For the more important promotional tracts on Pennsylvania, see Albert Cook Myers, ed., *Narratives of Early Pennsylvania, West New Jersey and Delaware* (New York, 1912).

23 Lockhart, *Aspects of Emigration*, 137; Marcus Wilson Jernegan, *The American Colonies, 1492–1750* (New York, 1929), 306; *Pennsylvania Archives*, 2nd ser., 19 vols. (Harrisburg, 1879) vii, 97, Logan to John Penn, 25 Nov. 1727. Carroll's visit is quoted from Hardy, "Papists in a Protestant Age," 122–3. In the early-eighteenth century, the Scottish owners of a tract in East New Jersey also maintained an agent in Belfast to recruit settlers; see Griffin, *People with No Name*, 89. Between 1641 and 1651, 134 imprints "relating to the New World" were published in Ireland; for a general discussion of the *European Americana* project, of which these are part, see Richard C. Simmons, "Americana in British Books, 1621–1760" in Karen Ordahl Kupperman, ed., *America in European Consciousness* (Chapel Hill and London, 1995), 361–87.

24 G. Alsop, *A Character of the Province of Maryland* (London, 1666) in *Fund Publications of the*

admitted that life in America could be difficult, this did not mean that *in extremis*, servants would be abandoned to the mercies of their masters. Intending servants were reminded that their indentures usually protected them in colonial law. In New York, for example, the colonial courts invariably awarded servants their freedom if a master was held to be in breach of contract while in Pennsylvania, a law of 1700 stipulated

> That no servant, bound to serve his or her time in this province, or counties annexed, shall be sold or disposed of to any person residing in any other province or government, without the consent of the said servant, and two justices of the peace of the county wherein he lives or is sold.

The law could also be invoked to prevent "Barbarous usage," to keep a servant's family together, to improve "a miserable Condition," or to ensure the payment of freedom dues.[25] For many aspiring Irish emigrants, such a benign culture seemed to confirm that Pennsylvania was "a good poor man's country where there are no oppressions of any kind whatsoever." It also suggested that servitude was not necessarily an invidious path towards the "promise" of the new world. As Job Johnson recalled, his "only encouragement" to go to Pennsylvania

> was because Many Go to America worth nothing yet some of them servants and [I] hear or see them Come back again, in two or three years worth more than they would have been by staying at home while they lived and yet they would Not Content themselves at home, but went back again which was sufficient to Convince any one that the Country was Good.[26]

Maryland Historical Society xv (Baltimore, 1880), 57; Alun C. Davies, ed., "'As Good A Country as Any Man Needs to Dwell in:' Letters from a Scotch-Irish Immigrant in Pennsylvania,, 1766, 1767, and 1784," *PH* c (1983), 320. For Alsop and other commentators on colonial Maryland, see James Horn, "Servant Emigration to the Chesapeake in the Seventeenth Century" in Thad W. Tate and David L. Ammermann, eds., *The Chesapeake in the Seventeenth Century. Essays on Anglo-American Society* (Chapel Hill, 1979), 51–95; and Richard S. Dunn, "Seventeenth-Century Historians of America" in James Morton Smith, ed., *Seventeenth-Century America: Essays in Colonial History* (Chapel Hill, 1959), 195–225.

25 John Bioren, publ., *Laws of Pennsylvania* 4 vols. (Philadelphia, 1810) i, 10, c.xlix. The last two quotations are from two petitions to Chester County Quarter Sessions Court in 1735, for which see Miller, Schrier, Boling, and Doyle, eds., *Irish Immigrants in the Land of Canaan*, 269, 271. For a discussion of the organisation and sale of indentures, see David W. Galenson, "The Market Evaluation of Human Capital: The Case of Indentured Servitude," *JPE* lxxxix (1981), 447–51, and *White Servitude in Colonial America: An Economic Analysis* (Cambridge, Mass., 1981). For a concise historical note on the evolution of indentured servitude, see the same author's "The Rise and Fall of Indentured Servitude in the Americas: An Economic Analysis," *JEH* xliv (1984), 1–13.

26 PRONI, D2092/1/3, T3700/1.

Servitude also gave access to America. For Johnson, given that during the eighteenth century, the passage could cost up to £6 at a time when a labourer's daily wages were from four to six pence, it enabled many to leave when it would have been otherwise impossible for them to do so. In return for a berth, the colonial servant signed what was usually a four-year labour contract with the ship's captains, "or his assigns," and this was then sold to the highest bidder after arrival in America. Servitude also served the broader strategies of the colonies to attract settlers to British North America. Between 1636 and 1683, for example, Lord Baltimore's *Conditions of Plantation* linked the distribution of the more substantial land allotments in Maryland to the importation of servants: promotion had to appeal to settlers as well as to investors and speculators. In June 1680 George Talbot of Co. Roscommon was awarded 32,000 acres "for transporting 640 persons within twelve years" while, in Pennsylvania, the London Society of Free Traders was given 20,000 acres on the understanding that imported servants would develop the fishing and fur trades on its tract. Most colonies also offered servants "headrights" of between fifty and eighty acres when their indentures expired. However, during the course of the eighteenth century, these arrangements were usually used to attract settlers to the frontier in the hope that they might help to secure those parts from hostile attack. During the 1720s Logan justified giving frontier land in Pennsylvania to Ulster Presbyterian immigrants because they had already "proven" their "bravery" when Derry and Enniskillen were attacked by Jacobite supporters in 1689. With such settlers, he argued, the colony would be secure against "any disturbance" in the future.[27]

A number of southern colonies also promoted other schemes to encourage immigration from Ireland. In 1731 South Carolina embarked on a programme of assisted emigration that included land grants, exemptions from taxation, the supply of provisions and tools to sow a farm, or the wherewithal to develop a trade in the colony. On 31 January 1734 and following application to the legislature, a number of Ulster Presbyterians who had recently arrived in the colony, were given eight hogsheads of corn, two of peas, two of salt, and

27 James Horn, *Adapting to a New World: English Society in the Seventeenth-Century Chesapeake* (Williamsburg, 1994), 65; McCormac, "White Servitude in Maryland," 21, 12–13; Gary B. Nash, "The Free Society of Traders and the Early Politics of Pennsylvania," *PMHB* lxxix (1965), 147–73; James G. Leyburn, *The Scotch-Irish: A Social History* (Chapel Hill, 1962), 191. For the *Conditions of Plantation*, see Russell R. Menard and Lois G. Carr, "The Lords Baltimore and the Colonization of Maryland" in David B. Quinn, ed., *Early Maryland* (Detroit, 1982), 167–9. For similar attitudes in contemporary South Carolina and New York, see "White Servants as a Measure of Defence" in Warren B. Smith, *White Servitude in Colonial South Carolina* (Columbia, S.C., 1961), 27–37; and McKee, *Labour in Colonial New York*, 94.

eighteen barrels of beef. By 1761, however, some argued that the concessions were not having "the desired Effect" and in 1766, 1767, and 1768 (a period during which the importation of black slaves was also prohibited), a second promotion promised exemption from taxes for ten years, one hundred acres of land for each head of household and fifty for each family member, as well as payment of passage money. These "projects" appealed to pre-arranged groups rather than to individuals and as such, they had a seventeenth-century ring to them. Moreover, the fact that they were restricted to Protestants and effectively focused on Ulster, suggested that the confessional undertones of the earlier Irish plantations were now being applied to the development of the Anglo-American south. Protestant clergymen took a conspicuous role in organising their communicants to take advantage of the concessions. However, the expected surge in the number of Irish servants did not happen and in January 1768 one of Carolina's leading political and commercial personalities, Henry Laurens (1724–92), concluded that he would have to make "an end of the account of the [Irish] servants by giving them away to save great expense."[28]

The appeal of such initiatives was complemented by the ways in which emigrants' letters and published "letters of advice" often pitted the socioeconomic troubles of Ireland against the advantages of contemporary America. At various points during the century the enclosure of common lands, the reorganisation of the tithe system, increasing prices and rents, and the greater expectations, "vigorous methods," and percentage demands of tithe agents had encouraged a number of popular protest movements to seek "justice for the poor." Some of these protests, especially those that were directed against increased rents and high renewal fines, coincided with periods of high emigration. In Ulster, many of the leases that had been set under the terms of the Williamite Settlement expired during the late-1710s and 1720s and renegotiated at higher rates. In these circumstances, emigration became "a practical alternative" to life in Ireland and in the opinion of one of the lords justices, Thomas Wyndham, the emigration of the 1720s was particularly high because of those "who make merit of raising rents as high as possible, setting them by cant to the highest bidder, without regard to the true value of the lands, or the goodness of the [existing] tenant." In 1766 the *Belfast News-Letter* outlined the alternative in America:

28 Smith, *White Servitude in Colonial South Carolina*, 54–5, 64–5, 42–3; Jean Stephenson, *Scotch-Irish Migration to South Carolina, 1772* (Strasburg, 1971), 7; Philip M. Hamer et al., eds., *The Papers of Henry Laurens*, 15 vols. (Columbia, S.C., 1968–2003) v, 567, Laurens to Alexander Gray, 26 Jan. 1768. See also Erna Risch, "Encouragement of Immigration as Revealed in Colonial Legislation," *VMHB* xlv (1937), 1–10; Robert L. Meriwether, *The Expansion of South Carolina, 1729–1765* (Philadelphia, 1964); E.R.R. Green, "Queensborough Township: Scotch-Irish Emigration and the Expansion of Georgia, 1763–1776," *WMQ* xvii (1960), 183–209.

It would swell the advertisement too great a length to enumerate all the blessings those people enjoy who have already removed from this country ... from tenants they are become landlords, from working for others they now work for themselves, and enjoy the fruits of their own industry.

Thus, as Henry Johnston wrote in 1773, Irish emigrants could come "out of a Land of Slavery [and go] into A Land of Liberty and freedom."[29] In such circumstances, America became less an "adventure" than an escape.

The Push from Ireland

As suggested by Bernard Bailyn's detailed analysis of the British Register of Emigration, a comprehensive data set which covers the years between 1773 and 1776, one can only indicate, rather than be certain, as to why people left for eighteenth-century America. Emigrants' letters can help to fill a gap in primary information but, as is clear from a recently published analysis of letters and memoirs which covers the years between 1675 and 1815, only a relatively small number of such sources survive from the colonial period and most of these were written from the middle colonies. A few are of dubious authenticity, including James Murray's letter to the Rev. Baptist Boyd, minister at Aughnacloy, Co. Tyrone. However, whether intended for private reading or public recitation, Murray's letter was widely circulated in Ireland and included the central themes of the *genre*. It described the flora, fauna, and produce of the "very strong Lan[d] [and] rich Ground" of New York and listed not only his own wages for keeping "a Skulle for wee Weans," but also those for carpenters (6s. a day), labourers (4s.6d. a day), spinners (4s.6d. a week), and tailors (20s. per suit of clothes). The price of land in his vicinity was given as "£10 a Hundred Acres for ever, and Ten Years Time tell yᵉ get the Money, before they wull ask ye for it." America was indeed "a bonny Country" and "I beg of ye aw to come [over] here."[30]

29 Lecky, *Ireland in the Eighteenth Century* ii, 7, n.1; Maurice J. Bric, "Priests, Parsons, and Politics: the Rightboy Protest in Co. Cork, 1785–1788," *Past and Present* c (1983), 117; Dickson, *Ulster Emigration*, 24, 40–5; PRONI, T659, Pelham Correspondence, Wyndham to unknown, dated 11 Jan. 1728–9; *BN*, 3 June 1766; PRONI, T3578, Johnston to Moses Johnston, dated 28 Mar. 1773.

30 Barnard Bailyn, *Voyagers to the West: A Passage in the Peopling of America on the Eve of the American Revolution* (New York, 1986), 189 *et seq.*; Miller, Schrier, Boling and Doyle, eds., *Irish Immigrants in the Land of Canaan*; Earl Gregg Swem, ed., *Letter of James Murray of New York to Rev. Baptist Boyd of Co. Tyrone, Ireland* (Metuchen, 1925), 1; James T. Lemon, *The Best Poor Man's Country: A Geographical Study of Early Southeastern Pennsylvania* (Baltimore, 1972); Davies, "As Good a Country," 320; Albert Cook Myers, *Immigration of the Irish Quakers into Pennsylvania, 1682–1750* (Swarthmore, 1902), 77. Murray's letter was originally published in *PG*, 27 Oct. 1737 but is regarded as "a public

Similar letters also presented Pennsylvania and New York as "the best poor man's country" although they also stressed that wherever emigrants chose to go, success and hard work went hand in hand. Job Johnson suggested that America was "as Plentifull a Country as any Can be if the People will be Industrious." Robert Parke added that if this was understood, one "could not do better than to come here [to Pennsylvania]." In 1767 William and Job Johnson wrote that their brother in Derry would

> make Well out at Making of Broomes [to] sweep Houses with [in Pennsylvania], their Being a Great Call for Such Tradesmen [at] sixpence per Broom … He Might Make Easily six of them Each Day Besides [having] Meat and Drink as Slatabogie [near Maghera, Co. Derry] Never can Afford.

David Lindsey was convinced that he also should set sail for "Pennsilvena." Writing to his cousin in 1758 he remarked that the "good Bargains of your lands in that Country Doe greatly encourage me to pluck up my spirits and make Redie for the Journey." Thirty years earlier, the Westmeath Quaker, James Wansbrough, suggested to his cousin in New Jersey that "if you or your sons Doe write unto me and give me good Encouragement I will transport my sellf and family and soninlaw … but pray tell me what is ye best Comodyty to teake into yt Contrey." He also noted that he had just read "a history of america which gave me a very [h]onest account of all your Contrey." Thus, it is clear that advice from and about America were not without influence on those who were thinking of leaving Ireland. Indeed, it was with this in mind that Murray's letter had been "printed and dispers'd in Ireland" in the first place. "Tell aw the poor Folk of your Place," it had asked Boyd, "that God has open'd a Door for their Deliverance." In 1725 Parke promoted Chester County, Pennsylvania in a similar fashion and added that although his was "as full an Account as Possible," he knew that "other Letters might Suffice" if it fell short.[31]

Some alleged that such "advices" were too one-sided and that unflattering accounts of America were often censored by those who managed Ireland's passenger trade. As one observer put it in 1729:

letter" rather than "an authentic letter" which was intended to be read by Boyd from his pulpit; see Michael Montgomery, "On the Trail of Early Ulster Emigrant Letters" in Fitzgerald and Ickringill, eds., *Atlantic Crossroads*, 13–26, 133–7. For general comment, see Trevor Parkhill, "Philadelphia Here I Come: A Study of the Letters of Ulster Emigrants in Pennsylvania, 1750–1875" in H. Tyler Blethen and Curtis W. Wood, eds., *Ulster and North America* (Tuscaloosa, 1997), 118–33, as well as the authoritative work by Miller, Schrier, Boling, and Doyle, eds., *Irish Immigrants in the Land of Canaan*.

31 Davies, "As Good a Country," 318; PRONI T2493, David Lindsey to Thomas Fleming, 19 Mar. 1758; Swem, *Letter of James Murray*, 1–2. Parke is quoted in Myers, *Immigration of the Irish Quakers*, 78; and Wansbrough in Miller, Schrier, Boling, and Doyle, eds., *Irish Immigrants in the Land of Canaan*, 22, 21.

I believe the people are imposed on and deceived by the accounts they receive from their relations and correspondents ... and by the indirect practices and insinuations of masters of ships ... [who] go about and send their factors and agents round the country, tempting and ensnaring them.

Four years later, another writer charged that while "the richer sort" were being assured that "their posterity will be for ever happy" in America, "the poorer sort" were being deceived by the accounts of the great wages given there to labouring men." However, perhaps the most publicised cautionary tale was what Kerby Miller has described as "the first Irish emigrant's guidebook:" McSparran's *America Dissected, Being a Full and True Account of All the American Colonies*, published in Dublin in 1753. Among other aspects of life in America, the author noted the

> Intemperance of the Climates, excessive Heat and Cold, and sudden Changes of Weather, terrible and mischievous Thunder and Lightening; bad and unwholesome Air, destructive to Human Bodies; Badness of Money; Danger from Enemies; but, above all, the Danger to the Souls of the Poor People that remove thither, from the multifarious wicked and pestilent Heresies that prevail in those Parts.[32]

Rather like Alsop a century earlier, Job Johnson addressed such conflicting accounts in 1767 and ascribed the "Desire to hear ill" of Pennsylvania to those who "would keep their friends there [in Ireland] with them in Bondage and Slavery" while Parke wrote that "talk [that] went back to Ireland that we were not Satisfied in coming here" was "false." As a result of this commentary, intending Irish emigrants did not lack for advice on life in America, negative as well as positive, legal as well as personal. They were also aware that circumstances varied from colony to colony. However, reaction to the promotion of America was also influenced by the distinctive cultures, traditions, and economies of Ireland's four provinces. As **Jean Hector St. John de Crèvecoeur** (1735–1815) observed of Irish settlers in New York in 1782, "the Irish themselves, from different parts of the kingdom are very different ... One would think, on so small an island, an Irishman would be an Irishman; yet it is not so.[33] These differences were reflected in both the regional origins and cultural character of

32 E.R.R. Green, "The 'Strange Humours' That Drove the Scotch-Irish to America, 1729," *WMQ* xii (1955), 118; "Roscommon," *To the Author of Those Intelligencers printed at Dublin* (New York, 1733), 2; *America Dissected* as quoted from Miller, Schrier, Boling, and Doyle, eds., *Irish Immigrants in the Land of Canaan*, 59.

33 Davies, "As Good a Country," 320; Myers, *Immigration of the Irish Quakers*, 71; Dickson, *Ulster Emigration*, 24, 181–200; Lewis Lewisham, ed., J. Hector St. John de Crèvecoeur, *Letters from an American Farmer* (New York, 1904), 83.

those who emigrated to colonial America as well as in the choice of the colonies to which these emigrants went.

For historical and cultural reasons, colonial America was not a vital part of the Irish Catholic world. Instead, as J.G. Simms has observed, "the real history" of contemporary Irish Catholicism was being traced in Europe rather than in America. It is true that since the early-seventeenth century, Irish Catholics had either gone, or been sent, to the Caribbean, especially if they had revolted against the government. The West Indies was the place for such "rebels," priests, and "rogues, vagrants, sturdy beggars, idle and disorderly persons," those who

> may not be at liberty to return again into this nation [Ireland], where that sort of people are able to do much mischief, by having so great an influence over the popish Irish here, and of alienating their affection from the present Government.

As such, the islands did not suggest the opportunities which colonisation and plantation offered in continental North America. Rather were they, as Andrew White described Montserrat in 1634, "a noble plantation of Irish Catholiques whom the virginians *would not suffer to live with them*." They were also seen as places of crude commercial exploitation and, if a choice could be made, of temporary exile, or "sojourning," rather than of permanent settlement. Around 1670 the three Blake brothers had gone there from Galway, in the words of one of them, to "recruite my great losses whereby I should be enabled to pay my debts at hoame." The image of the West Indies as a place of "slavery" and "dissoluteness" persisted throughout the colonial period and, as Dunn and Bridenbaugh have observed, the islands remained the "social failures" of the British Atlantic world.[34]

34 Moody and Vaughan, eds., *Eighteenth-Century Ireland*, 643; Aubrey Gwynn, "Cromwell's Policy of Transportation," *Studies* xix (1930), 616–7; Sean O'Callaghan, *To Hell or Barbados* (Dingle, 2000), 63; Miller, Schrier, Boling, and Doyle, eds., *Irish Immigrants in the Land of Canaan*, 123. For Jack P. Greene's disagreement with the views of Dunn and Bridenbaugh on the nature of society in the West Indies, see his "Society and Economy in the British Caribbean during the Seventeenth and Eighteeenth Centuries," *AHR* lxxix (1974), 1499–1517. White is quoted in Charles M. Andrews, *The Colonial Period in American History* 2 vols. (new ed., New Haven, 1964) ii, 259. The phrase "sojourning" is taken from Alan L. Karras, *Sojourners in the Sun: Scottish Migrants in Jamaica and the Chesapeake, 1740–1800* (Ithaca, 1992) which argues that white Europeans who went to the West Indies "never had any intention of integration, let alone prolonged residency" and as such, reflect a different paradigm of the immigrant experience in America. See also Hilary McD. Beckles, "A 'Riotous and Unruly Lot:' Irish Indentured Servants and Freemen in the English West Indies, 1644–1713," *WMQ* xlvii (1990), 503–22. Carl and Roberta Bridenbaugh noted that no promotional literature on the Caribbean was

While the islands developed a sizeable community of Catholic merchants, administrators, and servants during the seventeenth century, Irish Catholics did not completely ignore the continental colonies. However, whether at home in Ireland or abroad in America, they were often wary of the British empire and realised that engaging with it could limit rather than promote their ambitions unless they were willing to make concessions. In the Carolinas, the Dublin-trained Anglican minister, Charles Woodmason (c.1720–c.1776), noted that in the 1760s many Irish Catholic immigrants were "very desirous to do better." However, in order to do so, "many" had chosen to live as "concealed Papists" or to make the strategic decision to convert to Protestantism.

In 1715 Lord Baltimore's heir had converted to Anglicanism in order to secure the proprietorship while Dr. Charles Carroll (1691–1755) served in the colonial assembly for seventeen years after he had done the same in 1738. Writing to his son in Eton the following year, the assemblyman advised that "In point of Religion, be not too much attached to any [opinions] grown up with you [for] Bigotry and superstition in Religion is a grand Error [and t]he Church of England *as by Law Established* is worthy of your consideration." Such attitudes reflected those of Catholics in contemporary Ireland, some of whom sought "refuge" in the "convert rolls," especially when their positions, estates, or prospects were threatened. Accordingly, Irish Catholics who emigrated to the continental Americas traded one "fragment of empire" for another where the Penal Laws were applied just as unpredictably over time and place as in Ireland and where, as the more general laws on immigration and settlement suggested, old world prejudices were never far away.[35]

In Ireland, Quakers were also subject to the Penal Laws and like the members of other religious communities, they had to pay tithes to the Church of Ireland. After 1681, they could look to the Delaware where a group of Dublin Quakers had established the "Irish Tenth" on the eastern ride of the river, opposite Philadelphia. There, as well as in the provincial capital itself, they would find encouragement and security. Most of Ireland's Quaker emigrants left the

<hr />

published before 1645 and that this suggests that "the kinds of individuals whom they sought ... could not be attracted by pamphlets and sermons, for most of them were either illiterate or rootless or both;" see their *No Peace beyond the Line: The English in the Caribbean, 1624–1690* (New York, 1972), 11.

35 *Arch. Md.* xxxiii, 287–9. Woodmason is quoted in Leroy V. Eid, "Irish, Scotch and Scotch-Irish, a Reconsideration," *JPrH* cx (1986), 219, 222 and Carroll in Miller, Schrier, Boling and Doyle, eds., *Irish Immigrants in the Land of Canaan*, 458. Conversions from Catholicism to Anglicanism in connection with promotion and office are discussed in Miller, *Emigrants and Exiles*, 150–1. For "crypto-Catholicism" in contemporary Ireland, see T.P. Power, "Coverts" in T.P. Power and Kevin Whelan, eds., *Endurance and Emergence: Catholics in Ireland in the Eighteenth Century* (Dublin, 1990), 101–27.

country during the first quarter of the eighteenth century when the Penal Laws were being keenly enforced. Some of them were people of substance and some were not although it has been estimated that, in total, they did not exceed 2,500 in number. However, because all of them emigrated within networks and community structures that were only geographically split by the Atlantic, and usually had with them letters of identification and introduction (the so-called certificates of removal), emigration was a more positive experience than it was for many other communions.[36] In this, they were closer to the Atlanticism of Ulster Presbyterians than to the European focus of Irish Catholics.

Ulster Presbyterians had long been attracted by America. Because they did not belong to the established Church of Ireland, they were excluded from holding civil office in Ireland. The obligation to pay tithes to the established ministry was especially resented and, as Alexander Crawford wrote from Donegal in 1736, Presbyterians were "as Bound Slevs to Bishop [and] minestor By thire hurying yus into Bis[h]ops Corts." As a result, they were also, in the words of their memorial of 1728, "put on a level with the Papists." Against this background, many prepared to join their cousins in America and to enjoy there what "is denied them in their own country." This they would often do with the support of ministers such as Ezekiel Stewart of Fortstewart, Co. Donegal who noted in 1729 that

> The Presbiteirien Ministers have taken their shear of pains to seduce their poor ignorant heare[r]s by bellowing from their pulpits against y[e] landlords and y[e] [Episcopal] clargey, calling them rackers of rents and screwers of tythes, with other reflections of this nature which they know is pleasing to their people; at y[e] same time telling them that God had appoynted a country for them to dwell in (nameing New England) and desires them to depart thence, where they will be freed from the bondage of Egipt and to y[e] land of Canaan etc.

Many Irish Presbyterians responded to such appeals without diffidence. Historically, their view of colonisation and settlement was Atlantic in its scope and as such, it was relatively easy for them to make the second step to permanent settlement in America.[37]

36 Myers, *Immigration of the Irish Quakers*, 81–2; Miller, Schrier, Boling and Doyle, eds., *Irish Immigrants in the Land of Canaan*, 14. See also Richard S. Harrison, "The Evolution of the Irish Quakers" in Kevin Herlihy, ed., *The Religion of Irish Dissent 1650–1800* (Dublin, 1996) 69–75, and "'As a Garden Enclosed:' The Emergence of Irish Quakers: 1650–1750" in Herlihy, ed., *Irish Dissenting Tradition*, 81–95.
37 E.R.R. Green, "Scotch-Irish Emigration: An Imperial Problem," *Western Pennsylvania Historical Magazine* xxxv (1952), 198; PRONI, Castleward Letters, Book 3, D2092/1/3/141,

Ireland's American connections were also facilitated by patterns of trade. Provisions constituted the country's most important staple and exports were particularly high from the ports of **southern** and eastern Ireland. Consignments to America peaked during the 1760s and early-1770s, encouraged by the repeal of the Cattle Acts in 1759 as well as by increased orders during the Seven Years' War. By 1770, as Thomas M. Truxes has observed, Cork had become "home to the most highly developed provisions industry in the Atlantic economy" and was the major source of beef entering colonial New York and Philadelphia. During the seventeenth century the city had already developed a valuable trade with the islanders of the Caribbean who were "so intent upon planting sugar that they had rather buy foode at very deare rates [from Britain and Ireland] than produce it by labour, soe infinite is the profitt of sugar." Cork's merchants shipped many of their accounts either in their own vessels or in the several hundred others that weighed anchor there *en route* to the West Indies from British and other European ports. As a result, pastoral farming was a profitable business in the counties of southern Ireland although as the population increased, some tenants found the increased rents for what they were directly interested in (arable land) hard to bear. Thus, it was no coincidence that Munster and Leinster were the epicentres of the **Whiteboy movement** during the 1760s and 1770s, or that in 1753 thirty five emigrant vessels left Cork for America when there was a reputed "want of tillage" in the region. However, those who managed the export of provisions from Munster did not usually seek passengers for America. Moreover, their trade in servants was largely incidental to their commercial interests.[38]

In one sense, the departures in 1753 were an aberration because in Munster, economic hardship, however acute, rarely produced the same impulse to emigrate as it did in Ulster. In part, this is because *spailpínteacht*, or seasonal labour outside the locality, usually provided opportunities for employment which were not available closer to home. The cod fisheries of Newfoundland were part of this world and between March and November every year, several thousand workers were attracted there from Ireland, especially from Munster and southern Leinster. On 1 June 1765 *Faulkner's Dublin Journal* "noticed that

Ezekiel Stewart to Michael Ward, 25 March 1729 (hereafter cited as Castleward Letter). Crawford is quoted in Miller, Schrier, Boling, and Doyle eds., *Irish Immigrants in the Land of Canaan*, 26. For an analysis of Presbyterian disabilities as well as the background to the memorial of 1728, see J.C. Beckett, *Protestant Dissent in Ireland, 1687–1780* (London, 1948).

38 Truxes, *Irish-American Trade*, 147, 154; John J. McCusker and Russell R. Menard, *The Economy of British America, 1607–1789* (Chapel Hill, 1985), 155; Lockhart, *Aspects of Emigration*, 50. See also R.C. Nash, "Irish Atlantic Trade in the Seventeenth and Eighteenth Centuries," *WMQ* xlvii (1985), 229–56; Francis G. James, "Irish Colonial Trade in the Eighteenth Century," *WMQ* xx (1963), 574–84.

many thousand fishermen and servants who are employed at Newfoundland, live in the county of Waterford, and parts adjacent." Visiting Waterford in October 1776, one of the leading agricultural writers and travellers of the time, Arthur Young (1741–1820), observed that

> the staple trade of the place is in the Newfoundland trade ... there is more of it here than any where. The number of people who go as passengers in the Newfoundland ships is amazing; from sixty to eighty ships, and from three thousand to five thousand annually ... An industrious man in a year will bring home twelve to sixteen pounds with him, and some more.

About the same time, the Quaker traveller, James Jenkins, also reported that he had seen "shoals of them half-starved men, go on board [for Newfoundland], and in a few months, return well clad, & of healthful appearance." Newfoundland was not unlike similar seasonal workplaces in Ireland and in this sense, it was not perceived to be part of North America at all. More often than not, the region's *spailpíní* were working visitors, not potential settlers.[39] Nonetheless, their introduction to north America, on whatever basis, underlined how commercial structures could determine the nature, direction, and flow of passengers for America. This was even more apparent within the networks of Ireland's linen industry.

The linen industry was officially supervised by the Linen Board (founded in 1711) and encouraged by export bounties. The Linen Act of 1705 permitted the direct shipment of Irish white and brown linens to the British Americas while the Bounty Acts of 1743 and 1745 subsidised their export through English ports. As the linen industry grew, Ireland also became a major market for American flaxseed. Although there had been a long tradition of growing flaxseed in some parts of Ireland, the managers of the early-eighteenth-century linen industry concluded that the importation of foreign flaxseed was more efficient and practical since, in the words of one contemporary, "Flax-seed of our own growth sometimes degenerates, by reason of bad seasons and bad husbandry." After the Navigation Acts were amended in 1731 to allow the direct importation of flaxseed from America to Ireland, Irish purchases of American flaxseed grew dramatically, rising eight fold by 1740 alone, while in America, the *per capita* consumption of Irish linens also increased, doubling between 1751

39 *Arthur Young's Tour in Ireland ... with General Observations on the Present State of that Kingdom* (London, 1780), ed. Arthur W. Hutton, 2 vols. (London, 1892) i, 406; J. William Frost, ed., "The Records and Recollections of James Jenkins" in *Texts and Studies in Religion* xviii (New York and Toronto, 1984), 123. See also Cyril Byrne, "The Waterford Colony in Newfoundland, 1700–1850" in William Nolan and Thomas P. Power, eds., *Waterford: History and Society* (Dublin, 1992), 351–72.

and 1771. These developments had a particular impact on Ulster where in 1757, in the words of one of the Linen Board inspectors, Robert Stephenson,

> if the whole account of all of the linen manufactures promoted by the Linen Board in Leinster, Munster and Connaught, and a considerable part of Ulster, were valued ... they would not equal the returns made by one of the northern districts, where the manufacture was generally established.[40]

Even allowing for Stephenson's comments, considerable quantities of linen were shipped to America not just from Ulster but from all the major ports of Ireland. After 1745 Dublin and, to a lesser extent, Cork also shipped increasing consignments of linen *indirectly* to America through English ports. The export bounties that were paid by this diversion were, in the words of Benjamin Fuller, one of Philadelphia's leading merchants in the trade, "a considerable thing and will more than pay all Charges in getting them [Irish linens] to this Market." As a result, leading American houses in Dublin and Cork looked at the colonies through British ports and acted as commission agents on behalf of principals in Britain, the West Indies, and North America, in addition to managing their own interests. In Ulster, however, the flaxseed/passenger roundabout had a different culture which was indicated by the constant flow of vessels, most of which sailed directly to colonial America, especially to the middle colonies. This trade was all the more systematic because it was managed by families and commercial interests that spanned the Atlantic. It was also more self-contained than it was in the rest of Ireland and was to give a special character to the passenger trade between Ulster and America during the eighteenth century.[41]

In eighteenth-century America, Philadelphia and New York soon emerged as the major American importers of Irish linen. By 1767 as much as 96% of Ireland's import of American flaxseed also originated in the two ports. It was a lucrative business for American merchants and one that helped to redress an

---

40 Truxes, *Irish-American Trade*, 176–7, 34–5, 193–200, 284 and ch.9; W.H. Crawford, *Domestic Industry in Ireland: The Experience of the Linen Industry* (Dublin, 1972), 3–5; Dickson, *Ulster Emigration*, 8. Stephenson is quoted from John J. Horner, *The Linen Trade of Europe* (Belfast, 1920), 98, and the supposed superiority of foreign flaxseed from Thomas Prior, *An Essay to Encourage and Extend the Linen-Manufacture in Ireland, by Premiums and Other Means* (Dublin, 1749), 23, as quoted in Truxes, *Irish-American Trade*, 193. For the Linen Board and its promotions, see Harry Gribbon, "The Irish Linen Board, 1711–1828" in Marilyn Cohen, ed., *The Warp of Ulster's Past* (New York, 1997), 71–92.

41 Truxes, *Irish-American Trade*, 184–5, 74–8, 46–55. Fuller is quoted in *ibid.*, 179. For the wide geographical range of one American firm, with interests in Ireland, Britain, the West Indies and elsewhere, as well as the credit arrangements and bills of exchange which sustained its networks, see Thomas M. Truxes, ed., *Letterbook of Greg & Cunningham 1756–57* (Oxford, 2001), 1–3, *et passim*.

unfavourable balance of trade with Britain and Ireland, "especially," as the American writer Jared Elliot (1685–1763) noted in 1760, "when we consider how difficult it is for us to make Returns to Europe." Consignments of flaxseed could be paid for in bills of exchange in Ireland and these could then be used to purchase and ship goods through ports in Britain. Alternatively, the holds of the returning vessels could be filled with servants (as well as linen) for transportation back to America. Shipping servants was a cash business and "an advantageous returning freight," as one house put it in 1774, "& is *all paid ready down at Shipping*."[42] Given that merchants normally received between £10 to £20 for each servant, at a time when the cost of passage was about £5, the profit was not insignificant. It is clear from the contract that was made between the Belfast merchant, Daniel Mussenden and John Fowler, captain of the **ship** *Bruerton* (Belfast to Philadelphia, 1729), that even in a year when servants were in plentiful supply, Mussenden expected to make a profit of £100 from the sale of thirty two servants. Fowler was also allowed the difference if the servants were sold at a higher price. Thus, for those who managed America's flaxseed trade with Ireland, servitude had a commercial importance that was crucial to its success and profitability, especially in the northern part of Ireland.[43]

Most of the £1½ million that was allocated to support the linen industry between 1700 and 1775 was spent in Ulster. By 1770 the province was producing more than 80% of Ireland's total linen output and buying most of America's flaxseed export to Ireland. Belfast had a particularly active trade and by the middle of the 1770s, as much as two thirds of Ulster's direct linen export passed through the port. Derry developed an important connection with the Delaware and between 1736 and 1776, over fifty of the city's merchants had shares in vessels that were registered in Philadelphia, in addition to others that were owned exclusively on the Foyle. Newry's links with America were boosted after the Newry Canal was opened in 1742 and as a result, the port became second to Derry in importing American flaxseed within eight years. Indeed, the flaxseed and linen trades became so central to the regional economies of these

42 Truxes, *Irish-American Trade*, 198–9, 37–8; LC, Blair McClenachan Papers, letter dated 15 Aug. 1774. Elliot is quoted in Thomas M. Truxes, "Connecticut in the Irish-American Flaxseed Trade, 1750–1775," *Eire-Ireland* xii (1977), 37. For bills of exchange, see Jean Agnew, *Belfast Merchant Families in the Seventeenth Century* (Dublin, 1996), 153–9. For the ways in which these bills promoted "elaborate" commercial networks, see Cathy Matson, *Merchants and Empire: Trading in Colonial New York* (Baltimore and London, 1998), 145–6, 152–4, 328–9.

43 PRONI, D354/477. In 1762, 4-year indentures for boys fetched at least £20 each while those for girls were priced at between £16 and £20, see PRONI T138. *BN*, 24 Mar. 1767 claimed that servants from Waterford were sold in Philadelphia at the even better prices of between £30 and £35.

ports that as early as July 1728, Archbishop Hugh Boulter of Armagh (1672–1742) suggested that "the least obstruction in the linen manufacture *by which the North subsists*, must occasion the greater number following." The patterns and flow of emigration confirm this.[44]

Between 1750 and 1775, as many as 442 *direct* sailings to America were advertised from the principal ports of Ulster, of which 32.5% were from Belfast, 28.8% from Derry, 19% from Newry, 13% from Larne, and 6.8% from Portrush. It is difficult to be precise about the number of passengers who actually sailed in these ships. Few official sources have survived. In their absence, historians have relied on other accounts, including the marine entries and clearances which were published in contemporary newspapers and which often gave specific numbers of passengers for individual vessels. Newspapers also advertised a vessel's tonnage, structural features, and agents. Historians have used these sources in different ways. In his seminal *Ulster Emigration to Colonial America 1718–1785* (1966), R.J. Dickson used such published data to estimate that between 1720 and 1774, some 120,000 left the ports of Ulster for colonial America, of whom 37,600 departed between 1771 and 1774. He arrived at his figures after slightly amending the contemporary rule of thumb that "the number of Passengers [is] supposed equal" to a vessel's advertised tonnage. Such tonnages were used to similar purpose by the M.P. for Dublin (1776–97), **Sir Edward Newenham** (1713–1814), when he published his "Accounts of Emigrations from Ireland to America, 25 July 1769 to 25 July 1774" in the (Dublin) *Freeman's Journal* on 5 July 1774. In recent years Dickson's figures have been challenged, especially for the four years before the American Revolution, for which Dickson provided the most detailed data. The main point of Dickson's critics is that because a vessel's tonnage, as advertised in newspapers such as the *Belfast News-Letter* and *Londonderry Journal,* was usually higher than what was *officially registered* for the purposes of levying customs and other duties, it is a poor indicator of passenger flow. As a result, researchers have been encouraged to use officially compiled lists rather than the type of public data which Dickson and others have used to estimate the extent of emigration.[45]

---

44 Truxes, *Irish-American Trade*, 82–3, 276–7, ch. 9; John J. McCusker, "The Pennsylvania Shipping Industry in the Eighteenth Century" (1973), unpublished study in HSP, 285; Gill, *Rise of the Irish Linen Industry*, 185–6. Boulter is quoted from his letter to the duke of Newcastle in Beckett, *Protestant Dissent in Ireland*, 88.

45 Dickson, *Ulster Emigration*, 98, chs. 3–5, 62–4; *Gentleman's Magazine* xliv (1774), 332; *FDJ*, 13 Apr. 1773. For Dickson's detailed "Synopsis of Emigrant Shipping Advertisments, 1771–1775," see his *Ulster Emigration*, 238–71. Criticism of Dickson's figures comes from two sources. Historians such as David Doyle and Kerby Miller believe that Dickson's figures are too low and that, in Doyle's words, up to 10,000 *per annum* left

Such arguments are often overstated. Given the absence of official passenger records, advertised tonnage is an important and accessible way to calculate passenger flow (see Appendix I). However, it must be used with caution. Even Dickson himself recognised that the assumption that the "Number of souls may be reckon's equal to the Tons" should be made only at times of high emigration and that even then, it was not always accepted uncritically by contemporary observers. In this respect, an important qualification was made by the linen inspector, Robert Stephenson, who recorded the vessels which left for America from the ports of Derry, Belfast, Portrush, Larne, and Newry between March 1771 and March 1773. What makes this list uniquely important is that for the port of Belfast, Stephenson recorded not only the *advertised tonnages* of the relevant vessels (4,450 in total) but also the number of *passengers* on board each one (3,161 in total). The result was a ratio not of 1:1, although he was aware of the convention, but of 0.7 passengers per ton. By applying Stephenson's formula, one can thus argue that 26,320 rather than Dickson's figure of 37,600 left Ulster for the continental colonies during the four years (1771–74) which Dickson analysed in detail. Of these, some 3,500 sailed from Belfast between October 1771 and October 1773. Departures from Derry were higher, with about 3,000 leaving during 1773 alone.[46] However, the main conclusions are clear. Firstly, most of those who left Ireland for colonial America did so from Ulster. Secondly, during the decade prior to the American Revolution Ulster's merchants and brokers developed their passenger trade with

Ulster ports between 1771 and 1775; see Doyle, *Irishmen and Revolutionary America*, 53; Miller, *Emigrants and Exiles*, 152. On the other hand, Aaron Fogleman suggests that only some 108,600 left the island *as a whole* between 1700 and 1775; see his "Migrations to the Thirteen British North American Colonies, 1770–1775: New Estimates," *JIntH* xxii, no.4 (1992), 704–9. Fogleman's conclusions have been partly based on Wokeck's research on the Delaware Valley which suggests that on the basis of official statistics for the port of Philadelphia, Dickson's data are too high and that only "about 10,000" immigrants arrived in Philadelphia from *all* Irish ports "in the decade before the Revolution;" see Wokeck, *Trade in Strangers*, 183, 184–5. For a list of the better-known assessments of emigration from Ireland to colonial America, see Henry A. Gemery, "European Emigration to North America, 1700–1820: Numbers and Quasi-Numbers," *Perspectives in American History* new ser. i (1984), 286.

46 Dickson, *Ulster Emigration*, 64, ch. 5; *BN*, 6 Apr. 1773; PRONI, D562/8450; Leroy V. Eid, "'No Freight Paid So Well:' Irish Emigration to Pennsylvania on the Eve of the American Revolution," *Eire-Ireland* xxvii (1993), 39. PRONI has also published Stephenson's lists in *18th Century Emigration* (Belfast, 1972), document no.131. The figure for Derry was arrived at by applying Stephenson's ratio to Derry's advertised outward tonnage (4,250) for 1773. For further consideration of this migration and its estimated flow, see my "Emigration from Ireland to Colonial America, 1760–1775," forthcoming in *Irish Economic and Social History*.

an energy and concentration that was not equalled anywhere else on the island of Ireland.

The data are less detailed for ports outside Ulster where the passenger trade was less tightly organised. However, there was an important seasonal migration to Newfoundland from Waterford and other ports along the southern coast. The numbers involved rose from 2,000 *spailpíní* a year in 1750 to 5,000 in the late-1770s, some of whom later travelled southwards to New England and the middle colonies rather than return to Ireland. Southern brokers also promoted long-term emigration from other southern ports. During the 1720s, for example, Dublin became an important point of departure. However, it was difficult to counter the negative images with which emigration was often associated outside Ulster or to promote the emigrant experience as an alternative to seasonal labour. In any event, the passenger trade in the southern ports was not as integrated into the broader commercial culture as it was in Ulster if only because available cargo space in Dublin and Cork could be filled from a broader commercial inventory. From the middle of the eighteenth century, however, it is clear that the passenger trade, and the servant trade, in particular, was beginning to be managed along increasingly specialist lines in Dublin, Cork, Limerick, and Galway. The number of vessels involved in the American trade also began to increase and, as Audrey Lockhart has recorded, of the 439 ships that left southern ports for America between 1681 and 1775, the majority did so after 1750.[47]

Some of these vessels carried passengers, especially to Philadelphia, New York, and Baltimore. While on his tour in Ireland in the early-1770s, Young noticed this increased flow from southern Ireland. He also noted that during the early-1770s two vessels sailed from Limerick every year with emigrants for America and that there was also a "considerable" emigration from Kerry about the same time. In 1774 it was reported to Parliament that an estimated 1,000 families had "gone beyond the seas" from Galway during the previous two years. Treasury records from the early-1770s reveal that many Irish emigrants often followed the triangular commercial patterns of southern Irish trade and travelled to America through English ports. It is difficult to compute the number of such passengers but together with the direct traffic to America, emigration from southern Ireland amounted to at least 100,000 between 1700 and 1775, including the surge which occurred after 1760.[48]

47 Truxes, *Irish-American Trade*, 135, 137; Dickson, *Ulster Emigration*, 66; Lockhart, *Aspects of Emigration*, 43; Doyle, *Irishmen and Revolutionary America*, 65. The figures for Newfoundland are quoted in John Mannion, "The Waterford Merchants and the Irish-Newfoundland Provisions Trade, 1770–1820" in L.M. Cullen and P. Butel, eds., *Négoce et Industrie en France et en Irlande aux xviiie et xixe siècles* (Paris, 1978), 27.
48 *Arthur Young's Tour of Ireland*, ed., Constantia Maxwell (Cambridge, 1925), 50, 121; *Commons Journals. Ireland* xvi, 412–415; Gerald Fothergill, ed., "Emigrants from

Whether from the north or the south, these emigrants included not just "the poorer sort" who left Ireland "for Want of Work" but also "Farmers whose beneficial Bargains are now become a Rack-Rent too hard to be born [*sic*]." With Ulster in mind, Ezekiel Stewart noted in 1729 that

> y[e] richer sort say that if they stay in Irland their children will be slaves and that it is better for them to make money of their leases while they are worth something to inable them to transport themselves and familys to America, a place where they are sure of better tratment.

The same year, the *Dublin Intelligencer* reported that

> those who have any *ready Money*, or can purchase any, by the Sale of their Goods or Leases, because they find their Fortunes hourly decaying, that their Goods will bear no Price, and that few if any have any *Money* to buy the very Necessaries of Life, are hastening to follow their departed Neighbours.

By 1770 commentators again began to complain about the departure of richer emigrants and on 4 May 1773 the earl of Donegall was informed that what "makes this country wretched ... [is that] we are losing not only considerable sums of money, but a number of the principal manufacture of linen."[49]

This is not to suggest that all those who emigrated during the century were financially secure, a point which was made as follows by the *Londonderry Journal* on 9 April 1773:

> the greatest part of these Emigrants paid their passage, which at £3 10s. each, amounted to £690,725, most of them people employed in the Linen Manufacture or Farmers, and of some property which they turned into money and carried with them; in Evidence of this, it was computed that one Ship last Year, had no less than 4000l. in Specie on board ... till now, it was chiefly the very meanest of the people, that went off mostly in the station of indented servants and such as had become obnoxious to their mother Country.

England, December 1773 to April 1776," *New England Historical and Genealogical Register* lxii–lxv (1908–1911); Doyle, *Irishmen and Revolutionary America*, 61. The Treasury records have been analysed in Bailyn, *Voyagers to the West*, 67–239. For the role of Liverpool in "tapping" the ports of Dublin and Drogheda for colonial emigrants, see Paul G.E. Clemens, "The Rise of Liverpool, 1665–1750," *English Historical Review* 2nd ser, xxix (1976), 213.

49 *The Intelligencer* (Dublin, 1729), 210–11, letter dated 2 Dec. 1728, copy in TCD; PRONI, Castleward Letter; Miller, *Emigrants and Exiles*, 154; PRONI, T1893, George Portis to Donegall, 4 May 1773. For sentiments similar to those expressed by *The Intelligencer*, see Green, "Strange Humours," 17.

Like the 1720s, therefore, when, according to Stewart, "the raisons those unhappy people give for their goeing are as varied as their circomstances," the emigration of the 1770s was drawn from the "middling" sort, as *added* to what continued from the "lower" sort. This kind of social mix characterised the complement of several vessels that sailed for America during the 1770s. The three hundred "passengers and servants" who went on the ship *Wallworth* (Derry to South Carolina, 1773), for example, had been "obliged to leave their country, not for their misbehaviour, but on account of the great distress among the middling and lower class of people." However, whether or not economic misfortune had put them in poor circumstances, many of these emigrants were neither unskilled nor illiterate. Indeed, between 1772 and 1775, the number of skilled emigrants dramatically increased as the troubled linen industry pushed as many as 10,000 weavers out of the country from southern as well as Ulster ports. In 1769 it was reported from Cork that 3,000 looms had "within a very few years fallen into disuse." Small wonder that in the same year, many textile workers sailed on the twenty passenger vessels that were advertised in, or left from Cork for America, or that the Irish House of Commons was told in 1773 that many of those who were then emigrating were taking the reeds and gears of their looms with them.[50] From all parts of Ireland, the "drain" was clear and as the (Philadelphia) *Pennsylvania Journal* suggested on 12 July 1773, "great numbers of vessels from Dublin, Londonderry, Belfast, Learn [*sic*], Cork and other ports, have lately sailed or are soon expected to sail, full of passengers, for different parts of North-America." Thus, the years before the American Revolution not only confronted the imperial presence in government. They also challenged Americans to deal with an influx of immigrants from contemporary Ireland.

The Pull of America

Of the major destinations in colonial America, Maryland was the least appealing. Although Baltimore had been founded in 1729, Annapolis remained the colony's major entry point for most of the eighteenth century and its port books reveal that whereas only 972 Irish arrived there between 1764 and 1769, 5,868 did so during the following six years. 5,104 of these came from non-Ulster ports as opposed to only 764 who did not. This immigration included convicts

50 PRONI, Castleward Letter; *PG*, 11 Aug. 1773; Catherine S. Crary, "The Humble Immigrant and the American Dream: Some Case Histories, 1746–1776," *MVHR* xlvi (1959–60), 49; Lockhart, *Aspects of Emigration*, 58, 54; William O'Sullivan, *The Economic History of Cork City from the Earliest Times to the Act of Union* (Cork, 1937), 194; *Commons Journals. Ireland* xvi, 394.

who were sent to "the only province into which [they] ... may be freely imported," as the surveyor of customs at Annapolis, William Eddis (1738–1825), noted in 1776. It is impossible to give accurate figures for convict immigrants except to observe that the majority were of southern Irish origin and shipped through the ports of Dublin and Cork, the main centres of the convict trade before 1776.[51] Unlike Maryland, Charleston drew most of its emigrants from Ulster, especially through Larne. This traffic owed a lot to the promotions of the 1760s and as a result, the port became the second most attractive American destination for vessels of Ulster origin during that decade. During 1767 and 1768 at least 1,453 and 1,089 Irish settlers availed themselves of South Carolina's programmes of assisted emigration while many others went to Georgia under similar promotions. Although South Carolina cancelled these official initiatives in 1768, the link between Charleston and Larne endured and with the exception of the years of the War of Independence, four to five vessels sailed the route every year until the end of the century, each carrying some two hundred passengers. On 22 October 1772 the *South Carolina Gazette* reported an arrival from Larne, observing that "some other vessels, with a great Number on board, will soon follow this." Many of these passengers travelled in family units and were organised by Presbyterian ministers such as William Martin and William Beatty who acted as local agents for the American trade. However, as Jacob M. Price has put it, Charleston was more a "shipping point" than a "commercial center" or "general *entrepôt*" and many of its Irish immigrants passed through the port *en route* to the backcountry of the Carolinas and Georgia where their presence put a particular cultural stamp on the region.[52]

Colonial New York was also an important destination for Irish emigrants. During the early-1760s, one Robert Pillson sailed there from Newry with "the Encouragement of several of my friends in Ireland." These "friends" included the well-known local American traders, the Corrys, who, as Pillson wrote from New York in 1764, had

> manifested their good Inclinations to serve me, by giving a considerable order for shipping Flaxs[d] ... and for the better enabling me to send my Irish friends such Flaxseed as I know answers that [Irish] Market ... I mean to continue in

51 Eid, "No Freight Paid So Well," 48, n.39, 46, n.34; Doyle, *Irishmen and Revolutionary America*, 98; Ekirch, "Bound for America, 186–7. Eddis is quoted in McCormac, "White Servitude in Maryland," 98.

52 Smith, *White Servitude in Colonial Carolina*, 65–6; (Dublin) *Sleator's Public Gazetteer*, 21 May 1765. Price is quoted in McCusker and Menard, *Economy of British America*, 95. For the Carolina "projects," see Dickson, *Ulster Emigration*, 49–57. For similar schemes in Georgia during the 1760s, see Harold E. Davis, *The Fledgling Province: Social and Cultural Life in Colonial Georgia, 1733–1776* (Chapel Hill, 1976), 22–6.

doing business in the Commission way [and] shall always endeavour to transact it in such a manner as to give my Friends Satisfaction, by holding their property Committed to my care in the highest Esteem, and pay due attention in all respects to their Interest, which I hope will entitle me to the favour of their Commands.

Pillson never became a major figure in New York. However, there were a number of other merchants in New York who traded with Ireland with profit and energy. These included the city's largest house during the 1760s, Greg, Cunningham & Co., which was directed by three partners who had been born in Belfast, while the fourth, Waddell Cunningham, was a native of Co. Antrim. As their colleagues did in Philadelphia, they engaged servants and sold indentures in the usual way. Other agents provided supplementary services. In 1764 one John Coghill, a New York attorney, offered not only "encouragement to servants" and houses to let, but to enter names in "the books of this office gratis, in order to supply Masters and Mistresses who are in want of such [servants], to their satisfaction." By 1774 Solomon Griffiths was involved in a similar business and on 25 April of that year, his firm announced in the *New York Mercury* that it had opened

> a General Registry Office ... [because] great inconveniences hath and does very frequently happen to masters and mistresses of families, for want of knowing where to apply for good servants; and likewise servants where they may get good places ... [and] have their names entered in a book; and servants who desired places paid two shillings for registering.[53]

Although Governor William Tryon (1771–80) reported in 1774 that "passengers and servants" were coming out "annually" from Ireland, it is difficult to quantify the passenger flow into New York. Moreover, other evidence suggests that whereas most of the vessels that sailed from Ulster to Philadelphia carried emigrants, the reverse is true of most of those that left there for the Hudson. Of the twenty advertisements for New York that were carried in the *Belfast News-Letter* between 1771 and 1775, only three sought passengers. Twelve others shared the voyage with destinations in the Delaware which meant that in all probability, at least half the passengers disembarked at Newcastle or Wilmington before the vessels proceeded onwards to the Hudson. However,

---

53 NLI, Ms 10,360 (4), Robert Pillson to Henry Brabazon, dated New York, 5 April 1764; Norman E. Gamble, "The Business Community and Trade of Belfast, 1767–1800" (Ph.D. dissertation, Trinity College, Dublin, 1978), 297 *et passim*; NYHS, Letterbook of Greg & Cunningham, microfilm copy in NLI; *NYGWPB*, 13 Sept. 1764. The *New York Mercury* is quoted in McKee, *Labor in Colonial New York*, 50.

even those who chose to sail directly to New York were often either restricted (in the case of one sailing, to fifty people) or relatively small in number. This confirms other evidence that prior to the American Revolution, the vessels that entered New York from Ireland carried fewer passengers and servants than those that entered Philadelphia and Baltimore. Accordingly, during the last peak of Irish emigration prior to the Revolution (1771–75), New York remained a distant third choice to Philadelphia and Maryland, and may have attracted as few as 3,000 Irish immigrants during that time. As emigration began to rise during the late-1760s the reality was that most Irish emigrants preferred to go to Philadelphia or Maryland, or to the sponsored schemes of Carolina and Georgia, especially if they were "without estate."[54]

By 1760 any significant Irish passenger flow to New England was a distant memory. During the first high point of Irish emigration (1717–20), some 2,600 of the estimated 4,000 people who left Ireland for the continental Americas had sailed from Ulster to New England. Most of these emigrants were Presbyterians who, in the words of one of their ministers, the Rev. James MacGregor, pastor of Aghadowey, Co. Derry, sought in America "an opportunity of worshipping God according to the dictates of conscience and the rules of His inspired Word." In 1718 alone five vessels landed six ministers and 750 people in Boston, of whom the majority were, in Cotton Mather's words, "of so Desirable a character ... [and] from ye north of Ireland." At the time Mather also believed that "Much may be done for the Kingdom of God in these Parts of the World by this Transportation." However, the congenial welcome that these emigrants expected from their co-religionists in America was soon replaced by conflict and friction. As Patrick Griffin's research has shown, the newcomers resented that in America they had to pay the kind of ecclesiastical taxes to a Congregational establishment which they had paid to an Anglican one in Ireland. In any event, as a Boston customs official, Thomas Lechmere put it, it was feared that the "confounded Irish will eat us all up" at a time when provisions "were most extravagantly dear, and scarce." As a result, by 1722/23 even Mather had changed his mind about these new arrivals and regarded as "a marvellous grief unto us ... our United Brethern who have lately come from Ireland unto us ... there have been some who have indecently and ingratefully given much disturbance to the peace of our churches."[55]

54 Tryon, "Report on the State of New York," as quoted in Eid, "No Freight Paid so Well," 53; *BN*, 1 Sept. 1772.
55 Graeme Kirkham, "Ulster Emigration to North America, 1680–1720" in Blethen and Wood, *Ulster and North America*, 76–117; Dickson, *Ulster Emigration*, 23. McGregor is quoted in Miller, Schrier, Boling, and Doyle, eds., *Irish Immigrants in the Land of Canaan*, 436 and Lechmere in Griffin, *People with No Name*, 91. Mather is cited in Charles K.

TIME : Tue 14 Jul 2015 10:05AM
TERMINAL : /28
TITLE : Indians in colonial America /
the forgotten story of America 1750-1800 /
CALL NUMBER : 970.3 Sheff
BARCODE : S10000001153
STATUS : In Transit
PICKUP AT : South Dublin in Ballyroan

Received. Item has hold to be picked up
at South Dublin in Ballyroan.
When it arrives at South Dublin in Ballyroan
to, please check-in item to activate hold

When Irish emigration to New England surged again during the late-1720s, a Boston mob refused to allow vessels from Belfast to land their passengers. Little wonder that in 1729 the Revds. Cornwell of Clogher and Taylor of Ardstraw, Co. Tyrone, two of the Presbyterian ministers who had led the earlier emigration to New England, returned to Ulster, "not finding their acct. in the project:" too many "scandalous & unjust reflections" had been cast on them. The fading appeal of New England was also highlighted by the collapse of a number of settlement schemes which had been promoted in Ireland by "undertakers" such as Robert Edwards and Samuel Waldo. As a result, the governor of Massachusetts, Jonathan Belcher (1730–41), reported that by the time he assumed office, there were "but few Irish" in his colony "and indeed, the people of this country seem to have such an aversion to them, so they find but little encouragement" to go there. In these circumstances, the more tolerant codes of the middle colonies had an even greater allure.[56]

The Attraction of the Delaware

On 25 November 1727 Logan informed his proprietor that "we have from the North of Ireland, great numbers yearly, 8 or 9 ships this last ffal [sic] discharged at Newcastle ... [they] say there will be twice the number next year." Two years later, as some 1,865 entered Philadelphia, he noted that "it looks as if Ireld is to send all its inhabitants hither, for last week not less than six ships arrived." The city's newspapers also commented on the passenger flow from Ireland. On 13 January 1730 the *Pennsylvania Gazette* reported that some "forty five hundred persons, chiefly from Ireland," had arrived during the previous year while two months earlier, it warned that "swarms" of Irish "were being driven over into America" because "their griping avaricious landlords exercise over them the most merciless Racking Tyranny and Oppression." Irish traffic to the Delaware Valley dipped during the 1730s but then, it did from Ireland as a whole and remained relatively low until the years leading up to the American Revolution when nearly a quarter of America's European arrivals were Irish.[57]

Bolton, *Scotch-Irish Pioneers in Ulster and America* (Boston, 1910), 109; and in Griffin, *People with No Name*, 90 and 91. For the entrances into Boston, see James G. Leyburn, "Presbyterians and the American Revolution," *JPrH* liv (1976), 13.

56 Petition of John McMurphy to the lieutenant governor of New Hampshire (1730), as cited in Miller, Schrier, Boling, and Doyle, eds., *Irish Immigrants in the Land of Canaan*, 440; Dickson, *Ulster Emigration*, 127. Belcher is quoted in Truxes, *Irish-American Trade*, 363, n.119. For Cornwell and Taylor, see PRONI, Castleward Letter.

57 *PG*, 20 Nov. 1729. Logan is quoted in Karl Geiser, *Redemptioners and Indentured Servants in the Colony of the Commonwealth of Pennsylvania* (New Haven, 1901), 37, and in HSP, Logan Papers, Letterbook iii, 302, Logan to John Penn. See also Leyburn, *Scotch-Irish:*

By 1765 pre-Revolutionary Philadelphia was, in the words of Adam Gordon, "one of the wonders of the world." Despite its relatively recent foundation (1682–83), the city had bypassed Boston and New York to become the largest city in colonial America with a population of between 20,000 and 30,000 people. It was in a "flourishing Condition" when a French agent visited the city in 1765 with "great numbers of people abound[ing] to it." It had a lucrative flaxseed trade with Ireland, especially after the restrictions on non-enumerated goods were removed in 1731. Whereas in 1729 only 2,000 bushels were exported from Philadelphia to Ireland, by 1739 the volume had increased to 40,000 bushels. It continued to expand and in 1771 the 110,412 bushels that were shipped to Ireland accounted for a seventh of Philadelphia's total overseas export. The tonnage involved also rose and at its height, between 1768 and 1772, the commitment to Ireland (17,404 tons) was only 332 tons less than what cleared for Britain. The managers of these vessels sometimes sold their consignments for bills of exchange that were then used to return manufactured and other goods from British ports. As a result, the inward tonnage from Ireland (9,402 tons) between 1768 and 1772 was much less than the corresponding figure for vessels of British origin (33,407 tons).[58]

Whether by direct or indirect routes, Irish linen and provisions had easy access to the Delaware Valley where they found a ready market. The servant trade was part of this flaxseed-linen circuit and by providing predictable return freights from Ireland, it also gave the region's flaxseed merchants a modicum of security. The Philadelphia firm of Orr, Dunlope & Glenholme spoke for many

---

A Social History, 1962), 236–41; Wayland F. Dunaway, *The Scotch-Irish of Colonial Pennsylvania* (Chapel Hill, 1944), 47–9.

58 Howard H. Peckham, ed., "Journal of Lord Adam Gordon" in *Narratives of Colonial America, 1704–1765* (Chicago, 1971), 259, 262; "Journal of a French Traveller in the Colonies, 1765," *AHR*, xxvii (1921) as quoted in Whitfield J. Bell Jr., "Some Aspects of the Social History of Pennsylvania, 1760–1790," *PMHB* lxii (1938), 282; HSP, Society Miscellaneous Collection, Box 13-A, fol. 1; Regin F. Duvall, "Philadelphia's Maritime Commerce with the British Empire, 1783–1789" (Ph.D. dissertation, University of Pennsylvania), 6, 29–30; James G. Lydon, "Philadelphia's Commercial Expansion, 1720–1739," *PMHB* lxxxi (1967), 408–9; Virginia D. Harrington, *The New York Merchant on the Eve of the Revolution* (New York, 1935), 359–68; Stuart Bruchey, ed., *The Colonial Merchant: Sources and Readings* (New York, 1966), 16–18. For figures on the population of Philadelphia, Southwark and the Northern Liberties, see Billy G. Smith "Death and Life in a Colonial Immigrant City: A Demographic Analysis of Philadelphia," *JEH* xxxvii (Dec 1977), 863–889. Here, Smith gives a figure of 25,744 for 1769, rising to 32,073 in 1775. For more general comment on the evolution of Philadelphia, see Carl and Jessica Bridenbaugh, *Rebels and Gentlemen: Philadelphia in the Age of Franklin* (New York, 1942) and Gary B. Nash, *The Urban Crucible: Social Change, Political Consciousness, and the Origins of the American Revolution* (Cambridge, Mass., 1979).

when in July 1767 it directed its Dublin correspondent, Lane, Benson & Vaughan, to

> use your utmost endeavours to dispatch her [the ship *Philadelphia*] out here again as she will have little enough time to return here before the Flaxseed season comes on, which is very material to us … We expect you'll do what lies in your power to procure all the servants you can for her.

Accordingly, merchants, ship captains, and their agents traded in people as they did in any commodity. As Dickson has noted,

> In the eighteenth century the sale of a passage to America was regarded in the same light as the sale of household goods, and both lines of business were transacted by the same merchants in the same shop. For example, a person could purchase, according to inclination, a pound of garden seeds or a passage to America from McKedy and Elder at the sign of the Orange Tree in High Street, Belfast.[59]

In Philadelphia, the merchants who were involved in this trade operated through networks of personal, family, and church connections that spanned the Atlantic. By 1775 at least thirty of the city's merchants had established interests in the Irish trade. Of these, George Dunlope and William Glenholme corresponded with Andrew Orr as well as with their extended families and friends in Belfast and Dublin; Benjamin Fuller with, among others, his brother in Cork; and the Derry-born Blair McClenachan with a number of agents in his native city and beyond. Samuel and Thomas Morton were but two of Philadelphia's Quaker merchants who traded with Ireland. Their main Irish connection was a cousin, Thomas Greer of Dungannon, with whom they developed "commodity exchanges" that, in J.W. McConaghy's words, "displayed in miniature" some of the characteristics of Irish American commerce in general, especially after the bounty acts were passed in 1743 and 1745.[60] As in New York, the interests of

---

59 HSP, Orr, Dunlope & Glenholme Letterbook (1767–9), letter dated Philadelphia, 26 July 1767; Dickson, *Ulster Emigration*, 110.

60 Robert East, *Business Enterprise in the American Revolutionary Era* (New York, 1938), 17; Truxes, *Irish-American Commerce*, 121; J.W. McConaghy, "Thomas Greer of Dungannon (1724–1803), Quaker Linen Merchant" (Ph.D. dissertation, Queen's University, Belfast, 1979), 124–52. For a general treatment of the context and importance of these networks, see Bridenbaugh, *Rebels and Gentlemen*, ch. 6; Thomas M. Doerflinger, *A Vigorous Spirit of Enterprise: Merchants and Economic Development in Revolutionary Philadelphia* (Chapel Hill, 1986); Frederick B. Tolles, *Meeting House and Counting House: The Quaker Merchants of Colonial Philadelphia, 1682–1763* (Chapel Hill, 1948), 85–143, and *Quakers and the Atlantic Culture* (New York, 1960), especially ch. 2. For the importance of family,

these merchants were dominated by flaxseed which by 1737, had, in the words of John Reynell, "grown a very considerable branch of [the] trade" of the Delaware. During the 1740s and 1750s much of this business was handled by two Ulster-born immigrants, Samuel Carson and Andrew Caldwell. Writing in October 1748, the firm of Davey & Carson listed four agents in Strabane and three in Derry to whom it sent flaxseed and rum in return for linen and woollen goods. In November 1749 the firm acknowledged the arrival of the ship *City of Derry* "with Redemptioners on board." In return, 500 to 600 hogsheads of flaxseed, rum, lumber, and pig-iron were sent to Vance, Gregg and Caldwell in Derry. In 1766 Davey & Carson was reconstituted as Carson, Barclay & Mitchell but it was soon superceded as Philadelphia's principal Irish house by Conyngham & Nesbitt which had also been founded by two Ulstermen, John Maxwell Nesbitt and Redmond Conyngham.[61]

The Irish trade also involved the Delaware ports of Newcastle and Wilmington, especially where indentured servants were concerned. These two outer ports had grown in importance, firstly, after Pennsylvania imposed duties on incoming servants in 1729 and secondly, because Delaware's quarantine regime for incoming immigrants was not as strict as that of Pennsylvania. As a result, a number of passengers disembarked in Delaware and completed their journeys to Philadelphia overland or by tender. Because of its location, Newcastle was the more important first port of call. By 1682 it had a weekly market, by 1704, the seat of Delaware's government and in 1765 it was reputed to be "next to Philadelphia." It also developed early and enduring commercial and religious links with Ulster merchants and had the oldest Presbyterian church in the greater Philadelphia area. Indeed, the connection with Ulster was so strong that in 1723 an Anglican missionary reported that "the Church at Newcastle is environed with great numbers of Dissenters than ever, by reason of these fresh recruits sent [to] us of late from the north of Ireland." Thus, it was not unusual for Irish vessels, especially those which had sailed from Ulster, to stop at Newcastle and although it is impossible to quantify the disembarkation rate there in any definitive way, scattered sources suggest that in some cases from the 1750s, it may have been as high as 50% of the ship's list. To quote one example among many, half of the 500 passengers who sailed on the ship *Needham* (Newry to Newcastle and New York, 1773) landed at Newcastle

religious ties, acquaintances, and friendships in determining factoral relationships, see Arthur L. Jensen, *Maritime Commerce of Colonial Philadelphia* (Madison, 1963), 18, 85–7.

61 LC, Davey & Carson Letterbook (1745–50), letters to David Harvey, dated 28 Oct. 1748 and 21 Nov. 1749. Reynell is quoted in Jensen, *Maritime Commerce of Colonial Philadelphia*, 86. For Conyngham & Nesbitt, see *The Reminiscences of David Hayfield Conyngham*, ed. Horace Edwin Hayden (n.p., n.d.), copy in HSP.

before the vessel proceeded to New York.[62] However, many others proceeded onwards to Philadelphia with their complete complement.

The port of Wilmington was better appointed than Newcastle although in 1750 it was dismissed as an "upstart village lying in a neighbouring creek." However, like Newcastle, it had become a major *entrée* into the Delaware Valley by 1770 and in all likelihood, the vessels that stopped there also landed up to half their passengers. Wilmington had important commercial ties with Ireland. The ship *Wilmington*, built in 1741 to inaugurate the port's trade with the West Indies, was a joint venture with a group of Belfast merchants. The port was also part of the broader commercial culture of Philadelphia and its hinterland and there were close links between the two places. Although the relationship between the two Delaware ports and Philadelphia varied, there is no doubt about the intermediary importance of both Newcastle and Wilmington for traffic upriver as well as to other points to the north, west, and south. This two-step approach to cities like Philadelphia and Baltimore was not always welcomed. In 1722, for example, the preamble of Pennsylvania's Convict Act complained that

> it hath been a practice for masters of vessels, merchants and others trading in this province, with intent to avoid complying with the payment of duties, and giving the security [in Pennsylvania] ... to land their passengers, servants and convicts in some of the adjacent governments [Delaware], which passengers, have afterwards been secretly brought into this province.

Along similar lines, a law that was passed by Maryland in 1755 to prevent the "importation" of Catholics, "Popish Priests and Jesuits" noted that

> great Complaint has been made to this General Assembly of the great Number of Irish Papists imported into this Province [Maryland], by way of New-Castle, on Delaware, where they are purchased and brought into this Province, and sold ... particularly [in] ... the Northern Parts, where the said Irish Papists are chiefly disposed of, and by which means the several Laws for preventing too great an Importation of Irish Papists into this Province, are in great Measure evaded.[63]

62 James A. Monroe, *Colonial Delaware: A History* (Millwood, N.Y., 1978), 94, 23; "Journal of a French Traveller in the Colonies, 1765," 77; Guy S. Klett, "The Presbyterian Church and the Scotch-Irish on the Pennsylvania Colonial Frontier," *PH* viii (1941), 98–9; *PP*, 5 Aug. 1773. For contact between Delaware and Ulster, see Eid, "No Freight Paid so Well," 47; Sally Guertler Ferris, "The Wilmington Merchant, 1775–1815" (M.A. dissertation, University of Delaware, 1961), 23 *et passim*; and Monroe, *Colonial Delaware*, 161–7.

63 Ferris, "Wilmington Merchant," 8; Ramon S. Powers, "Wealth and Poverty: Economic Base, Social Structure, and Attitudes in Pre-Revolutionary Pennsylvania, New Jersey and

In eighteenth-century Irish newspapers, especially in Ulster, the preference for the Delaware and, in particular, for Philadelphia, is obvious and consistent. Between 1750 and 1775, 53.5% of the American-bound vessels that advertised for "passengers and freight" in the *Belfast News-Letter* gave Philadelphia as their destination. Ulster's passenger traffic also rose during this period. This was especially true for the period between 1771 and 1774, for which Dickson estimated that some 20,680 left for the Delaware. Marianne Wokeck has suggested that this figure has been exaggerated and that only 6,902 arrived there during these four years. In part, the differences between the two calculations can be explained by Dickson's use of advertised tonnage, or *tonnage burden*, and other published data, to calculate the passenger flow. Wokeck relied on officially-recorded tonnages as well as on a passenger list which the prominent Philadelphia physician, Thomas Cadwalader (1707–74), compiled for his home port between 29 August 1768 and 13 May 1772. The sources which each of these historians has used have limitations and these are discussed in Appendix I. In making my own calculations of emigration from Ulster, I have used passenger figures for individual vessels which in the main, were published in contemporary news-papers, to suggest that at least 18,600 left the northern province for the ports of the Delaware valley between 1771 and 1774 (see Appendix III). From these figures, it is clear that regular shippers of emigrants preferred to focus on Ulster ports. Leroy V. Eid has noted that the converse is true of emigration to contemporary Annapolis, with which the ports of southern Ireland had long-established connections. Thus, traditional links and preferences continued to colour the regional origins of Irish emigrants to America in the late-colonial period.[64]

As the Delaware Valley includes the ports of Newcastle and Wilmington, as well as Philadelphia, my figures for Ulster's late-eighteenth-century emigration

Delaware" (Ph.D. dissertation, University of Kansas, 1971), 125–7; Dickson, *Ulster Emigration*, 225; *Stats. at Large Pa.* iv, 135–60; Richard J. Purcell, "Irish Settlers in Early Delaware," *PH* xiii (1947), 95; *Stats. at Large Pa.* iv, 137; *Arch. Md.* lii (1755–6), 92. For the political and economic origins of the rivalry between Philadelphia and Delaware, see Robert W. Johannsen, "The Conflict between the Three Lower Counties on the Delaware and the Province of Pennsylvania, 1682–1704," *DH* v (1952), 96–132; and Mary Alice Hanna, *Trade of the Delaware District before the Revolution* (Northampton, 1917).

64 Dickson, *Ulster Emigration*, 225; Wokeck, *Trade in Strangers*, 173, 179–84; HSP, Cadwalader Collection. Box 15T (Thomas Cadwalader Section), Philadelphia Custom House, Passenger Lists, 29 Aug. 1768–13 May 1772. Dickson's figure for the Delaware has been computed on the basis that it is 55% of his total; see his *Ulster Emigration*, 64, 225. Eid, "No Freight Paid So Well." For the complexities and varieties of tonnage, and their relevance to the passenger trade, see Doerflinger, *Vigorous Spirit of Enterprise*, 88–9; McCusker, "The Pennsylvania Shipping Industry in the Eighteenth Century;" and Appendix I.

are for the region as a whole. However, while the general importance of the
Delaware stopover is clear, beyond that, it impossible to quantify in any
definitive way a preference to continue from there to Philadelphia, as opposed
to one to New Jersey, Maryland, the backcountry of Pennsylvania, Maryland,
or even the Carolinas. All that can be said is that at least 18,600 passengers of
Ulster origin sailed into the ports of the Delaware Valley between 1771 and 1774
and that it is likely that at least half of these continued their journey upriver to
Philadelphia. Over the same period, at the very least, another 1,683 entered
Philadelphia from southern Irish ports although given the shortcomings of the
sources from which this figure has been derived, it is probable that the flow from
southern Ireland may have been two or even three times that figure (see
Appendix IV). In total therefore, at least 11,600 entered Philadelphia from both
parts of Ireland during the four years, 1771 to 1774. However, given the custom
to count "passengers" rather than "souls", this is a conservative estimate.[65]

The merchants who managed this traffic also promoted the burgeoning city
of Philadelphia, especially after 1730, when Pennsylvania's booming economy
created opportunities for unskilled as well as skilled labour. As a result, many
Irish servants advertised their skills as craftsmen and tradesmen both before and
after they sailed for America. For example, after the **snow** *Betsey* (Dublin to
Philadelphia, 1766) docked in Philadelphia, the *Pennsylvania Journal* noted that
the vessel had carried

> a parcel of Healthy likely SERVANT MEN, WOMEN, AND BOYS, Mostly Country
> bred; among whom are the following tradesmen, Carpenters, Bricklayers,
> Masons, Blacksmiths, Taylors, Coopers, Hatters, Silversmiths, Weavers,
> Shoemakers, Barbers, Butchers, Brushmakers, &c. &c.[66]

As the Revolution approached, such reports became more common in the city's
newspapers as the flow of Irish emigrants increased. These emigrants possessed
varying skills and abilities, some of which are reflected in the two official lists of
indenture which survive from colonial Philadelphia. The first of these covers
the period between 23 October 1745 and 7 October 1746 and lists the indentures
of servants and redemptioners which were agreed before the then mayor of
Philadelphia, James Hamilton. Of the 498 Irish servants whose names were
taken at that time, 39.75% were bound to purchasers in Philadelphia city and

---

65 Eid, "No Freight Paid so Well," 38, n.14, 48 n.39. See Appendices III and IV.
66 *PJ*, 19 May 1766. Various skills were also assigned to the passengers of the ship *Needham*
    (Newry to Philadelphia, 1773) in *PJ*, 14 Aug. 1773; the brig *Conolly* (Dublin to
    Philadelphia, 1772) in *PJ*, 21 Oct. 1772 and the brig *Patty* (Cork to Philadelphia, 1772) in
    PG, 30 April 1772 while from the ship *Neptune* (Dublin to Philadelphia, 1764), no less
    than 28 different occupations were listed in *PJ*, 15 Aug. 1765.

county, 32.93% to Chester and Lancaster counties, and 6.63% to Burlington and Gloucester counties, New Jersey. It is clear that while there was a demand for general labourers to service the development of the agricultural hinterland, most of the contracts of these servants were redeemed in the greater Philadelphia area. In 1772 the times of several farmers from the **brig** *Patty* (Cork to Philadelphia) were also offered alongside those of "sundry tradesmen, such as smiths, nail-makers, shoe-makers, taylors, skinners [and] carpenters" and some of these immigrants are listed in the second official record which covers the period between October 1771 and October 1773. Of the 846 servants who were named in this particular list, Irish and Germans accounted for roughly equal proportions of 40%. However, the urban preferences of Irish servants is even more striking than it was in 1745–46. The same can be said of the 273 Irish redemptioners who were documented during the early-1770s.[67]

These two official records of indentures also show that by 1772–73 Irish servants were more likely to come from Ulster than from elsewhere in Ireland. This is not surprising, given the extent to which the passenger trade was organised in the province, as well as the high number of vessels which sailed from there for America. Ironically, the relatively low number of vessels which were engaged in the passenger trade from southern Ireland also helps to explain why the number of servants per vessel was higher on vessels from that part of Ireland. Thus, Farley Grubb's analysis of the regional origins of the servants whose indentures and ports of origin were registered between May 1772 and October 1773 shows that although only 16% of Irish vessels came from southern ports during these months, they ferried 31% of the listed servants. On the other hand, vessels of Ulster origin carried 28% of the servants but in this case, they were scattered over 44% of the vessels. Moreover, whereas emigrant

67 HSP, AM. 3091, "List of Servants and Apprentices Bound and Assigned before James Hamilton, Mayor of Philadelphia, 1745–46"; *PG*, 7 May 1772; HSP, "Record of Indentures ... October 3 1771 to October 5 1773"; Farley Grubb, "Immigrant Servant Labor: Their Occupational and Geographic Distribution in the Late-Eighteenth-Century Mid-Atlantic Economy," *Social Science History* ix (1985), 257, 253, 256; Grubb, "The Market for Indentured Immigrants: Evidence on the Efficiency of Forward-Labor Contracting in Philadelphia, 1745–1773," *JEH* xlv (1985) 859, n.12; Robert O. Heavner, "Economic Aspects of Indentured Servitude in Colonial Philadelphia" (Ph.D. dissertation, Stanford University, 1976), 43–4; Nash, *Urban Crucible*, 247; Doyle, *Irishmen and Revolutionary America*, 68–9; Grubb, "British Immigration to Philadelphia," 123, 121. Although differing from Grubb in her numerical conclusions, Salinger's analysis of the indentures led her to conclude that by the middle of the eighteenth century, servitude in the Philadelphia area "seems to have been overwhelmingly an urban institution"; see Sharon V. Salinger, "Colonial Labor in Transition: The Decline of Indentured Servitude in Late Eighteenth-Century Philadelphia," *Labor History* xxii (1981), 167–8.

vessels from Ulster carried a better mix of rich and poor, servant, and "passenger," those from southern Ireland took people who were more likely to be poorer than their Ulster counterparts. Southerners were also more likely to be single, a status that contemporary writers often equated with being poor. In contrast, commentaries on emigration from Ulster sometimes referred to the high number of families who were leaving. Since families were generally deemed to be able to pay the costs of passage, reporters characterised at least some of Ulster's emigrants as people "of substance." This point is also suggested by the fact that of the relatively high number (34.5%) of *Irish* redemptioner contracts in the 1771–73 records, the vast majority had come from Ulster.[68]

In Philadelphia, those who traded in indentures did not mind where their Irish servants came from. However, they were clear what type of person they wanted. In November 1765, Benjamin Marshall advised Dublin's Barnaby Egan that "should thee have a mind to send a Vessel this way [Philadelphia] … Stout able Labouring men & Tradesmen out of the Country with *Young Boys & Lads* answers best." Marshall's preferences were neither new nor peculiar to him. Indeed, they were already reflected in the 1745–46 records which show that only 13.5% of the recorded indentures relate to women or girls. Egan gave Marshall what he wanted but it is also worth noting that during the 1760s, some American masters were beginning to prefer German servants and to regard the Irish as unreliable. Given that the Germans were more likely to have arrived as redemptioners, many supposed that family and other ties made them less likely to run away. In contrast, many of the Irish were single and thus, presumably less attached to their master or the terms of their contracts. During the 1760s and 1770s these biases were borne out by the fact that the tendency to abscond was highest among the Irish. Of the list of runaways that Robert Heavner compiled from the *Pennsylvania Packet* (1771–73), 51 of the 90 who were labelled by nationality were Irish. More pointedly, David Doyle has concluded that of a sample that he has studied from the early-1770s, two thirds were "native" as opposed to **Scots-Irish**. The implication is that southern Irish servants had a poorer reputation than those from Ulster and that as the numbers increased from Dublin and Cork, they tainted the name of the Irish as a whole at a time when increasing numbers of German immigrants were competing for contracts.[69]

---

68 Grubb, "Immigrant Servant Labor," 274, n.10; Farley A. Grubb, "Immigration and Servitude in the Colony and Commonwealth of Pennsylvania: A Quantitative and Economic Analysis" (Ph.D. dissertation, University of Chicago, 1984), 323, 170; Doyle, *Irishmen and Revolutionary America*, 70.

69 "Extracts from the Letter-Book of Benjamin Marshall, 1763–1766," ed. Thomas

In these circumstances, those who were involved in the Irish servant trade were asked to ensure that their charges were aware of their contractual responsibilities. Agents and brokers in Ireland were also advised that "the best times for [sending] servants is about the month of May." To arrive at this time of the year was advantageous for the merchant as well as the servant. For the former, it was the most profitable time to sell Irish linens; for the latter, labour contracts were usually of shorter duration than those that were offered in the Autumn. Shippers also preferred a landing in May because it would allow two trips to be made in a given year, thus helping to maximise profits. As one correspondent put it, "follow the Example of our Londonderry merch[ts]" who more than most others, thrived on Ulster's connections with Philadelphia by managing such twice-yearly voyages. Given that between 1771 and 1773, only about 19% of Philadelphia's vessels from Ireland arrived during May and June, it seems that Marshall's advice was not heeded. This is also reflected in the indices of monthly servant sales for 1771–73 which show that the busiest months for registering the contracts of Irish servants were September (26.1%), July (23.2%), August (18.4%), and June (11%), followed by May (4.8%) and October (4.2%). However, Irish servant labour remained competitive and the flow from Ireland continued into the Delaware Valley until the outbreak of the American Revolution, and beyond.[70]

During the colonial period each American destination generated its own appeal for Irish emigrants. However, the ways in which they were perceived by potential emigrants did not stand still. The fate of those Irish Presbyterians who settled in early-eighteenth-century New England is a reminder of how, on both sides of the Atlantic, things could change. Massachusetts was not unique in this respect. The immigration policies of colonial South Carolina and Maryland also reflected their respective cultures while the more pluralist attitudes of the

Stewardson, *PMHB* xx (1896), 210; Marianne Wokeck, "Irish Immigration to the Delaware Valley before the American Revolution," *Proceedings of the Royal Irish Academy* xcvi (1996), 117; Heavner, "Economic Aspects of Indentured Servitude" 78; Doyle, *Irishmen and Revolutionary America*, 70. Of the 165 runaways who were advertised in New Jersey newspapers between 1751 and 1755, 60 were Irish, 30 were black slaves, and 22 were English; see Geiser, *Redemptioners and Indentured Servants*, 81.

70 Benjamin Marshall (Philadelphia) to Thomas Murphy (Dublin), November 1765, as quoted in Heavner, "Economic Aspects of Indentured Servitude," 38; LC, Davey & Carson Letterbook, to Robert Travers, dated 5 June 1746; Eid, "No Freight Paid So Well," 39–40; Heavner, "Economic Aspects of Indentured Servitude," 39. The correspondent is quoted in Truxes, *Irish-American Trade*, 136. In a similar vein, New York's Hugh Wallace advised Daniel Mussenden in Belfast in 1755 that while demand for linens was especially keen in April and May, "in y[e] Fall there is no selling Linnens at any Advantage," quoted in Truxes, *Irish-American Trade*, 188.

middle colonies influenced the terms on which people might settle there. In each of these regions, economic and commercial connections added a further dimension to the ways in which the colonies were perceived and for the travelling public, provided an access that was easier and wider than what was available a century earlier. To this extent, the ideological inheritance of the old world planter was slowly superseded by the pragmatism of the new world entrepreneur. These developments were also reflected in the ways in which the passenger trade changed, especially during the final quarter of the eighteenth century.

CHAPTER TWO

Immigrants and the Polity in Pennsylvania, 1760–90

Despite the crucial and acknowledged influences of Boston, New York, and Charleston on the development of colonial America, it was Philadelphia which provided the stage from which the new republic was proclaimed and moulded. As a city which was roughly halfway between Boston and Charleston, it was a natural choice for the Continental (1774–81) and Confederation (1781–89) Congresses and thereafter, for the nation's capital (1790–1800). However, it was also the centre of active city and provincial governments which, true to the intentions of their founder, had tried to encourage the expectations and status of the individual while ensuring the stability and harmony of the community as a whole. To this extent, Penn's creation was more than a casual choice as the Founding Fathers tried to redesign the polity of America. As George Washington recognised "the unequalled privilege of choosing our own political institutions, and of *improving upon the experience of mankind* in the formation of a confederated government," he could see how Pennsylvania had handled similar challenges, especially during the 1760s and 1780s, and how it had responded when the inherited languages, perceptions, and cultures of politics and representation had been put under strain. He could also learn from the ways in which it had managed contemporary debates on who could, or should, participate in public life. In a city such as Philadelphia which continued to attract a steady stream of people from Ireland, the implications for the political status of immigrants are obvious, especially as "ethno-cultural" rhetoric and organisation increasingly interacted with the evolving "first party system."[1] To this extent, Philadelphia was more than a mere theatre for the orators and thinkers who emerged from the American Revolution. It was a laboratory where local, regional, and national politics interacted.

---

1   Jared Sparks, ed., *The Writings of George Washington* 12 vols. (Boston, 1834–7) ix, 400, Washington to Newenham, 20 July 1788. The italics are mine. For Newenham, including his influential connections in America, see James Kelly, *Sir Edward Newenham, M.P., 1713–1814: Defender of the Protestant Constitution* (Dublin, 2003). For the historiography of the first party system, see xvii, n.18, above.

Colonial Legacies

A number of historians have examined the English origins of colonial politics and, in particular, the experience of "party" and "faction."[2] Many of these accept J.C.D. Clark's view of party as a collection of individuals who sought to further their respective interests but who were also influenced by ideology as well as by political practice. The Whigs and Tories of the early-eighteenth century satisfy these criteria.[3] However, the broad acceptance of the Whig ascendancy during the course of the century discouraged the development of competing parties and promoted instead the growth of factional associations based on friendships, family, mutual likes and dislikes, or common interests as a more effective means to achieve political influence and advancement. Such factions were fickle as well as pragmatic, coming together to get into power and then, once there, to reward their "connections" with office. They also reinforced the oligarchic character of English politics and the system of deference and clientilism that informed it. In these circumstances, a classic party system was anathema for most of the eighteenth century and, where party was regarded at all, it was discussed as part of a bland political or "anti-party" landscape.[4]

2 For an edition of selected writings, together with critical commentary, on eighteenth-century English political organisation, see Alan Beattie, *English Party Politics, Volume I, 1660–1906* (London, 1970); and J.A.W. Gunn, *Factions No More: Attitudes to Party in Government and Opposition in Eighteenth-Century England* (London, 1972). Pasi Ihalainen, *The Discourse on Political Pluralism in Early Eighteenth-Century England* (Helsinki, 1999) offers a conceptual study of "party" and "faction" as well as an analysis of relevant historiography, as does the J.C.D. Clark, *English Society, 1688–1832* (Cambridge, 1985), 8–41. See also Terence Ball, James Farr, and Russell L. Hanson, eds., *Political Innovation and Conceptual Change* (Cambridge, 1989); and H.T. Dickinson, *The Politics of the People in Eighteenth-Century Britain* (London, 1977).

3 J.C.D. Clark, *The Dynamics of Change: The Crisis of the 1750s and English Party Systems* (Cambridge, 1982), and *English Society, 1688–1832*. Some of the relevant historiography is assessed in Richard R. Johnson, "Politics Redefined: An Assessment of Recent Writings on the Late Stuart Period of English History, 1660 to 1724," *WMQ* xxxv (1978), 691–732; and J.V. Beckett, "Introduction: Stability in Politics and Society, 1680–1750" in Clyve Jones, ed., *Britain in the First Age of Party, 1680–1750: Essays Presented to Geoffrey Holmes* (London, 1987), 1–18. See also Geoffrey Holmes, *British Politics in the Age of Anne* (New York, 1967); J.H. Plumb, *The Growth of Political Stability in England, 1675–1725* (London, 1967); Robert Willman, "The Origins of 'Whig' and 'Tory' in English Political Language," *HistJ* xvii (1974), 247–64; and Tim Harris, "From Rage of Party to Age of Oligarchy? Rethinking the Later Stuart and Early Hanoverian Period," *JMH* lxiv (1992), 700–20.

4 For a review of relevant writings, see Frank O'Gorman, "The Recent Historiography of the Hanoverian Regime," *HistJ* xxix (1986), 1005–20, and "Approaches to Hanoverian Society," *ibid.* xxxix (1996), 521–34. The literature on this topic is extensive. For the classic interpretation, see Lewis B. Namier, *The Structure of Politics at the Accession of George III* (London, 1955) and *England in the Age of the American Revolution* (New York, 1966), in which Namier argued that political organisation was driven by individualist

In colonial America, the polity reflected many of these characteristics of old England and, in the words of Benjamin Newcomb, its leaders derived from English thought and practice "ambivalent moral lessons about parties."[5] This was especially true in Pennsylvania where the Quaker founders of the colony took up the single-interest paradigm with relative ease. Not only were they committed Whigs but implicit in their "holy experiment" was the claim that society needed only one "morally superior" interest group, a view that was also held within the contemporary Irish establishment. As already discussed in the first chapter, this notion had been central to the ideological impetus to empire during the sixteenth and seventeenth centuries and had justified the metropolis as the oracle of the political constitution of both centre and periphery. Even as the political elites of the colonies began to question aspects of their broader relationships within the empire, their commitment to the idea of the single-interest polity continued even after the original characterisation of "natural leadership" had apparently lost much of its relevance and where, as in eighteenth-century Pennsylvania, those who had initially promoted the colony, in this case, the Quakers, were no longer the largest community. However, the terms "majority" and "minority" are more appropriate to more modern times than to colonial America. In the event, the Quaker leadership continued for much of the century, if only because, as Alan Tully has suggested, the other significant groupings within Pennsylvania, the Scots-Irish and Germans, "simply attached themselves to *existing* interest networks and worked *within* the established parameters of political behavior."[6]

rather than ideological concerns. For an assessment of Namier's views, see John A. Cannon, *Parliamentary Reform, 1640–1832* (Cambridge, 1973); and Frank O'Gorman, *The Emergence of the British Two-Party System* (London, 1982). Among other works, see also Archibald S. Foord, *His Majesty's Opposition, 1714–1830* (Oxford, 1964); John Brewer, *Party Politics and Popular Politics at the Accession of George III* (Cambridge, 1976); Linda Colley, *In Defiance of Oligarchy: The Tory Party, 1714–60* (Cambridge, 1982); Frank O'Gorman, "Party in the Later Eighteenth Century" in John A. Cannon, *The Whig Ascendancy: Colloquies on Hanoverian England* (London, 1981), 77–89; B.W. Hill, *British Parliamentary Parties, 1742–1832* (London, 1985); and Geoffrey Holmes and Daniel Szechi, *The Age of Oligarchy: Pre-Industrial Britain, 1722–1783* (London, 1993).

5   Benjamin Newcomb, *Franklin and Galloway: A Political Partnership* (New Haven, 1972), 9. See also J.R. Pole, *Political Representation in England and the Origins of the American Republic* (New York, 1966); J.C.D. Clark, *The Language of Liberty 1660–1832. Political Discourse and Social Dynamics in the Anglo-American World* (Cambridge, 1994); and Greene, *Peripheries and Center*, and "The Plunge of Lemmings: a Consideration of Recent Writings on British Politics and the American Revolution" in *South Atlantic Quarterly* lxvii (1968), 141–75. For a discussion of the English background to partisan politics in America and in particular, the influence of Bolingbroke's *Idea of a Patriot King*, see Elkins and McKittrick, *Age of Federalism*, 257–302; and H.T. Dickinson, *Bolingbroke* (London, 1970), 260–6.

6   Richard Bauman, *For the Reputation of Truth: Politics, Religion, and Conflict among the*

Within this system, politics in colonial Pennsylvania were also driven by rivalries between factional interests, each of which was internally linked by family, business, and other ties. Since the colony was founded, Quakers had controlled the assembly and co-operated with the proprietors, the Penn family, on the understanding that they were allowed to dominate local government and the patronage which this brought. The supporters of the proprietor drew their strength from the provincial council. As William Hanna has observed, their interest was "a loose, very informal congeries of men, interests, and factions ... Similar to an English political group, it was formed out of a collection of independent interests directed by some great man or aristocratic clique desiring power." Relationships between the two interests were practical but never secure or predictable. Thus, when Thomas Penn (1702–75) tried to reassert his family's influence over the province and at least initially, refused to pay taxes on his estates and claims, the Quaker interest asked London in 1764 to end the proprietorship altogether and to designate Pennsylvania as a royal province. What on one level was a major proposal on governance was on another, little more than a stratagem to control the disposal of remunerative offices and positions. Moreover, while the relevant personalities changed from time to time, this "narrow" system of political leadership continued in Pennsylvania until the outbreak of the American Revolution which for many "proprietors and proprietary officers, their dependents and connexions" amounted, in the words of Thomas Gordon, to no more than a "loss of official emolument and influence."[7]

Pennsylvania Quakers, 1750–1800 (Baltimore, 1971), 2, 13–17; Alan Tully, "Englishmen and Germans: National Group-Contact in Colonial Pennsylvania, 1700–1755," *PH* xlv (1978), 240, italics mine. For the single interest polity, as applied to Pennsylvania, see Douglas M. Arnold, *A Republican Revolution: Ideology and Politics in Pennsylvania, 1776–1790* (New York and London, 1989); and Ryerson, "Republican Theory and Partisan Reality in Revolutionary Pennsylvania," 95–132.

7 Gordon is quoted in Bauman, *For the Reputation of Truth*, 94. See also William Hanna, *Benjamin Franklin and Pennsylvania Politics* (Stanford, 1964); Theodore Thayer, *Pennsylvania Politics, and the Growth of Democracy, 1740–1776* (Harrisburg, 1953); Wayne L. Bockelman, "Local Government in Pennsylvania" in Bruce C. Daniels, ed., *Town and Country: Essays on the Structure of Local Government in the American Colonies* (Middletown, 1978), 216–37; and Tully, *Forming American Politics*. For Thomas Penn's use of "remunerative office" to reinforce his interest, see G.B. Warden, "The Proprietary Group in Pennsylvania, 1754–1764," *WMQ* xxi (1964), 367–89. See also Alan Tully, "Quaker Party and Proprietary Policies: The Dynamics of Politics in pre-Revolutionary Pennsylvania, 1730–1775" in Bruce C. Daniels ed., *Power and Status: Officeholding in Colonial America* (Middletown, Conn., 1986), 75–105; and James H. Hutson, "The Campaign to Make Pennsylvania a Royal Province, 1764–1770," *PMHB* xciv (1970), 427–63. For the Quaker and Proprietary interests, see Gary B. Nash, *Quakers and Politics in Pennsylvania, 1681–1726* (Princeton, 1968); and Stephen Brobeck, "Revolutionary Change in Colonial Philadelphia: the Brief Life of the Proprietary Gentry," *WMQ* xxxiii (1976), 410–35.

Pennsylvania was also a "mixed multitude" of ethno-cultural groups, something that became more obvious after 1760.[8] The notion of the single-interest polity fitted awkwardly with such a diversified culture. However, Pennsylvania's Quaker elite hoped that the new and emerging sectors of the polity would be absorbed into existing factional structures and that in these circumstances, it could continue to satisfy the political expectations of those who had recently settled in the colony. Those who saw themselves as Pennsylvania's natural leaders saw no contradiction between serving the interests of a multicultural community and preserving the organic polity as they knew it. Indeed, they recognised that the contemporary political system, as well as their own ascendancy within it, could be preserved only if they incorporated new clients especially because, as a 1764 broadside suggested, some of these "have thought themselves too long denied the equal privilege of having some of *their own people* among their representatives." During the 1750s the "ticket" had been introduced to the electoral process to satisfy some of these expectations but it was done in ways which would also attach new ethno-cultural interests to established leaders without necessarily compromising the single-interest polity in which most of the older settlers had a vested as well as an historical interest. Until the Revolution, therefore, a certain level of accommodation was accepted on all sides and this encouraged what Benjamin Franklin's daughter Sally (1743–1808) termed the "half 'n halfs" system of Pennsylvania politics.[9]

This was also a system which ethno-cultural leaders broadly supported. Henry Melchior Muhlenberg recalled the verses of Jeremiah that "if ye be willing and obedient, ye shall eat the good of the land but if ye refuse and rebel, ye shall be devoured with the sword." However, even if some Germans allowed themselves to become, as Glenn Weaver has put it, "tools" of the colony's Quakers, the established leadership was expected to protect their interests in return. The Scots-Irish were also prepared to defer to Quaker leaders *provided*

8   The phrase "mixed multitude" is taken from Schwartz, *Mixed Multitude.* For the cultural dimension of political behaviour in colonial Pennsylvania, see the various articles by Alan Tully and Owen S. Ireland that are cited *in passim* and in particular, Ireland's "The Ethnic-Religious Dimension of Pennsylvania Politics, 1778–1779," *WMQ* xxx (1973), 423–48; Wayne L. Bockelman and Ireland, "The Internal Revolution in Pennsylvania: an Ethnic-Religious Interpretation," *PH* xli (1974), 125–59; and Alan W. Tully, "Ethnicity, Religion, and Politics in Early America," *PMHB* cvii (1983), 431–536. In 1995, Ireland and Tully also published important monographs which have extended the arguments of these articles; see Owen S. Ireland, *Religion, Ethnicity, and Politics: Ratifying the Constitution in Pennsylvania* (University Parks, Pa., 1995); and Tully, *Forming American Politics.*

9   Supplement to *PJ*, 25 Sept. 1764. Sally Franklin (to her brother in 1766) is quoted in Bernard Faÿ, *The Two Franklins: Fathers of American Democracy* (Boston, 1933), 4. For the introduction of the "ticket," see Dieter Rothermund, "The German Problem in Colonial Pennsylvania," *PMHB* lxxxiv (1960), 5.

that the overbearing characteristics of the old world would not be replicated in the new. Moreover, while they criticised the "higher" established leadership from time to time, they did not want to supersede it as much as to complement it. Therefore, for much of the colonial period, their political involvements were passive rather than active and would remain thus, as long as the more established interests "deserved" their support. This is not to suggest that Pennsylvania's Scots-Irish and Germans did not have political views of their own and that they did not articulate them if they felt that their interests were not being protected. This happened when the Quaker-controlled assembly tried to end the proprietorship. The Scots-Irish saw the application for royal status as a breach of faith and, accordingly, began to develop a distinct political interest which would threaten and ultimately confront that of the Quakers.[10]

Despite their apparent willingness to work within existing political structures, the Scots-Irish were regarded with mixed feelings by the establishment. As early as 1727 James Logan reported that "a settlement of five families from the North of Ireland gives me more trouble than fifty of any other people." However, the province's Quaker leaders did not worry unduly about the new arrivals until the late-1750s and early-1760s when, as Richard Alan Ryerson has noted, their historical "concern" about the political views and activities of the Scots-Irish began to grow into "an obsession." Many of these new tensions were precipitated by a view among the Scots-Irish that as the French and Indian Wars (1754–63) unfolded during the 1750s and, thereafter, Pontiac's Rebellion (1763–64), the Quaker-controlled provincial assembly was not willing to allocate increased resources to protect their more recently established settlements on the frontier. One pamphleteer bemoaned the fact that as he saw it, "the Quakers would be so liberal to Savages, & at the same Time [would] not contribute a single Farthing as a Society to help our Distresses last Summer [of 1763] although applied to for this Purpose." As a result, there was "an unjustifiable Attachment in the Quakers to Indian Savages, a fixed Resolution to befriend them & an utter Insensibility to [the] human Distresses" of the Scots-Irish. The simple implication of this policy was, as the Scots-Irish complained to the lieutenant governor, John Penn (1763–71; 1773–76), that their "Lives and Liberties" had been affected and "Great Numbers of the back Settlers were murdered, scalped & butchered" while hostile Indians had been indulged and even "protected, cherished, and maintained in Luxury and Idleness." The

10 Henry Melchior Muhlenberg, *The Journals of Henry Melchior Muhlenberg*, trans. and ed., Theodore Tappert and John W. Doberstein 3 vols. (Philadelphia, 1945) ii, 701; Glenn Weaver, "Benjamin Franklin and the Pennsylvania Germans," *WMQ* xiv (1957), 541; Charles H. Lincoln, *The Revolutionary Movement in Pennsylvania, 1760–1776* (Philadelphia, 1901), 24; and Tully, "Ethnicity, Religion, and Politics," 497, 513.

simple explanation for the policy was that Quakers had conscientious objections to committing public funds for military activities, even when these were for defensive purposes. For the Scots-Irish, however, the assumption was that the assembly, by abandoning them to the Indians, were trying to keep their emerging interest in check and so satisfy their "insatiable Thirst of Domination." Thus,

> Quakers may talk what they will of the Happiness & Justice of their Administration, but these are such glaring Evidences of their unjustifiable Usurpation, their thirst of Power, their Want of their Principles of Justice & the common Feelings of human Nature for the distressed; that we cannot but blame them at the Cause of many of our Sufferings.[11]

For some commentators, it was clear that however argued, and however benign the intentions of the original founders of the colony had been, the Quaker interest could no longer sit as a government for *all* the people of the province and act for the common good. Quaker apologists may have stressed the fact that "as a Religious Society [they had] ever carefully avoided admitting Matters immediately relating to civil Government into our Deliberations." However, for the Scots-Irish, the political realities of the 1750s and 1760s suggested that the Quaker interest had "made light of our Sufferings" and that a confessional limitation on public policy was neither acceptable or desirable. Neither was the corollary that in 1765 the interests of the three major eastern counties of Bucks, Philadelphia, and Chester, where most of the colony's Quakers lived, were disproportionately represented in the assembly and had "resolved at any Rate to fill the House of Assembly & rule the Province" so that the counties where the Scots-Irish lived did not have "an equal Share with them in the very important Privilege of Legislation."[12]

The **Conestoga massacres** (December 1763) and **Paxton riots** (1763–64) provided an important catalyst for these changes of temperament. As Tully has

11 Richard Alan Ryerson, *The Revolution is Now Begun: The Radical Committees of Philadelphia, 1765–1776* (Philadelphia, 1978), 17. The remaining quotations are taken from John Dunbar's edition of the principle pamphlets concerning the Paxton disturbances, *The Paxton Boys* (The Hague, 1957). Unless otherwise noted, all references are taken from this source and all the relevant pamphlets were published in Philadelphia in 1764. Where known, the authors have also been listed. See *An Apology of the Paxton Volunteers Addressed to the Candid & Impartial World*, as in Dunbar, *Paxton Boys*, 190, 191; *A Declaration and Remonstrance …*, as in *ibid.*, 108; *An Apology of the Paxton Volunteers*, as in *ibid.*, 185; Thomas Barton, *The Conduct of the Paxton Boys, Impartially Represented*, as in *ibid.*, 274; and *An Apology of the Paxton Volunteers* as in *ibid.*, 189. Logan is quoted from Schwartz, *Mixed Multitude*, 95. The words "Scots-Irish" and "Presbyterian" are used interchangeably; see note on the **Scots-Irish** in "Biographical Notes and Further Information."
12 *An Address of the People Called Quakers*, as in Dunbar, *Paxton Boys*, 138; *An Apology of the Paxton Volunteers*, as in *ibid.*, 187, 188; and *Declaration and Remonstrance*, as in *ibid.*, 105.

suggested, "Pennsylvanians who had identified with Quaker or Quaker-associated legislative leadership were quickly to perceive the massacre and march on Philadelphia as flagrant Presbyterian attacks on the principle of Quaker government." Thus, what was at stake was the survival of the Quaker interest as a "natural" ascendancy. This explains why the *Pennsylvania Journal* noted in 1764 that the colony's Presbyterians "tho' they are well entitled to their share of representatives, they have constantly declared that it is indifferent to them of which persuasions the new members are, provided *the present betrayers of our* [Quaker's] *rights* are turned out." By May of the following year, the wealthy Quaker merchant, John Reynell suggested that the Scots-Irish wanted to go even further and "get into the Seat of Government [and] tho *not fit to be trusted with it ...* [they] have been continually abusing and calumniating the Quakers in Order to *weaken their Interest* here with the People and represent them [as] Odious to the Government at home."[13]

In this context, suggestions that new settlers were undependable and disruptive grew stronger. However, while these focused on one particular group, the Scots-Irish, they were also used to express reservations about the overall nature and pace of change in an increasingly complex political and social economy. This was especially so as pressures grew to broaden Pennsylvania's political structures and to make them less exclusive. They linked the social, economic, and political changes of the 1760s – as well as insecurities and uncertainties about the future – to those who had hitherto remained on the periphery of provincial politics but who now wanted to take a more active part in political discussion as well as avail themselves of the rewards of office. The scurrilous pamphlet war of the mid-1760s was not just another exchange between the two interests of Quaker and Presbyterian. Ethno-cultural stereotype, as well as unflattering descriptions and caricature, not only focused on Presbyterian "disruption from outside" but encouraged the regrouping of those who felt threatened "inside" the establishment. As such, the exchanges of the 1760s encouraged a broader political discourse which reflected the growing complexities of American life.

Benjamin Franklin was a strong supporter of the Quaker leadership and in 1764 his influential *Narrative of the Late Massacres* included many of the themes of what would become a major pamphlet war during the following few years. His immediate targets were the "barbarous Men who committed the atrocious

---

13 Tully, *Forming American Politics*, 184; *PJ*, 27 Sept. 1764. Reynell is quoted from Bauman, *For the Reputation of Truth*, 116. For the development of the Paxton Boys during the 1760s, see Brook Hindle, "The March of the Paxton Boys," *WMQ* iii (1946), 461–86; Peter A. Butzin, "Politics, Presbyterians and the Paxton Riots, 1763–4," *JPrH* li (1973), 70–84; and George W. Franz, *Paxton: A Study of Community Structure and Mobility in the Colonial Pennsylvania Backcountry* (New York, 1989).

Fact [at Conestoga], in Defiance of Government, of all Laws human and divine, and to the eternal Disgrace of their Country and Colour, then mounted their Horses, huzza'd in Triumph, as if they had gained a Victory, and rode off – *unmolested.*" Ironically, it was an Ulster-born Anglican clergyman, the Rev. Thomas Barton (*c.*1728–80), who, on St. Patrick's Day 1764, published one of the better-known responses to the *Narrative*. In his *Conduct of the Paxton Men, Impartially Represented*, Barton suggested that the Quaker-controlled assembly had neglected those on or near the frontier so that the events at Conestoga, however crudely they were portrayed, were in self-defence. In his view, where government had "neglected and despised the Complaints of an injured and oppressed People," the Bible, English and Irish history, and constitutional theory justified rebellion while two civil wars provided precedents for such actions. This did not mean that the Scots-Irish were fickle or undependable, because for them, the historical record showed that they had "never" been

> concern'd in promoting or countenancing any Plots or Insurrections against the Government, but on the Contrary, when ambitious Men thirsting for Power have embroiled the State in intestine Commotions and Blood-shed, subverting the Order of Government, our Forefathers ... manifested their Abhorrence of such traitorous Proceedings.[14]

For some, Barton's historical references were nonsensical, arrogant, "false ... and horred Misrepresentations." However, for many Scots-Irish, they reflected two types of separate but complementary views about the nature of the polity. The first of these concerned the cultural purposes of British colonisation and the promotion of "civilisation" as these had been transmitted from the generations who had "planted" Ulster over a hundred years earlier. There was something familiar about their descriptions of Pennsylvania's Indians as "treacherous, faithless [and] rascally," as well as "villainous, [and] faithless Savages" and "*Heathens*" who could never be truly converted to either the reformed religion or a supposedly better political order. In Ireland, similar descriptions had been used to justify the harsh treatment of the indigenous inhabitants there, to highlight the self-supposed superiority of the planters, and to legitimise a reformed polity which since the sixteenth century, had been promoted to "civilise" as well as to subjugate the island. Thus, as Isaac Hunt (*c.*1742–1809) suggested, Barton "woul'd feign make us believe too that as God formerly gave the Land of *Canaan* by a Charter from Heaven to the Jews; so he

14 Franklin's *Narrative* is quoted from Dunbar, *Paxton Boys*, 61, and Barton from his *Conduct of the Paxton Boys* in *ibid.*, 298, 280, 274 *et seq.* For Barton's pamphlet, and the context in which it was written, see James Myers, "The Rev. Thomas Barton's Authorship of *The Conduct of the Paxton Boys, Impartially Represented (1764)*," *PH* lxi (1994), 155–84.

has given *Pennsylvania* to the *Presbyterians* by Virtue of the same Commission."
The corollary was, as Franklin argued in his *Narrative*, that "If it be right to kill
Men for such a Reason [as] ... revenge ... it seems these People think they have
a better Justification; nothing less than the *Word of God* ... and justify their
Wickedness, by the Command given *Joshua* to destroy the Heathen." Along a
second line of thought, the Scots-Irish also believed that the polity was
maintained by contract and that, as influential writers such as Algernon Sydney
(1622–83), James Harrington (1611–77), and John Locke (1632–1704) argued,
those who corrupted governance were without virtue and as such, had to be
chastised. The civil wars of the seventeenth century suggested that such people
had been treated no differently than the "wild Irish" had been during the
campaigns of the previous century; in both cases, neither had virtue and as
such, they had no status within the polity.[15]

These two streams of thought had come together during the 1640s when
Presbyterians were said by their opponents to "exceed all other People in acts of
brutality." For anti-Presbyterian writers in mid-eighteenth-century Pennsylvania,
the most notorious example of such behaviour was a massacre which had taken
place in January 1642 when "without the least Remorse," Presbyterians were
said to have"murder'd four thousand of the native *Irish*, men, women and
children in the *Isle Mc-Gee*," near Carrickfergus in Co. Antrim. For many
colonists at the time, the fact that the "native Irish" were giving strong support
to Charles I (1600–49) suggested that they were "without virtue." As such, the
established polity was no longer being solely defined by reference to the
supposed superiority of "English" civilisation over indigenous cultures – the
"war of two civilisations" – but also by the extent to which it promoted
harmony and thus, the virtue of its leadership. Across the Atlantic, the events
of the 1760s in Pennsylvania provided an American setting for a similar polemic
on the integrity of "a body Corporate"

> which body composes a Society in civil Government; and every Loyal Person,
> a real Member of that Society. Thus we are bound together by Unanimity and
> Concord, under the sanction of Laws, to support our civil and Religious Rights
> in Government ... by which this body Corporate is formed into a Society.[16]

15 *An Answer to the Pamphlet Entitled The Conduct of the Paxton Men*, as in Dunbar, *Paxton Boys*,
   320; Barton, *Conduct of the Paxton Boys*, as in *ibid.*, 280, 278, 293; Isaac Hunt, *A Looking Glass
   for Presbyterians, or A Brief Examination of their Loyalty, Merit, and other Qualifications for
   Government. With Some Animadversions on the Quaker Unmask'd, Number II*, as in *ibid.*, 303;
   Franklin, *Narrative*, as in *ibid.*, 63. For the influence of the plantation of Ulster on Barton's
   attitudes, see Miller, Schrier, Boling,and Doyle, eds., *Irish Immigrants in the Land of Canaan*,
   487, 510. For Barton's use of biblical and historical references, see *ibid.*, 497.
16 Hunt, *A Looking Glass*, as in Dunbar, *Paxton Papers*, 251, 248; *An Answer to the Pamphlet
   Entitled The Conduct of the Paxton Men*, as in *ibid.*, 325. The phrase "war of two

Such a polity could be guaranteed only by virtuous leaders. For the Scots Irish, as the author of an *Apology of the Paxton Volunteers* suggested in 1764, Quakers might

> talk what they will of the Happiness & Justice of their Administration, but these are such glaring Evidences of their unjustifiable Usurpation, their thirst for Power, their Want of the Principles of Justice & the common Feelings of human Nature for the distressed; that we cannot but blame them as the Cause of many of our Sufferings.

Thus, as *The Quaker Unmasked* put it, "I hope my Countrymen will cooly consider whether Quakers are fit to be their Representatives, or not, after such glaring and positive Proofs of their Insincerity; and whether we ought to continue to entrust them with our Lives and Liberties." An opposite view was put as follows:

> The Quakers have ever virtuously exerted themselves in favour of the just Rights and Liberties of Mankind, and have endeavoured to restrain the Proprietary Power within its proper Bounds: You [Presbyterians], on the other Hand, have join'd with that Power, in the foolish and vain Expectation of usurping the Whole. – The Quakers have ever supported the Government, its Laws and Constitution, and that against all rebellious Riots and Attempts to tread it under Foot: You, and those under your Influence, have been either the Principals or Abettors of all the Riots that have been insolently raised in Defiance of Government and its Laws, as your many insidious Writings, and the Letter now before me will testify.

For their part, Quaker apologists suggested that "the Religious as well as Civil Character of the *Quakers*, is well known, and too well established to suffer any Injury from false Invidious Representations and Slanderous Calumniations." That character was also "well known through the British Dominions above a Hundred Years, and was never concerned in promoting or countenancing any Plots or Insurrections against the Government." Moreover, they argued that the Quaker interest had always believed in Penn's commitment to develop "the most extensive Privileges both civil and religious of any People in the World" and agreed

civilisations" has been quoted from Hayes-McCoy, "Gaelic Society in the late-Sixteenth Century," 61. The writing on "virtue" is extensive. Among others, see Richard K. Matthews, ed., *Virtue, Corruption, and Self Interest. Political Values in the Eighteenth Century* (Bethlehem, 1994); J.G.A. Pocock, *The Machiavellian Moment: Florentine Republican thought in the Atlantic Republican Tradition* (Princeton, 1975); and Gordon S. Wood, *The Creation of the American Republic, 1776–1787* (Chapel Hill, 1969).

> like true *Britons*, [to] warmly oppose any that would presume to deprive us of
> them ... let us exert all our influence and power to keep the reigns of
> Government out of the Hands of *Presbyterians* ... as we are convinced,
> thoroughly convinced, of their Unfitness to govern both by Experience and
> undeniable Instances from History.[17]

It was argued that, in contrast, Presbyterians were so introspective in their
culture of government that they threatened the viability of a polity where "no
one Profession in particular can be established by Law." This was especially true
of New England where, according to some Quaker commentators, the
"sanguinary intolerance" of "Boston government" had been, in Reynell's
words, "inconsistent with all good Government." Thus, "from undeniable
facts," the Scots-Irish were "by no Means proper Men to hold the Reigns of
Government, either in War or Peace ... [they] have always been enemies to
Kingly Government, and consequently not fit to be trusted with any share of the
civil power, when a King reigns." As the state representative, George Clymer
(1778–82; 1784–88), observed in 1783, he would not have "our legislatures made
up of men of narrow souls."[18] At issue was where the greater civic virtue lay
and as such, who best could guarantee the harmony of the polity as a whole. As
many of Clymer's colleagues saw it, the choice which Presbyterians had was
clear: to be either confrontational or congenial, and to reflect either their own
interests or to subordinate those interests to those of the wider community. As
the Revolution loomed, many Quakers saw them leaning to the former.

Whatever the merits, or otherwise, of these arguments, elections and
"*political Designs*" gave Quakers an influential presence within the polity. As the
elections of 1764 approached, Presbyterians decided to organise themselves in
a more effective manner. As Peter A. Butzin has suggested, Presbyterians
associated their Quaker antagonists with "a closed oligarchy" for which their
religious networks had become a "political engine." Thus, in September 1764
Franklin suggested to Richard Jackson, who at the time (1763–65) was secretary
to the British Chancellor of the Exchequer, that "The Irish Presbyterians too,

17 *Apology of the Paxton Volunteers*, as in Dunbar, *Paxton Boys*, 189; David James Dove, *The
   Quaker Unmasked*, as in *ibid.*, 214; *An Address to the Rev. Dr. Alison, the Rev. Mr. Ewing,
   &c. Being a Vindication of the Quakers* (Philadelphia, 1764), 14; (Anon), *The Author of
   Quaker Unmask'd. Strip'd Stark Naked, or the Delineated Presbyterian Play'd Hob with*, as
   in Dunbar, *Paxton Boys*, 262; (Society of Friends), *The Address of the People call'd
   Quakers, In the Province of Pennsylvania, to John Penn, Esquire*, as in *ibid.*, 133; Hunt,
   Looking Glass as in Dunbar, *Paxton Boys*, 255.
18 Hunt, *Looking Glass* as in Dunbar, *Paxton Boys*, 245; *The Quakers Assisting to Preserve the
   Lives of the Indians in the Barracks Vindicated, Number II*, as in *ibid.*, 392; Hunt, *Looking
   Glass*, as in *ibid.*, 246, 249; HSP, Gratz Collection, case 1, box 19, Clymer to Fitzsimons,
   24 May 1783. Reynell is quoted from Bauman, *For the Reputation of Truth*, 116.

piqu'd at the Reflections thrown on them by the Quakers for the late Riots &
murders, have join'd the **Proprietary Party**, by which they hope to acquire the
Predominancy in the Assembly and subdue the Quakers." In more practical
terms, they also assembled a committee of ministers and elders, "deputed from
all Parts of Pennsylvania," which met in Lancaster on 28 August of that year.
This meeting recommended a "firm Attachment" to the proprietor because
among other things, this would, at least in their view, lead to the appointment of
judges from among their own interest "who will have it in their Power to be
revenged upon all the Enemies of *Presbyterianism*" and to pass "several Laws in
Favour of *Presbyterianism*." It also agreed to hold an annual meeting of a sub-
committee of the Synod "in order to settle and regulate all future Elections."
Recalling one of Barton's points, it also resolved that

> *Presbyterians* have as good a Right to *Pennsylvania* as the Children of *Israel*
> had formerly to the Land of *Canaan*, and that it is right and lawful for
> *Presbyterians* to make use of the same Means in extirpating *Quakers*, Indians,
> or any other of their Foreign or Domestic Enemies, that the *Israelites* did
> to extirpate the *Canaanites* … the sole right of civil and ecclesiastical
> Jurisdiction in this *Province*, belongs to *Presbyterian* Ministers.[19]

For unsympathetic commentators, such behaviour suggested that "all Means
are to be used between this, and the next Election to unite the *Presbyterians* as
one Man to choose such Persons for Assemblymen who (upon certain
Conditions) will grant any Thing the P[resbyterian]s demand." This set off an
alarm which should "awaken the Attention of every true Lover of his Country,
and rouse all other Persuasions, to unite as one Man against them, being the
most formidable and dangerous Enemies we have to cope with." Anti-
Presbyterian writers hoped that such arguments would be seen as reasonable as
well as a caution against compromising the pluralism and toleration for which
Pennsylvania was so well known. On occasion, however, such observers made
their point in more emotive terms: that in Pennsylvania, no less than in Ireland,
Presbyterians were a "lawless banditti" who had "murdered the *Indians* at
Lancaster," as their ancestors had done "much in the same manner" at
Islandmagee. While in both jurisdictions some had justified these actions by
portraying the native people as "barbarous," the wider point was that

19 *Address to the Rev. Dr. Alison* …, 7; Butzin, "Politics, Presbyterians and the Paxton Riots,"
   81; Leonard Labaree, ed., *The Papers of Benjamin Franklin*, 31 vols. to date (New Haven,
   1959-) xi, 327, Franklin to Jackson, 1 Sept. 1764; *Address to the Rev. Dr. Alison*, title page, 4,
   17–18, 17. The resolutions of the Lancaster meeting also revealed the continuing fear that an
   Anglican episcopate might be imposed on the province; see Carl Bridenbaugh, *Mitre and
   Sceptre: Transatlantic Faiths, Ideas, Personalities, and Politics, 1689–1775* (New York, 1962).

government, whether reflected in the British, Irish, or Pennsylvania legislatures, had abandoned "the people." To this extent, the attack on the Indians at Conestoga was both a real massacre and a symbolic statement against a legislature which the Scots-Irish regarded as having compromised its ability to promote and secure the happiness of society. As such, it had abandoned the end of all government. In this context, the controversies of the 1760s rehearsed the Revolution of the 1770s, albeit with this omission: they were articulated in terms of ethno-cultural factionalism rather than in the ideological language of Whiggery.[20]

In any event, the attempt to create a royal colony failed. The Quaker leadership survived the episode as did the factional arrangements that had characterised the colony before 1760. In 1767 the lawyer Joseph Galloway (1731–1803) informed Franklin that "We are at present very Quiet ... and I am satisfied, that, the watchword Among P[resbyteria]ns is Moderation." However, the controversies left an enduring legacy. They had caricatured political "outsiders" and especially recent immigrants, as disruptive, troublesome, unreliable, irresponsible, "unpatriotic," and lacking in any "*merit* ... for government." For his part, the author of *A Looking Glass* let it be known that at least he was "an *American born*" and, therefore, supposed to be "free from prejudice and partiality." While Scots-Irish leaders were annoyed by the negative reflections that were being cast on their character and, in particular, by allegations that they had inflamed events at Conestoga, the events of the 1760s helped to heal the disunity that the **First Great Awakening** had caused within their own ranks. As the proprietary interest failed to capitalise on the increasing deprecation of the Quaker interest, especially when it remained aloof from the revolutionary movement, the Scots-Irish were self-confident enough to articulate for themselves Whiggish concerns about the nature and integrity of public representation. They also insisted that as plans were revealed during the 1760s to establish an Anglican bishopric in America, old world abuses and grievances, especially in relation to tithes, would not take root in America:

> Our forefathers, harassed by spiritual Courts and the power of lordly Prelates ... being likewise denied the Privilege of peaceably worshipping God in a Way the most agreeable to their Consciences, at last wearied out with Persecution, resolved to leave their Native Country, and seek Shelter in the Wilds of America. The Power of the Church of England by Law established, they imagined was confined to England.

20 *Looking Glass II*, as in Dunbar, *Paxton Papers*, 305, 306; *Looking Glass*, as in Dunbar, *Paxton Papers*, 248.

Such people emerged from the controversies of the 1760s as a community which was comfortable in its new home and at ease in opposing the imperial legislation of the 1760s. As Tully has put it, "dissatisfaction with the old parties meant self-assertion and a higher political profile for the politically active."[21]

As Scots-Irish leaders moved from being what Ryerson has called "frustrated outsiders" to "angry idealists," they helped to organise a network of committees of correspondence, as well as a complementary roster of occasional meetings, to air colonial grievances. On a more popular level, they were also active in the unfolding protests against the "new imperialism" of the British government. In Ryerson's words, these activities were "of the first importance in the coming of the Revolution in Philadelphia." They also helped to set the putative revolutionary leadership apart from the more traditional colonial elite. Indeed, as the framing of Pennsylvania's state constitution drew close, James Cannon (1740–82), reputed to be the author of the state constitution of 1776, advised the people "to choose no lawyers or other professional characters called educated or learned men, but to select men uneducated with unsophisticated understandings." Both the Provincial Conference (18 to 25 June 1776) and the Constitutional Convention (15 July to 28 September 1776) contained a number of Presbyterian "new men," with 22 members (or 39%) in the former and 26 (or 40%) in the latter. Thus, as the Presbyterian minister, Dr. Francis Alison (1732–79), informed his "cozen Robert" in 1776, although the delegates to the convention were "honest well meaning Country men, [they were] entirely unacquainted with such high matters ... [and were] hardly equal to the Task to form a new Plan of Government." In a similar vein, the secretary of the Continental Congress (1774–81), the Ulster-born **Charles Thomson** (1729–86), bemoaned the retirement of John Dickinson (1732–1808) from Congress in 1776 as it had "thrown the affairs of this State into the hands of men totally unequal to them." However, the Scots-Irish spearheaded the "anti-establishment ambiance" of the colony towards the revolution of the 1770s and as they did so, they knew that as they continued the quest for political recognition on their own terms, it was only a matter of time before they could demand it, with or without reference to London. Between 1776 and the adoption of Pennsylvania's revised state constitution in 1790, the **Constitutionalists** made this possible.[22]

21 Hunt, *A Looking Glass ... II* in Dunbar, *Paxton Boys*, 302; Tully, *Forming American Politics*, 184; and "Ethnicity, Religion, and Politics," 529. Galloway is quoted in Thayer, *Growth of Democracy*, 137, and Alison in Miller, Schrier, Boling, and Doyle, eds., *Irish Immigrants in the Land of Canaan*, 516–7.

22 Ryerson, "Republican Theory and Partisan Reality," 107, and *Revolution is Now Begun*, 64; James H. Hutson, *Pennsylvania Politics, 1746–1770: The Movement for Royal Government and its Consequences* (Princeton, 1972), 209. Cannon is quoted in Ellis Paxton Oberholtzer, *The Literary History of Philadelphia* (Philadelphia, 1906), 98; Alison in

Revolution

The Constitutionalists were led by the Dublin-born Presbyterian merchant, **George Bryan** (1731–91), and his "Irish colonels." During the 1760s most of them had supported the Penns but now, a decade later, they became involved in the transition from colony to state. Their Republican opponents were largely Anglicans who were linked in various ways to merchants like Thomas Willing (1731–1821), Robert Morris (1734–1806), and James Wilson (1742–1813). Ryerson has concluded that by 1776 in Philadelphia,

> Political power began to flow downward to men who were less affluent, less well educated and far more obscure ... For the first time in Philadelphia's history, wealthy merchants and elegant lawyers in greatcoats and waistcoats were thrown together with obscure mechanics in shirtsleeves and leather aprons to perform a public service.[23]

The Constitutionalists typified such changes. They were taken to represent the "new men" of Pennsylvania politics: one side of the contrast between "the few and the many ... [the] aristocraticks and democraticks," as the chief justice (1777–99), **Thomas McKean** (1734–1817), put it in 1779. As such, they were resented by those who had governed the former colony and who were now "altogether out of the scale." As the artist Charles Wilson Peale (1741–1827) observed, the "political Genius" of the Quaker interest had been consigned to times past. Thus, the Philadelphia merchant William Shippen (1745–77) did not

> wonder to see some of our Friends offended and full of resentment upon the change — who have heretofore been at the head of affairs and in short have behaved as though they thought they had a sort of Fee simple in them, and might dispose of all places of Honor and Profit to such as pleased them best.

Instead, the new regime was dominated by political upstarts who had rejected "those Great leading characters whose Abilitys would command Respect & Carry with them the N[umber] *that are only fit to Follow*, from assuming public office."[24] As the diarist, Alexander Graydon (1752–1818), noted, political power

PMHB xxvii (1904), 379; and Thomson in Elisha P. Douglass, *Rebels and Democrats: The Struggle for Equal Political Rights and Majority Rule during the American Revolution* (Chapel Hill, 1955), 272–3. For the composition of the provincial conference and convention, see table iv in Bockelman and Ireland, "Internal Revolution in Pennsylvania," 143.

23 Ryerson, *Revolution is Now Begun*, 203. For the "Irish colonels," see Ronald M. Baumann, "The Democratic-Republicans of Philadelphia: the Origins, 1776–1797" (Ph.D. dissertation, Pennsylvania State University, 1970), 20; and Burton Konkle, *George Bryan and the Constitution of Pennsylvania, 1731–1791* (Philadelphia, 1922).

24 APS, Peale Family Papers, Charles Wilson Peale to David Ramsay, dated Aug./Sept.

"had fallen into low hands." Nonetheless, Bryan resented the presumptions of the "aristocratic juntos of the *well-born few*" to "lord it over their fellow creatures" and humble the "offensive *Upstart*." As Graydon suggested, he had a "passion or policy to identify himself with the *people* ... in opposition to those who were termed the *well-born*."[25]

The Constitutionalists were also thought to be men of modest circumstances. Because of this, the Republicans' opponents suggested that the state would have to pay the new leaders a "vast sum of money" in wages and "contingent expenses." According to a contemporary broadside, most of them were "skulkers under petty officers," people whose offices were "making numbers of gentlemen who had never been so before." As "An Enemy to Aristocracy" put it in 1783, "with a few under-lings," they had "confine[d] all the honors and posts of profit of the State to a few hands" and as such, were a new "aristocracy" in the sense that "power [was] lodged perpetually in the hands of a few men." The factional language of the past had not gone away. The Lancaster-based Judge Yates (1745–1817) had his own cynical view of the matter: while "the clamours of the red-hot patriots have subsided into easy places and offices of profit ... posts of *mere* trust go a-begging. No one can be found to accept *them*." Moreover, because they were not supposed to be "very eminent," Constitutionalists were easily associated with "mob government." What this implied, as one writer suggested, was that they neither had, nor ever could have, the "*virtue* sufficient to support a Republican Government in that purity and dignity which the [new] system of government required." As a result, they would corrupt "the simple morals" of late-eighteenth-century Americans. In 1776 an exasperated John Adams had suggested that

> Virtue and Simplicity of Manners are indispensably necessary in a Republic among all orders and Degrees of Men. But there is so much Rascality, so much Venality and Corruption, so much Avarice and Ambition, such a Rage for Profit and Commerce among all Ranks and Degrees of Men even in America, that I sometimes doubt whether there is public virtue enough to Support a Republic.[26]

1776; HSP, Shippen Papers xii, William Shippen to Edward Shippen, dated 27 July 1776, as quoted in Jackson Turner Main, *Political Parties before the Constitution* (Williamsburg, Va., 1973), 178–9; HSP, Gratz Collection, case I, box 5, George Fitzsimons to Benjamin Rush, 12 May 179. McKean is quoted in Main, *Political Parties*, 20.

25 Alexander Graydon, *Memoirs of His Own Time, with Reminiscences of the Men and Events of the Revolution* (Philadelphia, 1846), 283; Saul Cornell, ed., "Reflections on 'The Late Remarkable Revolution in Government'," *PMHB* cxii (1988), 115; "Centinel," as quoted in Joseph S. Foster, *In Pursuit of Liberty: George Bryan and the Revolution in Pennsylvania* (University Park, Pennsylvania, 1994), 144, 145; Graydon, *Memoirs of His Own Time*, 287.

26 "One of the Minority of Censors," "An Alarm. To the Freemen and Electors of Pennsylvania" (broadside, Philadelphia, 1 Oct. 1784); "An Enemy to Aristocracy" in *PG*,

The politics of the new state of Pennsylvania did not ease his fears on this account.

By characterising Constitutionalists as "numsculs," "outsiders," and "foreign-born" who were moved by "ambition," "malice," and "avarice," the rhetorical criticisms of the "new men" of the 1760s reappeared. The political uncertainties of the 1780s were not unlike those of some twenty years earlier. Neither were the leaders of Revolutionary Philadelphia willing to abandon the underlying assumptions of the single-interest polity. As Joseph Foster has noted, "expanding core groups" rather than "shifting voting patterns" best explain the configurations of contemporary politics, especially in the city and county of Philadelphia.[27] Thus, Ryerson has noted that "Reading in the radical Whig tradition ... [the Scots-Irish] encountered both the country myth of the *single-interest* society and the precept that the highest form of human endeavour is the defence of one's country against enemies, both external and internal." Moreover, Bryan was not uninfluenced by the British axiom that the interests of society should be reflected in the constituted government, as if, as Foster has suggested, "the socio-political needs of the community were a single interest unto itself." Crucially, these needs were also reflected in the unicameral character of the state constitution of 1776 which the Constitutionalists had sponsored. Bryan believed that the interests of a diversified society could be "work[ed] in the name of all the people." However, in many ways, this was an old world assumption and as the former colonies moved towards the new status of independent states, the hypothesis that a new world polity could be governed according to the criteria of the old was increasingly questioned.[28]

15 Jan. 1783; Yates to Col. Burd, dated at Lancaster, 29 Mar. 1777, as quoted in Samuel B. Harding, "Party Struggles over the First Pennsylvania Constitution" in *Annual Report of the American Historical Association* (1894), 380; HSP, Yates Papers, Correspondence and General Papers, Sarah Yates to Jasper Yates, dated Lancaster, 14 Sept. 1776; HSP, Henry Drinker Letterbook, Henry Drinker to John Canaan, 15 October 1795; John Adams to Mary Warren, 8 Jan. 1776 in "Warren-Adams Letters," *Collections of the Massachusetts Historical Society* lxxxiii (1925), 202.

27 Foster, *Pursuit of Liberty*, 138. For the characterisation of the "new men" of Pennsylvania politics, see HSP, Yates Papers, Correspondence and General Papers, Sarah to Jasper Yates, dated at Lancaster, 14 Sept. 1776; Baumann, "Democratic-Republicans of Philadelphia," 17–18, 21, 28; Konkle, *George Bryan*; Foster, *Pursuit of Liberty*; Charles Page Smith, *James Wilson: Founding Father, 1742–1798* (Chapel Hill, 1943), 108–9; Main, *Political Parties*, 206–11 and, most especially, Gordon Wood's chapter, "The Worthy against the Licentious" in *Creation of the American Republic*, 471–518.

28 Ryerson, "Republican Theory and Partisan Reality," 114; Foster, *Pursuit of Liberty*, 78. For Bryan's spirited defence of the unicameralism of the Pennsylvania assembly as the best statement of the "commonwealth" of Pennsylvania, see "Whitlocke" in *PEP*, 24 May 1777. For a discussion of context, see Wood's chapter, "Mixed Government and Bicameralism" in *Creation of the American Republic*, 197–255.

Republicans argued that unicameralism would endanger liberty and demanded that the constitution of 1776 should be reviewed and a two-chamber system established. They also made an obvious criticism that

> If the members of a Single Branch of Legislature, were invested with unlimited wisdom & Integrity of Conduct,— & if their View were always devoted to the public Good, without the Possibility of undue Influence operating, or the prevalence of Favor, Interest, or Affection, then might the Advocates of this Form of Government advance incontrovertible Reasons for the Support of it.

In their view, a two-branch legislature would provide a balanced forum for what "Demophilus" described in 1776 as "the most learned and experienced members of the state." Republicans also criticised what was even a more contentious area of the polity – the Test Acts – even if, by so doing, they were also sounding its death-knell as a harmonious community. Through the various Test Acts (1777–86), Constitutionalists had specifically excluded certain types of people from political participation. The earlier act of 1777 supplemented the oath of loyalty to the new revolutionary state which had been prescribed in the state constitution. It formally repudiated "all allegiance, subjection and obedience to the King or Crown of Great Britain" and obliged every citizen to reveal any "treasonable activities of which they were aware." It also listed a number of civil disabilities, as well as exclusion from certain professions and double taxation, for those who refused to subscribe to it. The act had been justified on the basis that "those who declined to participate in the toils, the sacrifices, and the hazards of the late revolution, should not enjoy all the benefits and advantages arising from, that inestimable blessing." In an address *To the Inhabitants of Pennsylvania* in 1782, Bryan, writing under the pseudonym of "A Freeholder," argued that those who had not supported Washington during the War of Independence had, in effect, "hid themselves in the times of difficulty." Thus, as the *Pennsylvania Journal* put it, "those who declined to participate in the toils, the sacrifices, and the hazards of the late revolution, should not enjoy all the benefits and advantages arising from, that inestimable blessing." For the Constitutionalist president (1778–81), Joseph Reed (1741–85), such people could not "really ... know ... the value of our present [liberty ... instead,] Treason, Disaffection to the Interests of America and even assistance to the British Interest is called openly only Error of Judgment, which Candour and Liberality of Sentiment will overlook." In May 1776 one correspondent to the *Pennsylvania Gazette* went even further than Reed, linking a failure to support the Revolution with attempts to derail the republic to which it had led. As a result, as he put it, "an enemy is at our gates and an enemy is within our doors" and this had to be recognised for what it was.[29]

However, Constitutionalists could also use the Test Acts as a crude political lever against their opponents and in favour of their friends. Thus, while Bryan may have originally regarded the acts as a strategic device to keep a presumed Loyalist fifth-column in check, in many ways, he allowed the exigencies of a war situation, as he had painted them, to continue inflexibly into a period when peace was being consolidated. As a "Citizen of Philadelphia" noted in 1785, the tests "are as often made use of as engines of the ruling party, to entrap and punish such people as they suppose inimical to themselves." Thus, as the new republic was being defined, Constitutionalists wrapped themselves in a rhetoric of nationalism in which there was no place for the "native" Quaker elite of colonial politics which had objected to the War of Independence. In contrast, they pointed to the prominent support which the "foreign born" had given to the Revolution and suggested that these could now be depended on to promote and secure the new republic. This cast of mind was reflected in the liberal terms of section 42 of the new state constitution under which the foreign-born could become citizens:

> every foreigner of good character, who comes to settle in this state, having first taken an oath of allegiance to the same &c., after one year's residence, shall be deemed a free denizen thereof, and entitled to all the rights of a natural born subject of this state, except that he should not be capable of being elected a Representative until after two years residence.

However, this provision was not introduced without controversy, especially when so many others remained restricted under the terms of the Test Acts. "One of the Majority" observed in 1784 that while he did not wish to discourage the settlement of "strangers" in Pennsylvania, he did

29 HSP, Gratz Collection, case I, box 3, William Bingham to Rush, 3 May 1784; *PJ*, 25 Sept. 1776, 2 Oct. 1784; "A Freeholder" (Bryan), *To the Inhabitants of Pennsylvania* (Philadelphia, 1782); *PJ*, 2 Oct. 1784. *PG*, 22 May 1776, as quoted in G.S. Rowe, *Thomas McKean: The Shaping of an American Republican* (Boulder, 1978), 95. The quotation from the 1777 act is in [Benjamin Rush], *Considerations upon the Present Test-Law of Pennsylvania: Addressed to the Legislature and Freemen of the State of Pennsylvania* (Philadelphia, 1784), 3. Reed is quoted in John F. Roche, *Joseph Reed. A Moderate in the American Revolution* (New York, 1957), 145. See also Robert M. Calhoon, *The Loyalists in Revolutionary America, 1760–1781* (New York, 1973), 382–407: and Arnold, *Republican Revolution*, 173–86. For the growth of opposition to the tests, see J. Paul Selsam, *The Revolutionary Constitution of 1776: A Study in Revolutionary Democracy* (Philadelphia, 1936), 221–2.

object to giving them all the privileges of citizens after only two years' residence among us. I conceive this section of the constitution to be injurious even to strangers themselves. It effectually prevents the establishment of a government by habits and prejudices, which often bind mankind more powerfully than laws.

As such, the status of the foreign-born highlighted the paradoxes or even contradictions of a bill of rights which promoted the right to elect, and be elected, among "all freemen, having a common interest with and attachment to the community." However, under existing circumstances, such a culture could not be developed, and the nature of the American republic itself secured, unless the constitutional provisions on naturalisation were addressed:

> Think then what must be the consequence of admitting men with such principles to share immediately in the power and offices of our republic. The admission of strangers too suddenly to the rights of citizenship has been mentioned by all writers, as one of the principal causes of the destruction of the Roman commonwealth. The laws of Pennsylvania formerly required seven years residence to entitle a foreigner to a vote. I conceive some limitation of the right of suffrage as established by the constitution to be more necessary now than ever. Most of the foreigners who will settle among us will probably migrate from the British empire. They will as in former times, bring with them their natural prejudices in favor of the British form of government, and perhaps of British power too. Think of the consequences of their votes, and influence upon our government.[30]

Owen S. Ireland is the modern authority on these points. He has pointed out that "relatively few" people voted in the annual elections to the assembly between 1776 and 1780 and that, when they did so, they usually elected Scots-Irish Presbyterians and their allies. The test laws effectively ensured that it could be little different. After 1780 the modification of the Test Laws meant that increasing numbers of Quakers qualified for the vote. As a result, the representation of the Republicans grew and between 1780 and 1783, Republicans had a majority in the state assembly. Their influence became even more apparent after 1783 when, by international agreement, the Treaty of Paris absolved Americans of their previous allegiances. Those who until then had conscientiously felt that they could not break their oaths to the British king, not least by supporting or waging a war against him, or by denying him through the test oaths, could now pledge loyalty to the new republic without compromising

---

30 "A Citizen of Philadelphia" is quoted from Ireland, *Religion, Ethnicity, and Politics*, 227.
  All the other quotations have been cited from "One of the Majority" in *PG*, 11 Feb. 1784.

principle and conscience. This brought sizeable numbers of new voters to the Republican interest which had always denounced the exclusionary provisions of the Test Acts and except for 1785 and most of 1784, Republicans duly retained a majority in the state assembly until 1790. They were less successful with the Council of Censors, a body which was mandated to meet every seven years to review the constitution. Despite the reconfiguration of Pennsylvania politics which followed the Treaty of Paris, Republicans did not have the two-thirds majority which was required to support constitutional change. Thus, they looked to the adoption of the federal constitution to strengthen their role in Pennsylvania politics. As Ireland has put it, they saw it as "an indirect way of undermining a powerful political opponent they had failed to defeat in direct battle."[31]

In any event, the days of the organic polity were numbered. The Constitutionalists were then being so driven back on their political base that they were often identified as "the Presbyterian party." In 1784 Franklin who a year later became president of Pennsylvania (17 October 1785 to 5 November 1788), even suggested that "Irish emigrants and their children are now in possession of the government of Pennsylvania by their majority in the Assembly, as well as of a great part of the territory." However, even a number of their interest felt so uncomfortable with the Test Acts that in early-1785 they petitioned the assembly observing that "the only ground upon which America could justify her first opposition to Great-Britain was, that she was attempted to be bound by laws made by a Parliament, in which she was not represented." The campaign to repeal these laws provoked a debate that not only challenged the assumptions of the single-interest polity of the past but suggested that the politics of the future would have to be influenced by all those who paid taxes, regardless of their history.[32]

Benjamin Rush (1746–1813) understood the implications of these developments. Arguing in 1785 why the Test Laws should be repealed, he observed that as they stood, they were "big with evils of a most alarming nature":

> The government, in a few years, must necessarily fall into other hands. Men with European ideas of government will soon occupy the seats of our present rulers ... Rome was undone by strangers getting her government into their

---

31 Ireland, *Religion, Ethnicity, and Politics*, 219, 225, 242, 249, 16.

32 Franklin to William Strachan, 19 Aug. 1784 in John Bigelow ed., *The Complete Works of Benjamin Franklin* 10 vols. (New York, 1887–1904) x, 416; *PJ*, 2 Oct. 1784; *IG*, 7 May 1785. For the rise of Presbyterians within the Constitutionalists and their supposed "triumph" in 1779, see Bockelman and Ireland, "Internal Revolution in Pennsylvania," 142–54; Owen S. Ireland, "The Crux of Politics: Religion and Party in Pennsylvania, 1778–1789," *WMQ* xlii (1985), 474; and Robert Brunhouse, *The Counter-Revolution in Pennsylvania, 1776–1790* (Philadelphia, 1942), 35.

hands, and introducing foreign prejudices, customs and vices among them. If our constitution cannot be altered, let us remedy that defect in it, by admitting the non-jurors to a share in the government, in order to balance the undue and dangerous weight of foreigners. The non-jurors are attached to our soil by birth, education and property ... These men can have no interest unconnected with our own. Born under the protection of the same laws with ourselves, educated in the same schools, and connected with us by the ancient ties of friendship and business, they are our natural friends and fellow-citizens. Our liberties, and the constitution of the state, will therefore be safe in their hands.

Three years earlier, John Montgomery (1722–1808) suggested that

When members of the same state divide into parties, the partialities of ancient citizenship moderate their rancour and defend them from the last extremities of revenge. Nay more, they often bring them back again to good fellowship. But this can never happen where parties are headed by strangers. They can feel for nothing but themselves. They see no old schoolmates, no relations, no members of the same church or of the same clubs among those who are opposed to them to plead for charity and forbearance towards their errors or conduct, and hence their fury is unmixed and without bounds.

As the debate on the repeal of the Test Laws developed, a Republican broadside asked the "Citizens of Pennsylvania" that while the state had "open[ed] the doors of freedom to the oppressed and distressed of all nations, even to those British subjects who have dyed their weapons with British blood, shall we shut them against men, who are bone of our bone, and flesh of our flesh?" Thus, the *Pennsylvania Evening Herald* recognised that whatever views non-jurors had held in the past, it was "of much more importance to know what opinions they now hold, and to consider by what means they may be most useful to the community" in the future. As the themes of the traditional polity were being increasingly challenged during the 1780s, McKean suggested that Pennsylvania "was not a nation at war with another nation, but a country in a state of *civil war*" within itself. In these circumstances, many argued that the virtue of the new regime could be developed only by "good Americans," regardless of where they were born. Once again, such thoughts suggested obvious questions about the "adopted son" in contemporary Pennsylvania and led to a further infusion of ethno-cultural language into the political discourse of the day.[33] During the

33 Rush, *Considerations upon the Present Test Law*, 8–9; Lyman H. Butterfield, ed., *Letters of Benjamin Rush* 2 vols. (Princeton, 1951) i, 291–3, Rush to Montgomery, 5 Nov. 1782; "To the Citizens of Pennsylvania. Friends and Fellow-Citizens, The Majority of the House of Representatives of the Freemen of Pennsylvania beg leave to Address you ..." (broadside,

middle of the 1780s these issues came to a head in a heated paper war between Mathew Carey and his fellow newspaper editor, **Eleazer Oswald** (1755–95) of the (Philadelphia) *Independent Gazetteer*.

"Adopted Sons"

The focus of the exchanges between Carey and Oswald was one of the Constitutionalists' more influential clubs, *The Society of the Lately Adopted Sons of Pennsylvania*. Although the Sons had held "several meetings" before agreeing on a constitution on 2 January 1786, few details of their structure and membership survive. However, on 28 January 1786, the *Independent Gazetteer* printed their "principles, articles and regulations," most of which reflected Bryan's commitment to an organic polity. The second article proposed that "all foreign distinctions shall forever be abolished amongst us" while in a similar vein, the preamble suggested that "jealousies, engendered by national distinctions," "invariably" weakened that "principle of common attachment, which is the firmest support of every country." Such views mirrored those of the Constitutionalists at large that "the idea of forming a separate class from the body of the people" should be rejected in all circumstances. The society's sixth article specifically prohibited its members from using their "collective influence" politically by "induc[ing] the members of this association to adopt the sentiments and support the measures of any particular party." Instead, the Sons were encouraged to "strenuously exert" themselves on behalf of the prosperity, independence, laws and welfare of the state as a whole.[34]

Also on 28 January 1786, "An Old Inhabitant" castigated these sentiments and resolutions. He ignored the Sons' stated aspirations and suggested instead that their very existence had created "an artificial and odious distinction between those who have been kindly received as adopted sons, and the old inhabitants of Pennsylvania." In his view, the Sons had developed an "unavoidable tendency" to encourage "absolute hatred," "dislike," and "prejudices" between immigrants and "the true and natural citizens of the commonwealth." As such, they were

> a body of a declared *political* cast and character — a combination not indeed directly prohibited by, but very offensive to, the laws of this or any other well regulated government ... Is it not rather to be feared that these worthy

Philadelphia, 1784); "A Pennsylvanian" in *PEH*, 28 Dec. 1785. McKean is quoted in Calhoon, *Loyalists in Revolutionary America*, 399.

34 In addition to the reports in *IG*, see *Adopted Sons of Pennsylvania: Principles, Articles and Regulations ... of ...* (Philadelphia, 1786).

strangers will, by their association, foster and encourage in each other, sentiments of dislike and prejudices against the natural citizens of Pennsylvania? – an association which appears not only to be ungrateful, but seditious, inasmuch as it has a tendency to disturb the tranquillity of government ... [they were] a combination of foreigners, formed manifestly for the purposes of interfering, as a compact body, in the politics of the state.

The "Old Inhabitant" also alleged that he had uncovered five unpublished articles of the Sons' constitution and although these had been concocted by the writer himself, they indicate how the society could be perceived and portrayed. These alleged articles suggested that the Sons were an exclusive group through which immigrants would have "as little connection as possible" with the "native-born." Thus, they included an oath whereby members were obliged to swear that they would associate only with those who had been born and educated "in one of the *three kingdoms*" while another proposed that the Sons should buy only from one another, meet in one another's taverns and inns, and deal only with lawyers who themselves were "adopted sons." It was also assumed that they would vote only for tickets that had been "approved by this society" and indeed, the "Old Inhabitant" alleged that the Sons would offer a "one shilling reward" to any member "who shall persuade twenty persons" to vote for candidates they recommended. Moreover, members who were elected to public office should "never do any act, matter or thing, without the consent and approbation of this society first." As a result, in the words of "A Foreigner," the Sons would threaten "domestic tranquillity," "raise sedition," and show the very "highest ingratitude to the country in which we receive our bread." They were a latter-day "Powder-Plot combination" of "foreign renegadoes" who were unworthy of any public trust in the new republic, including citizenship."[35]

Such commentaries led Oswald and others to taunt the Sons' leaders. However, despite reports that "the persons who set this scheme [of the Sons] on foot are very well known," few of them were, or can be, identified. Samuel Finlay, a recent immigrant from Ireland and his friend, Jean Marmie, a partner in the merchant shippers, Turnbull, Marmie & Co., were named as secretary and chairman, respectively. The political involvements of the Sons are also unclear. However, Finlay and Bryan were friends and on 28 January 1786 the *Independent Gazetteer* reported that Bryan had "won" the Sons for the Constitutionalists.[36] Also in 1786 Dr. James Hutchinson (1752–93) asked the

35 *IG*, 28, 7 Jan. 1786. "A Foreigner" is quoted in *PP*, 2 Dec. 1785. For the earlier meetings, see *IG*, 7 Jan 1786; 17 Dec. 1785; and *PP*, 2 Dec. 1785.
36 *PP*, 2 Dec. 1785; *IG*, 7 Jan. 1786; Vernon O. Stumpf, "Colonel Eleazer Oswald: Politician and Editor" (Ph.D. dissertation, Duke University, 1970), 200, 211–12, 192. For Finlay's "frequent" visits to Bryan's home, see Stumpf, *ibid.*, 200. Marmie had come to America

Sons for their votes and influence in the Assembly elections of that year and in September 1787 the Sons' swan-song mentioned their "important services" to the Constitutionalists. Over forty years later Carey recalled that the society had accorded "in political opinions with the constitutional party, to which it became an auxiliary." During the 1780s, however, he kept the Sons at arm's length and while the Irish-born Carey was himself an "adopted son," before 1800, he never commented publicly on the society, stating in December 1785 that he would leave "the defence of their cause to themselves." Carey realised that the broadsides against the Sons, as well as the discussion on the supposed influence of the foreign-born, were being used to promote broader concerns, including anxieties about the emergence of "new" leaders within the state. By that time, Oswald had already published a number of attacks on leading Constitutionalists. It was also alleged that on 17 December 1785 he had attacked Finlay with a club as he walked down Chesnut Street, one of the main streets of Philadelphia. Three years earlier Oswald had also been arrested and tried for libelling Reed. He was now convinced that Carey and the Sons had "enlisted under the banners of Mr. Bryan" and accordingly, he began to challenge and abuse them publicly through pamphlets as well as in his newspaper.[37]

Oswald's views were being expressed at a time when the political conflict between Constitutionalists and Republicans was particularly acute. As already stated, Rush had published an influential pamphlet in 1785 in which he argued

as secretary to Lafayette and later acted as Carey's second in his duel with Oswald in January 1786; Edward Carter II, "The Political Activities of Mathew Carey, Nationalist, 1760–1814" (Ph.D. dissertation, Bryn Mawr, 1962), 14–16. He became a leading flour merchant in Philadelphia and his company, formed in association with the Scottish immigrant, William Turnbull, had the city's highest tax assessment in 1781; see Duvall, "Philadelphia's Maritime Commerce," 159, 136–7. In his autobiography, Carey listed the leading Pennsylvania lawyer, Alexander Dallas, his colleague, Counsellor Heatly and one Mr. Coulthurst as members of the Adopted Sons; see Mathew Carey, *Autobiography* (Brooklyn, new ed., 1942), 13. Carey's biographer identifies Dallas as a founding member of the Sons; see Carter, "The Political Activities of Mathew Carey," 150. Dallas was a protegé of Bryan. He was also assumed to be "Harlequin" who had attacked Oswald during the elections of 1785; see (Philadelphia) *Freeman's Journal*, 5 Oct. 1785; *PP*, 5 Oct. 1785; and *IG*, 1, 8 Oct. 1785.

37 Raymond Walters, Jr., "The Origins of the Jeffersonian Party in Pennsylvania," *PMHB* lxvi (1942), 443; *PEH*, 1 Sept. 1787; Carey, *Autobiography*, 13; *PEH*, 31 Dec. 1785; *IG*, 7 Jan. 1786; *PEH*, 17 Dec. 1785; Stumpf, "Colonel Eleazer Oswald," chs. 5–7. Carter states that Carey was not only a member, but the secretary of the Adopted Sons; see Carter "Political Activities of Mathew Carey," 119. Brunhouse also refers to the Sons' role in the 1786 elections in his *Counter-Revolution*, 192. On the relationship between the Sons and the Constitutionalists, see J.T. Scharf and Thompson Westcott, *History of Philadelphia* 3 vols. (Philadelphia, 1884) i, 443. Charles Biddle suggested that the Sons disbanded after the Carey/Oswald duel; see *Autobiography of Charles Biddle* (Philadelphia, 1883), 231. In Dec. 1785, Carey alleged that Oswald's attacks had been occasioned because the *Herald* had not espoused "his [Oswald's] party," *PEH*, 7 Dec. 1785.

that the Test Acts should be repealed. For his part, Oswald also reminded his readers in January of that year that the acts had excluded from public life all those who had been pacifists during the Revolutionary war and that as a result, Pennsylvania's new Constitutionalist establishment had emerged from circumstances that were contrived, artificial, and immoral. However, attitudes to the acts were beginning to change on all sides. In April 1785 even Bryan and "100 more of the Constitutionalist party" signed "the Petition to the Assembly of Pennsylvania ... for the repeal of the Present Test Laws" while the following December, Carey's *Pennsylvania Evening Herald* stated that he

> could not conceive it a matter of much political consequence to government, what political opinions the nonjurors held nine or ten years ago; it is of much more importance to know what opinions they now hold, and to consider by what means they may be most useful to the community.

A few months later the paper even suggested that the Test Laws had "produced more disorders, by making enemies in this state, than have cursed all the union besides ... The best way to make men honest, is to let them enjoy equal rights and privileges." Because of these shifting political sands, Carey suggested that the October 1785 elections to the state legislature would "bid fair to produce a most violent contest" and observed after they began that "no exertions are spared on either side." The state's "adopted sons" were deemed to be vital to Bryan's success and as such, they were attacked in increasingly graphic language. They were, as one correspondent to the *Independent Gazetteer* put it, "such Arabs and Vipers of organized society, such Baboons of ingratitude and objects of Pennsylvania detestation [who] should be treated by every American and connaturalised American, with the contempt and infamy they deserve." In Oswald's eyes, Carey personified these "scourings of nations and the very refuse of mankind."[38]

Oswald commenced his attacks on Carey by suggesting that he had greatly overstated his involvement in the **Volunteer movement** in Ireland. He also challenged his portrayal as a champion of a free press there. In his autobiography, Carey recorded that he had been forced to flee to France in 1779 following the publication of a pamphlet which urged "the immediate repeal" of the Penal Laws in Ireland. Despite the "considerable alarm" which the pamphlet had caused, he was allowed to return, only to have to leave again after his newspaper, the (Dublin) *Volunteer Journal*, was accused of libelling the speaker of the Irish

---

38 Main, *Political Parties*, 204; *IG*, 7 May 1785; *PEH*, 28 Dec., 5 Oct. 1785; *PEH*, 11 Mar. 1786; Stumpf, "Colonel Eleazer Oswald," 184; *PP*, 2 Dec. 1785; *IG*, 7 Jan. 1786. The *Independent Gazetteer* is quoted in Fäy, *Two Franklins*, 77.

House of Commons. Oswald questioned Carey's account of this affair, suggested that he had never even owned the newspaper that was cited in the charge, and maintained that the circumstances of Carey's subsequent emigration from Ireland (supposedly disguised as a woman) had been far from honourable. Oswald also laced his charges with vitriolic references to Carey's background and personality and even linked the lameness of this "new-imported *petticoat*" to his "*crooked politics* [which] are corresponsive to *the deformity of your person:*" "Your being a cripple is your main protection against personal insults, which your *oblique insinuations* would otherwise challenge."[39]

Carey made every effort to refute the "most wanton, unjustifiable, and libellous" attempts "to destroy my character for ever." As one response to "the virulent libeller of Philadelphia" whose "crude [and] undigested" writing he likened to "the ravings of a lunatic, and the abuse of a Billingsgate fishwoman," he published affidavits concerning both his ownership of the *Volunteer Journal* and his **Patriotic** activities in Ireland. In the *Pennsylvania Evening Herald*, he also gave a detailed account of why and how he had left Dublin. Oswald had also accused Carey of "co-operating with our [America's] enemies to dishonour and degrade us, in *Hibernia*." Carey rejected this bluntly and was able to show that Oswald's alleged evidence for the charge had been "mutilated" from edited reports that had originated in the *London Evening Post*. If Oswald's allegation suggested anything, according to Carey, it was the extent to which British newspapers had been used as a tool of imperial propaganda during the Revolution. Carey also revealed that after he arrived in America, Lafayette asked him to visit and in recognition of his Patriotic activities in Ireland, gave him "a sum in bank notes sufficient to place me once more in business." He would "defy any *credible* person to produce a single line, or prove a single word, that I have ever written or said, derogatory to the honour or dignity of Pennsylvania." To the contrary, he had always been far from "crying down the country that gives me bread ... [or] dropping any malevolent odiums and stigmas on it." The Carey-Oswald exchanges reached their nadir on 16 January 1786 when Carey published the 294-line *Plagi-Scurriliad: A Hudibrastic Poem. Dedicated to Colonel Eleazer Oswald*. This was considered by at least one contemporary to be "the most *bitter* thing that has appeared in America." Carey himself admitted that his "piece will be styled severe; perhaps with justice; but I trust, in this case, as in various others, severity will not be found incompatible with candour and truth." Two days after it was published, it led to a duel between the two men as a result of which Carey was seriously injured. On 28 January 1786 his *Pennsylvania Evening Herald* finally published statements from the two men

39 Carey, *Autobiography*, 5; *PEH*, 25 Jan. 1785; Carey, *Autobiography*, 11; *IG*, 10, 3 Nov., 10 Dec. 1785.

which terminated at least the personal side of their quarrel. Carey recognised Oswald's "honour" and retracted "what I have asserted derogatory to this character" while Oswald acknowledged Carey's "candour and generosity [and] request[ed] that he may be considered in the same honourable point of view the public held him in, previous to the commencement of our disagreeable controversy."[40]

Carey acknowledged that the outcome of the debate with Oswald gave "great offence to the Irish, who had taken great interest in the affair on my side, many of whom never forgave me for what they called a degradation." Despite the castigation of his own reputation, he had always been aware of the broader dimensions of the exchanges. Oswald, he argued, "with no small artifice [had] endeavoured to make this a matter of party. But I hope the public will despise the subterfuge. It is a cause between two individuals, wherein I disclaim all interference of party in my favour, and beg that party may not operate against me." As a result, although he had bristled at suggestions that he had aided the "enemies of America" in Ireland, Carey understood that Oswald was also questioning the commitment and loyalty of all Irish immigrants to the Atlantic revolution. As Oswald had sarcastically put it, "the *lip* of patriotism is of late become so fashionable that every *vagrant* stranger and *new-coming* imposter, every *grasshopper* and *renegado*, can accommodate, as occasion requires, himself thereto." Carey thus presented himself less as an immigrant than as a Patriot whose "oppression" in Ireland should provide a "sufficient introduction" in a country which had recently fought for and obtained its own independence:

> From old Hibernia's troubled isle,
> where oft the Graces deign'd to smile,
> An injur'd, humble VOLUNTEER,
> I follow FREEDOM's fortunes here,
> To guard her rights, espouse her cause,
> Assert her claims, and guard her laws.

An ode which Carey published in honour of George Washington's birthday in 1786 made a similar point:

> From various lands and climes we come
> Invited to this common home,

---

40 *PEH*, 10 Dec. 1785; *The Plagi-Scurriliad: A Hudibrastic Poem. Dedicated to Colonel Eleazer Oswald* (Philadelphia, 1786), iii, iv; *PEH*, 10 Dec. 1785; *IG*, 7 Jan. 1786; *PEH*, 11, 25 Jan. 1786; *PEH*, 7, 31 Dec. 1785; *PEH*, 9 Nov. 1785; HSP, Lea & Febiger Collection (Incoming, 1785–96), x, Aneas Lamont to Carey, 22 Jan. 1786; *Plagi-Scurriliad*, iii; *PP*, 19 Jan. 1786. The retractions are also referred to in Carey, *Autobiography*, 16.

Resolv'd to guard the sacred rights you gave,
In Freedom's cause to persevere,
To hate a tyrant, and to scorn a slave.[41]

Carey argued that immigrants in general, and those who had come from Ireland, in particular, had played an active, acknowledged, and "a very great (perhaps I might say the major) part" in the fight for American independence. They had "proven" their patriotism in deed as well as in word and as such, they could be trusted to consolidate the new nation for which they had fought. As such people were now being crudely termed "aliens" or "foreigners," and were "the subjects of obloquy and reproach," Carey suggested that it was "Americans" who were "ungrateful to the highest degree." Oswald rejected any attempt to recognise Irish immigrants among the fathers of the Revolution and although he acknowledged some obligation to France, he argued that Carey's assertions were "such arrogant gasconade, as would disgrace the lips of an idiot" and that if anyone was ungrateful, it was the immigrants themselves. His *Independent Gazetteer* concluded that the "stranger" had "reviled the country that feeds him instead of treating it with respect" and that the involvement of immigrants in Pennsylvania politics could lead to nothing "other than ... separating the foreigners from the natives."[42]

Carey had always feared that the labelling of the Constitutionalists as "novel" and "outsider" would lead to a "most wanton attack on *new comers*." This was even more apposite because the conflict between Republicans and Constitutionalists was being presented in the terms of traditional political factionalism: "ins" and "outs," or the "old" competing with the "new" or "aspiring" wealth." Carey had always strongly opposed such contrasts, especially between "newcomers and residents," and later recalled that his "dispute" with Oswald had "originated from some illiberal remarks written in his [Oswald's] paper against new-comers. As a new-comer, I thought myself called upon to answer them." Carey argued that "national reflections ... are in every case, as *illiberal* as they are *unjust*." In August 1786 the *Pennsylvania Evening Herald* suggested that even to dwell on the issue was to "divide the people of this country, and create dissensions and ill-blood between the old citizens, and those who are on every occasion spoken of with a kind of superciliousness and impertinent obloquy and contempt as '*new comers — new comers*'." Carey was uncomfortable with such

---

41 *Autobiography*, 16; *Plagi-Scurriliad*, iv; *PEH*, 11 Jan. 1786; *IG*, 7 Jan. 1786; *PEH*, 25 Jan. 1785; LCP, Broadsides Collection, "Ode on the Birth-day of his Excellency, General Washington, celebrated by the Adopted Sons."

42 *PEH*, 9 Nov. 1785; Carey, *Autobiography*, 13; *IG*, 3 Dec. 1785; *IG*, 5 Nov. 1785; *PP*, 2 Dec. 1785.

language and although Oswald accused the newspaper of publishing the "discordant notes" of "every detestable faction and party in the state," Carey's personal views on political culture were traditional and conservative. True to the idealism of the Irish Reform Movement, Carey believed that political progress was possible only if it incorporated class and interest. His understanding of the polity was inclusive and comprehensive and because of this, it would also be unified and strong, tolerant, and benevolent. Towards the end of 1786 he also began to feel increasingly limited by Constitutionalist policies and to support the repeal of the Test Acts. In October 1785 Carey wrote that it was

> a most mortifying consideration that private views and prejudices have gained such an ascendancy over the good of the community, in the breasts of a majority of both the great parties that agitate and divide the state, [and] that no man or body of men comes forward from either side, to suggest any mode of effecting any accommodation.[43]

By the middle of the 1780s even emotional issues such as the Test Acts were a thing of the past. As the founders of the republic sat down to write a new federal constitution, political discourse was more pragmatic and positive than it had been five years earlier. In January 1789 Tench Coxe (1755–1824), the distinguished political economist and assistant secretary of the treasury (1790–92), spoke for many others when he wrote that he was "still a federalist & a republican, but I am no longer a *party man*." Pennsylvania's new state constitution reflected such a spirit of compromise between Republicans and Constitutionalists, letting the "old" absorb the "new" so that the document's promise of what one broadside called "security to life, liberty and property, and which has already restored harmony to our long distracted State" could be realised. However, by adding that "it will be necessary that the government should be administered by wise and good men," it also warned that the transition towards what Rush described as a "revolution in our principles, opinions and manners" might not be an orderly and balanced process.[44] The larger implications of the paper war between Carey and Oswald had highlighted

---

43 *PEH*, 10 Dec., 9 Nov. 1785; *Plagi-Scurilliad*, iii; *PEH*, 9 Nov. 1785, 30 Aug. 1786; *IG*, 14 Jan. 1786; *PEH*, 8 Oct. 1785.

44 HSP, Tench Coxe Papers, microfilm reel 52, Rush to Coxe, dated Philadelphia, 13 Jan. 1789; (broadside), *Philadelphia, September 6th, 1790. Gentlemen, Permit us* (Philadelphia? 1790); Butterfield ed., *Letters of Benjamin Rush* i, 39, Rush to Richard Price, 25 May 1786. For the constitution of 1790, see Harry M. Tinkcom, *The Republicans and Federalists in Pennsylvania, 1790–1801: A Study in National Stimulus and Local Response* (Harrisburg, 1950), ch.2; Joseph S. Foster, "The Politics of Ideology: The Pennsylvania Constitutional Convention of 1789–90" in *PH*, cix, no. 2 (Apr. 1992), 122–58.

some of the difficulties that the leaders of the new republic would face in comprehending "old" and "new" and showed that, even at a time of pragmatism, this was a complicated and at times, an uneasy challenge. However, Carey appreciated that if the situation in Philadelphia was anything to go by, the regulation and status of immigrants had to be clearly addressed as an aspect of consolidating the new republic.

"Meritorious Strangers"

In general terms, attitudes to immigrants had been shaped by the catchwords of the Country tradition: industry, frugality, public spiritedness, and independence and by the view, as repeated by Franklin in 1787, that "only a virtuous people are capable of freedom."[45] However, given a continuous passenger flow from Europe, they were also affected by how the old world was being seen from the new. Franklin had been greatly influenced by what he had experienced and observed during his visit to Scotland and Ireland in 1771 and he made his views known. As he wrote to the Rhode Island jurist, Joshua Babcock (1707–83), in 1772, the "savage state" of the peasantry exemplified a "horrible maxim" of the old world that in the interests of "tyranny and of commerce, [the people] must be poor" and forced labourers, urban as well as rural, into "pauperism," "beggary," "depravity of morals," and "almost every crime." As a result, the peasantry would remain forever "in subjection" and lack initiative and productivity. Franklin's opinions were not without influence as the Founding Fathers debated the status of immigrants in the new republic. In December 1774 Alexander Hamilton, later to become the first secretary of the treasury (1789–95), noted that the "continual emigrations" from Britain and Ireland were from two kingdoms that were "a good deal impoverished." At least for him, the warning to the new world of what to avoid of the old was obvious.[46]

---

45 Franklin to the Abbés Chalut and Arnaud, 17 Apr. 1787, as quoted in Drew R. McCoy, "Benjamin Franklin's Vision of a Republican Political Economy for America," *WMQ* xxxc (October 1978), 606. In a similar vein, Washington suggested to William Tilghman on 21 July 1793 that "perfect honesty, sobriety, and industry are indispensable" to freedom and independence; see John C. Fitzpatrick ed., *The Writings of George Washington* 39 vols. (repr. Washington, D.C., 1931–44) xxxiii, 26. For a discussion of the merits of virtue as an insurance against the dissipation of American potential, see Drew R. McCoy, *The Elusive Republic: Political Economy in Jeffersonian America* (Williamsburg, 1980), 619–22.

46 Franklin to Joshua Babcock, 13 Jan. 1772 in Labaree *et al.*, eds., *Papers of Benjamin Franklin* xix, 7; "Reflections on the Augmentation of Wages" in Jared Sparks ed., *The Works of Benjamin Franklin* 10 vols. (Boston, 1836–40) ii, 441–5; Hamilton, "A Full Vindication of the Measures of Congress from the Calumnies of their Enemies (New York, 1774)" in Harold C. Syrett *et al.*, eds., *The Papers of Alexander Hamilton* 27 vols. (New York, 1961–87) i, 58. For an analysis of Franklin's views on political economy, see

By December 1791 Hamilton had changed his ground somewhat and as Franklin had done earlier, he suggested in his *Report on the Subject of Manufactures* that America would benefit from the contribution that immigrants could make to economic and agricultural development although they had to be "made sensible" of what awaited them in America. Many agreed with him. Coxe argued that "European superiority in manufacturing technique could be overcome [in America] only by borrowing it" through its skilled workers.[47] Private organisations such as the New Jersey Manufacturing Society took up this point and offered premiums to encourage skilled people to emigrate from Europe while individuals such as Thomas Digges reprinted Hamilton's *Report*, "confident that the distribution of it, in the way I intend, will induce many to move towards the manufacturing parts of America." Some states also gave "premiums upon the introduction into the United States of all *kinds of manufacturing machinery*" and these were duly noted in the *Freeman's Journal* on 3 April 1790. After 1787 Virginia exempted incoming artisans

> from the payment from any tax or duty on his or their tools or implements of trade, which he or she shall bring into this Commonwealth ... and shall moreover be exempted from all taxes whatsoever, except the land tax, for the space of five years next thereafter, if he or they shall so long continue the actual exercise of his or their trade or occupation therein.

This act also repealed previous legislation, including the "Bill for the Naturalization of Foreigners" (1776), which had offered twenty shillings "to every foreigner" who came to Virginia "for the purpose of defraying his passage hither over the sea," as well as fifty acres of unappropriated land.[48]

Paul W. Conner, *Poor Richard's Politics: Benjamin Franklin and His New American Order* (New York, 1965); and Gerard Stourzh, *Benjamin Franklin and American Foreign Policy* (Chicago, 1969). Franklin's visit to Ireland is discussed in Bernard Nolan, *Benjamin Franklin in Scotland and Ireland* (Philadelphia, 1938).

47 Syrett ed., *Papers of Hamilton* x, 259. Coxe is quoted from Maldwyn Jones, *American Immigration* (Chicago, 1968), 68. For considered discussion of Hamilton's *Report*, see McCoy, *Elusive Republic*, 148–65; Elkins and McKittrick, *Age of Federalism*, 158–63; and Doron Ben-Atar, "Alexander Hamilton's Alternative. Technology Piracy and the Report on Manufactures" in Ben-Atar and Barbara B. Oberg, eds., *Federalists Reconsidered* (Charlottesville and London, 1998), 41–60. For an excellent analysis of the political economy of the period, see also Cathy D. Matheson and Peter S. Onuf, eds., *A Union of Interests: Political and Economic Thought in Revolutionary America* (Lawrence, 1990).

48 *FJ*, 3Apr. 1790; "An Act to Explain, Amend, and Reduce into one Act, the Several Acts for the Admission of Emigrants to the Rights of Citizenship ..." as in the *Virginia Gazette*, 10 Jan. 1787. For the 1776 act, see Julian P. Boyd *et al.*, eds., *The Papers of Thomas Jefferson* 31 vols. (Princeton, 1950–2004) i, 559. Digges is cited from Syrett, ed., *Papers of Hamilton* xi, 243, 241, n.1, Digges to Hamilton, dated in Belfast, 6 Apr. 1792.

The change in terms was significant because the 1787 legislation effectively redirected state encouragement and support for immigration away from "the peopling of America" *per se* and towards those "artists and their tools" who could promote the country's economic infrastructure. Before the Revolution, many colonies had sponsored schemes of assisted immigration that had been crucial to their development and security. During the 1770s public representatives were more cautious about such schemes. In 1775 Congress rejected a plan to promote immigration from Ireland by offering access to cheap land while in the 1780s it indicated that it would not support Jefferson's plans to develop the Northwest Ordinance and refused to sanction favourable concessions to those who might settle there. Its reasoning in these two instances was clear. Irrespective of colonial precedent and what Marilyn Baseler has termed "the contradictory principles and impulses embodied in the American asylum," there was general agreement that Congress and the various state governments should not promote emigration from Europe, at least in any formal manner.[49]

Franklin had long been in favour of a more discriminating policy on immigration and counselled against the "fruitless removals and voyages of *improper* persons" from Europe. He also felt that there was a need to correct the "wild imaginings" and "mistaken ideas and expectations" that some Europeans had of America and, in particular, to confront the "very assiduous ... endeavours [that were being made] to blacken America" in Britain and Ireland. This led him to write one of the principal expositions on eighteenth-century American immigration, the *Information to Those who Would Wish to Remove to America*. This was published in Philadelphia in 1782 and contained, in Washington's words, "every thing that needs to be known on the subject of migrating to this Country."[50] Franklin argued that opportunity in America had to be seen on its own terms and not on those of contemporary Europe. As Rush put it, "strangers of birth" were respected in America if they possessed a "useful art" and "behave[d] well," not because of their ancestry. In many ways,

For the New Jersey Society, see NA, FO/4/14, Hammond to Dundas, 4 Jan. 1792. See also Carroll W. Pursell, "Thomas Digges and William Pearce: an Example of the Transit of Technology," *WMQ* xxi (1964), 551–60.

49 *FJ*, 3 Apr. 1790; Marilyn C. Baseler, *"Asylum for Mankind:" America 1607–1800* (Ithaca and London, 1998), 146, 213–4,1. The phrase "peopling of America" is taken from Bernard Bailyn's work, *The Peopling of British North America: An Introduction* (New York, 1986).

50 "Information to Those who Would Remove to America" in Sparks ed., *Franklin's Writings* ii, 468–72, italics mine; "To the Printer of the Evening Herald" in *ibid*. x, 329–30. Washington's view of Franklin's *Information* is quoted in Saul Padover, ed., *The Washington Papers* (New York, 1955), 358. For the *Information* itself, see Sparks, ed., *Franklin's Writings* ii, 467–77. It was also published in Ireland in *BN*, 26 Oct., 2 Nov. 1784 and *HJ*, 8 Nov. 1784.

Rush's *Information to Europeans who are Disposed to Migrate to the United States* (Philadelphia, 1790) complemented Franklin's *Information*. It also characterised those "who ought *not*" to emigrate as well as those who "may better their condition by coming to America." Among the latter, the two writers suggested that husbandmen, indentured servants, mechanics, artisans "of all the necessary and useful kinds," and "good workmen" could "remove with advantage to America." Rush also discussed a number of practical points, such as the capital that was needed to settle in America as well as the types of holding that could be acquired there. The central point was familiar: "success depends upon industry." In his *Letters from an American Farmer* (London, 1782), Crèvecoeur made a similar point:

> If thou wilt work, I have bread for thee; if thou wilt be honest, sober and industrious, I have greater rewards to confer on thee ease and independence … the immunities of a freeman … Go thou and work and till thou shalt prosper, provided thou be just, grateful and industrious.

"In short," as Franklin concluded, "America is the land of labour."[51]

For Jefferson, Franklin's *Information* contained "cogent views" which he had reprinted to save "needless repetition" in answering letters he received on the subject. For his part, Franklin stated that he would personally give "no encouragement" to the "multitude of People" who "continually" applied to him for advice. Jefferson indicated that he also would be evasive, "having no charge from the United States on this subject." Adams was as cold. In 1788 he answered queries from the Dutch reformer, Francis van der Kemp (1752–1829), only in the most conventional terms, remarking that he had been "scrupulous of advising strangers to emigrate to America." Two years earlier, as the serving American minister to London (1785–88), he had made the same point in a more terse fashion to John Wooddrop of Glasgow: "I am not come to this Country, sir, to solicit emigrations to the United States of America, nor to offer any Kind of Encouragement to such as wish to go." In 1793 Washington also stated that he either made no answer, or replied only "in very general terms" to the "number of letters" that he received on emigration. To do otherwise "might be represented that I was officiously using the arts of seduction to depopulate countries, for the sake of peopling our own." In any event, such encouragement

51 (Benjamin Rush), *Information to Europeans who are Disposed to Migrate to the United States. In a Letter from a Citizen of Pennsylvania, to his Friend in Great Britain* (Philadelphia, 1790), 3, 10; J. Hector de St. John Crèvecoeur, *Letters from An American Farmer*, ed. Ludwig Lewisohn (Garden City, N.Y., 1904), 73. The quotations from Franklin are from his "Information to Those who Would Remove to America," as in Sparks, ed., *Franklin's Writings* ii, 468–72.

was inconsistent with the type of self-reliance that Franklin was trying to inspire through his *Information*. The "good laws and liberty" of America should speak for themselves.[52]

However, many of America's new leaders regarded "freedom of emigration" to be in "the general interests of humanity." Even as Washington recalled Hamilton's earlier fears that poorer immigrants might prove to be a liability rather than an asset to the new republic, he suggested that attracting "the oppressed and needy of the Earth" was neither untenable nor *ultra vires* in America, especially if it was balanced by the encouragement of "industrious characters from all parts of Europe." Work would generate its own rewards. In Franklin's view, this would lead immigrants of even "moderate fortunes and capitals" to "secure estates for posterity." For Rush, it would also enable the industrious to "make respectable connexions in marriage" and "ascend to the first ranks in society" and office. America offered not merely an opportunity for upward mobility. It also encouraged the kinds of individuality and competitiveness that were regarded as indispensable for the creation of the new republican experiment. Settlers would be able to stand on their own and would not be intimidated by the social, religious and political hierarchies of their ethno-cultural communities. They would also overcome the supposed political and religious absolutisms of the old world to "love this country [America] much better than that wherein [their] ... forefathers were born." As immigrants became more "American," they would dedicate themselves, in Washington's words, to "our customs, measures and laws."[53]

In 1727 this view of civic society had influenced a hostile memorial on immigration that was presented to the Pennsylvania legislature. Referring to Swedish immigrants, the document stated that "These preach to and instruct

---

52 Jefferson to Gallimard, 29 July 1788 in Boyd *et al.*, eds., *Papers of Thomas Jefferson* xiii, 431 and footnote to the same; Franklin to Robert Livingston, 15 April 1783 in Albert Henry Smyth, ed., *The Writings of Benjamin Franklin* 10 vols. (New York, 1907) ix, 34; HSP, Letters of John Adams, Am. oo6 (1781–1825), John Adams to Van der Kemp, 1 Jan. 1788 and to John Wooddrop, 3 February 1786, as quoted in a footnote to Boyd *et al.*, eds., *Papers of Thomas Jefferson* xiii, 432; Washington to Arthur Young, 12 Dec. 1793, "Miscellaneous Writings" in Fitzpatrick, ed., *Writings of Washington* xxxiii, 182; "Information to Those who would Remove to America" in Sparks ed., *Franklin's Writings* ii, 436. For Franklin's correspondents on the subject of emigration, see Merrill Jensen, *The New Nation* (New York, 1950), 122–3.

53 "Population and Emigration" in *NG*, 21 Nov. 1791; Washington to Robert Henderson, 19 June 1788 in Padover, ed., *Washington Papers*, 358; Washington to Jefferson, 1 Jan. 1788 in Fitzpatrick, ed., *Writings of Washington* xxix, 351; "Information to Those who Would Remove to America" in Sparks, ed., *Franklin's Writings* ii, 472; Rush, *Information to Europeans*, 8–9; Crèvecoeur, *Letters from an American Farmer*, ed. Lewisohn, 50; Washington to Adams, 27 Nov. 1794 in Sparks, ed., *Washington's Writings* ii, 1–2.

their People and perform all their worship in the Swedish Tongue. Few of them intermarry with any others than amongst themselves, but carefully *keep up a national Distinction.*" Such concerns were little different from those of Franklin twenty six years later when he berated Pennsylvania's German settlers because

> Few of their children in the county learn English; they import many books from Germany ... Advertisements intended to be general are now printed in Dutch and English; the signs in our streets have inscriptions in both languages, and in some places only German. They begin of late to make all their bonds and other legal writings in their own language which are allowed good in our Courts.

In 1750 James Hamilton, lieutenant governor of Pennsylvania (1748–54), had expressed the somewhat similar view that the province "would be better pleased with the speedy settlement of this by persons who understood our Laws and our Language. But these [German] people do neither nor will they for as long time to come." The fear was that as a result, the polity, as "founded by the English," would be compromised and that in Tully's words, "a significant de-Anglicization of Pennsylvania culture and politics" would follow.[54]

Such sentiments were not uncommon. They reflected the English origins and character of America's political culture which supposed the homogeneity of the polity and the reconcilability of its members. In his *Notes on Virginia* (1782), Jefferson thus aired his worries about the immigration of people from "absolute monarchies:"

> They will bring with them the principles of the governments they leave, imbibed in their early youth; or, if able to throw them off, it will be in exchange for an unbounded licentiousness, passing as is usual, from one extreme to another. It would be a miracle were they to stop precisely at the point of temperate liberty ... They will infuse into it [legislation] their spirit, warp and bias its direction, and render it a heterogenous, incoherent, distracted mass.

Jefferson was not alone in holding these views. Franklin also implied that because many European immigrants were "not used to liberty, they know not how to make a modest use of it" when the came to America. As a result, they

---

54 HSP, Society Misc., Box 4-B, a memorial; Franklin to Peter Collinson, 9 May 1753 in Bigelow, ed., *Works of Franklin* ii, 291; Tully, "Englishmen and Germans," *PH* xlv (1978), 245. Hamilton is quoted from A.G. Roeber, " Citizens or Subjects? German-Lutherans and the Federal Constitution, 1789–1800," *Amerikastudien* xxv (1989), 50–1. The context of the 1727 memorial is analysed in Swartz, *Mixed Multitude*, 88–92.

often assumed "airs" that threatened social peace and cohesion as well as the development of an undifferentiated society and polity. Thus, the *Pennsylvania Evening Herald* concluded that "water and oil may as easily be made to unite as the subjects of monarchies with the citizens of the republics of America." Not everybody agreed. One writer suggested that "Emigrants from the old world, flying from oppression, carried along with them ... minds emancipated from the tyranny of custom, and [as a result, were] open to the most enlarged views of the most liberal policy and jurisprudence." They were precisely the kind of people that the new republic needed.[55]

In *The Federalist*, John Jay described his "one connected country to one people" as follows: "a people descended from the same ancestors, speaking the same language, professing the same religion, attached to the same principles of government, [and] very similar in their manners and customs." This was an ideal community that had already been described somewhat differently by Crèvecoeur as a set of "individuals of all nations ... melted into a new race of men" and which justified a view of America as "the most perfect society now existing in the world." Others saw the development of the new republic in different terms. In *Common Sense*, Thomas Paine stressed that the integrity of the individual should not be fenced within a particular tradition, however noble, and famously suggested that "Europe, and not England, is the parent country of America. This New World has been the asylum for the persecuted lovers of civil and religious liberty from every part of Europe." For Paine and others, such sentiments would challenge America to develop *whatever* social and political model would best serve its interests. However, all were agreed that the ethno-cultural rivalries of the old world should not be reproduced in the new and that as Jefferson put it, "It is for the happiness of those united in society to harmonize as much as possible in matters which they must of necessity transact together." Thus, it is symbolic that as Congress agreed on the Great Seal of the United States in 1782, it accepted the motto of Eugène du Simitière (1737–84), *E Pluribus Unum*, but rejected his inclusion of national symbols from Ireland, the Germanies and France as part of the design. The establishment of "the national character of America" demanded no less.[56]

---

55 "Notes on Virginia" in Andrew A. Lipscomb ed., *The Writings of Jefferson* 20 vols. (Washington, D.C., 1903–4) ii, 120–1; Franklin to Collinson, 9 May 1753 in Bigelow ed., *Works of Franklin* ii, 413; "English Versus Germans" in "Notes and Queries," *PMHB* xvi (1893), 120; *PEH*, 30 Aug. 1786; *SN*, 4 Oct. 1785.

56 The quotations in this paragraph are cited in Willi Paul Adams, "The Founding Fathers and the Immigrants" in *La Révolution Américaine et l'Europe* (Paris, 1979), 138, 139, 137 and 146. For du Simitière, see Roeber, "Citizens or Subjects?," 50. The final quotation is from *NYP*, 24 Aug. 1787.

For some, the use of non-English languages in America represented a continuing challenge to progress. It also prevented the acquisition of a type of "useful knowledge" that was "necessary" for personal improvement and encumbered "not only the form of government, but the temper, the sentiments, and manners of the people." In August 1788 "Philanthropos" made an obvious point:

> Our elections are very frequent and by ballot, our electors free and equal, and no qualifications but local residence and citizenship are requisite in the elected. In a government so democratic it is necessary that the citizens should possess an uncommon portion of information. It is dangerous they should be uninformed. Their tickets may be changed at the door of the house of election, if they cannot read them. They will be constantly deceived by artful and designing men.

In 1785 the *Pennsylvania Gazette* suggested that the establishment of "a German College" might help to "prepare the way for the Germans to unite more intimately with their British and Irish fellow-subjects, and thus to form, with them, one homogenous mass of people." During the 1790s Washington's support for "establishing a National University" was influenced by a similar view that "the more homogenous our Citizens can be made in these particulars [education], the greater will be our prospect of permanent Union." However, such projects could be controversial. In the 1750s a scheme to educate German immigrants in charity schools in Pennsylvania failed because of allegations that the schools were being used to convert pupils to Anglicanism.[57]

Rush was not troubled by such proposals. Moreover, he actively encouraged the immigration of as many sects and groups as possible, however different they were from one another, and suggested that together, they could promote "the grand, supreme truth of universal salvation" which for him, had been heralded by the Revolution. However, Rush's "republican theology" was untypical and most of the Founding Fathers did not support immigration *en bloc* from Europe. In 1794 a worried Washington suggested to Adams that a proposed colony of Genevans "taking place in a body ... may be much questioned; for, by so doing, they retain the Language, habits, and principles (good or bad) which they bring with them." Jefferson also believed that it was "better to discourage

57 "Philanthropos" in *PG*, 6 Aug. 1788; "A Friend to Liberty and Learning in Pennsylvania" in *PG*, 31 Aug. 1785; Washington, "Eighth Annual Address to Congress," 7 Dec. 1796 in Fitzpatrick, ed., *Writings of Washington*, xxxv, 316–7. For the charity schools, see I.D. Rupp, ed., Benjamin Rush, *Account of the German Inhabitants of Pennsylvania in 1789* in *The Pennsylvania German* x (May, 1909), 80–1n. See also Schwartz, *Mixed Multitude*, 186–93 *et passim*. Adams' views are quoted from Roeber, "Citizens or Subjects," 52.

["foreigners"] settling together in large masses, wherein, as in our German settlements, they preserve for a long time their own languages, habits and principles of government." Robert Morris expressed similar concerns and even as he sought European settlers for his extensive lands in western Pennsylvania in 1795, he recognised that "should many of them *come together*, they [would] encourage each other in discontent."[58] Franklin and Adams agreed but their reservations were never absolute. While Franklin acknowledged that Germans were usually "sober, industrious and frugal," he also suggested that when people settled in a new country, there were responsibilities on *both* sides. Otherwise, Americans would not be able to preserve "all the advantages we will have ... and even our government will become precarious." Adams also proposed that immigrants had a civic obligation to promote the conventions of their new home, as well as "*our* language, *our* laws, *our* customs, and ... humours of *our* people." An apparent exception was when "families of the same religion [came] to settle a country together." The reasoning here was clear: "Without restraints of religion and social worship, men become savages much sooner, than savages become civilized by means of religious and civil government." However, religion was still a private matter. For Hamilton, homogeneity and harmony were inseparable and "must tend as much as any other circumstance to the permanency of ... [our] union and prosperity."[59] He also believed that "Foreign influence is truly the Grecian horse to a republic." In response, America's "adopted sons" continued to stress their loyalty to the new republic. At its simplest, they had only to mention the distinguished careers in the service of America of soldiers like the German-born Friedrich von Steuben (1730–94), the French Marquis de Lafayette (1757–1834), the English-born Horatio Gates (1727–1806), and the Irish-born Richard Montgomery (1736–75).[60]

58 Donald J. D'Elia, "The Republican Theology of Benjamin Rush," *PH* xxxiii (1966), 200–2, 197; Washington to John Adams, 15 Nov. 1794 in Worthington C. Ford, ed., *The Writings of George Washington* 14 vols. (New York, 1889–93) xii, 489; LC, Robert Morris Private Letterbook, Morris to Christian Gollob Frage, 7 May 1795 and to Amyard & Osborne, 7 May 1795, as quoted in Norman B. Wilkinson, "Land Policy and Speculation in Pennsylvania, 1779–1800" (Ph.D. dissertation, University of Pennsylvania, 1958), 116 and 110. Jefferson is cited from his letter to George Flower in 1817 in A.G. Roeber, "Citizens or Subjects?," 52.

59 Charles Francis Adams, ed., *The Works of John Adams* 10 vols. (Boston, 1850–6) vii, Adams to the President of Congress, 29 June 1780, 209 (the italics are mine); "Advice to American Farmers" in *NYDG*, 10 Mar. 1789. Franklin is quoted in Rothermund, "The German Problem in Colonial Pennsylvania," 11. Hamilton's views on homogeneity are taken from part of the first draft of Washington's speech to Congress (7 Dec. 1796) which he wrote; see Henry Cabot Lodge, ed., *The Works of Alexander Hamilton* 12 vols. (New York, 1904) viii, 218.

60 Lodge, ed., *Hamilton's Works* iv, 481, as quoted in Madison Grant and Charles Stewart Davidson, *The Founders of the Republic on Immigration, Naturalization and Aliens* (New York, 1928), 41.

Views from the Legislatures

With or without the benefit of such testimonials, most legislators felt that the inward flow of the "new immigrant" had to be regulated more effectively. Otherwise, those who were being attracted by the opportunities of America might threaten the viability of the state. After all, as Hamilton recalled, the downfall of Rome and Syracuse had happened in part after "a great number of foreigners were suddenly admitted to the rights of citizenship." In 1791 Coxe suggested that Americans should thus retain the right "to restrain that influx" of immigrants, especially "whenever it is found likely to prove hurtful to us," while four years earlier the *Dublin Evening Post* reported that William Findlay (1741–1821), one of Pennsylvania's delegates to the Constitutional Convention, had even suggested that Congress should "lay an impost" on all incoming immigrants. Although Congress had the power to act in this way, there is no evidence that it ever considered Findlay's proposal seriously, if at all. While legislators appreciated the challenges which immigrants posed to the reinvention of America, most of them believed that if only for economic reasons, immigration was desirable. Restriction would also be seen as a breach of faith as it would break the "equal privileges [that] had been pledged" by individual states to "foreigners" who wanted to emigrate to America and Congress had to respect the *bona fides* of the states in this respect. **James Madison** (1751–1836), one of the delegates from Virginia, disagreed. He believed that the United States should be "free to discriminate as they should think necessary" although he also appreciated that the conventions which governed the admittance and later life of immigrants had to be handled with great care.[61]

The agreement to establish a uniform rule of naturalisation across all thirteen states was a practical solution if only because, as Madison's fellow-delegate from Virginia, Edmund Randolph (1753–1813), noted, "obnoxious aliens" would not be able to travel from one state to the next as a result. Nonetheless, fears persisted that Congress might use the issue to decide the procedures and qualifications for voting and office-holding at state as well as at federal level. This was a sensitive issue, not least because there were important ideological differences on how these matters should be decided. For Jefferson and his supporters, the "genius of republican liberty" was that power derived from the people and not from background, birth, or class, as was the case in

---

61 Hamilton, "Examination of Jefferson's Message to Congress of December 7th, 1801 in Grant and Davidson, eds., *The Founders of the Republic on Immigration*, 48; *Dublin Evening Post*, as quoted in *PEH*, 5 Dec. 1787; F.G. Franklin, "The Legislative History of Naturalization in the United States, 1776–1795" in *Annual Report of the American Historical Association* (1901) i, 307, 305. Coxe is quoted from Baseler, *Asylum for Mankind*, 195.

much of the old world. However, Jay argued that too much power should not be given to those who were "unused to public affairs" or if born outside the United States, to those who had not experienced "a long residence in the country ... to appreciate the genius of the American government." To do otherwise would unduly challenge the attempts which in his view, were necessary to interrelate the stability, harmony, homogeneity, and "natural leadership" of the new republic. During the debates on the constitution, he therefore suggested that the indirect election of the president and senate would guarantee more "virtue" and objective concern for "the public good" than any representative chosen by the people in their "collective capacity." For some, to suggest that such a democratic deficit could secure the new polity was strange. As one writer noted in 1797, to be "true" Federalists, "we [the citizens] must be at once deaf, dumb and blind; we must hear nothing, say nothing, see nothing." However, it was agreed that the president would be indirectly chosen (by an Electoral College) and senators nominated by their respective state legislatures.[62]

Differences persisted on the role of the citizen in day-to-day politics and these did not cease with the adoption of the constitution. In part, they were informed by precedent. Since the colonies were established, suffrage had not been seen as an *independent* right but was linked to landownership. As an urban and commerce-based class grew, the freehold qualification for the franchise was *de facto* extended to recognise personal as well as real property. This may have reflected the realities of the times but by slowly departing from the inherited view of how the franchise was usually determined, it also questioned whether property should be even associated with the franchise in the first place. Adams had a number of reservations about these trends and in 1776 he cautioned that if the connection between property and the franchise were ended, it would "confound and destroy all distinctions" and "prostrate all ranks to one level." During the debate on Pennsylvania's first state constitution in 1776 Rush made a similar point on the proposed qualifications for the vote there: he could not "perceive the propriety or prudence of putting *these inhabitants* [in this case, worth fifty pounds] upon a level with the indigent or prodigal, who have not acquired such a small sum as *fifty* pounds." Therefore, the polity should not involve the poorer or unsubstantial sectors of the community because citizens should have, as the Maryland Declaration of Rights put it on 3 November 1776, a "property in, a common interest with, and an attachment to, the community."[63]

62 *Annals of Congress* i, 988 (5 Mar. 1790); Jonathan Eliot, ed., *Debates on the Adoption of the Federal Constitution* (Philadelphia, 1861) v, 398–9; M.N.S. Sellers, *American Republicanism* (London, 1994), 238–40; James Morton Smith, *Freedom's Fetters: the Alien and Sedition Laws and American Civil Liberties* (Ithaca, 1966), 177.

63 Franklin, "Legislative History of Naturalization," 310; Adams to Sullivan, 26 May 1776 in Adams, ed. *Adams Works* ix, 378; Chilton Williamson, *American Suffrage: From*

As the debates on the franchise developed, another important set of issues was posed by Hamilton: "Does the right to *asylum* or *hospitality* carry with it the right to *suffrage* and *sovereignty*?" Thus, as had happened before, immigrants continued to be part of the debates on citizenship as well as on one of its most important privileges, the right to vote. In Virginia, "the act to explain, amend and reduce into one act, the several acts for the admission of Emigrants to the rights of Citizenship" (January 1787) recognised that

> wisdom and safety suggest the propriety of guarding against the introduction of secret enemies, and of keeping the offices of government in the hands of citizens intimately acquainted with the spirit of the constitution, And the genius of the people, as well as permanently attached to the common interest.

At the Constitutional Convention in Philadelphia, even the Irish-born **Pierce Butler** (1744–1822), one of South Carolina's delegates, recalled that had he been "called into public life within a short time after his coming to America, his foreign habits, opinions, and attachments, would have rendered him an improper agent in public affairs." He now felt that in the new republic, immigrants needed time to divest themselves of their "foreign attachments," especially if they were to act as public representatives. As George Mason (1725–92), his colleague from Virginia, put it, immigrant legislators needed time to develop "local knowledge" in order to become effective representatives.[64]

For most of the other delegates, such aspersions on those who had not been born in America were a proven nonsense. Even Mason recognised that those who were "not natives of this country, had acquired great credit during the revolution." Similarly, Franklin, this time speaking in his capacity of one of Pennsylvania's delegates, observed that

Property to Democracy, 1760–1800 (Princeton, 1968), 101. Rush is quoted in Alexander, *Render Them Submissive*, 30, and the Maryland Declaration in David Curtis Skaggs, *Roots of Maryland Democracy, 1753–1776* (Westport, Conn., 1973), 191. For the historical background to the association between the franchise and freehold, see J.G.A. Pocock, "Machiavelli, Harrington, and English Political Ideologies in the Eighteenth Century," *WMQ* xxii (1965), 549–89. The more general evolution of the franchise is discussed Williamson, *American Suffrage;* and Jack Pole, *Political Representation in England and the Origins of the American Revolution* (New York, 1966).

64 Hamilton, "Examination of Jefferson's Message to Congress of December 7th, 1801 in Grant and Davidson, eds., *The Founders of the Republic on Immigration,* 46–7; Elliot ed., *Debates on the … the Federal Constitution* v, 398, 411. A copy of Virginia's 1787 act was included in one of Bond's reports (see NA, FO/4/5) and was published in, among other places, the *New York Independent Journal,* 27 Jan. 1787.

> We found in the course of the revolution that many strangers served us faithfully, and that many natives took part against their country. When foreigners, after looking about for some other country in which they can obtain more happiness, give a preference to ours, it is a proof of attachment which ought to excite our confidence and affection.

It was eventually accepted that membership of the U.S. senate should not be closed to the foreign-born provided that they were, in the words of Oliver Ellsworth (1745–1808), one of Connecticut's three delegates, "meritorious." The debate on whether to require four, seven, or even eleven years' residence of such citizens before they could be elected still revealed important reservations among some of the country's leaders that the newcomers could ever become "true Americans." However, most regarded the opinions of Butler, Mason, and others as being incompatible with the inclusive nature of their new republic and as implying a vote of no confidence in the ability of immigrants to commit to their new home with honour and distinction. Madison wanted to avoid any "tincture of illiberality" on the issue and felt that the law should reach out to all prospective citizens, even if they had been born overseas, as otherwise, it would "discourage the most desirable class of people from emigrating to the United States." In almost similar terms, one of Pennsylvania's delegates, James Wilson, himself an immigrant from Scotland, also cautioned against any "illiberal complexion ... to the system" and stressed "the effect which a good system would have in inviting *meritorious foreigners* among us."[65]

There was also a related debate on the conditions under which immigrants and, in particular, those who were not citizens, could hold land in America. This issue was somewhat controversial after 1783 partly because land which, before the Revolution had been used to secure loans from British creditors, was now being demanded *in lieu* of defaulted repayments. This was highlighted by a petition which the English-born Samuel Vaughan made to the Pennsylvania assembly in December 1786. In his submission, Vaughan argued that aliens should have the right to own land in America without taking the relevant oaths of allegiance or becoming American citizens. His supporters suggested that unlike commerce and trade,

> land has this particular property, that it attaches the owner to the country where it lies, and many a foreigner who never otherwise would have thought of leaving his native country, will be induced to come and reside upon his own

65 Elliot, ed., *Debates on ... the Federal Constitution* v, 393, 398, 399. The reference to "true Americans" is taken from a letter from Adams to the citizens of Arlington & Sandgate, Vermont., as in Adams, ed., *Works of John Adams* ix, 202.

estate while others will send over colonies of industrious peasants to cultivate their farms.

His opponents replied that by definition, exceptional arrangements were undesirable because they would "operate to defeat the generous and politic adoption of our constitution" and would "disseminate the odious distinctions and jealousies of alienage." It was also suggested that if Vaughan's proposal were supported, it would "put our real estate in the hands of aliens who might sell our lands to enemies in times of war." However, Vaughan's petition was accepted as a statement of "liberality and good sense." Mirroring Hamilton's later views on the promotion of manufactures, it was also argued that the positive outcome would lead to "the wealth of Europe being transferred to America" and that as a result, everybody, "whether citizens, or foreigners, [could] hold real property in this Commonwealth." Such optimism did not ease reservations that the foreign-born who either owned, or had a lien on American property, might place their interests at the disposal of "enemies in times of war." In these circumstances, investment by aliens in the state bank of Pennsylvania was forbidden in 1785 because it "would introduce European politics into their republic."[66]

Even with such caveats, policy makers took the practical view that as a result of Vaughan's success, increased foreign investment would follow. A Pennsylvania law of 1787 also supported the principle of alien ownership of land and as a result, in the words of William Bingham (1752–1804), one of the country's richest land speculators and, later, U.S. senator for Pennsylvania (1795–1801),

> the incentive to purchase is much stronger than in the other states, from a liberality that has prevailed in our system of legislation, admitting aliens to hold lands in their own names, [and] on the same terms, in every respect, as resident citizens. This gives a permanence, in the opinion of foreigners, to this State, in the purchase of lands.

The French traveller, the Duc de la Rochefoucault-Liancourt (1747–1827), also suggested that this law "will, no doubt, induce foreigners to settle in that fine country [Pennsylvania], in preference to every other" while William Maclay, one of the state's first federal senators (1789–91), noted that the law put

66 "A Friend to Emigration," *PP*, 6 Jan. 1787; *PEH*, 18 Sept. 1787; "Another Friend to Emigration," *PP*, 6 Jan. 1787; *Annals of Congress* i, 1147–67 (3 and 4 Feb. 1790). The two quotations from the petition are taken from a commentary in "Another Friend to Emigration," *PP*, 6 Jan. 1787. See also Sarah P. Stetson, "The Philadelphia Sojourn of Samuel Vaughan," *PMHB* lxxiii (1949), 459–74; Franklin, "Legislative History of Naturalization," 310. For the debate on the bank, see Baseler, *Asylum for Mankind*, 221.

Pennsylvania "far ahead of her sister states" in these matters. The preamble of a similar act in New York in 1798 stated that it would be "lawful for any foreigner to purchase lands, tenements, and hereditaments, within this State." As a result, there would be "a tendency to advance the public good and benefit, not only by introducing large sums of money, but also by promoting emigration, and the consequent settlement of this state." In Europe, these laws were often cited by speculators and brokers to support emigration to America. However, they were not typical of every state and from Philadelphia, the British consul general, **Phineas Bond** (1786–1812), warned his countrymen not to be duped into believing that it was otherwise.[67]

As the first Congress (1789–91) evolved from the Constitutional Convention, Congressman James Jackson of Georgia (1789–90) stated that he would not have foreigners owning land in America without either residence or a commitment to become a citizen because it would "be totally subversive of the old established doctrine, that allegiance and land go together." Even if, as Thomas Tudor Tucker of South Carolina (1789–92) proposed, Congress agreed to allow aliens to hold real estate and enjoy the rights of citizenship other than elected office, his colleague, William Smith (S. Carolina, 1789–97) suggested that "to let aliens come in, take the oath, and hold lands without any residence at all" would entitle them to the electoral rights which were, and always had been, intrinsic to freehold property. However, Thomas Hartley (Pa., 1789–1800) pointed out that it was the granting of the franchise *ab initio* rather than the right to own lands that was being objected to and with this in mind, he would not oppose the proposition that foreigners might hold land "on a qualified tenure" rather than on freehold. In Tucker's words, this would have the desired effect of "excluding them from the performance of duties annexed to that class of citizens" who could be elected to govern. This also essentially mirrored what was being done at state level, even in states with liberal immigration policies such as Pennsylvania and New York. Thus, as George Clymer of Pennsylvania (1789–91) suggested, "it might be good policy to admit foreigners to purchase

---

67 Duc de la Rochefoucault-Liancourt, *Travels through the United States of North America* 2 vols. (London, 1799) i, 352; Edgar S. Maclay, ed., *Journal of William Maclay* (New York, 1890), 217. Bingham is quoted in Wilkinson, "Land Policy and Speculation," 108. For Bond's warning, see his letter to Leeds, 3 May 1791, 481–3 and later, his letter to Grenville, dated 23 Nov. 1794 in J. Franklin Jameson, ed., "Letters of Phineas Bond, British Consul at Philadelphia, to the Foreign Office of Great Britain, 1787, 1788, 1789," *AHR* ii (1897), hereafter cited as "Bond II," 566–8. The Pennsylvania "Act to Enable Aliens to Purchase and Hold Real Estate within the Commonwealth" was passed in 1787 for a period of two years; see *Stats. at Large Pa.* xiii, 179. It was extended in 1789 and again, in 1792, for which, see *ADA*, 25 Feb. 1792. For New York's "Act to Encourage Emigration to this State," see [New York] *Argus*, 28 Feb. 1798, from which the quotations have been taken.

and hold hands in fee simple, without ever coming to America; [and] it would, perhaps, facilitate the borrowing of money of Europeans, if they could take mortgages, and be secure." He also noted that Pennsylvania had already "granted this liberty to aliens" and reflected the advice of the (Philadelphia) *General Advertiser*, "not [to] embarrass the trade of new comers, or obstruct their holding any property as freely as citizens."[68]

Part of the debate on the first federal naturalisation bill also looked at residence rather than the definition of the freeholder as a criterion for citizenship. This issue was less complex if only because it was not argued in terms of the relative competences of Congress and the states. Some members felt that a "bare oath" of loyalty was not sufficient for the purposes of naturalisation and insisted on a residency requirement because "an opportunity of esteeming the Government from knowing its intrinsic value, was essentially necessary to assure us of a man's becoming a good citizen." Madison was also in favour of residence of some type. In the event, many of these issues were not addressed in the naturalisation act. The bill was referred to a committee of the whole on 3 February 1790. An "amendatory bill" was presented fourteen days later and passed on the following 26 March. Under the terms of the act as passed, an immigrant who wished to apply for naturalisation had to be resident in America for at least two years, give one year's notice of his intentions to a common law court, satisfy the court as to good character, and swear to support and defend the constitution of the United States. By thus agreeing to a period of probation for citizenship, or to "citizenship by progression," Congress had in effect ignored the principle of "no taxation without representation" in the name of which its own Revolution had been partly fought. The law did not refer to the relationship between citizenship and land ownership, another important part of its constitutional legacy; this was left to the states.[69] While the first federal naturalisation act thus acknowledged the competence of Congress to regulate a common code for naturalisation and citizenship, it raised as many questions as it answered. It also recognised that the states could regulate and impose restrictions on the franchise as they saw fit and this remained the case until the fourteenth amendment was passed in 1868. Until then, one was first and foremost, a citizen of his state and thereby, of the United States.

68 *Annals of Congress* i, 1161, 1150, 1147–8, 1151, 1154–5, 1160 (3 and 4 Feb. 1790).
69 *ibid.*, 1147–8, 1284; *NYP*, 1 Apr. 1790; Baseler, *Asylum for Mankind*, 257; Albert J. McCulloh, *Suffrage and its Problems* (Baltimore, 1929), 31–3. For Washington's view, that "various considerations … render it expedient that the terms on which foreigners may be admitted to the rights of citizens should be speedily ascertained" by Congress, as in his first State of the Union message (8 Jan. 1790), see James D. Richardson, ed., *Messages and Papers of the Presidents* 10 vols. (Washington, 1897) i, 34.

The exchanges on these matters had focused on the process as well as on the form of contemporary politics and, in particular, on how these could not be separated from citizenship and public representation. Both during and after the colonial period Philadelphia had given a distinctive twist to the debates on these issues. Its immigrants had been crucial to these matters. By placing themselves, however inadvertently, in an influential position *vis-à-vis* both the discourse and the nascent organisation of contemporary politics, they challenged the ways in which the polity was understood not just in Philadelphia, as one of America's great cities, but in a place which, as the nation's erstwhile capital, was deciding what was best for the country as a whole. It was also the port which, as during the colonial period, continued to attract the majority of Irish immigrants after the Revolution. It was these "new Irish" who would give an even greater reality to the "new politics" of city and nation and provoke a more thorough debate during the later-1790s on the role of the immigrant in American life.

CHAPTER THREE

The "New Irish," 1783–1800: Perceptions, Management, and Flow

After 1783 the success of an apparently democratic revolution enhanced the attractions of the new American republic and strengthened its image as a "land of liberty." War-time interruptions to the passenger trade came to an end and Ireland's American traders rebuilt their interests with confidence and enthusiasm. However, the Irish emigration of the later-eighteenth century was often seen in terms which were different from those of fifty years earlier. It was "new." Potential emigrants examined their options more carefully and critically and, as a result, those who thought about leaving Ireland had a fuller and better understanding of both the emigration process and what lay ahead. They were also treated more benignly by managers and ship captains and regarded as clients to whom a reasonable service should be given. In part, this was because many of those who emigrated after 1783 were solvent and paying passengers; indentured servitude had all but disappeared. Emigrants also had their own effective ways to condemn their brokers if the management and circumstances of their journeys were not "proper." Thus, these "new Irish" landed in Philadelphia as people who were more self-assured than their colonial cousins. They also had an optimism about the "promise" of their adopted homeland and would engage in "every useful art ... to grow rich by."[1]

Letters from America

The attitudes of these "new Irish" have been carefully analysed in a scholarly study that was published in 2003 by Kerby Miller, Arnold Schrier, Bruce Boling, and David Doyle. This work complements a small but important collection of similar documents in the Public Record Office of Northern Ireland as well as various "letters of advice" which were published in contemporary

---

1 *BN*, 23 May 1786. For shipping advertisements which described America as a "land of liberty," see, for example, those of the brig *Rose and Betty* (Belfast to Virginia and Baltimore, 1783) and the ship *Congress* (Derry to Philadelphia, 1784) in *BN*, 7 Mar. 1783 and 21 May 1784, respectively. For the general points raised in this paragraph, see Maurice J. Bric, "Patterns of Irish Emigration to America, 1783–1800," *Éire-Ireland* xxxvi (2001), 17–35.

newspapers. In some ways, the tensions between the undoubted "pull" of later-eighteenth-century America and the "push" from contemporary Ireland had a familiar ring to them. For example, some emigrants felt that they "would do better in America" than in Ireland where they "could not earn bread sufficient to support [a] family." However, as Louis M. Cullen has concluded, the decline of the woollen and linen industries which had forced so many to emigrate before the American Revolution, had been arrested by 1783. Nonetheless, economic revival in these areas did not necessarily better the lot of those who depended on the land, especially as the population continued to increase. As the *Belfast News-Letter* remarked sarcastically on 23 May 1786,

> Dear rents, exorbitant taxes, and scarcity of work, as well as of the necessaries of life, are not the best methods of keeping the people at home, or of rendering them other than enemies of their rulers, and despisers of that land, in which they cannot subsist, without feeling the most intolerable oppression, and the most flagrant injustice.

Two years earlier, a published "letter from Wilmington" had suggested an alternative:

> there is great opportunity in almost every part of this country for a man of small capital, and the least abilities or industry to raise himself into affluence ... Though my property, when I left Dublin, was but small, yet it has done more for me here in nine months, than I could have expected from five times the money in Ireland; and I have every prospect of making a fortune in a few years. When I contrast this situation with that of Ireland, I am not surprised at the distress of your people. You are complete hewers of wood and drawers of water to the demagogues of the land.[2]

More often than not, emigrants thus looked on America as a place where they could better their lot and carefully explored what America had to offer. In 1790, for example, James and Thomas Young asked their brother-in-law Moses Johnston in Lancaster County, Pennsylvania, "if there would Be any encouragement for Weavers in America for we hear in this Country that One Man Can Make as Much as four Men Can Make here At Weaving." There is no record of Johnston's reply. The previous year, however, one John Denison wrote from Franklin Township, also in Pennsylvania, that his wages as a weaver were ten shillings a day and, perhaps anticipating the curiosity of his readers in

2 Miller, Schrier, Boling and Doyle, eds., *Irish Immigrants in the Land of Canaan*; Bailyn, *Voyagers to the West*, 195, 194; Louis M. Cullen, *An Economic History of Ireland since 1660* (London, 1972), 62–4; *HJ*, 20 Aug. 1784.

Dromore, Co. Down, he added those of shoemakers and millwrights, the yield per acre and market prices of various crops, as well as the price of land in his locality. For another Irish settler in Pennsylvania, Andrew Martin, America was a "Plentiful Country" and one which "before a year or two ... will be extremely enviable." It also offered a haven from what the *Dublin Evening Post* saw as the grievances which late-eighteenth-century Ireland "smart[ed] under," together with "the blessings of freedom in a country where sober, honest industry is sure of reward" and a chance to participate in building a new nation that would be an example to the world.[3] In all these observations, one can sense that the wider culture of emigration encouraged an optimism and confidence that overrode the mere rejection of the old world.

However, emigrants were urged not to leap into the dark. As "A Friend to Ireland" put it in the *Freeman's Journal* in 1788, they should be "wise to the consequences of [their] conduct" as well as practical about what to expect in America and what they could offer in return. Robert Simpson recalled in 1793 that, ten years earlier, America

> was really a good country for tradesmen of every description, when there were high wages and provisions cheap; but the knowledge of this has brought tradesmen of every description to this country in such numbers, that that time is now gone.

Simpson's caution was juxtaposed with a reminder of the cost of the "necessaries of life," rent, and fuel, as well as the uncertainty (as opposed to the level) of wages in America. From New York, another writer warned that rents were very high, if only "to gratify the inordinate desires of exorbitant landlords." Samuel Brown also gave detailed information on income and expenditure in Philadelphia and added that while labourers could earn from four shillings five pence a day there, boarding costs were "very dear, from two dollars [15 shillings] to three pr. week." Moreover, he observed that even where carpenters, for

3   PRONI, T2294, John to Samuel Denison, 15 Jan. 1789; PRONI, T1752, Andrew Martin to his father, 10 Aug. 1785; *DEP*, 5 July 1787. The Youngs are quoted from Miller, Schrier, Boling and Doyle, eds., *Irish Immigrants in the Land of Canaan*, 35. Irish emigration after 1783 has not received as much attention as that of the colonial period. However, in addition to the study by Miller, Schrier, Boling and Doyle, see Maldwyn A. Jones, "Ulster Emigration, 1783–1815" in E.R.R. Green, ed., *Essays in Scotch-Irish History* (New York, 1969), 55; Doyle, *Irishmen and Revolutionary America*; Miller, *Emigrants and Exiles*, 169–92; Canny, ed., *Europeans on the Move*; and Bric, "Patterns of Irish Emigration to America, 1783–1800." In *The Adaptation of English and Scottish Immigrants in Nineteenth-Century America* (Leicester, 1972), Charlotte Erickson analyses a run of nineteenth-century British letters and observes that like the Youngs, while some emigrants may have had "fears about the future ... No other goal was mentioned so frequently as that of independence," 27.

example, could earn as much as a dollar a day, they worked from "Sun up to Sun down." As such, rewards followed only from hard work and commitment. In 1785 the Ulster-born printer of the Declaration of Independence, John Dunlap (1747–1812), suggested to his brother-in-law in Strabane that "there is no place in the world where a man meets so rich a reward for *good conduct* and *industry* as in America." A published letter from Baltimore also advised Irish tradesmen that if they were "good ... [they could] make money in plenty, but a bad one need not come here." Along similar lines, "a letter from New York" stated in 1789 that although America "offers at present the most unbounded encouragement to the artificer and labourer ... we want *sober and diligent* tradesmen." The *Belfast News-Letter* accepted that even servants received better wages in America "but then they work much harder."[4] In public as well as in private, therefore, emigrants were urged to see America as a place to work and not simply as a refuge.

Emigrants were also advised to plan ahead. On 5 March 1784 Henry Johnston wrote to his brother, Moses, that "my son Jack is Talking of going to America, but I would be glad to know how things go before he would do it." He did not want Jack to find "a land of briars and thorns," as the *Freeman's Journal* characterised America the following year. However, even with "letters of introduction" and advice, one writer from New York suggested that "nothing can be more disagreeable than the letters given to young men who come out to this country without any specific plan." Yet it is clear from the edited collection of letters and memoirs cited above that potential emigrants were usually given practical information and advice rather than blindly encouraged to leave. On 10 August 1785 Andrew Martin wrote from Philadelphia County to his father that although he had not been "at a loss for work nor lost no time since I came to America ... As for encouraging any person to come here, I will not, but if any friends or acquaintances comes, I would be glad to see them." Similar views were expressed by John Denison although Samuel Brown informed his brother that after arrival, "a great many wishes to be in Ireland again. So from this, you'll be a gugge [*sic*] yourself."[5]

4 "A Friend to Ireland," as in *FJ*, 30 Aug. 1788; HSP, Am. 1528, Letters of Robert Simpson (1790–1807), Robert Simpson to his father, 1 June, 23 Dec. 1793; *BN*, 18 Apr. 1783; "Letter from Philadelphia," as in *BN*, 22 Feb. 1785; *VEP*, 11 Sept. 1784; *NYP*, 6 Feb. 1786; PRONI, T3525, Samuel to David Brown (in Belfast), 23 Dec. 1793; PRONI, T1336, John Dunlap to Robert Rutherford, 12 May 1789; *BN*, 22 Feb. 1785. The letters from Baltimore (dated 6 Dec. 1784) and New York (dated 3 May 1789) were published in *SN*, 8 Feb. 1785 and *PP*, 12 May 1789, respectively. The italics in the "letter from New York" are mine. For the importance of the notion of industry in American republican thought, see McCoy, *Elusive Republic*, 77–85, 237–43 *et passim*.
5 *FJ*, 7 May 1785; "Extract of a letter to a Merchant in Belfast" in *DEP*, 9 Oct. 1794; PRONI, T1752, Andrew Martin to his father, 10 Aug. 1785; PRONI, T2294, John to

Brown's letters to Ireland reflected the personal responsibility which individual immigrants felt to family and friends in Ireland. They understood that after arrival, some of them might be "driven back" to their native places as a result of unrealised ambitions, broken promises, high rents, and increasing taxes. Moreover, as one writer to the *Belfast News-Letter* dramatically warned on 28 November 1783, "Hospitality and friendship, the former characteristics of America have fled the land." For their own reasons, Dublin's major newspapers agreed. They suggested that America was a land of extreme climates, hot summers, fevers, and "numerous … poisonous insects, vermin and serpents," as well as a place where Irish immigrants were "tomahawked, scalped and murdered by the Indians." Thus, *Saunders* [Dublin] *News-Letter* advised that "no Irishman acts prudently to leave his own fine, wholesome, natural climate, to come to America, let the circumstances be what they may." The (Dublin) *Volunteer Evening Post* warned that many of those who had emigrated had been "taught to expect a Paradise, [with] lands flowing with milk and honey, perpetual spring, and great abundance and encouragement without any taxes." For such newspapers, the conclusion was clear: Irish people could live "more happily in their native country than in any part of the United States."[6]

Unappealing descriptions of the climate in America were sometimes trumped by emotive allegations that Irish servants were being sold "like beasts of burden, in the open market." On 4 January 1785, for example, the *Volunteer Evening Post* published the following "eye witness" account from Philadelphia:

> A vessel from the North of Ireland loaded with servants, arrived … the poor Irish were brought bound to the public market place, and, placed successively in pairs at the end of a hogshead, were sold by public auction. The history of their various miseries, aris[es] from excessive labour, in a most unwholesome climate – the want of every convenience that could soften their distress – their half-naked bodies exposed to pinching cold or scorching heat – the bloody punishment of the whip, and every ignominious circumstance of oppression that can abase human nature.

In 1786 the parents of one Daniel Kent, who had emigrated from Limerick to Chester County, Pennsylvania, wrote to tell him that "some of those People

Samuel Denison, 15 Jan. 1789; T3525, Samuel to David Brown, 23 Dec. 1793. Henry Johnston is quoted from Miller, Schrier, Boling and Doyle, eds., *Irish Immigrants in the Land of Canaan*, 34.

6   *VEP*, 4 June 1785, 29 Mar. 1787, 14 May 1785; *HJ*, 12 Dec. 1789; *SN*, 8 Feb. 1785; *VEP*, 14 Sept. 1784; *SN*, 29 Aug. 1786; *NYP*, 23 Feb. 1786. The writer to *BN*, 28 Nov. 1783 has been quoted from Baseler, *Asylum for Mankind*, 179. Baseler also explores the ways, positive and negative, in which the American "asylum" was presented in the contemporary press.

[servants] who sailed with you have met since their arrival in America with the severest Cruelty and hardship." Although Kent denied that he had been poorly treated as a servant, he admitted that "there are but four or five out of twenty And Upwards that Came to this part of the Country With me that have Stayed with their Masters, the Rest ran away. Some have Been taken up and Condemned to serve a Longer time."[7]

As if to underline this point, runaway notices and advertisements for the sale of servants were occasionally reprinted from American papers and although invariably focused on Maryland and Virginia, they suggested that Irish servants were subjected to "frequent examples of cruelty," held in the "most ignominious contempt," and "universally despised" in America as a whole. The following report cast these allegations in racial terms:

> The common Irish, who go as redemptioners, are sold in open market, and afterwards used worse than Negroes; for Black Sam, who obtained his freedom, absolutely buys up the Irish slaves, which he calls his White Negroes; and afterwards disposes of them to other free Blacks, of any property, throughout the country.

As the *Belfast News-Letter* suggested, "free negroes ... want to retaliate cruelty for cruelty." Therefore, as the *Volunteer Evening Post* saw it, America was a "land of pretended freedom, but, in reality, of abject slavery." As many Irish men and women relied on indentured servitude to pay their passage, anti-emigration correspondents hoped that if they circulated such sensational stories, the passenger flow would ease even if, as John Adams put it, such writings were usually "lost in ... vituperary Insolence." However, as Marilyn Baseler has noted, although such negative observations fostered "lasting misconceptions" of America, they were often seen for what they mostly were: "falsehoods, invented and proclaimed to dissuade emigration to America."[8]

---

7 *BN*, 18 Apr. 1788. For Kent, see Miller, Schrier, Boling and Doyle, eds., *Irish Immigrants in the Land of Canaan*, 189, 190.

8 *BN*, 5 Feb. 1790; *VEP*, 11 Sept. 1784; *HJ*, 7 July 1787; *BN*, 18 Apr. 1788; *VEP*, 14 Sept. 1784; "Letter from Philadelphia," as in *BN*, 29 Nov. 1783; *VEP*, 14 Sept. 1784; Baseler, *Asylum for Mankind*, 189; *SN*, 1 Oct. 1784. Adams is quoted in Baseler, *Asylum for Mankind*, 188. The generic descriptions of recruiting agents are quoted from *FJ*, 9 June 1789, *HJ*, 3 Dec. 1784, and *VEP*, 14 May 1785. Among the reports of the alleged mistreatment of servants which were published in Irish newspapers, see *BN*, 5 Feb. 1790, which reprinted from the *Maryland Gazette*, a petition from a servant, one Thomas Buckley, detailed "maltreatment" and whipping by his master despite orders from the local (Baltimore) justice of the peace to "use me well." For one of many citations of the term "white negro" to suggest the supposed inferior status of immigrant Irish servants, see *HJ*, 9 July 1787; for a similar reference, as drawn from the contemporary theatre, see

Commercial Networks

Regardless of propaganda, the recruitment and management of emigrants was a difficult business and needed the support of the wider commercial networks which bound Ireland and America. For all sorts of trade, these connections were even more important after 1783 if only because the Revolution had disrupted the common economic area which they had long shared with the former colonies. Irish merchants knew that the American market would be more challenging and that they would have to develop more considered approaches to both the commercial needs and market potential of the various American states. As one correspondent remarked in 1786, the considerable increase in transatlantic trade at the time gave "singular satisfaction ... [and] if due attention is paid to the *goods proper for the American market*, it must in time be productive of the highest advantages to this country." The Cork-born Philadelphia merchant, Benjamin Fuller, advised Doyle & Rowe of Dublin on 15 May 1784 that linen and coarse woollens were "very lucrative" in Philadelphia although he added that they should be "particularly attentive to colour, for none but high whites, will sell to advantage."[9]

Like other merchants, Fuller wanted to revive his commercial links with his Irish "kinsmen" after the hiatus of the Revolutionary war. In Ireland, Harvey & Lecky of Cork, Edmund Forbes of Dublin, and James Holmes of Belfast also resumed their correspondence with, among others, one of New York's leading merchants, Isaac Hicks (1767–1820). In 1783 the Belfast firm of Thomas Hardin & Co. sent two agents to Philadelphia "at least partly with the intention of re-establishing contacts there" while the following year, Fuller introduced to his cousin Abraham in Dublin, the distinguished Philadelphia merchants, John Donnaldson and Francis West who would be visiting "most of the principal places [in Ireland] ... in order to form connections." Also in 1784 American agents visited Kilkenny and "bought up most of the blankets ... and have given commissions for a great deal more," while **Blair McClenachan** (d.1812), one of Philadelphia's leading pre-Revolutionary correspondents with Ulster, visited his native city of Derry in June. McClenachan made a conspicuous display of his "opulence" and entertained two hundred of the city fathers to "an elegant breakfast [and] a dance, enlivened by good humour and a joyous innocence" aboard his "remarkable fine" vessel, the ship *Congress*. The *Freeman's Journal*

Bailyn, *Voyagers to the West*, 299. For reports on the purchase of Irish servants by free blacks, see for example, *SN*, 5 Jan. 1785; *FJ*, 16 Apr. 1785; *VEP*, 4 Jan. 1785.

9 *SN*, 15 July 1786; HSP, Benjamin Fuller Letterbook iii (1784–7), italics mine. For published advice on taking a considered approach to trade with America, see *PP*, 12 Oct. 1784; *FJ*, 12 Oct. 1790; and *HJ*, 9 Oct. 1789.

concluded that if Ireland made "proper use" of such American interest in Irish trade, Ireland "must unavoidably become, in less than half a century, great, rich, and flourishing." As if to underline the point, it was reported in 1786 that Captain Ferguson of the ship *The General Wolf* (New York to Galway) had brought home so many "orders for goods manufactured in this kingdom ... [that they] have caused some hundreds to be set to work, who before were out of employment."[10]

Cullen has observed that Ireland's linen industry responded to such orders with confidence and enthusiasm and that after 1783 it underwent a remarkable revival. Between 1783–84 and 1791–92 linen exports almost doubled and they continued at unprecedented levels of growth until the end of the century. In an assessment of the industry on 18 January 1788, the (Dublin) *Hibernian Journal* noted that

> a greater demand for linens of all prices, has been experienced here of late than for the last twenty years. The principal commissions are said to be from America; a market, which, from the rapidity of its growth, from the emigrations to it, that take place from all parts of the globe, may with due attention and cultivation, speedily become of infinite consequence to the trade of this country.

More than 135,000 yards of linen were shipped from Dublin to Philadelphia and New York on 12 April 1784, the year in which New York opened its own Irish linen warehouse. From Philadelphia, one Irish merchant wrote in July 1783 that he had sold his consignments at over 30% "clear profit" at the city's "very great market," adding that "Irish linens will always have a preference" there. From New York, the ship *Juno* (Dublin to New York, 1786) had "scarcely arrived when almost the entire cargo had been purchased." Thus, as had been the case during the colonial period, Philadelphia and New York remained the industry's main American *entrepôts* while in Ireland, the expansion of the flaxseed and linen trades brought more business to the ports of Dublin and Ulster. As a result, the familiar routes of the colonial passenger trade were also revived and new ones encouraged.[11]

10 HSP, Benjamin Fuller Letterbook iii, *passim*; *BN*, 15 Apr. 1783; HSP, Benjamin Fuller Letterbook iii, 24 June 1784; *VEP*, 26 Feb. 1784; *FJ*, 25 Nov. 1788. Ferguson is quoted in a letter from Galway in *NYP*, 7 Sept. 1786. For McClenachan's visit, see *BN*, 25 May, 15 June 1784 and *LJ*, 8 June 1784. See also Robert A. Davidson, *Isaac Hicks, New York Merchant and Quaker, 1767–1820* (Cambridge, Mass., 1964) and Doerflinger, *Vigorous Spirit of Enterprise*, 58–59 *et passim*. For the involvement of Cork merchants in transatlantic trade, see David Dickson's magisterial study of the city, *Old World Colony: Cork and South Munster 1630–1830* (Cork, 2005), 410 *et passim*.
11 Cullen, *Economic History of Ireland*, 62–3; Duvall, "Philadelphia's Maritime Commerce

These connections were also developed in pragmatic ways. As Norman Gamble's unpublished work shows, in the northern ports of Belfast and Derry, floating partnerships became more common after the Revolution. Because such joint enterprises concentrated capital, or could aggrandise it for a particular voyage, they gave merchants added financial security. They also enabled them to participate in a larger number of sailings. These arrangements were not confined to those who were perceived to be financially insecure or commercially insignificant. For example, two of Belfast's leading traders with colonial America, Thomas Greg and Waddell Cunningham, had associated in such ventures since 1756. After 1783 Cunningham managed a number of voyages on his own account while in others he associated, on either a separate or joint basis, with the city's other leading American houses, William & John Brown and John Campbell, in transporting passengers to Philadelphia (1783, 1788), Virginia (1783, 1784, 1784), and Baltimore (1784, 1786, 1787, 1788). As the venture demanded, he also promoted his interests in partnership with Greg, Cunningham & Co. As a result of these arrangements, Belfast's late-eighteenth-century passenger traffic to America came to be dominated by a number of principals in the city who, for their own strategic reasons, often associated with one another to realise their private interests in a number of enterprises.[12]

Especially in Ulster, these undertakings were advanced through a variety of personal, business and factoral relationships, some of which were reflected in the lists of sub-agents which were often published in connection with a proposed voyage. For example, the network of the ship *Independence* (Belfast to Philadelphia, 1783) involved people who had business or personal ties with the vessel's main promoters, Samuel Brown and John Cunningham of Belfast. These included Neal McCook and James Gamble of Ballymoney, George Brown, "near" Ballycastle, James Hamill of Coleraine, Samuel Brown and John Singleton of Armagh, and Michael Ranken of Newtownards. The published network of these "friends" suggested that proximity to the port of embarkation was sometimes less important in advertising a vessel than the relationship between the outlying agents and the principals involved. However, the wide geographical range of those who promoted the *Independence* was unusual.

with the British Empire," 455; *NYP*, 9 Feb. 1784; "Extract from a letter from Philadelphia, dated 26th July, 1783," as in *SN*, 2 Oct. 1783; *FJ*, 20 July 1786.

12 Norman E. Gamble, "The Business Community and the Trade of Belfast, 1767–1800" (Ph.D. disseration, Trinity College, Dublin, 1978), 25–41, 45. Information on the business partnerships of Cunningham and other Ulster merchants who were involved in promoting voyages to America has been drawn from the shipping advertisements of the *Belfast News-Letter* and *Londonderry Journal*. Cunningham's joint-ventures with Campbell are also discussed in Gamble, "Business Community and the Trade of Belfast,," 45–6, 305.

Belfast's sub-agents usually operated within a thirty to thirty five mile radius of the port and although there were exceptions, most sailings concentrated their advertising on Antrim, north Down, and east Tyrone. To the south, Newry's emigration brokers operated within about twenty five miles of the port, ranging westwards to Monaghan, northwestwards to Coalisland, Banbridge, and Armagh, and southwards to Drogheda. Derry's vessels were publicised westwards into Donegal and Inishowen, southwards to Omagh, southeastwards to Maghera and eastwards to Coleraine.[13]

While the management of any voyage drew on such local networks, it was also affected by an American decision in 1784 to double the tonnage duty on foreign-owned shipping and thus, to mirror British regulations. As a result of the order, some Europeans chose to co-own vessels with merchants in America or to register them there. Such strategies suggest that new partnerships, including some which spanned the ocean, could be developed to buy, lease, or operate vessels for the Atlantic routes. In no small measure, they also helped to re-establish and secure the passenger trade, especially in Ulster ports, and to spread it across a number of houses which otherwise might have never become involved in the business. As a result, local commercial structures after 1783 facilitated rather than retarded the growth of emigration in a variety of ways. Moreover, the actual residence of those who managed these voyages could determine a ship's destination. For example, John and James Holmes's ship *Brothers* sailed between Belfast and the Delaware, principally because a third brother, Hugh, was a partner in the Philadelphia firms of Holmes & Ralston and Holmes & Rainey. Indeed, the popularity of the Delaware was assured by the fact that joint-ownership or agencies with partners in Ireland were more common in Philadelphia than in any other American port. This reflected the city's long involvement in the Irish trade, especially with Ulster. It also underlined the fact that a number of Philadelphia's investors in the trade were Irish-born and accordingly, not put off by the new transatlantic structures and arrangements, whether these were inspired by Congress or not. As a result, whereas in 1784 Philadelphia's port entry books record that a mere sixth of the vessels was owned locally, by 1787 the figure had jumped to over a half with a further sixth co-owned with partners in other parts of the United States. Among these vessels, the house of the Ulster-born James Crawford, Haines & Crawford, co-owned the 300-ton brig *Penelope* (Belfast to Philadelphia, 1787) and the 300-ton brig *Betsey* (Cork to Philadelphia, 1787) and acted for nine of

13 *BN*, 29 Aug. 1783. For the pre-Revolutionary background of these networks, see Dickson, *Ulster Emigration*, ch. 7. For the analysis of the catchment areas of the vessels recorded in the British Register of Emigration, including London and Bristol, see Bailyn, *Voyagers to the West*.

the thirty one Irish entries in that year: five from Derry, one from Belfast, two from Dublin and one from Cork.[14]

In Derry, the doubling of the city's vessels between 1775 and 1785 seemed to strengthen the belief that its American trade would grow quicker and larger than that of any other Irish port. In April 1784 one newspaper reported that on the Foyle, "there are now more American vessels than ever at any one time in the memory of man." Like their Belfast colleagues, Derry's merchants did not welcome the new duties that the United States had placed on foreign-owned tonnage and as in Belfast, they sometimes promoted their American enterprises in association with connections in Philadelphia with whom they had built strong ties during the colonial period. Even where new vessels were being "purposely built" for the passenger trade, the decline in the number of Irish owners was less marked than it was on Belfast's river Lagan. Derry's merchants continued to own a number of the ships that were involved in the emigrant business and made special and widely-advertised efforts to secure this traffic. As a result, their business did not suffer. If anything, it increased.[15]

Between 1783 and 1798 the strength of the link between Derry and the Delaware was reflected in its high number of clearances for the region: 156. This accounted for 58% of the total from Ulster ports for that part of America, or nearly 37% from Ireland as a whole (see Appendix V). Of these, twenty were promoted as joint ventures to the Delaware, New York, Baltimore, or Virginia. From Belfast, the route to the Delaware was also the most popular and over the same period, fifty sailings, or 19% and 12% of the regional and national totals, respectively, were advertised for the Delaware, all but five of which were managed as direct connections. Thus, as in Derry, multiple destinations on the same voyage were the exception rather than the rule and underlined the culture of these ports to conduct business directly with individual destinations. Ulster's other major port, Newry, also had strong links with the Delaware (thirty eight sailings). It split a number of additional voyages between the Delaware and the Hudson (five) and developed a significant and enduring link with New York

14 Information on the ownership of Philadelphia-bound vessels from Ireland is taken from HSP, Port of Philadelphia, Outward Entries (1784–7). For 1784, Lloyds also gave the breakdown of Irish-owned vessels for Philadelphia as follows: Belfast (5), Derry (4), Larne (2), Dublin (2), Newry (1) and Cork (1); see *Lloyds' Register* (London, 1785). The data for 1787 are taken from HSP, Port Entry Books (hereafter, PEB) (Philadelphia) I (1 June 1786 to 29 Dec. 1787). The doubling of the tonnage duty is discussed in Duvall, "Philadelphia's Maritime Commerce," 113.

15 *SN*, 22 April 1784. References to vessels which were "purposely-built" for passengers are common in shipping advertisements at this time and, at least in Ulster, reflect the increasing specialisation of the passenger trade. See, for example, the notice of the ship *William and George* (Derry to Newcastle and Philadelphia, 1787) in *BN*, 2 Mar. 1787.

during the 1780s, a time when this route was not being as directly or actively pursued from other Ulster ports. The number of American sailings from Larne was small and after sending one ship to Philadelphia in 1783, 1784 and 1785, Charleston was almost the only American destination that was advertised from the port.

Until 1800, Dublin was Ireland's seat of government as well as its most important commercial and administrative centre. The Treaty of Paris (1783) had been seen as an opportunity to increase the "commercial enterprise of our traders." On 4 March 1786 *Saunders News-Letter* remarked that there were "more American ships now in the port of Dublin than have ever been known since the Revolution and the encouragement for the export of our manufacturers wears a more favourable aspect than it has ever done." Between 1783 and 1798 the city had the country's highest number of sailings from southern Ireland to the Delaware (ninety two) or 60% and 23% of the regional and national totals, respectively. After 1795 however, New York became Dublin's most popular American destination. Few of the letterbooks of the firms that were involved in Dublin's American trade have survived, and advertisements that were published in the capital city contain less detailed information that those of Belfast and Derry. The amount of locally-owned tonnage on the American routes was also small compared to what was committed to Britain which, for most of Dublin's merchants, was a more accessible market and a safer and cheaper investment. However, there were a number of regular traders. Until it was captured by "the Moors" in 1788, the 350-ton ship *Dublin Packet* was the best-known vessel on the Delaware route. It was co-owned by Leckey & Wilson and the Philadelphia firm of Haines & Crawford and usually made two trips every year. Although the ship usually took a small number of passengers, it also carried considerable merchandise and even adapted its times of sailing "to suit the Seasons of Demand for Irish Manufactures" in Philadelphia. In 1791 the ship *Philadelphia and Dublin Packet* advertised two sailings for Philadelphia, the first leaving in April, the second in September.[16]

That the numbers who travelled from Dublin were smaller than those who left Ulster is partly explained by the fact that in Dublin, the American passenger trade was not as well established and that the port had under-networked catchment areas on which its emigrant brokers could draw. Thus, when Philadelphia's Joseph Pringle and Josiah & Samuel Coates chartered the brig *Mary* (Philadelphia to Dublin to Philadelphia, 1789), Captain Henry Lunt was asked to "deliver cargo and receive [such] freight or passengers as the Agent of John Pringle may order, and with the same as soon as possible return to

16 *NCEP*, 19 Mar. 1791.

Philadelphia." The best that Coates and Pringle could hope for were passengers who were recruited piecemeal rather than assembled for the voyage by an organised system of sub-agents. However, there were occasional suggestions that the city's American trade was not an entirely bland affair. Some light was thrown on this when allegations of incompetence were made against the captain of the ship *Success* (Dublin to Philadelphia, 1783) and its Dublin-based owners, Galloway & Stillas, after the vessel docked in Philadelphia. The charges were widely publicised at the time but there were also hints that some houses were "malicious[ly] reporting" the affair in order to get an edge on their rivals in the passenger trade.[17] The affair highlighted the new energy with which Dublin's merchants were approaching the American routes after 1783 and, in particular, how they were competing for emigrants.

In Munster and south Leinster, the passenger trade was organised and advertised on a more casual basis. In part, this can be explained by the fact that emigrants were often recruited at hiring fairs as well as within other networks that were used to engage short-term labourers for the Newfoundland fisheries and the potato and slaughtering seasons. Because of its informality, this recruitment system is difficult to define. Moreover, shipping advertisements in southern Ireland were less common and detailed than in contemporary Ulster. Although it dates from the nineteenth century, the passenger list of the ship *Plato* (Cork to New York, 1816) suggests that Cork attracted emigrants from over a wide area: from Skibbereen (Cork) and Kenmare (Kerry) to the west, Bandon (Cork) and Nenagh (Tipperary) to the north, Limerick to the north-west, to Kilkenny and Meath to the north-east and far north-east, respectively. I have come across no comparable list for Dublin although of all Irish ports, it is probable that the capital city recruited passengers from all over Ireland. Dublin and Cork were also part of the catchment area of British ports such as Liverpool, Bristol and London and routed many Irish passengers to America from there. As Bailyn's analysis of the British Register of Emigration has shown, this had also been the case in Bristol during the early-1770s. Occasionally, ports in Munster were also included in American trips that originated in Britain. In 1792, for example, the *New Cork Evening Post* announced that the ship *Diligence* (Liverpool to New York) would "touch Cork" and that prospective passengers should book their berths with a local broker, one Edward Pope. After 1783 the city also renewed its passenger traffic with Baltimore. However, vessels which sailed from Cork were particularly vulnerable to privateers and impressment. While its geographical location gave the port good access to the convoys which travelled between Europe and America at the time, regional folklore about

17 HSP, Josiah & Samuel Coates Letterbook i (Nov. 1784 to July 1790), 11 July 1789; *IG*, 3, 4 Oct. 1783; *SN*, 23 Oct., 29 Nov. 1783. For the charges against the *Success*, see below, 116.

piracy and kidnapping discouraged traffic on the south Atlantic routes and during the 1790s most of Cork's Atlantic voyages were redirected northwards to the Delaware, New York, and New England. As a result, Cork's shipping connections with the Delaware were also strong between 1783 and 1798 (fifty five sailings). Leycester & McCall was especially important in promoting Philadelphia and managed among others, the ship *Nestor*, for which it engaged servants and redemptioners in 1791.[18]

Whatever their location, merchants were crucial to the viability of Ireland's eighteenth-century passenger trade. However, other personalities also appear from time to time. Among these were clergymen who became more involved in these activities during the colonial period, especially after Carolina and Georgia decided to offer land grants and other concessions to attract Protestants to their shores. Even after these schemes were retired in the late-1760s, clergymen continued to organise and advise prospective emigrants, especially if they wanted to sail to Charleston. During the 1780s and 1790s a number of sailings to Charleston were advertised by the Revds. Douglas of Clough and Acheson of Ballymena while the Rev. John Park of Buckna helped to recruit passengers on behalf of the merchants Anthony Sinclair of Larne and Narcissus Batt of Belfast. In 1790 the Rev. Bryce Miller of Ballymena was among six agents who advertised the ship *Irish Volunteer* (Belfast to Charleston) and indicated that he could "accommodate a number of people with lands of excellent quality." Henry Kerr was not a minister but in August 1783 he sought single servants and redemptioners to travel *via* the ship *Independence* (Belfast to Philadelphia) to his lands in Chester County, Pennsylvania while in 1792 the promoters of the ship *Sally* (Cork to Baltimore) advertised that its owner, Richard Lemmon, "a Native of Ireland," would oblige their passengers by renting "for ever to Persons well recommended and industrious, 300 Acres of Land, in the State of Virginia, all free of Taxes, at Three-Pence an Acre."[19] However, despite the importance of such people in influencing individuals to emigrate, especially in Ulster, the reality was that the flow of people from Ireland to America after 1783 was largely determined by commercial links. In these circumstances, the advertisement and promotion of the emigrant ship also assumed a new and more strategic importance.

18 Dickson, *Old World Colony*, 265–6, 312–4, *et passim*; NA, "List of Aliens Arriving in New York and Perth Amboy, 1799–1862;" Bailyn, *Voyagers to the West*, 122, 78; *NCEP*, 2 Sept. 1792; Bailyn, *Voyagers to the West*, 112. Like the *Diligence*, the ship *Nestor* (Whitehaven to Philadelphia, 1792) also sought passengers in Cork; see *NECP*, 26 Mar. 1792. For reports on convoy protection from Cork, see for example, *CHC*, 26 Mar., 29 Apr. 1798. On 11 Mar. 1786, *Lloyds' Lists* reported that 100 vessels had sailed from Cork for the West Indies "under convoy of the Canada Man of War." For the place of Cork in Bristol's American trade, see Kenneth Morgan, *Bristol and the Atlantic Trade in the Eighteenth Century* (Cambridge, 1993), 123–4; and Dickson, *Old World Colony*, 154–6.

Preparations and Passage

As the emigrant trade became more competitive from the late-1760s, and the major brokers promoted their vessels more widely and keenly, shipping advertisements became the focus of attention. Most of these invariably promised "to lay in plenty of good provisions and water for the voyage." The owners of the ship *Independence* (Belfast to Philadelphia, 1783) declared that "strict attention" would be paid to "the *quality* of the provisions, to have the Ship well stored with every thing proper and necessary for the voyage, so as to render the passage agreeable." If they were to attract passengers, vessels also had to be "in perfect repair." During the late-1720s many emigrants had been obliged to sail on what had "before been only Coasters ... because they cannot always get those that have been used to long Voyages." By the 1780s, however, passengers had a wider choice of vessels and were regularly assured that the advertised brig or ship was "stout," or newly and "well built of live Oak and Cedar." For example, the ship *Anne and Susan* (Newry to Philadelphia and New York, 1786) was said to have made only one previous voyage. The ship *Hannibal* (Belfast to Philadelphia, 1789) was especially "sturdy." It had been "built for a Ship of War" and as such, was supposed to be "superior in accommodation for passengers, to any other in the trade." Other vessels, such as the ship *Mary* (Derry to Philadelphia, 1783), had been "built entirely for the Passenger Trade" while the ship *Friendship* (Belfast to Philadelphia, 1785) had been "built *purposely* for carrying passengers." During the 1720s potential emigrants did not have such detailed descriptions before they sailed. By the 1780s it was more the exception than the rule that they had this kind of information and that they drew on it to decide with whom they would travel to America.[20]

Aside from hearing about the physical features of a particular vessel, the public wanted to be reassured that the captain was a man of "humanity" and "experience." After all, the captain was "King, Judge, and Governor aboard his own vessel" and at times, the "Desire to do Justice" could lead him to extremes. In November 1729 Captain Mercer of the ship *Drogheda* (Ireland to Philadelphia) was indicted before the Court of Admiralty in Philadelphia for abusing Thomas Flory, one of his passengers, whom he had accused of stealing one hundred guineas.

19 *BN*, 7 Apr. 1789, 23 Jan. 1791, 2 July, 29 Jan. 1790, 15 Aug. 1783; *NCEP*, 14 June 1792. For general comment on the role of clergymen in Irish emigration, see Miller, *Emigrants and Exiles*, 159–60; and Stephenson, *Scotch-Irish Migration to South Carolina, 1772*, 17–24.

20 *BN*, 20 Apr. 1792; *BN*, 11 July 1783; *PG*, 20 Nov. 1729; *BN*, 28 Mar. 1786; *BN*, 29 Dec. 1789; *LJ*, 11 Mar. 1783; *BN*, 8 Feb. 1785. The generic quotations are taken from the advertisements of the ships *Emelia* (Belfast to Philadelphia, 1783) and *Three Brothers* (Derry to Philadelphia, 1783), as printed in *BN*, 7 Feb. 1783; and *LJ*, 22 July 1783.

By the Captain's Order, a Rope [had been] put about his [Flory's] Neck, and a Prayer Book put in his Hand; he afterwards had Irons put on his Hands, by which he was hoisted up from the Deck, Matches dipped in Brimstone were put between his Fingers, and Toes, and being set on Fire, they burnt the Flesh to the Bones ... Flory was afterwards thrown over-board ... [and] with a rope round his Middle ... he languished ... several weeks, and at length died.

Within the more competitive passenger trade of the 1780s, such behaviour was less likely to be repeated or indulged. Instead, the "care and attention" of captains such as James Jeffries of the brig *Brothers* (Belfast to Philadelphia, 1790) was lauded and trumpeted. Captain William Cheevers of the ship *Anne and Susan* (Newry to Philadelphia and New York, 1786) was also an accomplished sailor; he was "long in the passenger trade" and had already made sixty nine voyages "across the Western Ocean" by 1786. Captain Francis Knox of the ship *Congress* (Derry to Philadelphia, 1784) conveyed his expertise in a more familiar way: "he is a Derry Man and served his Apprenticeship in the City in the Passenger Trade." He also personally helped to engage his passengers before departure and came to know them individually; as such, the *Congress* was "the best ship for America." Such claims were reassuring if only because it was the captain who determined whether a journey would be agreeable or not.[21]

While it was in the captain's interest to land his charges in a healthy state, for most of the eighteenth century, the poor regulation of the passenger trade in general, and of the servant trade, in particular, meant that the emigrant was often reduced from the status of being a mere traveller to that of someone whose primary importance was the passage money. However, from the mid-1760s, the building of purposely-designed passenger ships, as well as changes in the management of emigrant traffic, foreshadowed a trade that would become more specialised and passenger-centered after 1783. As a reflection of this, promoters assured their clients that vessels would not be overcrowded, even for those who travelled in steerage. On one level, it was easy to avoid overcrowding: promoters simply announced that they would limit the numbers they engaged. In 1784 the ship *Richard and Thomas* (Belfast to Philadelphia) promised that it

21 *BN*, 2 Mar. 1790; *PG*, 1 Dec. 1729; *BN*, 2 Mar. 1790, 28 Mar. 1786; *LJ*, 4 May 1784. Like Knox, capt. Charles Forrest of the brig *America* (Newry to Philadelphia and New York, 1783) was also said to be "long in the Passenger Trade from Derry;" *LJ*, 24 June 1783. For a general discussion of the voyage to America, see Melvin H. Jackson, "Ships and the Sea: Voyaging to the Chesapeake" in David B. Quinn, ed., *Early Maryland in a Wider World* (Detroit, 1982), 33–57; Ian K. Steele, *The English Atlantic, 1675–1740: An Exploration of Communication and Community* (New York and Oxford, 1986); Dickson, *Ulster Emigration*, ch.10. Although it focuses on the mid-nineteenth century, and aside from Dickson's chapter on the voyage, Terry Coleman, *Passage to America* (London, 1972) offers the only detailed treatment of the transatlantic voyage (in his case, from Liverpool).

would not be "Crouded with too many Passengers" while the ship *Alexander* (Derry to Philadelphia, 1788) warned that it would close its register at "a certain Number of Passengers" after which "none" would be taken. It was more difficult to guarantee that those who travelled in close quarters could do so in a healthy environment. However, many emigration brokers did try and, especially from the 1770s, they began to give more attention to ventilation on board their ships. Portholes were included in the designs of new vessels and were widely touted by the advertisers. The ship *Mary* (Derry to Philadelphia, 1783) was reported to be "very lofty" between decks, with six portholes on each side, while on the ship *Betsey* (Derry to Philadelphia, 1790) there were "6 Feet between Decks, Cabin and Steerage, Ditto." The ship *Three Brothers* (Belfast to Philadelphia, 1783) promised "several large rooms, and is in every other respect one of the best adapted Ships for this trade, that ever sailed from the kingdom." Advertisers knew that they could not make such claims lightly because passengers could preview the vessels for themselves before making any commitments. For example, there were boats to "take down any persons desirous of seeing" the ship *Richard and Thomas* (Belfast to Philadelphia, 1784) "every Friday during her stay" in port. Captain William Forrest of the brig *Joseph* (Newry to New York and Philadelphia, 1793) asked prospective travellers to call on him at Warrenpoint "that he may go with them on board the JOSEPH, in order to have any Birth insured to them in the Vessel, that they may wish to have during the Passage." If they were satisfied with what they saw, they could secure a berth by paying a deposit.[22]

Even with increasing attention to comfort and sanitation, disease was never far away, especially on long voyages. Smallpox, ague, and fever were particularly feared and indeed, a number of well-publicised tragedies occasionally reminded everybody that contracting an illness on the high seas was not a trivial matter. In 1774 it was reported that during a voyage between Newry and Philadelphia, "upwards of 140" emigrants had died "with sickness and for want of proper accommodation," while in a second vessel, a "very considerable" number perished in similar circumstances on the same route. Children were particularly vulnerable to disease at sea. In 1773 twenty five children died of smallpox on the ship *James and Henry* (Larne to New York). However, such a high level of mortality was unusual. Moreover, while the Irish-born American diplomat, David Bailie Warden (1772–1845), suggested that "the number of those who die

22 *BN*, 15 June 1784; *LJ*, 8 Apr. 1788; *BN*, 27 May 1783; *LJ*, 4 May 1790; *BN*, 15 July 1783; *BN*, 15 June 1784; *NS*, 15 Apr. 1793. It should also be noted that without a deposit, there was no guarantee that a berth would be available. Thus, the ship *Alexander* (Derry to Philadelphia, 1787) "refused upwards of 100 at sailing who had not given Earnest before the Books were Shut;" see *LJ*, 8 Apr. 1787.

at sea is not greater in proportion than those who die at land," some captains
tried to prevent such losses by insisting that children should be inoculated
before they went on board. The ship *Three Brothers* (Belfast to Philadelphia and
Baltimore, 1784) declared that it would not engage any children who had not
had the smallpox already. Such precautions were important and innovative and
although they were not thorough, surviving data for Irish voyages suggest that
mortality levels for both children and adults were not as high as on vessels
which carried German immigrants, slaves, convicts, or British troops to the
West Indies. However, intending emigrants did not disregard advertised promises such as those of the ship *Volunteer* (Dublin to New York and Philadelphia,
1783) that there would be a "Doctor and [a] Medicine Chest" on board or that
the ship *Three Brothers* (Belfast to Philadelphia, 1783) had engaged "a Physician
of eminence (who will be properly supplied with medicine) ... to pay a regular
attendance on every person on board requiring his assistance."[23]

Although passengers were influenced by promises of adequate food and good
conditions, they were also impressed when a particular vessel was reputed to be
"a remarkable fast Sailer." Under normal conditions, the voyage from Ireland
to America took anything from six to eight weeks, depending on the port of
origin, season of travel, and destination. On average, the trip to colonial
Philadelphia took from sixty four days in the early-Spring to forty nine during
the high season of July to September, with vessels from Dublin and Cork taking
a little less time than those from Ulster. For the route to New York, the data are
similar. The longer journey to Charleston was usually undertaken in the
autumn and took from eight to nine weeks, seven to ten days more than the trip
to Baltimore. During the 1780s and 1790s better-built ships sometimes did the

---

23 *FLJ*, 5, 18 Oct. 1774; *NYJ*, 21 Oct. 1773; MHS, David Bailie Warden Papers, ms. 871,
as in LC, microfilm copy, roll 1 (hereafter cited as "Warden Papers"); *BN*, 27 Apr. 1784;
SN, 20 Oct. 1783; *BN*, 2 Sept. 1783. Farley Grubb summarises comparable mortality
rates as follows: 11% for 8,400 British troops who were sent to the West Indies between
1775 and 1782; between 10% and 15% for English convicts sent to Maryland between
1718 and 1775; and for German immigrants, 5.5%: 3.8% "passage mortality" and 1.7%
from shipwrecks; see Grubb, "Morbidity and Mortality on the North Atlantic Passage:
Eighteenth-Century German Immigration," *JIntH* xvii (1987)," 568, n.6, 571, n.11. See
also James C. Riley, "Mortality on Long-Distance Voyages in the Eighteenth Century,"
JEH xli (1981), 651–7. For slaves, mortality rates varied from a low of 8% to a high of
30%. For a summary of the estimates, see Herbert S. Klein, "The Trade in African Slaves
to Rio de Janiero, 1795–1811: Estimates of Mortality and Patterns of Voyages," *Journal
of African History* x (1969), 533–35; and Joseph C. Miller, "Mortality in the Atlantic Slave
Trade: Statistical Evidence on Casualty," *JIntH* xi (1981), 385–423. For a general
discussion of ship diseases, see John Duffy, *Epidemics in Colonial America* (Port
Washington,1972) and "The Passage to the Colonies," *MVHR* xxxviii (1951), 21–38; and
Steele, *English Atlantic*, 252–59.

journey more quickly and this was recognised in some advertisements. For example, the ship *Dublin Packet* (Dublin to Philadelphia) trumpeted its quick passages of thirty to thirty five days to Philadelphia while "more than once, it performed its voyage from Philadelphia to Dublin, in 21 days." The ship *Paca* (Cork to Baltimore, 1785) was so fast and so ably organised that it managed "twice yearly sailings" from Ireland and on 25 January 1785 the *Belfast News-Letter* noted that its

> last voyage ... [had been] made in seven weeks and three days with 459 souls on board, who arrived at Baltimore all well, being the same number he took in at Belfast; and a circumstance which scarce has been equalled, the passengers not being able to use their full allowance of provisions during the voyage.

Playing another card, the promoters of the *Paca* also pointed out that the vessel's quick turnarounds were possible because it left port on the advertised day.[24]

Even with the best will and management, departures were often delayed. While this caused additional anxiety, trouble, and expense for those who were travelling, it was the rule rather than the exception for most of the colonial period. In 1735 those who had booked the ship *George* (Dublin to Carolina) had "spent what money they had" even before they sailed and accordingly, they petitioned Parliament for assistance. During the high emigration of the 1770s and 1780s postponements could last for up to four weeks. In 1783 the brig *Rose and Betty* (Newry to Baltimore and Virginia) had been advertised to sail on 20 April but was delayed no less than three times before it finally left on 23 May. This was not always the fault of a vessel's promoters but rather a reflection of the erratic ways in which passengers were sometimes engaged. Moreover, families were not always ready to leave on the appointed day. In 1795 the ship *Leeds Packet* (Belfast to New York) deferred its voyage by two weeks, "in order to accommodate a number of families." As the emigrant trade became better organised, such cases became more infrequent. However, as there is often no accounting for human failings, managers still had to allow for delays and tried to redress the resulting inconveniences in a professional manner. As a result, passengers were often provisioned from the day on which they were issued with a "positively final" notice to depart, even if ensuing delays were "at the request of a number of passengers." In 1784 the managers of the ill-fated ship *Faithful Steward* (Derry to Philadelphia) announced that their passengers "will have two free Houses at each side of Culmore Point until said Ship sails" while the brig *Rachel* (Newry to Philadelphia and New York, 1792) promised that "should the

24 *LJ*, 22 July 1783; *BN*, 9 June 1789; *CHC*, 8 Mar. 1785; *BN*, 25 Mar. 1785.

vessel be detained after the 14th April, any passengers who have then engaged, will be maintained on board from that day."[25]

Despite such undertakings, promoters wanted to keep their profits as high as possible, not least because fares were also being affected by an increasingly competitive passenger trade. Emigrants from Cork, Dublin, and Limerick usually paid higher rates than their equivalents from Ulster. In 1783 the fares from Cork to Philadelphia were listed as follows: "10 guineas in the cabin—6 in the Steerage—and 4 in the hold." For the steerage passengers who sailed on the ship *Ruth and Nelly* (Limerick to Philadelphia, 1783) the passage money was also six guineas while ten guineas bought a cabin from Dublin. As usual, provisions were included although some vessels also gave those in the steerage the option of paying three guineas for the berth only, provided that they brought their own food. From Ulster, however, the Atlantic voyage became cheaper during the course of the eighteenth century. Between the 1730s and 1760s the cost of a steerage passage from the province fell by almost half to £3 10s. From time to time, competition among shippers resulted in even lower prices. For example, the ship *Newry's Assistance* (Derry to Philadelphia, 1772) charged "not more than" £3 for the trip and this included basic provisions. However, while lower fares were welcomed, promoters often made up for lost profits by being "as frugal as Possible" with supplies. Blair McClenachan spoke for many owners in 1774 when he encouraged his captain "to keep the ship's disbursements ... as small as possible [as] the Small Sum of three Pounds for Each Passenger will not Admit of Going to Great Expence."[26]

Although McClenachan's advice was not always acted on, passengers were often urged to carry their own provisions for the journey and depending on their circumstances, many of them did, especially if they had children. This was even more important because at official level, governments had been slow to regulate the treatment of passengers on the high seas. Pennsylvania was a pioneer in this regard. During the colonial period it had passed a number of laws to ensure that the voyage would be, in the words of its act of 1749, "good and wholesome." This law, as well as a supplementary act that was passed in 1765, also provided for the "necessary room and accommodations" on board,

25 Dickson, *Ulster Emigration*, 122, 202–3; "Report from the Committee Appointed to take into consideration the Petition of Robert Oliver and others, Passengers, Unlawfully Detained on Board the Ship, called the George, of Dublin, Thomas Cumming, Master," *Commons Journals. Ireland* iv, appendix, lxiii; *BN*, 7 Mar., 30 May 1783; *BN*, 30 Mar. 1795; *LJ*, 20 Apr. 1784; *BN*, 6 Mar. 1792.

26 *IG*, 30 Sept. 1783; *CHC*, 21 July 1783; *SN*, 29 June 1784; *BN*, 29 July 1772; LC, Blair McClenachan Papers, McClenachan to Andrew Thompson, 10, 31 Dec. 1774. For a discussion of the decreasing fare over the course of the century, see Dickson, *Ulster Emigration*, 86.

that vessels should be "thoroughly smoked" and "well washed with vinegar," and have a "well recommended surgeon ... [as well as] a complete assortment of medicines ... [without] any pay or satisfaction" to nurse passengers who might need them. The 1765 act stated that passengers and managers should formally agree on the terms and conditions of the voyage before a vessel sailed. As a result, cases of breach of contract began to feature in court lists. In New York, a case was brought against the managers of the brig *Nancy* (from Scotland) in 1774. The trial underlined the importance of pre-embarkation agreements and suggested that those who did not have a "*written* contract, mentioning the principal articles of provision, and allowance" had suffered particular distresses during the voyage and had been reduced to "black raw musty meal, and stinking water." Seven years earlier, Captain Nathaniel Russell had been charged in South Carolina with breaking a pre-departure agreement that every passenger was to have "nineteen inches room in width for each person but scarcely had seven, there being so much crowded." Therefore, substantive steps were being taken through the colonial courts and targeted legislation was introduced to protect the health and comfort of European immigrants during their voyage across the Atlantic. The result protected everybody: the wider community as well as the immigrant. It also underlined the fact that passengers could no longer be dismissed as casual players in transatlantic commerce.[27]

The voyage across the Atlantic was a great leveller. As he sailed from Belfast to Boston in 1795, one John Cunningham suggested that "those on shore" did not fully appreciate the dangers of the trip to America and that if they did, contemporary emigration would have been much less than it was. Although by no means the norm, it was not uncommon to read accounts of "tempestuous voyages" from Ireland, of ships springing leaks, masts being split, pumps failing, waves crashing through portholes, and passengers and crewmen being swept overboard as they battled the elements to secure their vessels. In 1786, for example, it took the brig *Happy Return* ninety four days to sail from Dublin to Providence, during which time the vessel "met with many severe gales of wind, in which all her sails were split, the main-sail, main and jib-booms lost, and her rigging so much torn and otherwise injured as to be unfit for future service." The biographies of such trips is a reminder that poor weather could render the terms of a vessel's advertisement meaningless.[28]

Aside from the vagaries of the weather, another natural and constant threat to a safe passage was hidden beneath the sea. Delaware Bay presented one of the

27 *Stats at Large Pa.* v (1749–50), c.ccclxxxi, 94–7; *ibid.*, vi (1764–5), c.dxxvii, 432–40; *Virginia Gazette*, 10 Feb. 1774; HSP, Gratz Papers, Nathaniel Russell to Rev. Ezra Stiles, 19 July 1767; Smith, *White Servitude in Colonial South Carolina*, 42. See also Schwartz, *Mixed Multitude*, 193–4.

28 PRONI, D. 394/2; *BN*, 21 Mar. 1786.

greatest challenges to captains and their pilots; even Henry Hudson had been "forced to stand back" from it in 1609. At its entrance, the Delaware River spans sixteen miles and is bordered on the northeast by Cape May (New Jersey) and on the southwest by Cape Henlopen (Delaware). Here, it is eighty one miles or about a day's sail, from Philadelphia. Half-way upriver, the course narrows below Newcastle and then near Wilmington, both of which were ports-of-ease to Philadelphia. The bay was notorious for its shoals and shallows, especially at Reedy Island, Mud Island, Red Bank, and Cross Ledge Shoals, so named to suggest their dangers. However, it was not until 1759 that the noted surveyor, Joshua Fisher of Lewes, published the first detailed hydrograph of the "Shores, Creeks, Harbours, Soundings and Shoals" of Delaware Bay. This was welcomed at the time although even into the 1790s, many charts did not mark the bay's many wrecks. Moreover, given that the range between high and low tides was between four and six feet, the bay was always treacherous and vessels continued to run aground there until better charts were produced in the early-nineteenth century.[29]

Until a breakwater was erected at Cape Henlopen in the 1830s, the fresh-water ports of Phladelphia, Newcastle, and Wilmington were also troubled by enduring winter ice. Merchants complained that they often had to wait until the Spring to ship their consignments as navigation could be impossible for four to five months of the year. In 1783–84 the Delaware Valley experienced its worst winter since 1750, forcing "several" incoming vessels to divert to New York. As late as March 1784 the river was so frozen that it was reported to be "a common highway for the people of New Jersey and Pennsylvania to pass and repass – wagons, teams, sleds, and sleighs all pass with the greatest safety." When the ice eventually began to break, the ship *Three Brothers* (Philadelphia to Dublin, 1784), to take but one example, spent "near one third of [its passage of six weeks] … getting down the river Delaware, the navigation of which was impeded by the breaking up of the frost." Thirteen years later, the ice was reported to be "so strong as to carry travellers across; it was as common to walk over the river to New-Jersey as to walk the streets of Philadelphia." A number of merchants also turned the situation to their advantage and erected a number of temporary taverns on the riverbank to serve the unexpected custom.[30]

---

29 George Geib, "A History of Philadelphia, 1776–1780" (Ph.D. dissertation, University of Wisconsin, 1969), 208. Hudson is quoted in Marion V. Brewington, "Maritime Philadelphia, 1609–1837," *PMHB* lxiii (April 1939), 96. A list of charts and surveys of the Delaware is given in Priscilla M. Thompson, "Navigation of the Delaware Bay, 1790–1830," *DH* xix (1980), 73, 84–5.

30 *NYJ*, 25 Mar. 1784; *HJ*, 19 May 1784; *BN*, 10 Apr. 1797. For an early, if unsuccessful, petition from "the merchants of the city of Philadelphia … for the purpose of protecting vessels from the ice," see *NYP*, 25 Dec. 1790, 22 Jan. 1791. For the blockages of 1728–9, when 36 vessels were detained in Philadelphia for several weeks, see Nash, *Urban Crucible*, 10.

In 1785 a combination of bad weather and the natural obstacles of the Delaware led to one of the greatest tragedies of the late-eighteenth-century Irish passenger trade: the loss of the ship *Faithful Steward* (Derry to Philadelphia). On 9 July the vessel had left Derry with 249 passengers. On 1 September it ran aground on Mohaba, one of the many underwater banks off Cape Henlopen, obliging the captain "to cut away her masts, &c. all of which went overboard."

> Every effort was made to save the unhappy sufferers, who remained in the wreck during the night, the sea ... [being] extremely high ... the boats were with difficulty disengaged from the wreck, but before they could be got manned, they drifted ashore, therefore all relief was cut off, except by swimming or getting ashore on pieces of wreck, and we are sorry to add, that of the above, only 68 persons were saved.

Of the one hundred women and children who were on board, only seven women survived. The tragedy evoked a number of responses, from encouraging a subscription to relieve the "unfortunate" survivors, to demands that ship captains and pilots should have a thorough knowledge "of the practice and theory of navigation in its modern improved state." The fate of the *Faithful Steward* was not unique. Two years earlier, the ship *Philadelphia Packet* (Belfast to Philadelphia, 1783) had also run aground off Cape Henlopen and, although its 250 passengers made it ashore, seventy were later drowned when a schooner that had been hired to complete the journey to Philadelphia, keeled to one side and sank. In 1783 the bars off Cape Henlopen also claimed the ship *Success* (Dublin to Philadelphia). On 9 September, while still at sea, the vessel had been struck by lightning; eleven days later, it ran aground near the cape. When thirty one passengers later charged that the captain "did *knowingly* and *willing*[*ly*] run [the] said ship on a shoal," it was clear that this particular story had a twist. Some alleged that Captain John Cadenhead had been "difficult" during the voyage and that there had been "several disputes" about berths. Although Cadenhead was later publicly vindicated by seventeen Dublin merchants, there were suggestions that the affair was being used to discredit the Dublin brokers for whom Cadenhead worked. Thus, the episode suggests that Dublin's houses were beginning to keenly compete for the city's developing passenger trade with the Delaware.[31]

Aside from natural catastrophies and incompetent captains, passengers were also exposed to attack by "ALGERINES." After 1783, however, they could find

31 *PG*, 14 Sept. 1785; *NYJ*, 15 Sept. 1785; *BN*, 22 Nov. 1785; *PP*, 12, 23 Sept. 1785; *HJ*, 26 Jan. 1784.

some protection in the "Mediterranean Pass," a document which supposedly guaranteed safe passage as a result of an annual "tribute" that was paid to the rulers of Morocco, Algiers, Tunis, and Tripoli. However, these tickets were not issued to vessels of American registry because, in the words of John Fiske, the newly established United States was "too poor to build a navy, and too poor to buy off the pirates." Thus, when the American-registered ship *Paca* sailed from Belfast in March 1785, it was obliged to take its 300 passengers on the northern route to Baltimore "to avoid the Algerine cruisers, who continue to be very troublesome." Reports of the "Barbary danger" sometimes discouraged American-registered traffic from sailing on the southerly routes to America. They also resulted in higher insurance rates that British and French owners hoped would be unsustainable for American carriers. As one American reporter ruefully put it in 1787,

> the British make the danger appear greater than it really is, by which means the American bottoms are insured at a very high rate ... I am inclined to think that it would not be very agreeable to the French to see us have a very extensive trade in the Mediterranean.

Two years earlier, Spain had also decided to "make peace with those people [of North Africa]." The *New York Packet* predicted that thereafter, "the Algerines ... will be all over the Atlantic" to target the vessels of those countries which had not concluded treaties with them.[32]

On occasion, Americans were even taken to Africa as prisoners. In 1786 several merchants protested against the "bondage and misery" in which some of these were held but were assured by Congress that "the most effectual measures are taking" against the Emperor of Morocco "as well as the other predatory powers." However, the United States could do very little about threats from North Africa and contemporary newspapers warned Americans to "*beware!* Let nothing tempt you to come in the way of those people, for they are worse than can be imagined." Such advice again underlined the importance of the Mediterranean Pass for would-be emigrants as well as the more favoured British vessels over those which were registered in America. When the *Londonderry Journal* noted that the ship *Nancy* (Derry to Philadelphia, 1791) had such a pass, it added that "none but British Ships can have [one] – a pleasing Circumstance for Passengers to have themselves secured from the Danger of Captivity, to which all Foreign Ships are subject." Notice of these passes was

32 *LJ*, 8 Apr. 1788; John Fiske, *The Critical Period in American History, 1783–1789* (Boston and New York, 1888), 161; *NYP*, 4 Aug. 1785, 13 Feb. 1787, 17 Apr. 1786, 21 Nov. 1785. *BN*, 28 Jan. 1794 reported that insurance on "American bottoms" had increased by between 20% and 25% "in consequence of the Algerine captures."

also incorporated into shipping advertisements. For example, the promoters of the ship *Joseph* (Newry to New York and Newcastle, 1794) suggested that for

> those Passengers that intend going in her ... it must be satisfactory [to] them at present, going in a British bottom with a pass, as they will not have to fear being captured by those dreadful Savages now at War with America (the Algerines) that have of late captured so many of their Ships going out.[33]

Robert Simpson later recalled that in choosing to sail on the ship *Sally* (Derry to Philadelphia, 1788), he was greatly influenced by the fact that the vessel had a pass and that as a result, he presumed that his voyage would be safer. It was alleged that from time to time, some ships "belonging to the United States" clandestinely "procured" "Mediterranean Passes ... to cover these vessels against those piratical rovers." Others simply forged them. As these practices both gave American vessels an advantage which British and Irish vessels felt should be theirs alone and threatened the delicate agreements that had been made with the North African states, Parliament tried to halt the irregular use of Mediterranean passes in 1787. Vessels coming into New York were also asked to verify their passes with the British consul. In the 1790s the United States finally concluded its own agreements with Algiers (1795), Tripoli (1796) and Tunis (1797). Because of Ireland's interest in such matters, the *Belfast News-Letter* published a detailed report of the Congressional debate on the first of these treaties on 15 April 1795.[34]

After February 1793, when Britain and France went to war, there were other motives for searching and impressing passengers on the high seas. In 1795 British frigates took the captain and thirty two passengers off the brig *Harmony* (Cork to Philadelphia) because "they were in want of men for their fleet cruising off this coast." The following year forty were taken from the brig *Elizabeth* (Waterford to New York), "leaving only men who had large families" on board. Forty six passengers were impressed from the brig *Susanna* (Belfast to Philadelphia, 1796) while on 20 August 1795, and only "a few hours' sail from the American coast," a similar number, and all but one of the crew, were taken from the brig *Cincinnatus* (Belfast to Philadelphia) by three British frigates which were based in Halifax. Wolfe Tone was on board at the time and has left the following account of the encounter:

33 *SN*, 10 Mar. 1786; *BN*, 9 June 1789; *SN*, 5 June 1789; *NYP*, 21 Nov. 1785; *LJ*, 17 Feb. 1791; *BN*, 15 Apr. 1794.
34 HSP, Am. 1528, Letterbook of Robert Simpson (1790–1807), Simpson to his father, 1 Aug. 1788; *HJ*, 19 May 1785; *DEP*, 15 Mar.1787.

they pressed every one of our hands, save one, and near fifty of my unfortunate fellow passengers, who were most of them flying to America to avoid the tyranny of a bad government at home, thus most unexpectedly fell under the severest tyranny, one of them at least, which exists. As I was in a jacket and trousers, one of the lieutenants ordered me into the boat as a fit man to serve the King, and it was only the screams of my wife and sister which induced him to desist ... The insolence of these tyrants, as well to myself as to my poor fellow passengers ... I have not since forgotten, and never will.

Some two months earlier, his friend, Archibald Hamilton Rowan "had a narrow escape" in similar circumstances and avoided seizure only because he had been introduced to the officers of HMS *Melampus* as one "Mr. Thomson of South Carolina." In 1796 the American brig *Pearl* (Cork to New York) was boarded off Cape Clear and twelve passengers were impressed, "all Irishmen and Landsmen," despite the fact that they were travelling with papers which had been issued "under the sanction and with the permission of the Lord Lieutenant and Privy Council." Evidently, official protocols which had been agreed before departure were not always recognised on the high seas.[35]

Mid-Atlantic search and seizure were not confined to the actions of the British navy, especially after February 1793. Given American neutrality on the war in Europe, some assumed that because a particular vessel was an "American bottom," it would be safe. In August 1793 the promoters of the ship *Atlanta* (Newry to Charleston, 1793) suggested that passengers would have "nothing to fear from French Privateers, it being well known the respect they pay to American Ships" while the following year, those of the ship *Alexander* (Newry to Newcastle and New York) intimated that it was "unnecessary to mention the great security that Passengers, going to America, will experience in an American ship, at a time that a War exists between Great-Britain and France." However, given the poor relationship that existed between Revolutionary France and the governments of George Washington (1789–97) and John Adams (1797–1801), few were surprised that France, no less than Britain, did not regard American vessels as "neutral carriers," especially after Jay's Treaty was concluded in 1795.[36]

As revolutionary movements in Ireland developed close links with France during the later-1790s, French naval vessels often took a benign view of ships sailing from Ireland. In 1797, for example, it was reported that the brig

35 *ADA*, 7 May 1795; Bartlett, ed., *Life and Times of Theobald Wolfe Tone*, 109; *CHC*, 6 June 1796; *Argus*, 3 June 1796; *NS*, 29 Aug. 1796; *Aurora*, 12 Aug. 1796; *DJ*, 7 Jan. 1796; *Aurora*, 7 Apr. 1796. For the boarding of the vessels carrying Tone and Rowan, see also *BN*, 5 Oct. 1795 and the *Argus*, 8 Aug. 1795; and *CHC*, 10 Sept. 1795, respectively.
36 *NS*, 4 Sept. 1793; *BN*, 28 Mar. 1794.

Benjamin and Nancy (Dublin to New York) was boarded by a French sloop of war but "on being informed they were all Irish people who were his passengers, they treated them with every respect." However, nobody could rely on such benevolence to get them safely to America and the placement of floating batteries to protect the major ports of Ireland to reinforce "the numerous gun boats and the disposition of the military forces on or near the sea-coast" were an obvious reminder of the dangers current. Vessels were thus encouraged to carry a *rôle d'équipage* which was to Revolutionary France what the Mediterranean Pass was to the Moors. In 1798 the ship *Catherine* (Newry to Newcastle and Wilmington) announced that it was "furnished with a Role d'Equipage and every other paper accessary to secure her against capture by the French." Some vessels continued to give more traditional assurances. The ship *Betsey*, for example, announced that it would carry "16 six pounders" on its voyage between Dublin and America in 1799, while others stressed that they would sail in convoy.[37]

Destination Delaware

Although concerns for the safety of the Atlantic voyage occasionally affected the extent of the passenger flow from Ireland, it did not diminish the status of Philadelphia as the destination of choice for most contemporary Irish emigrants. In 1791 the (Philadelphia) *General Advertiser* reported that the number of vessels that were sailing with passengers "is astonishing, and shows that this country [America] is daily increasing in the opinion of the old world." Those which headed for the Delaware Valley as well as the numbers that they carried are reasonably well-documented in contemporary sources. In November 1784 the *Hibernian Journal* reported from Philadelphia that by the end of the previous July, "5,000 natives of [Ireland] had arrived in Philadelphia alone." The flow continued into the 1790s. In 1791, for example, the *Independent Gazetteer* reported that for the year ending 27 October of that year, 2,744 Irish immigrants had entered the city. Even in the "five or six sail of Vessels" that had arrived in American ports from Ireland in the late-season month of October 1784, "at least" seven to eight hundred passengers were said to have landed at Philadelphia.[38] Mathew Carey, the Irish-born secretary of the Hibernian

37 *SN*, 20 Dec. 1797; *GUS*, 30 May 1798, 20 Oct. 1798; *BN*, 19 Mar. 1798; *SN*, 20 Feb. 1799. In New York, a meeting of merchants in 1794 called on Congress to effect the "necessary measures" to vindicate "the wrongs done to the United States of America" on the high seas; see *NYDA*, 26 May, 5 Mar. 1794. For the resolutions of a similar meeting of "Masters and Mates of vessels belonging to the port" of Baltimore, see *NYDA*, 26 May 1794.

38 *GA*, 3 Aug. 1791; report from Philadelphia in *HJ*, 17 Nov. 1784; *IG*, 31 Dec. 1791; *HJ*, 7 Jan. 1785.

Society, paid close attention to these immigrants. On 9 September 1791 he informed the Dublin-based printer, **John Chambers** (1754–1837), that "the migrations from Ireland to this part within this year have been very great" and that already, between 3,000 and 4,000 had arrived in his adopted city. Anecdotal evidence confirms this assessment. In 1783, for example, it was reported that so many passengers had engaged for the sloop *Hibernia* (Newry to Philadelphia, 1783) that the owners had to apologise for refusing "so many" while the following year, the overflow from the brig *William* (Newry to Philadelphia, 1784) were referred to the ship *Hope* (Newry to Philadelphia).[39]

This "rage for emigration" was especially noticeable from Ulster and between 1783 and 1798, as many as 269 of the 422 vessels that sailed into the Delaware from Ireland originated in the province. During the late-1780s, however, Philadelphia's shipping entrances from Ulster and southern Irish ports grew closer (see Appendix V). After 1790 the predominance of the Ulster ports was more clearly re-established in the port's marine lists and, in particular, a strong connection with Derry. Derry never lost its place as the leading source for Irish immigrants and before 1800 a number of passenger vessels made regular runs from the Foyle. On 16 August 1797 the (New York) *Argus* noted that on the previous 1 June, Ulster newspapers had advertised thirteen vessels "in the passenger trade" from Derry to America; only two others were advertised from Belfast and one from Newry. Its conclusion was that even at the height of the "quasi-war" in 1797, "the desire of leaving the oppressed country was more prevalent than ever."[40]

Increased emigration from outside Ulster was also a feature of these years. From Dublin, one newspaper reported that "not less than 1,000 persons" had embarked for America in February 1784 while the ship *Favorite* (Dublin to Philadelphia, 1784) was said to be so over-subscribed that "more than 300 persons, male and female" were refused by both it and the other vessels that were in port at the time. In April 1784 over 300 passengers sailed on the brig *Convention* (Dublin to Philadelphia) while the previous year the promoters of the ship *Success* (Dublin to Philadelphia) got such a response to their advertisement that they announced that if the passage money was not completely paid before a certain date, deposits would be forfeited and the berths given to others. On 3 August 1784 the *Pennsylvania Packet* also underlined the popularity of the Delaware for Dublin's emigrants: "it is imagined ten more vessels could shortly

39 HSP, Lea & Febiger Letterbooks (1 Aug. 1788 to 10 Nov. 1794), Ledger D, Carey to John Chambers, 9 Sept. 1791; *BN*, 27 May 1783, 20 Feb. 1784.
40 PRO, FO/4/11, Phineas Bond to Grenville, 8 Oct. 1791. For context, see Alexander DeConde, *The Quasi-War: The Politics and Diplomacy of the Undeclared War with France, 1797–1801* (New York, 1966).

be filled, were they to sail with emigrants to that part of the world [Philadelphia] from the city and county of Dublin only." The heavy flow of people continued until war broke out in 1793, re-establishing Dublin as an important exit-point for free Irish emigrants. Indeed, the *Freeman's Journal* suggested on 10 January 1790 that emigrants from outside Ulster "would have gone off to America in ten-fold proportion, but could not possibly procure the means of providing their passage." From the other southern ports of Cork, Galway, Limerick, and Waterford, there were also several "alarming instances of emigration which continue to take place." Captain Benjamin Edmonston of the ship *Anne* (Cork to Philadelphia, 1784) announced that he would be "continuing ... [to] accommodat[e] passengers chiefly." As *Saunders News-Letter* reported on 3 June 1784, "the *sense* of people moving is almost tangible."[41]

Of the official observers of contemporary immigration into the Delaware Valley, the British consul for the middle states, Phineas Bond, had a special access to information because of the requirement that, on arrival, British and Irish captains had to record their registers and Mediterranean Passes at his office. His data for the 1780s are of particular interest and suggest that not only was the flow from Ireland higher than it was before the Revolution but that "the Migrations hither since the Peace ... have been much greater from Ireland than from all the other Ports of Europe ... An almost total Stop has been lately put to the Migration hither from the Palatinate, & other Parts of Germany." For the 1780s, Bond listed the figures as in Table 3.1:

TABLE 3.1: CONSULAR REPORTS ON IMMIGRATION INTO
PHILADELPHIA, 1783–89

Year	1783	1784	1785	1786	1787	1788	1789
Passengers	3508	9436	5866	2340	1220	1050	2296

Source: PRO, FO/4/7–8

Of these 25,716 arrivals, 23,823 were said to be "Scotch & Irish but chiefly Irish." In 1790 Bond thought that the number of incoming passengers, while still "important," had fallen "very short of the general expectation." However, although his lists for the 1790s are not as detailed as those of the previous seven years, in 1791, he was still reporting figures as high as 4,500 from Ireland, with "more expected." He was particularly struck by the continued immigration from Ulster and in 1791 he advised Lord Grenville, secretary of state for foreign affairs (1791–1801), that "The Rage for Emigration, which now prevails, excites well grounded Fears that some of the Northern Counties of Ireland will be

41 *SN*, 27 Feb. 1784; *PP*, 3 Aug., 10 May 1784, 30 June 1783; *PP*, 22 Nov., 30 Sept. 1784.

depopulated, unless a Seasonable Interposition be made to correct this alarming Evil."[42]

My own reconstruction from newspaper and other sources suggests that at least 66,000 passengers entered the Delaware Valley from Ireland between 1783 and 1798, half of them between 1783 and 1789 (see Appendix V). During that seven year period at least 21,800 came from Ulster and over 10,000 from southern Irish ports. For the 1790s, the contrasting origins of the immigrants is even more striking. From an annual average of some 1,455 between 1783 and 1789, the identifiable immigration from southern Ireland fell sharply to an annual average of a mere 165 between 1793 and 1799. In the meantime, emigration from Ulster ports continued throughout the 1790s and although it declined by nearly two thirds after 1797, its combined total between 1790 and 1798 was, at nearly 31,500, even greater than that for the preceding seven years, 1783–90. These figures represent a major flow of people although given that two children were usually "counted but one passenger," it is clear that they are understated. They also imply that while the Delaware Valley was a favoured destination from both parts of Ireland after 1783, war and fear of impressment had a greater impact on the passenger trade from southern Ireland. As *Saunders News-Letter* suggested in March 1796, because so many vessels had been pressed into Government service for the war, "and still the greater number which, since the war, have fallen into the hands of the enemy," the decline in the amount of shipping that was available to passenger brokers was "unexampled" notwithstanding the fact that "every ship builder's yard is full of work."[43]

For the port of Philadelphia, computing Irish immigration is complicated by the fact that, as during the colonial period, some passengers continued to disembark at the Delaware ports of Newcastle and Wilmington. The concessions that these two ports had offered over several decades were enhanced in 1786 when the state of Delaware enacted that

> all foreigners, merchants, seamen, manufacturers and artisans, as inhabitants of the United States, or any of them [except Loyalists], who may go, and reside in, either of the said towns [Newcastle and Delaware], and during the space of two months follow or practice any trade or occupation whatsoever therein, be admitted as freemen and citizens of the said towns.

The act also declared that, with the exception of slaves, goods imported into the two ports would be "exempt from all duties and imposts whatsoever," with the

42 PRO, FO/4/8, Bond to Leeds, 10 Nov. 1789; J. Franklin Jameson, ed., "Bond II," 464, Bond to Leeds, 1 Nov. 1790; *ibid.*, 488, Bond to Grenville, 10 Sept. 1791; PRO, FO/4/11, Bond to Grenville, 8 Oct. 1791.

43 *NYDA*, 6 Aug. 1800 (with reference to those on board the ship *Liberty* (Derry to Wilmington, 1800); *SN*, 17 Mar. 1796.

exception of those that were imposed for "the regulation" of domestic American commerce. Accordingly, the colonial practice of stopping in Delaware was still actively encouraged and many vessels, especially those of Ulster origin, continued to advertise for Philadelphia (and other destinations) "by way of" Newcastle. The ship *St. James* (Belfast to Newcastle and New York, 1789) indicated that it would not travel upriver to Philadelphia but that there were "frequent vessels" to take passengers there, if they so wished. With this is mind, "most" of the 400 passengers on its 1791 voyage expected to land at Newcastle while of the 350 who sailed on the ship *Nancy*, (Derry to Newcastle and Philadelphia, 1791), 200 "came ashore in New-Castle, [and] the remainder came up to this city [Philadelphia] in good health." In addition to these kinds of notices, the special relationship between the two ports is also implied by the 40% difference between my estimated figure of about 28,755 entrants for the first six years after independence and the 23,823 given by Bond for the same period. In one respect, this discrepancy is a matter of focus: mine on the Delaware Valley as a whole, Bond's on Philadelphia.[44] However, as during the colonial period, it again confirms that Newcastle was a port of dispersal through which passengers travelled both onwards to Philadelphia and to other ports, including New York to the north, and Baltimore and Charleston to the south. Nonetheless, the most popular destination for contemporary Irish emigrants remained clear: Philadelphia.

Changing Typologies

It is also clear that despite the decline in the number of emigrating servants after 1783, many of those who entered the greater Philadelphia area were neither unskilled nor illiterate. In 1784, for example, coopers, tailors, and weavers sailed on the ship *Friendship* (Belfast to Philadelphia) while "several" of the servants and redemptioners aboard the brig *William* (Newry to Philadelphia, 1784) were "acquainted with trades." On the ship *Providence* (Cork to Philadelphia, 1784), there were

---

44 *BN,* 14 Apr. 1789; *GA,* 19 Aug. 1791; *NYDG,* 27 July 1791. For the "Act to establish certain Free Ports within the Delaware State, for the encouragement of Commerce" (2 Mar. 1786), see *PP,* 20 Mar. 1786. For three other vessels that landed passengers at Newcastle before proceeding to Philadelphia, see the notices for the ship *Alexander* (from Newry, 1791) (110 at Newcastle and sixty onwards to Philadelphia); the brig *Sally* (from Derry, 1795) (170/100); and the brig *Betsey* (from Derry, 1796) (80/40) in *ADA,* 18 July 1791; *Argus,* 24 July 1795; and *Aurora,* 25 Oct. 1796, respectively. From these and other figures, one can infer that approximately between a third and a half disembarked at Newcastle.

carpenters, taylors, shoemakers, rope-makers, labourers, breeches-makers, clerks, farmers, coachmen, cutlers, weavers, butchers, joiners, harness makers, hairdressers, carvers, coach makers, white, black and coach smiths, glowers, masons, dyers, hatters, [and] brick makers.

For "the most part," many of Philadelphia's immigrants were also said to have paid their passage money before leaving Ireland. Indeed, there was such a demand for berths after 1783 that many captains were inclined "to take none but those who pay" and in their shipping advertisements, some of them openly discouraged servants and redemptioners. "No servants or redemptioners" would be taken on the ship *Providence* (Derry to Newcastle and Philadelphia, 1783), for example, while in Dublin only "tradesmen under a certain description" were being invited to "the different vessels now in our harbour." Those who sailed on the ships *Maria* (Dublin to Philadelphia, 1783) and *Congress* (Newry to Philadelphia, 1783) were "very respectable passengers" and "people of property, and manufacturers," respectively. For captains and passengers alike, such reports confirm both a declining demand for servants and redemptioners and a move away from the characteristics of the emigration of the colonial period.[45]

They were reflected also on the American side of the Atlantic, as Sharon Salinger has shown. Servants had always received "proper encouragement" to emigrate from Ireland and this continued after the Declaration of Independence, especially if they were young and single. In 1782, however, one Philadelphia merchant indicated that he would not accept servants from Ireland until he was clear "respecting the propriety of it, lest Congress may disapprove of such Men being carried out to America." In any event, Irish traders were being advised in 1784 that America was so "overstocked" with servants that "several" captains were unable to indent those who were already there. The following year, it was reported that Congress officially acknowledged this "glut" and forbade further traffic in servants, observing that "for want of employment, many of those [who had] already arrived here are in a starving condition, their indentures not being disposed of." Although the item was untrue, it was not denied in the contemporary Irish press. However, although some of Ireland's brokers continued to engage servants until the end of the century, the decline in this type of migration was irreversible and in November 1789 Bond wrote that "lately ... [but] few Redemptioners or Servants have arrived here from Ireland." In 1792 the brig *Mary* (Derry to Philadelphia) would recommend only "a few boys and

45 *PP*, 11 Sept. 1784; *PG*, 15 May 1784; *FJ*, 13 Aug. 1793; *BN*, 3 Aug. 1784; PRO, FO/4/8, Phineas Bond to the duke of Leeds, 10 Nov. 1789; "Letter from Dublin," as in *PG*, 4 Aug. 1784; *LJ*, 13 May 1783; *PG*, 3 Aug. 1784; *SN*, 28 Apr., 14 May 1783.

girls from 12 to 18 years of age, to go as servants" while the ship *Friendship* (Belfast to Philadelphia, 1786) advertised for "a number of fine healthy redemptioners of both sexes, from twelve to twenty-four years of age." Even as late as 1797, Captain John Delano of the ship *Delano* (Cork to Baltimore) sought "a few ... Stout, hearty, young Men and Women, as Redemptioners or Servants" and advisedly noted that they "may depend on being well treated."[46]

These years also saw an end to the convict trade between Ireland and America. Although the trade was one which we usually associate with the colonial period, at least nine convict transports left Ireland between 1784 and 1788, some of which were "much the subject of conversation" in New York. Some of these vessels had been organised by the Dublin merchants, J.H. Stockdale, and Bryan & Wild, who had official contracts to ship the city's convicts. In 1785 Stockdale sent 126 felons from Dublin and 50 from Cork on its vessel, the snow *Ann Mary Ann*, and although consigned to the Baltimore firm of Stewart & Plunket, they were actually sold in Georgetown and Alexandria "under the false colour of their being indented servants from Ireland." Each convict was usually valued at between £5 and £7 10s. in addition to the price of the indenture, which was worth anything from £8 to £10. In 1788 the felons on the snow *Dispatch* (Dublin to North America, 1788) were assessed at £5 17s.6d. per head but when this was "added to the usual mode of selling them as indented servants," the *Freeman's Journal* reported that it left "a great profit to those who are concerned." That same year, however, the newly-established Congress asked the states to pass "proper laws" to bring this business to an end. In Ireland, two years earlier, Sir Jeremiah Fitzpatrick's report on the Irish prison system had admitted that the then transportation system gave the ship captain "a power unwarrantable and illegal, of filling up the blanks as his interest directed, and contrary to the sentences of the Courts." As a result, some commentators suggested that convicts should be placed in public works programmes in Ireland rather than transported. However, these

---

46 APS, Franklin Papers, xxv, fol.72, 17 May 1782; *SN*, 1 Dec. 1784; *VEP*, 30 Nov. 1784; PRO, FO/4/8, Bond to Leeds, 10 Nov. 1789; *LJ*, 3 Apr. 1792; *PG*, 13 June 1786; *CHC*, 11 May 1797. For the encouragement of servants, see the advertisement of the ship *Hankey* (Dublin to Philadelphia, 1784) in *BN*, 27 Feb. 1784. For a report of the alleged Congressional debates on the flow of servants from Ireland, see *DEP*, 10 Sept. 1785 and *FJ*, 12 Sept. 1785; for its dubious nature, see Baseler, *Asylum for Mankind*, 181. For Salinger's observations on the servant trade, see her "'Send No More Servants:' Female Servants in Eighteenth-Century Philadelphia," *PMHB* cvii (1983), 29–48 and "Colonial Labor in Transition: The Decline in Indentured Servitude in Late-Eighteenth-Century Philadelphia," *WMQ* xl (1983), 83–84. From HSP, AM. 3039, "Indentures Recorded in the Office of Benjamin Paschall, Justice of the Peace," it is also clear that the number of recorded indentures began to decline noticeably after 1790.

were in a minority and as America disappeared as a possible destination for Irish and British convicts, Botany Bay became the new penal colony after 1790.[47]

In a further comment on the changing character of contemporary immigration, the *New York Daily Gazette* suggested in 1792 that "instead of servants by indenture, sent out from Great-Britain, Ireland and Germany, we find several respectable families from all these countries coming daily into our ports." Similar observations were made in the Irish press. At least four hundred families sailed from Munster and Connaught alone during 1784 while a further eight hundred were preparing to leave from Derry in July 1790. In 1783 the brig *Congress* and the sloop *Hibernia* brought "several families" from Newry to Philadelphia while three years later the ship *Nancy* (Newry to New York and Philadelphia, 1786) specifically advertised for families. As part of a strategy to attract such emigrants, agents wanted to assure them that their voyages would be comfortable. The ship *Nancy* (Newry to New York and Philadelphia, 1796) advertised that it had "commodious" space between decks for those "going with their families to America [and that they] can be very comfortably fixed in this ship" while in 1785 the ship *Charming Mary* (Dublin to Philadelphia) set "6 Rooms apart for private Families." For many commentators, something had to be done to prevent the departure of so many "persons in good circumstances" and the consequent impact on the national economy.[48]

Official Reactions

Such concerns were neither new nor confined to any one country and reflected the assumption that a country's industry and prosperity depended on a growing population. Hence, some Irish newspapers saw emigration, however it was characterised, as "inimical to the rising welfare of Ireland," especially after 1782 when Ireland was supposed to be politically and commercially independent. As the *Belfast News-Letter* put it in 1786, emigrants "must be a gain to the States in which they settle, in proportion to the loss sustained by their native country." From America, the complementary point was made in the (Philadelphia) *Aurora* on 4 November 1795 that "the practice of emigration among a people has ever

47 *NYP*, 22 May 1786, 17 Sept. 1789; *SN*, 20 Apr. 1787; *IG*, 3 June 1786; *HJ*, 15 Sept. 1788. For the nine transports, see *HJ*, 15 Sept. 1788, 15 June, 9 Nov. 1789; *FJ*, 17 May 1788. For a report that the convicts on the *Ann Mary Ann* had been "sham-indented" before they left Ireland, see *PP*, 26 July 1786. See also James Kelly, "Transportation from Ireland to North America, 1703–1789" in David Dickson and Cormac O Gráda, eds., *Refiguring Ireland: Essays in Honour of L.M. Cullen* (Dublin, 2003), 112–35; and Ekirch, *Bound for America*.

48 *NYDG*, 13 Aug. 1792; *PP*, 20 Apr. 1784; *FJ*, 10 July 1790; *PP*, 8, 12 July 1783; *SN*, 14 May 1783; *BN*, 21 Mar. 1796; *SN*, 30 June 1785; *FJ*, 3 Aug. 1793.

been thought a proof of national poverty, or discontent." Thus, the *New York Journal* concluded on 23 July 1791 that

> The revolutions and convulsions of the Transatlantic countries seem so designed by the hand of Providence, for the purpose of giving liberty to the old world, and peopling the new. From France and Ireland, we can expect to draw infinite resources of knowledge and improvement, by opening the bosom of America as an asylum to the worthy and oppressed inhabitants of each.

In Dublin, the *Freeman's Journal* and *Hibernian Journal* realised that they could use the issue to promote the Reform Movement and "divest ourselves of our absurd and illiberal Prejudices, and extend to our Fellow-Subjects, the Catholics, every Right of a free citizen." They argued that the government should "extend every encouragement possible to the lower orders of people in their respective districts" by regulating rents, tithes, and the "necessaries of life." After all, it was only as a result of the "languishing state of several of the Irish manufactures" that Americans had been able to target Irish artisans. As the *Hibernian Journal* observed, "they do not send to England [for them], for there it is well known trade flourished."[49]

Such concerns were heightened by reports that "agents" were "travelling about and inveigling away artists and their tools from England, Scotland and Ireland." In 1785 John Wardill wrote to the Connecticut Loyalist, Samuel Peters (1735–1826), then in exile in London, that "the American Emissaries are very busy here [in Dublin] ... to procure Emigrants." At an official level in Philadelphia, Phineas Bond understood these worries at first hand and in his diplomatic reports to London, he often put them down on paper. In November 1788 he wrote to the then secretary of state for foreign affairs (1783–91), Lord Carmarthen, that

> Artificers are often induced and encouraged to quit the Realm: – Our own manufactories have thereby suffered an essential loss, and foreign establishments, in various lines of Improvement, have derived a Benefit therefrom, which ought, in Justice and Policy, to be confined to the Country in which they originated.

49 *HJ*, 25 May 1785; *FJ*, 9 June 1789; *VJ*, 21 June 1783; *HJ*, 4 Jan. 1786; *BN*, 4 Sept. 1786. For similar sentiments, see *SN*, 2 Jan. 1786; *FJ*, 9 June 1789; report from Belfast in *PEH*, 11 Jan. 1787. For contemporary discussion of the link between population and prosperity, see *DEP*, 5 Apr. 1794, *PP*, 12 May 1789; and *NYJ*, 27 July 1786. On 11 August 1789, *FJ* also suggested that depopulation, as caused by emigration, was undermining the country's prosperity and accordingly warned that this "should be a serious warning to our legislators." For analysis of this theme, see Campbell, "Of People either too Few or too Many"; Bailyn, *Voyagers to the West*, 29–36; and McCoy, *Elusive Republic*. For the evolution of the more critical role of the contemporary press on these and other matters

Four years later the British minister to the United States (1791–95), George Hammond, went a step further and asked his government to halt the "seduction overseas" of skilled workers and wondered

> whether it may not be proper to employ Persons for the Purpose of discovering and convicting Agents who may be concerned in any such *illegal* Practice ... [who] were annually Employed in England for the purpose of engaging Artificers to emigrate to this country.[50]

Bond had already written to Carmarthen along similar lines and reminded him that

> The humanity with which the Government has interposed in the regulation of the slave trade has excited even the admiration of our enemies: – Something of a similar sort, my Lord, extended to ships which convey passengers from Scotland and Ireland particularly, would be naturally and beneficially applied.

Thus, he was "convinced" that if "strict attention" were paid to the management and shipping of emigrants, "artificers" as well as "other unwary natives" would be protected from unscrupulous agents who were "decoying them away from their native country" much to the detriment of its industry and prosperity. Bond advised that vessels carrying "above a certain number" should be inspected by customs officers, that the "quantity and quality" of the provisions on board, and the space allotted to each passenger, should be "ascertained" and "examined," that owners should post bonds to ensure "proper treatment" during the voyage, that magistrates should interview every departing passenger in order to verify their "voluntary consent to quit the Realm, & as to the Means used and practiced to obtain his assent to go beyond the Sea," that stiff penalties should be proscribed for "seducing" and "decoying" persons to emigrate, and that the disposal of the indentures of British subjects should be monitored.[51]

of public concern, see Brian Inglis, *The Freedom of the Press in Ireland 1784–1841* (London, 1954).

50 *FJ*, 3 Apr. 1790; Kenneth Walter Cameron, ed., *The Papers of the Loyalist Samuel Peters* (Hartford, Conn., 1978), 78; NA, FO/4/6, Bond to Carmarthen, 16 Nov. 1788; NA, FO/4/14, Hammond to Grenville, 2 Feb. 1792. Although the quoted extract from Hammond's memorandum refers to England, he usually lumped Britain with Ireland in assessing the problem (as he saw it) and in listing the ports where the proposed "discoverers" might be located, he cited Irish as well as British ports; see Bond to Nepean, 16 Nov. 1788, as in J. Franklin Jameson, ed., "Letters of Phineas Bond, British Consul at Philadelphia, to the Foreign Office of Great Britain, 1787, 1788, 1789," *AHR* I (1896), hereafter cited as "Bond I," 586.

51 NA, FO/4/6, Bond to Carmarthen, 16 Nov. 1788. For agents, see Dickson, *Ulster*

Other suggestions ranged from laws to prevent emigration completely to asking Parliament to investigate with "energy and vigor" why people left for America in the first place. Similar calls had been made during the colonial period but the response was, in R.J. Dickson's words, "latent rather than obvious" and few measures were implemented to curb or even regulate the passenger flow. During the late-1720s and early-1770s parliamentary committees had already enquired into the "real Causes" of emigration from contemporary Ireland. However, they achieved nothing. The first attempted to licence emigrants but this was thwarted by the lord lieutenant, the Earl of Carteret (1724–46), largely because he believed that the proposal would give too much power to local magistrates. The second was conducted at a time of high emigration but although it had the power to summon whatever persons, papers, and records it wanted, it never reported. In each case, political pragmatism had been more important than objective enquiry and as Dickson concluded, colonial emigration continued "uninterrupted by official intervention and, indeed, generally without apparent official consciousness."[52]

In 1783 customs officials were asked to list "the number and quality" of departing passengers. The following year one of Belfast's leading merchants, Waddell Cunningham (1730–97) wrote that he had tried to convince "the Patriots" in the Irish Parliament to introduce a bill to regulate the passenger trade "but I could not prevail." In 1785, however, a bill was passed "to Prevent the Practice of Seducing Artificers and Manufacturers from the Kingdom, into Parts beyond the Seas and of exporting the several Tools and Utensils made Use of in preparing and the working up the manufacturers thereof." This bill stipulated a fine of £500 and a year in prison if any person would "contract with, entice, persuade, or endeavour to persuade [to leave] ... any manufacturer, workman, or artificer of or in linen, wool, mohair, cotton, or silk ..." or any worker involved in iron, steel, brass, watches, or clocks because these "will enable foreigners to work up such manufactures, and thereby greatly diminish the exportation of this same from this kingdom." Sentences would be doubled for subsequent offences and penalties were also listed for officers who helped people to evade the law. In 1791 the act's provisions were extended to include the export of any professional "machine, engine, tool, press, utensil or

Emigration, ch.7. For Bond's career in America, see Joanne Loewe Neel, *Phineas Bond; a Study in Anglo-American Relations, 1786–1812* (Philadelphia, 1968).

52 *FJ*, 30 Aug. 1788; Dickson, *Ulster Emigration*, 182–9, 198–200; *Commons Journals. Ireland* ix, 59. For an overview of official attitudes to emigration during the colonial period, see Dickson, *Ulster Emigration*, 181–200. For the debate on setting up investigative committees, see *HJ*, 7 Aug. 1789; *FJ*, 6 Aug. 1789, 21 June 1787, 30 Aug. 1788 and *SN*, 14 June 1789. For attempts in contemporary Britain to regulate emigration, see Bailyn, *Voyagers to the West*, 49–57.

implement *whatsoever*." These two acts provided the first major legal restraint on Ireland's passenger traffic since the previous century when, at the height of English mercantilism, laws had been passed "to prevent the seducing of artificers," especially to "France and other foreign parts."[53]

Although the earlier laws had fallen into disuse, they were still on the statute books and together with the legislation of 1785 and 1791, they could still be invoked to check emigration as the authorities saw fit. In 1788, for example, the lord mayor of Dublin arrested a group of captains for attempting to ship "a number of artificers … secreted in different ships bound to America." They were fined £500 each, a huge sum at the time, and were still in prison in mid-1789, their fines not having been paid. In 1788 also, one Mr. Harrington was imprisoned for sixteen months "for engaging two weavers to emigrate to America" while in 1791 the collector of Belfast was formally requested to stop the many vessels that were known to be "preparing to proceed to America with Emigrants, among whom are several Manufacturers intending to take with them the Implements of their Trade, contrary to Law." On 13 May 1794 the *Dublin Evening Post* also reported that one William Cox had been remanded at the Court of King's Bench "on a charge of having attempted to seduce artificers to emigrate to America." However, such incidents were the exception rather than the rule. On 18 August 1791 the *Freeman's Journal* criticised the lord mayor of Dublin for failing to implement the laws on the emigration of "artificers" and wondered why he was not "more active in this important business." Two years earlier, the same paper had remarked that "the negligence of the magistracy in the North, or rather the connivance of some among them, suffers every thing to be passed over unnoticed."[54]

However, while Bond felt that it was "almost impossible" to implement the laws "entirely," he "rejoiced that prosecutions have been instituted to check the endeavours to seduce artificers from Great Britain and Ireland." For him, the

---

53 PRONI, T755, Pelham Papers, I, 138–41, dated Custom House, Newry, 5 Aug. 1783, J. Hamilton to the under-secretary, Sackville Hamilton; PRONI, D562/8479; *FJ*, 21 June 1787. For the 1785 and 1791 acts, see 25 Geo.III, c.xvii, as in *Statutes at Large (Irl.)* (1785), 118–22 and 31 Geo.III, c.xxiii, as in *ibid.* (1791), 681–3. For the former, see also *Commons Journals. Ireland* xi, 385, 390, 391, 394, 396, 404 and for the latter, see *ibid.*, xiv, 408, 424, 429, 430, 440. For the seventeenth-century legislation, see Baseler, *Asylum for Mankind*, 27–38.

54 *FJ*, 3 Mar., 28 June 1788; *HJ*, 10 June 1789; *FLJ*, 25 May, 9 Sept. 1789; PRONI, Customs & Excise Papers (Administration), 1A/43/5/1, dated 27 April 1791; *FJ*, 6 Aug. 1789. The continuing inadequacies of the 1785 legislation were highlighted when *FJ*, 20 Dec. 1792 published extracts from the act and stressed the penalties which it outlined, "information having been received that several Artificers and Manufacturers have been solicited and seduced to go out of this Kingdom into Foreign Countries not within the dominions of the Crown of Great Britain." See also Audrey Lockhart, *Aspects of Emigration*, 75, 82–3, 88–9.

important point was that the government was finally putting down markers for both the customers and managers of the passenger trade. Although several captains announced that they would not carry anybody unless their papers were in order, the legislation of 1785 did not halt the departure of "useful inhabitants." In 1789 there was such "a great number of artificers" on the brigs *Maria* and *Keziah* (both from Derry to Philadelphia) that the agents feared that they might "by law, [be] stopped from leaving." Even after the legislation was updated in 1791 the ship *General Washington* (Dublin to Philadelphia, 1794) "carried off a considerable number of artisans with their tools contrary to the laws of this kingdom," leading the *Freeman's Journal* to call for "the most pointed vigilance of the magistrates." The amendments of 1791 had left many loopholes. For example, by designating passengers as "yeomen" rather than as "artificers" or "manufacturers," ship captains could still assume that "this evasion sufficiently protects them from the lash of the law." On 15 August 1793 the *Freeman's Journal* alleged that this was especially true of the captains of American vessels: "the seducing away of artizans is a principle object with the Captains of those vessels, as well as for the purpose of securing profit to themselves, as additional population and property to the dominions of the American states." As a result, Washington's private secretary, William Jackson (1759–1828), thought that the introduction of tighter provisions was only a matter of time as "the jealousy of emigration is so great, on the part of government, in Great Britain and Ireland, that I shall not be surprised if some strong measures are resorted to prevent it."[55]

Jackson also recognised that

> The spirit of emigration is a source of serious perplexity to the ministry, as to allow it is to aid one of the causes of our [American] aggrandizement, and to check it would require an interference on the part of government which it would be dangerous to hazard—since an attempt, at the privation of loco-motive right, might operate a much more alarming discontent than has yet been manifested.

Government regulation also challenged ancient rights. As Bond remarked to Sir Evan Nepean, under-secretary at the Home Department (1782–89), on 16 November 1788, "It is not easy to tell how a man thinking himself free by

55 Bond I, 586, Bond to Evan Nepean, 16 Nov. 1788; J. Franklin Jameson, ed., "Letters of Phineas Bond, British Consul at Philadelphia, to the Foreign Office of Great Britain, 1787, 1788, 1789," *AHR* ii (1897), hereafter cited as "Bond II," 464, Bond to Leeds, 1 Nov. 1790; *HJ*, 10 June 1789; *FJ*, 12 Apr., 10 June 1794; Jones, "Ulster Emigration, 1783–1815," 55; *FJ*, 13 Jan. 1791; HSP, William Bingham Correspondence (Jan.-June 1795), William Jackson to William Bingham, dated at Derry, 9 Apr. 1795.

nature, to go to any part of the world, where he may flatter himself with a prospect of enjoying a greater portion of happiness, will reconcile to his feelings such restraint." A correspondent to the *Belfast News-Letter* urged his readers to rest easy. After all, he noted, Ireland was not Russia where a "Despotic power ... may by edict endeavour to prevent the emigration of its people ... [but here] no such power I trust will ever exist." In Ireland, the official response came on 14 April 1795 when Dublin Castle extended the existing regulations to "foreign ships or vessels" who engaged "divers artificers, manufacturers, and seafaring men ... for the purpose of quitting this kingdom." The proclamation also obliged ship captains to confirm the provisions of the earlier acts and to provide local customs officers and through them, the Privy Council, with a list of all their passengers under the headings of name, age, and occupation. If anybody affected by the terms of the 1785 act wanted to leave, "special permission" would be required before the vessel could depart.[56]

These new procedures were taken seriously, at least initially, and were sometimes included in shipping advertisements. In 1795 Captain Moore of the ship *Andromache* (Newry to Philadelphia) announced that he would take only those who had been "unaffected by the recent proclamation" while Captain James Robinson of the ship *Cincinnatus* (Belfast to New York) asked his passengers to convene before departure and give their names and occupations to satisfy the officials. The managers of the ship *Nancy* (Dublin to New York and Newcastle, 1798) advised potential passengers that "None need apply for passage who cannot obtain passes from Government." As this was a time of international war, the government would also prevent "any able bodied fellow that they think will or may be of use in assisting to defend the country in case of invasion" from leaving Ireland. In 1796 the agents for the ship *Eliza* (Cork to New York) "requested that Artificers or Seamen will not apply, as they cannot be taken," while the following year "no artificers or manufacturers" would be taken on either the brigs *Washington* or *Orion* (both from Cork to New York). Two years earlier the ship *Joseph* (Belfast to Philadelphia, 1795) announced its departure only after it had received official clearance to do so while the ship *General Washington* (Belfast to Philadelphia, 1795) would not sail "until it can be ascertained whether there are any artificers, mariners, or seamen on board." Such precautions were no mere formalities. The brig *Woolwich* (Cork to Philadelphia 1795) asked passengers, "tradesmen and sailors excepted," to "give

56 HSP, Bingham Correspondence (Jan.-June 1795), William Jackson to William Bingham, dated at Derry, 9 Apr. 1795; Bond I, 586, Bond to Evan Nepean, 16 Nov. 1788; "On the Proclamation to Prevent Emigration," a report from the *Wexford Chronicle*, as reprinted in the *Aurora*, 26 Nov. 1795; *BN*, 20 Apr. 1795. The correspondent to *BN* is quoted from Baseler, *Asylum for Mankind*, 168.

in their Names" five days before the scheduled sailing while the ship *Sally* had sailed from Limerick for Baltimore on 1 April 1795 but was unceremoniously "carried back and had 50 passengers, who were mechanics, taken from on board." The ship *American Hero* (Newry to New York, 1795) had a luckier escape: it had "got out only one day previous to the Proclamation for preventing artizans and manufacturers from emigrating." Such reports were not infrequent, especially in 1795 and as a result, the passenger trade was more tightly managed. In the longer term, however, Jones's view that the proclamation was a "dead letter" is probably accurate.[57]

In any event, there were technical problems with the proclamation also and these soon became clear. For example, the captain was asked to swear that "to the best of his knowledge," he had no artificers on board while passengers were asked merely to "agree with their description as set down in the [captain's] list." These procedures could lead to obvious abuses, some of which were cited in a report which a Derry customs officer made to the chief secretary in 1796:

> I feel it my duty to state to you the description of those persons who usually embark here for America, and to point out the difficulty of detecting such of them as are artificers and manufacturers. Many of them are merely cotters or labourers, some are the sons of farmers or farmers themselves, who having sold their leases take their families with them, and several of them are people who have been bred to some trade,—besides agriculture and manufacture are so connected in this country that many of those who come under the description of farmers and who actually are so, are also weavers ... They are generally described as farmers or labourers and it is almost impossible for the officer who examines them to detect them and if they are not so, there being no distinction among them as to dress or appearance.[58]

Despite these difficulties, the late-eighteenth-century Irish Parliament had tried to regulate the passenger trade from Ireland in an effective and practical manner.

It was not until 1803 that the "Act for Regulating the Vessels carrying Passengers ... with respect to the Number of such Passengers" was passed. This was the first British law to regulate the treatment of passengers in a

---

57 *NS*, 4, 14 May 1795; *SN*, 20 June 1798; *Argus*, 1 July 1795; *CHC*, 22 Sept. 1796; *SN*, 3 Apr. 1797; *CHC*, 6 Apr. 1797; *NS*, 15 June, 20 Apr. 1795; *CHC*, 20 Aug. 1795; *Aurora*, 17 July 1795; *The* [Philadelphia] *Minerva*, 27 June 1795; Jones, "Ulster Emigration," 55. For advertisements that carried advices similar to those cited, see also those of the ship *Swanwick* (Belfast to Philadelphia, 1795) and the ship *Young Eagle* (Belfast to New York, 1795) in *NS*, 4 May and 5 Oct. 1795, respectively. The latter's notice stated that it usually took about ten days to process a passenger list.

58 PRONI, T755/3, R.G. Hill to Thomas Pelham.

comprehensive manner and stated that everybody on board should have adequate water and provisions for at least twelve weeks, proper bedding, and access to medical assistance. The captain was ordered to fumigate his vessel twice a week, to keep "a regular and true Journal" of the voyage, to provide a list of his passengers under the headings of name, age, gender, destination, and conditions of passage, and to present these data before a customs officer and a justice of the peace. In order to prevent misrepresentation, these officials were also asked to interview the passengers before they embarked. While the detail of the legislation was welcomed, it is difficult to assess the extent to which it was either effective or enforced. While its tightened procedures did not reduce the number who wanted to "quit the kingdom," they did affect the profits of emigrant brokers and ultimately put those who managed the Irish servant trade out of business. This may explain why in 1816 Lord Castlereagh, then foreign secretary (1812–22), suggested to John Quincy Adams, the American minister in London (1815–17), that the 1803 act had effectively recast the type of emigrant who was leaving for the United States at that time.[59]

Testimonials

While emigrants welcomed the introduction of more humane provisions through the legislative process, they could draw on another instrument of their own to help ensure their comfort and safety on the high seas: public discussion on how they had been treated during their voyages. They could also publish formal notices recommending their vessel to the public. As an Irish parliamentarian who had a close interest in American affairs, Sir Edward Newenham welcomed such statements and saw them as an insurance against "the Cruelty of the Captains of the Ships … [which] hinder Some of the Better sort of People from going" to America. Although these memorials first appeared in the early-1770s, they became more common after 1783. In 1785 the passengers of the ship *Three Brothers* (Belfast to Philadelphia, 1784) thanked Captain James Gillis for his "humane, kind and friendly treatment of every individual of us,

59 Bond to Carmarthen, 10 Nov. 1788 in "Bond I," 581; Castlereagh to Adams, 30 July 1816, in Worthington C. Ford, ed., *The Writings of John Quincy Adams* 7 vols. (New York, 1913–7) vi, 54; Jones, *American Immigration*, 67–8. For the text of the 1803 act, see *A Collection of the Public General Statutes passed in the Forty-third year of the Reign of his Majesty King George the Third* (London, 1803), 451–62. For the background to, and a critical discussion of the act, see Oliver McDonagh, *A Pattern of Government Growth, 1800–60* (London, 1961), 54–65. For the related attempts to regulate the convict trade, including the health conditions on transports, see Oliver McDonagh, *The Inspector General. Sir Jeremiah Fitzpatrick and the Politics of Social Reform, 1783–1802* (London, 1981), 267–84 *et passim*.

during the whole voyage" while eleven years later those who praised the ship *North America* (Philadelphia to Derry, 1796) would "recommend it to all our Friends returning in the Spring to engage with the above, and we flatter ourselves that they will meet with the same good Treatment." In 1790 those who had come on the brig *Jeffries* (Belfast to Newcastle, 1789) published a seven verse encomium which acknowledged the vessel's advertised claim that it had been "adapted in every degree equal to carry on the passenger trade":

> She is as safe a vessel as ever cross'd the main,
> The captain who commands her, all fear he does disdain;
> The regulation kept on board, with victualling also,
> Exceedeth any other that in that trade doth go.[60]

These were not always spontaneous productions. However, they vindicated the management of a particular vessel and as such, were often incorporated into the notices of subsequent voyages. The advertisement of the ship *Three Brothers* (Belfast to Philadelphia, 1784) also added the following:

> We, the under-named persons who sailed from Belfast to Philadelphia on board the Three Brothers, should think ourselves wanting both in gratitude to our worthy Captain [Mr. James Gillis] as well as in regard to such of our friends and countrymen who at any future period may choose to visit America, were we to omit declaring, in the most public manner, the humane and friendly treatment we met with from that Gentleman during the whole of our passage.
>
> Philadephia, Nov. 20th, 1783.

The same year Captain William Cheevers of the brig *Congress* (Newry to Philadelphia, 1783) received what was perhaps the ultimate accolade: his "good treatment" of his passengers was too "well known" to bear detailed repetition. In 1788 Cheevers was also thanked by the passengers of the ship *Anne and Susan* (Newry to New York) for his "particular attention to the sick, [and for] having a medicine chest on board at his own expense." However, such remarks were received, as the [Philadelphia] *American Daily Advertiser* remarked on 16 August 1791:

---

60 APS, Franklin Papers xxx fol. 36, 20 Oct. 1786; *BN*, 25 Mar. 1785; *LJ*, 8 Mar. 1796; *DG*, 4 July 1790. For letters of thanks from the pre-revolutionary period, see *BN*, 26 Nov. 1771, 10 Aug., 10 Sept. 1773, and 7 July 1775. These letters relate to voyages between Belfast and Philadelphia.

the bare silence of the passengers would ... be looked on as sufficient condemnation of both the Captain and vessel ... and if once the Captain of one of these Ships, suffers the *"Mark of the Beast"* to be written on his forehead, or on the stern of the vessel, he will probably never again be able to procure a single passenger. It is therefore incumbent on him to guard against this, by taking care to lay in plenty of good wholesome provisions, and by treating the passengers with all possible tenderness and humanity during the voyage.

Testimonials thus protected both the captain and the passenger as well as vouched for the vessel itself. Some captains, such as William Forrest of the ship *Joseph* (Newry to New York, 1795), formally acknowledged a published "approbation" of "good conduct during the voyage" and as a result, publicly hoped to continue to "pursue that line of conduct which has merited your esteem."[61]

Not everybody could travel with Cheevers or Forrest. However, if they were "unhappy" with a particular voyage, they could resort to the courts as well as the quill. In 1794 the passengers of the ship *Port Mary* (Liverpool to New York, 1794) took their captain to court for reducing the agreed provisions after a mere six days at sea. The case had been taken "to obviate all passengers coming with him in future from England, from sustaining a repetition of like depredations." Six years earlier a Philadelphia court had also found against an Irish captain "for brutality and ill-treatment of his passengers." However, the city's most celebrated case of this sort was heard in February and March 1791 with the active support of the Hibernian Society for the Relief of Immigrants from Ireland, founded a year earlier. The charge was that Captain Robert Cunningham of the brig *Cunningham* (Derry to Philadelphia, 1790) had not honoured the terms of the pre-departure advertisement, that he had displayed "flagrant violations of the precepts of humanity," and that his vessel was overcrowded and understocked. According to a report of the proceedings which Bond compiled, the vessel also had little vinegar to keep it clean, and in one four-person berth, a passenger had stowed himself, his wife, and eight children and these "only drew the allowance of provisions for four people." After repeated representations by the Hibernian Society, Cunningham was indicted for mistreating his three hundred passengers. In March 1791 he was fined £500 by a Pennsylvania court and imprisoned for several months after he failed to pay. In a lengthy address "to the Friends of Humanity" that was published in various newspapers, the society recorded that "we cannot find language sufficiently expressive of the detestation in which we hold this inhuman

61 *BN*, 11 May 1784, 1 Apr. 1783; *IG*, 9 Feb. 1788; *Argus*, 23 Sept. 1795.

employer [Cunningham], who could accumulate wealth by sacrificing to his avarice the lives of his countrymen."[62] This case demonstrated that if passengers had cause to complain after they arrived in America, they would be heard.

The Hibernian Society also "certified" some of the emigrants' testimonials. In 1791, for example, the ship *Anne* (Derry to Philadelphia) advertised a "letter of thanks" which it received from the society for the captain's "becoming Attention and Humanity to the Passengers on Board." The previous year the Philadelphia and New York papers also published a comprehensive statement from the society in which it thanked the captains of the ships *Happy Return*, *Sally*, and *Anne* (all from Derry) "for their humane and kind treatment of the passengers, who lately arrived in their respective vessels from Ireland." A week later similar testimonials were addressed to the captains of the brig *Havannah* (Newry to Philadelphia), the ship *Alexander* (Derry to Philadelphia), and the ship *Sally* (Killybegs to Philadelphia) while in 1792 an address from the passengers of the ship *Tristram* (Derry to Philadelphia) was delivered to Captain Hallowell "in the presence of the Subscribers' Committee to the Hibernian Society for the Advice of Irish Emigrants." In Ireland, such testimonials were occasionally reprinted as part of a vessel's sailing advertisement. In 1791 the managers of the ship *Anne* (Derry to Philadelphia) stated that after his latest voyage, Captain Miller had "received a Letter of Thanks from the Hibernian Society established in Philadelphia for the Relief of Emigrants from Ireland for his becoming Attention & Humanity to the Passengers on Board."[63] Promoters were thus reminded that the support of the society was important to their reputation, especially at a time when the passenger trade was becoming more of a business than had been the case during the colonial period. For both broker and passenger, the emigrant trade had seen important changes since 1783.

The "new Irish" who travelled to Philadelphia after 1783 came into a new environment which would again test the ability of Americans to accommodate and absorb "adopted sons." This changing city would also challenge the ways in which political conventions and institutions could recognise an increasingly diversified society. Those who came from Ireland played an important role in these matters and even if the motives for leaving the country of their birth were

62 *NYDG*, 13 Dec. 1794; *FJ*, 30 Aug. 1788; *ADA*, 4 Mar. 1791; "Bond II," 472–3, 482, Bond to Leeds, 3 Jan., 3 May 1791. See also Erna Risch, "Immigrant Aid Societies before 1820," *PMHB* lx (1936), 30–2.
63 *LJ*, 22 Feb. 1791; *IG*, 11 Sept. 1790; *NYP*, 11 Sept. 1790; *IG*, 18 Sept. 1790; *ADA*, 3 Mar. 1792; *NG*, 19 July 1792; *LJ*, 12 Apr. 1791. In 1791, eight such testimonials were printed in Philadelphia's newspapers and fourteen in 1792. On 3 Mar. 1792 *ADA* made a "public approbation" of the Hibernian Society of the "humane and meritorious conduct" was addressed to the captains of no less than ten named vessels.

often economic, their arrival in such great numbers in the nation's capital spawned a more ethnocentric and self-conscious expression of their roles and identities in all aspects of life in their new homeland. Indeed, because the growth of a more self-confident "ethnicity" and "party" politics are mirror images of each other during this period, their conduct was to have major implications for the organisational life of a place which was central to both the leadership and direction of the new republic as well as the debates on how its polity might be broadened.

CHAPTER FOUR

Ireland, Irishmen and Philadelphia, 1783–95

On 13 February 1788 Benjamin Rush suggested to the influential writer and lexicographer, Noah Webster (1758–1843), that Philadelphia was "the primum mobile of the United States," a city which "from habit, from necessity and from local circumstances, all the states view ... as the capitol of the new world." Over four years later, in July 1792, it was agreed that the city would be the nation's capital for a period of ten years. It was also the country's major emporium, "indisputably the largest and most beautiful on the continent," as the Venezuelan revolutionary, Francisco de Miranda (1750–1816), put it when he visited in November 1783. Although this opinion was not shared by everybody, Philadelphia was conscious of its status in the new republic and as the Duc de la Rochefoucauld-Liancourt noted during his stay in 1795, it attracted "men of every class and of every kind of character, philosophers, priests, literati, princes, dentists, wits and idiots." Two years earlier Susannah Dillwyn was struck by the city's changing physical as well as social character:

> the town increases surprisingly ... thee would hardly know the upper ends of Market, Chesnut, Walnut, and Arch Streets, they are so built up with new houses—a Theatre, a Library, a Philosophic Hall and a Court House have all been built within a small distance from the State House.[1]

Such observations suggest that Philadelphia was both a city of "great diversity in the manner of the inhabitants" and a place that wanted to promote an American Enlightenment and become "the new Athens of the West," as the French revolutionary and writer, Jacques Brissot de Warville (1754–93), suggested in 1788. A number of philanthropic, educational, and socially-concerned societies reflected the new mood to the extent that in 1787 the (Charleston) *Columbian Herald* reported that there was a "rage of the spirit of

---

1 Rush to Webster, 13 Feb. 1788, as quoted in Eugene Perry Link, *Democratic-Republican Societies, 1790–1800* (New York, 1942), 10; Miller, *Philadelphia*, 34–6; LCP, Dillwyn Letters i, Susannah Dillwyn to her father, May 1793. De Miranda and de la Rochefoucauld-Liancourt are quoted in *The New Democracy in America: Travels of Francisco de Miranda in the United States, 1783–84*, trans. Judson P. Wood and ed. John S. Ezell (Norman, 1963), 41; and Ethel B. Rasmusson, "Democratic Experiment: Aristocratic Aspirations," *PMHB* xc (1966), 157, respectively.

association" in Philadelphia. These organisations can be broadly divided into five groups: the networks of the intellectual elite and socially-conscious; the older, "ethno-cultural" societies that had been founded before 1776; the immigrant-aid societies of the 1790s; and finally, the more ethnically neutral societies, such as Tammany. Between them, they charted the development of a city that slowly left its colonial culture behind and embraced instead the excitements of a nation that was not only reinventing itself but was intent on setting an "example to the world."[2]

"The New Athens of the West"

In 1788 de Warville observed that there were more learned societies in Philadelphia than anywhere else in America. Some of them, such as the *Library Company of Philadelphia* (founded in 1731) promoted "enlightenment" and "literary improvement" as ends in themselves. By 1790 the company had its own building as well as a collection of 8,000 books "whereby useful Knowledge has been more generally diffused in these remote Corners of the World."[3] Other societies emphasised what Carl Bridenbaugh has called "philosophy put to use." These included the *Philadelphia Society for the Promotion of Agriculture* (founded in 1785) which addressed "the very imperfect state of American Husbandry" and offered prizes for essays and experiments "relative to agriculture and rural affairs."[4] In a similar vein, the *Philadelphia Society for the Encouragement of Manufacturing and the Useful Arts* (founded in 1787) encouraged American manufactures to lessen what Tench Coxe called "the distresses ... from the commercial and manufacturing derangements produced by excessible importations from 1783 to 1787." It offered premiums to help the sector and also created a "manufacturing fund" to establish experimental

2 Isaac Weld, *Travels through the States of North America ... during the Years 1795, 1796, and 1797* (London, 1799), 12; and J.P. de Warville, *New Travels in the United States of America, 1788*, ed. Durand Echeverria (Cambridge, Mass., 1964), 253. The *Columbian Herald* is quoted in Alexander, *Render them Submissive*, 123.

3 De Warville, *New Travels*, ed. Echeverria, 253; *NYP*, 28 Jan. 1790; Labaree *et al.*, eds., *Papers of Franklin* x, 376, "Directors of the Library Company of Philadelphia to John Penn," 21 Nov. 1763. See also George Maurice Abbott, *A Short History of the Library Company of Philadelphia* (Philadelphia, 1913); and "A short account of the Library of Philadelphia" in *NYP*, 28 Jan. 1790.

4 *NYJ*, 16 Mar. 1786. Carl Bridenbaugh is quoted from his article, "Philosophy Put to Use: Voluntary Associations for Propagating the Enlightenment, 1727–1776," *PMHB* ci (1977), 70–88. See also Simon Baatz, *"Venerate the Plough:" A History of the Philadelphia Society for the Promotion of Agriculture, 1785–1985* (Philadelphia, 1985). *NYJ*, 16 Mar. 1786 also published the society's prospectus. Its premiums for 1790 were published in *NYJ*, 21 May 1790.

factories.[5] By 1787 the *American Philosophical Society* (founded in 1749) had also developed a practical as well as an intellectual interest in social and economic progress and in a public appeal for funds in that year, it revealed that its members wanted "to promote the ends of their useful institution, for the extension of *useful knowledge*, and for furthering the agriculture, manufactures and natural history of North America."[6]

Like the Philosophical Society, the *Society for Political Inquiries* also engaged with "the science of government," as the German physician and natural scientist, Johann David Shoepf (1752–1800), termed it after his visit in 1783. In "essays, facts, or observations" that were read to the members, it suggested that during the years of revolution and constitution-making, this "arduous and complicated" science had been "left to the care of *practical* politicians, or the speculations of individual theorists." This may have been unavoidable at that time but as the society saw it, it had given rise to an unwelcome "deficiency." Franklin had thus founded the society to examine how government could best promote commerce, manufacturing, agriculture, and the arts as well as discuss specific issues, such as municipal incorporation, immigration, and prison reform, matters which were of particular concern in contemporary Philadelphia. In 1788 it even offered a prize of "an oval plate of solid standard gold, of the value to ten guineas," for "the best essays" on topics which were selected by the society. The membership was confined to "fifty residing members" but, in effect, it was drawn largely from Franklin's own circle and usually met at his home. Most of the society's members had also been leaders of the American Revolution and men such as John Dickinson (1732–1808), Coxe, Rush, William Rawle (1759–1834), Robert Morris, and Edward Shippen (1703–81) saw it as helping to promote a more "complete" national independence. All told, the society sought to break through "the bounds, in which a dependent people have been accustomed to think" and to establish an America which would be independent of the "prejudices" and "fetters of foreign power."[7]

5   Jacob E. Cooke, *Tench Coxe and the Early Republic* (Chapel Hill, 1978), 102–3. For further information on the society, see LCP, Tench Coxe, *An Address to an Assembly of the Friends of American Manufactures* (Philadelphia, 1787); and Geib, "History of Philadelphia," 238–9.
6   *PP*, 18 May 1787. See also Carl Van Doren, "The Beginnings of the American Philosophical Society," *Proceedings of the American Philosophical Society* lxxxvii (1944), 277–89. For a general discussion of all these and similar societies, see Bernard Fay, "Learned Societies in Europe and America," *AHR* xxxvii (1932), 255–66; Adrienne Koch, "Pragmatic Wisdom and the American Enlightenment," *WMQ* xviii (1961), 313–29; Ernest Cassara, *The Enlightenment in America* (Boston, 1975), 146–9; Geib, "History of Philadelphia," 220–43; and Carl Bridenbaugh, *Cities in Revolt: Urban Life in America, 1743–1776* (New York, 1955).
7   LCP, *Rules and Regulations of the Society for Political Enquiries* (Philadelphia, 1787), 1;

The society also discussed immigration from Europe. In an address to the members, Rawle echoed Franklin's well-known opinions on the subject and proposed that the leaders of the new republic should encourage immigrants who were frugal, industrious, and self-sufficient and "incorporate" them into the contemporary polity. He argued that in such an environment, immigrants would be "free of any trace of their [European] origin" and all old world attachments would bow before the republican habits and structures of the new. Immigrants might then be recommended for American citizenship because any attempt to exclude them would merely "convince the newcomers [that] they were somehow separate from their neighbours." Rawle was again reflecting the notion of the community as a harmonious and integrated entity and frowned on any attempt to divide it. However, he also understood its responsibilities, including a commitment to help the "poorer sort." As one publication noted in 1787

> Charity not only desires the happiness of mankind, rejoices at their prosperity and grieves at their adversity, but being an active virtue, it prompts the mind to form with prudence, and execute with vigour, that plan that bids fairest for a happy attainment of the most generous and benevolent ends.[8]

Even before 1783 Philadelphia had a distinguished history of organised philanthropy. In 1732 the Quakers turned their almshouse into a public facility and a house of employment was added later. In 1767 the two institutions were brought together as a "bettering house," the very name of which underlined the optimism of the colony's Quaker leadership that marginals could become "useful members" of society. By 1788, however, de Warville reported that the house was being "kept alive only by immigrants and European travellers." As a result, some questioned its social purpose and wondered if it had any useful function other than assisting non-natives who might otherwise be a disruptive presence in their community.[9]

Johann David Schoepf, *Travels in the Confederation*, trans. Alfred J. Morrison (repr. New York, 1968), 78; Geib, "History of Philadelphia," 242; Michael Vinson, "The Society for Political Enquiries: The Limits of the Republican Discourse in Philadelphia on the Eve of the Constitutional Convention," *PMHB* cxiii (1989), 187, 193–4. For the society's membership, see *Rules and Regulations*, 5–18; and Kenneth Wayne Keller, "Diversity and Democracy: Ethnic Politics in Southeastern Pennsylvania, 1788–1799" (Ph.D. dissertation, Yale University, 1971), 5–7. The society's minutes (1787–9) are in HSP.

8 Klebaner, "Public Poor Relief in America," 71; *Rules of the Society for the Relief of Poor and Distressed Masters of Ships, their Widows, and Children* (Philadelphia, 1787), preface, i. Rawle is quoted from Keller, "Diversity and Democracy," 4–7 and from HSP, Rawle Papers, Journals of William Rawle I, private series, undated "memo on offices."

9 Klebaner, "Public Poor Relief in America," 132; Wiberley, "Four Cities: Public Poor Relief in Urban America," 14, 110–19; de Warville, *New Travels*, ed. Echeverria, 173. For

Apart from the reforming objectives of the overseers of the poor, others channelled a general concern for "justice and humanity" into specific areas such as Sunday schools (from 1791), the abolition of slavery (from 1774), and prison reform (from 1787). In the words of *The Philadelphia Society for Alleviating the Miseries of Public Prisons*, "the obligations of benevolence ... are not cancelled by the follies or crimes of our fellow creatures." The society thus brought together those who wanted

> to extend our compassion to that part of mankind, who are the objects of these miseries. By the aids of humanity, their undue and illegal sufferings may be prevented: the links, which should bind the whole family of mankind together under all circumstances, be preserved unbroken: and, such degrees and modes of punishment may be discovered and suggested, as may, instead of continuing habits of vice, become the means of restoring our fellow-creatures to virtue and happiness.

The *Society for Establishing Sunday Schools* saw its role in similar terms and noted that "opportunities of instruction ... [would] add to the prosperity and reputation of our country," especially if they were taken up by those "who might otherwise have added to its disgrace by their vices and to its taxes by its misery." In the words of the abolitionists, "it becomes us to consult and promote each other's happiness, as members of the same family, however diversified they may be, by colour, situation, religion, or different states of society."[10]

There were also more informal and ad hoc networks to assist the less fortunate. As the *Independent Gazetteer* noted in 1785, from "time immemorial ... collections have been made every winter, either by means of charity Sermons among the different Sects, or private subscriptions, for the poor." In 1791 after a "numerous and respectable meeting of citizens" had been told that the inclement winter had reduced many "industrious persons" to unemployment and want, collectors were appointed to solicit contributions in every ward of the city as well as in Southwark and the Northern Liberties. Their object was clear: to relieve

the 1766 legislation on the "bettering house," see Mitchell and Flanders, comps., *The Statutes at Large of Pennsylvania* vii, 9–17. For general discussion of public poor relief, see Alexander, *Render them Submissive*, 86–169; and Klebaner, "Public Poor Relief in America." For the origins and development of poor relief, see Gary B. Nash, "Poverty and Poor Relief in Pre-Revolutionary Philadelphia," *WMQ* xxxiii (1976), 3–30.

10 *The Constitution of the Pennsylvania Society, for the Abolition of Slavery ... Begun in the year 1774* (Philadelphia, 1787), 20; *Society of the Philadelphia Society, for Alleviating the Miseries of Public Prisons* ((Philadelphia, 1787), 1, 1–2; "Society for the Institution and Support of First Day or Sunday Schools, in the City of Philadelphia, and the Districts of Southwark and the Northern-Liberties" (broadside, Philadelphia, 1796); *Society for the Abolition of Slavery*, 5.

the distresses of such of their fellow citizens, as not being, or asking to become a general public charge … for want of employment, inability to carry out their usual business, from the rigour of the weather, or high price of fuel, or any other charge.

As one newspaper put it, those whom "Providence has blessed with the means of comfortable subsistence" had "obligations of benevolence" to "relieve their fellow creatures" and focus on the "deserving" poor. Again, the underlying object was to ensure that the fabric of society would not be unduly upset by various "awful crises" and thus, to restore the comfort and harmony of the community.[11]

During the colonial period a number of associations had been formally incorporated with similar goals in mind. One of these, the *Sea Captains Club* (founded in 1765), proposed that

> To relieve our fellow creatures in distress, and promote their welfare, is a most beneficent work, but few even of the most distinguished abilities can act in this respect beyond the limits of a narrower sphere. Numerous wants are neither readily nor easily supplied; hence individuals unequal of themselves apart to the noble task, combine together in Societies, [and] gain strength by their adherence.

Two others were founded to assist the widows, children, and poorer ministers of the Presbyterian and Anglican churches. In 1759 the *Corporation for the Relief of Poor and Distressed Presbyterian Ministers* argued that "subsistence is generally so small & precarious in this new planted countrey, that it is with great difficulty [that] many of them can maintain their familys with any Decency; much less make any provision for them after their decease." These societies levied "stated contributions" on their clerical members which would be "laid out in the purchase of small annuities … [and] kept in reserve for their wives and children, in case they should come to be *widows* and *orphans*." Although they also sought (and received) financial assistance from Britain and Ireland, the two societies were principally funded by their own members. In times of hardship, payments would be made to those ministers who had given to the society's funds and in the event of the clergyman's death, annuities were paid to widows and children but only "in consideration of these contributions." Despite the reservations that

11 *IG* is quoted in Alexander, *Render them Submissive*, 16. The other references are cited from *GA*, 11, 15, 7 , 18 Jan. 1791; Klebaner, "Public Poor Relief in America," 12; *GA*, 29 Nov. 1793 and *MDA*, 3 Nov. 1797. The notion of "repaying" Providence is quoted from *GA*, 7 Jan. 1791. For a public acknowledgment of the work of one such committee of "respectable inhabitants" that was formed to provide relief during the yellow fever epidemic of 1793, see *ADA*, 26 Mar. 1794.

Franklin and others had about "private" societies of this type, they promoted the kind of mutual assistance and self-sufficiency that Franklin admired. They suggested a desire not to become a burden on anybody else and thus, how individuals could strengthen the wider community and promote the harmony and interdependence of its members.[12]

Networks of private individuals and merchants, as well as those of local churches, complemented those of Philadelphia's benevolent societies. However, these served a variety of purposes, some of which could be personal. For example, when Sir Edward Newenham considered emigrating to America in 1784, he asked his friend, Benjamin Franklin, among others, for letters of introduction "as I shall land as a *stranger* in person & Character, but not congenial Principles, on that Land of Liberty." Similarly, when Mathew Carey arrived in Philadelphia in 1784, he did so with letters from Lafayette to two of the city's leading political and commercial personalities, Thomas Fitzsimons and Robert Morris. In 1791 William Bingham wrote to his friend, the Wexford-born **Commodore John Barry** (1745–1803), in the hope that it would "gratify your Feelings to be instrumental in relieving the Distress of a poor reduced Irish Family, who have nothing but the charitable Exertions of their Friends." To accommodate this family, Bingham asked for repossession of a "small tenement" that he had let to Barry "and which I find they will be very happy in being accommodated with."[13] More generally, support for Philadelphia's Irish immigrants reflected the transatlantic interests of the city's houses. During the 1760s James Crawford and David Lapsey travelled from Ulster to Philadelphia with introductions to Conyngham & Nesbitt. Some years earlier John Nesbitt himself had arrived in the city with similar recommendations to Redmond Conyngham and ended up becoming his partner in 1765. After 1783 such contacts also revealed the ways in which the passenger trade was being reorganised at the time. In 1784 the promoters of the ship *General Washington* (Derry to Newcastle and Philadelphia) promised its passengers that "Care will be taken to accommodate such as take their Passage in this Ship on their Arrival

---

12 "The Sea Captains Club" as in *PG*, 4 Apr. 1771; "The Corporation for the Relief of Poor Ministers, 1759" (part 1), *JPrH* xxx (1952), 24, 22. As with similar societies, it restricted its *largesse*, in its case, to those who contributed 40 shillings on admission and 20 shillings thereafter. For the appeal for funds to Ireland, see "Address to the Presbytery in the North of Ireland" in *ibid.*, (part 2), *JPrH* xxx (1952), 127–32; and Anon., *The First Two Hundred Years, 1747–1947, of the St. Andrew's Society of Philadelphia* (Philadelphia, 1947), 140–7. For a separate fund that was operated by the First Presbyterian Church, see *Corporation of the Widows Fund* (Philadelphia, 1784). For a similar society within the Anglican church, see *Corporation for the Relief of the Widows and Children of Clergymen, in the Communion of the Church of England in America* (Philadelphia, 1773).

13 APS, Franklin Papers xxxii, fol. 123, Newenham to Franklin, 29 Sept. 784; Carter, "Mathew Carey," 52; HSP, Dreer Collection, William Bingham to John Barry, 17 June 1791.

at Philadelphia by the Owners who reside there." With a similar interest in helping their Irish clients, Philadelphia's leading houses sometimes sought employment for their incoming passengers. In 1785 they also appealed for "benefactions" for the survivors of the ill-fated ship *Faithful Steward* (Derry to Philadelphia) which had foundered in Delaware Bay in September of that year. Thus, while such assistance did not make merchants an alternative to immigrant-aid societies, it underlined how far things had changed from the time of Captain Mercer during the 1720s.[14]

Among the churches and religious societies, the Quakers had the most organised charity networks. Since the late-seventeenth century, they provided considerable assistance to those in distress on both sides of the Atlantic through a triangle that linked the yearly meetings of London, Dublin, and Philadelphia. During the Revolutionary period Irish Quakers had established "the Irish Fund" "to promote liberal subscriptions for their [the colonists] relief." For their part, the American Friends continued to assist immigrants who landed from Ireland after 1783. In 1784, for example, James Pemberton of Philadelphia wrote to his brother in Ireland that one Jacob Stenson, "whom thou desirest to be noticed," had been introduced to his family and "continues to visit us, he with several of his Country-men lately arrived ... and I believe has been preserved from harmful company" as a result. The Presbyterian church also spanned the Atlantic and during the mid-1770s the Ulster Presbytery contributed £400 to the Presbytery of Philadelphia to help it during the uncertainties of the American Revolution. It also assisted needy immigrants after 1783.[15]

Unlike other faiths, Catholicism had not played a prominent role in Philadelphia during the colonial period. It maintained two chapels in the city, St. Joseph's, founded in 1733 and enlarged in 1757, and St. Mary's, opened in 1763. The number of communicants was small. Even in 1785 America's first

14 John H. Campbell, *The Friendly Sons of St. Patrick and the Hibernian Society of Philadelphia, 1771–1892* (Philadelphia, 1892), 108–9, 449; *LJ*, 13 Apr. 1784; *PP*, 16 Sept. 1785; *BN*, 22 Nov. 1785; *PG*, 14 Sept. 1785. For the introduction of the Constitutionalist leader, George Bryan, through a similar network, see Konkle, *George Bryan and the Constitution of Pennsylvania*, 18–23. For another recommendation, later processed through Bryan's own connections in Philadelphia, see HSP, Bryan Papers, box 4, fol.6, George Mollin to Bryan, Dublin, 5 Mar. 1794. Merchant houses in Philadelphia which were involved in relieving the survivors of the *Faithful Steward* included Campbell & Kingston and Conyngham & Nesbitt.

15 Kenneth L. Carroll, "Irish and British Quakers and their American Relief Funds, 1778–1797," *PMHB* cii (1972), 441–2; HSP, Pemberton Papers xli, 22, James Pemberton to John Pemberton, 23 May 1784; J.S. Reid, *History of the Presbyterian Church in Ireland*, 3 vols. (Belfast, 1851) iii, 324. For the Quaker networks, see also McConaghy, "Thomas Greer of Dungannon," 120–4; Tolles, *Meeting House and Counting House*; and "Letter of Friends in Philadelphia to Friends in Ireland, Soliciting Aid during the Occupation of Philadelphia by the British," *PMHB* xx (1896), 125–6.

bishop, John Carroll (1735–1815) of Baltimore, recorded that there were a mere 7,000 Catholics in Pennsylvania and 24,000 in the "United States Province" as a whole. However, these figures do not reflect what Carroll called "the special milieu" of American Catholicism: a church that was organisationally weak and whose clergy were not as visible within the wider community as those of other churches. This culture also suggested the understated circumstances of Catholicism in contemporary Ireland where many of Carroll's priests and communicants had been born. For most of the eighteenth century, the penal laws had left Irish Catholicism with poor ecclesiastical structures, uneven codes of belief and ritual, and inconsistent church-going. As the **Rightboy** movement of 1785–88 showed, many Irish Catholics were also unwilling to maintain their church on an open-ended basis and would challenge their priests if the circumstances warranted it. As increasing numbers of Irish Catholics left for America after 1783, they often brought with them their ambivalent feelings about their priests and church structures, thus adding to Carroll's task of retrieving his church from the peripheral position it had occupied during the colonial period.[16]

All types of ethno-cultural organisations, whether religious or secular, began to express themselves more openly after 1783. In May 1789 Philadelphia's German Lutherans stressed in an address to George Washington that "though as individuals we can be but very little known to you, yet *as representatives* [italics mine], in some respect, of a numerous people in this city" they were part of a new political landscape. The emergence of the African Church of Philadelphia also underlined a new toleration for individual congregations when it announced in 1791 that it would develop its own building for "Africans and the descendants of Africans." Before 1791 the members of this particular church had been

> scattered and unconnected appendages of most of their religious societies in the city ... That the attraction and relationship which are established among the Africans and the descendants, by the sameness of colour; by a nearly equal and general deficiency of education, by total ignorance, are only humble attainments in religion, and by the line drawn by custom as well as nature, between them and the white people, all evince the necessity and propriety of their enjoying separate, and exclusive means, and opportunities of worshipping God, of instructing their youth and taking care of their poor.

16 Carroll's observation is quoted in Ellis, *Catholics in Colonial America*, 447. For Carroll's 1785 report to Rome, see John Tracy Ellis, ed., *Documents of American Catholic History* (Milwaukee, 1956), 151–4. For the early history of the Catholic church in Philadelphia, see Ellis, *Catholics in Colonial America*, 370–80; and Joseph Kirlin, *Catholicity in Philadelphia* (Philadelphia, 1909). Scharf and Westcott, *History of Philadelphia* i, 1372–6

In reply to an address from the Episcopal Church, Washington recognised the distinctiveness of the city's churches. However, he also encouraged the "edifying prospects ... to see christians of different denominations dwell together in more charity, and conduct themselves in respect of each other with a more christian-like spirit, than ever they have done in any former age or in any other nation."[17] Thus, while recognising the new circumstances in which all churches functioned after 1783, he still promoted the harmony of the community of the whole.

The Catholic Church was also emerging from its own "hidden" world after 1783. In 1791 the historian Charles Plowden (1749–1829) observed that since the Treaty of Paris was agreed,

> catholics enjoy an equal participation of the rights of human nature with their neighbours, of every other religious denomination. The very term of *toleration* is exploded: because it imports a power in one predominant sect, to indulge that religious liberty to others, which all claim as an inherent right.

In Philadelphia, Fr. Robert Molyneaux also began to develop his own system of parochial education and poor relief which occasionally attracted legacies and gifts, including one from Commodore Barry "for the use of and benefit of the poor." In 1792 the Hibernian Society formally acknowledged the role of the church in assisting Irish immigrants when Fathers Christopher Keating and Anthony Fleming of St. Mary's were "unanimously" thanked for "sundry acts of humanity and benevolence ... [and] unsolicited, but well timed and generous exertions ... as well by pecuniary aids as by personal attendance" on behalf of the passengers of the ship *Queen* (Derry to Philadelphia, 1792). As a result, "several" people had been "saved from the ravages of an infectious disease, which unhappily prevailed in the ship."[18] Thus, at the very time when immigrant-aid societies were projecting a new sense of ethnocentricity, the Catholic Church was asserting its own integrity and managing its flock in a more open and direct manner than had been the case during the colonial period.

By 1790 the internal organisation of the Catholic Church was also being driven in other directions. Because some of the German parishioners of St.

also lists the names of the late-eighteenth-century clergy and gives a short biography of each of the city's churches. For Catholicism in contemporary Ireland, see S.J. Connolly, *Priests and People in Pre-Famine Ireland* (Dublin, 1982); and Bartlett, *Fall and Rise of the Irish Nation*.

17 *NYDG*, 18 May 1789; *ADA*, 30 Aug. 1790; *IG*, 3, 10 Sept. 1791; *NYP*, 22 Aug. 1789. The address from the Roman Catholics was published in *NYDG*, 18 March 1790. In it, bishop Carroll explained that this was because "our scattered situation prevented the communication and the collecting of those sentiments which warmed every breast."

18 Charles Plowden, *A Short Account of the Establishment of the New See of Baltimore* (Philadelphia, 1791), 4; Campbell, *Friendly Sons*, 98; *DG*, 8 Sept. 1792.

Mary's were afraid that their language and traditions might be swamped by their Irish-born priests, Holy Trinity Church was started in 1789 and completed six years later. However, Irish priests continued to come to Philadelphia and in 1796

> the Right Reverend Doctor CARROLL ... recommended to the Reverend Mr. [Matthew] CARR, superior of the AUGUSTINIAN ORDER IN DUBLIN, to settle in this City. In consequence whereof, this gentleman offers to their service, himself, and other men of zeal and abilities; who only await the tidings of his reception to join him.

As a result of Carr's move to Philadelphia, the foundation stone of St. Augustine's Church was laid in 1796. Contributions were sent by, among others, Mathew Carey, John and Jasper Moylan, and Thomas Fitzsimons, who had long been associated with both St. Mary's and the city's Irish community. By that time, what John Tracy Ellis has termed "the virus of nationalism" had already established itself among Philadelphia's Catholics. However, while German immigrants may have developed Holy Trinity as the city's "first national church," its foundation gave other Catholic immigrants and, in particular, Irish Catholics in the other parishes a clearer sense of their own identity than had been the case in the more undifferentiated culture of the colonial years.[19]

Another indication of the new attitudes of the Catholic Church came in 1795 when Washington recommended to

> all Religious Societies and Denominations, and to all Persons whomever within the United States, to set apart and observe Thursday the nineteenth day of February next, as a day of Public Thanks-giving and Prayer; and on that day to meet together and render their sincere and hearty thanks to the Great Ruler of Nations, for the manifold and signal mercies, which distinguish our lot as a Nation; Particularly for ... liberty with order; for the preservation of our peace Foreign and Domestic; for ... the suppression of the late insurrection [in Western Pennsylvania]; and generally for the prosperous course of our affairs public and private.

A correspondent to the *Aurora* observed on 28 March 1795 that Catholics were "bound, in conscience, to observe no ordinance or command, that does not, in religious matters, come from their own church." But the Catholic Church in America never developed the ultramontanism that characterised it in much of

19 HSP, Lea & Febiger Collection, Incoming Correspondence (1785–96), box 4. Carr/ Carothers Folder, 1792–96, "Address to the Inhabitants of Philadelphia;" John Tracy Ellis, *American Catholicism* (Chicago, 1969), 44. See also Kathleen Gavigan, "The Rise and Fall of Parish Cohesiveness in Philadelphia," *RACHS* lxxxvi–lxxxvi (1975–6), 107–31.

Europe in later years and, for the moment, even its critics recognised that American Catholics "openly disavowed" the type of "interference" which the Pope had pursued for several centuries in Europe and that to this extent, comparisons between Catholicism in Europe and America were "in error" and "ill-founded." The notion of Catholicism as an institution which existed within, but apart from, the state was already beginning to take hold in the new republic. Thus Madison "did not approve the ridicule attempted to be thrown out on the Roman Catholics" and rejected suggestions that their religion was inconsistent with republicanism. In advancing his case, he pointed to the viability of Switzerland, where over half the population was Catholic, as well as the recent history of America when Catholics "had, many of them, proved good citizens during the Revolution."[20] As such, there was no inconsistency between being true to private beliefs and being devoted to the greater good. This was also seen in the ways in which Philadelphia's ethno-cultural societies came to be perceived after 1783.

Ethno-Cultural Societies, Old and New

For Philadelphia's immigrants and their children, the city's five main "national societies" were also sources of assistance and advice. These societies had been founded before the Revolution and included the Welsh *St. David's Society* (founded in 1729), the Scottish *St. Andrew's Society* (founded in 1747), the *Deutsche Gesellschaft von Pennsylvanien*, or the German Society (founded in 1764), the Irish *Society of the Friendly Sons of St. Patrick* (founded in 1771), and the English *Society of the Sons of St. George* (founded in 1772).[21] America had given prosperity and success to many immigrants; these societies enabled such people to assist the less fortunate, especially those who had come from their own native countries. Although the biographical details of the early members of

20 "M.F." in *ADA*, 9 Jan. 1792; "A Catholic" in *ADA*, 7, 10 Jan. 1792; "A Roman Catholic" in *ADA*, 14 Jan. 1791. Madison is quoted from the debates on the 1795 naturalisation act in *Annals of Congress* iv, 1035. For Washington's proclamation, see *Aurora*, 2 Jan. 1795. For a recent analysis of "the emerging free marketplace of religion," see Frank Lambert, *The Founding Fathers and the Place of Religion in America* (Princeton, 2003); the quotation is from page 8.

21 For these societies, sometimes referred to as "national societies" in the contemporary press, see Howard B. Lewis, *The Welsh Society of Philadelphia* (Philadelphia, 1926); Anon., *First Two Hundred Years, 1747–1947, of the St. Andrew's Society of Philadelphia* (Philadelphia, 1947); Harry W. Pfund, *A History of the German Society of Philadelphia* (Philadelphia, 1944); Campbell, *Friendly Sons*; and Anon., *A History of the Society of the Sons of Saint George* (Philadelphia, 1923). For a review of these societies, see Risch, "Immigrant Aid Societies before 1820," 15–33; and Scharf and Westcott, *History of Philadelphia* i, 1464–8.

some of these societies are sketchy, it is clear that the members were drawn from the Philadelphia elite who were motivated by the spirit of the Enlightenment as well as by what they understood to be the best of their own "civilised nations," now transplanted to the new world. However, they were committed to their new home in America and as such, they did not want to overly indulge either "Love of their native Soil" or their altruism in ways that would emphasise their old world origins. Most of them had ambivalent feelings about organisations and networks that were too ethno-culturally identifiable. In the words of the Sons of St. George, "pity, social love, and charity, are *citizens of the world* [italics mine] and extend their benign influences to the whole human race." Moreover, in a sentiment that it shared with the other British and Irish societies, the preface to its constitution boldly stated that

> National attachments and prejudices are for the most part idle and unnecessary; and when they operate so far as to make us injure or despise persons born in a different country from ourselves, they are indeed very reprehensible.

For similar reasons, none of these societies paraded as a designated group in the Federal Procession of 4 July 1788 although some of their officers had prominent roles in organising and managing the event.[22]

Although "strangers in America" who needed support and relief could attract criticism and disapproval, the Sons of St. George recognised that such people should be helped. If only for this reason, "although national distinctions should on most occasions be avoided," a society like the Sons might, in circumstances of want and distress, "answer the best purposes." For the members of the St. Andrew's Society, the urge to assist fellow-country men and women "who must otherwise have suffered, without Friends, in a Place where they were Strangers," was also understandable, as was the belief that immigrants in distress would turn first to "those who were originally from the same Country" as themselves. However, as the Sons of St. George put it, this was not to be taken as "the effect of narrowness of sentiment." Some of those who arrived from England had been "disappointed in their expectations" in Philadelphia and as a consequence, "sank into [a] ruin almost unnoticed, when perhaps a little good counsel, or a small pecuniary assistance, would have saved them from destruction." The Sons offered to help but pointedly advised that they would "succor only the worthy." "Proper Testimonials of Character" were

22 *The Constitution and Rules of the St. Andrew's Society in Philadelphia* (Philadelphia, 1769), 4, 3; constitution of the Sons of Saint George, as adopted on 23 April 1772, as in *History of the Society of the Sons of Saint George*, 15, 16. For the federal procession, see Simon P. Newman, *Parades and the Politics of the Street* (Philadelphia, 1997), 40–2.

required of its beneficiaries while in 1774 the society added that it would offer relief "more especially if [the applicant] be found an honest worthy Tradesman or Manufacturer."[23] In developing such a policy, the Sons were clear about what they wanted to achieve:

> Many thousands have been relieved in Distress, and restored to Comfort and Happiness who were before destitute and miserable objects. Many who, with their Posterity, might have been lost to the Community, have thereby become useful and valuable members of Society, and sometimes been able to assist their kind Benefactors.

The St. Andrew's Society also recognised that "when particular Cases become the Care of particular Societies, the whole will be better provided for." As with the benevolent corporations of the Presbyterian and Anglican ministers, these societies would help only the "deserving." As John Alexander has argued, these societies wanted to ensure that in an era of change, the poor would behave in a "proper way" and blend into the wider community of the new republic. For the Friendly Sons of St. Patrick, this agenda was depicted symbolically in a medal which depicted "Liberty" joining the hands of "Hibernia," represented by a female holding a harp, and "America," which was portrayed as an Indian with a bow drawn and a quiver on his back.[24]

Given Philadelphia's strong links with Ireland, it is not surprising that the Friendly Sons evolved from among the city's many Irish traders. The society grew out of the *Irish Club*, an elite fraternity which had been founded during the 1750s to strengthen the links between these merchants. It was essentially a social club and hosted weekly games of cards and backgammon, followed by supper. On one of these occasions the members decided to establish the Friendly Sons as a charitable club. The twenty four founding members were men of financial importance in the city and were expected to pay fifty shillings for admission, three guineas for the society's medal, occasional levies as well as fines for non-attendance at meetings (five shillings) and for failing to wear the society's medal on designated occasions. They were also wealthy merchants who

---

23 *History of the Society of the Sons of Saint George*, 17; *First Two Hundred Years*, 161; *The Constitution and Rules of the St. Andrew's Society ... 1769*, 3; *History of the Society of the Sons of Saint George*, 16; *Rules and Constitutions of the Society of the Sons of St. George ...* (Philadelphia, 1788), 4; Anon., *An Historical Sketch of the Origin and Progress of the Society of the Sons of St. George* (Philadelphia, 1897), 7, 60–3; *Sons of St. George, Philadelphia. Rules and Constitutions of the Society of Englishmen* (Philadelphia, 1774), 19, vii.

24 *Sons of St. George ... 1774*, iii–iv; *The Constitution and Rules of the St. Andrew's Society ... 1769*, 4; Alexander, *Render them Submissive*, 164. For the Friendly Sons' medal, see Campbell, *Friendly Sons*, 35–6.

were involved in the rum, tea, and linen trades and were tied to one another in a variety of business and personal ways. The group included Thomas Barclay and his partner, William Mitchell of (Carsan), Barclay & Mitchell, Samuel Caldwell, and James Mease of Mease & Caldwell, and Thomas Fitzsimons and his brother-in-law, George Meade of Meade & Co. (see Appendix VI). The two Mitchells, John and Randall, were also business partners, the former being also a nephew of another founding member, Andrew Caldwell, cousin of Samuel and associate of a future member, James Caldwell (1778). The partner of the linen merchant John Boyle, Robert Glen, joined in 1772 as did Samuel Carsan, a sometime partner in (Carsan), Barclay & Mitchell. Other founding members such as Benjamin Fuller and John Shee also had extensive business contacts in Ireland as had John Nesbitt (1771) of Conyngham & Nesbitt. Indeed, the society's historian has noted of David Hayfield Cunningham (1775) and John Nesbitt that "quite a number of the Friendly Sons owe[d] their change of residence from Ireland to America by reason of the business connections of [their] firm in the North of Ireland."[25]

Those who joined the Friendly Sons between 1771 and 1790 reinforced the privileged character of the founding members. Of the eighty seven members whose professions can be identified, fifty nine were merchants (see Appendix VI). Stephen Kingston of Campbell & Kingston joined the society in 1790, six years after his partner James Campbell, while Hugh Holmes and Robert Rainey of Rainey & Holmes both enlisted in 1791. The honorary members were drawn from similar circles. Of the six original honorees, four were merchants of one type or other. Of these, the commercial network of the dry goods importer, John Cadwalader (1771), must have been particularly close to the established officers as it provided no less than five of the society's honorees in 1771 and 1772. As the Sons' official historian, John Campbell, has dryly observed, these men all "belonged to the same set." Similarly, William Constable knew many of his fellow-members "for many years" before he became a Friendly Son himself in 1781.[26] Philadelphia's closely-knit business community facilitated these kinds of connections. Some of the Friendly Sons also knew one another through other elite societies, especially the *First City Troop* (founded in 1774) and the *Hibernia*

25 Campbell, *Friendly Sons*, introduction, 107. The date in brackets refers to the year of induction into the society. Unless otherwise noted, general information on the Friendly Sons and its members has been drawn from the introduction and biographical sketches in this work. For Conyngham & Nesbitt, see also PGS, Family Archives, "Conyngham," 5–7; HSP, *Reminiscences of D.H. Conyngham* (n.p., n.d.); and Doerflinger, *A Vigorous Spirit of Enterprise*, 59, 236–8, 17.

26 Campbell, *Friendly Sons*, 140; William A. Davis, "William Constable: New York Merchant and Land Speculator, 1772–1803" (Ph.D. dissertation, Harvard University, 1955), ch.1.

Fire Company (see Appendix VI). The second of these societies had been founded on 20 January 1752 as a mark of the "special trust and confidence" that the members held "in each other's Friendship ... [and] for the purpose of preserving our own and our neighbours' houses from fire." It restricted its membership to forty, of whom eight were founder members of the Friendly Sons. It met every month and spent its income on repairing and maintaining fire engines as well as on suppers and other entertainments. Small amounts of money were also given to the poor and in 1769 the company presented an engine to the house of employment. In 1791 the Hibernia Fire Company was listed as the sixth oldest of Philadelphia's thirty five fire companies and was reported to have better fire-fighting equipment than most of the others.[27]

Many of the Friendly Sons were also related to one another. James Mease (1771) was the brother of John (1771) and Matthew (1771), and David Caldwell (1794) was the son of Samuel (1771). The merchant William Barclay (1781) was the brother of Thomas (1771) while the society's first president, the merchant and general of the American Revolution, Stephen Moylan (1771), was the brother of the lawyer Jasper (1781) and the merchant John (1781). George Campbell (1771) married a sister of John Donnaldson (1778) and the daughter of Blair McClenachan (1777) married her father's business partner, Patrick Moore (1786). The importance of the extended family as an introduction to the Friendly Sons was also reflected in the probate records of some of the leading members. For example, when the will of one of the original members, William West, was proven in January 1786, it listed five members as executors and two others as witnesses while that of another founder, James Mease, listed John Maxwell Nesbitt (1771), John Barclay (1779), and Samuel Caldwell (1771), "all merchants of Philadelphia," as executors. Alexander Nesbitt (1778) and George Hughes (1781), also merchants, acted as witnesses. After James Campbell's (1784) death from yellow fever in 1797, his daughter became the ward of George Latimer (1784), while in a will that was written before he left for France in 1803, the West India merchant, Michael Morgan O'Brien (1781), entrusted his daughter to Thomas Fitzsimons (1771). His will also named three other "particular friends," including Stephen and Jasper Moylan, as guardians of his family. Samuel Carsan (1772) stipulated that if there were any disagreements over his estate, his "worthy and much esteemed friends," William West (1771)

27 Anon., *The Hibernia Fire Engine Company* (Philadelphia, 1859); LCP, Broadsides Collection, Ab. (1786)–13, "Articles of the Hibernia Fire-Company in Philadelphia." The quotations are from "Articles of the Hibernia Fire-Company" (1786). See also *The Book of the First Troop, Philadelphia City Cavalry, 1774–1924* (Philadelphia, 1915). The other elite networks are discussed in Ethel B. Rasmusson, "Capital on the Delaware: The Philadelphia Upper Class in Transition, 1789–1801" (Ph.D. dissertation, Brown University, 1962), 57–69; 158–82.

and Benjamin Fuller (1771) were to be told and his beneficiaries advised that "upon all and every emergency [to] consult these gentlemen, and do not by any means go to law, but abide by their decision, and let their opinion be definitive."[28]

The links which bound the Friendly Sons were strengthened by the decision to confine the membership to "the descendants of Irish parents by either side in the first degree" as well as to "the Descendants of every Member, *ad infinitem*, [who] shall have a *natural Right* of Application [italics mine] to be admitted Members of this Society." Indeed, of those who joined in 1771, twenty were Irish-born and the four others were the sons of Irishmen. Of sixty others who joined between 1772 and 1790 and whose place of birth can be identified, forty three were born in Ireland while the other seventeen were the sons of an Irish parent (see Appendix VI).[29] Despite the society's regulations on the parentage of its members, the ethno-cultural character of the Friendly Sons remained somewhat understated. Like the Sons of St. George, the Friendly Sons were content to be "a Comfort to the Afflicted, an Honour to our Country, and a Worthy Example to Posterity." However, their comfortable networks were to be challenged by the "new" immigrants of the 1790s. Since these immigrants were often seen as potentially disruptive, members of the established elite wondered if the "new Irish" and their "new leaders" should or indeed, could be absorbed cleanly and comfortably into the polity that they knew and respected at a time when America was being shaken by the "loosening force" of the American Revolution. Given that in all walks of life, the concept of "natural leadership" seemed to have been diluted during the 1780s, the "transforming hand" of revolution had challenged not just the political but also the social pre-eminence of the families and networks that had ruled America for several decades. For societies such as the Friendly Sons, there were two responses to this situation. On the one hand, the "old leaders" could accommodate the "new men" and thus contain the "awakened democracy." On the other hand, the "old" could decide to exclude the "new," thereby obliging those who were economically, ethnically, and socially "outside" to develop their own institutions. During the 1790s the evolution of "new" societies such as *The Hibernian Society for the Relief of Emigrants from Ireland* (incorporated as the *Hibernian Society* in 1792) would force the choice.[30]

---

28 Campbell, *Friendly Sons*, 139, 129, 104. For a flattering portrait of Moylan, see Marquis de Chastellux, *Travels in North America in the Years 1780, 1781 and 1782*, trans. and introd. Howard C. Rice, (Williamsburg, 1971), 284–5.

29 HSP, Amb. 8899, Papers of Benjamin Fuller, "Rules to be Observed by the Society of the Friendly Sons of St. Patrick;" Campbell, *Friendly Sons*, 66, 127.

30 *Sons of St. George ... 1774*, ix; J. Franklin Jameson, *The American Revolution Considered as a Social Movement* (Princeton, 1926), 11; Alexander, *Render them Submissive*, 1, 32–3,

In terms of its social composition and outlook, the Hibernian Society was different from the Friendly Sons. It soon eclipsed the older society although by 1790 it was clear that the Friendly Sons were having their own problems. Firstly, as Samuel Caldwell, the Sons' treasurer, reported on 6 March 1793, the collection of fines and even admission dues was becoming increasingly difficult. There were also irregularities in the election of officers. Thirdly, despite their declared agenda, the Friendly Sons had never been actively involved in assisting immigrants. As a result, members such as Hugh Boyle (1787) felt that there was a certain irrelevance about their activities, especially as high numbers of Irish immigrants were pouring into Philadelphia at the time. Boyle was particularly socially-conscious and when he died in 1791 the *American Daily Advertiser* stated that "his exertions as a member of the Hibernian Society in relieving the distressed and protecting the oppressed and injured are too well known to need repetition." For "several years," Boyle had been making "many efforts" to set up a society with goals which were similar to those to which the Hibernian Society finally agreed in its stated objectives of March 1790:

> that as no object can be more laudable, so to a benevolent mind none can be more grateful than the relief of distress; perhaps no institution can afford a more ample scope for the effectuation of this purpose than the national societies established in this country for the protection of those emigrants whom misery, misfortune or oppression has compelled to foresake their native country and fly to the "asylum" established here "for the oppressed of all nations." By these societies, emigrants have been not only rendered more happy in their situations, but more useful members in society; oppression has been punished, migration hither encouraged, misery alleviated, and consequently the temptations to wander from the paths of rectitude diminished. These reasons and others equally forcible, have induced the subscribers, natives of Ireland, or descendants of Irishmen, to associate themselves under the title of "The Hibernian Society for the Protection of Irish Emigrants.[31]

Of the twelve men who were present on the occasion, six were Friendly Sons, including the Sons' then-president, John Nesbitt, and its secretary, John Brown. Later in the year, the Hibernians' first secretary, Mathew Carey, published a list of members which included a number of lawyers and judges, as well as doctors, wardens, surveyors, customs officers, and collectors of the port

104–5, 120–1, 160–74, *et passim*. For a discussion of Philadelphia's elite, Rasmusson, "Capital on the Delaware" and Geib, "History of Philadelphia."

31 Caldwell to J.M. Nesbitt, 6 Mar. 1793, as quoted in Campbell, *Friendly Sons*, 90–1; *ADA*, 13 Sept. 1791; *PP*, 3 Mar. 1790. In his autobiography, published in 1837, Carey suggested that it was he who had called this initial meeting "having previously prepared a constitution;" Carey, *Autobiography*, 29.

of Philadelphia – professions on which the Hibernians could draw to provide a practical local service to Irish immigrants. Although the society's early minutes (1790–1813) do not survive, the biographies of the early members have been compiled by the Hibernians' official historian, John H. Campbell, and these suggest that the society's membership was less exclusive than that of the Friendly Sons. As William Martin put it on 6 June 1790, "all degrees of Persons might have the liberty of subscribing." Of the 146 men who were members between 1790 and 1800 and for whom information is available, there were three innkeepers, including Patrick Byrne (1790) of "Byrne's Tavern" and his brother James (1790), ten "grocers" and seven "schoolmasters," professions that were not recorded by the Friendly Sons. Edward Hanlon was involved in the bottling business, Robert Bridges was a sailmaker, and John Savage and Edward Nugent were among six "shopkeepers." Edward Scott was one of two tailors, Robert Fitzgerald a blockmaker, John McElwee "a painter and color man," and Owen Morris a "comedian." Over a third of the members were listed as "merchants," the profession which also dominated the Friendly Sons. However, the overlap between the membership of the two societies was less than 20%. The Sons who became leading Hibernians tended to be those who had wanted to broaden the activities of the older society. The wider agenda was also reflected in an amendment which was made to the Hibernians' constitution in September 1790 to allow that

> The *actual* members of the Society shall consist of Irishmen, or descendants of Irishmen only; but persons of character, natives of other countries, who shall subscribe to this constitution, and comply with the rules of it, may be admitted as *honorary* members.[32]

The first draft of this constitution had been adopted on 5 April 1790 and while based on that of the Friendly Sons, it included important changes. The most notable of these were procedures for assisting immigrants. In order "to prevent and punish [the] imposition and oppression of emigrants by owners, masters, or freighters of vessels," at least two Hibernians were to visit every passenger vessel that arrived from Ireland. These men were also empowered "to call for the advice" of lawyers and physicians if the situation so demanded and indeed, article III stipulated that two members from each of these professions should be among the society's officers. These articles were not empty rhetoric, as the indictment of Captain Richard Cunningham of the brig *Cunningham*

---

32 HSP, Lea & Febiger Collection, Incoming Correspondence (1785–96) ix, Martin to Carey, dated 6 June 1790; *IG*, 4 Sept. 1790. Carey's list is in Campbell, *Friendly Sons*, 62. The biographical data in this paragraph have been taken from the same source. For the society's original constitution, see *ibid.*, 153–6.

(Derry to Philadelphia, 1790) showed.[33] The Hibernians' visits to immigrant vessels were also widely reported on both sides of the Atlantic while their committee of correspondence publicised the society's activities in the different ports of Ireland "whence emigrants generally come." On 7 November 1791 the *Hibernian Journal* picked up on their activities and described the society as one which had been founded "for the protection and relief of such as quit this country and may require pecuniary and other assistance." As a result of this publicity, the Hibernians were soon receiving applications from hapless Irish immigrants in Philadelphia. A number of such requests survive in the letterbooks and papers of Mathew Carey. While each petition tells its own story, one theme which runs through most of them was the distress which had been caused as a result of broken promises. For example, Mary Dunn had come from Derry in 1793 to become a housekeeper for her brother, a Philadelphia doctor. She had been forced into service after he had "broke[n] loose and since led a dissipated life" and proved unable to engage her, "agreeable to his encouragement & her expectations." As a result, Mary fell into poor health and was unable "to use any more efforts of Industry." Writing on Dunn's behalf, Charles O'Hagen asked Carey to use his influence to raise a "private" collection to send her back to Derry in the confidence that "God will reward your laudable interference in heaven & can only be acknowledged on earth by the Applicant." John Justice found himself in a similar predicament. He had been stranded "without either friend or Relation, house or home nor no place of residence" after "a Gentleman from Cork" who had "meant to do for me ... told me he had no further occasion for me, and desired me to go and provide for myself."[34] Again, the society's good offices were requested.

Other immigrants alleged that they had been cheated after arriving in Philadelphia. Stephen Fotterall explained that he had been advised to emigrate by Captain Blair of the ship *Rising Sun*. Under their arrangement, Fotterall agreed to bind himself to Blair for five years, after which he would be placed as a clerk in the offices of the vessel's owners, Gurney & Smith of Philadelphia. However, after he landed in America, Fotterall was "ill used" by Blair and later sold to one Mr. Hubley for 15l. After two years and three months, Fotterall ran away from his master and although he sent Hubley 15l., "thinking that it would satisfy him for any time" and promised "to remit him more when I could afford it," he was not released from his indenture. Fotterall asked the Hibernian

33 Risch, "Immigrant Aid Societies before 1820," 23–30; *ADA*, 4 Mar. 1791. The constitutional references are taken from Campbell, *Friendly Sons*, 155, 153. For the *Cunningham* case, see also Risch, "Emigrant Aid Societies," 30–2, as well as the previous chapter.
34 HSP, Lea & Febiger Collection, Incoming Correspondence (1785–96) xii, 5 Nov. 1796; *ibid.*, ix, Petition of John Justice to the Hibernian Society, n.d.

Society to intervene. The young Patrick Morgan also had cause for complaint. Before setting out for Philadelphia, his mother had lodged a sum of money with one Mr. Farrel, from which occasional allowances were to be paid to him. However, Farrel would not recognise Morgan after he arrived and refused to answer his requests to draw on the account. As a result, Morgan was left "without a single shilling." In these circumstances, he wrote to Carey and although an interim arrangement was made, Morgan was writing again a year later. By this time, Morgan seems to have had enough of America and asked Carey for assistance "to either alter my occupation or leave a country which has not been propitious to me." On the other hand, William Sotherin was the author of his own misfortune. Sotherin had been in prison for nineteen months for fraud and indebtedness when he wrote to Carey asking him to encourage the Court of Common Pleas to review his case. In the meantime, his wife and family needed help from the overseers of the poor with whom, as with Sotherin's three creditors, Carey was also asked to use his "influence."[35]

Most of the applications to the Hibernian Society were from Irish immigrants who sought assistance and advice on how to survive in Philadelphia. John Justice asked Carey to procure "some little employment, for a livelihood" while the two Blake brothers stated that they wanted "countenance and advice" rather than "any pecuniary assistance" to put their "very good education" to use in America. When the druggist James Pierce failed to attach himself to an established house in Philadelphia, he wanted help to set up his own business, adding that any money that Carey "should please to advance, shall be duly and honestly repaid at such times and in such payments as they [the Hibernians] will be pleased to appoint." The Hibernians also continued to process introductions for newly-arrived immigrants. For example, Carey's Dublin friend, the printer John Byrne, introduced one Hugh Morris as a sometime clerical student and Latin teacher who, "being in a strange place without friends," might be "put in the way of getting honest bread." In a similar letter to Carey in 1794 James Carsan introduced a teacher from Ireland who

> in his migrations from Ireland has been much distressed by means of his placing too much Confidence in one of his Countrymen who had been in this Country for some years, stripped of every thing as he can inform you, he came here with a wife and one child destitute even of clothes to cover them.

Even Carey's own cousin, the engraver, Alexander Carey, wrote to him as "Sect^y to the Honble Society for the relief of Irish passengers." Knowing of "the

35 HSP, Lea & Febiger Collection, Incoming Correspondence (1785–96) vii, 15 June 1791; xii, 5 Oct. 1795; 17 Dec. 1796; xv, 17 Mar. 1791.

repeated instances" of his "humanity extended towards so many of our *Hibernian* Adventurers," Alexander Carey asked "what encouragement one of my profession might have a probability of meeting with within the extended circle of your acquaintance in America."[36] Thus, the services which the Hibernians offered to Irish immigrants set them apart from the Friendly Sons.

In a similar vein, the *Scots Thistle Society* (founded in 1796) set itself apart from the older St. Andrew's Society. While its aim to assist "each Scots emigrant whose circumstances require, and Character is deserving" corresponded with that of the older society, this was now being pursued more vigorously and consistently. It also included the resolve "to procure employment" for immigrants and to promote a mutual assistance programme that would provide funding on the death of a member or a member's wife. Members were also obliged, on pain of fine, to attend the funerals of their colleagues. The society's constitution observed that "Humanity calls the Society to attend to this last tribute of respect."[37] Such resolutions were yet another manifestation of a more assertive ethno-culturalism with which so many public figures were uncomfortable after 1783. In 1799 the Welsh Society was reinvented as the *Welsh Society of Pennsylvania for the Advice and Assistance of Emigrants from Wales*. As one might expect, it committed itself to assisting its own nationals. However, in so doing, the society suggested that "to have especial fellowship with the descendants of our ancestors, is perfectly consistent with true patriotism and universal philanthropy." In 1790 the decision of the *German Lutheran Aid Society* that "all business, orally or in writing, must be transacted in the German language" was perhaps the most obvious gloss on the increasing cultural introspection of national networks and clubs in the Philadelphia of the 1790s. Five years later the *Mosheimian Society* was founded

> for the purpose of keeping up the knowledge of the German language, and to preserve it in its purity. It was named after Mosheim, a celebrated writer in Germany, who made the most strenuous exertion to purify this elegant language from every foreign word and name, in order to simplify it as much as possible.[38]

36 *Ibid.* xiii, 24 July 1791; vii, n.d.; xviii, 24 July 1791; Byrne Folder (1785–96), n.d.; box 3, 4 Nov. 1794; Alexander Carey and James Carey File (1791–93).

37 *Scots Thistle Society of Philadelphia. Constitution of the ... Instituted November 30, 1796* (Philadelphia, 1799), 18–20, 16–17, 18. See also "Extract from a Memorial Read before the Scots Thistle Society, Dec 21st 1796," *The Minerva*, 4 Mar. 1797. A comparison between the membership lists of the Scots Thistle Society (1799) and the St. Andrew's Society (1791) suggests that there was only one member common to the 65 members of the first and the 93 of the second; see *Scots Thistle Society* (1799) and *St. Andrew's Society of Philadelphia. The Constitution and Rules of ...* (Philadelphia, 1791), 11–12.

38 *Welch Society of Pennsylvania. Constitution and Rules of the ...* (Mount Holly, 1799), 4;

On 11 July 1792 the *Aurora* noted that the French were still "unprovided with an Institution" of the type that the Irish and British had. However, this was redressed on the following 28 December when a number of Frenchmen founded the *French Patriotic Society of Friends to Liberty and Equality*

> to fix on a proper mode of celebrating the happy success of their fellow patriots in France, [and] unanimously agreed, instead of a festival, fireworks or illuminations, to open a subscription for the relief of the distressed of that nation here, or of any other, should the funds be equal to this double object.

The society also ensured that Bastille Day (14 July) and the Franco–American alliance (6 February 1778) would be remembered. Neither did it forget the pivotal dates of the recent French Revolution. In May 1795 the society held a "civic festival" to mark "the late glorious successes of the French Republic, and the emancipation of the people of Holland" while in April 1797 it met to honour "the victories of the French Republic in Italy, and the surrender of Mantua." Such celebrations, together with their slogans and toasts, celebrated the heroes and milestones of contemporary European republicanism, marking a new type of event on the festive calendar in Philadelphia. As such, they had an international appeal which transcended the particular interests of any one society or network and their toasts manifested this. For example, at the April 1797 celebration, the eighth salutation was to "Ireland – may the Irish harp be speedily torn from the British willow, and its strings be made to vibrate to a revolutionary air." In many ways, such toasts were not ethno-cultural at all because, as David Waldstreicher has suggested, "Precisely because the extent of America's democratic transformation remained unclear, the French Revolution addressed the insecure achievements of the American Revolution, providing a language for rekindling, or securely ending, that struggle."[39] As such, the celebration of what on one level might be seen in narrower ethno-cultural terms was, on another, a challenge to the ways in which the American republic itself was being defined during the 1790s.

John G. Frank and John E. Pomfret, "The German Lutheran Aid Society of 1790," *PMHB* lx (1939), 61–4; Benjamin Schultz, *Oration Delivered before the Mosheimian Society on July 23rd, 1795* (Philadelphia, 1795), 3, n.1. The latter society, drawn from the largest congregation in Philadelphia, had been founded "to take care of the poor and the sick, to provide them, according to their needs, with food, and to grant them all, necessary aid," *ibid.*, 61.

39 *NG*, 2 Jan., 9 Mar. 1793; *ADA*, 1 May 1795; *ADA*, 21 Apr. 1797; Waldstreicher, *In the Midst of Perpetual Fetes*, 19. For the establishment of the society itself, see *NG*, 2 Jan. 1793 and Francis James Dallet, "The French Benevolent Society of Philadelphia and the Bicentennial," *RACHS* lxxxi (1979–80), 63–8.

American Societies

During the 1770s as the debate developed on "who should rule at home," some insisted that the new republic would exhibit an "American spirit." In the associational world of Philadelphia, this was reflected in the evolution of the *Society of the Sons of St. Tammany* (founded in May 1772) which in many ways also became a foil for the ethno-cultural societies of Saints David, Andrew, George, and Patrick. In 1773 the society noted that

> As all nations have for several centuries past adopted some great personage remarkable for his virtues and loved for civil and religious liberty as their tutelar saint, and annually assembled at a fixed day to commemorate him, the natives of this flourishing Province [Pennsylvania], determined to follow so laudable an example, for some years past have adopted a great warrior sachem and chief named Tammany, a fast friend to our fore fathers, to be the tutelar Saint of this Province.

It also provided a *vita* for America's own "native-born saint," St. Tammany. The leading hagiographer was Samuel Latham Mitchell whose *Life, Exploits, and Precepts of Tammany* was published in full in 1795. Mitchell mourned that he was no Homer. However, he stressed that Tammany was a heroic figure: an "*American* sage" who, with "his people," had lived in an uncharted land west of the Allegheny Mountains "whose antiquity no man knows, nor can ascertain." Thus, there was a sense of mystery about Tammany. However, Mitchell suggested that this was partly because he and his civilisation had been excluded from the canon of ancient history as this had been determined by the European academies: the indigenous leaders of America were no less civilised than the more familiar names of Europe.[40]

Tammany's story was told in allegorical terms. He had long led his people wisely and well. As a result, he had overcome "the evil spirit" and led his people to such "improvement," "industry," and "civilization" that even the Inca had sought to treat with him. However, after returning from the parlay, Tammany found that the "Old Enemy" ["evil"] had taken advantage of his absence" to introduce "idleness and depravity" among his people. The "evil influence" had also led them to reject Tammany's advice that America's early American Indians should "operate in concert, stand together, [and] support each other ... [because] disharmony would terminate in their ruin; and in union, consisted

---

40 Carl Becker, *A History of Political Parties in the Province of New York, 1760–1776* (Madison, 1960), 22; LCP, a card, "Sir, As all Nations have for Seven Centuries ..." (Philadelphia, 1773); Samuel Latham Mitchell, *The Life, Exploits, and Precepts of Tammany* (New York, 1795), 19, 5.

their salvation." Mitchell then made the obvious point with which he ended his "sermon:"

> Cease your prating about St. Patrick, St. George, and St. Louis; and be silent concerning your St. Andrew and St. David. Tammany, though no saint, was you see, as valiant, intrepid, and heroic as the best of them; and besides that, did a thousand times more good.

Although Mitchell presented a very idealised and anthropomorphic view of the history of the native-American Indian, his message echoed the official mantra of the new republic: the focus on America and what was native to it.[41]

Mitchell also stressed Tammany's other legacy: that America was best celebrated in an undifferentiated and integrated community where the descendants of Tammany and Columbus could live together in peace and harmony, and without corruption or autocracy. However, Tammany's inclination to associate native ("Indian") and imported ("European") conventions as a paradigm for the new republic reflects the history of the 1780s rather than the 1790s. However, while its members did not have any "ambition to be greater, they determined not to be less than their fellow citizens" either. In this spirit, they usually invited the officers of the other societies to their annual dinners (a practice common to all the societies) and toasted their good fortune and health. As a toast at its first dinner put it, "May the Sons of King Tammany, St. George, St. Andrew, St. Patrick, and St. David love each other as brethren of *one common ancestor*, and unite in their hearty endeavors to preserve *native* Constitutional American Liberties." Despite such aspirations, as well as Tammany's hopes that America might be "an Asylum to the oppressed of all countries," as put in one of its toasts in 1793, few of the Friendly Sons joined its ranks. This was a voluntary decision on their part because neither the Friendly Sons nor their "adopted brethren" in the other societies were ever specifically excluded from Tammany as was the case initially in New York.[42]

Tammany declined in Philadelphia during the 1790s. However, *The Philadelphia Society, for the Information and Assistance of Emigrants and Persons Emigrating from Foreign Countries* reflected a similar ethos. This society was established in August 1794 and was supported by modest initiation and yearly fees ($1 in both cases). It developed against a background of increasing immigration from Europe and expressing a goal that it deemed to be "worthy of every virtuous and benevolent mind," it resolved "to render emigration as

41 Mitchell, *Life ... of Tammany*, 6, 15, 16, 29, 21, 33.
42 *PP*, 5 May 1785; Von A. Cabeen, "Society of the Sons of Saint Tammany" (part I), 443–4; *ibid.* (part III), *PMHB* xxvi (1902), 218; *ibid.* (part II), *PMHB* xxvi (1902), 21.

advantageous as possible" for both the immigrants and "the country that affords them refuge." However, it also recognised that

> many of those who emigrate, although frequently endowed with talents and virtues the most valuable, arriving from an unknown shore, bereft of the means of support, and destitute of friends to whom to apply for advice or assistance, are lost, for a time, to society and to themselves.

Thus, the society would offer immigrants every assistance and "information to those who may stand in need of it" and would do so favouring "the relief of distress from no particular clime, considering all men as brothers." In 1797 it published a seventy two page pamphlet which included its constitution and by-laws as well as a number of public laws on the regulation of the passenger trade and the legal status of European immigrants in America. With respect to "the *immediate* comfort" of immigrants, the society provided different types of practical support, including a list of lodging houses and "their terms of accommodation." Its registrar was also designated to assist "cases of emigrants wanting employment," especially those who were mechanics, artisans, and "persons possessing certain degrees of capacity and talents." In October 1796 the then-registrar, Henry Heins, placed an advertisement in Philadelphia's papers on behalf of "a man lately arrived from Europe, who wishes to get Employment in the Distillery Line." An eighteen year old recent arrival was available "to bind himself as an Apprentice carpenter." Replies were to be sent to Heins at Number 103, North Third Street. The following year its acting committee reported that the society had already assisted sixty seven immigrants "to obtain for them almost immediate employment."[43]

The society also had its own physician who could "exert every legal endeavour" to prevent ship captains from endangering "the lives and health of passengers" and bringing "disgrace to human nature." It appointed committees to visit vessels. After one visit "relative to the objects of the society," Captain Geddes of the ship *General Washington* (Dublin to Philadelphia, 1795) was formally and in a "public manner," thanked "for his polite behaviour, & humane attention to the [passengers'] comforts during the voyage." Not every passenger

---

43 Princeton University Library, Am.11,613, "(Philadelphia) Society for the Information and Assistance of Emigrants ... CONSTITUTION" (broadside, Philadelphia, 1 April 1795); *Aurora*, 16 Oct. 1795; *GA*, 7 Oct. 1794; *Philadelphia Society for the Information and Assistance of Persons Emigrating from Foreign Countries. The Act of Incorporation, Constitution, and By-Laws of the ...* (Philadelphia, 1797), hereafter cited as *Act of Incorporation*; *GA*, 7 Oct. 1794; *Act of Incorporation*, 10; *GA*, 7 Oct. 1794; *GIG*, 7 Oct. 1796, 18 July 1797.

had a captain as benign as Geddes. However, if such people were not satisfied with the circumstances of the journey across the Atlantic, the society would offer them "every assistance to obtain justice" and in 1796 and 1797 it appointed sub-committees for these purposes. The society's nine man committee of conference and correspondence met weekly and ensured that these activities would be kept in the public eye, especially where immigrants had "well-founded complaints" against their captains.[44] The society was also actively involved in philanthropy, details of which were given in a report which was published in 1797. Aside from those whom the society had assisted to get employment, another 140 had been "afforded pecuniary assistance" either to alleviate "actual distress" or to purchase "working tools." "Pecuniary and medical aid" had been granted to "between 60 and 70 sick and needy emigrants, many of whom [had] laboured under infectious diseases." Although the society's first secretary, William Turner, observed that "pecuniary assistance" was one of its "two distinguishing traits," this was not granted without qualification. The society's revised constitution stated in 1797 that where sums of over $9 had been given to individuals, promissory notes to repay were required. Aside from these activities, Turner recorded that the society's "efforts ... [included] advice, to render the necessitous independent upon others to enable him to direct his talents to their proper ends, and to restore him at once to the community and himself."[45]

In 1796 the society also decided to look into "the various causes," course and impact of immigration through a number of public events, notably charity sermons. One of the more important of these was given on 22 May 1796 by the Welsh-born Baptist minister, Morgan J. Rhees (1760–1804). Drawing on the parable of "the good Samaritan," Rhees stated that since October 1794 the society had taken a "great number of Emigrants ... from the path of poverty and placed [them] in the field of plenty" and, in particular, had directed "the laborer, mechanic, and artist where to find employment." Rhees also referred to the society's "utility" in prosecuting rogue captains who had abused indentures and treated their passengers poorly; the society was "pledged to ... bringing such tyrants to a proper sense of their duty." He also saw immigrants as an undifferentiated mass: "Here every nation, kindred, and tongue under heaven, forget their ancient animosities, and form one race of *republicans*." This would have pleased Franklin and the Tammany Society but then, the Philadelphia Society had always taken the broad view of society and stressed the need for all slices of society to be assimilated into one. Thus, Rhees gloried in a society which

44 *Aurora*, 25 Dec. 1794, 30 May 1795, 25, 18 Dec. 1794.
45 *GIG*, 18 July 1797; *Act of Incorporation*, 11.

pays no respect to any national character ... thanks be to GOD, the day of *all Saints* has at last arrived, the PHILADELPHIA Society unites them all, in one fraternal band—all party stars disappear—the sun of Philanthropy has risen—and the morning heralds proclaim—*All Men are Brethren*.

Neither this pious hope nor Rhees's exhortation to immigrants to become "active members" of the society was realised. Moreover, despite an amendment that was made to the society's constitution in 1797 to enable officers to "confer and hold correspondence with individuals and similar societies," there is no evidence that this happened. Although it had tried to confront the increasingly ethnic character of societies such as the Hibernian Society, the Philadelphia Society ended as a splendid failure.[46] The reality was that as the 1790s unfolded, the city's immigrants, but especially the Irish, looked to their own.

National Days

Tammany's consensual approach to marking the achievements of the new American republic was also evident in its decision to inaugurate a "native American" festival on 1 May that would be "set apart to the memory of Saint Tamina." The 1784 celebrations were held at an estate on the Schuylkill River and were typical of most of the others. After the state flag was raised, a burst of cannon fire introduced "the festivity," the society's "Chief & Sachems" were elected, and the "law of liberty proclaimed." The company then gave thirteen toasts, the first of which recognised "St. Tammany and the day." Most of the others recalled personalities and events of the Revolution, including Washington and "the citizen soldiers of America." In a gesture towards the broad geographical canvas of Patriotism, the society also expressed the hope that "the people of Ireland [would] enjoy the freedom of Americans." However, in line with Tammany's origins, the activities of 1 May focused on celebrating America, including the promotion of "free trade in American bottoms." The high-point of the day was the reading of the Declaration of Independence. A "Song for St. Tammany's Day" was also usually composed for the occasion and celebrated "great Tammany's feats" above those of any other. From 1783, for example,

46 Morgan J. Rhees, *The Good Samaritan. An Oration delivered on Sunday Evening, May 22nd, 1796, in behalf of the Philadelphia Society for the Information and Assistance of persons Emigrating from Foreign Countries* (Philadelphia, 1796), end advertisement; *GIG*, 18 July 1797; *Aurora*, 16 Oct. 1795; Rhees, *Good Samaritan*, 11, 12, 14, 12, 16, 17; *Act of Incorporation*, 5. Occasionally, the society's meetings were held at the African School at Willing Alley; *Aurora*, 3 Jan., 1 May 1798. For Rhees's involvement in the society, see also *GA*, 30 Sept. 1794 and *GIG*, 6 Oct. 1796.

> Of Andrew, of Patrick, of David, and George,
> What mighty achievements we hear!
> While no one relates great Tammany's feats,
> Although more heroic by far, my brave boys ...
> These heroes fought only as fancy inspired,
> As by their own stories we find;
> Whilst Tammany, he fought only to free
> From Cruel oppression mankind, my brave boys,
> From cruel oppression mankind.

Acclaiming America was common to all these songs, as a further sign of which revellers usually wore "a piece of buck's tail on their hats or in some conspicuous situation" in much the same way as the Irish wear shamrock on St. Patrick's Day.[47]

During the 1780s Tammany's commemorations also displayed a rhetorical commitment to bring old and new together: to "keep fast the chain of friendship, and put the same around us." In April 1786 the society entertained members of the Seneca "on the banks of the Schuylkill" and reminded those present that their respective ancestors had encouraged them "to live in union and friendship with all their children, and to bury the *hatchet* forever." Moreover, not only had Tammany "so kindly and cordially welcomed our [European] ancestors to this fruitful country," as their orator put it in 1784, but as the American equivalent of the European saints, he had heaped on him the characteristics that were dearest to Revolutionary Americans: industry, frugality, honour, virtue and patriotism, all of which were celebrated at Tammany gatherings. The company was urged to embrace the new American flag as a symbol of these traits and to ensure that the society would promote the kind of republican polity for which it stood.[48]

Such commemorations, and the rituals and attitudes which they embodied, had a long history within the wider British world. At a time when the new republic was inventing its own symbols as well as refining those which it had inherited from the past, these colonial traditions now helped to re-establish

47 Quoted from Eddis, *Letters from America* in Von A. Cabeen, "Society of the Sons of Saint Tammany" (part I), 441; report from Philadelphia in *NYP*, 13 May 1784. The 1783 song is quoted from Scharf and Westcott, *History of Philadelphia* ii, 560–1. The wearing of bucktail is quoted from Eddis, *Letters from America* in Von A. Cabeen, "Society of the Sons of Saint Tammany" (part I), 441. For other examples of Tammany songs, see *PEP*, 30 April 1776; (Philadelphia) *Freeman's Journal*, 7 May 1783, 2 May 1785; *PEH*, 6 May 1786; and *IG*, 21 Apr. 1787. For the resolution that only "American beer and cider" should be served during the 1788 federal procession, see Lee Travers, *Celebrating the Fourth: Independence Day and the Rites of Nationalism in the Early Republic* (Amherst, 1997), 86.

48 *PP*, 20 Apr. 1786; *NYP*, 13 May 1784.

them as part of contemporary popular culture. They also helped the new American republic to find what Len Travers has called its own "myth of origins." From 1777 the adoption of the national flag, and the designation of 4 July as the day on which American independence was officially commemorated, facilitated this process. The toasts and orations that were offered at Tammany's celebrations were not just *pro forma* but were also, as Travers suggests, a "form of oath-taking, in which an individual signifies his fidelity ... to a set of beliefs to which the group subscribes." As Americans participated in these rites as a "shared" exercise, they were conscious that they were thus identifying the symbols, and inventing the rituals, through which the new citizens might celebrate their new republic. Waldstreicher and others have argued that these ceremonies also helped to promote the "myth of consensus" of the contemporary polity as well as its "all-embracing ideology." These activities not only marked out new heroes, but by saluting their past activities and current positions, they also helped to shape the nature and direction of the contemporary polity, including the meanings of republicanism and patriotism, "good government" and a virtuous citizenry. In a 4 July oration in Philadelphia in 1788 there was a familiar ring when James Wilson identified the "virtues and manners" that "justify and adorn" the good citizen: frugality, temperance, industry, and "a warm and uniform attachment to liberty, and to the constitution." Over time such characteristics became a "patriotic litmus test," as Travers has put it, and encouraged a conversation that would continue to promote the idealism of the organic polity as well as the need to avoid division and promote consensus and harmony, thus securing the republic and its polity. By 1788 the fourth of July rather than the first of May had become "the day, which ... will always on its *annual* return behold in us a people united, virtuous, free, and strictly independent." It would also be the day which would "prove an *annual witness* of our enjoying undiminished the blessings which it gave." Tammany had provided an important forum for celebrating the Revolution and its achievements. By 1790, however, the marking of American independence was no longer taken to be the preserve of any one society.[49]

This was inevitable not least because the American Revolution was often presented as part of an international movement which did not stop in 1783. Donald H. Stewart has observed that what was happening in contemporary France, in particular, was "watched with almost paternal pride" in America. As the *Gazette of the United States* noted on 28 October 1789 the French Revolution was "one of the most glorious objects that can arrest the attention of mankind" and, in its view, America had inspired it. Thus, at one of its

49 Travers, *Celebrating the Fourth*, 22, 52, 54–5; Waldstreicher, *In the Midst of Perpetual Fetes*, 2, 9; *PG*, 9 July 1788; Travers, *Celebrating t he Fourth*, 23; *NIJ*, 12 July 1788.

meetings in 1789, Philadelphia's German Society hoped that "the altar of Freedom now erecting in France ... [would] prove as eminent and illustrious as that established in America." Also, before Louis XVI was executed on 23 January 1793, the celebrations of the fourth of July often honoured republican France as vindicating "the sacred rights of mankind," just as the American Revolution had done during the 1770s. Nearly six months later, when the **Society of the Cincinnati** met in Philadelphia to mark the fourth of July, they saluted "universal liberty–religious, civil, and political" as well as the polities of the United States and "the Republic of France" which in its view, expressed it best. In this context, toasts to the "freedom of Ireland" became common outside the banquets of St. Patrick's Day as "The Sister Republics of America and France" were called upon to apply their united "efforts ... in the cause of liberty," then under a supposed threat from the "despots of Europe." The "civic feasts" of the 1790s also recognised the "Republic of France" as well as the achievements and heroes of the American Revolution, the officers of the federal and state governments and "the day." "The day" could mark anything from the anniversary of the Franco-American alliance and the fall of the Bastille to the celebration of individual French victories in Europe. Jeffersonians admired the march of revolution in Europe, both literally and ideologically, and hoped that "the arms of France [might] prove victorious over all the combined powers leagued against them." With a government which had declared its neutrality on the war in Europe, such resolutions did not sit well. Indeed, some Federalists began to question the assumption that the French and American revolutions were similar. Even before the French king was executed, one critical citizen wrote to the *Gazette of the United States* on 16 January 1793 that

> In America no barbarities were perpetrated – no men's heads were stuck upon poles – no ladies bodies mangled, were carried thro' the streets in triumph – their prisoners guarded and ironed, were not massacred in cold blood. The American did not, at discretion, harass, murder, or plunder the clergy – not roast their generals unjustly alive. – They set limit to their vices, at which their pursuits rested. And whatever blood was shed, [it] flowed gallantly in the field. The American Revolution, it ought to be repeated was not accomplished as the French has been, by massacres, assassinations, or proscriptions: battles, severe and honourable, were fought, and the chance of war left to decide.[50]

During the 1790s events in contemporary France thus provided a reference which could challenge a somewhat self-satisfied interpretation of revolution in

---

50 Stewart, *Opposition Press of the Federalist Period*, 116; *NYP*, 2 Jan. 1790; *ADA*, 10 July 1793; *GA*, 9, 12 July, 16 1794. For reactions in Philadelphia to the French Revolution, see Eric Foner, *Thomas Paine and Revolutionary America* (New York and Oxford, 1976).

America and the "spirit of French liberty" became an emblem for the changing ideals of American as well as French republicanism. As Waldstreicher has observed,

> Precisely because the extent of America's democratic transformation remained unclear, the French Revolution addressed the insecure achievements of the American Revolution, providing a language for rekindling, or securely ending, that struggle.

For the *General Advertiser*, the implications were more ominous: the "salvation of America depends on our alliances with France" and might even "bring a speedy end to American independence" if the French Revolution "failed." While most Americans were not as pessimistic as this, they began to think less about the international aspects of reform and revolution and more about the domestic needs of their own republic. This was not as easy as it seemed, not least because the two were not unconnected. **Philip Freneau** (152–1832), editor of the anti-Federalist *National Gazette*, had argued that the celebration of the French Revolution had initially "welded America's own solidarity." As Elkins and McKittrick have maintained, this became a metaphorical reference for leaving Britain behind and for encouraging the "self-estimation" of the new republic. However, by suggesting that the leaders of their sister revolution in France might have feet of clay, those who were sceptical about events there were also questioning how the legacy of 1776 was being managed in America. In these circumstances, their own Founding Fathers would no longer attract automatic deference as the oracles of the revolutionary idea. As Elkins and McKittrick have concluded: "they had identified their very personalities with a particular understanding of it [society], and this challenge to that understanding would be a fundamental challenge to *them*."[51]

Given that "patriotic" meetings were no longer confined to the fourth of July and that many of them were becoming more critical of the Federalist government, it would be difficult to contain less cautious interpretations of republicanism. Also, such critics all but appropriated the "liberty cap" and "national cockade" and increasingly expressed their views in partisan ways, especially during the second half of the 1790s. At an Independence Day "festival" in 1796 that was presided over by Philadelphia's congressman (1795–98), **John Swanwick** (1740–98), and attended by the French minister and consul general, "The French Republic" was saluted with "Victory to her arms and Universality to her

---

51 *GA*, 8 July 1794, 1 Jan. 1791; Elkins and McKittrick, *Age of Federalism*, 354, 343, 304, 306, 26, 34. The substantial quote is from *ibid.*, 78; the italics are mine. Freneau is quoted from Stewart, *Opposition Press of the Federalist Period*, 117.

Principles." The Batavian and Genevan republics were also recognised as well as "Injured Ireland: May all people remember that resistance to oppression is the first of duties." Even generic toasts often had a party-political colour to them. After Swanwick and his company saluted "Our Republican Representatives in the Federal Legislature," they added the hope that Congress would "never degenerate into a chamber for registering executive edicts." In a similar vein two years later, "a number of Members of Congress and other citizens" of Philadelphia expressed their "resistance to arbitrary power."[52]

They also saluted "Republicanism, pure, genuine and elective – May it never be poisoned by its sources, by the corruption of the people, nor be interrupted in its content by the infidelity of their agents." These two occasions had been clearly influenced by the highly partisan debates of the time, the first by those on Jay's treaty (see Chapter 5) and the second by those on the Alien and Sedition Acts (see Chapter 6). However, in more general terms, they also influenced a growing belief that the leadership of contemporary America was little short of an "aristocracy of pretence" which had abandoned the values for which the Revolution had been fought. One gathering on 4 July 1795 insisted that "Cincinnatus ... [Washington] [should] be called from his retirement, and by his virtues, his patriotism, and his wisdom, save us from the calamities which threaten us." Little wonder perhaps that on 7 July of the same year, the *Aurora* wrote of the "funereal solemnity" with which the fourth of July was celebrated in Philadelphia as a result of Jay's treaty: "it appears more like the internment of liberty than the anniversary of its birth."[53]

The ways in which Philadelphia's ethno-cultural societies marked their own national days did not ease worries about being challenged "from outside." In Philadelphia, the English, Scots and Welsh marked St. George's Day, St. Andrew's Day, and St. David's Day on 23 April, 30 November, and 1 March, respectively. The Friendly Sons held their "elegant dinners" and elected their officers on St. Patrick's Day (17 March) and celebrated with "the greatest festivity and good humour." Until the early-1790s, their toasts were cautious rather than critical of public policy, and tended to associate with the leaders and symbols of the new homeland. In 1791, for example, the Hibernian Society saluted Lafayette, **Henry Grattan** (1746–1820), "the Irish patriot," and "the immortal memory of Dr. B. Franklin." It also recognised the president of the United States, the federal constitution, and "the Government and people of Pennsylvania." Other toasts saluted "universal toleration" and the aspiration

---

52 *Aurora*, 12 July 1796, 9 July 1798. For the symbols and rites of celebrating both the American and French Revolutions, see Newman, *Parades and the Politics of the Street*.
53 *Aurora*, 9 July 1798; Waldstreicher, *In the Midst of Perpetual Fetes*, 65, 114–5, 89; *Aurora*, 7 July 1795.

that "the distressed sons of Hibernia [might] come to a speedy knowledge of this land of freedom – and may they crowd our shores." As a report of a St. Patrick's Day meeting in New York in 1789 put it,

> Many of those present doubtless experienced those sensations, which piety towards their former country must have excited; but all must have acknowledged the liberality of that land, which is willing to receive, and to convert into free Americans, the worthy natives of every region.[54]

Such celebrations thus tried to bridge the old and the new, the elite and non-elite, and the familiarities of the past and uncharted waters of the future. To this extent, as John Brooke has put it, they were part of "a counter public sphere" in which "the contest for power" sat easily with "the creation of culture." However, although they were effective only when what Sacvan Bercovitch has called the societies' "rites of assent" were not contested, this was not an "unthinking" process. As Albrecht Koschnik has suggested,

> political ritual in the early republic played a paradoxical role. Celebrations expressed factional conflict, but simultaneously denied that conflict by pointing to the consensus among participants, by describing the participants as representative of the community (a description that excluded their respective political opponents), and by attempting to subsume conflict under an all-encompassing ideal of national unity. In the end, political conflict and group consensus fed off each other.

The inevitable challenges were down to how these public occasions were presented and managed by Philadelphia's ethno-cultural societies. They were also influenced by the impact of the "new Irish" after 1783. These arrivals were less cautious than their colonial cousins about their behaviour and began to keep their national day in a more flamboyant manner than the Friendly Sons had done during the previous decades. There was more "hilarity and festivity" and occasionally, as the *Pennsylvania Evening Herald* reported in 1787, "it is to be lamented, that shameful excesses and customs prevail, more among certain classes on that day [17 March], than has been observed in the celebration of the Festivals of other nations." In 1785 the same newspaper reported that "several riots" had taken place on St. Patrick's Day during which "the mobility" had caused "black eyes, broken noses, [and] cut heads, with all the other insignia of club-law battles." One newspaper even proposed that "plentiful dose[s] of

54 *VEP*, 13 May 1784; *IG*, 9 Apr. 1791; *NYDG*, 18 Mar. 1789. The reference to "elegant dinners" is taken from the *Providence Gazette*, 1 Apr. 1769, with respect to the St. Patrick's day celebrations of that year in Philadelphia.

Shillelah" were becoming so common that a society should be founded "to suppress, or even totally prevent" the festivities and in the process, to "preserve" the Irish community from "the odium" which such "riotous and unlawful proceedings" were attracting. While most people did not take this kind of advice very seriously, they felt that ethno-cultural societies should conduct themselves in ways that would not attract too much attention to their European backgrounds. However, the "new" societies of the 1790s did not see anything unusual or disloyal about celebrating the old world on their own terms.[55]

Many of the songs that were composed for St. Patrick's Day also recalled Ireland's past glories, as well as present troubles, in a more robust way. So did the toasts that were given at festive dinners. By 1793 the Hibernians had moved from the relatively innocuous recognition of "the land of Shil[leh]ah" to salute "all who arm in the cause of the Rights of Man." The "cause" of Ireland was also linked with the fate of Revolutionary France and this became more assertive as many Irishmen saw events in Europe as a vehicle to help establish a republic in Ireland. Within five years the Society of the United Irishmen promoted these sentiments on both sides of the Atlantic. On St. Patrick's Day 1799 six of the seventeen toasts related to various aspects of the movement "and the army of martyrs to Irish liberty." Most Federalists regarded such resolutions as "un-American" and hardly a recommendation of the Irish as "good citizens." However, as Marilyn Baseler has pointed out, "the ramifications of the French Revolution [had] destroyed Federalist confidence in the benefits to be derived from foreign-born subjects" once and for all. By behaving in a more assertive manner, many such Irish-born "subjects" had rejected the myth of consensus and no longer saw anything un-American in contesting the symbols of American republicanism. Thus, no less than with their increasing involvement in party politics, and especially in Jeffersonian republicanism, their "rites of assent" were becoming more qualified.[56]

55 Waldstreicher, *In the Midst of Perpetual Fetes*, 14; Brooke, "Ancient Lodges and Self-Created Societies," 316, 281; Albrecht Koschnik, "Political Conflict and Public Contest: Rituals of National Celebration in Philadelphia, 1788–1815," *PMHB* cxviii, no.3 (July 1994), 210; *PEH*, 15 Mar. 1786, 17 Mar. 1787, 19 Mar., 1785, 15 Mar. 1786. Bercovitch is quoted from Waldsteicher, *In the Midst of Perpetual Fetes*, 9. For the early history of the St. Patrick's Day celebrations, see James Crimmins, *Early History of St. Patrick's Day* (New York, 1902). For a view on how similar festivities influenced aspects of contemporary Ireland, see Jacqueline Hill, "National Festivals, the State and 'Protestant Ascendancy' in Ireland, 1790–1829," *IHS* xxiv (1984–5), 30–51.

56 *IG*, 31 Mar. 1792; *ADA*, 19 Mar. 1793; *Aurora*, 20 Mar. 1799; Baseler, *Asylum for Mankind*, 243. For commemorative "odes," see for example, those published in *NYJ*, 17 Mar. 1788 (which lauded the record of Irishmen on the battlefield) and *IG*, 17 Mar. 1789 which mentions the sigificance of "shamaracks."

An Evolving Party System

After 1783 Philadelphia's immigrants also began to debate and contest political arrangements more keenly than they had done before. However, they did so in a political environment that in many ways, continued to reflect the colonial past. One of the state's first federal senators, William Maclay, even suggested that older networks had been merely rearranged after 1776 as "many revolutionists ... wished for the loaves and fishes of government," now that the "diadem and sceptre" had passed from London to Philadelphia. Pennsylvania's first gubernatorial election in 1790 reflected this kind of political culture and was largely a personal rather than an ideological contest between two prominent Federalists. It was also about clientilism. Some two years after **Thomas Mifflin** (1744–1800) had been elected as governor, one of his critics stated that in the next election, he would support **Frederick Augustus Muhlenberg** (1750–1801) because Mifflin did not manage "an open and candid distribution of offices". The process of selecting candidates also had a familiar ring to it. Although the relevant caucuses were supposedly more open after 1790, the reality was somewhat different, at least until the middle of the decade. On 20 September 1792 the Federalists proposed to hold a state-wide conference to pick candidates for the forthcoming congressional elections. The "conferees" were to be chosen at popularly-convened county meetings, the object of which was to suggest that "every motive, every pretext, for party, is at an end." But these meetings simply ratified candidates who had already been "clandestinely" chosen by "a set class ... [of] arbitrary nabobs ... [and] by private letters directed to none but the well-born junto." As a result, the *Aurora* concluded that the "conferees" were as elitist as their colonial predecessors: "*men* and not *measures* are the object."[57]

The emergence of a new Republican interest was no different. In September 1792 the *General Advertiser* reported that the Republicans had written to 520 "impartial and respectable Citizens" and asked them to choose delegates who might pick suitable candidates for the forthcoming elections. However, the decision on the slate was made in fact by the Republican leadership in "a secret conference." The paper also alleged that even some of the leaders were not happy with this and tried to overturn what had been decided. "A Plebeian" thus suggested that

---

57 Maclay ed., *Journal of William Maclay*, 12; Tinkcom, *Federalist and Republicans*, 33–44, 135; *ADA*, 14 Aug. 1793, 27, 31 July 1792; *NG*, 15 Sept. 1792; *GA*, 9 Aug. 1792. For the 1790 and 1793 gubernatorial elections, see respectively, "A Republican" in *IG*, 25 Sept. 1790; and Baumann, "Democratic Republicans of Philadelphia," 337.

> Whether the [selection] mode [is] by conference, or that by committee of correspondence ... the minority get the power into their own hands, by being united in opinion, and gaining some of the majority, for the day of the election hastening, prevents the majority who would wish to think for themselves, of fixing upon a ticket, and therefore dividing their interest throws the balance of power into the hands of the designing few.

Accordingly, the routes by which candidates came before the public were not dissimilar and this explains why Adams saw the 1792 elections in Pennsylvania as between "clashing grandees."[58]

It was inevitable that electoral tickets would coincide to some degree, a reminder that faction was still strong and party immature. In 1792 several partly overlapping tickets were published for Philadelphia's five seats in the state assembly. There were no major surprises at the result although Swanwick who was associated with the rising Republican, or "Rights of Man" interest, was elected over a Federalist favourite, William Lewis (1752–1819). For Congress, seven of the thirteen candidates were common to the two principal published tickets and may explain why "An Elector" complained that "inattention to elections for members of the Legislature too generally prevails." Although the Federalists won all the city's congressional seats, Coxe observed that their list "contained some representatives of an opposition sentiment" while that of the Republicans was a combination of moderate Federalist and "anti-government" names. Noting a proposed ticket in August 1792, another commentator wrote in the *Aurora* that "I abominate distinctions of every kind, unless, as I said before; they are the *solid* distinctions of fortune, or perhaps of family."[59] It was only a matter of time before such traditional views of the polity and public representatives would alter. Integral to this process were the changing ways in which candidates were characterised. As "An Elector" suggested in February 1792, it was "not improper" as candidates presented themselves for election, "to make some enquiry into their respective qualifications." "Another Elector"

---

58 *GA*, 24, 5 Sept. 1792; Walters, "Origins of the Jeffersonian Party in Pennsylvania," 445; *NG*, 18 Aug. 1792. Adams is quoted from Baumann, "Democratic Republicans of Philadelphia," 703.

59 Miller, *Philadelphia*, 48; *ADA*, 5 Dec., 11 Feb. 1792; and "A Federalist," "To the Independent Electors of Pennsylvania. Citizens and Friends (Philadelphia, 1792)" in *GA*, 27 Aug. 1792. The tickets for the city election were published in *ADA*, 9 Oct. 1792 and the results in *ibid.*, 22 Oct. 1792. Coxe is quoted in Miller, *Philadelphia*, 47. For a discussion of the relative merits of the candidates for office in Philadelphia, see the broadside by "Hambden," "To the Freemen of the City of Philadelphia;" and *ADA*, 11, 13 Feb. 1792. For the 1792 elections, see Walters, "Origins of the Jeffersonian Party," 440–58; Alan Nevins, *The American States during and after the Revolution* (New York, 1924), 295; and Baumann, "Democratic Republicans of Philadelphia," 239–40, 379–80.

observed that such a "task is not a pleasing one." Perhaps because of such reticence, candidate descriptions were usually presented in generic terms of experience, age, and ability. As one observer suggested, "it requires time to qualify a man for the arduous task of legislation and to give him a facility in public speaking." A candidate's honour and "integrity" were also often mentioned as were his service during the American Revolution, proven "whig principles," and the support of "numerous and respectable class[es] of citizens." As the published support of public caucuses and meetings became more common during the 1790s, they became increasingly personalised and inevitably, an agency of polarisation.[60]

These activities are usually, if somewhat vaguely, used to suggest "the rise of the first party system," a process which also saw foreign policy inform the nature and direction of domestic policy. Differences between Thomas Jefferson and John Adams were well known. However, even after Jefferson's criticisms of Adams's views of the French Revolution were published without his permission in May 1791, Jefferson suggested to the vice-president that "you and I differ on the best form of government [and] is well known to us both, but we have differed as friends should do, respecting the purity of each other's motives, and confining our differences to private conversation." Adams's reply is also instructive for the evolution of a different type of polity: he had not realised that they had "differed" at all. Although, as Elkins and McKittrick have pointed out, this kind of *politesse* had a long history, and was famously celebrated by Madison in *The Federalist*, it could not last. In March 1792 one commentator suggested that the governing Federalists were "bewitched & perverted" by contemporary Britain while others predicted that they would introduce an aristocracy and "hierarchical establishments" into America and, in the manner of the British monarchy, make the office of president "for life first, and then hereditary." Freneau criticised the increasing level of ceremonial which surrounded Washington's presidency as a "forerunn[er of] Monarchy and Aristocracy in the United States." Recording his attendance at one of Washington's levees, Maclay observed that "The practice however is considered as a feature of Royalty, is certainly Anti-republican ... [and] this escapes Nobody." Jefferson also reflected these sentiments when he wrote that

> In place of that noble love of liberty and republican government which carried us triumphantly through the war, an Anglican Monarchical and Aristocratical party has sprung up, whose avowed object is to draw over us the substance, as they have already done the forms, of the British Government.

60 *ADA*, 11, 13, 11, 14 Feb. 1792. A candidate's desired characteristics were quoted of Muhlenberg in *GA*, 11 Apr. 1793 and *ADA*, 14 Aug. 1792, respectively.

Jefferson believed that Britain still harboured a "deeprooted" hatred of America and that "nothing is wanting with her but the power to wipe us out of existence" and regain her "lost colonies." Such fears contrasted with his respect for France whose assistance during the Revolution he never forgot. Even in Ireland, similar views were not uncommon. In 1794 John Chambers informed Carey that

> some people [in Ireland] are angry at her [America] Apparent indifference towards the affairs of France, & accuse her of more than political ingratitude ... the number is not small who think they see a very strong British Influence over your Federal Government ... your drawing so near and cordially to England does not look well, and alarms the sensible and observant friends to general freedom.[61]

From Philadelphia, George Hammond, told his secretary of state, Lord Grenville, in 1793 that "publications daily appear ... insisting on the gratitude due from America to the people of France, and asserting the existence of a connection between the cause of liberty in that country and this." These newspapers usually supported Jefferson and included the *General Advertiser*, founded in October 1790 by **Benjamin Franklin Bache** (1769–98), and renamed the *Aurora* on 8 November 1794, and Freneau's *National Gazette* (founded in October 1791). Two others took a different view of events and supported the Federalists: the *Gazette of the United States* (founded in April 1789) and *Porcupine's Gazette* (founded in March 1792), edited by John Ward Fenno and William Cobbett, respectively. Whatever their biases, between them, these newspapers created a litany of political "buzz-words" which in the "blunt, vulgar language" of "the people," helped to create what Norman Blantz has

61 Elkins and McKittrick, *Age of Federalism*, 263–70; "Brutus" in *NG*, 15 Mar. 1792; Sisson, *The American Revolution of 1800*, 135; "Mirabeau" in *NG*, 12 Dec. 1792; Jefferson to Mazzei, 24 Apr. 1796 in Lipscomb, ed., *Jefferson's Works* ix, 335–6; Sisson, *Revolution of 1800*, 130; HSP, Lea & Febiger Collection, Incoming Correspondence (1785–96), box 4, James Chambers Folder (1792–1796), Chambers to Carey, 26 Mar. 1794. Maclay is quoted from Newman, "Principles or Men? George Washington and the Political Culture of National Leadership, 1776–1801," 486, and the Jefferson-Adams exchanges in Elkins and McKittrick, *Age of Federalism*, 238. The feared evolution of "hierarchical establishments" is discussed in Louise Burnham Dunbar, "A Study of 'Monarchical' Tendencies in the United States from 1776 to 1801," *University of Illinois Studies in the Social Sciences* x (1922), no.2. For an analysis of some of the more important political writings on the topic, see Marshall Smelser, "The Federalist Period as an Age of Passion," *AQ* x (1958), 391–419. For the views of Americans, including Jefferson, on France and the French Revolution, see Charles D. Hazen, *Contemporary American Opinion of the French Revolution* (Baltimore, 1897), 1–53; Bernard Faÿ, *The Revolutionary Spirit in France and America* (New York, 1927); and the letters of "Aratus" in *NG*, 14, 24 Nov. and 12 Dec. 1791.

termed "the political phenomenon of factions emerging as parties," especially during and after 1792. This is not surprising if one considers the determination of both Jefferson and Madison to establish the *National Gazette* and to counter Fenno's promotion of the "doctrines of monarchy, aristocracy, & the exclusion of the influence of the people." Thus, as "Hancock" observed in September 1795

> Even the common cant language of the ministerial agents of Great Britain, has been naturalized here [in Philadelphia] by the idolaters of the President, and the friends to the Constitution and enemies in usurpation, are in ministerial jargon, denominated *jacobins, disorganisers, democrats, levellers, traitors, rabble and mob*.[62]

These developments highlighted the increasingly important role of the press in the evolution of a more critical political culture especially where, as "Sidney" put it in January 1793, there were "many occurrences, properly within the sphere of public representation, on which the people cannot express their sentiments, by their representatives." For "Sidney," the press was not only "a means of diffusing useful knowledge" but "a check" on "the conduct of public servants ... which may be particularly beneficial in many cases, which no other constitutional remedy can reach." Thus, it was vital that it should "continue free ... [and] never be conducted by those who through factious or selfish views would sacrifice religion, morality, or their country." However, the 1790s saw the press become less altruistic and more partisan, a point captured in a toast given on 4 July 1796: "Immortality to the freedom of the press and Destruction to its venality." Two years later the Adams administration tried to curb the press to its own ends through the Sedition Act as one meeting on 4 July of that year saluted "The liberty of the press" and vainly hoped that "every attempt to abridge it, [might] be as ineffectual, as it is unconstitutional."[63]

The presidency, the original symbol of a united country, also began to lose its lustre during the 1790s. Before 1793 most Americans had been slow to criticise Washington. As Elkins and McKittrick have put it, the president was "the living symbol of non-partisan politics, [and] was an almost ideal republican

---

62 *British State Papers*, 10 June 1793, as quoted in Arthur Irving Bernstein, "The Rise of the Democratic-Republican Party in New York City, 1789–1800" (Ph.D. dissertation, Columbia University, 1964), 115; Miller, *Philadelphia*, 93; Norman Blantz, "Editors and Issues," 4; Elkins and McKittrick, *Age of Federalism*, 240; *Aurora*, 12 Sept. 1795.

63 *GA*, 23 January 1793; *Aurora*, 11 Oct. 1795, 12 July 1796, 9 July 1798. For wider discussion of the importance of newspapers in the formation of party, see Jeffrey L. Pasley, *"The Tyranny of Printers:" Newspaper Politics in the Early American Republic* (Charlottesville, 2001); and Robert W.T. Martin, *The Free and Open Press: The Founding of American Democratic Press Liberty, 1640–1800* (New York, 2001).

embodiment of the Patriot King." Even Adams observed during the debates on the federal constitution that "some of our members [were] disposed to idolise an image which their own hands have molten. I speak here of the superstitious veneration which is paid to General Washington." It may have been that Washington's future vice-president would "honour him for his good qualities" but as an elected member of the Continental Congress, he could still "feel myself his superior." However, that was in private. In public, it was not until 1793 that Freneau and Bache challenged Washington, the former suggesting that by not consulting Congress before he issued the Proclamation on Neutrality, the president had behaved in an arbitrary manner and was being buoyed by the "opiate of sycophancy." Washington was far from amused and in June 1793 wrote that "The publications in Freneau's and Bache's papers are outrages on common decency." In 1795 and 1796 Bache and Duane also published a number of pamphlets which portrayed Washington, in the words of the former, as a "mediocre general and a President who sanctioned monarchy and corruption." In 1795 Tone suggested to his friend Thomas Russell (1767–1803) in Belfast that it was "no longer a damnable heresy to doubt the infallibility of the President." The following year these attacks culminated in Paine's vitriolic address in which he argued that the president "had debauched the nation" and asked "whether you are an apostate or an imposter; whether you have abandoned good principles, or whether you ever had any." On Independence Day 1796 one newspaper writer pointedly asked Americans how long they would "suffer themselves to be *awed* by *one* man?" The mockeries of Washington, Hamilton, Adams, and other public figures were such that the *Gazette of the United States* suggested that a stranger would think that "the worst men in the country had crept into office during the first years under the Constitution." Such criticisms of eminent men influenced many of the public, including recent Irish immigrants who themselves had left behind a country that was in political and social turmoil. Others were attracted by the new Republican slogans, especially when they criticised the supposedly pro-British leanings and culture of the Federalist administration.[64]

64 Elkins and McKittrick, *Age of Federalism*, 266; Blantz, "Editors and Issues," 168; Thomas Paine, *Remarks Occasioned by the late Conduct of Mr. Washington as President of the United States*, as quoted in John R. Howe, "Republican Thought and the Political Violence of the 1790s," *AQ*, xix (1967), 149; *GUS*, 25 Feb. 1792. Adams is quoted from *The Autobiography of Benjamin Rush*, ed. George W. Conner (Princeton, 1948), 141; and Freneau (1793) and Washington in Stewart, *Opposition Press of the Federalist Period*, 147 and 521, respectively. The quotation from the celebrations of Independence Day 1796 is quoted from Stewart, *The Opposition Press*, 526–7. In addition to Paine's pamphlet, Jasper Wright [William Duane], *A Letter to George Washington* (Philadelphia, 1796) was also very critical of Washington's record as a public servant. See also Newman, "Principles or Men," 477–508. For Tone's comments, see his letter dated from

The mission to the United States of the French minister Edmond Genet (1793), the formation of the Democratic Society of Pennsylvania (1793), and the debates on Jay's treaty (1795–96) were also important signposts of political change. Genet arrived in Philadelphia on 16 May 1793, nearly one month after Washington had announced that the United States would remain neutral in the developing war between Britain and France. He was greeted by a large gathering at the State House and presented with a formal address. This memorial highlighted many themes of American republicanism and stressed that every citizen had the right to take part in public life, regardless of economic or social status. In a separate presentation to Genet two days later, the German Republican Society reinforced these views and suggested that it was "high time that they [Germans] should step forward, declare themselves independent of other influences, and think for themselves." Later, a call was issued to

> all able bodied seamen who are willing to engage in the cause of Liberty, and in the service of the French Republic ... Particular attention will be paid to the generous and intrepid natives of Ireland, who, it is presumed, will act like those warlike troops from that oppressed country, who took refuge in France.[65]

Between May and July 1793, Philadelphia saw so many pro-Genet meetings that even Genet remarked that the "voice of the people continues to neutralise the declaration of neutrality." Adams later recalled that "day after day," demonstrators had tried to compel Washington to declare war on Britain and "in favour of the French Revolution." As some Philadelphians celebrated the important dates of the French revolutionary calendar and the successes of the French armies, there was also an increase in what Alexander Graydon termed "*sans culotte* foolery" as they went about the city with chopped hair and in pantaloons, addressing each other as "citizens" and "citesses." As a result,

---

Philadelphia, 1 Sept. 1795, as in Bartlett, ed., *Life and Times of Theobald Wolfe Tone*, 451. For Washington's bitterness at newspaper coverage of his actions, and the ways in which these influenced his decision to retire from public office, see Elkins and McKittrick, *Age of Federalism*, 496–7 et passim. For the particular role of the *Aurora* in these matters, see ibid., 859, n.39.

65 *GA*, 16 May 1793; *GUS*, 17 May 1793; *NG*, 22 May 1793; *ADA*, 18, 20 May 1793; LC, Pennsylvania Broadsides, "They Steer to Liberty's Shore" (August 1793), 132. For the reception of Genet in Philadelphia, see also Faÿ, *Two Franklins*, 176–81; and Elkins and McKittrick, *Age of Federalism*, 342–3. The address from the German Republican Society is discussed in Link, *Democratic-Republican Societies*, 6–8. For general analysis of contemporary American foreign policy, see Charles S. Hyneman, *The First American Neutrality: A Study of Neutral Obligations during the Years 1792 to 1815* (Philadelphia, 1974).

William Bradford stated that "parties run very high [in Philadelphia] ... scarce any man can escape [without] ranking himself under, or in opposition to, the Genet Faction." He might have added that as Genet's visit energised public debate on the national and international issues of the day, it encouraged a political vocabulary which also fed the growing sense of ethno-cultural identity among groups such as the Germans and Irish. The "new politics" and the evolution of a more assertive and wider public sphere were inseparable.[66]

During 1793 the shape of politics was also influenced by the outbreak of yellow fever which, between 19 August and 15 November, caused the deaths of an estimated 45,000 people in the city. Although a health committee was put in place to manage relief on a non-partisan basis, its concerns soon became politicised, splitting on many of its more important concerns, including how best to treat those who became infected and why the pestilence had broken out in the first place. Most Philadelphia Federalists had no doubt that the fever was a "foreign disease" and as such, they used the tragedy to associate immigration with an alleged health threat to the nation's capital. To this extent, as Martin S. Pernick has pointed out, given that Philadelphia was "the medical capital of the United States," what Alan Kraut has called "the medicalization of politics" now evolved as an aspect of the rise of the first party system. This was especially so after differences became personalised between "Philadelphia's lone confessed Federalist physician," Dr. Edward Stevens, on the one hand, and Dr. Benjamin Rush, on the other. Moreover, as each of these doctors gathered testimonials from national figures, even if these were issued for political rather than scientific reasons, the debate on yellow fever in Philadelphia became part of the wider discourse on party, especially so after Alexander Hamilton chose to polarise what had initially been a "non-partisan jumble."[67]

66 Harry Ammon, *The Genet Mission* (New York, 1973), 55; Adams to Jefferson, 30 June 1813 in Adams, *Adams Works* x, 47; Graydon, *Memoirs of a Life*, 335; HSP, Wallace Papers, Bradford to Boudinot, 7 June 1793. For the use of the terms "citizen" and "citess," see *NG*, 30 Jan. and 23 Mar., 1793; for the wearing of the cockade, see *ADA*, 23 May 1793. The impact of Genet's visit on the changing nature and extent of public celebration in contemporary Philadelphia is also discussed in C.D. Hazen, "The French Revolution as Seen by the Americans of the Eighteenth Century," *Report of the American Historical Association* (1895), 455–66.

67 Martin C. Pernick, "Politics, Parties, and Pestilence: Epidemic Yellow Fever in Philadelphia and the Rise of the First Party System," *WMQ* xxix (1972), 559, 566, 560; Alan M. Kraut, "Illness and medical Care among Irish Immigrants in Antebellum New York" in Richard H. Baylor and Timothy J. Meager, eds., *The New York Irish* (Baltimore, 1996), 167; Pernick, "Politics, Parties, and Pestilence," 563, 574. For the general points discussed in this and the subsequent paragraphs, see Pernick, "Politics, Parties, and Pestilence," 559–87. I am grateful to David Doyle for bringing these references to my attention.

Differences between Federalist and Republican on the origins of the fever were almost immediately applied to electoral politics when the city's esteemed former mayor, Samuel Powel (1739–93), died during the fever epidemic, causing a vacancy in the state senate. On 12 December Philadelphia's Republicans nominated **Israel Israel** (1743–1822) to fill the vacancy as a man "whose philanthropy on a late melancholy occasion is well known, and whose firm and steady attachment to the people will, it is hoped, bring forth the united sufferings of the citizens in his favour." Israel belonged to the Democratic Society, of which he was vice-president. He was also an active member of the health committee and although he had been widely praised for his commitments to it, there was a fear that his good name and reputation might be used to develop the political presence of Jeffersonian republicanism in Philadelphia. The Federalists nominated William Bingham. However, although Bingham had sat out the epidemic from the comfort of his home in New Jersey, he was elected on 19 December with 62% of the vote. The contest had been far from clean. There had been allegations about the expenses and "arrogance" of the health committee and its members, one even suggesting that Rush had enriched himself from his treatments. Fears were also expressed that the committee might assume the role of duly elected bodies such as the guardians of the poor. Such concerns became all the keener because many felt that the committee reflected the social agendas of the emerging Republican organisation in Philadelphia. In 1794, for example, the health committee recommended that there should be an annual tax to maintain, educate, and apprentice orphans who had been "left by the late calamity." In any event, with Israel's defeat, the growing differences between the two parties were postponed rather than resolved. They would resurface in November 1797 when another by-election which also saw Israel carry the Republican banner during another outbreak of yellow fever, revisited many of the issues, as well as intensified the partisan atmosphere in which they were discussed.[68]

In 1794 differences between Federalist and Republican continued during the Congressional elections when, to the astonishment of all parties," and in what Madison termed a "stinging change for the aristocracy," Swanwick defeated the Federalist incumbent, **Thomas Fitzsimons** (1789–94), by 1240 votes to 1180. Despite a description of the contest as between the "Rights of the People," on the one hand, and "the advocate[s] for hereditary power and distinctions," on the other, there was much that was traditional about the election, including an ambiguity about the new congressman's political ideology, of which Adams wrote that "Swanwick may be for anything that I know as federal as his Rival."

68 Pernick, "Politics, Parties, and Pestilence, 582, 583; Miller, *Philadelphia*, 57–8; *GA*, 18 Mar. 1794.

Swanwick's selection as a candidate had been so tightly controlled that even the *General Advertiser* observed that "little time [would] remain after the result of this [nomination] meeting is obtained, to take any measures to counteract or modify that result." Moreover, his victory was less a vote *for* Swanwick "on his own merits" than *against* Fitzsimons and, in particular, against his support for duties on loaf sugar, snuff and liquor. Fitzsimons had made few efforts to answer his critics, sharing Coxe's "disinclin[ation] to the irritations and servility of personal politics." Of the election of 1790 he had already observed that

> for my own part, I should deem them [the candidates] unworthy of the station [office] *if they would stoop to solicit it* … if their fellow citizens think them the most eligible … they ought to give the one most fitting their suffrages. I should hope either of them had as many personal friends as would do all that was necessary in recommending them.[69]

In a similar vein, the *Gazette of the United States* observed four years later that the "established mode of electioneering" was still one where

> the friends of the candidates were satisfied to use their influence, *in private* amongst their own particular friends; whilst the objects of their choice observing a reserve and decorum, evinced a becoming respect for public opinion and permitted it to take its own direction without an unfair bias.

Such ambivalence was not Swanwick's recipe for success and, as he saw it, he would refuse to "practice any genteel hypocrisy" in how he campaigned. As a result, Federalists attacked him because he was "the first to move forward in [a] new style." For example, Cobbett recalled that the first time that Swanwick had "commended my notice" was

> when on the State-house ground in Philadelphia, he canvassed for a seat in the State legislature. This was an unusual sight: in all the elections for thirty

69 Madison to Jefferson, 16 Nov. 1794, as quoted in Martin I.J. Griffin, *Thomas Fitzsimons* (Philadelphia, 1887), 19; Miller, *Philadelphia*, 70, 58–60; HSP, U.C. Smith-William Jones Correspondence, Samuel Clark to Jones, 15 Oct. 1794; Miller, *Philadelphia*, 58–60; John to Abigail Adams, as quoted in Baumann, "John Swanwick: Spokesman for 'Merchant-Republicanism' in Philadelphia," 165; *GA*, 14 Oct. 1794; HSP, Wallace Papers ii, William Bradford to Elias Boudinot, 27 Oct. 1794; HSP, Tench Coxe Papers (microfilm), reel 61, Coxe to Francis Corban, 8 Nov. 1794; HSP, Gratz Collection, Old Congress, case 1, box 5, Fitzsimons to Rush, 12 May 1790. For the nominations of Swanwick and Fitzsimons for Congress, see *GUS*, 9 , 13 Oct. 1794. For the results of the tally, see *GUS*, 12 Nov. 1794. Statistics of the Pennsylvania elections of the 1790s are also cited in J.R. Pole, "Election Statistics in Pennsylvania, 1790–1840," *PMHB* lxxxii (1958), 217–20. For comment on the merits of the two candidates, see the letters from "Z" and "Civis" in *GUS*, 13 Oct. 1794.

years preceding I had never once seen a candidate, passing off his own ticket. In that space of time I had known some ambitious men, and many weak ones, solicitous for seats in the legislature, but modesty or some other old fashioned virtue generally kept them from the ground on the day of election, or if they attended, it was only as spectators, leaving it to their friends and well-wishers to take care of their interest. How shall we account for this novelty? Shall we suppose him vain enough to think himself above the common rules of decorum, or stupid enough to despise them?[70]

In any event, Swanwick and Fitzsimons were such different types of people that a sharp contest was inevitable. Fitzsimons was a member of both the elite Friendly Sons of St. Patrick and the "aristocratic junto" which had run Philadelphia for several years. Swanwick was neither. Although, as Elkins and McKittrick have observed, he was "among the richest men in North America," he was still seen as an *arriviste*. As such, he appealed to the outsiders of the city who were seeking to become insiders. Moreover, Swanwick's more combative electoral methods, including an effective use of rhetoric, was taken as pandering to the "awakened democracy" and giving it a hold over public representatives that was an anathema to the city's established political culture. "It is not in a croud [*sic*]," warned one observer, "that the small voice of reason is held." Nonetheless, Swanwick courted groups such as Irish immigrants who were emerging within the local polity at the time and his successful campaign established what were to be the most enduring pockets of Jeffersonian strength in Philadelphia: the settlements of the "new Irish" in the city's northern and southern Liberties as well as the socially peripheral wards of North and South Mulberry. Both before and after his election, Swanwick attended a number of public festivals which toasted an "Injured Ireland" while contemporary broadsides such as that addressed "To the Men of Ireland" (Philadelphia, 1794) repeated the "ills" that Britain had heaped on Ireland. Swanwick understood the significance of these ethno-cultural commemorations and how important they were, especially to those who had recently arrived in America. Whereas Fitzsimons had proposed "reprobating and stigmatizing 'self-created societies'," Swanwick associated himself with them, most notably with The Philadelphia Society for the Information and Assistance of Emigrants, of which he was sometime president. He also called for retaliation against Britain for its mistreatment of neutral American vessels on the high seas. These calls were tough and uncompromising and helped to revive anti-British slogans as

---

70 *GUS*, 7, 11, 13 Oct. 1794; Cobbett, *Tit for Tat, or, a Purge for a Pill*, 20. Representing himself as "Dick Retort," Cobbett wrote of Swanwick's election that "in all the elections for thirty years preceding, I have never once seen a candidate pressing his own ticket;" see *Tit for Tat*, 28.

expressions of political protest in the United States. They also linked the evolving political language of the supporters of Jefferson with the ethno-cultural vocabulary of the "new Irish" in a common cause against the supposed corruption and despotism of the British government. In this, Swanwick's campaign proved to be the harbinger of a new phase of political culture in Philadelphia, not least because it suited the social as well as the political underpins of Jeffersonian republicanism.[71]

"Self-Created Societies"

The clearest indication of coming change in public opinion came with the creation of the *German Republican Society of Philadelphia* (founded in April 1793) and the *Democratic Society of Pennsylvania* (founded in May/June 1793). The former was established to promote an informed, independent and virtuous citizenry and to guard "against every encroachment on the equality of freemen." Some weeks later, after the arrival of Genet on 18 May, the Democratic Society was founded with more explicit objectives to support "The Rights of Man ... [and] the legitimate principles of Government, [which] have been closely developed by the successive Revolutions of America and France." The pairing of the two revolutions was to be expected, as was the extended hope that French "arms [might] henceforth be ... successful in giving freedom" to the "patriotic citizens" of Ireland, Holland, and Poland, and that "remembrance" of the actions of "the martyrs in the cause of American independence ... [might] inspire us with a firm resolution to transmit to posterity that freedom for which they fought and bled."[72]

While these declared aims provided the two societies with concise statements of mission, their recognition of universal liberty also led them to stress what was common to all as well as the hope that in their evolving republic, "the

71 Miller, *Philadelphia*, 62–3; Elkins and McKittrick, *Age of Federalism*, 459, 520–1; *GUS*, 27 Oct. 1794; Miller, *Philadelphia*, 58–60; *Aurora*, 12 July 1796, 24 Dec. 1794. For the quoted broadside, see Link, *Democratic-Republican Societies*, 88–9. See also Baumann, "John Swanwick," 161–66. For Fitzsimons and the "junto," see Ethel E. Rasmusson, "Democratic Experiment — Aristocratic Aspiration," *PMHB* xc (1966), 163–4. For further discussion of the generic themes discussed in this paragraph, see also Thomas P. Govan, "The Rich, the Well Born, and Alexander Hamilton," *MVHS* xxxvi (1949–50), 675–80.
72 German Republican Society of Philadelphia, "To Friends and Fellow Citizens, April 11, 1793" as in Philip S. Foner, ed., *Democratic-Republican Societies, 1790–1800: A Documentary Sourcebook of Constitutions, Declarations, Addresses, Resolutions, and Toasts* (Westport, Conn., 1976), 54; *GA*, 31 July 1793; *Aurora*, 11 July 1795. Eugene Perry Link has estimated that forty six democratic societies were formed in the United States during 1793 and 1794; see his *Democratic-Republican Societies*, 13–15. Unless otherwise noted, "Democratic Society" refers to the Pennsylvania Society.

distinction of nation and of language, [would] be lost in the association of Freedom and Friendship, till the inhabitants of the various sections of the Globe shall be distinguished only by their virtues and their Talents." Even when the German Republican Society resolved to conduct its business in German because many of its constituents were "totally ignorant of the English language, and therefore ignorant of the most essential transactions of our government," it stressed, perhaps with more realism, that

> Being, in common with your brethren of other nations, but one people, we wish not to make national distinctions, but in so far as necessity may require; a kindred in language will necessarily draw men together, for we are as naturally inclined to those with whom we can hold communion in our own, as are distant from others, who are incapable of social intercourse with us from an ignorance of our language. – This will beget distinction, but as it is more the distinction of language than of nation, it will only remain until the English language shall become the mother tongue of every citizen in the state.

The Democratic Society also suggested that it was "unfettered by *religious* or *national* distinctions, unbiased by party and unmoved by ambition:"

> the *People of Pennsylvania* form but one indivisible community, whose political rights and interests, whose national honor and prosperity, must in degree and duration be forever the same; and, therefore, it is the duty of every freeman, and shall be the endeavour of the Democratic Society to remove the prejudices, to conciliate the affections, to enlighten the understanding, and to promote the happiness of all our fellow-citizens.[73]

Despite such proclaimed commitments to impartiality, the democratic societies were often seen as the mouthpieces of "French principles" and what for many, was an alternative interpretation of a republican order. On 9 January 1794 France was described as "our only true and natural ally." However, its fortunes were causing the Democratic Society "anxious concern, while she is greatly contending against a World, for the same rights which she assisted us to establish." It thus resolved to "view with inexpressible horror the cruel and unjust war carried on by the combined powers of Europe against the french republic." It also celebrated when this war was marked by French successes. On 1 May 1794, for example, the society organised a "civic festival" to mark "the

73 "Principles, Articles, and Regulations, Agreed upon, Drawn, and Adopted, May 30, 1793" as in Foner, ed., *Democratic-Republican Societies*, 64; German Republican Society of Philadelphia, "To Friends and Fellow Citizens, April 11, 1793" as in *ibid.*, 54; "Principles, Articles, and Regulations, Agreed upon, Drawn, and Adopted, May 30, 1793" as in *ibid.*, 65.

late glorious successes of the … French Democrats over the Royalists and Aristocrats associated for the purpose of expelling the Rights of Man from the World." Eight hundred people, including Pennsylvania's governor (1790–99), Thomas Mifflin and French diplomats, attended this event at "Democratic Hall," the country seat of the society's vice president, Israel Israel. Under the flags of France and the United States, toasts were given to "The Republic of France, one and indivisible," "The People of the United States," "the Franco-American alliance," the Republic of Genoa, "the constitution of the United States," the "Men of the People," "a Revolutionary Tribunal in Great Britain," "the armies of the French Republic," "the extinction of monarchy," "Reason," "Knowledge," "the fair daughters of America and France" and "the Democratic and Republican Societies of the United States." After all this, Jean Fauchet, the French minister to the United States (1794–96), was led back to the city to the accompaniment of music and song. Although the event had been attended by "several Officers of the Federal and State Governments," most Federalists regarded such behaviour as arrogant and suggested that the societies' celebration of "French principles," as well as the particular inter-pretation of republicanism which flowed from it, were neither compatible with loyalty to America nor in its best interests.[74]

To this extent, as in the 1760s, "foreign influence" in America was again being seen in the context of potential challenges to the single-interest paradigm. However, the Democratic Societies could not be ignored. They had committed themselves to "disseminating political knowledge" and giving the citizen the "natural privilege … to give his sentiments on all public measures." As the Democratic Society put it on 30 May 1793, the purpose was "to cultivate a just knowledge of rational Liberty, to facilitate the enjoyment and exercise of our civil Rights and to transmit, unimpaired, to posterity, the glorious inheritance of a *free Republican Government*." Over a year later the "Democratic asso-

---

74 Minutes of the Democratic Society, 9 Jan. 1794, as in Foner, ed., *Democratic-Republican Societies*, 69. For the civic festival, see Foner, ed., *Democratic-Republican Societies*, 102–3. Ascribing "French principles" to these societies is quite common in contemporary writing; the reference here is cited from "Anti-Club" in *GUS*, 23 Dec. 1794. The concept of the "associational world" has been taken from Peter Clark, *British Clubs and Societies, 1580–1800: The Origins of an Associational World* (Oxford, 2000), which also surveys the British background to the culture of the club. For a newer, and for many, a more "dangerous" type of society, see Michael L. Kennedy, *The Jacobin Clubs in the French Revolution. The First Years* (Princeton, 1982) and *The Middle Years* (Princeton, 1988). For the influence of clubs in promoting a more thoughtful public in contemporary Ireland, see Kevin Whelan, "The United Irishmen, the Enlightenment and Popular Culture" in Dickson, Keogh and Whelan, eds., *United Irishmen*, 269–95; and Nancy Curtin, "The Transformation of the Society of United Irishmen into a Mass-Based Revolutionary Organisation 1794–5," *IHS* xxiv (1985), 478–9.

ciations" were again saluted in the hope that they might "invariably possess discernment to applaud the virtuous, and spirit to arraign the corrupted officers of our government." They would thus encourage the freemen of Pennsylvania to "discuss without fear, the conduct of the public Servants, in every department of Government." As such, the societies convinced many public officials at city, state, and national levels, that they were setting themselves up not only as an "efficacious instrument" between government and people but to attack the *bona fide* of government itself. They would also resist "all attempts … to connect us more intimately with Great Britain" and obstruct "the progress of British influence in the United States [in that it] has endangered our happiness and Independence, that it has operated to make us tributary to Great Britain, and to engender systems and corruptions baneful to Liberty." However, as the societies sought to ensure that "Governmental misconduct" would not lead to "measures at enmity with our Constitution," they also seemed to have arrogated to themselves the discretion to decide who was or was not being true to "the glorious inheritance of the late Revolution," *as they understood it*. The fact that such resolutions were being adopted within the shifting circumstances of American foreign policy and related French, as opposed to English, interest in the United States and its republicanism, opened them to suspicion among Federalists. On 18 December 1794 the societies thus felt compelled to deny that

> They never have, as has been weakly advanced, attempted to usurp the powers of Government; they never did attempt to substitute their wishes for law; and never expected that their opinions would have more weight than their intrinsic merit demanded. They felt themselves, as a portion of the people, bound by the acts of the legal representatives of the whole, and ready with their lives and fortunes to maintain obedience to the laws; but the observance of this duty did not deprive them of the right of questioning their policy.[75]

Nonetheless, the reality was that the traditional "associational world" of sociability was developing a new role in civic society. This was often seen as

75 "Extract from the Minutes of the Democratic Society" as in *GA*, 10 Mar. 1794; (Democratic Society of Pennsylvania), "Principles, Articles, and Regulations, Agreed upon, Drawn, and Adopted, May 30, 1793" as in Foner, ed., *Democratic-Republican Societies*, 64; *GA*, 8 July 1794; Democratic Society of Pennsylvania, "Principles, Articles, and Regulations, Agreed upon, Drawn, and Adopted, May 30, 1793" as in Foner, ed., *Democratic-Republican Societies*, 64; (John Swanwick), *A Roaster; or, A Check to the Progress of Political Blasphemy* (Philadelphia, 1796), 7; minutes of the Democratic Society, 10 Apr. and 5 Jun. 1794, as in Foner, ed., *Democratic-Republican Societies*, 77; "The Democratic Society of Pennsylvania … to their Fellow Citizens … 18 December 1794" as in Foner, ed., *Democratic-Republican Societies*, 99.

inconsistent with its supposedly private *raisons d'être*. However, given their articulate and consistent attacks on the ideological, governmental, and political character of Federalist America, the democratic societies were often configured as an "improper influence" which was all the more troubling because they were evolving outside the conventional structures of contemporary politics and policy formation. Morever, as the role of opposition politics was still unclear, various writers to the *General Advertiser* saw these societies as mediators between government and society and as such, performing a role which, in itself, they saw as being perfectly compatible with a healthy republican society. As one of Bache's correspondents put it,

> If the laws of our Country are the echo[es] of the sentiments of the people, is it not of importance that those sentiments should be generally known? How can they be better understood than by a free discussion, publication, and communication of them by means of political societies?

After all, public officials should not assume that "public spirit and virtue are exclusively confined to themselves."[76]

Dispassion was easier to claim than to achieve because as Swanwick observed in 1795, the societies would not only "assert the majesty of the people" but would also be "vigilant in expunging the excesses of aristocracy, which spring up like weeds in every government." However, these were value judgements which could imply criticism of an older "natural leadership." They also suggested that there were alternative leaders who, if called upon to do so, were prepared to become more active in contemporary politics. After all, a virtuous polity could only be realised when there was an appropriate "choice of persons to fill the offices of government ... [and where] every citizen should act according to his own judgement" on the issues and political leadership of the day. Thus, few were surprised when, with an eye to the congressional elections of October 1794, the Democratic Society advised the public on 12 June "to deliberate and decide at the approaching elections, how far their Representatives are entitled to public confidence, by approving the good and dismissing the bad." It also helped to organise meetings and even advised its own members that it would do their "electioneering business" for them. By promoting the democratic societies as a reference point for virtue and republicanism and more pointedly, by linking these with particular events in the calendars of the French as well as the American revolutions, the societies both fed and fed off a changing public sphere and the emerging and multifaceted polity that would mould and

---

76 *GUS*, 4 Apr. 1794; *Aurora*, 27 Nov. 1794; minutes of the Democratic Society of Pennsylvania, 9 Oct. 1794, as in Foner, ed., *Democratic-Republican Societies*, 95.

lead it. It is not surprising that within a year of their establishment, these societies – and by association, some of the ethno-cultural societies discussed earlier – would be drawn into a more public debate on the nature and direction of the republican polity in America and criticised as being incompatible with its stability and harmony.[77]

Cobbett was among those who led the broadsides dismissing the leaders of the democratic societies as "men of [no] property, and such as were, owed their possessions to some casual circumstance, rather than to family, industry, or talents." Implicit in this view was the older notion that public representatives should be educated for leadership and be men of substance and "respectability." That the members of the democratic societies could be characterised as outsiders also introduced new elements into public ritual and, therefore, into its "metaphors of power," which could no longer be neatly accommodated within existing paradigms. The decision by the Democratic Society on 27 March 1794 to use the term "citizen" in all correspondence and "that all letters shall be dated from the Era of American Independence" underlined the challenge to the prevailing structures of power and authority. By adopting the term "citess," the society also implicitly recognised a new status for women within a wider polity. Thus, as Cobbett saw it, "the word *citizen* [became a] stalking-horse of modern liberty-men." It was but a short step from this to casting the societies as a kind of conspiracy. As "E.F." put it, where sovereignty rested in the people as a whole and where representatives were elected to govern for "the whole nation," no unelected club or society could supersede this by claiming a similar authority. Thus, "If our government is to be overturned, these societies are the best instruments to effect the work, [and] they can answer to no other purpose.[78]

In 1794 Edward Jennings Randolph developed the views of "E.F." in an influential series of thirteen letters. Writing as "Germanicus," he argued against "self-created societies … whose principle it is to condemn constitutional laws, or sap the confidence of the people in the government." Moreover, because they would "prepare, by the well concerted approaches of a *few*, to ensnare your affections, and thus become the directors of your power," there was no "propriety" in either "their *principle*" or actions. Instead, these societies were "baneful." As the *Gazette of the United States* saw it, they were not only "self-created centinels of liberty" which projected "a pompous display of wordy

77 John Swanwick, *A Rub from Snub, or a Cursory Analytical Epistle Addressed to Peter Porcupine* (Philadelphia, 1795), 41; *Aurora*, 11 July 1795; "Fellow Citizens," 12 Jun. 1794, as in Foner, ed., *Democratic-Republican Societies*, 86; *GA*, 17 July 1794.

78 [William Cobbett], *History of the American Jacobins* (Philadelphia, 1796), 22; Koschnik, "Political Conflict and Public Contest," 210–11; minutes of the Democratic Society, 27 Mar. 1794, as in Foner, ed., *Democratic-Republican Societies*, 74; Cobbett, *History of the American Jacobins* (Philadelphia, 1796), 24; "E.F." in *GUS*, 21 Jul. 1794.

patriotism" but "self-created clubs" of "private persons" which assumed, in the manner of an elected assembly, that they might engage in "offering addresses" to people like Genet or accuse Federal officials of an "amazing lack of republicanism." Cobbett had a similar difficulty with these societies. After all, as he saw it, "a political club, if it is not intended to strengthen the government, must be intended to act against it. The very foundation of such a club [as the Democratic Society] must imply a systematic opposition to the lawful rulers of the land."[79]

Cobbett's remark had been directed against the "mother club" of the democratic societies, the Democratic Society of Pennsylvania. However, it could also be taken as a challenge to other networks including the various "agricultural [and] mechanical ... associations" which had been established in Philadelphia to influence public policy in their respective areas. Although these societies had also been "self-created" in the sense that they had "no authority from the people," few could agree, even when sarcastically put, that they were "as dangerous to liberty, as literary societies are injurious to improvement." Even "Germanicus" accepted that there was no

> resemblance between societies, calculated to promote the energies of the soil by scientific culture; to abridge the dependence of the United States on foreign countries; and to acquire, if possible, a superiority by mechanism; ... and those, which labour to defeat the operation of the laws, and disseminate suspicions, jealousies, and accusations of the whole government?

However, the same could not be said of the democratic societies, especially when they became involved in politics or saw *themselves* as "the people." Indeed, as one writer put it in the *General Advertiser*, it was only a matter of time before such organisations, "however pure and well-intentioned ... in their commencement," would presume "to dictate as a body." This is precisely what Washington accused them of doing in September 1794 when he suggested that they had provoked the **Whiskey Rebellion** in western Pennsylvania. In his sixth annual message to Congress on 19 November 1794, he repeated these sentiments as follows:

> In the four western counties of Pennsylvania a prejudice, fostered and imbittered by the artifice of men who laboured for an ascendancy over the will of others by the guidance of their passions, produced symptoms of riot and violence.

79 [Edmund Jennings Randolph], *Germanicus* (Philadelphia, 1794) : letter iv, 17–18; letter iii, 15–16; letter i, 3; *GUS*, 4 Apr., 17 Jan. 1794. All the thirteen letters of "Germanicus" were published in pamphlet form in Philadelphia in 1794; the relevant quotations have been cited from this source.

Although Washington confined his criticism to the "seditious and treasonable purposes" of "certain self-created societies" who would "destroy a free government," Cobbett made the connection in less diplomatic language: "the influence that the Democratic Clubs had in *producing* the [western] Insurrection, and its consequent calamities" was clear and had "rendered the Democrats extremely odious."[80]

Between 21 and 26 November, the members of the House of Representatives debated their reply to the president's message and traded opinions on whether or not these societies had "led" the citizenry "by calumny and lies to despise ... dread and to hate" the government. Samuel Dexter (F., Mass., 1793–94) argued that not only were they trying to supersede the constituted authorities but that they were doing so surreptitiously:

> clubs ... being a small minority, have attempted to control the majority; to usurp a power which the people never delegated to them; to act as censors, nay, controllers of the Government and laws; they are responsible to nobody for the exercise of it, and are to continue in office as long as they shall please. Such societies have all the properties, except the power, of absolute despotism; yet these tyrants prate about liberty, and profane the name of Republicanism.

The debate, especially as seen from the Federalist benches, thus touched what Dexter called "the most essentials of Republicanism." What was at issue was whether or not, as Fisher Ames (F., Mass., 1789–96) put it, the "clubs" saw themselves ultimately "as a substitute for representation." In the meantime, the country was being subjected to "the continual contest of one organized body against another" which would only "produce the alternate extremes of anarchy and excessive rigor of Government." In short, "tranquillity would be out of the question," the harmony and security of the polity irreversibly undermined, and the country's seasoned leadership and government replaced by "popular Government."[81]

80 Cobbett, *History of the American Jacobins*, 18; *Germanicus*, letter iii, 13; *GA*, 18 Jan. 1794; *Germanicus*, letter v, 19; *GA*, 18 Jan. 1794; Richardson, ed., *Messages and Papers of the Presidents* i, 155; Cobbett, *History of the American Jacobins*, 33, 47.

81 *Annals of Congress*, 929 (26 Nov. 1794), 938, 937 and 938 (Dexter, 27 Nov. 1794), 923, 925 and 923 (Ames, 26 Nov.). Unless otherwise noted, references to the debate on the reply to Washington's message are taken from the debates of the 3rd Congress, 2nd session (3 Nov. 1794 to 3 Mar. 1795). For the purposes of identifying the broad political philosophy of this and other congressmen, *F.* denotes the Federalist supporters of Adams and Hamilton, and *R.* those of the Jeffersonian and Republican interest. *N.P.* refers to those who were not associated with either.

For Federalists, one way of overcoming this challenge was to denounce unequivocally those "self-created societies" which were, in the words of Thomas Fitzsimons, "misrepresenting the conduct of the government, and disturbing the operation of the laws ... and may actually be supposed to have stimulated and urged the insurrection" in western Pennsylvania. The acceptance of such an amendment would "echo" Washington's speech and support the president's desire to prevent "destruction to legitimate Government." However, despite reservations about the societies, there were many who were uncomfortable with such suggestions because they could be interpreted as "a point of deference and politeness to the President." "Now," as Robert Rutherford (R., Va., 1793–96) observed, "if anybody is in favour of societies, *the President is drawn across his face.*" Others drew attention to the fact that whatever their views of the president might be, Congress should exercise its own judgement in framing its reply to the message and not, as Thomas Carnes (N.P., Ga., 1793–94) put it, "make it an exact echo of the Speech itself." For him, as indeed for others, Fitzsimons's proposal questioned the integrity of the House just as, as Federalists argued, the clubs were challenging it in other ways. In the words of John Nicholas (R., Va., 1793–1800), Washington's "weight and influence" had been brought to bear on the debate in ways that stifled a free exchange of views. However, Ames focused on another reality: that "the self-created societies described in the clause, are calculated to destroy a free Government, that they will certainly destroy its tranquillity and harmony, and greatly corrupt the integrity of the rulers, and the morals of the people." Such a "disorganizing Spirit" had to be stopped at all costs. Supporting the views of the president was an effective way of doing this. Moreover, by rallying around Washington in this way, it would reinforce the notion of a political community that was at ease with itself, and without internal rancour or dissension. However, this did not conform to the political realities of the day. If anything, it helped to further reveal Washington's clay feet.[82]

The "checking or restraining [of] public opinion" also provoked a question from William Lyman (R., Mass., 1793–96) as to "where will this business of *censorship* end?" Echoing the eleventh amendment to the U.S. constitution (1791), James Madison (R., Va., 1789–96) reflected in a short but ominous observation that

> When the people have formed a Constitution, they retain those rights which they have not expressly delegated. It is a question whether what is thus

---

82 *Annals of Congress* iv, 899 (Fitzsimons, 24 Nov. 1794); *ibid.*, 908 (Fitzsimons, 25 Nov.); 906 (Vans Murray, 26 Nov.), 919 (Giles, 26 Nov.), 915 (Rutherford, 26 Nov.), 942 (Carnes, 27 Nov.), 940 (Nicholas, 27 Nov.), 931 (Ames, 27 Nov.), 906 (Vans Murray, 25 Nov.).

retained can be legislated upon. Opinions are not the objects of legislation. You animadvert on the abuse of reserved rights: how far will this go? It may extend to the liberty of speech, and of the press.

Madison did not realise at the time that within three years, the debate on Washington's speech would focus more precisely on these issues (for which, see Chapter 6). For the moment, the ways in which "the people" might express themselves outside Congress on the political issues and leaders of the day were being discussed in a substantive way for the first time since the constitution was adopted. In this context, all "associations ... religious, political, and philosophical" were up for debate and juxtaposed with the plethora of town meetings, petitions, and other platforms which citizens could also use to declare their views on public policy. While all these activities celebrated the sovereignty of the people, the recent histories of the democratic societies challenged the view that they, in particular, could exist *with* rather than *beyond* government. As Elias Boudinot (N.P., New Jersey, 1793–94) argued, America did not need the type of *Jacobin* club that had evolved in France where, in the absence of the type of Revolutionary committees that America had, they had helped, in the words of William Vans Murray (F., Md., 1791–96), "to break down and subvert the old bulwark of habitual authority." Moreover, while most congressmen accepted that these societies were "not strictly unlawful," they were taken by some to have implicitly questioned "good order" and "true liberty" as well as the "perfect political freedom" that was being promoted by government.[83]

As a result, as in some of the newspaper commentary, Federalists simply chose to demonise these societies as both "mischievous in their consequences" and a kind of conspiracy of people who "meet in darkness, [and] hide their names, their numbers, and their doings." According to caricature, they were supposed to meet at night when, according to Ames, "they shut their doors, pass votes in secret, and admit no members into the society but those of their own class." What Ames meant by this, as he warmed to his thesis, was that the membership of these societies had been drawn from "the outcasts of society" who were "usually ... the most inflamed party men" and who, under the guise of providing impartial "political information," met to "perform incantations against liberty ... to medicate their poisons, to whet their daggers, [and] to utter their blasphemies against liberty." Within the halls of Congress, therefore, Federalist descriptions of those who would "censure" government in any way were taking shape in Philadelphia.[84]

83 *Ibid.*, 900 (Giles, 24 Nov.), 901 (Lyman, 24 Nov.), 934 (Madison, 27 Nov.), 900 (Giles, 24 Nov.), 920 (Boudinot, 24 Nov.), 907 (Vans Murray, 24 Nov.), 899 (Fitzsimons, 24 Nov.).
84 *Ibid.*, 902 (Smith, 24 Nov.), 902 (Lyman, 24 Nov.), 926, 923 and 926 (Ames, 26 Nov.), 901 (Smith, 24 Nov.).

Among these was the view that the politics of the Federal capital itself were being unduly influenced by disruptive immigrants. In 1794, for example, the German Republican Society boldly announced that it was "high time" that Germans "should step forward, declare themselves independent of other influence, and think for themselves." The Irish were not shy either. Partly because they were English-speaking, partly because of their numbers and partly because they were immigrating from a country that was itself in the middle of a similar process of political upheaval, the Irish were also active within the Democratic Society. However, while, according to Jefferson, "a great many" of the society's members were Irish, they did not see the society in ethno-cultural terms. Instead, as Eugene Perry Link has put it, "any number of spirited Irishmen ... might be termed the fire brands of the popular societies because of their fervency and activist spirit" and commitment to a more universal discourse of liberty and democracy with which they were long familiar. In a similar vein, as "A Democrat" admitted that "*some foreigners*" were members of the Democratic Society, they were such as wanted to enjoy "all the sweets of liberty" in America, having fled there from the "despotism and slavery" of the old world. However, despite such a colourless cosmopolitanism, one cannot deny that the societies' anti-English and pro-French slogans appealed to the biases of the increasingly vocal Irish immigrants or that the Irish were not moved when the Democratic Society toasted "a speedy emancipation to the Sons of Hibernia— may they soon rank as a republic amongst nations." In such circumstances, especially when they are taken with the increasing currency of "foreign" symbols and toasts in the rituals of contemporary American republicanism, familiar debates between old and new reappeared. However benignly "A Democrat" might explain their motives, the reality was that the democratic societies were questioning America. Hence, Cobbett's criticism that "two-thirds of the Democrats were foreigners, landed in the United States since the war," would be used as a stick with which to beat the societies and divert discussion from their objective merits.[85]

The Naturalisation Act of 1795

One contribution to this resurrected debate was an article which "Pennsylvaniensis" published in the *General Advertiser* in April 1793 where he maintained that

85 German Republican Society of Philadelphia, "To Friends and Fellow Citizens, April 11, 1793" in Foner, ed., *Democratic-Republican Societies*, 54; Link, *Democratic-Republican Societies*, 71–99; *GA*, 4 Aug. 1794; *Aurora*, 11 July 1795; Cobbett, *History of the American Jacobins*, 27. For Jefferson's comment, see Maude H. Woodfin, "Citizen Genet and his Mission" (Ph.D. dissertation, University of Chicago, 1928), 183–5.

It would be a difficult matter to convince an unprejudiced mind, that foreigners merit the same degree of public confidence, which is due to the natives of our country ... The Romans ... were so scrupulous about admitting foreigners to even the common rights of citizenship, that they enacted the most rigorous laws against it, and these laws continued in force till it became the policy of *interested* men to relax them, and their abrogation, and the indiscriminate admission of foreigners [to] citizenship and the offices of government, are considered by *philosophers* as among the causes of declension of the Roman Commonwealth ... for if the interest of the country clash with the interest of the country which his private views have called him to, the presumption is that his original prejudices will determine his conduct.

"Philo-Sydney" disagreed and pointed out that whatever else, in the words of the former,

persons who were born in England, Ireland, Scotland, Germany and several other parts of Europe, were as much attached to the Revolution, and to the liberty and independence of America as any of the natives of the United States.

"An Unprejudiced American" also drew on recent history to make his point that without question, the foreign-born would be "good citizens" and "loyal" to the American republic. He suggested that such persons had come to America to escape "oppression" in the first instance and that they would hardly support the oppressions of the old world in the new. While such arguments had already been made in similar discussions over the previous thirty years, they were now being presented in more "awful" times, as "William Penn" put it. For this particular writer, the public role of America's immigrants was dragging the country into "the calamities of Europe, and having her soil circumscrib'd with the blood of her Citizens." For another, the cause of the problem was clear: "the facility by which foreigners have hitherto become citizens of the United States, [and which] has been productive of much mischief." The solution was equally clear: to revise the naturalisation act of 1790 under which aliens could acquire citizenship after two years' residence in the United States.[86]

Within Congress, the matter was taken up by a committee of the whole on 22 December 1794. Congressmen agreed that, in general terms, America needed immigrants but as Theodore Sedgwick (F., Mass., 1789–96) argued, not at the cost of undermining the republic. As it was, "as great a portion of freedom as was consistent with a social compact" had been "left to the citizen."

86 *GA*, 2, 5 *Apr.* 1793; *Aurora*, 12 *Oct.* 1795.

Recent events had now convinced him that under existing legislation, this could lead to "abuses" which could unravel the polity itself as well as the government which had been established to protect and promote it. Therefore, it was "indispensable to the continuance of our happiness" that government be "preserve[d] ... in its purity." This was no more than any legislator had wanted since 1776. However, while there had been few worries that this could be achieved, principally because Americans were "more wise and virtuous than any other people on earth," they could now be easily corrupted, as Vans Murray put it, by those who were "coming from a quarter of the world so full of disorder and corruption" and who as a result, "might contaminate the purity and simplicity of the American character." Few congressmen wanted "complete exclusion." Sedgwick accepted that even those who had but few assets "had a reasonable assurance ... of independence, competence, and respectability." However, such immigrants needed "industry and economy" in order to succeed in America, characteristics which could not be taken for granted. Moreover, as Dexter suggested, "the times" underlined the need to give immigrants time to acquire "the habits of temperate discussion, patient reasoning, and a capacity of enduring contradiction" so that American citizenship would be "guarded ... against adulteration by foreign mixture," especially when they came with "principles entirely different from ours." Thus, in addition to the challenges which came from newcomers who might not be as virtuous as themselves, there was also the potential divisiveness which an open door policy could cause in the new republic.[87]

Events, both at home and abroad, led Sedgwick to conclude that "the present ... [was] the most inauspicious time for the indiscriminate admission of aliens to the rights of citizenship" and that, in particular, "the existing state of things in Europe" had "increased" his "opposition" to the provisions of the existing Naturalisation Acts. His reasoning here was straightforward:

> A war, the most cruel and dreadful which had been known for centuries, was now raging in all those countries from which emigrants were to be expected ... [Thus,] could any reasonable man believe, that men who, actuated by such passions, had fought on grounds so opposite, almost equally distant from *the happy mean we had chosen*, would here mingle in social affections with each other, or with us? That their passions and prejudices would subside as soon as they should set foot in America? or, that, possessing those passions and prejudices, they were qualified to make or be made the governors of Americans?

87 *Annals of Congress*, 1006 (Sedgwick, 22 Dec.), 1023 (Dexter, 22 Dec.), 1066 (Sedgwick, 22 Dec.), 1023 (Vans Murray), 1006, 1008 and 1006 (Sedgwick, 22 Dec.), 1022 (Dexter, 22 Dec.).

By focusing on elections and public issues, these reflections could also be discussed in more conventional political terms. In 1794 the *Aurora* reported that in the recent elections for congress in Boston,

> the privileges of the citizens of this town [Boston] were never more violated in the business of election ... The citizens seemed to be overpowered by an extraneous body of voters, consisting of foreigners from on board vessels at the wharves, and persons from other towns.

Thus, Sedgwick argued that Congress had to "check the admission of foreigners in such a manner as might [not] be dangerous to our political institutions." As eventually agreed in the naturalisation act of 1795, the changes were not insignificant: potential citizens had to have lived in America for at least five years before applying for naturalisation, they should have a "good moral character," be "attached to the principles of the Constitution of the United States, and well disposed to the good order and happiness of the same," renounce "all foreign allegiance" and promise to support the constitution. Then, they had to wait a further three years before the process was complete.[88]

During 1794 and 1795, both inside and outside Congress, various commentators revived the public argument on the role of the foreign-born in the new republic. The ways in which immigrants were choosing to celebrate America and interpret the republicanism upon which it had been built added to the discussion, as did the notion that where ethno-cultural societies could not contain their own immigrants, they were catalysts of instability within the community at large. They were no longer merely the benevolent societies of the 1770s and 1780s which had chosen to promote the harmony of a wider and more integrated polity. Instead, the governing Federalists were presenting them as the agents of disruption. If, as Cobbett suggested, there "existed [in America] all the materials for a revolution, but they were scattered here and there; [and that] affiliated clubs were wanting to render them compact, and manageable, as occasion might demand," then the changing nature of the public sphere gave pause for thought. It is the case that this was a time of increasing insecurity both at home and abroad and that, as John Higham has concluded, it was at such points of uncertainty that the "foreign connections" of immigrant groups have always become a focus for what was "un-American." It may be that in this context, the emerging nativism of the 1790s was a negative phenomenon

---

88 *Ibid.*, 1008 and 1009 (Sedgwick, 22 Dec.); *Aurora*, 14 Nov. 1794; *Annals of Congress*, 1009 (Sedgwick, 22 Dec.). The act is quoted from Frank G. Franklin, *The Legislative History of Naturalization in the United States* (Chicago, 1906), 70.

because it promoted "Americanism" through suggesting what it was not. It also implied a lack of confidence that immigrants could be accommodated within, much less assimilated into, the mainstream of the American republic. After 1795 there was much to suggest that this was not merely a philosophical question. The increasingly assertive public behaviour of Irish immigrants through a range of "self-created societies" which seemed to be more threatening and conspiratorial than anything that been experienced until then drove the point home.[89]

89 Cobbett, *History of the American Jacobins*, 17; Higham, *Strangers in the Land*, 4.

CHAPTER FIVE

Irish Radicals in Philadelphia

By 1795 the rise of a more active and diverse polity in Philadelphia was irreversible. Many factors had influenced this process, not the least of which was an increasingly vocal Irish immigrant community which wanted to advance the "new politics" in the nation's capital. As a result, immigrant leaders became increasingly visible in the city's political networks, as did a more pointed ethno-cultural interpretation of public policy. Many Federalists were wary about these developments and also realised that the distresses and unfolding rebellion in contemporary Ireland powerfully reinforced Anglophobia within the Irish community in ways which neither reason nor policy could counter effectively. They also believed that the emotional ways in which these circumstances were sometimes presented and more particularly, how reform in Ireland was linked to French invasion, could destabilise their own fragile republic with the immigrant Irish as the vanguard of a potential second American Revolution. Therefore, the last five years of the 1790s was a period of political "phrenzy," as Marshall Smelser has termed it, for which events in Ireland, and their reception in America, provided important catalysts.[1]

Ireland and America: Revolutions Entwined, 1776–90

Before the American Revolution, many writers on both sides of the Atlantic had believed that the grievances of the colonies mirrored those of Ireland. Years earlier, when seminal Irish writers such as **William Molyneux** (1656–98) had written that the Irish polity was "bound" only by laws "to which the community have given its consent," they repeatedly struck a chord in America as well as in Ireland. During the course of the eighteenth century a succession of Patriotic writers developed a line of thought which in their view, would promote the integrity of the citizen and protect him from the intrusions of an increasingly overbearing executive. During the 1760s and 1770s the Revolutionary movement in America aired similar concerns while in contemporary Ireland, the erstwhile leader of the Patriots, Henry Grattan, regarded "the liberties of America" as

---

1 Marshall Smelser, "The Jacobin Phrenzy: The Menace of Monarchy, Plutocracy and Anglophobia, 1789–1798," *Review of Politics* xxi (1959), 239–58.

"inseparable" from those of his own country. Similarly, Molyneux's suggestion that being bound by English laws would "naturally" subject Ireland to taxation "without our Consent" was echoed by an American insistence on preserving "our Rights & Privileges as English Men, [and] of being taxed only by our Representatives." In 1776 the preface to a new edition of Molyneux's *Case of Ireland Being Bound by Acts of Parliament Stated*, originally published in Dublin in 1698, also identified a *bête noir* that was common to reformers in Ireland and colonial America:

> The same lust for domination, which hath led them [the British government] to encroach on the constitutional rights of our fellow subjects in America, may, if their attempt should succeed, lead them to desire to bind Ireland by their laws in all cases whatsoever.[2]

These feelings of a shared burden were also reflected in a network of Patriotic clubs, toasts, parades, and addresses which linked Ireland and America at this time. One of the more widely publicised connections was noted in 1784 when the Yankee Club of Stewartstown, Co. Tyrone, saluted George Washington and his army because they had "not only vindicated the freedom of your country but have also shed their benign influence over the distressed kingdom of Ireland." In reply, Washington suggested that "if in the course of our successful contest, any good consequences have resulted to the oppressed kingdom of Ireland, it will afford a new source of felicitation to all who respect the interests of humanity." Such exchanges were not unusual although Ireland's reactions to the American Revolution were often ambivalent. The recent work of historians confirms this. The leaders of the Catholic Committee, for example, which had been founded to repeal the Penal Laws, took a pragmatic view of the conflict and pondered how it might assist its own campaign for reform in contemporary Ireland. As a result, in July 1775 Bishop Sweetman of Ferns (1744–86) cautioned his communicants not to draw on "our holy religion, the odium of our mild government, and the gentlemen in power in our country." Similar protests of loyalty became louder after March 1778 when France announced that it would enter the Revolutionary War on the side of the colonies. In August 1779 two months after Spain also joined the Franco-American alliance, Catholic leaders in Kilkenny declared that they would

---

2   J.G. Simms, ed., William Molyneux, *Case of Ireland being Bound by Acts of Parliament in England Stated* (Dublin, 1977), 127; Daniel Owen Madden, ed., *The Speeches of the Right Hon. Henry Grattan* (Dublin, 1854), 93; Simms, ed., *Case of Ireland*, 116, 48. The quotation from the 1776 edition of the *Case of Ireland* is taken from the preface, a copy of which is in TCD.

"conduct ourselves in such a manner, as will fully evince our loyalty to his majesty, and satisfy our fellow Protestant subjects." However, as they did so, they were conscious, as Vincent Morley has noted, that "lower-class Catholics were equally unrestrained in celebrating British defeats" in America. Eighteenth-century Catholic Ireland was nothing if not the sum of its parts.[3]

Given that some of the Penal Laws had already been rescinded, and that commitments were being given to repeal others, the leaders of Catholic Ireland had every reason to hope that a reinvented polity, even if it was one which was being mooted by Dublin Castle, would have a place for them. They also believed that it was important to protect their own "natural leadership" from anarchy and revolution, both at home and abroad, especially as popular protest movements, such as the Whiteboys and **Defenders**, were offering an alternative cadre of leaders should the more established and conventional channels of redress prove ineffective in addressing agrarian grievance. Could the Catholic Committee manage what John Foster called the "race for the Catholic" in an effective and practical manner, especially given that the "disengagement of the gentry from popular culture ... [had] completely transformed the administration of law and order, which had been indulgent and personalised"? In a telling addendum to their address in 1779, Kilkenny Catholics observed that "where the honour and glory of these kingdoms are at stake, we know of no distinction of religion, but unite as British subjects in defence of his majesty's person and government." An influential member of the Catholic gentry, Charles O'Conor (1710–91) of Belanagare, hoped that this would be recognised in ways which would suit both the Catholic elite and Dublin Castle and that the government "should, indirectly, be confirmed in the important idea that a passive party among us [Catholics] deserves protection, not only from the *moral* injustice [*recte*: 'justice'] due to all parties but the *political* justice due to the republicans." Catholic leaders were thus no less steadfast in professing such sentiments than the established Anglican elite of contemporary Ireland, especially after free trade and legislative independence were granted in 1780 and 1782, respectively. The M.P. for Cork city (1761–90), John Hely Hutchinson, wrote from his port city in 1780 that the "citizens of Cork are, as they certainly ought to be, thoroughly contented and highly sensible of the advantages and favours they have obtained." Dublin Castle had come to realise that the polity could be renewed, and thus secured, only through the politics of accommodation, not by

3 *BN*, 17 Sept. 1784; *FJ*, 15 July 1775, 21 Aug. 1779; Morley, *Irish Opinion and the American Revolution*, 169. For evaluations of the ways in which the Revolution was seen in contemporary Ireland, see Morley, *Irish Opinion and the American Revolution;* and Bric, "Ireland, America and the Reassessment of a Special Relationship," 88–119. For context, see Neil Longley York, *Neither Kingdom nor Nation: The Irish Quest for Constitutional Rights, 1698–1800* (Washington, D.C., 1994).

insisting on the divisions of religion over the recognition of wealth, education, "experience," and property.[4]

It was more difficult to bring Presbyterian leaders within this framework, a problem highlighted by how they reacted to events in America where they had many family and church connections. Although Irish Presbyterians were actively involved in promoting Patriotism during the 1770s and 1780s, especially through the Volunteer movement, they were less interested in the constitutional basis of the established polity, of which they were an indulged rather than an intrinsic part, than in reforming its structures to give more recognition to the individual citizen. Thus, they often saw the American revolutionaries as mirror images of themselves. Support for the Revolution was strongest in Presbyterian Ulster, a point which Lafayette acknowledged when he advised the French foreign minister (1774–81), the Comte de Vergennes, that should France decide to open a second front of the Revolutionary War by invading Ireland, "the revolution should be made by the Presbyterians from the four counties of Down, Antrim, Derry, and Donegal who are all friends of liberty, strongly disposed to the Americans, and by their location (especially Londonderry) would be easy to assist." But Presbyterian reaction to events in America remained passive, "the venting of a spleen," as Maurice O'Connell has observed, "rather than a [show of] constructive interest in imperial affairs." Thus, for both Catholic and Dissenter, the "crucial impact" of the American Revolution on Ireland was, in the words of Breandán Ó Buachalla, "emotional and symbolic." Ireland largely ignored the theoretical basis of the colonial protest for the narrower use to which Anglo-American disagreements could be put to address what Benjamin Franklin termed "the heavy yoke of [imperial] tyranny."[5]

For their part, American revolutionaries also looked at events in contemporary Ireland in political terms. To be sure, as Franklin observed in 1773, two years after a visit to Ireland, there were "many Points in Similarity" in the "Cases" of

---

4 Kevin Whelan, "The United Irishmen, the Enlightenment and Popular Culture" in Dickson, Keogh and Whelan, eds., *United Irishmen*, 275, 295; *FJ*, 21 Aug. 1779; *Irish Opinion and the American Revolution*, 134 and 238.

5 Stanley J. Idzerda *et al.*, eds., *Lafayette in the Age of the American Revolution: Selected Letters and Papers, 1776–1779* 2 vols. (Ithaca, 1979), ii, 268–9; O'Connell, *Irish Politics and Social Conflict in the Age of the American Revolution*, 31; Breandán Ó Buachalla, "From Jacobite to Jacobin" in Bartlett, Dickson, Keogh and Whelan, eds., *1798*, 82. Franklin is quoted from Michael Kraus, "America and the Irish Revolutionary Movement in the Eighteenth Century" in Richard B. Morris, ed., *The Era of the American Revolution* (New York, 1939), 335. For the impact of the Volunteers on a changing public sphere in Ireland, see P.D.H. Smyth, "The Volunteers and Parliament, 1779–84" in Thomas Bartlett and David Hayton, eds., *Penal Era and Golden Age: Essays in Irish History, 1690–1800* (Belfast, 1979), 113–36.

Ireland and America. Indeed, he suggested that "our growing weight might ... be thrown into their [Irish] scale, and, by joining our interests with others, a more equitable treatment from this [English] nation might be obtained for them as well as for us." The first formal expression of such a link between these two imperial siblings was an address which Congress made to the "people of Ireland" in 1775 in which it listed the "undeserved injuries" which had been inflicted on America. In the view of Congress, "England" had established an "arbitrary sway" over the traditional rights and liberties of her citizens in America. It had allowed "evil and abandoned Ministers" to impose punitive trade and taxation laws "without our consent," to abolish trial by jury, to set up courts that were "unknown to the constitution," to establish a standing army, and to violate her "ancient charters ... [so that] their form of government [had been] mutilated and transformed." The warning for Ireland was clear: "The Ministry, bent on pulling down the pillars of the constitution, endeavoured to erect the standard of despotism in America; and if successful, Britain and Ireland may shudder at the consequences."[6]

Nonetheless, subsequent events showed that rhetoric would not be confused with reality. In 1775 Congress resolved to suspend all commerce with *both* Britain and Ireland "until our rights are fully restored to us." To an objection whether Ireland should be part of this move, Alexander Hamilton suggested that Irish "self-love ... would direct their resentment at its proper objects" in the British government. However, America later rescinded its ban on the export of flaxseed to Ireland because this had caused "a much greater Degree of Distress and Ruin to the poor of that Kingdom, than Congress apprehended." Following the "most serious attention" to Ireland's "misery and distress," Congress again addressed "the good people of Ireland" in 1778 and proposed "a reciprocal commercial interest." It also expressed the hope that "the liberation of your country" had already "been effected in America." However, the progress of revolution in America had encouraged Dublin Castle to kill a potentially similar phenomenon in Ireland with an appropriate kindness: free trade and legislative independence for **"Grattan's Parliament"** (1782–1800).[7]

6 Franklin is quoted from J.G. Simms, *Colonial Nationalism, 1698–1776* (Cork, 1976), 63; and Labaree *et al.*, eds., *Papers of Franklin* xix, 21, Franklin to Thomas Cushing, 13 July 1772, respectively. For the address from Congress, see *HJ*, 23 Aug. 1775, from which the quotations have been cited. For Franklin's visit to Ireland, see J. Bennett Nolan, *Benjamin Franklin in Scotland and Ireland* (Philadelphia, 1938).

7 "Third Resolution of the Committee on Trade, No. 1" (read on 2 Oct. 1775), as in Worthington C. Ford, ed., *Journals of the Continental Congress, 1774–1789* 34 vols. (Washington, D.C., 1903–37) i, 35; *A Full Vindication of the Measures of Congress* as in Syrett *et al.*, *Papers of Alexander Hamilton* i, 59, 60; Peter Force, *American Archives* 6 vols. (Washington, D.C., 1837–53) ii, 1631. The quotations from the 1778 address have been taken from *HJ*, 4 Oct. 1778.

Although the more conservative leaders of the Reform Movement were satisfied by what had been achieved, the reality was that however positively these concessions were presented, they were limited, if not "a most bungling imperfect business," in Wolfe Tone's colourful words. Moreover, in March 1784, after the failure of the reform bill which had emerged from their National Convention the previous November, many others believed that their main problem was less the link with Britain than with those in Ireland, and especially those in Parliament, who used this link to preserve their own ascendancy. For these more radical reformers, Grattan's Parliament was thus a beginning rather than an end. It also led to a renewed reform movement which would unite Presbyterian radicalism with those Catholic leaders who still felt that all they were being offered was, in the words of Henry Flood (1732–91), "all toleration to religion" but no "political power." This does not mean that Anglican Protestants completely faded from the reform movement. However, the movement after 1782 was different from its earlier manifestations, not least because its push for a thorough reform of Parliament, public representation, and patronage was being promoted through a network of dedicated Whig Clubs. As James Kelly has observed, an informal, if uneasy relationship with the Catholic Committee also gave the cause of reform an even wider appeal, as did tentative criticisms of the tithe system. However, despite such varied interests and support, and internal differences on the further repeal of the penal laws, the reform movement continued to pose a potential challenge to the established leaders of contemporary Ireland at a volatile time.[8]

Partly for this reason, by the early 1790s, the older aristocratic leaders of the Catholic Committee had withdrawn from the cause of reform. In any event Catholics whose estates were worth at least forty shillings a year (the forty-shilling freeholders) were given the vote in 1793. Despite these advances, Catholic leaders felt under increasing challenge from the "unnatural union" between radical Presbyterianism and reform-minded Catholics. An even greater threat loomed with the increasing influence of popular protest movements such as the Whiteboys (from 1761, principally in the southern half of Ireland), the Oakboys (1763, principally in Armagh and Tyrone), the Steelboys (1769–72, principally in Antrim and Down), the Rightboys (1785–88, principally in Cork, Tipperary and Kilkenny), and the Defenders (1790s, principally in Ulster and

8   James Kelly, "Parliamentary Reform in Irish Politics: 1760–90" in Dickson, Keogh and Whelan, eds., *United Irishmen*, 86. Tone and Flood are quoted from Thomas Bartlett, "The Burden of the Present: Theobald Wolfe Tone, Republican and Separatist" in *ibid.*, 11; and J.A. Froude, *The English in Ireland in the Eighteenth Century* 3 vols. (London, 1887) ii, 332, respectively. For the limitations of Grattan's Parliament, see James Kelly, *Prelude to Union: Anglo-Irish Politics in the 1780s* (Cork, 1992); and Gerard O'Brien, *Anglo-Irish Politics in the Age of Grattan and Pitt* (Dublin, 1987).

Leinster). Each of these movements represented its own version of "the wrongs done to the poor" and their grievances were clearly identified. These included oppressive payments for tithe and rent, as well as the failure to recognise any privileges which existing tenants might claim when leases came up for renewal. However, the proffered solution was not an absolute refusal to pay. Instead, the movements pointed to a hierarchy of agents and officials which had grown up in consequence of absentee landowners and the subdivision of holdings, the expectations of Catholic priests who wanted to rebuild their churches and schools now that the Penal Laws were being repealed, and the ways in which the tithe system had become corrupted by tithe farmers, proctors, and canters. Even Grattan claimed that some tithe farmers received as much as one third of a tithe that, as originally conceived, should have gone entirely to the church.[9]

The level of Catholic dues was easily addressed by an agreement in 1786 not to demand more than "the house can afford." Along similar lines Grattan made an appeal to settle the payment of tithes by a modus, or a fixed monetary payment. However, even as he introduced a parliamentary motion on the subject in 1787, he realised that the tithe question was not without its complications. Grievance not only focused on increased demands but highlighted how the payment of tithe had become a business where on a number of levels, different agencies had to be paid their share. Thus, he claimed that the tithe farmer

> collects sometimes at 50 *per cent.* he gives the clergyman less than he ought to receive, and takes from the peasants more than they should pay; he is not an agent who is to collect a certain rent, he is an adventurer ... he sometimes sets the tithe to a second tithe-farmer, so that the land becomes a prey *to a subordination of vultures.*

Despite the immorality of such a system, Grattan had to acknowledge that tithe was a type of property which its owners were entitled to enjoy. Tithe also provided the principal means by which the Church of Ireland was maintained,

9 Dáire Keogh, "Archbishop Troy, the Catholic Church and Irish Radicalism, 1791–3" in Dickson, Keogh and Whelan, eds., *United Irishmen*, 126; Froude, *The English in Ireland in the Eighteenth Century* ii, 27 n.6. Grattan is quoted from *The Speeches of the Right Honourable Henry Grattan*, edited by his son, 4 vols. (London, 1822) ii, 44. For popular protest, see Maurice J. Bric, "The Whiteboy Movement, 1760–80" in William Nolan, ed., *Tipperary: History and Society* (Dublin, 1985), 148–84; and "Priests, Parsons and Politics," 100–23; and James Donnelly, "Hearts of Oak, Hearts of Steel," *Studia Hibernica* xxi (1981), 7–73. For the evolution of the Defenders and their interaction with the United Irishmen, see Elliott, *Partners in Revolution*, 35–51 *et passim*; and Thomas Bartlett, "Defenders and Defenderism in 1795," *IHS*, xxiv (1984–5), 373–94. For the wider circumstances in which these movements evolved, see Jim Smyth, *The Men of No Property: Irish Radicals and Popular Politics in the Late Eighteenth Century* (Basingstoke, 1992).

despite the fact that the clergy provided no service to the majority of those who paid it. Thus, official Ireland tended to see the issue in terms that were wider than those of the Rightboys and Defenders. As Dr. Richard Woodward, Church of Ireland bishop of Cloyne (1781–94), put it in 1787, the established church was "so essentially incorporated with the State ... that the Subversion of one must necessarily overthrow the other." As a result, many regarded suggestions to reform the tithe system as a means to confront "the glorious revolution of 1688,'" from which the established polity had drawn its inspiration and *raison d'être*. As the *Dublin Evening Post* noted in 1787 that tithe had already "kept Ireland in a state of civil war for years," there was a feeling that this was not just an observation of the past but a premonition of the future.[10]

Proposals to reform the tithe system during the 1780s foundered on the supposition that similar arguments could be made to regulate rents and leases, neither of which were deemed to be appropriate areas for the intervention of Parliament. Parliament had an obligation to defend property at all costs including, if necessary, deploying increased numbers of army and police to protect landlords and clergymen, and to ensure that the various laws which had been passed to "prevent riotous and tumultuous assemblies," and their "illegal" activities, would be implemented. Parliament thus responded to the development of agrarian protest not by enquiring into the nature and extent of grievance but by passing measures which would strengthen the institutions of the state to deal with protest itself. However, as Parliament steered clear of objective enquiry and by extension, compromised its role as the court of ultimate redress, popular protest movements evolved as an alternative culture which stressed, in the case of tithe, the "public justice" that was due to the paying parishioner rather than the "private interests" of the tithe hierarchy. Such a moralistic presentation of their cause gave these movements an influence which was difficult to counter. Moreover, a network of local Whiteboy "captains," "adjutants," "chiefs," and "treasurers" emerged as a potentially powerful alternative to the newly-won official respectability of the Catholic Committee. This challenge to more conventional leaders was all the more real because the "Whiteboy oaths" bound parishioners together in "combinations" which consolidated the appeal of these new and more popular "under-leaders" in ways which could not be easily undone. The organisation and *modus operandi*

10 *FJ*, 1 Aug. 1786; Richard Woodward, *The Present State of the Church of Ireland* (Dublin, 1787), 14; *DEP*, 22 Jan. 1786. The reference to 1688 is quoted of Sir Edward Newenham in *The Parliamentary Register: or, History of the Proceedings and Debates of the House of Commons* 17 vols. (Dublin, 1782–1801) vii (debates of 13 Mar. 1787), and to Grattan from the his speech on his motion on the reform of the tithe system, 13 March 1787, in *Speeches of the Right Honourable Henry Grattan*, edited by his son, ii, 13 and 11, respectively.

of popular protest had awakened the peasantry to their own potential influence as discrete political actors as well as to an ability to assert themselves on their own terms.[11]

Removed from the controlling hand of both their landlords and the Catholic Committee, and partly because of their failure to solve their grievances through conventional channels, popular societies became more persistent in their demands, especially after the limited concessions of the **relief act of 1793**. While Tone acknowledged that Catholics deserved what had been granted, they also deserved what had been withheld. These societies thus became bolder and more furious in carrying out what the *General Advertiser* described in March 1793 as "great outrages." Over two years later the *Aurora* reported that the Defenders had become

> more numerous and more daring than ever ... These defenders have hitherto been considered as mere desperadoes, driven by extreme wretchedness and want to acts of violence and to pillage and rapine; but their systematic proceedings at this time warrant a conjecture, that they are now under leaders, a powerful political engine, which, however unworthy, may be the means and perhaps, the only means, of effecting a regeneration of Ireland, and ridding that fine country from the yoke of England and the tyranny of priests.

This report sums up how, by the middle of the 1790s, popular protest in Ireland was no longer being seen as merely a vehicle to articulate grievance. Others suggested that the networks of the Defenders were expanding and that in some parts of the country, their leaders were being interlocked at baronial, regional, and even provincial levels. Such wider networks were the exception rather than the rule and even where they probably did exist, in parts of Ulster and Leinster, they owed more to a new type of political protest which was being inspired by contemporary France rather than to one which had been home-grown. Because the Irish countryside had become more violent than it had been in 1761, when the Whiteboys first appeared, and the levels of distress were more acute and more pathetically evident, it was easy for supporters of the government to characterise popular protest in Ireland as a fifth column of Revolutionary France.[12]

---

11 Virginia Crossman, *Politics, Law and Order in Nineteenth-Century Ireland* (Dublin, 1996), 199–200; *DEP*, 21 June 1786; Bric, "Whiteboy Movement," 154. For the importance of the Whiteboy oath, see Bric, "Priests, Parsons and Politics," 111–12.

12 *GA*, 25 Mar. 1793; *Aurora*, 19 Oct. 1795. Tone has been quoted from Keogh, "Archbishop Troy, the Catholic Church and Irish Radicalism" in Dickson, Keogh and Whelan, eds., *United Irishmen* 133. For the francophobic theme in eighteenth-century Irish history, see Gerard O'Brien, "Francophobia in later eighteenth-century Irish history" in Gough and Dickson, eds., *Ireland and the French Revolution*, 40–51.

For Dublin Castle, the United Irishmen came to embody this "French disease" in Ireland. They were founded in Belfast in October 1791 and committed themselves to social, economic, and political equity. In recent years, historians have analysed the society more critically and as a result, its broader characteristics are clearer.[13] The society's diverse programme attracted different types of reformers, radicals, and revolutionaries, many of whom recognised that they could also promote their own agendas, however informally, through "internal politics." Such campaigns included the repeal of the remaining Penal Laws as well as the redress of social and economic grievances. The United Irishmen also developed a separatist colour insofar as they suggested that Ireland was "ruled by Englishmen, and the servants of Englishmen, whose object is the interest of another country, whose instrument is corruption, and whose strength is the weakness of Ireland." The society thus became all things to all people. In the words of the (Dublin) *National Journal*, it was "not only for the politician and man of letters but for the artisan, the mechanic and the husbandman." By bringing together radical politics and popular protest, it also offered opportunities for "new leaders" and promoted a more inclusive perception of the polity of late-eighteenth-century Ireland.[14]

The United Irishmen presented a different type of challenge to the Irish establishment together with a new vocabulary of protest. In addition, the society's role as an agent of civic education did not go unnoticed. Its newspaper, the (Belfast) *Northern Star*, had been founded in January 1792 "to give a fair statement of all that passed in France, whither every one turned his eyes [and] to inculcate union amongst Irishmen of all religious persuasions." As R.B. McDowell has written, the paper was "continually reminding [its readers] that they were part of a great world-wide political and moral movement destined to early victory." The propagandistic agendas of both the United Irishmen and the Defenders suggested that if the people could articulate their grievances in the

13 Much of this historiography has been discussed in Bartlett, Dickson, Keogh and Whelan, eds., *1798*. This volume followed from a five-day conference which was held in May 1998 and also contains a list of relevant works published on the 1790s; see Whelan, "Bibliography" in *ibid.*, 659–724. The reference to the "French disease" is taken from the title by Dáire Keogh, '*The French Disease': The Catholic Church and Irish Radicalism, 1790–1800* (Dublin, 1993).

14 Louis M. Cullen, "The Internal Politics of the United Irishmen" in Dickson, Keogh and Whelan, eds., *United Irishmen*, 187; *ADA*, 28 Mar. 1792. The *National Journal* is quoted in McDowell, *Ireland in the Age of Imperialism and Revolution*, 385. The sense of this comment is also present in Emmet's well-known suggestion that the United Irishmen aspired to "make every man a politician;" quoted in Nancy J. Curtin, "The United Irish Organisation in Ulster: 1795–8" in Dickson, Keogh and Whelan, eds., *United Irishmen*, 220. For an overview of how the United Irishmen have been seen, see Bartlett, "The Burden of the Present" in Dickson, Keogh and Whelan, eds., *United Irishmen*, 1–15.

language of protest and reform, their cause would gain a new edge. As the erstwhile M.P (1791–95) and United Irishman, Arthur O'Connor (1763–1853), put it, "the increase of information and improvement of intellect among the poor, not being accompanied by a proportionate amendment of their condition, [meant that] they became fully sensible of the wretchedness of their state." The facility with which United Irish agents promoted their programme through ballads, songs, broadsides, pamphlets, and other writings that were read in "clusters," thus led to a new phenomenon: what Kevin Whelan has described as the "creation of public opinion as a positive political force."[15]

Another distinguishing feature of the United Irishmen was their admiration of the French Revolution. It is difficult to assess the impact of this on the United Irish rank and file. In June 1798, when a parliamentary enquiry asked **Thomas Addis Emmet** (1764–1827) how the mass of the people understood the society's commitment to constitutional and parliamentary reform, he explained that they were not particularly interested in this agenda "till it was explained to them as leading to other objects which they looked to, principally the abolition of tithes." Another United Irish leader, **William James MacNeven** (1763–1841), told the enquiry on 8 August 1798 that "if tithes had been commuted according to Mr. Grattan's motion [of 1788], a very powerful engine would have been taken out of our hands." While some historians do not accept that the United Irishmen operated on two platforms with, in the opinion of some of them, "social" concerns "reactive to events," Emmet's comment is a reminder that as the United Irishmen plotted with France to stage a revolution based on the idea of the republic, they could not ignore the grievances of the Whiteboy tradition even if, much like the Jacobins, Tone had little intention of either interfering with property rights or promoting social change.[16]

15 McDowell, *Ireland in the Age of Imperialism and Revolution*, 385; Whelan, "The United Irishmen, the Enlightenment and Popular Culture," 276–7, 275. The *Northern Star* is quoted from McDowell, *Ireland in the Age of Imperialism and Revolution*, 385 and O'Connor from Whelan, "The United Irishmen, the Enlightenment and Popular Culture" in Dickson, Keogh and Whelan, eds., *United Irishmen*, 276. For the propaganda of the United Irishmen and the Defenders, see also Curtin, *The United Irishmen: Popular Politics in Ulster and Dublin 1791–1798*, ch.7; Whelan, *Tree of Liberty*; and James S. Donnelly, Jr., "Propagating the Cause of the United Irishmen" in *Studies* lxix (1980), 5–23. For the influence of the *Northern Star*, see Simon Davies, "The Northern Star" and the Propagation of Enlightenment Ideals" in *Eighteenth Century Ireland* v (1990), 143–52.

16 Cullen, "Internal Politics" in Dickson, Keogh and Whelan, eds., *United Irishmen*, 176; Bartlett, "The Burden of the Present" in *ibid.*, 7. Emmet and MacNeven are quoted from Thomas Addis Emmet, *Memoir of Thomas Addis and Robert Emmet* 2 vols. (New York, 1915) ii, 462; and John T. Gilbert, *Documents Relating to Ireland* (Dublin, 1913, new ed., 1970), 175. For the nature of the United Irish agenda, see Cullen, "Internal Politics" in Dickson, Keogh and Whelan, eds., *United Irishmen*, 176–96; Curtin, "The United Irish Organisation in Ulster" in ibid., 209–21; and James Quinn, "The United Irishmen and

For most of the 1790s what are usually taken to be the more "popular" aspects of public protest were mainly organised and led by the Defenders which, as had the Whiteboys and Rightboys in their time, protested against escalating tithes and rents as well as the high charges associated with the renewal of leases. They were also painted with the brush of conspiracy, due in part to a system of passwords and other types of mystical language and symbols, characteristics which the society shared with the United Irishmen. Unlike the United Irishmen, the Defenders were overwhelmingly Catholic. Their targets were often holdings which were owned by Protestants, or being vacated by Protestant emigrants. As a result, it was inevitable that in southeastern Ulster and northern Leinster, where the movement was strongest, their activities were sometimes presented in sectarian rather than in agrarian terms. As Whelan has pointed out, the "consciousness of dispossession," although deeply rooted in history, still retained a powerful appeal. The movement added to insecurities which had already been exacerbated among some Protestants by the repeal of the Penal Laws. One unsympathetic pamphleteer wrote in 1793 that "parochial meetings, county meetings, Catholic Committee, Societies of United Irishmen and Defenders were all jumbled together in one enormous mass of vice and wickedness." After 1795 such views would also be expressed through the Orange Order.[17]

As mutual distrust grew into fear, and prospects of a French invasion increased, Orangeism became as much a popular and armed instrument of the state as an outlet for expressing the agrarian grievances of Irish Protestants. In this climate, as Ian McBride has suggested, many who would otherwise have remained aloof joined either the Orange Order or the United Irishmen, depending on their background. It soon became clear that the original United Irish ideal that "no reform is practicable, efficacious, or just, which did not include Irishmen of every religious persuasion," would not be realised. The rise of sectarian rhetoric during the second half of the 1790s, as well as the draconian

---

Social Reform," *IHS* (2000), 113–28. For the place of the United Irishmen in late-eighteenth-century popular protest, see Curtin, *The United Irishmen: Popular Politics in Ulster and Dublin, 1791–1798* as well as her influential article, "The Transformation of the Society of United Irishmen into a Mass-Based Revolutionary Movement," *op. cit.*

17 Whelan, "The United Irishmen, the Enlightenment and Popular Culture" in Dickson, Keogh and Whelan, eds., *United Irishmen*, 274. In her "The Defenders in Ulster" in *ibid.*, 222–33, Marianne Elliot makes a similar point to Whelan's, that the evolution of the Defenders can be explained by, among other factors, the "relatively recent losses of land ... a sense of lost status ... [and] Protestant incursion into traditional Catholic territory" (the quotation is from 225). For a sense of how these memories had evolved, see Whelan, "An Underground Gentry? Catholic Middlemen in Eighteenth-Century Ireland," *Eighteenth-Century Ireland* x (1995), 7–68 and, from a different perspective, James Kelly, "'We Were all to have been Massacred:' Irish Protestants and the Experience of Rebellion" in Bartlett, Dickson, Keogh and Whelan, eds., *1798*, 312–30. The pamphleteer has been quoted from Smyth, *Men of No Property*, 66.

ways in which the agencies of government dealt with unrest and rebellion, wrecked Tone's ideal "to unite the whole people of Ireland, to abolish the memory of all past dissensions, and to substitute the common name of Irishman in place of the denominations of Protestant, Catholic and Dissenter." This was especially so from the later months of 1795 when the Defenders and the United Irishmen began to work more closely with one another, thus bringing the political and social emphases of protest together. This association also ensured that the "principles" of French republicanism would be interpreted in terms of social as well as political equality. Defenderism was, in the words of Jim Smyth, now "infused with an almost millenial zest." Catholics readily recalled the circumstances in which the island had been "planted" and "cleared" in the first place and how grievance had been piled on grievance. Thus, it was easy to characterise contemporary events in Ireland as "a formidable and extensive conspiracy" which posed a choice between two types of government, the first which existed with a British connection, the second, "a Republican form of government [which would be established] in conjunction with the French government." The "war of two civilisations" had been reignited in the rhetorical languages of the present.[18]

"The Present State of Ireland"

During and after 1796 American newspapers offered their own reports and analyses of "Irish affairs." In some cases, they relied on "authentic" or independent "letters" from "gentlemen" who had "just arrived" in Philadelphia. More usually, however, they printed their news from sources in contemporary Ireland and England although when they did, they often prefaced such columns with their own editorial observations. Thus, the reporting of Ireland in America not only conveyed news about events in Ireland but often how these were being interpreted in America.[19] For all editors, distress and disturbance in late-eighteenth-century Ireland were "shocking" and "perfectly astonishing." In 1797 the (Baltimore) *Maryland Daily Advertiser* described a country that was "in a state of hitherto unheard of wretchedness ... [with] villages ... burned to

---

18 Ian McBride, *Scripture Politics: Ulster Presbyterianism and Irish Radicalism in the late Eighteenth Century* (Oxford, 1998), 208–9; Elliott, *Wolfe Tone*, 140; Bartlett, ed., *Tone*, 46; Smyth, *Men of No Property*, 51; *IG*, 13 Apr. 1796. The concept of the "war of two civilisations" has been quoted from Hayes-McCoy, "Gaelic Society in the late-Sixteenth Century," 61 and is discussed in ch. 1 above.

19 Letters and reports on "the rise and progress of the late revolt in Ireland" are common in American newspapers. See, for example, those from "an Irish Emigrant" in the *Aurora*, 16 Mar. 1799, "a gentleman traveller through the North of Ireland" in *CR*, 15 May 1798 and "a Respectable Character in Ireland" in *Aurora*, 24 Dec. 1796. The title of the sub-section has been quoted from the *Aurora*, 1 Apr. 1798.

ashes ... [and] Many ... shot at their own doors." There were also reports
which described "the horrid outrages and murders which have been committed
by a savage British soldiery." The (New York) *Time-Piece* suggested that in part,
these brutalities had occurred because Ireland had been "divided into parties
who seem to breathe nothing but animosity against each other" and was, as a
result of the activities of the paramilitary yeomanry, in particular, "on the verge
of a terrible shock." In some cases, the accounts were quite vivid, especially
those from Ulster. In March 1799 the *Aurora* reported that the predominantly
Protestant yeomanry had "plundered, pulled down, and burned" the homes of
some eight hundred Catholics in Armagh, Down, and Tyrone, "killing some of
the principal heads of families." The raw sectarianism of such activities was
often reported in the American press, as was the peculiar nature of the yeomanry
as an agency of government. *Carey's* [Philadelphia] *Recorder* wondered

> What the end will be, God only knows: murder, robbery, plunder, burning,
> ravishment, &c. are daily and hourly committing by those who call themselves
> friends to government. Immediate death would be a pleasure to the tortures
> many suffer.[20]

Some newspapers also reminded their readers that there were two sides to
this coin and that the sectarianism of the oath of the Orange Order, for example,
was matched by that of the Defenders and the password by which it was known:
"EPIPHISMATIS ... Every Loyal Irish Protestant Heretick I Shall Murder And
This I Swear." Although Alan Blackstock and others suggest that sectarianism
in contemporary Ireland was a complex issue, the picture which American
newspapers conveyed at the time was that Ireland was a hopelessly divided
place. It was also a country where its divisions had developed into mutual
recriminations of a most violent and bloody kind. The progress of the rebellion
was reported, often in detail, with some American newspapers highlighting
differences between how it was impacting on various parts of the island. By and
large, the southern and western parts of Ireland were seen to be peaceful. In
March 1797 the *Time-Piece* suggested that even if the French expeditionary
force had successfully landed in Bantry Bay the previous December, "the

20 *MDA*, 5 Dec. 1797; *Aurora*, 1 May 1798; *Time-Piece*, 31 May, 30 June 1797; *Aurora*, 16
   Mar. 1799; *CR*, 24 July 1798. The generic descriptions have been quoted from *PorcG*, 2
   Jan. 1799; *GUS*, 2 Jan. 1799; and "Extract of a Letter from a Respectable Character in
   Ireland, to his friend in New-York, dated Oct. 4, 1796" in the *Aurora*, 24 Dec. 1796. For
   the theme of sectarianism in Ulster, see Kevin Whelan, "United and Disunited Irishmen:
   The State and Sectarianism in the 1790s" in his *Tree of Liberty*, 99–132; and Marianne
   Elliott, "Religious Polarization in the Ulster Rebellion" in Bartlett, Dickson, Keogh and
   Whelan, eds., *1798*, 279–97.

general good disposition of the people through the south and west was so prevalent, that ... their hope of assistance from the inhabitants would have been totally disappointed." The situation in Ulster was different although even from there, the *Aurora* was reporting that by August 1798 "every appearance of Rebellion ... seems to be at an end, and the leaders disposed of." Continuing "engagements" in counties Wicklow, Wexford, Kildare, Cork, [and] parts of Tipperary and Kilkenny proved that the country was anything but peaceful and Irish newspapers were still "filled principally with details respecting unhappy Ireland." On 4 January 1799 the same newspaper was still (erroneously) reporting that the rebellion "so far from being suppressed, is as formidable as it was six months ago – and that one of the most populous tracts in Ireland of several miles in extent was completely in the possession of the *rebels*." While American newspapers sometimes challenged the view that "the island in general meant to throw itself under the protection of the French Republic," it was generally difficult for Americans to distinguish fact from fancy. For the Federalist traveller, Joseph Allen Smith, it was because of its links with France that Ireland was a scene of "wanton cruelty and devastation" as the United Irishmen had no sense of moderation, "consideration or principle." In America, the dominant image of Ireland remained as "an incessant Golgatha" which had been partly caused by France.[21]

Such impressions of a country that was marked by atrocity and knee-deep in blood were reinforced in private correspondence, especially as public order deteriorated during 1798. In June 1798 the Irish-born American radical and educator, Daniel McCurtain (b.1745) informed Mathew Carey of the "horrid picture... [which] our ill-fated country presents to the friend[s] of Man" and in a more emotional link to the atrocities of an earlier rising, he suggested that "1641 vanishes before it." A British army doctor, Dr. George Pinckard (1768–1835), seemed to agree when, in March 1799, he wrote to his influential friend, Benjamin Rush, of "the horrid scenes of an enraged and savage Rebellion" in

21 *IG*, 8 June 1796; Alan Blackstock, "The Social and Political Implications of the Rising of the Yeomanry in Ulster: 1796–8" in Dickson, Keogh and Whelan, eds., *United Irishmen*, 234–43. *Time-Piece*, 27 Mar. 1797; *Aurora*, 31 Aug. 1798; *GUS*, 2 Jan. 1799; NYHS, King Mss., Smith to King, dated from Dublin, 1 June 1798; Mathew Carey, *A Plumb Pudding for the Humane, Chaste, Valiant, Enlightened Peter Porcupine* (Philadelphia, 1799), 22. The regional rebellions of 1797–8 are analysed in Bartlett, Dickson, Keogh and Whelan, eds., *1798*, 97–187. Smith, half-brother of congressman William Loughton Smith (F., S.C., 1789–97) and minister to Spain and Portugal (1797–1801), spent much of the time between 1793 and 1808 in London; see Michael O'Brien, *Conjectures of Order Set. Intellectual Life in the American South, 1810–1860* (Chapel Hill, 2004), 92. For the currency of EPIPHISMATIS in Ireland, see Curtin, "The Transformation of the Society of United Irishmen into a Mass-Based Revolutionary Movement," 478–81.

Ireland. Joseph Allen Smith's lengthy letter to **Rufus King**, then the American minister in London (1796–1803), was particularly graphic. Among other incidents, it referred to a "massacre" at Prosperous, Co. Kildare, summary executions in Co. Meath, "persons taken up, flogged & otherwise tortured ...dead bodies exposed in the [Dublin] Castle Yard ... several persons hanging at the lamp posts ... [and the] many servants [who] had purchased arsenic for the purpose of poisoning their masters." One can only imagine the impact which such a letter made on King at the very time when he was being asked to allow those who had participated in the 1798 rebellion to emigrate to America. It seemed to confirm the view of the United Irishmen as a French-inspired "conspiracy ... having for its object a general Insurrection & Massacre." For the Federalist press in the United States, the point was clear: that the brutality of the rebellion in Ireland was an example of what would happen when people supported "a Revolution on French principles." As Cobbett and Fenno observed, the cruelties of the Irish rebellion of 1798 were the "consequence of the principles and practices of the United Irishmen." Now, they suggested, "agents" of the same organisation had "coalesced with the Jacobins of France" to establish "a revolutionary state" in America and to subvert the democracy of the new republic. They had to be stopped.[22]

Irish Radicals in Philadelphia

The offer by the French Convention in November 1792 to "grant fraternity and assistance to all peoples who wish to recover their liberty" had already highlighted the potential threat of the United Irishmen in Ireland and it was only a matter of time before the society was proscribed there. This happened in May 1794 and many of its leading figures decided to leave the country even if, in some cases, only temporarily. America offered a secure, if distant, refuge as well as the comfort, fellowship, and company of congenial people who essentially believed in the same things as they did. As Tone wrote after his arrival in America in 1795, "the moment I landed [in America], I was free to follow any plan which might suggest itself to me, for the emancipation of my [own] country." Maldwyn Jones has thus described such leaders as "less immigrant than exile" in their temporary havens. In a similar vein, a United Irish "entertainment" in Philadelphia in 1799 toasted "The Emigrant Irish

---

22 HSP, Miscellaneous Correspondence of Dr. Benjamin Rush, xiii, 90, Pinckard to Rush, 10 Mar. 1799; NYHS, King Mss., Smith to King, dated Dublin, 1 June 1798; *GIG*, 30 June 1797; *PorcG*, 21 Dec. 1798; *GUS*, 22, 18 Nov., 18 Dec. 1798. McCurtain has been quoted from Miller, Schrier, Boling and Doyle, eds., *Irish Immigrants in the Land of Canaan*, 592.

Republicans—*Soon and successful be their return*" while the preamble to the constitution of the American Society of United Irishmen proclaimed that the "love of freedom has not been lessened ... for Ireland by our distance." A similar sentiment is also implicit in a curious story which Rush recalled in 1811 of a meeting with Archibald Hamilton Rowan: "'Our situation,' said I, 'Mr. Roan [*sic*], is a good deal alike in Philadelphia. We are both in an *enemy's* country.' 'No, sir,' said he, 'I am in a *foreign* country only.'"23

Of those who went to the Delaware Valley, Rowan was to have a particularly important influence over the Irish community and the Republican politics of the area. In January 1794 he had been convicted for "seditious conspiracy" and distributing "a seditious paper" in Dublin, as a result of which he was fined £500 and committed to Newgate prison for two years. The following May he escaped from "the Irish Bastil" to France. While in Paris, Rowan often met influential figures such as Paine, and became a close friend of the then American minister to France (1794–96) and future president, James Monroe (1758–1831), whom he later thanked for his "polite attentions." In 1795 Rowan sailed from Le Havre to Philadelphia. En route, his ship was searched by the British navy but posing as one "Mr. Thompson of South Carolina," Rowan safely arrived in the Delaware on 13 July with appropriate references and recommendations. Within a few days, he was staying at a boarding house in Philadelphia with several members of Congress, including the future presidents, John Adams (1797–1801) and Andrew Jackson (1829–37). He was also said to have received a letter from George Washington "complimenting him on his arrival in an asylum in which the Rights of Man created no alarm, but were practically enforced and supported by the Government."24

On 21 July 1795 Rowan dined with the Co. Carlow born Senator Pierce Butler (R., S. Carolina, 1789–96), a man he described as "of the patriotic party

23 Bartlett, ed., *Tone*, 105; Jones, *American Immigration*, 85; *Aurora*, 21 Mar. 1799; William Cobbett, *Detection of a Conspiracy, formed by the United Irishmen with the Evident Intention of Aiding the Tyrants of France in Subverting the Government of the United States of America* (Philadelphia, 6 May 1798), 6; Butterfield, ed., *Letters of Benjamin Rush* ii, Rush to John Adams, 26 Dec. 1811. The "propaganda decree" of Nov. 1792 has been quoted from Blanning, *French Revolutionary Wars*, 92.

24 William H. Drummond, ed., *The Autobiography of Archibald Hamilton Rowan* (Dublin, 1840, repr. Shannon, 1972), 184, 183; *DESA*, 4 June, 5, 26 July, 22 Oct. 1794; HSP, European Miscellaneous Papers, box 28, case 13, Rowan to Monroe, 13 Feb. 1800; Drummond, ed., *Archibald Hamilton Rowan*, 278; *CHC*, 10 Sept. 1795; Drummond, ed., *Archibald Hamilton Rowan*, 279, 282. Washington's supposed letter was reported in *DEP*, 17 Sept. 1795. Later, Tone also recalled that when he met Monroe in February 1796, the U.S. minister asked about Rowan and spoke of him "in terms of great respect;" see diary entry for 23 Feb. 1796, as in Bartlett, ed., *Tone*, 476. For a report to Whitehall on Rowan's arrival in Philadelphia in July 1795, see NA, FO 5/11, report dated 28 July 1795.

here" and who had been "very obliging" to him since he had arrived in Philadelphia. Indeed, his "kindness and friendship" were such that in 1796 Rowan's wife, Sarah Anne, wrote a highly personal letter to Butler in which she asked that because Rowan had not replied to her letters, if she had "displeased" her husband in any way. When Rowan heard of the letter, he berated Butler "for holding a secret correspondence with my wife" and, in particular, for supporting an official offer which had been made to Mrs. Rowan to settle in England. The Philadelphia printer, Thomas Stevens, dedicated the American edition of the *Proceedings of the Society of United Irishmen of Dublin* (Philadelphia, 1795) to Butler as "A Senator of the United States of America, An Enemy of Aristocracy; and a Friend of Man." However, it is clear that Butler's support of Rowan had been influenced by ancestral nostalgia rather than political ideology and there is no evidence that Butler supported the United Irish cause in America. Nonetheless, because of such influential contacts, Rowan faced "inquisitive questions" from British agents as a result of which he moved to Delaware in March 1796 where he established himself as a printer and dyer, and where **George Logan** (1753–1821) introduced him to his famous cousin, John Dickinson, as a man whose "political character is well known, & the sacrifices he has made in the cause of Liberty have been very great." Dickinson was to become an influential and loyal friend during Rowan's stay in America and indeed, when Rowan later filed his petition for a royal pardon, Dickinson and his own father were the only people to whom he sent copies of the correspondence.[25]

Rowan's other important American connections were the family of Caesar Rodney who had led the Revolution in Delaware and whom he had met during an earlier tour of America in the 1770s. Through Rodney, Rowan extended his social and political connections and as his subsequent correspondence shows, he befriended many of the leading Jeffersonians of the area. These included, in addition to Logan, Dickinson, and Rodney, William Poole, Dr. James Tilton (1745–1802), member of both the Continental Congress (1783–85) and several Delaware assemblies, and Robert Hamilton, each of whom regarded Rowan as another messenger of a movement that was not confined by class, interest, or

25 HSP, Butler Papers, Miscellaneous Correspondence, box 16, folder 9, letters from Mrs. Rowan to Butler, 22 Aug. 1796, and Rowan to Butler, 2 April 1797; *Proceedings of the Society of the United Irishmen of Dublin* (Philadelphia, 1795), dedication page; Harold Nicholson, *The Desire to Please* (New York, 1943), 162; HSD, John Dickinson Collection, box 3, Logan to Rowan, 28 Mar. 1796; HSP, Maria Dickinson Logan Family Papers, Rowan to Dickinson, 9 Sept., 26 Apr. 1803. For Rowan's sojourn in Paris and his campaign to return from America to Ireland (which was eventually successful in 1806), see RIA, 24 K 48 and PRONI, T823, "Pieces concernant le Sr. Archibald Hamilton Rowan, refugie Irlandais debarque a Roscoff;" and Durey, *Transatlantic Radicals and the Early American Republic*, 213–6.

national origin. Governor Mifflin was also "particularly attentive" and by September 1795, he had already entertained Rowan at his country retreat. On 6 September, Mifflin took him "down to the river to shoot reed-birds." Even before he had developed these contacts, Rowan's reputation had been widely discussed. As Mathew Carey informed a friend in Dublin in June 1795, "there are in this country thousands of kindly souls, who sympathize in his sufferings." There were others who were less taken by Rowan. In March 1796 John Fisher suggested to Rodney's son, Caesar Augustus (1772–1824), that "I fear he is making himself too cheap, by traveling about with every dunce, that aspires to his acquaintance." However, while it is true that Rowan involved himself in different campaigns, these often reflected the social concerns of the Reform Movement that he had left behind in Ireland and were far from casual. In August 1796, for example, he was so touched by the fact that forty passengers had died on the ship *Harriot* en route from Ireland to America, that thirty six had been impressed, and that several others had arrived "sick," that he "used the utmost exertions in procuring accommodations for the relief of those distressed emigrants." The following year, he also expressed his concerns about the "swarms of Irish" who continued to arrive in Philadelphia and bemoaned the city's "brisk trade for *Irish slaves* ... to make up for the low price of flax seed."[26]

In Philadelphia, Rowan renewed contact with the Tyrone-born Dr. James Reynolds who, as he, had been an active and radical member of the Dublin section of the United Irishmen and between 1792 and 1794, had served on the committee to draw up a plan for parliamentary reform. In 1794 Reynolds was among the United Irish leaders who met the French agent, William Jackson, to negotiate French support for the activities of the United Irishmen in Ireland. When these meetings were revealed by an English spy, he fled from Ireland on the ship *Swift* (Belfast to Newcastle and New York) in May 1794. During the voyage, according to Cobbett, he "assisted at the hanging of King George in effigy, on board the ship, in which he came passenger." Of his association with other United Irish exiles, Leonard MacNally, later to become notorious as an informer, reported in 1795 that

26 Nicholson, *Desire to Please*, 33–4, 43; Rowan's diary (September 1795), as in Drummond, ed., *Archibald Hamilton Rowan*, 284, 283; HSP, Lea & Febiger Collection, Letterbooks (1792–7), Carey to Chambers, 19 June 1795; HSD, John Fisher Papers (1794–1800), folder I, Fisher to Rodney, 2 Mar. 1796; *IG*, 6 Aug. 1796. Rowan's comments on Irish immigration in 1797 are quoted from James McLaughlin, *Matthew Lyon, the Hampden of Congress* (New York, 1900), 43. Although the report in *IG* identified the *Harriot* as the distressed vessel, it is clear from marine records that the relevant vessel was the *Henrietta* (from Derry to Newcastle and Philadelphia); see *Aurora*, 4 Aug. 1798. For Rowan's correspondence with his friends in Delaware, see HSD, Archibald Hamilton Rowan Manuscripts, Ms. 40.45, manuscript article by Lewis P. Bush, M.D.; and HSP, Gratz Collection, letters from Rowan to Rodney, 1779–1816.

A kind of seditious connection is now forming in America, composed of Hamilton Rowan, Napper Tandy, Doctor Reynolds, Wolfe Tone and other fugitives from Ireland. These men have it in their power, and no doubt it is their wish to give every possible information and assistance to France.

When he published the constitution of the *American Society of United Irishmen*, also in 1797, Cobbett associated the society with Reynolds. However, in his autobiography, Rowan placed Reynolds's arrival in Philadelphia much earlier and suggested that he had come to America before the enactment of the naturalisation act of 1795, most probably in May 1794, after the United Irishmen had been formally proscribed. In any event, once he had arrived in his new home, Reynolds would "amuse himself with the politics of America" and in Rowan's words, became "as busy, as sincere, and as zealous as he was in [Dublin's] Kilmainham" jail. Rowan and Reynolds remained close friends. Indeed, Rowan recalled in 1803 that he owed his life to a "certain vapour" that Reynolds had administered to him during the yellow fever epidemic of 1797.[27]

Having being implicated in charges of high treason against Jackson, Tone had left Ireland in June 1795 together with his wife, sister, and three children. On 1 August he arrived in Wilmington and within a week, journeyed to Philadelphia where he stayed with Rowan. In the same lodgings, he also found that his "old friend and brother exile," James Reynolds, was already "very comfortably settled." Rowan gave him a letter of introduction to the local French minister, Pierre Adet, who asked him "to throw on paper, in the form of a memorial, all [that] I [Tone] had to communicate on the subject of Ireland." In this document, Tone suggested that as Ireland was a major supplier of food to the army and navy, "England" would defend its position in Ireland to the last, all the more so because in his opinion, "England *cannot* exist without Ireland." However, Tone believed that English interests in Ireland could be "destroyed" by an invasionary force of 20,000 Frenchmen acting in concert with a domestic rebellion although for the moment, Adet ignored Tone's offer to take the memorial to France. Tone was not encouraged by the "selfish and interested" culture that he saw in Philadelphia, a view that was shared by Rowan and Reynolds. He settled on a 180-acre farm in Princeton, New Jersey, where he would

27 Wilson, *United Irishmen, United States*, 21; Durey, *Transatlantic Radicals*, 168; *PG*, 2 Feb. 1798; Cobbett, *Detection of a Conspiracy*, 5, 22–4; Drummond, ed., *Archibald Hamilton Rowan*, 284, 283; HSP, Maria Dickinson Logan Family Papers, Rowan to Dickinson, 9 Sept., 26 Apr. 1803. Although Cobbett did not publish the constitution of the American Society of the United Irishmen until 6 May 1798, he gave 8 Aug. 1797 as the date when the constitution was originally "printed for the Society;" see Cobbett, *Detection of a Conspiracy*, 6. MacNally's secret service report is quoted in Rupert Coughlin, *Napper Tandy* (Dublin, 1976), 110, n.8.

try ... [to] form a farmers club ... with a small annual subscription to be laid out in purchasing an Agricultural Library, importing seeds etc. from Europe, for experiments, introducing articles from other parts of the Union, and trying them here.[28]

Despite his disillusionment with Philadelphia politics, Tone consulted with **John Beckley**, Jefferson's close confidant and clerk of the U.S. house of representatives (1789–1807). Partly because of such contacts, he was convinced that he was "most probably watched" during his residence in the city by "English agents." After further encouragement from his friends in Ireland "that the state of the public mind in Ireland was advancing to republicanism faster than even I could believe," Tone again visited Adet. On this occasion, Adet gave Tone letters of introduction to the Committee of Public Safety in Paris. The Irish-born French government official, Nicholas Madgett, also advised Rowan, that Tone should leave Philadelphia "instantly, in order to confer with the French government and determine the necessary arrangements, and that he had done this by order of the French Executive." Beckley helped Tone to secure his passport and gave him a coded introduction to Monroe in which he described Tone as "an agent from Ireland, in whom you may justly confide." Having wound up his affairs in America, Tone left for France on 1 January 1796.[29]

Two weeks before he sailed, Tone spent a day with Rowan, Reynolds, and Tandy, his "old friend and fellow-sufferer" from Ireland. Tandy had been active in popular politics in Dublin during the 1770s and in 1775 he sent a pro-American address to the King. Later, while he was secretary of the Dublin section of the United Irishmen, he was forced to leave Ireland for "having, at a meeting of the Society of United Irishmen, armed with swords and bayonets, distributed libelous and seditious printed papers addressed by the Society to the Volunteers of Ireland, calling upon them to arm." He left for Hamburg and from there, for America, where he arrived in September 1795. On 10 September 1795 the *Aurora* reported that Tandy had been received in Philadelphia "with the greatest complimentary acclamations, and that the citizens [had] illuminated their houses at night for joy" on his arrival in their city. Because Tandy, like Tone, saw himself as an active agent of an international movement, he quickly established an "intimate and cordial relationship" with Adet. On 27 September

28 Bartlett, ed., *Tone*, 110, 111; J.J. St. Mark, "Wolfe Tone's Diplomacy in America: August–December, 1795," *Eire-Ireland* vii (1972), 8; Nicholson, *Desire to Please*, 160. For Tone's plans for his club, see TCD, Sirr Mss., Tone to Thomas Russell, 25 Oct. 1795. For Tone's time in America, see Elliott, *Tone*, ch.20.

29 Bartlett, ed., *Tone*, 111, 113, 114, 470; NYPL, Monroe Papers, Beckley to Monroe, 14 Dec. 1795. For a review of Tone's contacts with Adet, see TCD, Sirr Mss., Tone to Delacroix, 26 Feb. 1796.

1797 MacNally wrote that "the first solicitation to France, from the independent party in Ireland, was through the medium of the French Ambassador at Philadelphia—J.N. Tandy the Agent." During these years the pivotal role of Philadelphia in these "solicitations" was underlined when in 1796 the French minister for foreign affairs, Charles Delacroix (1795–97), suggested to Tone that any "military stores" the French might offer to the United Irishmen in Ireland might be channeled through America.[30]

For security and practical reasons, Tone disagreed with Delacroix although MacNally later claimed that the plans for the ill-fated Bantry Bay expedition were known in Philadelphia three months before it actually took place. While this is difficult to believe, by 1797, the United Irishmen were thought to be well-entrenched in a number of American as well as European locations. In this, they reflected what on 15 December 1792 the *National Gazette* had stated "as our opinion, that [radical] *Ireland* is deeply involved in the progress of liberty in France—and not only Ireland, but the *whole world*," including the United States. In a country which had recently seen the power of "democratic revolution," there were fears that radical Irish immigrants might promote another revolution "from below" or "from outside." A potential war with France did not diminish that fear and convinced Federalists that the United Irishmen were not just "disaffected Irishmen" but international conspirators who were also "disaffected with the government of the United States."[31]

National and International Networks

From the time they were founded, the United Irishmen had always seen themselves as part of an international brotherhood. Although this aspect of their history was recalled in the 1840s by R.R. Madden, it is only recently that it has been given due recognition.[32] The society corresponded with like-minded

30 Bartlett, ed., *Tone*, 114; Durey, *Transatlantic Radicals*, 87, 111–12; Coughlin, *Napper Tandy*, 111; Bartlett, ed., *Tone*, 470. The charges against Tandy have been quoted from Coughlin, *Napper Tandy*, 95. With respect to dating Tandy's arrival in Philadelphia, Tone recalled before he left for France on 1 Jan. 1796, that Tandy had "recently arrived from Hamburg;" see Bartlett, ed., *Tone*, 114. For the United Irishmen and France, see Elliot, *Partners in Revolution*.

31 Coughlin, *Napper Tandy*, 111; *PorcG*, 21 Dec. 1798. The other citation is from Palmer, *Age of Democratic Revolution*. For a more recent interpretation of the view that a war between America and France was a distinct possibility, and of the ways in which this impacted on contemporary American politics, see James Roger Sharp, *American Politics in the Early Republic: The New Nation in Crisis* (New Haven and London, 1993).

32 For the international aspects of the United Irishmen, see Elliott, *Partners in Revolution*; Durey, *Transatlantic Radicals*; Wilson, *United Irishmen, United States*; Paul Weber, *On the Road to Rebellion: the United Irishmen and Hamburg, 1796–1803* (Dublin, 1997); and

people abroad in a network that stretched from Edinburgh to London, and from Hamburg to Paris. The individual "sections" kept in contact with one another through their "delegates" as well as through a system of formal addresses. The United Britons, for example, sent a representative to Ireland to remind their colleagues there that

> from mutual sufferings & mutual commiseration, the prejudice of Nations is done away [with] and the English burn with desire to hail the Irish as Freemen & as Brethren ... the emancipation of both countries ... [was] the greater object ... we offer you our confidence and in return, demand yours.

On 17 January 1798 the society in Ireland was told that it had eleven delegates between Hamburg and Paris alone.[33] Wolfe Tone, resident of Philadelphia (June to December 1795) and then of Paris (February to September 1796), was often seen as the *éminence grise* of these international links. One of his more important contacts in Paris was Madgett. It was he who advised Tone that "such money as was indispensable" as well as "military stores ... in neutral bottoms" could be sent "through the medium of America" from France to Ireland. Although Tone thought that this plan was "impracticable," he did not doubt Madgett's influence with the Directory. Tone was also "very politely" received by Monroe on 15 February 1796. By this time his coded letter of introduction from Beckley had been deciphered and he had "no difficulty" in getting access to the American minister. Monroe's influence in Paris was not inconsequential and he was willing to use it on Tone's behalf. When, at a subsequent interview with Tone on 23 February, Monroe advised his Irish friend that he should "go at once to the Directoire Executif and demand an audience," he told him that he "may go so far as to refer to me for the authenticity of what you may advance, and you may add that you have reason to think that I am, in a degree, apprised of the outline

Maurice J. Bric, "The United Irishmen, International Republicanism and the Definition of the Polity in the United States of America, 1791–1800" in *Proceedings of the Royal Irish Academy* civ, no.4 (2004), 81–106. For Madden, see C.J. Woods, "R.R. Madden, Historian of the United Irishmen" in Bartlett, Dickson, Keogh and Whelan, eds., *1798*, 497–511.

33 PRONI, D714/2/13, "United Britons to the United Irishmen," n.d.; PRONI, D714/2/14, 17 January 1798; *GUS*, 30 Mar. 1799. See also "Address from United Britons to United Irishmen" and "Address of the London Corresponding Society to the Irish Nation" in *Report of the Committee of Secrecy of the House of Commons of Great Britain* (Dublin, 1799), 68–70 and 70–3, respectively. For the society's system of international delegates, see also Gerlof D. Homan, "Palmer vs. Brown: the Society of United Irishmen in the Batavian Republic," *Eire-Ireland* xiv (1979), 30–4. For the connections between the United Irishmen and the United Britons, see Durey, *Transatlantic Radicals*, 126–7. For the United Irishmen in Britain, see *Report of the Committee of Secrecy*, 9–16, 24–35, 43–73, 75–87. For the United Irishmen in Hamburg, see *ibid.*, 35–6.

of your business." The two men often dined together and became such good friends that Monroe also assisted Tone financially.[34]

American sections also latched on to these networks and on 18 December 1798 the *Gazette of the United States* reported that "A permanent committee of correspondence has existed for three years [in America], with the executive directory of France, and another with the revolters in Ireland. With both, constant intercourse and communication is maintained." In America, the fact that such well-known radical *émigrés* as Paine, Joseph Priestley, Joseph Callender, and Thomas Cooper moved in the same political and social *milieux* as the United Irishmen made a similar point. Although he probably never visited Ireland, Paine was elected as a member of the United Irishmen in Dublin and let this be known after he arrived in America in 1794. Cobbett thus made the crucial observation, as he saw it: "Americans, then, and Britons, and Frenchmen, and men of every country being eligible to the society. Can any one be silly enough to suppose that the [United Irish] conspiracy had only Ireland in view?" Given their international understanding of contemporary reform, most of his adversaries did not disagree. In 1793, even Rowan observed that the "votarys [*sic*] of liberty are of no country, or rather of every country."[35]

In Philadelphia, the first published version of the constitution of the American Society of United Irishmen was agreed in August 1797. However, it is clear from other sources that the society had been active for some time before this. In May 1798 one writer recalled that it had been founded in Philadelphia "more than three years" earlier by "a number of men who had fled from the north of Ireland." In August 1797 a report to the House of Commons had also suggested that even by then, there were "a number of [United Irish] societies formed in North America." Membership was open to all "as have suffered in the cause of freedom" and who were known for "their zeal for THE RIGHTS OF MANKIND," "civism, "a free form of government, and uncontrouled [*sic*] opinion on all subjects." These themes were repeated in the test which each member was obliged to take:

> I A.B. in the presence of the SUPREME BEING, do most solemnly swear, that I will, to the utmost of my power, promote the emancipation of Ireland from the tyranny of the British Government. That I will use the like endeavours

34 Tone's Journals, 17, 15, 23 Feb. 1796, as in Bartlett, ed., *Tone*, 470, 466, 468, 476 *et passim*.
35 Richard Twomey, *Jacobins and Jeffersonians: Anglo-American Radicalism in the United States, 1790–1820* (New York, 1989), 218, 42; Cobbett, *Detection of a Conspiracy*, 8. Rowan is quoted from Durey, *Transatlantic Radicals*, 331, n4. For Paine's membership of the Dublin section of the United Irishmen, see LC, Paine Papers. For Paine and Ireland, see David Dickson, "Paine and Ireland" in Dickson, Keogh and Whelan, eds., *The United Irishmen*, 135–50.

for increasing and perpetuating the warmest affections among all religious denominations of men, and for the attainment of LIBERTY AND EQUALITY TO MANKIND, IN WHATEVER NATION I MAY RESIDE. Moreover, I do swear, that I will, as far as in me lies, promote the interest of this and every other society of United Irishmen, and of each of its members; and that I will never, from fear of punishment, or hope of reward, divulge any of its SECRETS given to me as such.

"Emancipation" was also linked to the view that the British government would never be "disposed to acknowledge, or assent, to the freedom of Ireland" and that as a result, it should not "of right" govern Ireland. In order to promote these aims, the society usually met every week in sections of no more than forty members, each of which was presided over by a chairman, secretary, and treasurer. Despite its essentially secret character, a committee of correspondence ensured internal and intersection contact. A delegate and sub-delegate were also chosen to attend the meetings of neighbouring sections and to "report proceedings." If a member wanted to relocate, or travel abroad, this committee would also furnish "certificates" of introduction to people in the new abode.[36]

Financially, the United Irishmen were maintained by initiation and monthly fees as well as by fines. Although there were allegations that by August 1797 $211 had been remitted from "the Brotherhood in North America" to "the Irish Union," payments both to and from the society were irregular and were nothing like the similar remittances of the following century. The American society also hosted readings from contemporary radical works, many of which were published in Philadelphia during the 1790s. These included Thomas Stephens's *Proceedings of the Society of United Irishmen of Dublin*, a work which brought together various resolutions, addresses, circulars, and reports of radical meetings that had take place between 1791 and 1794. When it was published in Philadelphia in 1795, it was described by one regional newspaper as being "of high importance to the cause of Civil and Religious Liberty." It was complemented by American editions of other radical publications from Ireland as well as by the

36 Cobbett, *Detection of a Conspiracy*, 6; "Montgomery" in *CR*, 19 May 1798; Cobbett, *Detection of a Conspiracy*, 7, 9, 9–10, 9, 14, 16, 14, 17, 16. The reference to the Irish parliamentary report is cited in *PorcG*, 18 May 1798 (hereafter cited as "*Irish Report*"). See also "Of the origin, character and views of the societies of UNITED IRISHMEN, in Philadelphia, and elsewhere in the United States" in *GUS*, 5 Dec. 1798. For a detailed contemporary account of the "nature and system of United Irishmen, as fully established in Ireland," see *Report of the Committee of Secrecy*; the quotation is from the heading of section I, 7. The oath of the Belfast society, while not unlike that of Philadelphia, by promoting "a brotherhood of affection" and a commitment to reform, does not have the sense of international reference; for the Irish oath, see A. T. Q. Stewart, *A Deeper Silence: The Hidden Origins of the United Irishmen* (Belfast, 1998), 162.

republication in America of important articles by and about the United Irishmen in Ireland. In March 1792 for example, the *Declaration and Resolutions of the Society of United Irishmen of Belfast* of October 1791 were published in the *American Daily Advertiser* while a month later the Dublin resolutions, as signed by Napper Tandy, were carried in the same newspaper. Thomas Ledlie Birch's influential *Account of the Rise and Progress of the Commotions in Ireland* was also published in Philadelphia in 1799. Other publications were sent directly from Dublin. In March 1794 John Chambers sent Mathew Carey "two Copies of the *published* Proceedings of the *much abused United Irishmen* [that] ... were finished only this day." Such writings reflected not only the "character and views of the societies of United Irishmen" but also the society's commitment to political education.[37]

Although each section was obliged to keep minutes and a "roll," and to make quarterly returns of the "*numbers, names, residences, and occupations of its members*" to its state committee, none of these detailed records seem to have survived. However, it is clear that there were state committees and district sections in Pennsylvania, Delaware, Maryland, and New York. On 20 August 1798 the *Aurora* even carried a notice calling "an aggregate meeting" of "the several sections of this Society as are now in Philadelphia." Thus, Cobbett did not have "the least doubt" that there was a "General EXECUTIVE Committee" or "Directory" which "is now sitting in Philadelphia" and which connected the "exertions of ... individuals ... in different parts of the United States ... under one ... superintending guidance." Various sources suggest that its "chief agent" was either Rowan or (more probably) Reynolds and that the "mother society" was located in Philadelphia. Without an "exact register" of its members, it is impossible to quantify the movement's numerical strength in the city. However, in May 1798 Cobbett suggested that in the greater Philadelphia area, the membership of the United Irishmen had grown to some 1,500 and that as a result, its usual meeting-place at the African School had to be abandoned because "their number was become too great for so small a room."[38]

37 Cobbett, *Detection of a Conspiracy*, 13, 15–16, 15; *ADA*, 26 Mar. 1795; *DESA*, 18 Feb. 1795; *ADA*, 28 Mar., 4 Apr. 1792; HSP, Lea & Febiger, Incoming Correspondence (1785–96), box 4, Chambers to Carey, Dublin, 26 Mar. 1794; *GUS*, 5 Dec., 1798. The remittance figure is quoted from the *Report of the Committee of Secrecy*, app. xiv, as in *PorcG*, 18 May 1798. For the re-publication of United Irish addresses, see *NG*, 7 Apr., 22 June 1792 and 27 Apr. 1793.

38 Cobbett, *Detection of a Conspiracy*, 15, 16, 27, 19; *GUS*, 18 Dec. 1798; *PorcG*, 3 Nov. 1798; *GUS*, 27 Nov. 1798; Cobbett, *Detection of a Conspiracy*, 16; *PorcG*, 15 May 1798. For reports of United Irish activities in Maryland, see *GUS*, 18 Dec. 1798, and Maryland Diocesan Archives, Vertical Files, Rev. Archibald Walker to Bishop John Thomas Claggett, where Walker complained that the "United Irish preachers" were provoking

It is difficult to comment authoritatively on the accuracy of Cobbett's information. *Carey's Recorder* rejected his figure, also in May 1798, although it did admit that

> several hundreds of industrious men have been taken from their wives, children, and firesides in Ireland, and have had the alternative of the gallows, or to transport themselves in a given time to America. Many have effected their passage hither by the sale of their effects, and others by the sub-scriptions of their countrymen at home ... Some of those who had been united Irishmen and had obtained employment here, resolved to associate to aid and assist their brethern; and such as had been compelled to save their lives by indenting themselves, were principally the objects of the society.

Only seventeen were specifically identified as members of Philadelphia's Society of United Irishmen and some of these denied the connection. Cobbett and Fenno published the list in December 1798. It included two schoolmasters, Thomas MacAdam and John O'Reilly, a shoe-seller, Daniel Clark, and Samuel Parke, who kept a tavern in Zachary's Court. Clark was the person to whom "brethern" were usually invited to apply for "cards of admission" to meetings of the United Irishmen in Philadelphia. I have been unable to identify four others although Mathew Carey later described two of them as tailors and the others as tavern keepers. In any event, Fenno's description of one of these four as a Mr. Lloyd "of Newgate" was intended to suggest that such people whoever they were, were of questionable background. The list also included Mathew Carey and his brother, James (also a printer and editor), James Reynolds, the editors **John Daly Burk** (1775–1808) of the *Time-Piece* and William Duane of the *Aurora*, and Samuel Wiley and John Black, both of the College of Pennsylvania, all of whom were familiar in Jeffersonian networks. **Matthew Lyon**, Vermont's Irish-born Republican congressman (1797–1801), and James Callender were also mentioned. Five of those who were named formally denied that they were affiliated with the United Irishmen although in doing so, James Carey insisted that even if Cobbett's allegations were true, there was nothing wrong with belonging to the society and that, in any event, no "supposed odium [should] attach to the members of that, society." Thus, addressing the *Gazette of the United States* on 18 January 1799 Reynolds stated that he felt "no insult to

differences and difficulties within the Maryland clergy. For a report of "secret meetings" in Wilmington, see *GUS*, 11 Dec. 1798. *GUS*, 29 Jan. and 7 Mar. 1799 also reported on "the alarming extent and increasing virulence of the United Irishmen" in Montgomery County, Pennsylvania. For the United Irishmen in New York, see Massachusetts Historical Society, Pickering Papers (microfilm), (hereafter cited as Pickering Papers), dated Albany, 21 Dec. 1798. For a general survey, see Wilson, *United Irishmen. United States.*

be called an United Irishman. I glory in the illustrious epithet." However, he did demand "satisfaction" from Fenno for publicly alleging that he was one. Fenno declined, denouncing Reynolds as "a traitor and an outlaw."[39]

Whether those named were actually United Irishmen or not is less important than that they were supposed to be shady characters who were incapable of giving any loyalty to any government. It was in this context that Federalist newspapers also dubbed the well-known Jeffersonians, George Logan, James Tilton, Caesar Rodney, and Thomas McKean as United Irishmen. By connecting the United Irishmen with the secretive masonic order and, in particular, with the development of the Illuminati, they also linked the society with a "conspiracy ... [aimed] at the overthrow of religion & government throughout the world." Not only was this supposed threat "*well-founded*" according to Dwight Foster (F., Mass., 1793–1800), but its Jacobin "political missionaries," "infidels," and "disciples of Tom Pain [*sic*]" had established masonic lodges in America "ostensibly ... for other purposes, [but which] are really political." As to Ireland, and despite the country's deeply-rooted tradition of popular protest, the **Abbé Barruel** (1741–1820) saw the origins of the United Irishmen there as "couched in the style and exact terms of the Hierophants of Illuminism." The society's structures, test, and organisation were also taken to be masonic in origin and character. In America, the secretary of the treasury (1795–1800), Oliver Wolcott, thus believed that because of their broadly-based membership and "mystery," masonic societies were ideal vehicles for Jacobin agents to pursue "a general plan of *Secret Mischief*" in the United States.[40] **Uriah Tracy** (F., Conn., 1793–96, Senator, Conn., 1796–1807) also announced that he had seen "very many Irishmen and with a very few

---

39 "Montgomery" in CR, 19 Aug. 1798; GUS, 18 Dec. 1798; *Aurora*, 20 Aug. 1798; *GUS*, 20 Dec. 1798, 18 Jan. 1799. For denials that James Carey, Parke, Reynolds, Black, and Wylie were United Irishmen, see *GUS*, 20, 22 Dec. 1798, 18 Jan. 1799, 22, 26 Dec. 1798, respectively. In a letter to John Adams, Pickering also denounced Duane as a United Irishman; see Pickering Papers, 24 July 1799. See also Durey, *Transatlantic Radicals*, 144, 193, 334 n.50. For the influence of radical Irish editors on the politics of contemporary Philadelphia, see Michael Durey, "Thomas Paine's Apostles: Radial Emigrés and the Triumph of Jeffersonian Republicanism," *WMQ* xliv (1987), 661–88. For Callender and others, see Richard J. Twomey, "Jacobins and Jeffersonians: Anglo-American Radical Ideology, 1790–1810" in Margaret C. Jacob and James R. Jacob, eds., *The Origins of Anglo-American Radicalism* (Atlantic Highlands and London, 1984), 313–28.

40 HSP, Gratz Collection, American Clergymen, case 2, box 9, Abbot to Dr. Jedediah Morse, dated 9 Dec. 1798; HSP, Gratz Collection, case 1, box 36, Foster to Jedediah Morse, dated Washington, 30 Mar. 1802; and case 9, box 2, Rev. Joseph Badger to Morse, dated 8 July 1799; HSP, Gratz Collection, American Miscellaneous Collection, case 8, box 20, Wolcott to Morse, dated Philadelphia, 2 May 1799. Barruel is quoted in *PorcG* 18 May 1799. For the Federalist fear of the Illuminati, as fanned in particular, by some New England clergy,

exceptions, they are United Irishmen, Free Masons, and the most God-provoking Democrats on this side of Hell."⁴¹ For Tracy, such descriptions were interchangeable; they alluded to the same world. Accordingly, Cobbett was not surprised to conclude that "the ceremonials of the [United Irish] compact are essentially the same as those of freemasonry" and both he and Fenno examined the "mystical meanings" of the society's passwords and paraphernalia with this in mind. They also offered morphological analyses of what they termed the United Irish *'Rising Parole and Countersign'*: the Irish words *codraomaght* and *saoirseaught*. These were translated respectively, as *equality* and *liberty*, although the *Gazette of the United States* added that the latter, "like the word *notorious*, is for the most part used in a bad sense; for it also means Baseness and Licentiousness," while the former could be translated as *leveller* as well as *equality*, at least in the type of Tory rhetoric which many Federalists were using to damn the French Revolution and a world which for them, was being turned upside down.⁴²

By November 1798 Fenno reported that Philadelphia already had its share of "vagabonds, and renegades of Ireland, [as well as] outlaws, assassins, traitors, and fugitives from justice of every description." These were dubbed "the United Dagger-Men of Philadelphia," a band of "dark and desperate, unnatural and bloodthirsty ruffians" who were "without property, without principles, without country, and without character," and who were intent on importing

see Link, *Democratic-Republican Societies*, 186–200; Stauffer, *New England and the Bavarian Illuminati*. For the place of United Irishmen within these broader fears, see Stauffer, *New England and the Bavarian Illuminati*, 271–2. See also Amos Hofman, "Opinion, Illusion, and the Illusion of Opinion: Barruel's Theory of Conspiracy," *Eighteenth Century Studies* xxvii (1993–4), 27–60.

41 Tracy is quoted in James Morton Smith, *Freedom's Fetters: The Alien and Sedition Laws and American Civil Liberties* (Ithaca, N.Y., 1956) 24. For Rowan's initiation into, and relationship with the Freemasons, see Nicholson, *Desire to Please*, 39. In Dublin, the United Irishmen were founded and often met in Taylor's Hall which was also used for "regular meetings" of the Freemasons with whom, Nicholson concluded, "the United Irishmen were closely connected," *ibid.*, 91; see also Jim Smyth, "Freemasonry and the United Irishmen" in Dickson, Keogh and Whelan, eds., *United Irishmen*, 167–75. For Mathew Carey's Masonic connections, see Lea & Febiger Collection, Incoming Correspondence (1785–96) vi, John Dunkin to Carey, undated. Before emigrating, Reynolds had been president of the General Masonic Committee in Tyrone; see Wilson, *United Irishmen, United States*, 44.

42 *PorcG*, 21 Dec. 1798; *GUS*, 20, 21 Nov. 1798. Cobbett based his observations on a lengthy commentary on Barruel's *Memoirs Illustrating the History of Jacobinism*; John Robinson, *Proofs of a Conspiracy against all the Religions and Governments of Europe* ... (New York, 1798) and the *Report of the Committee of Secrecy*, which he published in *PorcG* on 17, 18 and 19 May 1798. For the impact of Freemasonry on the evolution of the Orange Order, see Petri Mirala, *Freemasonry in Ulster, 1733–1813: a social and political history of the masonic brotherhood in the north of Ireland* (Dublin, 2007).

their "wicked ways" into the nation's capital. On 11 February 1799 the *Gazette of the United States* suggested that if the inhabitants of Philadelphia did not recognise this "sense of their danger, they almost deserve all the direst consequences with which they are threatened." Left unchecked, the United Irishmen would subject Americans to "the greatest tyranny that has ever cursed the world and plunder them of their honest and well earned property." To tolerate the society at home, or to be sympathetic to its agenda abroad, was to invite into America the political and social confusion of contemporary Ireland and France. As the *Gazette of the United States* put it on 19 November 1798

> our own country [America] fosters in its bosom multitudes of wretches animated by the same infamous principles, and actuated by that same thirst for blood and plunder, which has reduced France to a vast human slaughter-house. The hordes of United Irishmen in America, are alone sufficient for a most extensive scene of ruin, and little doubt can be entertained that they are preparing for it.

The former chief justice of the United States (1789–95) and governor of New York (1795–1801), John Jay, added weight to the refrain and in August 1797 he told the secretary of state (1795–1800), **Timothy Pickering**, that if "the Clubs and their associates should acquire a decided ascendancy, there would be Reason to apprehend that our Country would become the Theatre of Scenes resembling those which have been exhibited by their Brethren in France." The United Irishmen were presented as fifth columnists of the French republic and supporters of everything for which it stood. Cobbett also argued that the unregulated and unchecked admission of United Irishmen into America amounted to the revival of the colonial policy of dumping British and Irish felons in the new world. "Botany Bay is the proper place for United Irishmen," he wrote, not the newly-independent United States.[43]

Charges that Irish immigrants, in general, and the United Irishmen, in particular, were a potential threat to the new nation were often repeated, usually in emotional and provocative language, leading Reynolds to deny, in a formally-phrased and strongly-worded statement, that "the subversion of the constitution of the United States, murder, rapine, and pillage, were the objects of my exiled countrymen." Mathew Carey regarded the publication of Fenno's list of December 1798 as an anti-climax: "when every body looked forward to see lists of hundreds of thousands of those Cannibals, the blood-thirsty United Irishmen,

---

43 *GUS,* 27 Nov., 5 Dec. 1798; *PorcG,* 8 May 1798; "A Loyal Irishman" in *GUS,* 22 Nov. 1798; Cobbett, *Detection of a Conspiracy,* 4; *GUS,* 22 Nov. 1798; Massachusetts Historical Society, Pickering Papers, Jay to Pickering, 17 Aug. 1797; *PorcG,* 19 Jan. 1799.

the mountain was heard to groan, and after many hard throes, the mouse crept out." However, the "reports of plots, combinations, and conspiracies, of United Irishmen" during the heady days of 1799 made it impossible "to live peaceably ... [and] to avoid controversies of every kind," particularly with Cobbett, especially when these "plots" were linked to a supposed United Irish resolve "to aid the French, if occasion should serve, against the Government of the United States." As a result, "the name of *Irishman* is become, and not without reason, detestable in the ears of Americans."[44] In Federalist eyes, the United Irishmen, in particular, had nothing to offer America except social and political agitation and disloyalty to the republic.

Conspiracies, Real or Imagined?

If such published suggestions were true, Cobbett's writings had been particularly influential in making them so. He had published a series of pamphlets, as well as a newspaper, *Porcupine's Gazette*, in which he had taken it upon himself to confront Jacobinism in America and, in particular, those whom he regarded as its principal agents: the United Irishmen. His main themes were predictable: that a French "vortex" had determined to entrap the United States within its "savage system," that France was spending "millions" in what one of his pieces imaginatively called "the commerce of consciences," that a plan of "indirect operations" had been "fixed" on Washington after Jay's treaty with Britain had been ratified in 1795, and that as a result, the"partizans of France" in America were determined "to acquire a perfect command of the American government." For Cobbett, the United Irishmen provided a common link between these activities. The members of the society had "all [been] schooled in sedition, are adepts at their trade, and they most certainly bear as cordial a hatred to this government as they did to their own." They were nothing less than conspirators who were working for the French from within, just as their colleagues had done in Geneva and other parts of Europe. They were men of "bad moral character" with "a want of every real virtue" and of course, to complete the caricature, they were also assumed to be atheists and to enjoy whiskey.[45]

---

44 *GUS*, 18 Jan. 1798; Carey, *Plumb Pudding for the Humane*, 20; *PorcG*, 21 Dec. 1798; Cobbett, *Detection of a Conspiracy* as in Cobbett, *Porcupine's Works* viii, 197–229, with the quotation from page 228. This quotation was not included in the pamphlet which Cobbett published on 6 May 1798, from which all the previous quotations have been taken; *GUS*, 29 Jan. 1799.

45 William Cobbett, *History of the American Jacobins* (Philadelphia, 1796), 7–8, *A New Year's Gift to the Democrats* (Philadelphia, 1796), 6, *A Bone to Gnaw ... By Peter Porcupine*

For Cobbett and Fenno, Irish immigrants also had the "long habit" of opposing the government in Ireland. In their view, this could hardly recommend them to America especially because "the proceedings" of the United Irishmen in America, like those of the democratic societies before them, included "general accusations against *every branch* of the government." Further claims were made that the society was committed to universal suffrage in ways which would be socially divisive and economically untenable. Cobbett thus argued that "by an *equal partition of rights*, there is not the least doubt that the *United Irishmen* meant an equal partition of *property*." Such a "master wheel in the machine of reformation," whether applied in the world of politics or to the holding of property, had clear implications: "it must ever end," as morosely noted in the *Gazette of the United States*, "in the ruin of the rich, and its inevitable consequence, universal poverty" because "it transfers the power from the hands of the rich into the hands of the poor." Along similar lines, allegations were also made that United Irish "villains" had "begun *to tamper with our negroes*." However, although *Carey's Recorder* dismissed these reports as another "cock-and-a-bull story," it did not deny that the United Irishmen would support slaves if they asserted "their rights." Cobbett sarcastically concluded that an "advantageous distribution of the words *liberty*, *tyranny*, *slavery*, &c. does wonders with the populace." Supporters of the society responded that by liberty, "we never understood unlimited freedom, nor by equality, the levelling of property or the destruction of subordination." However, by referring to these highly charged issues in the first place, some Federalist writers stressed that the United Irishmen were a threat to the American constitution in more ways than one. Not only "French ways," but also "Irish ways," had to be resisted.[46]

With the "aspersions" which were being cast on the United Irishmen, the need to silence the "Porcupinian trumpet" became more obvious. By Cobbett's account, he had been receiving threats since 1796. By 1798 these amounted to "some hundreds" and included plans "to assassinate or poison me, or fire my house." Cobbett also attracted written ripostes to his journalism. For his part, Mathew Carey did not want to be drawn into another literary war with Cobbett. However, in September 1796 he wrote to his old antagonist that he "regret[ted] exceedingly the introduction of my name into your life ... My regret arises

(Philadelphia, 1795), 44, *A New Year's Gift to the Democrats*, 6, *History of the American Jacobins*, 9; *PorcG*, 15 May 1798; Cobbett, *History of the American Jacobins*, 3.
46 Cobbett, *History of the American Jacobins*, 8 and *A Bone to Gnaw*, 21, 11; *GUS*, 22 Nov. 1798; *PorcG*, 8 June 1798; *CR*, 11 June 1798; Carey, *To the Public* (broadside, Philadelphia, 5 Feb. 1799); Cobbett, *A Bone to Gnaw*, 21; Link, *Democratic-Republican Societies*, 117; Cobbett, *A Bone to Gnaw*, 11.

from the occasion it has since given to no less than four writers to couple our names together." He also described *Porcupine's Gazette* as the

> most infamous, blackguard newspaper, that ever disgraced a civilized country, & by a nefarious wretch, who combines in his detestable & detested person, qualities heretofore believed by natural & moral philosophers to be utterly incompatible ... [who has] advanc[ed] the most atrocious & villainous lies, to answer his black & detestable purposes [but] ... I shall never disgrace my paper with your detested name.

Carey was slow to address Cobbett's negative imagery directly. Instead, he stressed a general point that he had also made a decade earlier, that far from trying to overthrow the U.S. constitution, Philadelphia's Irish community would never compromise the very country that had given them hope as well as shelter and that their loyalty to the United States was both beyond question and historically proven. With these points in mind, he eventually responded to Fenno's published report of December 1798 in which the *Gazette of the United States* had named him and his brother, James, as United Irishmen. In Carey's eyes, this "list" had constituted an "unprovoked and very unjustifiable attack" on the integrity of naturalised Irish citizens in the United States. However, aside from this crisp denial, Carey's specific statements on the United Irishmen were few although it is possible that he contributed to the columns of Philadelphia's newspapers on the society and its purposes, especially after the *Aurora* had decided in May 1798 that Philadelphia's Irish community should not be subjected to "injured truth" any longer.[47]

In a similar vein, the *Aurora* suggested in 1799 that

> If we were to place implicit belief in some of those [Federalist] *oracles*, we should be persuaded that the Irish possess as perfect felicity, as any people on earth, that the English rule is the most moderate in existence, and that the complaints of the people are the most ungrounded and absurd that have ever formed a pretext for rebellion.

Among such "oracles," "Peter Porcupine" was seen as a writer who was motivated by a particular "hatred ... to Ireland, and Irishmen." From the middle of 1798 a number of articles appeared, especially in the *Aurora* and *Carey's Recorder* which, while reacting in part to Cobbett, presented a more

47 "A Friend to Liberty" in *CR*, 15 May 1798; [William Cobbett], *The Democratic Judge ... by Peter Porcupine* (Philadelphia, 1798), 14; Lea & Febiger Collection, 1st series, Letterbook iii (1792–7), Carey to Cobbett, d. 6 Sept. 1796; HSP, Lea & Febiger Collection, 2nd series, box 2 (July 1798–June 1799), Carey to Cobbett, undated; Carey, "To the Public;" "Brehoontas" in the *Aurora*, 16 May 1798.

benign view of Ireland's "determination to be free" than one which might be simply "construe[d] to be ... *French principled*." In addition to describing the "truly distressed situation" of Ireland at the time, as already noted, Philadelphia's republican editors sought "to place the state of English and Irish relations on its true ground" by publishing their own potted histories of Ireland and Anglo-Irish relations. On 14 February 1799 the *Aurora* published "a short abstract of the Irish penal code" which had been drawn up for the Catholic Committee in 1792 by, among others, Reynolds, Emmet, and Tone, "all of whom," it noted, "were either Presbyterians or of the Episcopal church." While the "debasing vassalage" of the laws was not ignored, the article wanted to stress that their "barbarous" effects were recognised by men of all religions and that the campaign to repeal them was not confined to the Catholic community. A number of others also traced the "afflictions" of Ireland from the Norman invasion in the twelfth century. Famines (some of which had been allegedly contrived by the state) plantation and colonisation, the violence of the wars of the seventeenth century, including graphic descriptions of half-hangings and other forms of personal violence, as well as a number of other cruelties, were all duly listed. "The whole history," as one of James Carey's writers put it in May 1798, was "an uniform picture of ... barbarity." As a result of such litanies, the editors hoped that "the American reader may be able to judge for himself upon Irish injuries and British tyranny."[48]

Although it was argued that events in Ireland had not been matched by anything that had occurred in America, several of Carey's articles stressed that this was a difference only of degree. Moreover, as they saw it, suffering and distress were universal features of empire, as was the denial of liberty. As *Carey's Recorder* put it in May 1798:

> England has been the scourge of Ireland ... [and] has never ceased to pursue the same barbarous system [everywhere else] ... the system of oppression pursued in Ireland is not confined to that island, but is common and universal in the transactions of England, in every part of the world where she obtains influence or power in any form or shape.

It was also true that those who had escaped from such "bondage" would hardly "destroy their guardians and hospitable protectors." Even for the most cynical of observers, the memories of the "galling and degrading slavery" that they had left behind in their "truly distressed" country would see to that. Thus, the

---

48 *Aurora*, 14 Feb. 1799; "An Old Irish Drummer" in *CR*, 19 May 1799; letter from Dublin, dated 1 June 1798, as in *Aurora*, 1 June 1798; *CR*, 17 May 1797; "De Profundis Clamavi" in *Aurora*, 16 Feb. 1799; "Brehoontas" in *Aurora*, 18 May 1798; *CR*, 17 May 1798.

danger to America was not from the United Irishmen who had come from outside the country but from the "sycophants" and Anglophiles who lived inside it. However, while Bache and James Carey pressed their own version of events in Ireland, they also saw their publications as part of a propaganda war in which they felt that they had long been the underdogs, not least because of the ways in which Irish history had been written in the past. In their view, such histories had led to distorted images of Ireland and the Irish. This was a particular worry when American public figures repeated "gross national aspersions" in Congressional debates. It may have been that when they did so, they were unaware that they were echoing the opinions of "ignorant men who have ceased to exist for a century." The political issues of the day were too controversial to allow for such shorthand.[49]

During the debate on the Alien Bill, for example, one writer to the *Aurora* was struck by "the manifest ignorance which prevails among persons who pretend to talk of Irishmen and Irish affairs." For the supporters of the "Plea of Erin" which had outlined Irish objections to this bill (for which, see below), this was hardly encouraging, especially as they expected Congress to examine their complaints objectively or thoroughly. For another writer to the same newspaper, some American Federalists had been even more calculating in characteristing the Irish in negative ways:

> let us enquire for a moment how it has come to pass that United Irishmen are affected to be made such an object of dread & alarm to the United States of America. Is it a necessary inference that men who have borne the galling yoke of British oppression, and wrenched their fetters from them, should come to America, so enamoured of tyranny, as to be ready to destroy the most free government in existence ... We must look to something deeper ... The people of America are united upon the principles of their government, and do not want a large standing army. A necessity for an army must be first created before an army can be raised ... The United Irish are therefore made the *raw-head and bloody-bones* to *scare* the American people ... they speak from experience of the fatal ills that have befallen their native country from want of union among its inhabitants.

The perceived crime of the radical Irish in America was that they spoke their mind and as a result, they were "liable to be branded with opprobrium the moment they dare to act or think differently from their flatterers." To this extent, their defenders in Philadelphia saw republicanism in general, and United Irishmen, in particular, as protecting free speech and ensuring that

49 *CR*, 22 May 1798; "Montgomery" in *CR*, 17 May 1798; *Aurora*, 1 May 1798; "A Friend to Liberty" in *CR*, 31 Mar. 1798.

opinion on government and public policy would not be corralled by, or into, any one interest or party.[50]

On 15 May 1798 "A Friend to Liberty" rejected the notion that the United Irishmen constituted a conspiracy "with the intention of overturning the government of the United States." Such "calumnies" were substantially no different from those which had been levelled against Washington and Adams before 1776 and were rejected by one James M'Guire, secretary of the American Society of United Irishmen in May 1798. In his view, the United Irishmen were no less honourable than the Founding Fathers and he reiterated their dedication to "a love of liberty itself, as recognized in the constitution of the union, and the several states." If anything, as the *Time-Piece* put it in November 1797, "America might shew her gratitude to the cause of Ireland by assisting such Irish emigrants as adventure here to become citizens of a free Republic." "Brehoontas" even went so far as to compare the Declaration of Independence and the constitution of the United Irishmen: "I find many features and sentiments which are common to both ... [including the notion that] *ALL men are created equal.*" His point was clear: "if true and just in America, it must be so every where ... [and] that if America's suffering was great and her danger imminent, that the oppression of Ireland has been ten million of degrees more horrible and stupendous." It only stood to reason, as *Carey's Recorder* suggested on 17 May 1798, that

> From the united Irishmen's principles, the constitution of America merits the most respectful and fond attachment ... and in associating for the purpose of relieving their fellow sufferers whom English tyranny has driven thither, they only exercise that generosity proverbial to their nation.[51]

In an ironic twist, such writers also turned the notion of French conspiracy on its head and intimated that in contemporary Philadelphia, the enemy was the same as it had been in Ireland: "English intrigue." In Ireland, this had already smashed the evolving union of Catholic, Protestant, and Dissenter as the basis of a more harmonious polity. In America, it would now cultivate divisions and "a jealousy in the bosoms of Americans against the Irish." Such comments could only encourage the growing Anglophobia of Philadelphia's Irish organisations although in any event, a change of mood was taking place within these networks which would sometimes be expressed in crisper and for some, a more uncomfortable language. This was especially so during and after 1797 when the Irish in Philadelphia were being powerfully influenced by their own

50 "Brehoontas" in *Aurora*, 18 May 1798; *Aurora*, 14 Feb., 13 Mar., 14 Feb. 1799.
51 *CR*, 15 May 1798; *Time-Piece*, 26 Nov. 1797; "Brehoontas" in the *Aurora*, 16 May 1798.

interpretation of the unfolding rebellion in contemporary Ireland. However, the toasts that were offered by both the Hibernian Society and the Friendly Sons on St. Patrick's Day 1799 were cautious and traditional. They included a hope for "peace and prosperity" in "Old Ireland" but no references to the United Irishmen, to its radical programme, or to its leaders. By way of contrast, a "festive meeting" that was chaired by Reynolds on 18 March 1799 gave eighteen toasts which recognised, among others, the United Irishmen, the "Hibernian Directory," and the "Army of Ireland." Familiar toasts were also offered, including one to St. Patrick, but even to this, the company added the codicil that "Our island wants again to be purged of wolves and reptiles."[52]

At another republican celebration, "agonizing reflections" were offered on the "bondage" of Ireland while "the pains of memory" were thematically outlined in ways that would become more familiar during the course of the nineteenth century. Audiences were also advised not to fear the memories of the past. Indeed, as the orator put it:

> retrospect is replete with anguish and horror: Will it inspire no other emotion? Yes, it will arouse indignation; it will give a new *edge* to our revenge – a new *spring* to our love of country; [lest] her sacrifices be forgotten. It ought to make us cling more closely to the sacred principle of our association, and to each other; it ought to blend itself with all our passions

Such St. Patrick's Day celebrations reflected the increasing ethnocentricity of Philadelphia's Irish community. James Carey left his readers in no doubt where he stood: the city's United Irishmen would "cherish in the hearts of their children the love of liberty and *a perpetual hatred of English government and usurpation*." On 13 March 1798 "Paddy" made a similar point in the *Gazette of the United States*: "the purpose of their [United Irish] meetings is to keep alive in their minds the sufferings of their country men under the British Government." Inevitably, such resolutions were linked with the "vagabond" presence of exiles such as Reynolds and Rowan. Fenno had already suggested that the number of Irish and French "agents" was increasing in the United States, especially since the arrival of several United Irish and Defender leaders who had participated in the failed rebellions of 1796 and 1798. Indeed, the *Salem Gazette* vividly reported on 18 September 1798 that "every ship vomit[ed] United Irishmen" on American shores. The warning to Americans was obvious, especially after diplomatic efforts to negotiate with France collapsed during the Spring of 1798.[53]

52 *CR*, 22 May 1798; *Aurora*, 20, 21 Mar. 1799.
53 *Aurora*, 23 Mar. 1799; *CR*, 17 May 1798; *GUS*, 27, 19 Nov. 1798. The *Salem Gazette* is quoted in Rex Syndergaard, "'Wild Irishmen' and the Alien and Sedition Acts," *Eire-Ireland* ix (1974), 16.

Official Views

President Adams had sent a three-person commission to France the previous year. However, Talleyrand, the French minister for foreign affairs (1797–99, 1799–1807), did not even meet them perhaps because they had been "avowed approvers of ... the British treaty" of 1795. Instead, he sent three officials (later dubbed X, Y, and Z) to demand that America aid France's war effort and provide a bribe of $250,000 for himself. When some of the commission's official papers were published in and after April 1798, it raised an outcry and as John C. Miller has noted, this removed the "last doubt that the United States must fight for its existence against revolutionary France." A "half-war" followed during which the Federal Government commissioned a number of armed vessels, established a department of the navy, and empowered the president to raise a provisional army. Supportive addresses flowed towards Adams and as Congress moved closer to war with France, Robert Liston, the British minister in Philadelphia (1796–1800), enthused that the "spirit of animosity" towards France was unmistakable. One of Jefferson's correspondents welcomed the outbreak of yellow fever in 1798 because it would "prove a happy check to a much worse one, the black Cockade fever, I mean the fever that, under the pretence of defending us from a *foreign* war, aims at promoting a *civil* one." Thus, the important question for Republicans was whether, as the *New York Commercial Advertiser* put it on 25 January 1798, "policy and interest [should] UNITE GREAT BRITAIN and the UNITED STATES, in the same SYSTEM OF DEFENCE." The militia of Montgomery County, Pennsylvania, had an answer and in June 1799 it suggested to the governor that

> the Perfidy and injustice by which the French government have recently disgraced its own character and violated our rights has cancelled all reciprocal attachment between the two Nations and [we] think it the duty of every Friend to this country to prepare for War.[54]

Such resolutions provided a boon for Cobbett and Fenno. Now, as they equated radical republicanism with France, and France with dishonour, they

---

54 Bernstein, "The Rise of the Democratic-Republican Party in New York City, 1789–1800," 221; John C. Miller, *Crisis in Freedom: the Alien and Sedition Acts* (Boston, 1951), 72; NYPL, Gordon Lester Ford Collection, Transcripts of British State Papers, 18 Apr. 1797; LC, Jefferson Papers, Stevens Thomas Mason to Jefferson, 26 October 1798; HSP, Papers of James Wilson, box 3, case 12, the militia officers of Montgomery County to Mifflin, 23 June 1798. For an overview of the XYZ affair, see Albert H. Bowman, *The Struggle for Neutrality: Franco-American Diplomacy during the Federalist Era* (Knoxville, 1974); and Elkins and McKittrick, *The Age of Federalism*, 549–79.

claimed to be vindicating the integrity of the United States. Accordingly, they wrapped themselves in the nation's flag. Such sentiments strengthened the resolve to identify what Adams later called "foreign meddlers" in America and, in particular, to pursue the United Irishmen. On 8 January 1798 the *Massachusetts Mercury* spelt out the danger from the society, as it understood it. Having reminded its readers of the Bantry Bay expedition of 1796, the newspaper wondered if the United Irishmen would "give the same invitation for our country." The "XYZ affair" had made this question less fanciful than it had been a year earlier. Irish leaders in America had hoped that the American government would see the cause of the United Irishmen in terms of its own path to independence. While few of them expected the United States to intervene directly in Ireland, they argued that the former colonies should shun Britain internationally, or that in a more practical gesture, they would welcome and assist those who had been forced to flee the tribulations of contemporary Ireland. The "quasi-war" with France quashed these hopes once and for all.[55]

Outside America, the views of the Adams administration on events in Ireland were officially expressed by Rufus King, the American minister in London. King watched the unfolding rebellion in Ireland closely and became even more interested in it when some of its leaders indicated that they would like to settle in the United States. He had maintained his own network of correspondents in Ireland through whom he followed the development of the rebellion and from whom he concluded that an "intimate connection subsist[s] between the Chiefs of the Malcontents and the Directory." Such judgements about Ireland were no mere academic or strategic observations of a foreign ambassador. They also reflected a concern about the direction and viability of the United States itself. King had long held the view that much of what he saw as the political "troubles" of contemporary America had been caused by "lower class" Irish immigrants who had been "organized for mischievous purposes." In December 1798 William Bingham reinforced that view by highlighting to King

> the danger that may arise from the emigration of so many Irish insurgents to this country; amongst whom it appears there are many professional char-acters, who will be able to make an impression on society, much greater than the common class of disaffected Irish. They will join the party in opposition to the Government and will vent their resentments against Great Britain by attacking those who are disposed to be on friendly terms with her. They will be discontented and therefore disorganizing characters whose residence

55 Adams, ed., *John Adams* ix, 584, Adams to Christopher Gadsden, 16 April 1801; DeConde, *The Quasi-War*.

amongst us cannot be otherwise than injurious in the present moment of political agitation.[56]

King regarded the United Irishmen as being "utterly inconsistent with any practicable or settled form of Government." Accordingly, he wrote several letters to British politicians, including the Irish lord lieutenant, objecting to any arrangement under which these "malcontents" might emigrate to America. As he explained to the British home secretary (1794–1804), the Duke of Portland,

> they will [not] be a desirable acquisition to any Nation, but in none would they be likely to prove more mischievous than in mine, where from the sameness of language and similarity of Laws and Institutions, they have greater opportunities of propagating their principles than in any other Country.

King made similar representations to his own government. On 14 June 1798 he suggested to Pickering that with the probable suppression of the rebellions in Ireland,

> thousands of fugitive Irish will seek asylum in our country. Their principles and habits would be pernicious to the order and industry of our people, and I cannot persuade myself that the Malcontents of any country will ever become useful citizens of our own.

Six weeks later he informed Pickering that the "Chiefs in the late Rebellion are to go into Exile for Life" and strongly urged that the Administration should exclude "those disaffected Characters who will be suffered to seek an asylum among us."[57] Pickering agreed with these views and as America and France moved closer to war, he indicated that he would co-operate with United States district judge Richard Peters, and William Rawle and Richard Harrison, the respective attorneys of Pennsylvania and New York, two states with liberal immigration policies, to watch closely "the internal Foes, who are plotting Mischief" and especially, "the secret projects" of the United Irishmen. However, Pickering admitted in August 1798 that he had no formal evidence

56 Charles R. King, ed., *The Life and Correspondence of Rufus King* 6 vols. (New York, 1894–1900), v, appendix iv, 637, King to Pickering, 11 May 1798; ii, 645–6, King to Jackson, 28 Aug. 1799; v, appendix iv, 644, William Bingham to King, 8 Dec. 1798. For the context of King's observations, see James Quinn, "The Kilmainham Treaty of 1798" in Bartlett, Dickson, Keogh and Whelan, eds., *1798*, 421–36.

57 King, ed., *Life and Correspondence of King* v, appendix iv, 639, King to Pickering, 13 June 1798; 637, King to Portland, 17 Oct. 1798; 640, King to Portland, 13 Sept. 1798; 637, King to Pickering, 14 June 1798; and 638, King to Pickering, 3 Aug. 1798.

against America's United Irishmen although he did suggest to Peters that "'something' would turn up" and that when this happened, he would not fail "'to avail of it'." This only compounded Republican fears that evidence would be concocted against the United Irishmen and, indeed, that those who provided such information would "be well taken care of."[58]

Pickering had his own reasons for prosecuting Reynolds. In 1798 Reynolds had accused the secretary of state of taking five dollars for issuing a passport, a service that was free. As a result, he was denounced for engaging "in a most base attempt to vilify" Pickering's character. Pickering admitted that he had accepted the money but only on the basis that it had been voluntarily offered. When an attempt to indict Reynolds followed, the *Aurora* asked if the British minister had

> any share in the plan ... for persecuting the already persecuted united Irishmen? Was the editor of Porcupine's Gazette or any other person authorised to engage, that if any two men could be procured to substantiate something effectual against Dr. Reynolds or any other United Irishman who was a Citizen of the U. States they and their families should be well taken care of? I can conceive no cause of dread from the injured friends of Irish Liberty unless we dread republicanism.

The move against Reynolds failed. However, since he was employed as a physician at the Philadelphia dispensary, "several" contributors threatened to withdraw their financial support if Reynolds remained there and as a result, he was turned out by the managers.[59]

King also recommended that the immigration process should be overhauled and that those who wished to settle in America should have testimonials to "their honesty, sobriety, and generally their good Character." These proposals were endorsed by Pickering as well as by Adams who saw them as "timely" and "extremely acceptable." Indeed, Pickering ordered that descriptive lists should be drawn up lest "United Irish Desperadoes" would immigrate indirectly into the United States. This plan was not very successful. **Thomas Ledlie Birch** (1754–1828) recalled that the ship in which he sailed from Belfast to New York in 1798 was "loaded" with political refugees. During his trial in Lisburn on 18 June 1798 for "treason and rebellion" at Saintfield, Co. Down, Birch had been

58 Massachusetts Historical Society, Pickering Papers xxiii, Peters to Pickering, 24 Aug. 1798; HSP, Peters Papers x, part i, 53, Pickering to Peters, 27 Aug. 1798; Massachusetts Historical Society, Pickering Papers xxiii, Peters to Pickering, 30 Aug. 1798 and Pickering to Peters, 27 Aug. 1798; *Aurora*, 27 Feb. 1798. For Pickering's "hysteria" about "French agents," especially after the XYZ affair, see Gerard H. Clarfield, *Timothy Pickering and the American Revolution* (Pittsburgh, 1980).
59 *PorcG*, 2 Feb. 1798; *Aurora* 27 Feb. 1798; *PorcG*, 7 June 1798. See also *GUS*, 26 Jan. 1798.

thanked for helping to bury soldiers who had been killed and for seeking, "as a man of humanity," the release of four men who had been taken prisoner. He had also announced that he "loved the King." For some of Birch's friends, this was something of a surprise given that he had been a supporter of the American Revolution and that in 1784 he had written a much publicised address from Ireland in which he had congratulated Washington on his victory over "slavery." In the charged circumstances of the late-1790s, however, and following the intervention of his influential brother, George, Birch decided to "remove himself … to America." Another United Irish leader, Richard Caldwell, was also allowed to emigrate to America in 1798 following his father's "humble petition" to the lord lieutenant in which he proclaimed his "warmest feelings of Veneration and gratitude" and acknowledged the "misconduct" of his "deluded" and "infatuated" son. Before his voyage, Caldwell was also warned

> not to enter into any Political disgusction (*sic*) with any person, and to have as little communications, with any persons on board the Vessel, – who may have left this country, in consequence of Political Embarrassments, as the nature of the case will admit.[60]

In 1797 the *Aurora* also noted that John Arnold, the Presbyterian minister of Ballybay, Co. Monaghan, had arrived in New York among "a number" of others who had also been "obliged to flee the country for espousing the popular cause" while the ship *Augusta* took "several of the United Irishmen" from Derry to Philadelphia the same year. Among the 450 passengers who were on board the ship *Mars* (Derry to New York) in 1797, there were also "a number who belonged to the United Irishmen." By September of the following year, it was reported from Derry that "several persons who had been convicted at different times of acts of treason or sedition [were] … suffered to transport themselves from his Majesty's dominions for life … and conveyed to the Ship New-York, bound to America" while on 24 July 1799 the *Aurora* recorded that no fewer than three vessels were preparing to leave Derry "with passengers (chiefly United Irishmen) for Wilmington, Delaware." In February 1798 Charles Nisbet (1736–1804), the Scottish-born Presbyterian founder of Dickinson College, had already expressed an obvious worry from Philadelphia that

60 King, ed., *Life and Correspondence of King* v, appendix iv, 638, King to Pickering, 14 June 1798 and 644, Pickering to King, 5 Feb. 1799; Robert Ernst, *Rufus King: American Federalist* (Chapel Hill, 1968), 264; Thomas Ledlie Birch, *Letter from an Emigrant ….* (New York, 1799), 1; *BN*, 29 June 1798; Durey, *Transatlantic Radicals*, 85; PRONI, T3541/6/2, "The Humble Petition of John Caldwell …" n.d.; PRONI, T3541/1/8, James Parks to [John] Caldwell, 18 Aug. 1798. For Birch's career in Ireland and the circumstances in which he left for America, see Wilson, *United Irishmen, United States*, 112–20 *et passim*; and Durey, *Transatlantic Radicals*, 84–6, 122–5.

> We are in danger of an Inundation of Irish Rebels among us ... nothing can hinder them from transporting themselves hither in private ships, while there is no law here to forbid their Reception, & while we are so ready to make them Citizens & Patriots as soon as they are among us.

Leaders such as Emmet, William Sampson (1764–1836), William MacNeven, Robert Adrian (d.1843), and Thomas O'Connor (1770–1855) were not able to come to the United States until after Jefferson was inaugurated as third president of the United States in 1801. They never forgave King for his intransigence and haunted his later political career in New York.[61]

Anglophiles and Francophiles

For all the focus on the United Irishmen, there was also a wider debate on whether political pluralism could be accommodated in a country, "the true and permanent interest" of which was defined in Washington's Farewell Address (1796) as being "without regard to local considerations, to individuals, to parties, or to [other] nations." However, during and after 1795, the polarisation of public opinion was unavoidable, especially after the conclusion of Jay's Treaty with Britain in 1795.[62] In 1794 when Jay left to negotiate a new treaty with Britain, most Jeffersonians had dismissed him as the envoy of America's "British party" and amid "the shouts of the people," they guillotined and blew up his effigy. When the treaty was agreed the following year, they felt that they had been vindicated because Jay had given too many concessions to the former mother country. They argued that the treaty did not oblige Britain to respect American neutrality or to pay compensation for the impressment of American citizens and ships that taken place since Washington's proclamation of April 1793. As Tench Coxe observed in a letter to Jefferson, "tho' some things are granted [in the treaty], they are mere Indian presents." Thus, when the *Aurora* published a *précis* of the treaty on 29 June 1795, James Madison made a predictable response:

> the Treaty, from one end to the other, must be regarded as a demonstration that the party to which the Envoy belongs, and of which he has been more the organ than of the United States, is a British party, systematically aiming at an exclusive connection with the British Government, and ready to sacrifice to

---

61 *Aurora*, 24 July 1797; *MDA*, 11 Sept. 1797; *Time-Piece*, 16 Aug. 1797; *BN*, 7 Sept. 1797; Charles Nisbet to William Marshall in "Letters to William Marshall, 1798–1800," *JPrH* xxxix (1961), 55.

62 The Farewell Address is quoted from James Thomas Flexner, *George Washington: Anguish and Farewell 1793–1925* (Boston, 1969), 29.

that object, as well as the dearest interests of our commerce, as the most sacred dictates of National honour.[63]

The treaty was widely denounced in Philadelphia. It also hardened political differences in the city and reflected the extent to which domestic politics were being informed by foreign policy.

As the election of 1795 approached, Republicans also used the anti-treaty protests to secure their Irish supporters. The previous year, Chambers had suggested to Mathew Carey that the number of Irishmen "who think they see a very Strong British Influence over your Federal Government" was "not small." Many of the Irish immigrants who were streaming into the Delaware at this time were in no doubt where they stood. For Tone, the "The Treaty with England ... [was] but a [pre]text. The real state is Aristocracy against Democracy, and I know you [Thomas Russell] will rejoice to hear that against all the weight of property and government influence, Democracy is daily gaining ground." Thus, the *Northern Star* reported that Philadelphia's "Aristocrats ... recollecting that Irishmen were the principal hands in fighting the battles which made America once free, seem very uneasy at their flocking out in such numbers latterly." In July 1795 the city's "new Irish" gave particular cause for such concerns as they helped to organise meetings against the Federalists' proposed *rapprochement* with Britain. During that month there were three major public protests against Jay's treaty in Philadelphia. The first happened on 4 July when a number of people from the outer suburb of Kensington marched through the city "amid the acclamation of hundreds of citizens" and burned Jay in effigy. The second occurred on 23 July when a committee that included **Alexander James Dallas**, who at the time was Pennsylvania's secretary of state (1791–1801), Blair McClenachan, Thomas McKean, and John Swanwick, was appointed to draft a address to Washington against the treaty. During a third gathering that took place two days later, the crowd listened to McClenachan's "fervid oratory" and afterwards, marched to the residences of the British minister and consul and burned copies of the treaty. Although Bache reported that between 5,000 and 6,000 attended the meeting, Wolcott suggested that only 1,500 were present. However, Wolcott had

---

63 Scharf & Westcott, *History of Philadelphia* i, 478; HSP, Tench Coxe Papers (microfilm), reel 62, Coxe to Jefferson, 30 July 1795; Madison to Robert Livingston, 10 Aug. 1795, as quoted in Daniel Sisson, *The Revolution of 1800* (New York, 1974), 232. For the arguments against Jay's appointment, see Margaret Woodbury, *Public Opinion in Philadelphia, 1789–1800, Smith College Studies in History* v (1919), 81–7. For the background to Jay's anti-French feeling, derived from his supposed mistreatment while he was a peace commissioner to France in 1778, see Jerald A. Combs, *The Jay Treaty* (Berkeley, 1970), 18–19.

gone not to count the number who turned up but "for the purpose of observing the proceedings." His conclusion was that those who had attended were "ignorant and violent." Fenno also proclaimed that "there were at this meeting about as many persons immediately round the scaffold as arrived in the two last ships from Ireland, interspersed with about 50 French Emigrants" and reported that the treaty was burned "by about 50 or 100 persons, composed chiefly of those who having just arrived in the country, might not know their throwing stones and other riotous proceedings, even in a republic, subjected them, to the particular notice of the Police!"[64]

The *Aurora* disagreed and suggested instead that the majority of the protesters were "respectable mechanicks:" the type of people who had served Washington and the continental army during the Revolutionary War. He did concede that the "complexion" of the audience was such that the recently-exiled United Irish leader, Archibald Hamilton Rowan, had received an enthusiastic welcome. McClenachan introduced his guest as a man who had just arrived to "take refuge amongst us, from the despotism of his native country." Given his recent career and reputation, Rowan had a powerful influence on his listeners. Federalists denounced his address and his proposition "that every good citizen … [should] kick this damned treaty to hell" was cited both at the time and long afterwards as an example of unwarranted and undesirable intrusion of immigrants into the substance and direction of American politics. Towards the end of July copies of Jay's Treaty were distributed throughout the city and by December 1795 2,300 had signed a petition urging Congress not to ratify the treaty. Washington was alarmed by these and similar developments which, in the words of one emigrant letter to Ireland in 1795, had "rendered [him] so odious, by striking such deep blows against the sacred rights of man that his name cannot be borne with in private, or public company." As Tone recalled in a letter to his Belfast friend, Thomas Russell, in 1795, it was "no longer a damnable heresy to doubt the

---

64 HSP, Lea & Febiger, Incoming Correspondence (1785–96), box 4, Chambers to Carey, Dublin, 26 Mar. 1794; Tone to Russell in Bartlett, ed., *Tone*, 451; "letter from Philadelphia" in *NS*, 27 Aug. 1795; *GUS*, 7, 9, 26, 27 July 1795; *Aurora*, 7, 9, 10, 24, 27, 29 July 1795; *IG*, 15, 19, July 1795; (Philadelphia) *Minerva*, 25 July 1795; *ADA*, 25, 27, 29 July 1795; and Tinkcom, *Republicans and Federalists in Pennsylvania*, 89. For the burning of Jay's treaty in front of Bond's house, see Bond to Grenville, 27 July 1795, as quoted in Bowman, *Struggles for Neutrality*, 218. Protests were also made outside the home of the pro-treaty senator, William Bingham and several of his windows were broken; see Scharf and Westcott, *History of Philadelphia* i, 481. For Wolcott's observations of the protests, see George Gibbs, *Memoirs of the Administrations of Washington and John Adams* 2 vols. (New York, 1846) i, 217–8. The background to the protests is discussed in Combs, *Jay's Treaty* and Samuel Flagg Bemis, *Jay's Treaty: A Study in Commerce and Diplomacy* (New Haven, 1962). For a discussion of the different estimates of those present at the third meeting, see "M" in *Aurora*, 29 July 1795.

infallibility of the President." These and similar reflections were critical factors in convincing Washington not to seek another presidential term.[65]

Against the backdrop of Jay's mission to Britain, the 1795 elections provided an even more important catalyst for changing times. William Bingham suggested that "the public mind is greatly agitated" about the proposed treaty while a Philadelphia merchant, Clement Biddle (1740–1814), foresaw a "very warm contest" over who would represent the nation's capital in Congress. The Republican and Federalist tickets were designated as "anti-treaty" and "treaty," respectively, and reflected the divisions between those who had publicly endorsed Jay and those who had led the demonstrations and petitions against him. In October 1795 the *Aurora* made the political point that "the name of a Federalist and an Aristocrat are now in connection." Thus, the "no treaty tickets" were seen as a challenge to the "*British* junto" who had "alienated [America] from ... the affections of the French Republic." Beckley expected that these would be carried "by a large majority" in both the city and county of Philadelphia. The result was not as sweeping as he had predicted although McClenachan was elected in place of Frederick Muhlenberg in the county. For Republicans, this victory was particularly sweet because Muhlenberg was not just the sitting congressman but also the speaker of the outgoing House of Representatives (1793–95). Thus, as Beckley explained to Irvine:

> a great victory [has been won]... over the united and combined forces of the British and Aristocrats ... to throw out Muhlenberg, who gave the casting vote for the British treaty and elect Blair McClenachan in his room, who recommended to kick the treaty to hell.[66]

65 *Aurora*, 22, 29 July 1795; *NS*, 27 July 1795; *GUS*, 27 July 1795; Miller, *Philadelphia*, 72; William Cobbett, *A Little Plain English ... By Peter Porcupine* (Philadelphia, 1795), 109–110; PRONI, T1012/3, Potts to Lemon, 17 Nov. 1795; Tone to Russell in Bartlett, ed., *Tone*, 451. Rowan had arrived in America from Le Havre on 17 July; see *NS*, 6, 31 Aug. 1795. For an anti-treaty petition from "the city and neighbourhood of Philadelphia," as presented to Congress by Swanwick and signed by some 1500 "persons, inhabitants of the city and neighborhood of Philadelphia," see *Annals of Congress* vi, 1114. Both the context and text of the attacks on Washington are analysed in two articles by Marshall Smelser, "The Jacobin Phrenzy: The Menace of Monarchy, Plotocracy and Anglophobia," *op.cit.*, and "Jacobin Phrenzy: Federalism and the Menace of Liberty, Equality, and Fraternity," *Review of Politics* xiii (1951), 457–82. See also DeConde, *Entangling Alliance*, 459–62. See also Simon P. Newman, "Principles or Men? George Washington and the Political Culture of National Leadership, 1776–1801," *Journal of the Early Republic* xii, no.4, 477–508.
66 HSP, Irvine Papers xiii, 22 Aug. 1795, Bingham to Presley Nevill; *Aurora* 9, 1, 19 Oct. 1795; HSP, Irvine Papers xiii, Beckley to Irvine, 15 Sept. 1796 and 17 Oct. 1795. Biddle is quoted in Miller, *Philadelphia*, 74. For the 1795 elections, see *Aurora*, 3, 6, 8, 13, 19 Oct. 1795.

During October 1795 there were also elections to the state senate and house of representatives. In the contest for the latter, Israel Israel, and Henry Kammerer, the president of the German Republican Society, stood as two of the six-man Republican ticket for the city. The two candidates were also linked to a number of immigrant and benevolent clubs and organisations, including those that had been set up to relieve the distresses of the yellow fever epidemic two years earlier. "Justicia" argued that it was precisely such altruistic and public-spirited men who should represent the public and, in particular, he mentioned Israel. Here was a man of "feeling and of humanity, who is the best guardian of our civil as well as private welfare," irrespective of "political cant." With this in mind, he asked his readers not to "let philanthropy like this go unrewarded." The result was determined less by such high-minded thoughts than by the social make-up of the relevant constituencies. Philadelphia county, which included sizeable enclaves of Irish and German immigrants, continued the pattern of previous years and elected a Republican ticket that included two members of the Democratic Society of Pennsylvania, Blair McClenachan and Michael Leib (1760–1822), whose "love of popularity" was said to be "without comparison." For the *Aurora*, the result had rejected the notion that members of the democratic societies were "a disorganizing, anarchical, sanguinary race of beings":

> The People have not taken warning; the citizens of Philadelphia county, in the face of those friendly admonitions have chosen the President of the Parent society and one member of the same to represent them in the next General Assembly.[67]

The pro-treaty Federalists consolidated their hold over the city itself and retained all six seats as well as the Senate seat for the district of Philadelphia. It was also clear that among the artisans, unskilled laborers, and Irish immigrants, Republicans had attracted a sizeable number of votes. Israel received the highest number of votes on the Republican slate for the city but even at that, he was 460 lower than the last Federalist candidate elected. These figures confirmed the dichotomy between the Federalist "nabobs" of the city and the "Independent Republicans" of the county. "Phocion" described the division as follows:

> hitherto the city and county of Philadelphia have considered their interest as inseparable; mutual interest being mutual assistance, and tho' the same relation continues, the Representatives from the county of Philadelphia have almost uniformly joined *in their votes* with an interest which has opposed itself to the city and its neighbourhood.

67 *Aurora*, 3, 5, 15 Oct. 1795. For the characterisation of Leib, see HSP, Meredith Papers, box 2, Elizabeth to David Meredith, 14 Apr. 1796.

Electoral success also gave Republicans a base from which, during the second half of the 1790s, they would successfully challenge the Federalist establishment in the Philadelphia area as a whole. There was no certainty about what lay ahead except that, in Mathew Carey's words, "it is more than ever desirable to the friends of mankind that the French may finally triumph over their enemies. If they fail, it requires little penetration to see that our Republicanism will perish with them." Like others, Carey was worried about the implications of Washington's retirement (1796) which was eloquently summed up by Caesar Rodney's brother, Thomas (1744–1811), as follows:

> There are two parties in America, one leans to the French the other to the British – the first approve your [Washington's] conduct in the Revolution but deprecate it since – the latter deprecated your conduct in the war but approve it since – the first are anxious to get hold of the government of America – which they could not do while you stood in the way – the other wants to bring America back to Great Britain which could not be done while you were in the way. Therefore, both parties converge in wishing your retirement.

While this may have been true, Carey was troubled about something else: that the election of John Adams would "plunge us into ... the worst of wars – a war with France ... our only sister republic on Earth."[68]

Washington's departure as well as Monroe's return from France, the publication of his *View of the Conduct of the Executive* (Philadelphia, 1797), and the subsequent paper war about his views on the direction of public policy, helped to galvanise Republican clubs in the nation's capital. Monroe had arrived back in Philadelphia on 1 July 1797, almost a year after Wolcott had advised Hamilton that "we must stop the channels by which foreign poison is introduced into our Country." He was greeted in the nation's capital by what John Rutledge (F., S. Carolina, 1797–1803) called a "heterogenous mixture:"

> Here you saw an American disorganizer and there a blundering wild Irishman – in one corner a banished Genevan and in another a french Spye ... brought together by a general invitation ... [although some] with all ... pretensions to Democracy, could not be prevailed upon to be of this party.

68 "Phocion" in *ADA*, 5 Oct. 1795; HSP, Lea & Febiger Letterbooks (1792–7), Carey to Chambers, 7 June 1796; HSP, Thomas Rodney Papers, Journals and Poetry (1796–7), diary entry from 24 Jan. 1797; Miller, *Philadelphia*, 590. Carey's worries about the consequences of Adams's election are cited from Miller, *Philadelphia*, 190. For further comment on the growing dichotomy between city and county, see also *Aurora*, 24, 27 Oct. 1795. The election results were published in the *Aurora*, 15 Oct. 1795. On 21 Oct., the *Aurora* also published the results of the senate race between Robert Hare (F.) and Jacob

Rutledge was not a sympathetic observer. He conveyed an image of Jeffersonian Republicanism as a mosaic of different parts, many of which were outside the political mainstream. Newspapers also noted the "elegant entertainment" and "Feast of Reason" that was held in Monroe's honour on 13 July and the toast that was offered to "*Ça ira!* on the Irish harp." Similar receptions had been given to Genet in 1793 and two years later when Rowan's arrival in Philadelphia coincided with the publication of Jay's treaty with Great Britain. Irish immigrants were particularly noticeable at these and similar political demonstrations and as one of Carey's correspondents observed five years earlier, these "seem[ed] to understand better, and to join more heartily in, true principles and support our democratical Governments, than any other European people." They were also assured of French support and before Monroe left Paris, Tone gave him an eight-page letter for Rowan "to assure him of the determination of the French government to persevere in our business."[69]

By 1797 the radical Irish in Philadelphia and the country from which they had come, attracted a web of conflicting and often emotionally charged views. Cobbett had played a key part in influencing the views of Federalists and had no doubt that at least in Philadelphia, "the whole of those [United Irish] gentry are held in the utmost detestation by every one, except by a few of Jefferson's party." Although not intended as a compliment, this observation suggested what to a greater or lesser extent, was accepted on all sides of Philadelphia politics: that the radical Irish and, in particular, those who were regarded as United Irishmen, were real influences on the rise of Jeffersonian Republicanism in the nation's capital. This was to become even more noticeable in Philadelphia during the campaigns for the state senate in late-1797 and early-1798 as well as during the renewed national debates on the status of the foreign-born in America which in no small way, these elections inspired.[70]

Morgan (R.). These show that Hare received 1501 and 512 votes in the city and county of Philadelphia, respectively. Morgan's corresponding votes were 1130 and 988, again highlighting the differing political dispositions of the two areas.

69 *Argus*, 14 July 1797; HSP, Lea & Febiger Collection, Incoming Correspondence (1785–96), box 2, Isaac Briggs to Carey, dated Savannah, 22 May 1787; Tone's Journals, as in Bartlett, ed., *Tone*, 24 Feb. 1797, 733. Monroe's supposed reception is quoted from George C. Rogers, *Evolution of a Federalist* (Columbia, S.C., 1962), 302; and Wolcott from Elkins and McKittrick, *Age of Federalism*, 856, n.39. For a Federalist criticism of Monroe's *View*, see Uriah Tracy, *Reflections on Monroe's View* (Philadelphia, 1798).

70 *PorcG*, 25 Mar. 1797.

CHAPTER SIX

Irish Radicals and Philadelphia Politics, 1797–1800

In 1799 the election of Thomas Jefferson as third president of the United States marked the culmination of a long debate on how America should be governed. It also vindicated the viability of the "first party system," not least because the result was accepted by all sides.[1] However, during the previous two years in Philadelphia, the wider issues which such a process involved had already been aired in the often heated circumstances of electoral contests there. This was especially so in October 1797 and February 1798, when, as in December 1793, there was a vacancy to represent the greater Philadelphia area in the state senate.

Philadelphia's Special Senate Elections, 1797–98

The electoral district included the city and county of Philadelphia as well as Delaware county. In the first election, held in October 1797, Benjamin R. Morgan (1765–1840) was the candidate of the Federalists while Israel Israel again stood for the Republicans. Morgan had been active in Federalist networks for a number of years and was senator *pro tem* since the previous December. To his supporters, Morgan's legal expertise had given him an ability and status which made him an effective public representative. As one of them declared in the *Philadelphia Gazette*, Morgan was the "only person of legal knowledge" in the senate and because "no other person of that description is expected to be elected this year in any of the other districts," he suggested that there was a strong case for retaining Morgan in office. Israel was painted in more plebian colours. As a tavern keeper, he was said by one writer to the *Gazette of the United States* to be "wholly improper" for such high office. As in 1793, he was a member of the health committee which had been set up in 1797 to deal with another outbreak of yellow fever. He was again widely praised for his work which would be "long remembered by the grateful citizens" of the city. As the *Aurora* put it, he had "risk[ed] his health in relieving the sufferings of his indigent fellow citizens" and was a worthy candidate. Such sentiments also gave Israel's candidacy a popular edge that transcended party politics. However, as

1   For the literature on the "first party system," see the notes to the Introduction.

the campaign unfolded, some Federalist commentators suggested that Israel's altruism was ephemeral and was little more than a crude political calculation. One critic even alleged that Israel had used his position on the relief committee to attract votes to himself and his causes. However, the *Aurora* made the telling point that "the true reason for the opposition ... to him, is that he is a Republican."[2] Israel ignored Federalist taunts and was elected by a margin of thirty eight votes on 9 October 1797. The outlying wards of the constituency, long associated with Irish immigrants and the poor, were crucial to this victory. In the Northern Liberties and Southwark, for example, the Israel/Morgan split was 678/144 and 498/75, respectively. Conversely, Morgan carried the more elite city wards but not North and South Mulberry, where there were also sizeable Irish pockets. It was only a matter of time before Federalists linked these results to the malevolent influence of recently arrived Irish immigrants on the electoral process and referred the outcome to a senate sub-committee.[3]

Under state law, the result of a senate election could be challenged if at least twenty qualified electors of the relevant district petitioned "complaining of an undue election or false return." For "A Bye Stander" in the *Aurora*, such a process was not always pursued because it "could have been ... made to speak a different language from that of truth by intrigue and faction." However, hearings on Israel's return were held on 22, 24, and 25 January 1798. Among other arguments, Morgan's counsel, George Keppele, suggested that because polling had taken place in, among other locations, a private house in Southwark, and not "at the place fixed by law," some electors were denied the opportunity to vote. In Keppele's view, the electoral commissioners could not arbitrarily choose to conduct an "election upon wheels" or to relocate the polling stations as they saw fit. Keppele argued that if this were conceded, such actions would corrupt the entire election process, possibly deprive some voters of the opportunity to vote, and cause confusion among the electorate. Alexander James Dallas, represented Israel. He did not recognise Keppele's arguments at all, pointing out that whether in America or in England, where many of the republic's political conventions originated, the actual places where the public

---

2   *PhilG*, 9 Oct. 1797; *ADA*, 19 Feb. 1798; *Aurora*, 9 Oct. 1797; LCP, broadsides, Ab (1798)–5, "A Dutch Man," "To the Inhabitants of the County of Philadelphia ... February 21st 1798." For the 1793 election and Israel's involvement in the health committees of 1793 and 1797, see Pernick, "Politics, Parties, and Pestilence", 559–87. For other references to Israel's philanthropic work, see Powell, *Bring Out Your Dead*, 178–93; and Miller, *Philadelphia*, 94–5.

3   For the election results, see Miller, *Philadelphia*, 94 and 96. The votes for Israel and Morgan for the city wards, and for North and South Mulberry, were 588/902, 110/78, and 120/143, respectively; see also *Aurora*, 12 Oct. 1797.

interest was formally decided, whether by elections, the courts or even the legislature, were often not fixed. The impact of war, fire, and adverse weather, as well as the often volatile political involvements of those who owned the polling places, could not render it otherwise. In the case of the contest between Israel and Morgan, the fact was that the "awful contagion" of yellow fever had effectively put some of the polling stations of the previous election beyond use. For Dallas, the point was not whether the conduct of the recent election had been inconsistent with experience but whether or not any fraud had been committed as a result of moving from the old stations.[4]

Keppele's second point, that the inspectors of election had not exacted "the necessary qualifications" from those who had voted, was more powerful. For those who had not been born in America, the right to vote was governed by the provisions of the various Naturalisation Acts. At federal level, the laws of 1790 and 1795 admitted the right after a residence of two and five years, respectively, provided that the applicant had also taken an oath "to support the constitution of the United States." At state level, Pennsylvania's constitution of 1790 had allowed the vote to all adult males who were over twenty one years of age, paid city or county taxes, and been resident in the state for at least two years. Keppele's main point here was that because Congress had been authorised to establish a uniform rule of naturalisation, federal law superseded state law on the subject. Accordingly, the electoral inspectors should have demanded actual proof that voters had taken the oath, as prescribed in *federal* law, rather than merely asked voters whether or not they paid taxes, or were resident in Pennsylvania, as prescribed in *state* law. Keppele claimed that as a result, up to fifty "illegal votes" had been cast and that the return was invalid: the legal and constitutional conventions had not been observed. Developing his earlier concerns about how the election had been managed among the immigrant communities of Southwark and the Northern Liberties, he suggested that the votes of these districts should be set aside and that the votes of the rest of the constituency should be taken as reflecting the sense of the whole.

In his rebuttal, Dallas argued that the inspectors were under no obligation to ask for "legal proof" of citizenship but merely that they should not "knowingly permit" anybody to vote who was not entitled to do so. In the *Aurora*, "A Friend to Justice" suggested in February 1798 that if it were otherwise, every legislator in Pennsylvania would have to vacate his seat. Dallas questioned what was

---

4 "An Act to regulate the Trials of Contested Elections" (23 Sept. 1791) in *Laws of the Commonwealth of Pennsylvania, 1700–1810*, 4 vols. (Philadelphia, 1803) iii, 48; "A Bye-Stander" in *Aurora*, 28 Dec. 1797. Unless otherwise noted, Keppele's contributions are quoted from the *PhilG*, 25, 26 Jan. 1798, and the *Aurora*, 26 Jan. 1798. Those of Dallas are quoted from the *Aurora*, 31 Jan. and 3 Feb. 1798.

actually meant by "legal proof" in this instance. Between 1777 and 1789 Pennsylvania's test laws had obliged the foreign-born as well as natives to take an oath which pledged allegiance to the United States as well as abjured George III. Dallas suggested that when these laws were abolished in 1789, so did the requirement to produce the certificates of loyalty which had been provided for under these laws. Where documentation was concerned, the main requirement on those who still lived in Pennsylvania was to prove that they were resident, paid taxes, and had abjured George III, not that they were citizens. Whether guided by history or the law, as Dallas understood them, while foreign-born voters still had to take an oath, they were not obliged to furnish a certificate of citizenship. Thus, as Dallas later observed, there was no charge against Israel except a "trivial one of a few persons having voted who had not taken an oath of allegiance." However, while it might be argued that on this point Dallas tacitly conceded the substance of Morgan's objections to Israel's election, he did not agree that they were founded in law and that therefore, the result of the election could be invalidated.[5]

Aside from making points of law, Dallas also used the investigation into the election to make wider political points, championing the right of everybody to participate in public life, provided they had "virtue" and "talents." In his view, Israel had both attributes. Dallas's arguments to the committee also addressed his character, reputation, and public service, especially during the two yellow fever outbreaks "when this gentleman was acknowledged to render such services to his fellow citizens as only an eternity can reward." Because this did not seem to matter to his opponents, Dallas could only conclude that the decision to contest the result of the election had been taken because of a "*Party spirit* which disregards every thing but its own gratification." Israel had been vilified and this showed

> how completely we are divided into parties, and how violently we are stimulated into action by party spirit [which was] calculated to disturb the harmony of society, to destroy the tranquillity and weaken the energy of our government ... [Thus] if on the one hand you are to preserve your elections from abuses, from fraud, corruption, violence, and perjury, on the other hand, you are to preserve them from cavil, from litigious exceptions, and from the persevering attacks of party spirit.

Dallas was conscious of the wider implications of the hearings and suggested that the outcome would affect "the whole fabric of our government. This is not a decision of a single election, but for future elections, [and] the principle will

5 *Aurora*, 16 Feb. 1798; *CR*, 17 Feb. 1798.

govern and overthrow every fair and impartial election thro' future generations; & in this point of view it is important indeed." Along similar lines, "Fair Play" argued in the *Aurora* that because foreign-born electors might be debarred from voting unless they had taken "the oath of allegiance, as prescribed by an act of Congress ... The precedent here attempted, if established, will lead to consequences, which perhaps at present are not foreseen."[6]

Dallas saw the contested election as part of a Federalist campaign to promote their own view of the polity and, in particular, to question the integrity of foreign-born citizens. Keppele had suggested as much when he stated that in the October election, "*American* interests [had been] neglected – and the *American* character ... degraded." The senate sub-committee agreed with Keppele that on election day, no enquiries had been made "as to the right of citizenship." Although the sub-committee accepted that this was not unusual,

> from the evidence produced to the committee, they are decidedly of opinion, that a greater number of persons who were not entitled to vote for members of the legislature, have been admitted to vote for Senator at the election held in the district of Southwark, than the difference in number between Mr. Israel and the person next highest in vote.

Israel's election was invalidated on 7 February 1798 and a special election called to coincide with Washington's birthday, on 22 February. The political calculations which affected the choice of this date were highlighted as follows in a broadside which was published in Philadelphia on 21 February 1798:

> To-morrow is the birth-day of WASHINGTON – it is ominous of the success of those who prefer this country to all others. Choose, therefore, a man who has not slandered our *American Hero* –who has not joined, with his enemies, to embitter the evening of his days with vile calumnies.[7]

Given the controversial circumstances in which the second election had been called, the preparatory meetings on both sides were set to be highly partisan. On Morgan's side, some supporters were impressed by their candidate's "talents and integrity," others by his "long and tried services in public life" and

6 "Fair Play" in *Aurora*, 18 Jan. 1798.
7 "Fellows and Fellow Citizens ... Philadelphia" (broadside, 21 February 1798). For the sub-committee's decision, see *PhilG*, 15 and 20 Feb. 1798. The outcome occasioned its own paper war, with many reflections on the make-up and attitudes of the senate sub-committee. For this, see *PhilG*, 14 Feb. 1798 as well as "A Freeman" and "A Citizen" in *GUS*, 21 Feb. 1798. "A Citizen of Pennsylvania" suggested that it was because of the warmth of these exchanges that the committee took the unusual step of later publishing a "true judgement" of its findings; see *PhilG*, 20 Feb. 1798.

"attachment" to "order and good government." On the Republican side, a "number of citizens" recommended Israel on 11 February 1798, having considered his "republican principles, and private virtues." For those in Philadelphia's North Ward, Israel was a man of "integrity and abilities." In Delaware County, George Logan supported Israel as "a true discipline on whom the Democrats might depend" while a meeting in the Northern Liberties cleverly stressed his "integrity as a citizen of the United States," "convinced" that he would "use his utmost exertions" to support the established laws and constitutions of both the federal and state governments. For some of his opponents, this was a somewhat ironic testimonial as it highlighted Israel's connection with the Democratic Society which in their view, had "fanned" the western insurrection into "a flame" that had allegedly cost more than $1 million to suppress. It did not make sense, at least to one writer, that "one of its most violent and active members" should be elected to the state senate.[8]

The candidates were also judged by reference to their supposed support for the interests of "the poor" (Israel) over those of "the rich" (Morgan). Although this was not an unfamiliar theme at election time, both reacted sternly to such caricatures and saw in them the hand of malevolence and rancour. For his part, Morgan strongly denied that he was the candidate of "an aristocracy." He shunned such a label and instead, stressed that he was as much a "new man" as anybody else and moreover, one who would not, as his opponents were implying, "seek to deprive the people ... of their rights." In a grand statement, the *Gazette of the United States* suggested that

> The enemies of the rich are the enemies of the poor ... [and] of all the arts practiced by demagogues to raise themselves to power, there is none so base, treacherous, mischievous and destructive, as that which draws a line of political distinction between the rich and the poor.

Writing in the *Aurora*, "Order" agreed and suggested that "If a combination against the poor has actually taken place, there is no calculating the result. It may lay the foundations of irretrievable evil. The seeds of hatred and discord may be sown by it." Nonetheless, the broader issue—that everybody, regardless of status and background, had the same integrity within the political system—remained controversial. Republicans rejected the notion that it was only those who had been born into the polity could have a "manifest and permanent interest in its welfare, [and thus] possess the right of suffrage."[9]

8 *GUS*, 19, 22, 20 Feb. 1798; *ADA*, 12, 14 Feb. 1798; *Aurora*, 21 Feb. 1798; LCP, broadsides, Ab (1798)–10, "A Pennsylvanian," "Friends and Fellow Citizens ... February 21st 1798."
9 *GUS*, 16, 22 Feb. 1798; *Aurora*, 22 Feb. 1798; "A Citizen of Pennsylvania" in *PhilG*, 15 Feb. 1798.

Also disputed were the meanings of the word "patriotism." Other than supporting the government in office, especially in its foreign policies, few were sure what the term actually meant. Federalists knew what it did not mean: unqualified support for the French Revolution, however benign and well-meaning, and the republic which had evolved from it. Thus, while writers to the *Gazette of the United States* presented Israel as "ready to surrender our independence" to France, Morgan "professes that America is an independent people possessing the right to govern themselves by laws of their own making without the controul [*sic*] of any sovereign nation, to make treaties and compose differences without the interposition of foreign public ambassadors or secret emissaries." While Morgan's testimonial was laced with innuendos informed by Genet's mission to America, for those who missed such subtleties, a broadside addressed "To the Inhabitants of Germantown" made the point explicitly for Morgan:

> Look before you leap! ... THOSE of you that wish to strengthen the French faction, come forward to-day and like a good Ox put your necks into the yoke of your own making, by voting for ISRAEL ISRAEL. Those of you that have sense enough to wish to remain your own masters, come forward like men and vote for BENJAMIN R. MORGAN.

A Morgan supporter, "One of the People," put the choice in even starker terms, advising the electorate that "If you *wish for war*, vote for Israel Israel by all means. If you prefer peace and good Government, vote for Benjamin R. Morgan." As in October 1797 the election thus offered a clear choice. "A Philadelphian" wrote in the *Gazette of the United States* that Morgan was marked by

> the great intercourse which he has at all times had with persons conspicuous for their talents and information [and] ... his habits of intimacy with people of literary character ... [Israel] never has appeared as a prominent character amongst his fellow-citizens, except in turbulent times, when he was made use of by others, more cunning and equally mischievous with himself, as a ladder to their individual promotion. In such times, he has ever been esteemed the *favorer of anarchy, the supporter of sedition*; his feeble attempts have been directed to the introduction of disorder into the state, and no means have been neglected, that promised success in promoting the views of the party, with which he acted ... [his exertions during the fever] would have due weight if urged as a qualification in a candidate for the appointment of a manager of the Hospital, or a guardian of the poor, but could by no means furnish proofs of his fitness for legislative functions ... Men, who could applaud the conduct of *Genet*, or any other foreign minister, when insulting their country in the person of their *beloved chief magistrate*, can know little of

that *love of country*, so essentially requisite in a Patriot. Such men may lay claim to the wages of a foreign faction, but are devoid of the principles which form the character, and, of course, undeserving of the name of good citizens.

The rhetoric was no less partisan in the *Aurora* since both newspapers were promoting different types of public representative as much as they were supporting two different men.[10]

Despite the energy and colour with which the candidates were presented, many voters felt that the people had already spoken in October 1797, that the challenge to the outcome had illegally deprived Israel of his seat, and that there had been "an attempt upon our rights." Morgan's supporters took a different view and argued that since so many of them had fled Philadelphia during the outbreak of fever, even if they had done so willingly, and on the basis that they could afford to do so, they had been disadvantaged electorally. Israel's supporters did not have the choice, being poor. However, having stayed in the city, they had distorted the election and in addition, allegedly enjoyed up to £30,000 from the health committee "by which, it is believed, he [Israel] got a great many votes." This time out, Federalists were anxious to see a "true" process, including a concerted effort "to secure the right of suffrage from foreign influence." The number of "illegal votes" which was said to have been cast at the previous election made the point for one writer in the *Gazette of the United States*, while another observed that a "large number of votes" had been cast in Southwark by "foreigners who had "no right" to do so. In Federalist eyes, these people were all the more threatening because they

> revile the heroes who effected the salvation of our country for all that is dear and sacred to freemen—they take part with the domestic and foreign enemies of the United States ... [and] they anticipate the time when the floods of licentiousness shall sweep away all the principles that gave peace and security in life, or hope in the hour of dissolution.

Simply put, they were "bloody and remorseless" foreigners who had an undue influence over American elections. Federalist newspapers also alleged, and their Republican colleagues were forced to deny, that Israel had said that he wanted to naturalise "hordes of United Irishmen, to be admitted to the rights of citizenship, in order to influence the election." Given the contemporary images

10 "Fellow Citizen" in *GUS*, 22 Feb. 1798; HSP, "Another of the People," "To the Inhabitants of Germantown" (broadside, Philadelphia, 1798); "One of the People" in *PorcG*, 21 Feb. 1798; "A Philadelphian" in *GUS*, 22 Feb. 1798. For the use of the word "patriotism" in candidates' notices, see for example, *GUS*, 20 Feb. 1798, where it was applied to Morgan.

of the society, as well as its origins in Ireland, it was a short step for "Truth" to put the forthcoming election in a certain context:

> the friends of peace and order [and of Morgan] ... will now behold the necessity of supporting the government and raising their country to that degree of national dignity, as not to be endangered by foreign influence, or exposed to be shaken by the acts of seditious foreigners ... [and] avert the dangers to which this country is exposed ... [otherwise] all power will be submitted to the hands of a mob ... insurrection will become the order of the day, our houses will no longer remain our castles, and peace, happiness and security will be banished from among us.[11]

In addition to coining their own electoral buzz-words, the two campaigns also established networks which would mobilise and manage their respective voters. A meeting in Philadelphia on 13 February urged "early and active exertions" among Morgan's friends to publish "the result of their deliberations, and by all such other means as shall suggest themselves as promotive of the same end." Four days later there was a similar gathering "to concert their measures" on Morgan's behalf. Another meeting urged its followers to follow Morgan's electoral interests with "united and unremitted exertion" and not only to vote for him on 22 February but to recommend him to their friends as "a proper character for the said office." A few days before the election Israel's supporters from "all the wards in the city" were also invited to meet "to devise measures for conducting to the best effect, their desires." The effect of such meetings was not only to co-ordinate the organisations of the two candidates but to initiate practices which would become more notorious in later generations: printing tickets with the name of one of the candidates excluded, contractors threatening to withdraw their custom from tradesmen if "they would not sacrifice their right of suffrage at the shrine of party rancour and desperation," landlords intimidating tenants, and employers visiting blacksmiths, sailmakers, labourers, joiners

> and those mechanics who were particularly concerned in the shipping line, and declar[ing] to them that a combination had been entered into by the merchants, to deprive any person employed by them of any more business, unless they voted as they did [in this case, for Morgan] at the election.

11 *Aurora*, 14, 15 Feb. 1798; LCP, Ab (1798)–25, "One of the People," "To the Friends of Israel Israel ... February 22, 1798;" "A Dutch Man," "To the Inhabitants of the County of Philadelphia;" *GUS*, 22 Feb. 1798; *PorcG*, 27 Nov. 1798; "Common Sense" in *PhilG*, 17 Feb. 1798; "Truth" in *GUS*, 20 Feb. 1798. For allegations that United Irishmen had a distorting influence on Israel's election, for example, see "Philopolites" in *GUS*, 19 Feb. 1798 and "Truth" in *ibid.*, 20 Feb. 1798.

It was also reported that ship captains would give preference to any "mechanic or labourer" who made himself "conspicuous" in Morgan's cause.[12]

Such intimidation was not confined to any one side. It could also take on a more violent character. On 17 February 1798, for example, the *Gazette of the United States* reported that pro-Morgan meetings had been upset by "*a numerous and daring mob*" and later, that a pro-Israel group had "attempted to deny the right [to assemble] to any but themselves." It also suggested that on election day, supporters of Israel had intimidated voters and had kept selected taverns open during the previous week, "free of expense to all precious republicans," while three days earlier, *Porcupine's Gazette* alleged that one pro-Israel meeting had collected money "to defray the expenses of drink, &c. for the Chairman and his Secretary." Federalists did not have a monopoly of virtue and as the election drew close, Israel's "friends" were warned that Morgan's "party" would "provoke riots, broils, and personal contest." All of this led one writer to the *Aurora* to warn electors to

> suspect the man who has no better argument to convince you of the purity of his motives than by aspersing the private character of his opponent – Despise those who attempt to gain an improper influence by their wealth, and dare to threaten, those whom they cannot convince ... who are for ever preaching up the necessity of a more efficient government, as though the people were not sufficiently enlightened to know, and virtuous to pursue, their true interest.

However, despite the fact that the *Aurora* always wanted to call the Federalists of Philadelphia to account, its comment was one which could be applied to all shades of opinion, and citizens were urged to vote so that "the truth may be once [and] for all fully ascertained." As "A Freeman" had put it in October 1797,

> *all* depends upon the exertions of the Democratical Republicans of Philadelphia ... Let not then a single republican voter omit exercising his important right of suffrage on this occasion, big with the fate of their country's best interests, under the delusive idea, that one vote more or less will be of no consequence.[13]

12 LCP, broadsides, Ab (1798)–1, "At a Meeting of a Number of Citizens ... February 12;" *Aurora*, 21 Feb. 1798; *GUS*, 20 Feb. 1798; *Aurora*, 20 Feb. 1798; *GUS*, 22 Feb. 1798; *Aurora*, 27, 28 Feb., 10 Mar. 1798; "Cassius" in *Aurora*, 22 Feb. 1798. Nearly forty electoral recommendations for the two candidates were re-printed on election day; see *ADA*, 22 Feb. 1798.

13 *GUS*, 20, 24 Feb. 1798; *PorcG*, 21 Feb. 1798; *CR*, 20 Feb. 1798; *Aurora*, 29 Aug. 1798; "Fellow Citizen" in *GUS*, 22 Feb. 1798; "A Freeman" in *Aurora*, 1 Oct. 1797.

Eligibility to vote had already proven to be contentious in October 1797 and it remained a live issue four months later. On 14 February 1798 the *Gazette of the United States* pointedly advised all naturalised citizens who intended to vote at the ensuing election to "take out their certificates," provided of course, that they were "of good moral character, and well attached to the constitution of the United States." It reported that "a number of Irish" had already done so and on the following day, published the names of sixty eight Irishmen who had taken the necessary oaths. Prior to election day, procedures for voting were also clarified in a number of public statements. As was usual, electoral judges and inspectors were appointed and these announced that they would ask electors: firstly, if they were native to Pennsylvania, or any other state, or had ever sworn allegiance to "any foreign power;" secondly, if they were citizens or had been legally naturalised; and thirdly, if they had lived in Pennsylvania for at least two years and paid the required county or state taxes. These questions were not without their own controversies and chief justice Thomas McKean felt obliged to question their validity in a broadside that was circulated on the day before the election. McKean also felt that voters were not legally obliged to produce certificates of citizenship on election day. However, the questions were asked, the election was held, and Israel lost by a margin of 357 votes (see table 6.1).[14] As in 1797, the Northern Liberties and Southwark had voted overwhelmingly for Israel while, for the most part, the city had stood with the Federalists.

TABLE 6.1: PENNSYLVANIA SENATE
Special Election for the First District (Philadelphia & Delaware Counties),
22 February 1798

	Morgan (F)	Israel (R)
City Return	2041	1498
Northern Liberties	441	1135
Southwark	322	746
Kinsessing & Blockley	96	77
Germantown	283	265
Bustletown	347	102
Delaware County	1010	360
	4540	4183

Sources: *Carey's Recorder*, 24 Feb. 1798; *Aurora*, 24 Feb. 1798

14 *PorcG*, 15, 18 Feb. 1798; Aurora, 22 Feb. 1798. McKean's views on the inspectors' questions are quoted from LCP, broadsides, Ab (1798)–9, "Fellow Citizens ... Carlisle 29

The Renewed Debate on the Polity

The outcome did not settle the controversies which had overshadowed the two elections, and the wider debate on the influence of the foreign-born continued. In February 1798 "An Enemy to Misrepresentation" asked the central question:

[should] every man whose private interests have brought him here, or whose public *crimes* have driven him from his own country ... the moment he touches the soil of America possess the power of legislating the rights of property, of personal liberty, and personal security [in America]?

At the time, Israel's supporters and, in particular, Irish immigrants, were the obvious targets of such comments. As might be expected, Republicans made every effort to defend the integrity of these recent arrivals because Federalist insecurities about a broadening polity were largely linked to the political organisation and presence of such people in Philadelphia. With Morgan's election, the city's Federalists had scored an important victory in their efforts to curb the role of the immigrant in contemporary politics. As they celebrated Morgan's victory in April 1798, it was reported that "the company" was "sheltered" not by "the tricolored emblem of gallic perfidy, but [by] the banner of freedom, the eagle of the United States." Among the twenty toasts which were offered on the occasion was one to "The *American* people – May they banish from their councils and their confidence, those who have shewn a disposition to degrade their country." Another expressed the hope that the debates of the house of representatives would be "uncontrouled (*sic*) and undefiled by imported doctrines, uncongenial with the American character, and inconsistent with its dignity." With this in mind, they expected that "those wretches among us, on whom France calculates for our destruction, [would] be speedily detected and punished" and that, in particular, the "mistaken" citizens of Southwark would be "undeceived" and that the district's "former Federal character [would] be speedily restored." The Federalist congressman from South Carolina (1793–1800), Robert Goodloe Harper, also attended the gathering and saluted America's "unconquerable will and courage ... never to submit or yield."[15] However, unlike the earlier election, and in the aftermath of

September 1798" and Ab (1798)–8, "Opinion of Chief Justice McKean." The inspectors' questions were also published in *ADA*, 21 Feb. 1798. On 21 Feb., *GUS* reported that Mathew Carey had taken out his certificate of naturalisation on 20 Feb. 1798; for the certificate, see HSP, Edward Carey Gardiner Collection, box 84–A.
15 "An Enemy to Misrepresentation" in *GUS*, 15 Feb. 1798; *PorcG*, 24 Apr. 1798. Harper's attendance at the event was reported in the *Aurora*, 15 Aug. 1798.

the yellow fever outbreak, the city voters were now back in their own homes. The result was there for all to see.

Energised by Morgan's electoral success, Philadelphia's Federalists pressed for new laws and regulations on naturalisation and what was vaguely described as "sedition." The object was little different from what it had been in the earlier part of the decade: to curtail one of the Republicans' vital sources of political support and deny them further electoral success. As part of this ambition, Federalists argued that the United Irishmen and their cohorts could never become "truly American." Moreover, during the months after Morgan's election, the flag of the United States was all but monopolised by them. As put by the *Gazette of the United States* on 7 March 1799,

> Believe one whose country is America, that these various tricks will not avail you towards forming a character which you were never intended for ... The American disposition delights in uprightness, and every specious of ingeniousness; the outcast Irishman in injustice and every species of low deception. The American uses every effort to promote the welfare of his country, and especially to support the laws and constituted authorities; the abandoned Irishman's chief pride, is to destroy his country's decreed rights, to trample down her laws, and overturn her legal power—ferocious by nature, licentious by inclination; no laws divine or human, will deter the one, or restrain the other—Lay these characteristics seriously to heart; they are such as experience will confirm; and say whether you think it possible [that] you [Irish] can become an American, by the practice of those arts which now hail you chief of a faction.[16]

The perception that many Irish immigrants were nothing more than "a detestable banditti of foreign invaders" was not new. However, as many countered, where one was born did not necessarily indicate a person's primary loyalties. The foreign-born were citizens by choice rather than by chance and had a personal and honourable interest in realising the opportunities which America offered them. Republicans, in particular, recognised that although America was a land of immigrants, the challenges of the past and shared interests in the present would in the future, promote an integrated nation. The *Gazette of the United States* was not so sure and urged Americans not to "import" the kind of "*national* prejudices" which were "a melancholy fact" in contemporary Europe. Instead, it suggested that Americans should

---

16 *GUS*, 7 Mar. 1799. For the evolution of "sedition" as an issue of legislative concern, see Smith, *Freedom's Fetters*; and Miller, *Crisis in Freedom*.

forever make a distinction between the *bad men* in a nation, and the *nation*; and not like absurd English and Frenchmen, condemn *whole nations* for the misdeeds of their rulers, or a number of bad individuals … consider all men as our brethern, until they have individually proved themselves unworthy of the appellation. It is much to be complained of that the evil complained of in other nations has been imported into this.

Such sentiments also surfaced in Noah Webster's commitment to develop a more uniform "national language" as well as in his strong belief in education as an instrument of cultural integration. By stressing the virtue and patriotism of the centre, the private, local, and regional biases of America's citizens, whatever their national, cultural, or religious backgrounds, would be replaced by the acknowledgment of "a pure American character [that would be] free from the vices and errors which have deluged the European world in crimes and miseries." Nonetheless, many Federalists remained uncomfortable about the apparent ease with which, as the *Gazette of the United States* saw it, the foreign-born acquired "the full and perfect right to citizenship" in America. In May 1798, Congressman John Allen (F., Conn., 1797–99) bemoaned the "vast number" of naturalisations which had recently taken place in Philadelphia and in an apparent reference to the Israel-Morgan contest, he suggested that those involved had supported "a particular party." He thought that the foreign-born had questionable judgement and that the Naturalisation Acts should be reformed. The security of America's fledgling republican polity demanded no less.[17]

Outside Congress, the relevant debates were energetic and wide-ranging. At a meeting in Philadelphia in July 1798, an unnamed "literary society" even discussed whether it was "just or impolitic" to prohibit immigration altogether. While it argued that "misery and death" in contemporary Europe had always made immigration a matter of "justice," it proposed that it was now time to consider whether or not the best "interests of the [American] people" were being served by inviting foreigners to settle in America. There were tensions between "the duties of humanity which we owe to strangers" and "the principles that bind us to our relatives, to our friends, to our country." After all, the society resolved, "self-preservation is the first law of nature." Moreover,

> foreign emigration has a tendency … to destroy the sentiments of national character, and … national honor … we should not lose sight of our country and ourselves … Men who differ widely in their opinions, in their principles,

---

17 *GUS*, 11 Feb. 1799, 6 Mar. 1798. The last quotation from the *GUS* is cited from Smith, *Freedom's Fetters*, 162 and Allen from the *Annals of Congress* vii (15 May 1797–19 July 1798), 1588 (3 May 1798). For Webster, see David Simpson, *The Politics of American English, 1776–1850* (New York, 1986).

and in their wishes can never continue long under one government. Their national counsels will present an eternal scene of confusion and discord.

The meeting was pushed in this direction as much by a fear of "furious demagogues ... who have fled from the countries that gave them birth [and were] ... unfit to mingle with the citizens of America" as by the hope that an "assimilation of manners" might promote the most "permanent union." While the latter comment indulged the older aspiration to the organic polity, there were many who still believed that immigrants brought with them "their peculiar habits, and their peculiar prejudices." As a result, they feared that a viable "national character can never be established." America was still in a "state of infancy," as a meeting of another "literary society" in Princeton put it in August 1798, but as a correspondent noted a month earlier, "the strength of a country consists in the attachment and love of its inhabitants." The challenge was how to define this in law.[18]

Newspapers had also been commenting on these points. From the mid-1790s domestic events and foreign wars ensured that they would continue to do so with even greater vigour than before. Various writers to the *Gazette of the United States* challenged the "impertinent intruder" from abroad for "arrogat[ing] to yourself the privilege of judging of the policy of the measures of our administration." Some also berated the "passiveness" of more settled Americans because the United Irishmen had "proceeded from insult to open outrage; they bid defiance to our laws, [and] they threaten our fellow creatures with assassination." As the debates on the Alien Laws of 1798 gathered momentum, the *Gazette of the United States* went even further and promoted the notion of "*exclusive patriots*," that is that citizenship should be exclusively tied to birth. Moreover, it argued that who still felt that "true" Americans should stress the "inextinguishable *nationality*" of America and not forever parade, however benignly, "Irish afflictions" and "the Irish character" as if the fate of the world was determined by them. A contrary view was offered by the *Aurora* on 5 February 1798:

> None but a proud, prejudiced and selfish being ... will quarrel with a man because he did not draw his first breadth on the same spot with himself, or will reproach him, because the consequence he has acquired in wealth and station, was not bequeathed to him by his ancestors, but earned by his own industry and merit.

18 *GUS*, 28 July, 29 Aug., 28 July 1798.

In June 1798 at the height of Franco-American tensions, the "natives of Great Britain and Ireland" also reflected on such themes in a letter to president Adams,

> impressed with a strong sense of the duties of obedience and support to that government, which so benignly protects them, and that they repose a full confidence in the integrity, firmness, and abilities, that have so eminently distinguished your administration.

By suggesting that loyalty and foreign birth were not incompatible, this petition was much more than what in contemporary Britain, would have been termed a "loyal address."[19]

Inside Congress, a number of Federalists were also responding to these issues by trying to restrict the provisions of the Naturalisation Acts of 1790 and 1795. They were motivated to do so by considerations that ranged from the party political to questions of national security, contested definitions of the polity, and the continuing debates on the representation and leadership of the public. During the special session of Congress which had been called for May 1797 to discuss the deepening crisis with France, it was clear that several congressmen were worried about the growing influence of the foreign-born. On 1 July 1797 the legislative debate on revised stamp duties and, in particular, a proposal to impose $20 on naturalisation certificates, gave them a preliminary opportunity to address these concerns. Among Federalist congressmen, David Brooks (N.Y., 1797–99) and Samuel Sewall (Mass., 1796–1800) agreed with the proposal, conscious that it would also help to restrict the ability of Republicans to draw on the votes of immigrants. From his bench, Sewall did not "wish to see foreigners [as] our governors" and in his view, "if they were admitted as voters at our elections, they in some degree became the governors of our country" as well. Among Republicans, **Albert Gallatin** (NP, Pa., 1795–1800) and John Swanwick (Pa., 1795–98) suggested that Brooks's proposal was, in the words of the latter, "too considerable a sum" for the purpose intended and that it would hit the "poor emigrant." Brooks also raised an important point of principle because if immigrants did not pay the proposed fee, "they would be living in the country as foreigners, and not as citizens of a free country." In Gallatin's words, "it would operate in a very improper manner," not least because

---

19 "M" in *GUS*, 7 Mar. and 11 Feb. 1799; *GUS*, 12 Feb. 1799; *Aurora*, 5 May 1798; *GUS*, 12 Feb. 1798. For the address to Adams, see *Argus*, 19 July 1798.

one-fourth, if not one-third part of the inhabitants of a country [would be] living as foreigners in its bosom … speaking the same language and having the same manners [as Americans], after they had been in the country ten or fifteen years, [and] would look upon the refusal to admit them to the common right of citizens, except upon the payment of twenty dollars, as unjust and oppressive.[20]

As Gallatin saw it, a measure that was being introduced "for the purpose of revenue" was not an appropriate basis on which to re-visit "the rights of citizenship" or "to throw obstructions in the way of emigration." Joseph McDowell (R., N. Carolina, 1797–98) suggested that what was being proposed represented

a departure from the spirit of our Government, and [was] derogatory to us as an enlightened nation. It had been remarked by gentlemen that we had fought and bled for our liberty. It was true, that we had fought for liberty, but, he trusted, we did not mean to confine it to ourselves, nor to sell it to others. On the contrary, people of other countries had been invited to come and partake with us in our blessings … but now, after vast numbers were come, and others were coming, all at once, we propose to make sale of our privileges. This he could not agree to. It was not the wealthy, the high-bred, the well-born, that he wanted to emigrate to our country; it was a different class of men, viz.: mechanics, farmers, and other industrious persons.

Although he tied the particular onus of the stamp tax to both an ability to pay and the potential invidiousness of a two-tiered system of naturalisation, the more general and broader issues were also there for all to see. As Matthew Lyon (R., Vt., 1797–1801) put it, the proposals were "injurious, cruel, and impolitic," especially after American legislators "had told the world, that there was in this country a good spring of liberty, and invited all to come and drink of it." The proposed tax was so restrictive in his view that it looked as if the administration was "entering a treaty offensive and defensive, with the Monarch of Britain, to prevent his subjects from leaving him and coming hither." The measure would prevent many immigrants from becoming fully active in American life and restrict immigration. In essence, it was, in the words of John Williams, (F., N.Y., 1795–98), "rather a tax upon liberty, than upon property." As finally agreed, the tax was limited to $5, despite Republican objections that this would be counter-productive and that it would detach immigrants from the

20 *Annals of Congress*, vii, 422 (Brooks), 426 (Sewall), 422 (Gallatin), 422, 429 (Swanwick), 422, 423 (Gallatin). All quotations in this and the following note have been taken from the debate of 1 July 1797.

very government to which they should always be looking without hesitation or discouragement.[21]

It was during this debate that Harrison Grey Otis (F., Mass., 1797–1801) had also expressed his wish not "to invite hordes of wild Irishmen, nor the turbulent and disorderly of all parts of the world, to come here with a view to disturb our tranquillity, after having succeeded in the overthrow of their own Governments." Otis's "wild Irish" speech was particularly offensive to Irish immigrants, not just because it castigated their part in the achievement and consolidation of American independence but because it had indulged "rancorous prejudices" that stretched back to the sixteenth century. On 13 September 1797 the *Time-Piece* recalled that

> The word 'wild' ... was a term of reproach bestowed on Ireland by Englishmen because of their impatience of bondage, her violent and bloody struggles for freedom ... it answers to the word rebel among [Americans] ... How ridiculous to call that nation [Ireland] which is as high advanced in improvements as any nation in Europe ... it does not apply even to peasantry in Ireland.

Despite its provocative language, Otis's speech reflected a widely-held view that the provisions of the naturalisation laws were too liberal or in Brooks's enigmatic words, that "the rights of citizenship [should not be] made too common." Moreover, because "there were foreigners [who] came here, fugitives from justice, and others, who never would be of any advantage to any country," the government was right to insist on "some security for the attachment of [foreign-born] persons" to it. Reflecting similar sentiments, an increasing number of congressmen were suggesting that longer periods of residence should be required of the foreign-born before they became citizens of the United States. Because these observations had been made in the aftermath of the special session of Congress, they were taken up by a committee which had been appointed "for the protection of commerce and the defence of our country." On 17 April 1798 it was proposed to extend the remit of this committee "to enquire whether it be not expedient to suspend or to amend the act for establishing an uniform rule of naturalization."[22]

The main debate on revising the Naturalisation Act took place during May 1798. The principal speakers were those who had spoken on the stamp duties the previous July. The main themes were also familiar although criticisms of the

21 *Ibid.*, 427, 428 (Gallatin), 427 (McDowell), 426 (Lyon), 426 (Williams).
22 *Ibid.*, 430 (Otis); "An Irishman," "To Harrison G. Otis, Esquire" in *CR*, 8 July 1797; *Annals of Congress* vii, 422 (Brooks); *ibid.* viii, 422 (Otis), 1427. All but the last quotation have been taken from the debate of 1 July 1797. The last has been taken from the business of 17 Apr. 1798.

existing arrangements for naturalisation, whereby one could become a citizen after five years, were particularly sharp. Despite further arguments that an extended waiting period would, in effect, lead to different types of citizenship, Senator William Bingham of Pennsylvania observed that it would at least deprive those who had not been born in the United States "of the power of influencing Elections" in the future. Otis agreed that it was desirable that the probationary period should be long enough to wean the foreign-born away from their supposed attachments to the old world and move them towards an unequivocal loyalty to their new homeland. As the subsequent debate unfolded during the earlier days of May 1798, some congressmen even suggested that citizenship was not a *sine qua non* to enjoy the opportunities that were on offer in America but rather a privilege which should be restricted to its own native-born.[23]

Others argued that citizenship could be made incremental for the foreign-born. As Marilyn Baseler has pointed out, loyalists had been given a "limited" form of citizenship after the Revolution while in states such as Virginia and South Carolina, citizenship did not automatically confer the right to vote or to seek office, even when the citizen paid taxes. Such arguments were as old as they were familiar. They rested on an assumption that since the U.S. constitution had been passed, partisan controversy had been spearheaded by immigrants. For Harper, this was to be expected because "strangers ... however acceptable they may be in other respects, could not have the same views and attachments with native citizens." For him and his Federalist supporters, this was a point of fact although Sewall suggested that in the case of the Irish, it had been intensified by the "distracted state of the country from whence they emigrated" which supposedly predisposed them to agitation, violence and disrespect for the institutions of the state and public order. Harper hoped that the outcome of the current discussion would enable the United States to "recover from the mistake [it] ... fell into when it first began to form its constitutions, of admitting foreigners to citizenship ... [a] mistake ... productive of very great evils to this country." Indeed, he believed that those "evils" would greatly increase if they were not corrected.[24]

Harper's views were extreme, especially when he suggested that while he had no objection to the foreign-born owning property in America, "nothing but birth should entitle a man to citizenship in this country." He appreciated why people moved to America "to better their condition" but "was it necessary," he

23 *Ibid.* viii, 1572 (Otis, 3 May 1798); vii, 422 (Sewall, 1 July 1797). Bingham is quoted from Smith, *Freedom's Fetters*, 33.
24 Baseler, *Asylum for Mankind*, 205–7; *Annals of Congress* viii, 1568 (Harper, 2 May 1798); 1778 (Sewall, 21 May 1798); 1567 (Harper, 1 May 1798).

asked, that "these persons should at once become entitled to take a part in the concerns of our Government?" Otis clearly believed that they should not, especially because they could be used by other countries to "gain an influence in our councils" at a time when the United States was "growing into a nation of importance." For James A. Bayard (F., Del., 1797–1803), the point was underlined by the supposedly disruptive influence of the "many Jacobins and vagabonds [who] have come into the United States during the last two years." In Sewall's view, all these reservations could be eased by requiring a long term of residence before naturalisation. Otis was still not happy and proposed that "no alien born, who is not at present a citizen of the United States, shall hereafter be capable of holding any office of honour, trust, or profit under the United States." Both Abraham Venable (R., Va., 1791–98) and Nathaniel Macon (R., N. Carolina, 1791–1816) doubted the constitutionality of such a motion on the basis that once a man was admitted as a citizen, Congress could not limit his rights as a citizen. This point was also discussed in an address "To Irish Emigrants and Particularly that Class Denominated Aliens" in July 1798: those who paid taxes should not be excluded from voting for government or precluded from enjoying "the benefits" of the laws to which they, like all citizens, were subject. The foreign-born had either to be refused citizenship altogether or, once naturalised, given their full rights. There was no half-way house.[25]

As America and France drifted towards war during the spring of 1798, concern about the status of the foreign-born led to fears of their ability to subvert the country from within. Otis was not alone in focusing on "that crowd of spies and inflammatory agents which overspread the country like the locusts of Egypt, and who were continually attacking our liberties." In Allen's view, such people were "ready to join a foreign Power" to "subjugate" America. Allegations that Holland, Switzerland, and Venice had fallen to Napoleon through the activities of internal agents, fanned Federalist anxieties during 1797 and 1798. Federalists were determined that nothing similar would happen in the United States. They would "restrain the evil," if necessary, by imprisoning or deporting "suspect" immigrants from countries which went to war with America. In Harper's words, the Alien Acts would "put a hook in the nose of persons who are leagued with the enemies of this country." These sentiments were also reflected in the Alien Enemies Act which would give the president sweeping powers in times of war and "quasi-war." While this act was still in

25 *Annals of Congress*, viii, 1567, 1568 (Harper, 2 May 1798), 1572 (Otis, 3 May 1798), 1566 (Sewall, 1 May 1798), 1568 (Otis, 2 May 1798). For the reservations of Venable and Macon, see *ibid.*, 1569–71 (3 May 1798). The address to "Irish Emigrants" is in *Aurora*, 4 July 1798. Bayard is quoted from Smith, *Freedom's Fetters*, 31.

committee, Congress received the "XYZ" *communiqués*. An immediate reaction was to adopt a bill in which Senator James Hillhouse (F., Conn., 1796–1810) had asked that all non-naturalized aliens who were "dangerous" to the country's "peace and safety" should be expelled, and that those who remained should be registered. Because Hillhouse's bill had been read and amended by mid-June 1798, it was swiftly adopted by both houses and signed into law as the Alien Friends Act on 25 June for an initial period of two years. The act enabled the president to deport any alien whom he suspected (with or without evidence) to be "in treasonable or secret machinations against the government." It also tightened immigration by obliging ship captains to give detailed reports to the office of the secretary of state, of the numbers, origins, and descriptions of the passengers they brought into America.[26]

Given the sweeping powers of the Alien Friends Act, due in no small part to the emotive atmosphere in which it had been mooted, as well as its "temporary" nature, Gallatin overcame objections to move the other legislation, the proposed Alien Enemies Act, out of committee, noting that "if this bill is not passed, the President of the United States will have the power of removing from the country all those aliens whom he may think it necessary and proper to be removed, whether they are alien friends or alien enemies." However, the legislation also had potentially serious implications for Jeffersonian networks and especially for those of the United Irishmen and others, who were easily identified as admirers of France and its particular brand of republicanism. Especially worrying were the act's provisions to deport anybody who had been convicted of a crime in his native country, as a result of which some of America's radical Irish immigrants felt particularly vulnerable. As signed into law on 6 July 1798, the act provided that resident aliens of a country with which the United States was in a state of "declared war" could be "apprehended, restrained, secured and removed, as alien enemies" by presidential proclamation. James Morton Smith has observed that "buried in the heart of this bill was a bold attempt to purify the national character by isolating all aliens from American society and from each other."[27]

The Sedition Act also dealt with the status and loyalty of the foreign-born in the United States. However, it also affected native-born Americans such as George Logan, whose private "peace mission" to France in June 1798 had provoked John Kittera (F., Pa., 1791–1801), to warn against "internal enemies" who were otherwise beyond the reach of the Alien Laws. Although specific

---

26 *Annals of Congress* viii, 1575 (Otis, 3 May 1798), 1578 (Allen, 3 May 1798), 1577 (Sitgreaves); *Annals of Congress* vii (Senate), 548 (25 Apr. 1798); *Stats at Large* i, 570–2.
27 *Annals of Congress* viii, 2035 (Gallatin, 25 June 1798); Smith, *Freedom's Fetters*, 52. For the act's provisions, see Smith, *Freedom's Fetters*, 440–1.

references to France were struck from the final draft, that the act was intended to target the supposedly hostile activities of "Jacobin agents" in America was unmistakable. The message which the act conveyed was that one could not be an apologist for France and a supporter of the American government at the same time. It also gave a platform to those who articulated a version of "patriotism" that was bound up with loyalty to the existing government and its visible head. Indeed, some senators who considered the act to be unconstitutional, voted for it in order "to evince [a] determination *to support Government*" at a time of supposed national danger. As Stevens Thomson Mason (R., Va., 1794–1803) suggested, it "was a lesser evil to violate the constitution than to suffer the printers to abuse the Govt."[28]

Such ideas were not new. Even within a month of Morgan's election to the Pennsylvania senate, the *Aurora* had noted that

> as soon as the administration began to feel an opposition to some of their measures, they attempted to artfully blend the idea of opposition to the constitution with that of opposition to the administration, and thus to brand as enemies of the constitution those who opposed their measures.

As adopted in July 1798, the Sedition Act stipulated

> That if any persons shall unlawfully combine or conspire together, with intent to oppose any measure or measures of the government of the United States ... or to intimidate or prevent [a person] from holding a place or office ... [or] from undertaking, performing or executing his trust or duty ... or attempt to procure any insurrection, riot, unlawful assembly, or combination ... [or] write, print, utter or publish ... any false, scandalous and malicious writing or writings against the government of the United States, or either house of the United States, or the President, with intent to defame the said government ... the said President ... or to aid, encourage or abet any hostile designs of any foreign nation against the United States ... stir up sedition ... or to excite any unlawful combinations ... for opposing or resisting any law of the United States, *or any act of the President* [my emphasis]... [or] encourage or abet any hostile designs of any foreign nation ... [they could incur a] fine not exceeding two thousand dollars ... [or] imprisonment not exceeding two years.

These provisions were wide-ranging and even threatening. Together with those of the Alien Acts, they were considered by many contemporaries to constitute

28 *Annals of Congress*, 2016 (Kittera, 21 June 1798); LC, Jefferson Papers, Stevens Thomson Mason to Thomas Jefferson, 6 July 1798. For Logan's mission, see Frederick B. Tolles, "Unofficial Ambassador: George Logan's Mission to France, 1798," *WMQ* vii (1950), 3–25.

an excessive interference with personal liberty, free speech, and freedom of assembly. Two major historians agreed: James Morton Smith in *Freedom's Fetters* and John C. Miller in *A Crisis in Freedom*.[29]

These laws also raised a number of other complicated and controversial constitutional issues at a time when checks and balances within American governance were jealously guarded. Even if the published measures were only "temporary," they showed how the respective roles of Congress and the states (which retained legal discretion with respect to migration until 1808) could be curtailed, in this case, because of a power that was being assigned to the executive to admit aliens to the status of citizenship, and to restrain or banish those "whose intrigues and malpractices" were deemed to threaten the government. The implication of the laws was that America's foreign-born were "strangers merely" and hence were neither fully protected by the U.S. constitution nor presumed to have the right to petition about matters of public concern. Such assumptions were offensive in that they discounted the roles of the foreign-born in the American War of Independence and called into question the loyalty which such people now wished to give to their adopted country. Others saw the laws as breaching faith with immigrants, tarnishing America's reputation abroad, and encouraging suspicions among the very people America needed to develop the new republic, especially in the west: "it [is] in our best interest to attach them to us," McDowell observed on 21 May 1798, "and not always to look upon them as aliens and strangers." Above all, the laws seemed to suggest that even assessments of service during the American Revolution, whatever their merits or necessity, were flawed by being referenced to the political views of one administration: that of the Federalists. They represented an apparent lack of confidence that the new republic could accommodate its disparities and that immigrants could ever become Americanised, irrespective of either their willingness to do so, or their formative cultural contexts. The Alien and Sedition Acts were thus based on strategies of exceptionalism and as such, challenged the long-held notion that diversity could be securely and harmoniously indulged in the new republic.[30]

"Pleas of Erin"

Given the language and focus of these debates, it was inevitable that the *Aurora* would urge each of its readers "to state his [*sic*] opinion" on the Alien Acts,

29 "A Citizen of Pennsylvania" in 21 Mar. 1798; Smith, *Freedom's Fetters* and Miller, *A Crisis in Freedom*. The text of the act is in *Statutes at Large* i, 596–7.

30 *Annals of Congress* viii, 1776 (McDowell, 21 May 1798). The characterisation of America's foreign-born is quoted of Timothy Pickering in the *Aurora*, 6 Nov. 1798.

"whether his opinion be true or false." On the electoral front, the first opportunity to do so came in December 1798 when a special election to the Pennsylvania assembly was held in Philadelphia county, following the resignation of the incumbent, John Huston. This local contest pitted George Logan against the former Federalist speaker of the U.S. house of representatives, Frederick A. Muhlenberg. Although the war hysteria and Federalist paranoia of the previous spring had receded considerably by that time, given the cultural complexion of the constituency, as well as the personalities who were involved, it was inevitable that the recently-passed legislation would be discussed during the campaign. Logan's supporters galvanised Republican objections to the acts and at a meeting in the Northern Liberties on 17 December 1798, they appointed a committee to prepare a petition against the "injurious, oppressive, and unjust" acts that had been passed some six months earlier. They also stressed that "public servants are amenable" to the people and that government policy could always be reversed despite suggestions that even in times of war, the country's "natural leaders" knew what was best for the country. Logan was elected and his victory hailed by the *Aurora* as "the best reply which could have been given by the people to the president" in the aftermath of Logan's disputed mission to France.[31]

Despite Logan's success, or perhaps even because of it, the protests and petitions against the Alien Acts continued and involved the United Irishmen. In March 1799, for example, it was reported that the United Irish section in Montgomery County had prepared a petition that would be carried by "appointed agents ... to go forth to obtain signatures." The anonymous "Captain John" was said to be "advanced to the rank of chief agent" and to be "riding about the country" trying to raise public interest in the acts. The *Gazette of the United States* was particularly critical of these activities which in its opinion, were

> for the purpose of discovering uninformed citizens into measures extremely prejudicial to government and their own interest ... [their leaders] are aliens and all unfriendly to our government – forgetful of the country that has long nourished and protected them ... judging the policy or impolicy of the measures of our administration ... [their] utmost wish is to realize [in America] the scenes of cruelty and confusion which a greater part of Europe has lately experienced ... [and] destroy those citizens, whose simplicity ... causes them to despise that authority which it is their chief advantage to

31 *Aurora*, 4 July, 19 Dec., 22, 24 Dec. 1798. For the election itself, see NYPL, Gordon Lester Ford Collection III, Liston to Grenville, 31 January 1799; *Aurora*, 22 Nov. 1798, 13 Feb., 13 Mar. 1799.

uphold ... [we should] purge our land of those who would sap the foundation of our government and raise themselves on its ruins ... as well might we attempt to tame the Hyena as to Americanize an Irishman.

In the *Aurora* of 19 February 1799, "A Citizen of Montgomery County" denied that the United Irishmen were involved in this business and suggested that the idea to collect signatures had originated at a private dinner of "a few citizens" who were unhappy with the new laws. The writer added that if one examined the names of the organising committees, it would be found that far from being "the emissaries of a disorganizing faction ... three-fourths and more" of them were "native American."[32]

The most publicised reaction to the Alien Acts from Philadelphia's Irish community came when the "natives of Ireland in the United States" addressed Congress in February 1799. In making its case, this "Plea of Erin" repeated the familiar theme that Irish immigrants had been "driven from our homes, like your venerable forefathers, by civil and religious oppressions" and had come to America to enjoy "a safe asylum from poverty, and, *in time, from oppressions also.*" The "plea" insinuated that the acts had unfairly singled out the "guiltless immigrant" who, despite his European origins, had the same constitutional rights to personal liberty, "tranquillity and safety" as the American-born. It expanded on this and other legal points, echoed concerns about the new "discretionary" powers that were now vested in the president, and insisted on the presumption of innocence until guilt was proven in court. It also addressed another concern: that at least in part, the Alien Acts may have resulted from "misrepresentations ... [that had been] incessantly propagated concerning us and our countrymen" as well as the "unjust impressions" of the Irish in America. This was ironic, if not insulting, given that

> the *blood* of the Irish flowed in your service here, as if it were *their own*, and that they *faithfully* acted in your highest public trusts ... of the Irish residents in the United States, a greater *proportion* partook of the hazards of the field, and of the duties of your independent republican councils, than of the Americans.

The memorial argued that the respective positions of America in 1775 and Ireland in 1798 were the same and suggested that more than most others, John Adams should have understood this because he had been a member of the Congressional committee which in 1775, had "deliberately prepared, and reported the touching address to Ireland, which openly excited them to approve, to assist, and to imitate the American struggle." Far from discriminating against

32 *GUS*, 7 Mar. 1799.

Irish immigrants, Congress should thus encourage them "to enjoy ... the peace, liberty and safety, which our gallant countrymen have helped to establish, till gracious Heaven, by dispensing to Ireland the same blessings, shall grant the remainder of our mutual prayers."[33]

The "Plea" had been prepared at a meeting in Philadelphia on Friday, 7 February, and signatures were taken at the Presbyterian and Catholic churches on the following Sunday, a day before several other petitions on the subject were to be discussed in the House of Representatives. The *Aurora*'s Clonmel-born editor, William Duane, the wealthy immigrant merchant, Robert Moore, a young Irish-born printer, Samuel Cuming, and Dr. James Reynolds were deputed to circulate the petition for signature. According to Duane, these men had been "judiciously chosen" to manage the morning's business, being either "Americans by birth," naturalised citizens, or the children "of respectable Emigrants." A considerable number of people had already subscribed on Saturday but because the Congressional debate was imminent, the organising committee decided to collect signatures at Sunday services. There was no opposition to the petition from the Presbyterian congregations. This was not the case at St. Mary's Catholic church where, although "three-fourths of the people who visit that church came under the penalties created concerning aliens," the petition was challenged after it was presented to the congregation after Mass. Shots were fired, scuffles broke out, and the *Gazette of the United States* reported that there occurred "a more daring and flagitious riot, than we remember to have outraged the civil law and the decorum of society for more than forty years." The four men who collected the signatures were later brought before the court of the Federalist mayor, Robert Wharton (1789–1800), and all but Cuming were remanded on bail of $4,000. However, when Cuming was refused bail because "he could not swear that he owed nothing," the Jeffersonian chief justice, Thomas McKean, intervened and overrode the mayoral court. This caused considerable controversy. Party interests were never far from the incident and while Wharton was criticised for fixing an unusually high bail for charges that were relatively minor, McKean was accused of displaying the

---

33 LC, Pennsylvania Broadsides (1799), "The Plea of Erin, or, The Case of the Natives of Ireland in the United States, fairly displayed." Unless otherwise noted, the quotations have been taken from this source. The petition was also published in the *Aurora*, 13 Feb. 1799. For the 1775 address, see Bric, "Ireland, America and the Reassessment of a Special Relationship," 110–11. In December 1798, a month after he became the new editor of the *Aurora*, Duane also observed that "the United Irishmen stand precisely in the same *odious circumstances* with relation to England that John Adams stood twenty years ago – they consider George III, an intolerable tyrant now, and he did *then*;" Smith, *Freedom's Fetters*, 278, n.3.

supposed arbitrary characteristics of the governments of Turkey and Algeria as he sought to re-balance the scales of justice.[34]

The trial for the "United Irish riot" took place on the following 21 February. The prosecution was led by Joseph Hopkinson (1770–1842), a prominent Federalist and author of the well-known anthem, "Hail Columbia." Alexander Dallas appeared for the four defendants who were charged with riot and assault. Reynolds faced an additional charge of riot "with an intent to kill" one James Gallagher. In confronting Reynolds, Gallagher claimed that he had been "hurt by the injury and insult done to my religion, making that a place of political meetings" and had thus asked members of the congregation to stay in the church after Mass and not to involve themselves in the proceedings outside. He had also torn down a copy of the petition from the walls of the church because "no *Jacobin* paper had a right to a place" there. As Duane put it, Gallagher had been "wholly engrossed … by holy rage against Jacobinism." With this in mind, Duane regretted that the opposing counsel had "by an involution of ideas connected Irishmen and Jacobinism" and that as a result, "the affection of his mind [had] jaundiced his eyes to every thing."[35]

During the trial many of the tired descriptions of America's "lately-adopted sons" were repeated and developed. It was alleged that those who had been indicted respected neither public nor church property, as the "profane" activities at St. Mary's had supposedly shown. One of the defence witnesses, Thaddeus McCarney, himself an immigrant in 1797, told the trial that because of the limited time that was available before the petition was sent to Congress, "a number" of the congregation had indicated that they would sign only if the memorial was brought to the church. While even prosecution witnesses accepted that divine service had not been interrupted, the local curate, Fr. Carr, added that in contemporary Ireland, it was "customary" to hold meetings of public interest after Sunday Mass, that petitions were "frequently" endorsed after services had concluded, and that this "was never considered [to be] any profanation of the church, or insult to the congregation." Thus, it was wrong to argue that the accused were blasphemous simply because they had met in the

---

34 William Duane, *A Report of the Extraordinary Transactions which Took Place at Philadelphia, in February 1799, in Consequence of a Memorial from Certain Natives of Ireland to Congress, Praying a Repeal of the Alien Bill* (Philadelphia, 1799), 12, 3, 13, 17, 3, 13; *GUS*, 11 Feb. 1799; Duane, *Report of the Extraordinary Transactions*, 3, 4; *PorcG*, 13 Feb. 1799. Wharton also served as mayor between 1806 and 1807, 1810 and 1811, 1814 and 1819, and 1820 and 1824, making him Philadelphia's longest serving mayor to date.

35 Duane, *Report of the Extraordinary Transactions*, 2, 5, 4, 6, 7, 25. *PorcG*, 12 Feb. 1799 dubbed the incident the "United Irish riot." See also "The Irish riot at St. Mary's Church, Philadelphia, 1799," *ACHR* xvii (1900), 86–8; and "The Story of St. Mary's," *ibid.* x (1893), 63–7.

precincts of the church. Simply put, Dallas suggested that the "habits and customs" which Irish immigrants had brought with them "from abroad" should be recognised without insult or condescension. Carr also noted that the practice was not unknown in America either, as Federalists occasionally held meetings in churches to organise addresses to Adams. Dallas stated that he himself had read accounts of such proceedings in "eastern newspapers." For him, the only difference between the one and the other was that while such Federalists were "complimentary" to Adams, those who had assembled at St. Mary's were not.[36]

Dallas also pointed out that the events at St. Mary's reflected the "party spirit [which] has very much prevailed in this city." For many Federalists, Reynolds had long represented the more undesirable face of political controversy. According to Dallas, he had been "pointed at by the party to whom he is opposed," disturbed in his lodgings, and even threatened with assassination which, as Dallas stated with "no doubt," accounted for the fact that Reynolds carried a pistol. Matthew Clay (R., Va., 1795–1812) who lodged with Reynolds, said that he had warned Reynolds that there was a plot to assassinate him and that as a result, Reynolds had got a gun to protect himself. Thus, on the Sunday in question, Reynolds was armed not because he intended to murder anybody but for reasons which "from the occasion of the times," were no different from those of "many gentlemen in this country who wear sword-canes." Dallas also denounced other "clamours and misrepresentations" of his clients and, in particular, their designation as Jacobins which, he claimed, was a "base ... epithet," the application of which was intended to deny them counsel and blacken their witnesses. For him, Jacobinism had an unacceptable "arbitrary and sanguinary character" which was inconsistent with "the principles of republicanism" which were the bedrock of the new republic. Dallas bemoaned the confusion between the two if only because, as the trial showed, it effectively tainted "any man who wishes to exercise the right of free opinion ... [as] marked out for party obloquy." He was particularly anxious to protect the right to petition and rejected the notion that when the foreign-born engaged in this process, it was often taken as a threat to undermine the constitution and laws of the United States. For Dallas, these biases reflected the abandonment of those

> most flattering views of freedom and independence, safety and security [which had brought the Irish] to the American shores, under the sanction of known laws and an admired constitution; [and where they] ... are taught to believe, that the moment they arrive [in America] they shall enter into a free participation of all these blessings.

36 Duane, *Report of the Extraordinary Transactions*, 9, 17, 8, 9, 24, 26, 24.

Accordingly, when the foreign-born chose to petition, it should not be taken as evidence of a "dark conspiracy formed to overthrow not alone the constitution but to subvert the very principle of our form of government." To suggest otherwise was to indulge "a party case, a party question altogether" and Dallas cautioned the jury that this was precisely what was before them.[37]

Prosecutor Hopkinson disagreed. However, this did not discourage him from portraying the trial as one which, in the words of Vans Murray, had been "engendered in a spirit of disappointed faction." Hopkinson had no qualms about arguing that "an involution of ideas [had] connected Irishmen and Jacobinism" and that in any event,

> aliens have no right whatsoever to petition, or to interfere in any respect with the government of this country; as the right of voting in elections is confirmed to our citizens, the right of petitioning is also ... it appears that a majority of the persons assembled to sign and procure signatures on this occasion are not citizens of the United States ... the greatest evils this country has ever endured, have arisen from the ready admission of foreigners to a participation in the government and internal arrangements of the country ... had the Americans been left to themselves, we should not this day have been divided and rent into parties.

Hopkinson suggested that it was in this context that in Congress, some believed that as much as fourteen years were necessary before a foreign-born person could be naturalised although he added that immigrants who settled in the United States should in any event, have to abide by "our laws ... they ought not to expect to bring with them their bad customs." The presiding judge decided not to comment on these and other issues which had been raised "extraneously on either side." Instead, he would "compare recital with law." Dallas won the case, largely because of his arguments, firstly, that there was "nothing in the manner or purpose" of the meeting at St. Mary's that was "improper" and secondly, with respect to Reynolds, that he had not gone to the church with an intention to murder.[38]

---

37 Duane, *Report of the Extraordinary Transactions*, 14, 33, 18, 30, 18, 13, 22, 18, 19.
38 Duane, *Report of the Extraordinary Transactions*, 25, 37, 38, 40, 45, 13. Vans Murray is quoted from William Cobbett, *Porcupine's Works* x, 108. Hopkinson himself was later to become a victim of party prejudices. He lost his official posts as clerk of both the Orphans' and Mayor's courts when "the tyrannical, political persecutor," Thomas McKean, became governor; quoted of Hopkinson in Burton Alva Konkle, *Joseph Hopkinson, 1760–1842* (Philadelphia, 1931). For the trial, see also *Annals of Congress* ix, 2884–2906, 12 Feb. 1799. For a report on the verdict, see *GUS*, 21 Feb. 1799.

Views from Editors

The trial had taken place at a time when Philadelphia's Federalist editors were being heavily criticised for both their portrayal of the city's Irish community and the negative influence over legislation which, in James Carey's view, "will allow of expelling the Irish emigrants." It was in this context that press attention to both the events at St. Mary's church and the petition to Congress provoked, according to the *Aurora*, "not a little of indecent language." For Fenno's *Gazette of the United States*, the Irish had displayed an "unprecedented indecency ... [by] pass[ing] censures on *our* government, *our* laws, *our* principles, and *our* conduct ... If they are Americans, what have they to do with the grievances, real or pretended, of Ireland?" The whole business merely underlined the need for Americans "to be upon our guard" against the "future operations" of the United Irishmen in America. Given the bloody "consequence of the principles and practices" of the society in Ireland, the *Gazette* again warned that it was "time for us to be alarmed" and to resist any attempts the United Irishmen might make to apply in America "the detestable principles" that they had adopted in Ireland. As Fenno put it on 11 February 1799

> If the daring outrages which have lately been committed by a banditti who invest this city, do not rouse its inhabitants to a sense of their danger, they almost deserve all the direful consequences with which they are threatened ... *The United Irishmen* have at length broken out into acts, which no longer render them the objects of uncertain suspicion. Encouraged by our passiveness, they have proceeded from insult to open outrage.[39]

During January 1799 there were a number of bitter exchanges between Reynolds and Fenno after the *Gazette of the United States* alleged that Reynolds had said that "the subversion of the constitution of the United States, murder, rapine, and pillage, were the objects of my exiled countrymen." After a series of further "unprovoked calumnies," Reynolds sued Fenno for libel, given that he had been refused "the satisfaction of a gentleman" for the newspaper's "unwarrantable conduct." However, Fenno did not escape unscathed because he was attacked with clubs and a "naked cutlass" by two "raw Irishmen, and filthy, dungeon'd looking villains" who had been "hired" for the purpose. On 28 March 1799 "a gang of United Irishmen" also "flogged in the most cruel and barbarous manner," Andrew Brown, editor of the Federalist-oriented *Philadelphia Gazette*, because of what they saw as a concerted campaign "to poison the public mind by the most daring calumnies continually poured out on the

39 *CR*, 10 May 1798; *Aurora*, 14 Feb. 1799; *GUS*, 30 Mar. 1798.

suffering and gallant people of Ireland, and the exiles who have been forced by the most bloody and frantic tyranny to take refuge in these states." Many had also been angered by the fact that while the trial of those who had been charged with the fracas at St. Mary's was pending, Brown's *Gazette*,

> in defiance of all forms of law, and decency, continued to publish falsehoods concerning the transaction [that were] calculated to convey false ideas of plain facts, and to stamp upon the proceedings of a court of justice, and a jury, a contempt to which neither can be subjected.[40]

Brown also published a number of "scandalous calumnies" about the celebration of St. Patrick's Day in 1799 and referred to a number of Francophile toasts that "a number" of United Irishmen had made as they "pushed about the *jorum* [drinking-cup]." He singled out Reynolds for particular mention and alleged that the company had a "degree of hardness and contempt for the public feeling of this country." An Irish immigrant, John Richard McMahon, who had arrived in America only two months earlier, was later found guilty of the assault on Brown. He was fined $280, deprived of his "rights of citizenship" for seven years, and obliged to give security for his good behaviour. At his trial, McMahon stated that he had carried out the attack because Brown had denigrated the United Irishmen. However, the *Gazette of the United States* intimated that the attack proved that there existed "in the midst of us, a combination of men, linked together by the most flagitious principles, and in pursuit of the vilest and most abandoned purposes." This made it all the more important, as the recorder put it at the end of McMahon's trial, that if and when "foreigners look for the countenance and respect of the citizens of this country, it becomes them not to interfere with our political concerns, and at least to treat the government with decent respect."[41]

The assaults on Brown and Fenno, together with others on Duane and the previous year, on Duane's predecessor as editor of the *Aurora*, Benjamin Franklin Bache, reflected the tensions which surrounded those who reported public affairs during these years. They also indicate that the media's presentation of the radical Irish in Philadelphia was not limited to literary exchanges or political caricature and provide part of the explanation as to why, despite the acquittal of Duane and his colleagues for the "United Irish riot" at St. Mary's church, Federalist newspapers did not substantially alter either the tone or

40 *GUS*, 31, 18 Jan., 31, 29 Mar. 1799; "The Man who Flogged Brown" in *Aurora*, 1 Apr. 1799; *Aurora*, 22 Feb. 1799.
41 *Aurora*, 1 Apr. 1799; *GUS*, 29 Mar., 16 May 1799; *GUS*, 30 Mar. 1799; *PorcG*, 10 Apr. 1799; *GUS*, 9 Apr. 1799.

content of their reports on the United Irishmen. The *Gazette of the United States*, for example, justified its continued focus on Duane on the grounds that he "was not an American but a foreigner, and not merely a foreigner, but an United Irishman." "An American" expressed a similar view in June 1799:

> While I am a friend to an unlimited freedom of the press when exercised by *An American*, I am an implacable foe to its prostitution to a *foreigner*, and would at the same time assist in hunting out of Societies, any meddling foreigner who should dare to interfere in our politics.

Of course, the Sedition Act could be used to curb editors such as Duane. On 30 July 1798 the editor of the *Aurora* was arrested for seditious libel for suggesting that British influence and secret service money was directing American foreign policy and that "the people must endeavour to identify as well as they can the channels in which this corruption of Britain has circulated." After what was often a farcical series of events, Duane was eventually indicted under the act on 17 October 1800.[42] However, he was never deported because the act had expired by the time the process was completed.

Events in the nation's capital also had serious resonances elsewhere. John Daly Burk, editor of the *Time-Piece*, also fell foul of the Sedition Act. In 1796 he had fled his native Ireland after some of his friends had been arrested for involvement in the United Irishmen. He became politically active among the Irish community in New York but on 6 July 1798 he was arrested for publishing "seditious and libellous" statements against the president. In the *Time-Piece*, Burk had also described Washington as a "meaner species of Aristocracy," a "mock Monarch ... [who] would extinguish the sentiment of Liberty." He was also expansive in his views about contemporary Ireland and according to "Themistocles," writing (perhaps inevitably) in the *Gazette of the United States* on 6 July 1798, on being informed

> that the French had effected their landing in Ireland – Burk, with marks of much approbation ... believed that the French would [also] come here, and he wished to God they would, and every scoundrel in favour of this government would be put to the guillotine.

---

42 *GUS*, 16 May 1799; "An American" in *Aurora*, 23 June 1799. Duane's allegation had been published in the *Aurora*, 24 July 1799. For the attack on Duane, perpetrated by John Ward Fenno, see *GUS*, 16 May 1799. In October 1797, Bache had also been assaulted by one Clement Humphreys, later a supporter of Morgan in the contest with Israel Israel. Bache was later arrested on charges of libelling the president but died of yellow fever on 10 Sept. 1798 before the trial could took place. Fenno also died during the epidemic and his son, John Ward Fenno, took over as editor of the *Gazette of the United States*; see also

The charges against Burk were not pursued following an undertaking that he would return to Ireland. However, he did not keep his word and instead, hid in Virginia until Jefferson became president. Matthew Lyon was less fortunate. Born in Ireland, he had been elected to Congress from Vermont in 1797. The following year, he and the Federalist congressman, Roger Griswold (F., Conn., 1795–1805), had a celebrated exchange on the floor of the house. After Griswold criticised Lyon's record during the Revolutionary War (a not uncommon event between Federalists and Republicans at the time), Lyon spat on Griswold's face and as a result, he was threatened with expulsion from Congress. Although the Federalists failed to muster the two thirds majority that was necessary to implement the motion, on 5 October 1798, Lyon was indicted for publishing letters that were critical of Adams. He was found guilty as charged and sentenced to four months in prison, from where he managed his re-election to the House of Representatives in February 1799. Federalist papers reported that his campaign had been managed by "contemptible characters" who had encouraged Lyon with a civic feast which, in supposedly typical fashion, had seen the guests get drunk, "as democrats generally do whenever they get a chance to swig."[43]

Electing the Governor, 1799

While Lyon's re-election was being celebrated in Vermont, McKean's decision to run for the governorship of Pennsylvania later that year meant that Republicans would mount one further challenge to Federalist power and influence and confront Federalist assumptions that after Morgan's victory in February 1798 they were a "decaying power" in Philadelphia. Their opponent was James Ross, since 1793, one of the state's two U.S. senators. The views of the two men on the nature and direction of the American polity were not only different; they were strongly held. Moreover, as they organised their supporters around an impressive array of meetings and networks, they were conscious that they were not only helping to crystallise the enduring debate on the future of America but that in doing so, they had an eye to the forthcoming presidential election.[44]

Norman Victor Blantz, "Editors and Issues. The Party Press in Philadelphia, 1789–1801" (Ph.D. disseration, Pennsylvania State University, 1974), 226–7.

43 *PorcG*, 27 Feb. 1799. Burk's comments on Washington are quoted from Smith, *Freedom's Fetters*, 208–9. For Burk, see Joseph I. Shulim, *John Daly Burk: Irish Revolutionist and American Patriot* (Philadelphia, 1964); and Durey, *Transatlantic Radicals*, 114–6 *et passim*. For Lyon, see *Matthew Lyon, the Hamden of Congress. A Biography* (New York, 1900).

44 "Cassius" in the *Aurora*, 22 Feb. 1798.

McKean had long been a target of the Federalists. The gubernatorial election provided another opportunity to castigate him in terms that by then, must have been wearingly familiar. Federalists linked McKean's "filthy embraces" of "the democrats of Pennsylvania" to his status among "the seditious horde" of Irish immigrants. Certainly, McKean was no stranger to the Philadelphia Irish and as a lawyer, he acted for a number of them. His presidency of the Hibernian Society (1790–1800) and his friendships with Duane, Reynolds, and the Carey brothers, among others, associated him with the city's Irish community and, in particular, with radical *émigrés*. Given the negative ways in which the Irish were sometimes portrayed in the Federalist press, Ross's supporters found it easy to suggest that McKean could not be trusted because of these connections. Still reflecting old stereotypes, the Republican candidate was also said to be "not only soliciting the votes of the *present citizens*, but he is absolutely making new ones" in order to ensure his election. However, if McKean had hoped to pervert the electoral clout of such immigrants, as had been alleged during the Israel–Morgan contest, he would be disappointed as the act "to Regulate the General Elections within this Commonwealth," passed on 15 February 1799, made the election process less open to abuse.[45]

During the election campaign, McKean was said to have expressed the hope that "twenty thousand United Irishmen would land in the United States, for they would teach us what true liberty was." Although McKean had made no secret of his admiration for their society, he stressed that this was "because he thought the people of Ireland [were] barbarously oppressed." However, when he denied that he had exalted the United Irishmen as reported, Federalists suggested that this

> merely imports a disbelief of the existence of those machinations, for the destruction of public order and private property, which had been imputed to the emigrants from Ireland, and a contempt for the system of alarm, which had recently [been] introduced here, in imitation of a similar system invited by the minister of another country ... the sentiment .. [of which] ... pervades every county of Pennsylvania, and every district of the union.

McKean also refuted these insinuations although he realised that the fact that his alleged comments had been reported in the first place suggested that the ambivalence with which the Irish community was viewed at the time as well as how the characterisation of a candidate in the ethno–cultural terms of the old

---

45 *GUS*, 16 Aug.1799; "An American," *To the Independent Electors of Pennsylvania* (Philadelphia, 1799), 1–3. For the electoral law, see *Statutes at Large. Pennsylvania* xvi (1798–1801), (Harrisburg, Pa., 1911), 163–181.

world, could be negative influences on the public perception of a candidate for public office. McKean thus tried to distance himself from factional tags. However, Cobbett appreciated this strategy also and poked fun at McKean for "disclaiming and abjuring all connection and relationship with a people, of whose national Society [the Hibernian Society] he is the President!"[46]

Some Federalists also described McKean as a member of the Catholic church, largely on the basis that McKean's daughter had married the Spanish ambassador, Don Carlos Martinez d'Yrujo. Even when this was dismissed and McKean's Presbyterianism affirmed, it was still being "asserted in the most confident manner" that McKean had "forced" his daughter "to wed a Papist, against her inclination, to do penance, be rebaptized. &c." McKean appreciated that for many Americans, the Catholic church represented a superintending power which existed outside their borders and that many regarded this as incompatible with both the origins and nature of the republic. Even as "An Apprentice" declared that these rumours were "absolutely false, and very publicly known to be so in the city," he recognised that their underlying purpose was "to prejudice the most zealous protestant" against McKean's candidacy. McKean knew that these and similar assertions about his personal life were part of a wider political ruse to isolate certain types of voters from him and that he had to neutralise it. Addressing McKean in August 1799 one hostile writer in *Porcupine's Gazette* thus mooted that McKean

> knew that the *Germans* were very numerous [in Pennsylvania], and that the part of them that you could hope to deceive, harboured no little antipathy against the *Irish nation* and the *Roman Catholic religion*; and this it was that made you resolve publickly to disclaim even the most slight connection with either the one or the other ... in order to ... blind, and still preserve the support of, the good-natured unsuspecting *Irish Catholics*, at the same time that you were sacrificing their reputation to the ungenerous prejudices of the Germans.[47]

46 "Milo" No. 6 in *GUS*, 31, 16 Aug. 1799; *Aurora*, 10 Aug., 3 Oct. 1799; An Irish Catholic" in *PorcG*, 16 Aug. 1799. McKean's alleged comments on the electoral use of the United Irishmen were also referred to in what was probably Ross's most important electoral publication; see the *Address to the Freemen of Pennsylvania from the Committee of Correspondence for the City of Pennsylvania, Appointed by the Friends of James Ross* (Germantown, Pa., 1799), 15. This pamphlet included documentation to "corroborate" its allegations and offered more if "necessary;" *ibid*, and was published in reply to the pro-McKean *Address to the Republicans of Pennsylvania ... Peter Muhlenberg ... 7 August 1799* which, among other things, alleged that Ross was using a partial press to "deceive and mislead," and that Ross's election committees had been formed "to become involved in the unpleasant task" of commenting on the conduct of McKean. As part of the developing exchanges between the two campaigns, on 15 Aug. 1799, *PorcG* formally asked McKean to deny his alleged statement about the United Irishmen.

McKean also had to resist efforts to dislodge Irish Presbyterians from his cause, especially as Cobbett was insinuating that within the wider Irish community,"cunning" Catholics were duping "stupid Presbyterians into a *net*" of McKean's making. However, while the number of Philadelphia's Irish Catholic immigrants increased after 1783, their political influence remained relatively minor in a city which had long attracted men and women from Ulster. For McKean, the challenge was how to walk adroitly between all these groups, especially as each of them had been developing its own sense of political importance and influence since 1776. Thus, his supporters described him less in the terms of a particular religion than as someone who "has always shewn the highest reverence for the Christian religion" and whose "religious principles and christian deportment are beyond the power of that blackening spirit, by which the Rossites are actuated." McKean did not have a monopoly on virtue either. His counter charge that Ross was "*an Infidel*, or in modern language, a DEIST," was hardly made for altruistic reasons. This allegation was no more credible than those that had been made about McKean's "domestic concerns" and only encouraged "certificates" to the contrary from the "pious and devout" elders of Ross's former Presbyterian community in York County.[48]

Federalist attempts to imprison the Republicans within specified constituencies were meant to convey the notion that if elected, McKean would not be able to appreciate the best interests of the state as a whole. The most emotive aspect of their argument was that McKean was not only "in both soul and body, devoted to the French" but that by defending "most of her measures towards this country ... [he] reprobates those of our own government." As a result, McKean had "a tendency prejudicial, if not ruinous, to the honor, independence and interest of our common country" at a time when many Americans supposed that war with France was still possible. On 17 July 1799 a Federalist meeting in the Northern Liberties spelt out the implications in a clear, if extravagant, manner: Americans had to confront

> the overwhelming ambition of France; the danger with which every republic on earth has been threatened; and many of them destroyed by her open

47 "Fontaine" in *GUS*, 3 Sept. 1799; "An Apprentice" in *Aurora*, 16 Sept. 1799; "An Irish Catholic" in *PorcG*, 16 Aug. 1799. McKean is buried in the cemetery of the First Presbyterian Church of Philadelphia.

48 "An Investigator of Truth" in *PorcG*, 19 Aug. 1799; *Aurora*, 16 Sept. 1799; *Address to the Republicans of Pennsylvania ... Muhlenberg*, 5–6; "A Pennsylvanian" in *Aurora*, 2 Oct. 1799; *Address to the Freemen of Pennsylvania ... by the Friends of James Ross*, 16. The testimonials from the elders of York County were published in *ibid.*, 19–23. For the rising number of Catholic immigrants after 1783, see Bric, "Patterns of Irish Emigration to America, 1783–1800," 17–35.

violence or secret intrigues; and the importance of filling our offices of public trust with men who were who have ever manifested an exclusive attachment to *our own country*; who have no connection with *foreign factions*, no bias from *foreign influence*, who are truly *republican* in their *manners and principles*, and truly *American* in their affections and patriotism.

Not surprisingly, Federalists regarded Ross as being more congenial in that he had actively supported the Adams administration, was not "tainted with the novel philosophy of France," and had "no bias from foreign influence." McKean's supporters could not accept this and without much irony, dismissed Ross and his friends as ardent "supporters of the British government" and advocates of the "curious," "extraordinary," "important and alarming" evolution of "the *British* party in America." They also alleged that not only was the British consul, Phineas Bond, involved in these political developments which were "*indecently* full of anti-American and anti-republican feelings and declarations," but newspapers such as the *Gazette of the United States* aggressively promoted a "*connexion with the English government people here.*" Thus, a prediction from one of Ross's supporters that the election would "determine whether we are to govern ourselves or be governed by foreigners" cut two ways.[49]

While such exchanges were part of the new political repartee, McKean could not ignore those who drew on them to question his patriotism, or to suggest that he and his fellow Republicans were the dangerous "domestic agents" of a foreign power. Thus, he denied that he had presided over the protests against Jay's Treaty because he wanted to promote a "rupture" between Britain and the United States. Quite the contrary. Not only was he "the enemy of *tyranny* and *monarchy*; [but far] ... being desirous of a war with Great Britain ... he was only solicitous of avoiding a war in concert with her and the despots of Europe." Thus, his objections to the treaty were on points of principle and not because he wanted to reinvent his country as a client of France. As a result, as one of his apologists put it, "for merely warning the government of its [the treaty] danger, Mr. *M'Kean*, and his friends, were, at that period, exposed to unmerited reproach and obloquy." On the other hand, merely by supporting the Federalist interpretation of Anglo-American relations, Ross's supporters had concluded that their candidate was "truly *republican* in *manners* and *principles*, and truly *American* in affections and patriotism." There were similar tones to the discussion of George Logan's mission to France, obliging McKean to reject

---

49 "An Irish Catholic" in *PG*, 18 Aug. 1799; *Address to the Freemen of Pennsylvania ... by the Friends of James Ross*, 6, 7; *GUS*, 26 July 1799; *PorcG*, 19 Aug. 1798; *Address to the Freemen of Pennsylvania ... by the Friends of James Ross*, 17; *Aurora*, 27 June 1799; "A Pennsylvanian," *To the Electors of Pennsylvania. When a Candidate ...* (Philadelphia, 1799).

charges that he had sought to circumvent the official channels of American diplomacy, specifically by giving Logan a letter of introduction to facilitate a "favourable reception" in Paris. Logan also rejected the allegation because he knew that Federalist "babblings" might adversely influence "the election of a citizen who deserves well of his country."[50]

McKean greatly resented the ways in which his involvement in these proceedings was being depicted as unpatriotic and that as a result, he should not be "exalted ... to places of trust and power." For him, a true concern for the integrity of the American government and the security of his nation obliged him to speak out when he felt that these were under threat. Moreover, when he did so, he saw no inconsistency between criticising the government and promoting what he considered to be the best interests of America. He was not a Jacobin in American garb. In these circumstances, as the discussion about the two candidates became expressly part of a larger ideological debate, or what one commentator called "a trial of the strength of the old whig spirit," both the descriptions of the two candidates and their campaign keynotes sought to suggest who was the "better republican" as well as the more "patriotic." While Ross had been relatively successful in painting himself in the colours of the second theme, he was less so with respect to those of the first. Indeed, one pro-Ross pamphleteer suggested that Republicans were "distinguish[ing] themselves, and their candidate, by the exclusive appellation of republicans" although he was not "acquainted with any just ground" why they should do so. As a result, McKean and his advocates had assumed that they had "the exclusive right of thinking and acting in the politics of our country, and proscribing as Traitors to it all the citizens who differ from them in relation to public men or public measures."[51]

McKean also stressed his public spirit in other ways. For example, he often said that he was "a friend of the poor" and that he "assisted" many "institutions of charity." His humanitarian work among the Irish community was also well-known although this could be turned against him, as Federalists played on fears that immigrants could become charges on the city and state. Moreover, given that the later-1790s was a time of recession, some argued that immigrants could deprive native-born Americans of jobs. In Philadelphia, Ross put this argument to good use and as a result, he received significant electoral support from the

50 "MLTO" in *GUS*, 17 Oct. 1799; *Address to the Republicans of Pennsylvania ... Muhlenberg*, 4; "A German" in *Aurora*, 10 Aug. 1799; *Address to the Republicans of Pennsylvania ... Muhlenberg*, 4, 5; *Aurora*, 9 Oct. 1799; "A Pennsylvanian," *To the Electors of Pennsylvania ... When A Candidate ...* (Philadelphia, 1799).

51 "An Irish Catholic" in *PorcG*, 18 Aug. 1799; *Aurora*, 9 Oct. 1799; "A Pennsylvanian," *To the Electors of Pennsylvania. When a Candidate ...* (Philadelphia, 1799) , 1; *An Address to the Freemen of Pennsylvania ... by the Friends of James Ross*, 6, 5.

artisans of the New Market and Lower Delaware wards. By drawing attention to McKean's role as legal counsel for the claim of the Penn family for compensation for appropriated lands, Federalists also criticised the Republican candidate for supporting the drain of much needed revenues out of the new republic. The response was predictable: to highlight McKean's involvement in the creation of American independence. On 4 July 1799 one company of his supporters thus hoped that "the gratitude of American Republicans [might] be evinced by electing him for our Governor at the ensuing election for the valuable services he rendered his country upon all occasions, particularly in our struggle for independence." Another stressed that McKean was not only "a republican, a patriot and a Christian ... [but] High on the list of republican worthies." Others routinely associated his name with those of Washington and Franklin. The message was clear: "With them he bore a part in a trying conflict ... the crime of ingratitude can never be charged to the freemen of the County of Philadelphia." Thus, McKean's "civic virtue" was a matter of historical record. Moreover, his campaign insisted that it was also reflected in his subsequent public life in Pennsylvania.[52]

As the election campaign developed, partisan broadsides, handbills, and caricatures polarised opinion even further and supporters distorted or promoted as the occasion demanded. Republicans characterised Ross as "a Monarchist ... [a] British Partizan ... [and] Patron of the Alien and Sedition Bills." McKean was "a Republican ... a true American ... [and] a Supporter of the Trial of Jury, and the Freedom of the Press." In developing these descriptions, there is no doubt that "rage and intemperance" featured on both sides and that some of them were channelled through a fiercely partial, or "tributary" press. As a result, one commentator observed that the influence of the press had been "notoriously destroyed ... The good and the bad were there reduced to a level; the good could reap no honor from public praise; the bad could suffer no disgrace from public censure." Thus, the press was no longer

> the source of public intelligence and instruction; and became an instrument to vitiate the taste, to mislead the understanding, to taint the virtue, and to undermine the independence of the People ... [by] boldly assailing the character of Mr. *M'Kean*, and sedulously extolling the character of Mr. *Ross*, in aid of men, whose private views and party passions, are directly opposed to the experience, judgement, and interest of the community.

52 *Aurora*, 9 Oct., 6 July 1799; "An American," *To the Independent Electors of Pennsylvania*. For references to McKean's supposed associations with Washington and Franklin "with whom he bore a part in a trying conflict," see the broadside by "Franklin," "To the Citizens if the County of Philadelphia. Friends and Fellow Citizens ... Philadelphia 1799;" *Aurora*, 6 July 1799.

The organisational apparatus of party was also more blatantly partisan than had been the case in the past. By May 1799 McKean had established a state-wide committee of correspondence "to circulate ... intelligence" and on the following 17 July this was replicated at local level in the Northern Liberties. Ross's supporters were also active and even within the Pennsylvania legislature, a number of their adherents proposed in May 1799 that election committees should be established in the different counties of the state. These introduced a new aggressiveness into the two campaigns as well as a keener approach to coordination and effectiveness. Ross's committee would "give a beneficial direction to our common efforts" to elect him, the urgency and pragmatism of which were particularly clear to one of his managers, Levi Hollingsworth, who advised Ross's supporters that

> The summer may slip away before a suitable plan of mutual support is adopted, and the hour of election may find us disunited and unprovided to resist those artificers and deceptions frequently exhibited by [McKean's] party, and long deplored by good citizens ... Let every man, therefore, call to mind his solemn obligations to his Country, to his Friends, his Family, and himself; let each consider himself as individually bound and answerable not merely for his own vote, but for his strenuous exertions to excite his neighbours to assist in securing, as far as the choice of a good Governor can do it, a continuance of our happiness and prosperity; let meetings of your good Citizens from the several townships be speedily convened, and your county be divided according to its election districts, and those again into smaller divisions, so that no man, having a right to vote, be passed over without an invitation to perform his duty on that most important day.[53]

Federalists agreed with the central point. Electors were encouraged to focus on a candidate's "fitness for the station" as well as his "just and uniform principles ... manners ... understanding ... accomplishments ... talents ... usefulness, integrity and capacity, in the important public stations to which he has been called." Although there was little new in such an inventory, and the popular use to which it was put, the invective was particularly sharp during this election. One pro-McKean address suggested that Ross's partisans had "exercised the art of blackening characters in its fullest extent ... they have entered the sanctuary of his [McKean's] house; and exhibited to the world a false picture of his domestic affairs." Ross's supporters were also advised to

53 "To the Electors of Pennsylvania. Take your Choice ... Philadelphia, 1799," as published in the *Aurora*, 8 Oct. 1799; *Address to the Republicans of Pennsylvania ... Muhlenberg*, 1, 2; *GUS*, 16 Apr., 26 July 1799; "Sir, Deeply Interested in the Approaching Election ... Levi Hollingsworth" (broadside, Philadelphia, 27 May 1799).

counter the "false rumours, [and] the groundless calumnies, which have already begun to be used as engines of political operations" and to "maintain our ground by the exclusive aid of moderation, truth and firmness." However, it proved almost impossible to do this without becoming involved in "the unpleasant task of commenting on the conduct of the opposite candidate, or that of his advocate," if only because "artful insinuation" rather than "direct charge" was part and parcel of both campaigns.[54]

McKean was duly elected governor of Pennsylvania in October 1799. In the greater Philadelphia area, his margin of nearly 700 votes over Ross was a decisive victory which was further enhanced by the fact that for the first time, Republicans won one of the city seats in the state assembly, in addition to sweeping the congressional as well as the state elections in the county. As Republicans celebrated their victories, they were clear what success meant to them. As the *Aurora* put it on 18 October 1799, "the citizens of Pennsylvania have stood up like men, and by chusing [*sic*] a man of '76, declared that – a *republic means something*." A congratulatory address to McKean, prepared under the chairmanship of Israel Israel, saluted not only "the triumph" but also the rescue of "the republican cause" and "the principle of Republicanism itself" at a time of "awful crisis in human affairs." "Had defeat attended the Republican efforts," it observed, "the consequences would have been fatal to the principles of our government." As it was, certain "artifices [had been] employed to underline our political fabric, and to prostrate in ruin the comforts, the interests, and the rights of the people," as well as to spread "indecency of conduct and traduction of character." By way of contrast, McKean's triumph meant the election of one whose "old fashioned principles of right, instruct you still to maintain a deference and respect for the only legitimate sovereign in the United States:" the people. In reply to these "republican citizens" of Philadelphia, McKean acknowledged that the intervening path had been neither smooth nor free and stated that the election campaign had seen "the most abominable lies," "intrigue," and "menace" where "nothing" had been forgotten "that could arrest a vote." Thus, most thought that the new governor would interpret "the general welfare" in a partial manner. Moreover, as he celebrated McKean's inauguration with a toast to "the United Irishmen [and] rebellion against tyrants," Israel had a feeling of both satisfaction and expectation as a "republican meeting God."[55]

54 *Aurora*, 8, 3 Oct. 1799; *PorcG*, 21 Aug. 1799; *Address to the Freemen of Pennsylvania ... by the Friends of James Ross*, 3, 4.
55 *Aurora*, 11 Nov. 1799. For the election returns from Philadelphia, see *GUS*, 9 Oct. 1799.

It was one thing to please the converted. It was another to placate a divided legislature. In particular, the state senate, where Federalists had a majority, took exception to McKean's suggestion that those who had supported Ross had not been "actuated by the purest motives" or that their "conduct ... [had not] been equally decorous and independent." In the House, the Federalist minority suggested, perhaps with intended irony, that McKean's "exercise in wisdom" would not "in the remotest degree, contribute to conciliate the opinions of the people generally." McKean took their criticisms as "premeditated insults" although he appreciated that, in part, these had also been inspired by his decision not to re-appoint several officials to the state positions which they had held under Thomas Mifflin. Nonetheless, the Republicans were now in the winner's enclosure and in 1800 they also saw their candidate, Thomas Jefferson, elected to the presidency. The "revolution of 1800" had been consolidated at federal as well as state levels.[56]

---

56 *Aurora*, 11 Jan., 1 Feb. 1800; *GUS*, 1 Feb. 1800. For the controversy surrounding the appointment of presidential electors, see Higginbotham, *Keystone in the Democratic Arch*, 27–31. Jefferson's assessment of the importance of the year 1800 is cited from his letter to Spencer Roane, 6 Sept. 1819, in Andrew A. Lipscomb and Albert Bergh, eds., *The Writings of Thomas Jefferson* 20 vols. (Washington, 1903) xv, 212.

Postscript

Jefferson's election confirmed the view that the American republic was entering a new phase in its development. However, perhaps it was less the "revolution" that Jefferson had characterised than the creation of a new "space" from which Americans could look to the future without deferring to the presumptions of the past, and where the polity could draw its energy from the flexibility of popular politics rather than from entrenched elites. In Philadelphia, the 1790s had seen not just the superceding of these elites as a "natural" leadership but also a successful challenge to the underlying assumptions which had made this political culture possible over several generations. Moreover, the extent to which the elite continued as a political force was based on its ability to accommodate itself to a type of politics that had evolved at a considerable distance from it rather than (as had been the case until then) by an ability to absorb new leaders within its own structural and rhetorical boundaries. As the new century dawned, the integrity of the political process, about which there had been such a "phrenzy" before 1800, had been reinforced and strengthened.[1]

Despite the controversies of the 1790s, party politics were brittle and in any event, as James E. Lewis has argued, they had been informed less by "party loyalty" than by "personal loyalty among persons of the same party." This became obvious after 1800 when Jefferson's nation settled down to try and recover the harmony and homogeneity of the eighteenth-century polity. As Elkins and McKittrick have suggested, Jefferson did not regard the elections of 1800 as "revolutionary" in the sense that they had "blessed" the currency of partisan politics, even if he had owed his election to them. Instead, he interpreted his election as both a popular choice for his "brand" of republicanism over that of the Federalists and an expression of the sovereignty of the people which had been somewhat obscured by the "artificial" government of the

---

1 Joyce Appleby, "Thomas Jefferson and the Psychology of Democracy" in James Horn, Jan Ellis and Peter S. Onuf, eds., *The Revolution of 1800* (Charlottesville and London, 2002), 155. For the peaceful character of the outcome of the election of 1800, see the essays in *ibid*. For the historiographical currency of Jefferson's understanding of the "revolution of 1800," see Sisson, *Revolution of 1800*, 3–22, *et passim*. See also John Ferling, *Adams vs. Jefferson: The Tumultuous Election of 1800* (New York, 2004). For the view that 1800 ended the notion that government by an enlightened and disinterested elite was necessary to a virtuous polity, see Gordon Wood, *The Radicalism of the American Revolution* (New York, 1992).

later-1790s. However, there were important differences with previous generations, not the least of which was that the enhanced role of the people generally in influencing the character and procedures of contemporary politics was seen as well as believed. The polity now moved back to the steady position of entrenching itself in the centre. Nothing better exemplified this than the inclusive spirit of Jefferson's first inaugural address (4 March 1801), the tone of which was set by the well-known comment that "We are all Federalists. We are all Republicans. Let us then break in pieces our idols, and laying our hands with pure and simple hearts upon the altar, unite in the worship of the true God." In Pennsylvania, McKean also sought to avoid extremes after 1800. As a result, those who continued to use the Jacobin slogans of the 1790s became outsiders once again, this time under a regime which they had helped to create. McKean and Jefferson were now the electorally acknowledged epitomy of a "true" republicanism which did not have to be validated any longer by reference to France. The "correctives" which French republicanism could offer to the newly-independent United States had been recognised within the body politic by virtue of the election of Republican slates in 1799 and 1800.[2]

On 4 July 1800 toasts and resolutions in the Northern Liberties also expressed the hope that "the virtuous principles of republicanism [might] predominate over this extensive empire to the entire destruction of the Alien, Sedition, and every other oppressive law." The "oppressions" of Ireland were not forgotten either nor the hope that "the inherent rights of Man" might be restored in Ireland and England. In the years that followed, Jefferson welcomed the defeated leaders of the United Irishmen and their disillusioned supporters to the United States as "republican brothers" who had also crucially informed the character of a new political culture in America. Within the narrower world of the Irish community in Philadelphia, the United Irishmen had been ethno-cultural as well as political heroes and during the 1790s, they had used this status not only to support Jefferson and his interest but to promote a new kind of ethnic consciousness among Irish immigrants. Blacks and German speakers apart, such people had been the most obvious sign of the city's diversity during the early national period. They symbolised the city's success as well as the

2 James E. Lewis, "What is to Become of Our Government? The Revolutionary Potential of the Election of 1800" in Horn, Ellis and Onuf, eds., *Revolution of 1800*, 22; Elkins and McKittrick, *The Age of Federalism*, 753, 693, 691; Peter S. Onuf, *Jefferson's Empire: The Language of American Nationhood* (Charlottesville and London, 2000), 78 *et passim*; Seth Cotlar, "Joseph Gales and the Making of the Jeffersonian Middle Class" in Horn, Ellis and Onuf, eds., *Revolution of 1800*, 331–59. Appleby, "Thomas Jefferson and the Psychology of Democracy" in Horn *et al.*, *Revolution of 1800*, 165. Jefferson's inaugural is quoted from Sisson, *Revolution of 1800*, 58. For the address, see Stephen Howard Brown, *Jefferson's Call for Nationhood: The First Inaugural Address* (College Station, 2003).

challenges which faced the metropolis of the new republic. Given their political experience and organisation, Irish immigrants in particular were not content with a passive role and both Federalists and Republicans recognised as much. But it does not follow that the Irish of the time saw their role in the "hyphenated" terms of the mid- to later-nineteenth century. No less than many of their American hosts, the Irish immigrants of early national Philadelphia saw themselves as citizens of a wider universe. Moreover, with *émigrés* from the United Irishmen in Ireland among them, their clubs and societies could reach into the "new politics" of the first party system in ways in which many other "new leaders" could not. Their presence in such societies, as well as in the Democratic Republican clubs, thus typified a wider political culture which in America was marked by the milestones of the decade, from contested elections to the debates on the Naturalisation, Alien and Sedition acts, and from party formation at state and local levels to the streamlining of a partisan and committed press.[3]

After 1800 the United Irishmen, as well as those who had supported them, wanted to enjoy the political changes which they had helped to create. A few saw these changes as a means to social as well as political "revolution." However, the paradox was that the success of the "revolution of 1800" depended on its ability to avoid any divisive reconstitution of American society as such, so that the more enduring Irish-born radicals were soon no more than lonely voices. The nineteenth-century tail of the United Irishmen was better exemplified by others who, like Jefferson on the grander stage of the presidency, wanted to avoid division, now that the legacy of 1776 had been placed in what he regarded as more secure hands and the putative counter-revolution of the Federalists halted. Carey also became a champion of the more mainstream "American system" and while he remained an eminence of Irish-America until he died in 1839, his views remained what they had always been: more typical of the calmer, passive world of the Society of the Lately Adopted Sons than of the perceived aggressiveness of the United Irishmen. The ethnocultural societies of Irish immigrants continued to enable the Irish to identify with the mainstream of political life and as such, and in no small way, contributed to the invention of the new America.

3 *Aurora*, 11 July 1800.

APPENDICES

Dickson and his Critics: A Note on Sources

Since it was first published in London in 1966, R.J. Dickson's *Ulster Emigration to Colonial America, 1718–1775* has been the central reference for the debate on assessing passenger flow from eighteenth century Ireland to colonial America. Because its conclusions were mainly derived from newspapers and in particular, from the advertised tonnages of the relevant vessels, it has attracted criticism from those who believe that these data are unreliable and unrealistic and that it is best to rely on official statistics. The interpretation of tonnage, and the ways in which it is often used to compute passenger traffic, is part of this debate.

Tonnage

Although tonnage was central to a range of shipping activities during the colonial period, it lends itself to several definitions. At its simplest, a vessel's "burthen" could be conveyed by at least three different types of tonnage: *registered, measured,* and *"cargo,"* and even each of these could be recorded inconsistently in respect of individual vessels.[1] Of the three, the second was the clearest in that it was calculated by shipwrights according to a legal formula which was passed in the English Parliament in 1695 for the building, buying, and sale of vessels. It was also used as a base from which to calculate a vessel's liability for a variety of harbour and customs duties. However, because many seventeenth century vessels carried less cargo than their measured tonnage suggested, it was customary to allow a discount when making these payments. As a result, the tonnage which was *registered* in respect of a particular vessel in a given part was invariably underestimated and, over time, lost its relevance to what a vessel could carry in fact.[2]

---

1 For this and the following paragraph, I have drawn on John J. McCusker, "The Pennsylvania Shipping Industry in the Eighteenth Century," unpublished manuscript (1973), HSP, and "The Tonnage of Ships Engaged in British Colonial Trade during the Eighteenth Century" in his *Essays in the Economic History of the Atlantic World* (London & New York, 1997), 43–75; Ralph Davis, *The Rise of the English Shipping Industry in the Seventeenth and Eighteenth Centuries* (London, 1962), and "Colonial Tonnage Measurement: Five Philadelphia Merchant Ships as a Sample," *JEH* xxvii (1967), 82–91; Joseph A. Goldenberg, *Shipbuilding in Colonial America* (Charlottesville, 1976) ; and Christopher J. French, "Eighteenth-Century Shipping Tonnage Measurements," *JEH* xxxiii (1973), 434–43. The 1695 formula was (length of keel x breadth of beam x ? breadth of beam) divided by 94; see 6 & 7 Wm. & M., c.12. For its adoption in Pennsylvania, see *Stats. at Large Pa.*, iii, 166–7.
2 The 1695 formula was (length of keel x breadth of beam x ½ breadth of beam) divided by 94; see 6 & 7 Wm. & Mary, c.12.

Measured tonnage and the formula on which it was based, also did not allow for improvements in the design and building of ships which evolved during the course of the eighteenth century. Thus, as John McCusker has written,

> measured tonnage, which all agree in the seventeenth century, overstated cargo capacity, had, by the mid-eighteenth, become a considerable understatement of the cargo capacity of merchant vessels ... [Nonetheless, it] followed a vessel from document to document like a faithful dog.

To address this issue, the British Parliament enacted a new formula in 1773. However, this did not come into effect in America and ship captains, often in cahoots with the customs authorities themselves, continued to use their registered tonnage to minimise payments to the custom house. This was acknowledged in a report to the British House of Lords in 1791. For most of the eighteenth century, therefore, a vessel's tonnage could be all things to all men.[3]

More crucially for calculating passenger flow, it is also clear that for assessing capacity, measured tonnage was of limited use and was being recognised as such during the course of the eighteenth century. With the extension of the carrying trade, potential consignors were looking for a clearer sense of what a vessel could carry and it was against this background that ship owners began to discuss volume rather than cubic feet and, as such, to revert to the medieval meanings of "tonnage." In the earlier usages, tonnage was calculated with respect to the number of casks of wine, or "tuns," which a vessel could hold and although as a supposed efficiency, this was later superceded by a formula-based method to compute duties and other levies, it was slowly revived as a more relevant way to assess a vessel's carrying capacity. As a result, *cargo tonnage* became part of the vocabulary of ships and shipping. Thus, not only were registered, measured, and cargo tonnages *functionally* different but the shortcomings of the first two in regard to carrying capacity were recognised, especially towards the middle of the eighteenth century.[4] Moreover, because cargo tonnage was traditionally understood as a means of suggesting capacity, merchants also developed tables of "commodity equivalents of one cargo ton" according to the type of consignment involved. It was in this context that

3 McCusker, "Tonnage of Ships," 46, 48. The British act of 1773 "for the Better Ascertaining the Tonnage and Burthen of Ships and Vessels" (13 Geo.III, c.74) stipulated a formula of ([length x 0.6 breadth] x breadth x 0.5 breadth) divided by 94. The House of Lords report of 1791 is quoted from Duvall, "Philadelphia's Maritime Commerce," 356.

4 Goldenberg, *Shipbuilding in Colonial America*, 3–4. McCusker reckoned the difference between registered, measured, and cargo tonnages as 3:5:6; see his "Pennsylvania Shipping Industry," 50.

advertised tonnages became part of the changing and complex world of indicating the capacity of a vessel to carry passengers, and that the conventions which were used by Dickson and Newenham for these purposes emerged as a reference for calculating passengers.[5]

Cadwalader's List

Officially-recorded tonnages served their own purposes which were not necessarily concerned with accuracy. As such, these are of limited use in assessing either passenger flow or a vessel's capacity to carry passengers. This is reflected in the ledgers which were compiled by Thomas Cadwalader for the period between 29 August 1768 and 13 May 1772.[6] Perhaps under the auspices of Pennsylvania's health acts, Cadwalader visited many of the vessels which docked in Philadelphia from Ireland and for each one that he visited, he recorded a number of passengers, as well as its origin and tonnage. For 1769, 1770, and 1771, the only years for which it gives complete figures, Cadwalader records 29, 23, and 25 sailings from *all* Irish ports and that these carried 826, 924, and 1,456 passengers for the respective years. However, it is clear from other sources that these figures, at least so far as they relate to passengers, are incomplete. For example, Cadwalader noted that only two passengers had sailed on the ship *Earl of Donegall* (Belfast to Philadelphia, 1769). However, as advertisements in Philadelphia later sought two runaways from this particular sailing, the suggestion that every person whom this vessel carried to America in 1769 had run away after it had docked there, despite the fact that it was a 300-ton vessel with an established reputation in Ulster's passenger trade, is hardly credible. Such underestimates are not confined to vessels of Ulster origin. From the southern port of Cork, also for 1769, Cadwalader assigned two and six passengers for the ships *Phoebe* and *Pennsylvania Farmer*, respectively, although other sources suggest that these figures are incomplete and that the two vessels had sailed from Ireland "with passengers." The 300-ton *Pennsylvania Farmer* ferried passengers on a regular basis. It made two trips in 1769 (from Newry and Cork), one in 1770 (from Newry), two in 1771 (from Cork), and one in 1773 (from Galway). With such a history in the passenger trade, it must have carried

5 McCusker, "Tonnage of Ships," 73, n.(j). In compiling his particular table, McCusker accepts Dickson's formula for computing a "load factor" for "men and women" although one should again note that Dickson used advertised, and not registered tons; *ibid.* For a recent rebuttal of Dickson's critics which arrives at conclusions which are not unlike mine, see also Miller, Schrier, Boling and Doyle, eds., *Irish Immigrants in the Land of Canaan*, 656–7.
6 For Cadwalader's list, see HSP, Cadwalader Collection, Box 15T (Thomas Cadwalader Section). Philadelphia Custom House. Passenger Lists, 29 August 1768–13 May 1772.

more than six passengers on a given trip. Such suggested underestimates are even more striking when contrasted with the figures which Robert Stephenson gave for emigration from Belfast. For four other vessels which sailed between Belfast and Philadelphia in 1771, Stephenson recorded 80, 300, 270, and 150 passengers while on 20 June 1771, the *Pennsylvania Journal* listed 320 passengers on a fifth, the ship *Newry Packet* (Newry to Philadelphia, 1771).[7] The Cadwalader list matches these figures as follows: 48, 148, 65, 80, and 79. Although it should be noted that some passengers from the second vessel disembarked in Delaware, the differences between the two sets of figures is so striking as to caution against relying on only one.

Although it is less satisfactory, it is also possible to question Cadwalader's record of incoming passengers by looking at the wider histories of individual vessels. For example, it is without question that the 300-ton ship *Jupiter* (usually from Derry) was involved in the passenger trade. Cadwalader acknowledged this by ascribing the following number of passengers to it for the years between 1769 and 1771: 87, 115, and 88. However, for two years beyond the list's remit, 1772 and 1773, the *Pennsylvania Journal* reported that 430 and 513, respectively, had sailed on the vessel. A similar contrast can be drawn with respect to the record of the ship *Rose* (also from Derry). For 1769, 1770, and 1771, the respective figures in Cadwalader are 120, 59, and 123, in contrast to 340 (for 1772) and 350 (for 1773), as also reported in the *Pennsylvania Journal*. For the ship *Philadelphia* (from Belfast), the list records the following: 92 (1769), 54 (1770), and 148 (1771) while a local newspaper recorded 300 for 1772.[8] As Cadwalader's under-recording of passengers suggests, whether highlighted directly in the cases of the *Earl of Donegall*, the *Phoebe*, and the *Pennsylvania Farmer*, or implicitly, in the other cases, lists which record information on passenger flow, whether they have been officially or artificially compiled, are of limited value if they are not used together.

Marine Lists

This is also true when tabulating actual shipping entries from Ireland into the Delaware. For example, it is clear that the marine entries which were recorded

---

7   Lockhart, *Aspects of Irish Emigration*, appendix c, 202; Dickson, *Ulster Emigration*, appendix c, 234–7; Leroy V. Eid, "No Freight Paid So Well," 36 n.4. Stephenson's figures are in PRONI, D562/8450. Although published in *PG*, 23 Jan. 1772, the notices about the runaways from the ship *Earl of Donegall* refer to the vessel's 1769 voyage, the arrival of which was noted in *PG*, 2 Mar. 1769.

8   *PJ*, 18 June 1772, 4 Aug. 1773, 26 Aug. 1772, 22 Sept. 1773. For the commissioning of the *Jupiter* to transport emigrants to Alexander McNutt's tract in Nova Scotia, see Dickson, *Ulster Emigration*, 141, 143, 113 n.4.

in the *Pennsylvania Gazette* alone are incomplete and should be supplemented
not only by the data in Dickson and Audrey Lockhart, but also by similar lists
which were published in other contemporary newspapers, notably in the
Pennsylvania Journal and the *Pennsylvania Packet*. A comparison between the
marine lists which were compiled by Dickson, Lockhart, and Cadwalader also
underlines the point that they are most useful when related to one another and
indeed, for their overlapping years (1769–1771, inclusive), a number of sailings
are unrecorded in the latter: nine from Lockhart (for 1769), one from Lockhart
and four for Dickson (for 1770), and one from Dickson (for 1771). As it is likely
that some of these vessels carried passengers, these identifiable exclusions,
together with the nature of measured tonnage, the underreporting of passenger
numbers, and the limits of officially-recorded tonnages to compute immigration,
suggest that historians should use Cadwalader's list with care.[9] Moreover, they
should discourage historians from using the specifics of this list, including the
number of passengers per ship, to make broader conclusions about the general
passenger flow from Ireland. These data are most useful only when read in
conjunction with information from other sources, especially with respect to
assessing passenger flow, and then only with a sense of the purposes which each
of these sources served, as well as the extent to which these purposes had been
either corrupted or superceded over time.

In the following appendices, the data have been compiled by collating a
number of sources, and modify other figures which have been produced
elsewhere for the purposes of assessing the flow of vessels and passengers from
late-eighteenth-century Ireland to contemporary Philadelphia.

---

9 It is clear from Lockhart, *Aspects of Emigration*, appendix c, and Dickson, *Ulster
   Emigration*, appendix d, that at least four of the vessels which are nor recorded by
   Cadwalader had left Ireland with passengers. These vessels were the brig *Polly* (two
   sailings) and the ships *Philadelphia*, and *Kitty and Peggy*. See also *PJ*, 20 June 1771.

Voyages between Southern Ireland (S) and Ulster (U), Delaware, and Philadelphia, 1760–75

	1760	1761	1762	1763	1764	1765	1766	1767	1768	1769	1770	1771	1772	1773	1774	1775
Cork		1	1	1	6	4	6	9	8	21	13[a]	11[b]	6	4	3	4
Dublin	4		2	5	2	3	13	9	8	11	7	7	6	4	2	3
Waterford			1		2		2	3		3	3[c]	6[d]	3	2	2	1
Others (S)[1]	1			2	2	1	1		1		2	1		1	1	
Belfast	1	2	4	2	2	4	9	3	2	3	2	4[e]	5	8	4	3
Derry	8	6	7	7	6	6	10	11	5	11	7	7[e]	8	10	8	7
Newry	2			2		1	1	2	3	3	2	2	7	3	6	6
Others (U)[2]		1		2	1	1	2	1		1	1					1
Total (S)	5	1	4	8	12	8	22	22	17	35	25	25	15	11	8	8
Total (U)	11	9	11	13	9	12	22	17	10	18	12	13	20	21	17	18
"Ireland" *via* Delaware[3]										3	4	3	3	4	3	3
Total Ireland	16	10	15	21	21	20	44	39	27	56	41	41	38	36	28	29
Delaware[4]	17	13	6	7	2	2	6	5	5	1	4		3	6	7	4

a Includes one entry from Cork and Tenerife; and two from Ulster and Cork

c Includes one entry from Belfast and Waterford

b Includes one entry from Liverpool and Cork

d Includes two entries from Ulster and Waterford

e Includes vessel that stopped *en route* at Cork

1. Included in this column are entries from the ports of Sligo (one for 1760 and 1765, and two each for 1763 and 1764); Limerick (one for 1766 and 1774); Dingle (one for 1768, and two for 1770); and Galway (one for 1771 and 1773).

2. Included in this column are entries from the ports of Killybegs (one for 1763, 1766, 1767, and 1769); Coleraine (one for 1763, 1764, and 1765); Larne (one for 1766); Lough Swilly (one for 1761); and Portrush (one for 1770 and 1775).

3. This line refers to vessels for which, although listed in the marine notices as entering from "Ireland," the port of origin there is unclear.

4. Vessels from the Delaware ports of Lewes and Newcastle are often mentioned in the marine lists, and are listed in this line. In most cases, it is impossible to identify whether or not these vessels were acting as tenders for ships of Irish origin which, in some cases, stopped in Delaware before proceeding to other destinations, such as New York, Baltimore, and Charleston. Where such vessels can be identified as serving vessels which came from either Ulster or the southern ports, they have been listed in the relevant line of regional origin in Ireland.

Sources: The figures in this appendix have been assigned to their specific ports of origin in Ireland on the basis of the custom-house notices as published in the *Pennsylvania Gazette*. Where relevant, supplementary figures have been drawn from similar notices in the *Pennsylvania Journal* and

Pennsylvania Packet; the Cadwalader List; Lockhart, *Aspects of Emigration*, Appendix D; and Dickson *Ulster Emigration*, Appendices B, C, and D. However, these supplementary data were used only when they did not appear in the columns of the *Pennsylvania Gazette*. Between them, they give a reasonably full picture of the extent of the traffic between Ireland and the colonial Delaware.

Although the published marine notices also list entries from ports in Delaware, such vessels were not included in this table except where such entries "from Delaware" have been identified from Irish sources as having left from a specific place in Ireland. Such sailings have been included in the column of the relevant port of origin in Ireland.

Ulster and the Delaware Valley: Passenger Traffic, 1771–75

1	2					3					4				
Port of origin	Known Number of passengers					Vessels "with passengers"					Unclassified vessels				
	1771	1772	1773	1774	1775	1771	1772	1773	1774	1775	1771	1772	1773	1774	1775
Belfast	800 (4)	824 (3)	2930 (7)	850 (2)	730 (3)				490 (700/2)		2	1			
Derry	483 (5)	1710 (5)	2703 (3)	1400 (3)				385 (550/2)	420 (600/2)	280 (400/1)	2	1	7	3	7
Newry	140 (2)	823 (2)	720 (3)	1020 (3)	150 (1)			700 (1000/3)	490 (700/2)	595 850 (2)		2		1	3
Ulster and Delaware		400 (2)	400 (2)	117 (1)				350 500(2)	455 650(2)	613 875(3)	2		2		3
Total	1423 (11)	3757 (12)	6753 (15)	3387 (9)	880 (4)			1435 (7)	1855 (8)	1488 (6)					

Note: The above data on immigration have been compiled from passenger and other shipping information, as published in the sources listed in Appendix II, especially in Philadelphia's newspapers, and have been presented under three broad headings, depending on the nature of the information. The figures in Column 2 have been compiled from specific passenger figures which were published for individual vessels in the newspapers of the period. As such, they are "Known Numbers of Passengers." The numbers in brackets refer to the number of vessels to which these passenger figures refer. Those in Column 3 are known to have been "primarily involved in the passenger trade," and published notices that they carried passengers. As such, I have applied Stephenson's ratio of 0.7:1 (for which, see Chapter I, 27–28) to their tonnages to calculate their complements. The figures in brackets refer to the number of vessels and their combined tonnage. Because of the nature of their advertisements, and the absence of notices that they were either involved in the passenger trade, or had left Ireland "with passengers," those vessels listed in Column 4 are impossible to assess for the purposes of computing passenger flow.

APPENDIX IV

Southern Ireland and Philadelphia:
Passenger Traffic, 1771–75

1	2					3					4				
Port of origin	Known number of passengers					Vessels "with passengers"					Unclassified vessels				
	1771	1772	1773	1774	1775	1771	1772	1773	1774	1775	1771	1772	1773	1774	1775
Cork	269 (4)	152 (4)	80 (1)	200 (1)		1	2	2	1	1	6		1	1	3
Dublin	40 (4)	66 (2)	220 (3)			1	3				2	1	1	1	3
Waterford	299 (5)	89 (1)	80 (1)	100 (1)		1	1			1	1	1	1	1	
Others (South)	8 (1)		80 (1)						1						
Total	616 (14)	307 (7)	460 (6)	300 (2)		3	6	2	2	2	9	2	3	3	6

Note: The passenger table for these vessels refers to ships which landed in Philadelphia. The cited data do not refer to stops in Delaware which, in any event, was much rarer for vessels for southern Irish origin than it was for those which had sailed from Ulster. For the sources used for this table, see Appendix III. Column 2, "Number of Known Passengers," has been compiled on the same basis as its counterpart in Appendix III. While it is known that the vessels listed in Column 3 carried passengers, it is impossible to apply Stephenson's ratio as the contemporary newspapers do not give tonnages for the relevant vessels. However, as the Cadwalader list, or notices seeking the return of runaway servants, or general newspaper references reported that these vessels carried passengers, they are included here in a discrete column. As with the similar column in Appendix III, it is impossible to classify the numbers listed in Column 4 for the purposes of computing passenger flow.

Ulster (U) and Southern Ireland (S) and the Delaware Valley: Shipping and Passenger Figures, 1783-98

1		2	3	4	5	6	7
Year/Regional origin		Number of vessels	Passengers: known figures	Additional passenger vessels (A)	Minimum figures	Vessels sailing "with passengers" (B)	Unidentified
1783	U.	22	3222 (16)	385 (2)	3607	284 (2)	2
	S.	11	420 (3)		420	874 (4)	4
1784	U.	26	5781 (19)	770 (3)	6551	140 (1)	3
	S.	13	1995 (8)		1995	315 (2)	3
1785	U.	11	1771 (7)	385 (2)	2156		2
	S.	9	1010 (4)	560 (2)	1570		3
1786	U.	14	1885 (8)	420 (2)	2305	140 (1)	3
	S.	9	1400 (6)		1400		3
1787	U.	17	1405 (7)	700 (3)	2105		7
	S.	14	1620 (6)	630 (3)	2250		5
1788	U.	13	1943 (8)	455 (2)	2398		3
	S.	12	2000 (6)		2000		6
1789	U.	15	2561 (12)	140 (1)	2701	300 (1)	1
	S.	11	270 (1)	280 (1)	550	1600 (5)	4
1790	U.	16	3537 (15)	140 (1)	3677		
	S.	12	720 (3)	245 (1)	965		8
1791	U.	19	3833 (14)	630 (4)	4463		1
	S.	10					10
1792	U.	22	5577 (22)		5577		
	S.	9	500 (3)	245 (1)	745		5
1793	U.	18	3323 (14)	228 (2)	3551		2
	S.	7	180 (3)		180		4
1794	U.	14	2075 (9)	175 (1)	2250		4
	S.	7	183 (2)		183		5
1795	U.	17	3159 (12)	175 (1)	3334		4
	S.	13	351 (8)		351		5
1796	U.	17	3532 (14)	438 (1)	3970		2
	S.	7	110 (1)		110		6
1797	U.	20	2600 (9)	560 (2)	3160	805 (3)	6
	S.	2	11(1)		11		1
1798	U.	8	80 (1)	1344 (6)	1424		1
	S.	7		154(1)	154		6
Total	U.	269	46284	6945 (33)	53229	1669 (8)	
	S.	153	10770	2114 (9)	12884	2789 (11)	

Note: The information tabulated in Appendix V has been drawn from Irish and U.S. sources, especially from the marine lists and other shipping information contained in contemporary newspapers. In Ireland, these sources include (for Ulster), the *Belfast News-Letter*, the *Londonderry Journal*, and the (Belfast) *Northern Star*. For the ports of southern Ireland, I have used *Saunders* [Dublin] *News-Letter* and the *Cork Hibernian Chronicle*. These newspapers have been used as my source of first call and have been supplemented, especially for computing passenger figures, by the following Philadelphia newspapers: the *Pennsylvania Packet*, *American Daily Advertiser*, the *General Advertiser* and *Aurora*, the *Pennsylvania Evening Herald*, and the *Independent Gazetteer*. I have also drawn on Philadelphia's Port-Entry Books, Pilots' Lists, and Health Reports.

The table lists the regional origins of the 422 Irish vessels which entered the Delaware Valley between 1783 and 1798 (Column 2). Column 3 presents the passenger figures for those vessels for which such details were published, usually in U.S. rather than in Irish newspapers, as well as the number of vessels (in brackets) to which these passenger figures refer. Column 4, "Additional Passenger Vessels (A)," also refers to vessels which carried emigrants. However, in the absence of a published passenger figure for the relevant vessels, Stephenson's ratio has been used to identify the complement by reference to advertised tonnage in accordance with the arguments listed in Chapter I, 27–28 and Appendix I, and because they were "primarily involved in the passenger trade." As such, the data listed in Column 5 can be regarded as minimum figures for Irish emigration to the Delaware Valley between 1783 and 1798.

It is clear that the vessels to which Column 6 (Vessels sailing "with passengers' (B)) refers also carried passengers, and were noted as having done so in contemporary newspapers. However, as the advertisements of these vessels were not as detailed as those of Column 4, it is not clear if they were "primarily involved in the passenger trade." Thus, while the ratio has been used to compute the figures in Column 6, it is more difficult to apply them with certainty to passenger flow. As such, these figures represent a "second," if somewhat less sure, lower threshold for the passenger flow of this period.

The vessels listed as "unidentified" in Column 7 seem to have been primarily involved in trade and while they may have carried some passengers, it is impossible to quantify the numbers involved.

The Friendly Sons of St. Patrick of Philadelphia: Membership List, 1771–90

No.	Name	Date of Induction	Place of Birth	Profession	Other memberships	Other information
1.	All	1781		ship captain		ship owned by 20
2.	John Barclay	1779	1	merchant banker	1, 4	mayor, 1791
3.	Thomas Barclay	1771	1	merchant		brother of 4; uncle of 24; partner of 68
4.	William Barclay	1781	1	merchant		brother of 3
5.	John Barry	1779	1	ship captain	1	59 mentioned in will
6.	Thomas Batt	1773		merchant		
7.	Ephraim Blaine	1780	1	public servant		
8.	John Bleakley	1794	2	"gentleman"	1	
9.	William Bourke	1783				
10.	Robert Boyd	1774	1	doctor		
11.	Hugh Boyle	1787		merchant	1	
12.	John Boyle	1771	1	merchant	4, 2, 3	partner of 44
13.	John Brown	1779	1	merchant	1	
14.	William Browne	1787				
15.	Richard Butler	1781	1	agent		
16.	Andrew Caldwell	1771	1	merchant	4	cousin of 20; partner of 18
17.	David Caldwell	1794	2	public servant		son of 20
18.	James Caldwell	1778	1	merchant	4, 3, 2	partner of 16
19.	John Caldwell	1787	2	lawyer	4, 3	
20.	Samuel Caldwell	1771	1	merchant	4, 2, 1	father of 17; partner of 63
21.	William Caldwell	1786				
22.	George Campbell	1771	1	lawyer	4	brother-in-law of 34
23.	James Campbell	1784	1	merchant	1	daughter ward of 57 after Campbell's death
24.	Samuel Carson	1772	1	merchant		partner of 3 and 65
25.	Daniel Clark	1784	1	merchant		
26.	John Cochran	1781	2	doctor		
27.	James Collins	1783	1	merchant		
28.	John Connor	1783	1			
29.	William Constable	1781	1	merchant	2, 4	
30.	David H. Conyhgham	1775	2	merchant	4, 2	partner of 79
31.	James Crawford	1779	1	merchant	2, 4, 1	recommended to 30; broker with 34
32.	George Davis	1771	1			
33.	Sharp Delany	1772	1	druggist		executor of 94
34.	John Donaldson	1778	2	merchant	4, 2, 1	brother-in-law of 22
35.	John Dunlop	1778	1	printer	4	
36.	William Erskine	1780	1	merchant		witnessed will of 22
37.	Thomas Fitzsimons	1771	1	merchant	1, 2	brother-in-law and partner of 61
38.	Alex Foster	1794	1	merchant		
39.	Tench Francis	1771	2	merchant	3, 2	niece married 58
40.	Tubbit Francis	1771	2	army	3	
41.	Benjamin Fuller	1771	1	ship broker	2	executor of will of 68
42.	George Fullerton	1771	1	merchant	4	
43.	Arch Gamble	1782		academic		
44.	Robert Glen	1772				partner of 12
45.	Robert Gray	1781	1			
46.	John Green	1783		merchant		
47.	Edward Hand	1782	1	doctor	1	
48.	James Hawthorn	1792	1	merchant	1	nephew of 79
49.	Charles Heatly	1783	1		1	52: witness to will

No.	Name	Date of Induction	Place of Birth	Profession	Other memberships	Other information
50.	George Henry	1775	1	merchant	2, 4	
51.	Alex Holmes	1780				
52.	Hugh Holmes	1791	1	merchant	1	partner of 86; 59, 57 acted as sureties
53.	George Hughes	1781	1	merchant	1, 2, 4	
54.	William Irvine	1781	1	army		
55.	Francis Johnston	1779	2	public servant	4, 1, 2	
56.	Henry Knox	1782	2	merchant		
57.	George Latimer	1792	2	public servant; merchant	1	married niece of 39
58.	Thomas Lea	1785	2	merchant	1, 2	
59.	John Leamy	1792	1	merchant	1	relative of 79
60.	Ulysses Lynch	1771	1			brother-in-law of 37
61.	George Meade	1771	2	merchant	1	partner of 20; executor of 2, 20
62.	James Mease	1771	1	merchant		partner of 20; executor of 2, 20
63.	John Mease	1771	1	merchant	4, 2, 3	brother of 62
64.	Matthew Mease	1771	1	merchant		brother of 62
65.	John Mitchell	1771	1	merchant	2, 3, 4	nephew of 16
66.	Randall Mitchell	1781	2	merchant	1	son of 65
67.	William Mitchell	1771	1	merchant	1	partner of 65
68.	Hugh Moore	1771		merchant	41, 3	executors
69.	James Moore	1783	1	merchant		31 an executor
70.	Peter Moore	1785		druggist		
71.	James Moylan	1786		merchant	4, 1	married daughter of 7
72.	Jasper Moylan	1772	1			brother of 73, 74, 75
73.	John Moylan	1781	1	lawyer	1, 4	brother of 72, 74, 75; married widow of 62
74.	Stephen Moylan	1781	1	merchant		brother of 72, 73, 75
75.	Stephen Moylan	1771	1	merchant	2, 3	brother of 72, 73, 74
76.	John Murray	1772		merchant	2	
77.	Blaine McClenachan	1777	1	merchant	1, 2, 3	daughter married 92
78.	Alex Nesbitt	1778	1	merchant	1, 2, 3, 4	brother of 79; partner of 94
79.	John M. Nesbitt	1771	1	merchant	5	95 executor; brother of 78
80.	Francis Nichols	1784	1	army	4	
81.	John Nixon	1771	2	merchant	1	
82.	Michael Morgan O'Brien	1781	1	merchant	1, 2, 3	75, 39, 49 mentioned in will, and given wardship of daughter
83.	John Patterson	1772	1	printer		
84.	John Patton	1779	1	merchant	1, 2, 3	
85.	Oliver Pollock	1783	1	merchant	1	
86.	Robert Ramsey	1791	1	merchant	1, 2, 4	
87.	Thomas Rea	1782	2	ship captain		
88.	Thomas Robinson	1782		judge	3	
89.	John Shea	1771	1	merchant		
90.	Hugh Shiell	1780	1	doctor	2	
91.	Charles Stewart	1782	1	surveyor	1	cousin of 92
92.	Walter Stewart	1779	1	army	1, 2	son-in-law of 77
93.	William Thompson	1778	1	surveyor		
94.	Anthony Wagner	1771	2	surveyor		
95.	Francis West	1786	2	merchant	4, 2	son of 97; brother of 96
96.	John West	1786	2	merchant	4, 2	son of 97; brother of 95
97.	William West	1771	1	merchant		executor of 41, 98, 81; daughter married 30; uncle of 98
98.	William West Jnr.	1772	2	merchant		nephew of 97
99.	John White	1772		merchant	3	
100.	Joseph Wilson		1		4	

Note: The following indicators have been used. For "Place of Birth" in Column 4, those members who were born in Ireland are identified by (1), and those who were born in Philadelphia of Irish parentage by (2). For "Other Memberships" in Column 6, the following have been used: Hibernian Society (1), Hibernian Fire Company (2), Gloucester Fox Hunting Club (3), and First City Troop (4).

Biographical Notes and Further Information

John Adams (1735–1826) was born in Braintree, Massachusetts, and graduated as a lawyer from Harvard university. Having written against the Stamp Act (1765), he became active in the Revolutionary movement and eventually, a member of the First (1774) and Second (1775–66) Continental Congresses. Having been a member of the committee which had been appointed to draft the Declaration of Independence (1776), he was sent to France to promote what became the Franco-American Alliance of 1778. After playing a pivotal role in the Massachusetts Constitutional Convention (1780), he was again sent overseas, first to Holland and, thereafter, to London (1785–88), the latter experience leaving a lasting impression on him. He was elected as Washington's vice-president in 1789 and succeeded him as second president of the United States in 1797. His term as president was dominated by the so-called "quasi-war" with France and the passage of the Alien and Sedition Acts (1798) which aimed to silence his critics. In 1800 he was defeated for re-election by Thomas Jefferson. For a critical biography, see David G. McCullogh, *John Adams* (New York, 2001). See also Richard Alan Ryerson, ed., *John Adams and the Founding of the Republic* (Boston, 2001).

The **battle of Aughrim** (1691), Co. Galway, finally broke the Jacobite resistance to William III in Ireland, leading ultimately to the exile of its leader, Patrick Sarsfield. See J.G. Simms, *Jacobite Ireland* (London, 1969).

Benjamin Franklin Bache (1769–98) was the grandson of Benjamin Franklin who trained him as a printer. In 1790 he founded Philadelphia's *General Advertiser* which in 1794 was re-named the *Aurora*, the principal paper of Jeffersonian republicanism. Such was his opposition to the presidency of John Adams that in 1798 Bache was arrested under the Alien and Sedition Acts but died during Philadelphia's yellow fever epidemic of that year. See James Tagg, *Benjamin Franklin Bache and the Philadelphia Aurora* (Philadelphia, 1991).

The Jesuit **Abbé Augustin Barruel** (1741–1820) fled from the French Revolution to Britain in 1792. He wrote a number of books and pamphlets, including his *Memoirs Illustrating the History of Jacobinism* (1796) which argued that the French Revolution had been inspired by an anti-Catholic and Masonic conspiracy. See Vernon Stauffer, *New England and the Bavarian Illuminati* (New York, 1918).

Commodore **John Barry** (1745–1803) was born in Wexford and emigrated to Philadelphia in or about 1760, where he developed his career as a ship captain. On the outbreak of the Revolution, he placed his expertise at the disposal of the revolutionary cause and was given various commands in the fledgling navy of the Continental Congress. In 1794 Washington appointed him as Senior Captain of the United States

Navy, from which his popular designation of "Father of the American Navy" derives. See Leonard Wibberley, *John Barry, Father of the Navy* (New York, 1957).

Although **John Beckley** (1757–1807) emigrated from London as an indentured servant, he amassed considerable tracts of western lands and in 1789 became clerk of the house of representatives, in part, due to his friendship with James Madison. During the 1790s he also became what Noble Cunningham has called "an early American party manager." In this capacity, he was indispensable to the evolution of Jeffersonian republicanism in Pennsylvania and for these exertions, the Federalists ousted him from his post in 1797. Following Jefferson's election, he was reinstated and, in addition, he was appointed Librarian of Congress. See Edmund Berkeley and Dorothy Smith Berkeley, *John Beckley: Zealous Partisan in a Nation Divided* (Philadelphia, 1973); Noble Cunningham, "John Beckley: An Early American Party Manager," *WMQ* xiii (1956), 40–52; and Jeffrey L. Pasley, "A Journeyman, Either in Law or Politics': John Beckley and the Social Origins of Political Campaigning," *Journal of the Early Republic* xvi (1996), 531–69.

Thomas Ledlie Birch (1754–1828) was a Presbyterian minister in Saintfield, Co. Down. He supported the American Revolution and the campaigns to repeal the Penal Laws, and became chaplain to the local Volunteer corps and later, a member of the United Irishmen. Following his role in the 1798 rebellion, he was exiled to Pennsylvania where he became a controversial and very public apologist for "Old Side" Presbyterianism. See Michael Durey, *Transatlantic Radicals and the Early American Republic* (Lawrence, 1997).

Phineas Bond (1749–1815) served as British consul for New York, New Jersey, Pennsylvania, Delaware, and Maryland from 1786. He was based in Philadelphia and also acted as British commissioner for commercial affairs in the United States. Following a reorganisation of Britain's representation in America, he was appointed consul general for the middle and southern states in 1793 and served in this capacity until his return to Britain in 1812. See Loanne Loewe Neel, *Phineas Bond: A Study in Anglo-American Relations* (Philadelphia, 1968).

Although it had an important international context, the **battle of the Boyne** (1 July 1690) is one of the more remembered military engagements in Irish history. It was where the forces of William III effectively broke those of James II who departed for France three days later. See J.G. Simms, *Jacobite Ireland* (London, 1969).

The **brig** had a triangular fore-sail and was also square-rigged. However, it was only two-masted and varied only slightly from the **snow**, with which it was often equated.

George Bryan (1731–91) was born in Dublin, from where he emigrated to Philadelphia in 1752. There, he soon emerged as a prominent merchant and member of the Presbyterian church. In politics, he was also involved with the Proprietary interest during the 1760s and in 1776 he became the first vice-president of the new state of Pennsylvania. Thereafter, he became the leading defender of the state's new constitution and leader of the Constitutionalist party (1776–90). See Joseph Foster, *In Pursuit of Equal Liberty: George Bryan and the Revolution in Pennsylvania* (University Park, 1994).

John Daly Burk (1772–1808) joined the United Irishmen while he was a student in Trinity College, Dublin. Following his expulsion from the university in 1794, he became active in radical politics in Dublin. In 1796 he fled to Boston after several of his political associates had been arrested for seditious activities and subsequently settled in New York where he edited the Republican paper, the *Time-Piece*. He had always been an ardent supporter of Jefferson and was arrested in 1798 for his criticisms of the Adams administration. He fled to Virginia where he remained until after Jefferson had been elected in 1800. He was the author of the influential play, *Bunker-Hill; or the Death of General Warren* (1797) as well as the *History of the Late War in Ireland* (1799), and the *History of Virginia* (1804–5, 1816). He was killed in a duel in 1808. See Joseph I. Shulim, *John Daly Burk. Irish Revolutionist and American Patriot* (Philadelphia, 1964).

Pierce Butler (1744–1822) was born in Carlow, Ireland. Having emigrated to South Carolina, he was a member of the state legislature during the 1770s and 1780s. In 1787 he was elected to the U.S. Constitutional Convention and two years later, to the U.S. senate, where he remained until 1796 when he became disenchanted with Hamilton and resigned. He was later re-elected in 1802 and served until 1806. See Lewright B. Sikes, *The Public Life of Pierce Butler, South Carolina Statesman* (Washington, 1979).

James Carey (1762?–1801) was brother of Matthew. He emigrated to Philadelphia where, like his brother, he became a publisher and newspaper editor. See Kerby A. Miller, Arnold Schrier, Bruce D. Boling, and David N. Doyle, eds., *Irish Immigrants in the Land of Canaan* (Oxford, 2003), 592 n.30.

In 1779, after **Mathew Carey** (1760–1839) wrote a contentious pamphlet in support of the repeal of the Penal Laws, he fled to France. There he met Lafayette and Franklin, who engaged him for several months as a printer at Passy. Following his return to Dublin in 1780, Carey established the *Volunteer Journal* in 1783 "to defend the commerce, the manufactures, and the political rights of Ireland, against the oppression and encroachments of Great Britain." However, in September 1784, he was again obliged to emigrate, this time to Philadelphia, after his paper was charged with libelling the Speaker of the house of commons. There, with the help of Lafayette, Carey continued his career as a publisher, founding the *Pennsylvania Evening Herald* in January 1785, the *Columbian Magazine* in October 1786, and the *American Museum* two years later. Although his activities as editor and publisher drew him into a number of controversies during the 1780s and 1790s, he was not an enthusiastic supporter of partisan politics. See Edward C. Carter II, "The Political Activities of Mathew Carey, Nationalist, 1760–1814" (Ph.D. dissertation, Bryn Mawr College, 1962).

John Chambers (1754–1837) was a leading Dublin printer and publisher during the last twenty years of the eighteenth century. He was also one of the founders of the Dublin Society of United Irishmen and was arrested in March 1798. Between 1798 and 1802, he was imprisoned in Fort George, Scotland, from where he emigrated to France and thereafter, to New York, in 1805. See Miller, Schrier, Boling, and Doyle, eds., *Irish Immigrants in the Land of Canaan*, 589, n.13.

William Cobbett (1763–1835) was editor of Philadelphia's *Porcupine's Gazette* which, together with a number of pamphlets, castigated the "foreign influence [that] ... directed, ruled, and managed all our divisions;" *PorcG* 12 May 1797. In particular, Cobbett targeted Irish and French immigrants as undesirable citizens and became one of the most steadfast supporters of the Federalist administrations of the 1790s. See Mary Elizabeth Clark, *Peter Porcupine in America: the Career of William Cobbett, 1793–1800* (Gettysburg, 1939).

Although the **Conestoga** Indians lived peacefully near Lancaster among the white settlers, the Scots-Irish accused them of assisting the more unfriendly tribes on the frontier to launch a number of hostile raids. On 14 November 1764 a Scots-Irish party attacked the Conestoga settlement and killed six Indians. Over a month later a further fourteen Conestogas were killed in Lancaster, where they had taken refuge. See John Dunbar, ed., *The Paxton Papers* (The Hague, 1954).

Jean Hector St. John de Crèvecoeur (1731–1813) was born in France but as a young man, emigrated to New York where he became a successful farmer and author of the influential portrayal of late-eighteenth-century America, *Letters from an American Farmer* (1782). After the international recognition of the United States in 1783, he served as French consul general in New York but continued to be better known as an agriculturalist and writer. See Gay Wilson Allen and Roger Asselineau, *St. John de Crèvecoeur: The Life of An American Farmer* (New York, 1987).

Alexander James Dallas (1759–1817) was born in Jamaica and admitted to the Pennsylvania bar in 1785. As Pennsylvania's secretary of state (1791–1801), Dallas was one of the more important and influential managers of Jeffersonianism in the state. He later became U.S. secretary of the treasury (1814–6) under President James Madison. See Raymond J. Walters, Jr., *Alexander James Dallas: Lawyer – Politician – Financier, 1759–1817* (Philadelphia, 1943).

The **Defenders** was a Catholic society which originated in Armagh in the mid-1780s, partly in reaction to the Protestant Peep of Day Boys. As it spread throughout the northern part of Ireland, as well as into Leinster, it targeted surging rents and tithes, at a time when high emigration from Presbyterian Ulster and the reform of the Penal Laws were giving Catholics new opportunities to acquire land, thus causing insecurities among Protestants. Organisationally, the movement was cell-based but was tighter and more secretive than the Whiteboys. During the 1790s it co-operated closely with the United Irishmen in pursuit of political reform. See Jim Smyth, *The Men of No Property: Irish Radicals and Popular Politics in the Late Eighteenth Century* (London, 1992).

William Duane (1760–1835) became editor of the Philadelphia *Aurora* following Bache's death from yellow fever in September 1798. Born in New York of Irish parents, he went to Ireland with his mother in 1774. In 1786 he settled in Calcutta, where he subsequently edited the *World* but was deported in 1795 after a stream of criticisms of the East India Company. Following a short period in London as editor of the anti-government *Telegraph*, Duane returned to Philadelphia where he began work for the *Aurora* in 1796. See Kim Tousley Phillips, *William Duane: Radical Journalist in the Age of Jefferson* (New York, 1989).

Like his father and grandfather, **Thomas Addis Emmet** (1764–1827) trained as a doctor but later abandoned medicine for law. During the 1790s he was an active member of both the Dublin Society of United Irishmen and the society's Leinster Directory. For these involvements, he was arrested in March 1798 and deported to Fort George, Scotland, together with seventeen other "state prisoners." After spending three years there, largely because the Federalist Rufus King, the then U.S. minister to London, blocked permission to emigrate to America, Jefferson's administration allowed Emmet to leave for New York in 1804, a year after Emmet's brother, Robert (1778–1803) was executed for leading an abortive rebellion in Dublin. In New York, Emmet became active in city politics, one of the state's best known and respected lawyers, and state attorney general in 1812. During the gubernatorial election of 1807, when King was the Federalist candidate, King's attitude to the 1798 rebellion in Ireland, and to those who had been involved in it, were highlighted by Emmet. The resulting controversy proved to be a crucial factor in ensuring Emmet's defeat. See Thomas Addis Emmet, *Memoir of Thomas Addis and Robert Emmet with their Ancestors and Immediate Family* 2 vols. (New York, 1915).

The word **ethno-cultural** has been used in this text to suggest, in Tully's words, "a far greater range of characteristics than the religion or ethnicity with which writers have largely been concerned" in describing the activities and interests of immigrants and their communities. See Alan W. Tully, "Ethnicity, Religion, and Politics in Early America," *PMHB* cvii (1983), 492n.

As a political interest, the **Federalists** believed in strong central government and a federal constitution which would promote it. As events began to unfold after 1789, they favoured the British rather than the French model of government as well as a distinctive role for a "natural leadership" rather than an "uncontrolled democracy."

John Ward Fenno (1751–98) became publisher of the *Gazette of the United States* in 1789. He died during the yellow fever epidemic in Philadelphia in 1798. See Donald H. Stewart, *The Opposition Press of the Federalist Period* (Albany, 1969).

The **First Great Awakening** was an evangelical revival which evolved between the 1730s and the 1760s. Defenders of the movement were termed "New Light," as opposed to the "Old Lights," who saw it as both a religious and a social threat. See Perry Miller and Alan Hiemart, eds., *The Great Awakening* (Indianapolis, 1967).

Thomas Fitzsimons (1741–1811) was born in Dublin. After emigrating to Philadelphia as a young man, he joined the firm of George Meade & Co. and became active in the city's Revolutionary committees and later, a member of various state bodies, including the state assembly. In 1782 he was elected to the Continental Congress and in 1787, to the U.S. Constitutional Convention. Between 1789 and 1795, he served as a Federalist member of Congress and was recognised as a member of the Federalist-dominated "junto" which ran Philadelphia until 1800. Fitzsimons was also one of the original members of the Friendly Sons of St. Patrick. See John H. Campbell, *History of the Friendly Sons of St. Patrick* (Philadelphia, 1892), 100–111.

Benjamin Franklin (1706–90) is often regarded as America's greatest eighteenth-century *philosophe*, even before he represented Pennsylvania as its agent in London (1757–62), and thereafter, Massachusetts, New Jersey, and Georgia (1765–75). In 1775 he was elected as a member of the second Continental Congress but the following year, he was sent to France to negotiate an alliance. He remained there until 1785 when he was elected as president of the Executive Council of Pennsylvania. In 1787 he was also elected as a delegate from Pennsylvania to the Constitutional Convention. See Edmund Morgan, *Benjamin Franklin* (New Haven, 2002).

For the achievement of **"free trade"** in Ireland, see the note on **Henry Grattan**.

Philip Freneau (1752–1832) was educated at Princeton where he became a close friend of Madison and Henry Brackenridge (1748–1816). With Brackenridge, he collaborated in publishing poetry and later, a number of critical writings in support of the American Revolution. In July 1791, with the support of Madison and Jefferson, he founded the *National Gazette* which became one of the most vitriolic critics of the Federalist administrations. After Jefferson was elected in 1800, Freneau retired to his farm from where he lived the remainder his life indulging his private interests, including writing and farming. See Philip Axelrod, *Philip Freneau: Champion of Democracy* (Austin, 1967).

Albert Gallatin (1761–1849) was born in Switzerland and emigrated to Pennsylvania in 1780. He soon became a champion of "the frontier" and, by extension, an opponent of the Federalist interest which drew its strength from the more established and more populous eastern counties of his adopted state. In 1790 he was elected to the assembly and in 1793 to the U.S. senate. However, following Federalist objections that he did not satisfy the terms of the Naturalisation Acts, he was refused his seat. Two years later he was elected as a member of Congress and became one of the more influential leaders of Jeffersonian republicanism during the 1790s. He also served as secretary of the treasury (1801–14). See Edwin G. Burrows, *Albert Gallatin and the Political Economy of Republicanism, 1761–1800* (New York, 1986).

Edmond Genêt (1763–1834) was the first minister of the French republic to the United States. On 16 May he arrived in Philadelphia from Charleston, where he had landed the previous 18 April. His undiplomatic criticisms of Washington's policy of neutrality between Britain and France drew loud criticisms from the contemporary Federalist administration and he was soon recalled. He later settled in the United States. See Harry Ammon, *The Genet Mission* (New York, 1973).

Henry Grattan (1746–1820) trained as a lawyer. He was elected as an M.P. in 1775 and became the leader of the **Reform Movement** in the Irish Parliament, the highpoints of which came in 1779 with the removal of the restrictions on the external trading capacity of Ireland (**"free trade"**) and more notably, in 1782, with the repeal of Poyning's Law, which had curbed the legislative competence of the Irish Parliament (**"legislative independence"**). However, what became known as **Grattan's Parliament** (1782–1800) was disappointing in carrying forward the reform agenda and led to the emergence of a more radical movement, culminating, firstly, in the rise of the United Irishmen, and secondly, in the abolition of the Irish Parliament altogether and the passage of the Act of Union in 1800. Between 1805 and 1820, Grattan sat in the united parliament as M.P. for Dublin; see R.B. McDowell, *Grattan: A Life* (Dublin, 2001); and Danny Mansergh, *Grattan's Failure: Parliamentary Opposition and the People of Ireland, 1779–1800* (Dublin, 2005).

Alexander Hamilton (1755–1804) was born in the West Indies but educated in New York. He served in the Continental army, becoming an aide-de-camp to George Washington and later (1782), a member of the Continental Congress, an influential member of the Constitutional Convention, and with Jay and Madison, an author of *The Federalist Papers* in which he argued the case for a strong central government. While Washington's secretary of the treasury (1789–95), Hamilton had an unenviable task but used his position to establish his preferred paradigm of government. After 1790, and more than any other "high" Federalist, he was the *bête noire* of the alternative Jeffersonian view of political behaviour and an unapologetic Anglophile. On 12 July 1804 he died following a duel with Jefferson's principal lieutenant in New York, Aaron Burr. See Jacob Cooke, *Alexander Hamilton* (New York, 1982).

The massacre at **Islandmagee** , or "the **Isle Mc-Gee**," followed the decision by the settler lords of south Antrim, Sir Edward Chichester and Sir Edward Conway, and the Catholic lord Antrim, whose estates lay further to the north, to arm their tenants following the outbreak of civil war in Ulster in October 1641. Islandmagee was a Catholic enclave which lay between the two spheres of influence and was attacked by the retainers of Chichester and Conway in what Raymond Gillespie has described as an act of "gratuitous violence." However, the numbers killed were between sixty and seventy rather than 4,000. I am grateful to Dr. Gillespie for this information. For the context of the attack, see Raymond Gillespie, "Destabilizing Ulster" in Breandán Mac Cuarta, ed., *Ulster 1641. Aspects of the Rising* (Belfast, 1993),107–22; the quotation is from page 113.

Israel Israel (1743–1822) was a tavern keeper who hosted meetings of various societies and networks which were committed to social and political reform. He was also an active member of the Democratic Society of Pennsylvania and served as its vice-president. His contest with Benjamin Morgan for election as one of Philadelphia's state senators (1797–88) became one of the most celebrated in the history of the eighteenth-century city. He was also a prominent Mason. See Richard G. Miller, *Philadelphia – The Federalist City: A Study of Urban Politics, 1789–1801* (Port Washington, 1976).

John Jay (1745–1829) was the first chief justice of the United States. In 1795 he was appointed as a special envoy to negotiate a treaty with Great Britain that is usually called after him. **Jay's Treaty** sought to "complete" the Treaty of Paris by addressing various points that were not settled in 1783. Among these were American compensation for debts incurred by British merchants, British compensation for the seizure of American ships and cargo, the evacuation of British posts on the western frontier, and the place of American trade in the British West Indies. However, because Jay also made a number of concessions on the status of neutral vessels as carriers of provisions and other goods, the treaty caused great controversy in the United States. See Samuel Flagg Bemis, *Jay's Treaty: A Study in Commerce and Diplomacy* (New Haven, 1962).

After being elected to the second Continental Congress (1775–56), **Thomas Jefferson** (1743–1826) was appointed to chair the committee to draw up the Declaration of Independence, after which he served in the Virginia legislature where he introduced his controversial bill on religious liberty. In 1779 he was elected governor but retired in 1781. In 1785 he succeeded Franklin as minister to France and remained there for four years. His observations on the unfolding French Revolution made him a life-long admirer of France, a sympathy which would bring him into celebrated clashes with Adams and Hamilton. He was appointed as Washington's secretary of state in 1789 but resigned in 1793. Although he lost the presidential election of 1796 by three electoral votes, he succeeded four years later, defeating the incumbent, John Adams. The second half of the 1790s saw an increasingly bitter division between him and the Federalists. This was typified by the evolution of **Jeffersonian republicanism**, a view of the polity which stressed states' rights over those of strong central government, as well as the integrity of the individual voter over that of a "natural leadership." See Merrill D. Peterson, *Thomas Jefferson and the New Nation* (New York, 1970), and *Adams and Jefferson: A Dialogue* (Oxford, 1978).

Rufus King (1755–1827) represented Massachusetts in the state general assembly (1783–5), Congress (1784–86), and the Constitutional Convention (1787). Following his marriage to the daughter of a wealthy New York merchant, he moved to his wife's native city in 1789 and represented his adopted state in the U.S. senate (1789–96). Between 1796 and 1803, he served as U.S. minister to Britain. Always a staunch Federalist, he was his party's vice-presidential candidate in both 1804 and 1808. After failing to get elected as the Federalist candidate for governor in 1807, he served as senator from New York between 1812 and 1824 and was the Federalists' candidate for the presidency in 1816. See Robert Ernst, *Rufus King. American Federalist* (Chapel Hill, 1968).

For the achievement of "**legislative independence**" in Ireland, see the note on **Henry Grattan**.

George Logan (1753–1802) was a grandson of **James Logan** and graduated as a medical doctor from the University of Edinburgh. After returning to Philadelphia, he was a member of the Pennsylvania legislature at various points during the 1780s and 1790s and also became well known as a writer and promoter of scientific agriculture and reform. In 1799 he went on a personal mission to France to defuse deteriorating relations between France and America. As a result, the Federalist government passed the so-called Logan Act which forbade such acts of private diplomacy. He later represented Pennsylvania in the U.S. senate (1801–7). See Frederick B. Tolles, *George Logan of Philadelphia* (New York, 1953),

James Logan (1674–1751) was born in Ulster but left for Scotland with his family in 1688. After settling in Bristol and befriending William Penn, he later accompanied Penn to his new colony in 1699 and remained the principal advisor to the Penn family until his death. In this capacity, he held most of the major provincial offices and while President of the Council, became the effective governor of the colony between 1736 and 1738. He also had immense influence on the disposal of land, later developing important interests on the frontier through his involvement in the fur trade. See Federick P. Tolles, *James Logan and the Culture of Provincial Pennsylvania* (Boston, 1957).

Matthew Lyon (1749–1822) emigrated from Ireland as a redemptioner in 1765, settling first in Connecticut and then, in a part of New Hampshire which later became known as Vermont. After serving in the Revolutionary militia, he was a member of the house of representatives between 1779 and 1783, when Vermont became a state, and thereafter, until 1796. Between 1797 and 1801, he also represented his state in Congress and was cited for contempt when he spat on Roger Griswold (F., Conn., 1795–1805) on 30 January 1798 after Griswold had questioned his record of service during the Revolutionary War. He was also arrested under the Alien and Sedition Acts for his criticisms of president Adams and was re-elected to Congress from his prison cell in 1799. In 1801 he emigrated to Kentucky which he also represented in Congress between 1803 and 1811. See Aleine Austin, *Matthew Lyon: "New Man" of the Democratic Revolution, 1749–1822* (University Park and London, 1981).

Blair McClenachan (d.1812) emigrated from Derry to Philadelphia. By the time of the American Revolution, he had already established a prosperous commercial house in his adopted city, specialising in transatlantic trade. He became vice-president of the Democratic Society of Pennsylvania and one of the earlier and most identifiable leaders of the emerging Jeffersonian movement in Philadelphia. In 1796 he was elected to Congress, having served in the state assembly since 1790. His election was a major milestone in the emergence of Jeffersonian republicanism as a political force in the nation's capital. See Miller, Schrier, Boling, and Doyle, eds., *Irish Immigrants in the Land Of Canaan*, 588–9, n.11.

Thomas McKean (1734–1817) was born of Presbyterian parents in Chester County, Pennsylvania. He was a member of the colonial, revolutionary, and independent legislatures of Delaware, the Stamp Act Congress (1765), one of the signatories of the Declaration of Independence, a member (1774–83) and President (1781) of the Continental Congress, and Speaker (1772–73) and President of Delaware (1777). He was a member of the Constitutional Convention. He was also involved in Pennsylvania politics, serving as chief justice (1777–99) until he was elected as its second governor (1799–1808) as the candidate of the Jeffersonian republicans, following Mifflin's retirement. See G.S. Rowe, *Thomas McKean: The Shaping of an American Republican* (Boulder, 1978).

William James McNeven (1763–1841) studied medicine in Prague and Vienna, where his uncle was a physician to the empress Maria Theresa. After returning to Ireland in 1784, he became involved in radical politics and a member of the Leinster Directory of the United Irishmen. As a result, he was arrested and interned in Fort George, Scotland. He later emigrated to New York where he practised as a doctor and became a leader of the city's Irish-American networks, most notably those which supported Daniel O'Connell. See Durey, *Transatlantic Radicals and the Early American Republic*.

James Madison (1751–1836) became a close associate of Thomas Jefferson during the 1770s and represented Virginia in the Continental Congress (1780–83). Together with Jay and Hamilton, he wrote *The Federalist Papers* which championed a federal constitution for the new republic. Following his election to Congress in 1789, he sponsored the Bill of Rights. He remained in the house of representatives until 1797, becoming one of the leading lights of Jeffersonian republicanism, a role which was recognised in 1801 when Jefferson appointed him as his secretary of state. In 1809 he succeeded Jefferson as fourth president of the United States (1809–17). See Drew R. McCoy, *The Last of the Fathers: James Madison and the Republican Legacy* (New York, 1989).

Although a Quaker, **Thomas Mifflin** (1744–1800) became one of the most ardent supporters of the American Revolution in his native state of Pennsylvania. He joined the continental army, rising to the rank of quarter master general. He was a member of the first Continental Congress and later, of the Constitutional Convention. He succeeded Franklin as President of the Executive Council in 1788 and following the adoption of the revised state constitution in 1790, he became the first governor of Pennsylvania, a post which he occupied for two terms until 1800. See Kenneth Rossman, *Thomas Mifflin and the Politics of the American Revolution* (Chapel Hill, 1952)

William Molyneux (1656–98) was educated at Trinity College, Dublin and the Middle Temple, London. Although he represented his old university in Parliament in 1692 and again, in 1695, his principal interest was the study of science. He also became an admirer of John Locke and in 1698 published his *Case of Ireland's Being Bound by Acts of Parliament in Ireland, Stated* which had a powerful influence on the cause of reform on both sides of the Atlantic. See J.G. Simms, *William Molyneux of Dublin (1656–1698)* (Dublin, 1982).

Frederick Augustus Muhlenberg (1750–1801) was born in Pennsylvania of German immigrants. A Lutheran minister, he was a member of the Continental Congress (1779–80), the Pennsylvania state legislature (1780–83), President of the Pennsylvania Constitutional Convention (1787), and a member of Congress (1789–97), where he was also Speaker between 1789 and 1791, and between 1793 and 1795. During his second term as Speaker, he gave the casting vote to pass Jay's treaty. See Oswald Seidensticker,

"Frederick Augustus Conrad Muhlenberg: speaker of the House of Representatives in the First Congress, 1789," *PMHB* xiii (1889), 184–206.

During the 1770s and 1780s, **Sir Edward Newenham** (1734–1814) had been an active member of the Volunteer and Reform Movements, the Irish expressions of "Patriotism." He sat as M.P. for Co. Dublin (1776–97) and corresponded with a number of the Founding Fathers, including Washington, Jefferson, and Franklin. See James Kelly, *Sir Edward Newenham, M.P., 1713–1814: Defender of the Protestant Constitution* (Dublin, 2003).

Having emigrated from England to New York, **Eleazer Oswald** (1750–95) was apprenticed to John Holt, the printer of the *New York Journal* as well as the state printer, whose daughter he also married in 1772. He took an active part in the Revolutionary War, notably at Fort Ticonderoga (May 1774), the attack on Canada, and the battle of Monmouth. Back in Philadelphia, he established the *Independent Gazetteer* on 13 April 1782. He also sided with the Anti-Federalists and became a vocal critic of Thomas McKean who was, at that time, a strong Federalist. In 1792 he went to France where he became involved in the Revolution and was sent to Ireland the same year on a reconnoitring mission. He died in Philadelphia. See Vernon O. Stumpf, "Colonel Eleazer Oswald: Politician and Editor" (Ph.D. dissertation, Duke University, 1970).

Patriotism is a contemporary term which was used on both sides of the British Atlantic to identify those who wanted to secure the legislative independence of their respective representative assemblies, free trade, and political reform. As such, it encapsulates movements in America as well as Ireland during the 1770s and 1780s. In the text, the word is capitalised to distinguish it from its more popular meaning of love of country.

The **Paxton Boys** were formed in response to a presumed lack of official interest in, and funding for, the protection of the frontier during Pontiac's Rebellion (1763–64). This rebellion, called after an Ottawa chief of that name, was a powerful Indian attempt to halt European expansion west of the Allegheny mountains. The "Boys" took their name from Paxton, a Scots-Irish frontier settlement, and blamed their defenceless position on an assembly that was dominated by Quakers. However, they vented their revenge by massacring a number of Susquehanna Indians who had settled in Lancaster County. Thereafter, some 1,500 of them marched on Philadelphia where Franklin promised that their grievances would be examined; see Dunbar, ed., *The Paxton Papers*.

After serving his native state of Massachusetts in a number of Revolutionary committees, and as a colonel and later (1780–85), quarter master general in the Continental army, **Timothy Pickering** (1745–1829) moved to Pennsylvania where he was a member of the state's Constitutional Convention (1789–90). After Washington was elected, he appointed Pickering as his postmaster general (1791), secretary of war on 2 January 1795 and later that year, secretary of state. His tenure of this post (until 1800) coincided with one of the most controversial periods of American foreign policy during which Pickering adopted a High Federalist antipathy to revolutionary France and an admiration for contemporary Britain. Like Rufus King, he adopted a tough attitude to those who were involved in the 1798 rebellion in Ireland and its supposed "agents" in the United States. See Gerald Clarfield, *Timothy Pickering and the American Republic* (Pittsburgh, 1980).

The **Proprietary party** was the political interest of Pennsylvania's governors, the Penn family, within the provincial legislature.

For the **rebellion of 1798**, see the note on **United Irishmen**, below.

For the **Reform Movement**, see the note on **Henry Grattan** above.

The **relief act of 1793** admitted Catholics to the franchise, provided they possessed a freehold worth at least forty shillings a year. See Thomas Bartlett, *The Fall and Rise of the Irish Nation: The Catholic Question, 1690–1830* (Dublin, 1992).

Dr. James Reynolds (d.1808) was a physician from Tyrone. He was also a leading Mason and member of the United Irishmen in Ulster and Dublin. He was imprisoned in March 1793 but later managed to flee to Philadelphia in 1794 after he had become implicated in plans for a French invasion of Ireland. In Philadelphia, Reynolds became the person most often associated with the United Irishmen in that city and as such, was subject to constant harassment and criticism from the city's Federalists. See Durey, *Transatlantic Radicals and the Early American Republic*.

For the **Rightboys**, see the note on the **Whiteboys** below.

Archibald Hamilton Rowan (1735–1834) was born to a family with an extensive estate in Co. Down. He went to America in 1771 as secretary to Charles Montague, the governor of South Carolina, but soon returned to England as a supporter of the colonial cause and with the friendship of the Rodney family in Delaware. He joined the United Irishmen in Dublin in 1792 and became its secretary. After the society's *Address* was published, he was fined and sentenced to two years in prison, from which he escaped, first to France, and thereafter, to America. He lived in Delaware until 1806 when he was pardoned and returned to Ireland. See Harold Nicholson, *The Desire to Please* (New York, 1943)

Benjamin Rush (1745–1813) graduated from the University of Edinburgh as a doctor in 1768. After returning to Philadelphia, he was elected to the Continental Congress in 1776, signed the Declaration of Independence, and attended the wounded during the Revolutionary War. However, he became better known as a writer in support of the Revolution as well as on public health issues, especially during the yellow fever epidemic of 1793 when, amid great controversy, he explained in his *An Account of the Bilious Remitting Fever, as It Appeared in the City of Philadelphia, in the Year 1793* (Philadelphia, 1794) that the outbreak was due to domestic rather than imported factors. See Donald D'Elia, *Benjamin Rush: Philosopher of the American Revolution* (Philadelphia, 1974).

The term **Scots-Irish** (or "Scotch-Irish") is usually applied to those of Scottish and Presbyterian origin who settled in Ulster during and after the plantation and thereafter, emigrated to America. While it is difficult to trace the history of the term, as early as 1730, a variant was used by Penn's Ulster-born secretary, James Logan, to refer to the Irish immigration of the 1720s which was largely of Ulster origin. In 1720 a petition from Ulster Presbyterians who had settled in Massachusetts objected to being called "*Irish people* when we so frequently ventured our all for the British crown and liberties against the Irish papists;" as quoted in Miller, Schrier, Boling, and Doyle, eds., *Irish Immigrants in the Land Of Canaan*, 264. These distinctions were formalised when the Scotch-Irish Congress was founded in 1889 "to preserve the history and perpetuate the achievements of the Scotch-Irish race in America." The predominantly Catholic American-Irish Historical Society was founded eight years later as a counterbalance. See Leroy V. Eid, "Irish, Scotch and Scotch-Irish, a Reconsideration," *JPH* cx (1986), 211–25; and Guy S. Klett, *Presbyterian in Colonial Pennsylvania* (Philadelphia, 1937).

Shillelah is a village in Co. Wicklow which was well-known for its oak forests. The name was later developed as a sobriquet for the distinctive sticks that were often used for purposes other than walking. I am grateful to Professor Tom Garvin for this information.

The **Society of the Cincinnati** was originally established in New York in May 1783 for officers who had fought in the Continental army. Similar societies were soon established in other states, including Pennsylvania. George Washington remained closely associated with the Cincinnati and served as the first President General between 1783 and 1799. See Minor Myers, Jr., *Liberty Without Anarchy: A History of the Society of the Cincinnati* (Charlottesville, 1983).

References to "**southern Ireland**" and "**southern ports**" have been taken to apply to those parts of Ireland outside Ulster where the passenger trade was not as well organised as it was in the northern province. As used in the text, the "southern ports" refer to the region's main ports: Dublin and Cork and, to a lesser extent, Limerick and Galway.

Although the term **ship** was colloquially applied to all vessels, it had a technical meaning also: a three-masted vessel whose square sails hung from wooden cross-laths on the fore and main masts. It also had a triangular fore-sail. During the course of the eighteenth century, the number of sails was sometimes increased in order to improve sailing time. The ship was the most familiar of all the vessels which travelled between Ireland and America.

For **snow**, see the note on the "**brig**" above.

John Swanwick (1740–98) was a merchant who became active in Jeffersonian politics in Philadelphia and represented the city in Congress between 1795 and 1798. See Ronald M. Baumann, "John Swanwick: Spokesman for 'Merchant-Republicanism' in Philadelphia, 1790–1798," *PMHB* xcvii (1973), 131–82.

James Napper Tandy (1740–1803) became a member of Dublin corporation as a representative of the guild of merchants. He soon became a fierce critic of municipal corruption and later, the first secretary of the Dublin Society of the United Irishmen. He also became involved with the Defenders. After being charged with sedition in 1793, he fled to Philadelphia and thereafter, to France (1798). After the failure of the French expeditionary fleet to land in Ireland, he fled to Hamburg, where he was arrested and returned to Ireland for trial. Although he was sentenced to death in 1801, this was later reprieved and was exiled to France where he later died. See Rupert Coughlan, *Napper Tandy* (Dublin, 1976).

Charles Thomson (1729–1824) was born in Maghera, Co. Derry and emigrated to America with his family in 1740. Following the death of his father just before his vessel reached America, Thomson was taken in and educated by Dr. Francis Alison. After his involvement with the Revolutionary cause, he was elected as secretary of the Continental Congress in September 1774 and remained in this post until 1789. See J. Edwin Hendricks, *Charles Thomson and the Making of a New Nation, 1729–1824* (London, 1979).

Theobald Wolfe Tone (1764–98) was born in Dublin and educated in Trinity College, Dublin. Although Protestant, he became secretary of the Catholic Committee in 1792 which had been set up to promote the repeal of the Penal Laws. During the 1790s he became the principal figure in Irish radicalism and the mentor of the United Irishmen. He also understood that republicanism was an international crusade and to this extent, he was prepared to negotiate for French assistance to realise his own domestic revolution in Ireland. With this in mind, he also fled to Philadelphia, from there to France, and returned to Ireland with the French expedition which was led by admiral Hoche in 1796. The expedition was not successful and Tone was arrested. However, before his prosecution for treason could be processed, he was found dead in his cell, as a result of poison. See Marianne Elliot, *Wolfe Tone: Prophet of Irish Independence* (New Haven, 1989).

Uriah Tracy (1755–1807) graduated as a lawyer from Yale university. After some years as a member of the state legislature, he represented Connecticut as a member of the U.S. house of representatives (1793–6) and senate (1796–1801).

The **United Irishmen** was a radical society founded in 1791, later (in 1795) becoming a secret revolutionary organisation committed to overthrowing the political establishment. Though attracting thousands of supporters from all religions, its **rebellion of 1798** was unsuccessful. It faded away following a more small-scale rebellion in 1803. See Marianne Elliott, *Partners in Revolution: The United Irishmen and France* (New Haven, 1982).

The late-eighteenth-century Irish **Volunteers** were a paramilitary movement which had been founded to protect the Irish establishment from possible invasion from France and Spain during the American Revolutionary War. However, it also developed a political programme which was not unlike that of the Sons of Liberty in America and through its network of regiments and companies, gave both organisational and military backing to the campaigns for "free trade" and the establishment of an independent Irish parliament. See P.D.H. Smyth, "The Volunteers and Parliament, 1779–84" in Thomas Bartlett and David Hayton, eds., *Penal Era and Golden Age: Essays in Irish History* (Belfast, 1979), 113–36.

George Washington (1732–99) was appointed as commander in chief of the Continental Army in June 1775. Following Cornwallis's surrender at Yorktown (1781) and the effective independence of the new American republic, he later chaired the Constitutional Convention which drafted a constitution for the new republic. As such, he was a natural and unanimous choice as first president of the United States (1789–97). Despite his insistence on neutrality in foreign affairs, as between the pro-French sympathies of Thomas Jefferson and the pro-British inclinations of Alexander Hamilton, Washington was perceived to be wary of France because events there suggested ways in which a fragile republic could be de-stabilised, if not unravelled. Although not everybody agreed, he was not actively criticised until the middle of the 1790s. For Washington, these criticisms were both unexpected and hurtful and he declined to run for re-election in 1796. See John E. Ferling, *The First of Men: A Life of George Washington* (Knoxville, 1989); and Don Higginbotham *et al.*, *George Washington Reconsidered* (Charlottesville, 2001).

The **Whiskey Rebellion** broke out in western Pennsylvania during the summer of 1794 in protest against a 25% tax which the Treasury had imposed on the sale of alcohol. It was quickly suppressed by a militia which Washington recruited and commanded for the purpose. See Thomas P. Slaughter, *The Whiskey Rebellion, Frontier Epilogue to the American Revolution* (New York, 1986).

The Whiteboys was a popular society that had been founded in the early-1760s to protest against enclosure as well as increasing rents and tithes. Although it had originated in Tipperary, it had spread to most of the counties of Munster and Leinster by 1785, by which time it was more usually known as the **Rightboy** movement and was also questioning many of the charges which were being imposed by the Catholic clergy. For the management and articulation of these protests, as well as their effects on the relationship between priest and parishioner, see Maurice J. Bric, "The Whiteboy Movement in Co. Tipperary, 1760–1780" in William Nolan, ed., *Tipperary: History and Society* (Dublin, 1985), 148–84; and Bric, "Priests, Parsons and Politics: The Rightboy Protest in Co. Cork, 1785–1788," *Past and Present* c (1983), 100–23.

Select Bibliography

PRIMARY SOURCES IN MANUSCRIPT

UNITED STATES OF AMERICA
Baltimore, Maryland. The Maryland Historical Society

David Baillie Warden Papers
Maryland Diocesan Archives. Vertical Files
William Wilson Account Book, 1788–95

Boston, Massachusetts. The Massachusetts Historical Society

Pickering Papers

New York. The New York Historical Society

Broadsides Collection
Rufus King Papers

New York. The New York Public Library

Gordon Lester Ford Collection. Transcripts of British State Papers, 1789–1801
James Monroe Papers, John Beckley to Monroe, 14 Dec. 1795
Charles Nisbet Correspondence, 1793–97

Philadelphia. The American Philosophical Society

Franklin Papers
Peale Papers

Philadelphia. The Historical Society of Pennsylvania

Letters of John Adams
American Miscellaneous Collection
William Bingham Collection
George Bryan Papers
Butler Papers
Cadwalader Collection
Caldwell Papers
Coates-Reynell Papers
Tench Coxe Papers (microfilm)
Ferdinand Dreer Autograph Collection
Henry Drinker Letterbooks
European Miscellaneous Collection
Benjamin Fuller Papers and Letterbooks
Thomas FitzSimons Papers

Edward Carey Gardiner Collection
Simon Gratz Autograph Collection
Greer Collection
Hawthorn & Kerr Letterbooks, 1789–1800
Hibernia Fire Company. Minutes
Hollingsworth Papers and Letterbooks
Irvine Papers
Lea & Febiger Collection (including Mathew Carey Papers)
List of Servants and Apprentices Bound and Assigned before James Hamilton, Mayor of
    Philadelphia, 1745–1746
Maria Dickinson Logan Collection
Logan Papers
John J. McCusker, "The Philadelphia Shipping Industry in the Eighteenth Century"
    (unpublished manuscript, 1973)
Thomas McKean Papers
Meredith Papers
Orr, Dunlope & Glenholme Papers
Richard Peters Papers
Philadelphia Custom House Papers
Port of Philadelphia Books
William Rawle Papers
Record of Indentures … October 3 1771 to October 5 1773
Thomas Rodney. Journal and Poetry, 1796–97
Letters of Robert Simpson, 1790–1807
Society Miscellaneous Collection
Society Small Collection
Society for Political Enquiries. Minutes
Stewart & Nesbitt Letterbooks, 1783–1803
Wallace Papers
Wayne Papers
Francis & John West Letterbooks, 1783–98
James Wilson Papers
Wister Family Papers, 1804
Yates Papers

Philadelphia. The Library Company of Philadelphia

Broadsides Collection
Dillwyn Papers

Philadelphia. The Free Library of Philadelphia

Carsan Collection

Princeton University, New Jersey. The Firestone Library

Broadsides Collection.

Washington, D.C. The Library of Congress

Davy & Carson Letterbooks

Thomas Jefferson Papers
Blair McClenachan Papers
Miscellaneous Manuscript Collection
James Monroe Papers
Pennsylvania Broadsides

Wilmington, Delaware. The Historical Society of Delaware

H.F. Browne Collection
John Dickinson Papers
John Fisher Papers
Rodney Papers
Rowan Papers

IRELAND

Belfast. The Public Record Office of Northern Ireland

Caldwell Papers and Memoirs
Custom and Excise Papers (Administration), 1791
Emigrant Letters:
    Brown Correspondence
    Denison Correspondence
    Dunlap Correspondence
    Johnson Correspondence
    Martin Correspondence
Archibald Hamilton Rowan. Parts of a Manuscript Diary
Correspondence between the United Irishmen and United Britons
Pelham Papers. Copies of Transcripts from Add. Mss., British Museum

Dublin. Library of the Royal Irish Academy

Memorial of Archibald Hamilton Rowan

Dublin. Library of Trinity College

Sirr Manuscripts

ENGLAND

London. National Archives

FO/4 and FO/5. Reports from Diplomatic Posts in the United States to the Foreign Office.

NEWSPAPERS

IRELAND

Belfast News-Letter
Cork Evening Post
Cork Hibernian Chronicle
Dublin Evening Post
(Dublin) *Faulkner's Dublin Journal*

(Kilkenny) *Finn's Leinster Journal*
(Dublin) *Freeman's Journal*
(Dublin) *Hibernian Journal*
Londonderry Journal
New Cork Evening Post
(Belfast) *Northern Star*
(Dublin) *Volunteer Evening Post*
(Dublin) *Volunteer Journal*
(Dublin) *Saunders News-Letter*

PHILADELPHIA

Aurora
Carey's Recorder
Dunlap's American Daily Advertiser
Gazette of the United States
General Advertiser
Independent Gazetteer
National Gazette
Pennsylvania Evening Herald
Pennsylvania Gazette
Pennsylvania Journal
Pennsylvania Packet
Pennsylvania Gazette
Porcupine's Gazette

OTHER

(New York) *Argus*
New York Daily Advertiser
New York Daily Gazette
New York Journal
New York Packet
(New York) *Time-Piece*
(Wilmington) *Delaware and Eastern Shore Advertiser*
(Wilmington) *Delaware Gazette*

PUBLISHED PRIMARY SOURCES

BROADSIDES

The following broadsides and pamphlets are listed in chronological order and unless otherwise noted, were published in Philadelphia. Most of them are also available in Evans, *Early American Imprints*. Series I (New Canaan, Ct., 2002).

LCP, a card, "Sir, As all Nations have for Seven Centuries ..." (1773).
Constitutional Society, "To the Citizens of Pennsylvania" (1780).
"A Freeholder"[Bryan], "To the Inhabitants of Pennsylvania" (1782).

"To the Citizens of Pennsylvania. Friends and Fellow-Citizens, The Majority of the House of Representatives of the Freemen of Pennsylvania beg leave to Address you ..." (1784).

LCP , Ab (1786)–13, "Articles of the Hibernia Fire-Company of Philadelphia" (1786).

HSP, "Philadelphia, September 6th, 1790. Gentlemen, Permit us ..." (1790).

"Hambden," To the Freemen of Philadelphia ... Oct. 9, 1792.

"Mentor," "To the Freemen of Philadelphia ..." (1792).

"A Federalist," "To the Independent Electors of Pennsylvania. Citizens and Friends ..." (1792).

LC, Pennsylvania Broadsides, "They Steer to Liberty's Shore" (August 1793).

Princeton University Library, Am.11,613, "(Philadelphia) Society for the Information and Assistance of Emigrants ... CONSTITUTION" (1 April 1795).

"Society for the Institution and Support of First Day or Sunday Schools, in the City of Philadelphia, and the Districts of Southwark and the Northern-Liberties" (1796).

HSP, "Another of the People," "To the Inhabitants of Germantown" (1798).

LCP, Ab (1798)–1, "At a Meeting of a Number of Citizens ... February 12" (1798).

Fellows and Fellow Citizens ... Philadelphia" (21 February 1798).

LCP, Ab (1798)–5, "A Dutch Man," "To the Inhabitants of the County of Philadelphia ... February 21st 1798."

LCP, Ab (1798)–8, "Opinion of Chief Justice McKean." (1798).

[William Cobbett], "The Detection of Bache ... June 18, 1798."

LCP, Ab (1798)–9, "Fellow Citizens ... " (Carlisle, 29 September 1798).

LCP, Ab (1798)–10, "A Pennsylvanian," "Friends and Fellow Citizens ... February 21st 1798."

LCP, Ab (1798)–25, "One of the People," "To the Friends of Israel Israel ... February 22, 1798."

Mathew Carey, "To the Public ... It is Difficult to Account ... 5 February 1799."

LC, Pennsylvania Broadsides, "The Plea of Erin, or, The Case of the Natives of Ireland in the United States, Fairly Displayed" (1799).

"May 27th, 1799. Sir, Deeply Interested in the Approaching Election ... Levi Hollingsworth."

"Franklin," "To the Citizens if the County of Philadelphia. Friends and Fellow Citizens ... James Ross" (1799).

LCP, Ab-1799–3, "To the Electors of Pennsylvania ... Alpha ... 3 October 1799."

"To the Electors of Pennsylvania. Take Your Choice! Thomas McKean – or – James Ross" (1799).

PUBLISHED PRIMARY SOURCES

PAMPHLETS (in chronological order, all of which were published in Philadelphia unless otherwise noted)

"Roscommon," *To the Author of Those Intelligencers printed at Dublin* (New York, 1733).

An Address to the Rev. Dr. Alison, the Rev. Mr. Ewing, &c. Being a Vindication of the Quakers (1764).

An Address to the Freeholders and Inhabitants of the Province of Pennsylvania. In Answer ro a Paper Called the Plain Dealer (1764).

Remarks upon the Delineated Presbyterian ... Philo-Veritatis (1764).

Remarks on the Quaker Unmask'd (1764).

[Isaac Hunt], *No. IV. A Continuation of the Exercises, in Scurrility Hall* (1765).

The Constitution and Rules of the St. Andrew's Society in Philadelphia (1769).

Corporation for the Relief of the Widows and Children of Clergymen, in the Communion of the Church of England in America (1773).

Sons of St. George, Philadelphia. Rules and Constitutions of the Society of Englishmen (1774).

[Joseph Galloway], *Historical and Political Reflections on the Rise and Progress of the American Rebellion* (London, 1780).

[Benjamin Rush], *Considerations Upon the Present Test-Law of Pennsylvania: Addressed to the Legislature and Freemen of the State of Pennsylvania* (1784).

[Benjamin Bush], *Considerations upon the Present Test Law* (1785).

Adopted Sons of Pennsylvania. Principles, Articles and Regulations ... of ... (1786).

[Matthew Carey], *The Plagi-Scurriliad: A Hudibrastic Poem. Dedicated to Colonel Eleazer Oswald* (1786).

The Constitution of the Pennsylvania Society, for the Abolition of Slavery ... Begun in the year 1774 (1787).

Tench Coxe, *An Address to an Assembly of the Friends of American Manufactures* (1787).

Rules and Regulations of the Society for Political Enquiries (1787).

Society of the Philadelphia Society, for Alleviating the Miseries of Public Prisons (1787).

Rules and Constitutions of the Society of the Sons of St. George ... (new ed., 1788).

[Benjamin Rush], *Information to Europeans who are Disposed to Migrate to the United States. In a Letter from a Citizen of Pennsylvania, to his Friend in Great Britain* (1790).

Charles Plowden, *A Short Account of the Establishment of the New See of Baltimore* (1791).

St. Andrew's Society of Philadelphia. The Constitution and Rules of ... (1791).

[Edmund Jennings Randolph], *Germanicus* (1794).

[William Cobbett], *A Bone to Gnaw, For the Democrats ... By Peter Porcupine* (1795).

—— *A Little Plain English ... By Peter Porcupine* (1795).

Samuel Latham Mitchell, *The Life, Exploits, and Precepts of Tammany* (New York, 1795).

Proceedings of the Society of the United Irishmen of Dublin (Philadelphia, 1795).

Benjamin Schultz, *Oration Delivered before the Mosheimian Society on July 23rd, 1795* (1795).

John Swanwick, *A Rub from Snub, or a Cursory Analytical Epistle Addressed to Peter Porcupine* (1795).

[James Carey], *A Pill for Porcupine* (1796).

Matthew Carey, *Miscellaneous Trifles* (1796).

—— *To the Public* (1796).

[William Cobbett], *History of the American Jacobins* (1796).

—— *A New Year's Gift to the Democrats* (1796).

—— *The Political Censor, or Monthly Review* (1796).

—— *A Kick for a Bite* (1796).

—— *The Life and Adventures of Peter Porcupine* (1796).

—— *Tit for Tat; or, a Purge for a Pill ... By Dick Retort* (1796).

[A. Henderson], *The Adventures of a Porcupine* (1796).

Paddy's Resource: being a Select Collection of Original and Modern Patriotic Songs (1796).

[John Swanwick], *A Roaster ... as a Brief Reply to Peter Porcupine ... By Sim Sanscolotte* (1796).

—— *British Honour and Humanity* (1796).

Jasper Wright [William Duane], *A Letter to George Washington* (1796).

Morgan J. Rhees, *The Good Samaritan. An Oration delivered on Sunday Evening, May 22nd, 1796, in behalf of the Philadelphia Society for the Information and Assistance of persons Emigrating from Foreign Countries* (1796).

[John Swanwick], *A Roaster; or, A Check to the Progress of Political Blasphemy. Intended as a Brief Reply to Peter Porcupine* (1796).

Philadelphia Society for the Information and Assistance of Persons Emigrating from Foreign Countries. The Act of Incorporation, Constitution, and By-Laws of the ... (1797).

[William Cobbett], *The Democratic Judge ... by Peter Porcupine* (1798).

—— *Detection of a Conspiracy, formed by the United Irishmen with the evident intention of Aiding the Tyrants of France in Subverting the Government of the United States of America* (6 May 1798).

John Robinson, *Proofs of a Conspiracy against all the Religions and Governments of Europe* ... (New York, 1798).

Uriah Tracy, *Reflections on Monroe's View* (1798).

"A Pennsylvanian," *To the Electors of Pennsylvania. When a Candidate* ... (1799).

Address to the Republicans of Pennsylvania ... Peter Muhlenberg ... 7 August 1799 (1799).

Address to the Freemen of Pennsylvania from the Committee of Correspondence for the City of Pennsylvania, Appointed by the Friends of James Ross (Germantown, Pa., 1799).

"An American," *To the Independent Electors of Pennsylvania* (1799).

Thomas Ledlie Birch, *Letter from an Irish Migrant* .... (1799).

John Daly Burk, *History of the Late War in Ireland* (1799).

Mathew Carey, *A Plumb Pudding for the Humane, Chaste, Valiant, Enlightened Peter Porcupine* (1799).

—— *The Porcupiniad. A Hudibrastic Poem in Three Cantos. Addressed to William Cobbett Canto I* (1799).

—— *The Porcupiniad. A Hudibrastic Poem in Three Cantos. Addressed to William Cobbett Canto II & III* (1799).

Duc de la Rochefoucault-Liancourt, *Travels through the United States of North America* 2 vols. (London, 1799).

William Duane, *A Report of the Extraordinary Transactions which Took Place at Philadelphia, in February 1799, in Consequence of a Memorial from Certain Natives of Ireland to Congress, Praying a Repeal of the Alien Bill* (1799).

Report of the Committee of Secrecy of the House of Commons of Great Britain (Dublin, 1799).

Scots Thistle Society of Philadelphia. Constitution of the ... Instituted November 30, 1796 (1799).

Welsh Society of Pennsylvania. Constitution and Rules of the ... (Mount Holly, 1799).

Isaac Weld, *Travels through the States of North America ... during the Years 1795, 1796, and 1797* (London, 1799).

William Cobbett, *Porcupine's Works* 12 vols. (London, 1801).

EDITED PRIMARY SOURCES

Charles Francis Adams, ed., *The Works of John Adams* 10 vols. (Boston, 1850–56).

Thomas Bartlett, ed., *Life of Theobald Wolfe Tone: Memoirs, Journals and Political Writings, Compiled and Arranged by William T.W. Tone, 1826* (Dublin, 1998).

Albert E. Bergh and Andrew A. Lipscomb, eds., *The Writings of Thomas Jefferson* 20 vols. (Washington, D.C., 1905).

John Bigelow, ed., *The Complete Works of Benjamin Franklin* 10 vols. (New York, 1887–1904).

Julian P. Boyd *et al.*, eds., *The Papers of Thomas Jefferson* 31 vols. (Princeton, 1950–2004).

William H. Browne *et al.*, *Archives of Maryland* 68 vols. (Baltimore, 1883–1959).

Lyman H. Butterfield, ed., *Letters of Benjamin Rush* 2 vols. (Princeton, 1951).

Mathew Carey, *Autobiography of Mathew Carey* (Brooklyn, 1942).

George W. Conner, ed., *The Autobiography of Benjamin Rush* (Princeton, 1948).

A.C. Davies, ed., "'As Good a Country as Any Man Needs to Dwell In:' Letters from a Scotch-Irish Immigrant in Pennsylvania, 1766, 1767, and 1784," *PH* c (1983), 313–22.

Durand Echeverria, ed., J.P. de Warville, *New Travels in the United States of America, 1788* (Cambridge, Mass., 1964).

John Dunbar, ed., *The Paxton Boys* (The Hague, 1957).

William H. Drummond, ed., *The Autobiography of Archibald Hamilton Rowan* (repr. Shannon, 1972).

Jonathan Elliot, ed., *Debates on the Adoption of the Federal Constitution in the Convention held at Philadelphia* (Philadelphia, 1861).

John Tracy Ellis, ed. *Documents of American Catholic History* (Milwaukee, 1956).

Thomas Addis Emmet, *Memoir of Thomas Addis and Robert Emmet* 2 vols. (New York, 1915).

John S. Ezell, ed., and Judson P. Wood, trans., *The New Democracy in America. Travels of Francisco de Miranda in the United States, 1783–84* (Norman, 1963).

John C. Fitzpatrick ed., *The Writings of George Washington* 39 vols. (repr. Washington, D.C., 1931–44).

Philip S. Foner, ed., *Democratic-Republican Societies, 1790–1800: A Documentary Sourcebook of Constitutions, Declarations, Addresses, Resolutions, and Toasts* (Westport, 1976).

Paul Leicester Ford, ed., *The Writings of Thomas Jefferson* 10 vols. (New York, 1895).

Worthington C. Ford, ed., *The Writings of George Washington* 14 vols. (New York, 1889–93).

—— ed., *Journals of the Continental Congress, 1774–1789* 34 vols. (Washington, D.C., 1904–37).

Joseph Gales and W.W. Seaton, eds., *The Debates and Proceedings of the Congress of the United States* 42 vols. (Washington, 1834–56).

Madison Grant and Charles Stewart Davidson, eds., *The Founders of the Republic on Immigration, Naturalization and Aliens* (New York, 1928).

J. Franklin Jameson, ed., "Letters of Phineas Bond, British Consul at Philadelphia, to the Foreign Office of Great Britain, 1787, 1788, 1789," *AHR* i (1896) and ii (1897).

Charles R. King, ed., *The Life and Correspondence of Rufus King, Comprising His Letters, Private and Official, His Public documents, and His Speeches* 6 vols. (New York, 1894–1900).

Leonard W. Labaree *et al.*, eds., *The Papers of Benjamin Franklin* 37 vols. (New Haven, 1959–).

Ludwig Lewisohn, ed., J. Hector de St. John Crèvecoeur, *Letters from An American Farmer* (Garden City, 1904).

Henry Cabot Lodge, ed., *The Works of Alexander Hamilton* 12 vols. (New York, 1904).

Edgar S. Maclay, ed. *Journal of William Maclay* (New York, 1890).

Kerby A. Miller, Arnold Schrier, Bruce D. Boling and David N. Doyle, eds., *Irish Immigrants in the Land of Canaan: Letters and Memoirs from Colonial and Revolutionary America, 1675–1815* (Oxford, 2003).

James T. Mitchell and Henry Flanders, comps., *Statutes at Large of Pennsylvania from 1682 to 1801* 17 vols. (Harrisburg, 1896–1915).

Howard C. Rice, trans. and introd., Marquis de Chastellux, *Travels in North America in the Years 1780, 1781 and 1782* (Williamsburg, 1971).

James D. Richardson, ed., *A Compilation of the Messages and Papers of the Presidents, 1789–1897* 10 vols. (Washington, 1896–99).

J.G. Simms, ed., William Molyneux, *Case of Ireland Being Bound by Acts of Parliament in England Stated* (Dublin, 1977).

Albert Henry Smyth, ed., *The Writings of Benjamin Franklin* 10 vols. (New York, 1907).

Jared Sparks, ed., *The Works of Benjamin Franklin* 10 vols. (Boston, 1836–40).

—— ed., *The Writings of George Washington* 12 vols. (Boston, 1834–47).

L.F. Stock, ed., *Proceedings and Debates of the British Parliament Respecting North America* 5 vols. (Washington, D.C., 1924–41).

Earl Gregg Swem, ed., *Letter of James Murray of New York to Rev. Baptist Boyd of Co. Tyrone, Ireland* (Metuchen, 1925).

Harold C. Syrett *et al.*, eds., *The Papers of Alexander Hamilton* 27 vols. (New York, 1961–87).

Thomas M. Truxes, ed., *Letterbook of Greg & Cunningham 1756–57* (Oxford, 2001).

Richard Walsh, ed., *The Mind and Spirit of Early America: Sources in American History, 1607–1789* (New York, 1969).

SELECTED SECONDARY SOURCES

Given the various subject areas and regions on which this study touches, it would be impossible to give a comprehensive list here of the books and articles which have influenced it. The following is a selective list.

1. For *Late-Eighteenth-Century Ireland*, many of the relevant readings have been listed in the following two bibliographies: David Dickson, "Bibliography" in T.W. Moody and W.E. Vaughan, eds., *Eighteenth Century Ireland, 1691–1800* (Oxford, 1986) vol. iv of *A New History of Ireland* 9 vols. (Oxford, 1976–2005), 713–95; and Kevin Whelan, "Bibliography. A Check-List of Publications on the 1790s, the United Irishmen and the 1798 Rebellion, 1900–2002" in Thomas Bartlett, David Dickson, Dáire Keogh and Kevin Whelan, eds., *1798: A Bicentenary Perspective* (Dublin, 2003), 659–724. The following publications are those which are either not listed in these bibliographies or are recognised because of their importance for this study.

Bartlett, Dickson, Keogh, and Whelan, eds., *1798: A Bicentenary Perspective* includes important articles by those who have defined the interpretation of the period. See also the following two collections: Hugh Gough and David Dickson, eds., *Ireland and the French Revolution* (Dublin, 1990); and David Dickson, Dáire Keogh and Kevin Whelan, eds., *The United Irishmen, Republicanism, Radicalism and Rebellion* (Dublin, 1993). For the debates on reform and other constitutional issues, see James Kelly, *Prelude to Union: Anglo-Irish Politics in the 1780s* (Cork, 1992); R.B. McDowell, *Ireland in the Age of Imperialism and Revolution* (Oxford, 1979); and Neil Longley York, *Neither Kingdom nor Nation: The Irish Quest for Constitutional Rights, 1698–1800* (Washington, 1994). For the evolution of the "French disease" in Ireland and, in particular, how it influenced the United Irishmen, see Rosamund Jacob, *The Rise of the United Irishmen, 1791–4* (London, 1937); Marianne Elliott, *Wolfe Tone: Prophet of Irish Independence* (New Haven, 1989); Dáire Keogh, *'The French Disease': The Catholic Church and Irish Radicalism, 1790–1800* (Dublin, 1993); A.T.Q. Stewart, *A Deeper Silence: The Hidden Origins of the United Irishmen* (Belfast, 1998); and Kevin Whelan, *The Tree of Liberty: Radicalism, Catholicism and the Construction of Irish Identity: 1760–1830* (Cork and Notre Dame, 1998). For the tradition of popular protest in Ireland before 1791, see my own "Priests, Parsons and Politics: the Rightboy Movement in Co. Cork, 1785–8," *Past and Present* c (Aug. 1983), 100–23 and "The Whiteboy Movement, 1760–80" in William Nolan, ed., *Tipperary: History and Society* (Dublin, 1985), 148–84. For an overview of these and other movements, see Jim Smyth, *The Men of No Property: Irish Radicals and Popular Politics in the Late Eighteenth Century* (Basingstoke, 1992) and, for the 1790s, Marianne Elliott, *Partners in Revolution: The United Irishmen and France* (New Haven and London, 1982) which, despite its title, contains a good analysis of the Defenders. See also Nancy J. Curtin, *The United Irishmen: Popular Politics in Ulster and Dublin 1791–1798* (New York and Oxford, 1998). For the society's social agenda as an aspect of its own commitment to reform, as opposed to one which owed its *raison d'être* to the Defenders, see James Quinn, "The United Irishmen and Social Reform," *IHS* xxxi (1998), 188–201. David Dickson, *Old World Colony: Cork and South Munster 1630–1830* (Cork, 2005) gives a superb account of the place of one important Irish port in terms of its own urban structures, hinterland, and external connections. James Kelly's biography of *Sir Edward Newenham, M.P., 1713–1814: Defender of the Protestant Constitution* (Dublin, 2003) outlines one parliamentarian's commitment to reform in Ireland while for an earlier period, Nicholas Canny, *Making Ireland British* (Oxford, 2001) examines the clash of cultures and solutions as Ireland was subjected to the new regime of what would become the first British Empire.

2. For **Ireland and the wider world**, see Nicholas Canny, ed., *The Origins of Empire*, vol. i of William Roger Louis, editor-in-chief, *Oxford History of the British Empire* 5 vols. (Oxford, 1998–9). This work cites most of the major secondary sources for the study of Ireland and the first British Empire during the sixteenth and seventeenth centuries, including his own extensive writings on the topic, as well as those of David B. Quinn and others. See also Canny's "Fashioning a British Atlantic World" in Canny, Joe Illick and Gary B. Nash, eds., *Empire, Society, and Labor: Essays in Honor of Richard S. Dunn*, special supplement to *PH*, lxix (1997), 6–45. For the later connections between the two sides of the Atlantic during **the period of the American Revolution**, see Vincent Morley, *Irish Opinion and the American Revolution, 1760–1783* (Cambridge, 2002) which contains an extensive bibliography of the relevant secondary literature published until then. See also my own "Ireland, America and the Reassessment of a Special Relationship, 1760–1783," *Eighteenth-Century Ireland* xi (1996), 88–119; and Maurice O'Connell, *Irish Politics and Social Conflict in the Age of the American Revolution* (Philadelphia, 1965). For the commercial connections of the period, see Norman E. Gamble, "The Business Community and the Trade of Belfast, 1767–1800" (Ph.D. dissertation, Trinity College, Dublin, 1978); R.C. Nash, "Irish Atlantic Trade in the Seventeenth and Eighteenth Centuries," *WMQ* xlvii (1985), 229–56; and Thomas M. Truxes, *Irish-American Trade, 1660–1783* (New York, 1988). For context, see the authoritative John J. McCusker and Russell R. Menard, *The Economy of British America, 1607–1789* (Chapel Hill, 1985).

David Noel Doyle, *Ireland, Irishmen and Revolutionary America, 1760–1820* (Cork and Dublin, 1981) has also examined this period as well as the years of the early American republic. For the 1790s see Marianne Elliott, *Partners in Revolution: The United Irishmen and France* (New Haven and London, 1982) as well as the following which focus on contemporary America: Richard Twomey, *Jacobins and Jeffersonians: Anglo-American Radicalism in the United States, 1790–1820* (New York, 1989); Michael Durey, *Transatlantic Radicals and the Early American Republic* (Lawrence, Kansas, 1997); and David A. Wilson, *United Irishmen, United States: Immigrant Radicals in the Early Republic* (Dublin, 1998). See also my own "The United Irishmen, International Republicanism and the Definition of the Polity in the United States of America, 1791–1800" in *Proceedings of the Royal Irish Academy* civ (2004), 81–106 and "The Irish Immigrant and the Broadening of the Polity in Philadelphia, 1790–1800" in

Eliga H. Gould and Peter S. Onuf, eds., *Empire and Nation: The American Revolution in the Atlantic World* (Charlottesville, 2005), 159–77.

For the links which bound America and Ireland through **emigration**, see especially R.J. Dickson, *Ulster Emigration to Colonial America, 1718–1785* (London, 1966); Audrey Lockhart, *Some Aspects of Emigration from Ireland to the North American Colonies between 1660 and 1775* (New York, 1976); David Doyle, *Ireland, Irishmen and Revolutionary America*; Bernard Bailyn, *Voyagers to the West: A Passage in the Peopling of America on the Eve of the American Revolution* (New York, 1986); Aaron Fogleman "Migrations to the Thirteen British North American Colonies, 1770–1775: New Estimates," *JIntH* xxii, no.4 (1992), Leroy V. Eid, "'No Freight Paid So Well:' Irish Emigration to Pennsylvania on the Eve of the American Revolution," *Eire-Ireland* xxvii (1993); Marianne Wokeck, *Trade in Strangers: The Beginnings of Mass Migration to North America* (University Park, 1999) as well as my own "Patterns of Irish Emigration to America, 1783–1800" in Kevin Kenny, ed., *New Directions in Irish-American History* (Madison, 2003), 17–35. Maldwyn A. Jones, "Ulster Emigration, 1783–1815" in E.R.R. Green, ed., *Essays in Scotch-Irish History* (New York, 1969) also deals with the period after 1776. See also Miller, Schrier, Boling and Doyle, eds., *Irish Immigrants in the Land of Canaan* which, in addition to compiling several letters and memoirs on Irish emigration, provides a critical analysis of that emigration as well as important observations on the historiography of the passenger flow. For the convict trade, the more important works include Roger Ekirch, *Bound for America: The Transportation of British Convicts to the Colonies, 1718–1775* (Oxford, 1987) as well as the older, but still useful Abbot Emerson Smith, *Colonists in Bondage. White Servitude and Convict Labor in America* (Chapel Hill, 1947). For recent commentary on the Irish convict trade, see Patrick Fitzgerald, "A Sentence to Sail: The Transportation of Irish Convicts to Colonial America in the Eighteenth Century" in Patrick Fitzgerald and Steve Ickringill, eds., *Atlantic Crossroads: Historical Connections between Scotland, Ulster and North America* (Newtownards, Irl., 2001); and James Kelly, "Transportation from Ireland to North America, 1703–1789" in David Dickson and Cormac Ó Gráda, eds., *Refiguring Ireland: Essays in Honour of L.M. Cullen* (Dublin, 2003), 112–35.

The Scots-Irish dimension of these movements of people are discussed in a number of well-known works by, among others, Wayland F. Dunaway (1944) and James G. Leyburn (1962). Guy S. Klett, *Presbyterians in Colonial Pennsylvania* (Philadelphia, 1937) and "The Presbyterian Church and the Scotch-Irish on the Pennsylvania Colonial Frontier," *PH* viii (1941), focus on the major American destination for Irish emigrants during the eighteenth century. For general commentary, see the more recent H. Tyler Blethen and Curtis W. Wood, eds., *Ulster and North America* (Tuscaloosa, 1997); and especially Patrick Griffin, *The People with No Name: Ireland's Ulster Scots, America's Scots Irish, and the Creation of a British Atlantic World, 1689–1764* (Princeton, 2001). For the status of immigrants in eighteenth-century America, see Chilton Williamson, *American Suffrage: From Property to Democracy, 1760–1860* (Princeton, 1968); and E.P. Hutchinson, *Legislative History of American Immigration Policy 1798–1965* (Philadelphia, 1981). Marilyn C. Baseler, *"Asylum for Mankind:" America 1607–1800* (Ithaca and London, 1998) is indispensable to understanding the evolution of official attitudes to emigrants and emigration before 1800 as is Sally Schwartz, *"A Mixed Multitude." The Struggle for Toleration in Colonial Pennsylvania* (New York, 1987) for colonial Pennsylvania.

3. The literature of the issues, policies and personalities which shaped this period at *Federal level* is voluminous. For the *period before 1790*, see the following, among others, by Jack P.

Greene: *Peripheries and Center: Constitutional Development in the Extended Politics of the British Empire and the United States, 1607–1788* (Athens, 1986), *Intellectual Construction of America: Exceptionalism and Identity from 1492 to 1800* (Chapel Hill, 1993), *Negotiated Authorities: Essays in Colonial Political and Constitutional History* (Charlottesville, 1994), and "Empire and Identity from the Glorious Revolution to the American Revolution" in Peter Marshall, ed., *The Eighteenth Century* (Oxford, 1998o. See also Gordon Wood, *The Creation of the American Republic, 1776–1787* (Chapel Hill, 1989).

For the *period after 1788*, much of the relevant literature is cited in Stanley Elkins's and Eric McKittrick's magisterial *The Age of Federalism* (New York and Oxford, 1993). The following historiographical essays are also useful: Robert E. Shalope, "Towards a Republican Synthesis: the Emergence of an Understanding of Republicanism in American Historiography," *WMQ* xxix (1972), 49–80; and Peter S. Onuf, "Reflections on the Founding: Constitutional Historiography in Bicentennial Perspective," *WMQ* xxxxvi (1989), 341–75. For the ways in which republicanism evolved during the 1790s, see Joyce Appleby, *Capitalism and a New Social Order: The Republican Vision of the 1790s* (New York, 1984) and *Inheriting the Revolution: The First Generation of Americans* (Cambridge, Mass., and London, 2000). For a wider umbrella, see Isaac Kramnick. *Republicanism and Bourgeois Radicalism: Political Ideology in Late Eighteenth-Century England and America* (Ithaca, 1990).

The literature on the evolution of "party political" ideologies is vast. For a useful overview, see Linda K. Kerber, *Federalists in Dissent: Imagery and Ideology in Jeffersonian America* (Ithaca, 1970); Richard J. Buel, Jr., *Securing the Revolution: Ideology in American Politics, 1789–1815* (Ithaca, 1972); and Robert Shalope, *The Roots of Democracy: American Thought and Culture, 1760–1800* (Boston, 1990). For a closer focus on the Jeffersonian movement, see Lance Banning, *The Jeffersonian Persuasion: Evolution of a Party Ideology* (Ithaca, N.Y., 1978); and Noble E. Cunningham, Jr., *The Jeffersonian Republicans: The Formation of Party Organization, 1789–1801* (Chapel Hill, 957). For the Federalists, see Ben-Atar and Barbara B. Oberg, eds., *Federalists Reconsidered* (Charlottesville and London, 1998); and the older Manning Dauer, *The Adams Federalists* (Baltimore, 1953) as well as the biographies of Robert Ernst, *Rufus King: American Federalist* (Chapel Hill, 1968); and David McCullough, *John Adams* (New York, 2001)

Historians do not agree on the extent to which "party" processes were distinctive and as a result, there are differing views on the organisational expressions of "party." See William N. Chambers, *Political Parties in a New Nation: The American Experience, 1776–1809* (New York, 1963); Joseph Charles, *The Origins of the American Party System* (Williamsburg, 1956); William N. Chambers, *Political Parties in a New Nation: The American Experience, 1776–1800* (New York, 1963); Richard Hofstadter, *The Idea of a Party System: The Rise of Legitimate Opposition in the United States 1780–1840* (Berkeley, 1969); Roy Nichols, *The Invention of American Political Parties* (New York, 1967); John Zvesper, *Political Philosophy and Rhetoric: A Study of the Origins of American Party Politics* (New York, 1977); and James Roger Sharp, *American Politics in the Early Republic: The New Nation in Crisis* (New Haven and London, 1993). In *The Revolution of 1800* (New York, 1974), Daniel Sisson draws on the opinions and writings of the Founding Fathers in his analysis of the evolution of "party."

Alexander DeConde, *The Quasi-War: Politics and Diplomacy of the Undeclared War with France, 1797–1801* (New York, 1966); Albert H. Bowman, *The Struggle for Neutrality: Franco-American Diplomacy during the Federalist Era* (Knoxville, 1974); and Matthew Q. Dawson, *Partisanship and the Birth of America's Second Party, 1796–1800: Stop the Wheels of Government* (Westport, 2000) review the issues of contemporary foreign policy which had such an impact on the domestic politics of the period. For specific topics, see Harry Ammon,

The Genet Mission (New York, 1973); William Stinchcombe, *the XYZ Affair* (Westport, 1981) and for Jay's treaty and its aftermath, see Jerald A. Combs, *The Jay Treaty. Political Battleground of the Founding Fathers* (Berkeley, 1970); and Bradford Perkins, *The First Rapprochement: England and the United States, 1795–1805* (Philadelphia, 1985). More recent literature is reviewed in Todd Estes, "Shaping the Politics of Public Opinion: Federalists and the Jay Treaty Debate," *Journal of the Early Republic* xx (2000), 393–442.

For the wider context in which "foreign interests" were influencing contemporary views, see Marshall Smelser, "The Jacobin Phrenzy: The Menace of Monarchy, Plutocracy and Anglophobia, 1789–1798," *Review of Politics* xxi (1959), 239–58; John Howe, "Republican Thought and the Political Violence of the 1790s," *AQ* xix (1967), 147–65; John C. Miller, *Crisis in Freedom. The Alien and Sedition Acts* (Boston, 1951); and especially, James Morton Smith, *Freedom's Fetters: The Alien and Sedition Laws and American Civil Liberties* (Ithaca, 1956). In so far as these laws were as much about "defining" America, as about curtailing a supposed foreign influence in the United States, see James W. Caesar, *Reconstructing America: The Symbol of America in Modern Thought* (New Haven, 1997); Edward Countryman, *Americans. A Collision of Histories* (New York, 1996); and Drew R. McCoy, *The Elusive Republic. Political Economy in Jeffersonian America* (Chapel Hill, 1980).

4. For *Pennsylvania politics prior to 1790*, the citations and bibliographies in Douglas M. Arnold, *A Republican Revolution. Ideology and Politics in Pennsylvania, 1776–1790* (New York and London, 1989); Alan Tully, *Forming American Politics: Ideals, Interests, and Institutions in Colonial New York and Pennsylvania* (Baltimore, 1994); and Owen S. Ireland, *Religion, Ethnicity, and Politics. Ratifying the Constitution in Pennsylvania* (University Park, 1995) list the more important works, including, in the case of the last two authors, their own influential articles as well as the work of J. Paul Selsam (1936), Robert Brunhouse (1942), Alfred Theodore Thayer (1953), Dietmar Rothermund (1961), David F. Hawke (1961), William S. Hanna (1964), Paul W. Conner (1965), James H. Hutson (1972), Benjamin H. Newcomb (1972), Stephen E. Lucas (1976), and Richard Bauman (1981). The most recent article on the Paxton Boys is Peter A. Butzin, "Politics, Presbyterians and the Paxton Riots, 1763–4," *JPrH* li (1973), 70–84.

For revolutionary Pennsylvania, see also Richard Alan Ryerson, *The Revolution is Now Begun: The Radical Committees of Philadelphia, 1765–1776* (Philadelphia, 1978). The same author's "Republican Theory and Partisan Reality in Revolutionary Pennsylvania: Toward a New View of the Constitutionalist Party" in Ronald Hoffman and Peter J. Albert, eds., *Sovereign States in an Age of Uncertainty* (Charlottesville, 1981) offers an important assessment of the years between the first (1776) and second state constitutions (1790) as do Joseph S. Foster's biography of George Bryan, *In Pursuit of Liberty. George Bryan and the Revolution in Pennsylvania* (University Park, 1994); and Ronald M. Baumann, "The Democratic-Republicans of Philadelphia: the Origins, 1776–1797" (Ph.D. dissertation, Pennsylvania State University, 1970). The celebrated exchanges between Mathew Carey and Eleazer Oswald, and their part in the politics of contemporary Philadelphia, are best discussed in Edward C. Carter II, "The Political Activities of Mathew Carey, Nationalist, 1760–1814" (Ph.D. dissertation, Bryn Mawr College, 1962); and Vernon O. Stumpf, "Colonel Eleazer Oswald: Politician and Editor" (Ph.D. dissertation, Duke University, 1970).

For the social and cultural character of contemporary Philadelphia, see George Winthrop Geib, "A History of Philadelphia, 1776–1789" (Ph.D. dissertation, University of Wisconsin, 1969); Gary B. Nash, *The Urban Crucible: Social Change, Political Consciousness, and the Origins of the American Revolution* (Cambridge, Mass., 1979); Ethel B. Rasmusson, "Capital on the Delaware: The Philadelphia Upper Class in Transition, 1789–1801" (Ph.D. dissertation, Brown University, 1962); Billy G. Smith, *"Struggles of the Lower Sort." Philadelphia's Laboring People, 1750–1800* (Ithaca, 1990); John K. Alexander, *Render Them Submissive: Responses to Poverty in Philadelphia, 1760–1800* (Amherst, 1980); Sharon V. Salinger, *"To Serve Faithfully and Well:" Labor and Indentured Servants in Pennsylvania, 1682–1800* (New York, 1987); and Simon P. Newman, *Embodied History: The Lives of the Poor in Early Philadelphia* (Philadelphia, 2003), each of which has relevant bibliographies. For Philadelphia's commercial life and external connections, see Thomas M. Doerflinger, *A Vigorous Spirit of Enterprise: Merchants and Economic Development in Revolutionary Philadelphia* (Chapel Hill, 1986).

5. *During the 1790s*, the politics of the nation's capital were greatly influenced by those of the federal government. As such, the more general monographs listed in section 3 above are directly relevant to any study of the interpretation and organisation of Philadelphia political activity during this period. Ronald M. Baumann, "The Democratic-Republicans of Philadelphia: the Origins, 1776–1797"; and Richard G. Miller, *Philadelphia. The Federalist City: A Study of Urban Politics, 1789–1801* (Port Washington, NY, 1976) document the ways in which these interactions influenced the city's own elections, for both its own assemblies and Congress. Martin C. Pernick, "Politics, Parties, and Pestilence: Epidemic Yellow Fever in Philadelphia and the Rise of the First Party System," *WMQ* xxix (1972), 559–87, adds an important perspective before the Democratic Societies became the reference for the growth of party in the nation's capital. For studies on contemporary New York, see Arthur Irving Bernstein, "The Rise of the Democratic-Republican Party in New York City, 1789–1800" (Ph.D. dissertation, Columbia University, 1964); and Alfred Young, *The Democratic Republicans of New York: The Origins, 1763–1797* (Chapel Hill, 1967).

These studies also trace the evolution of political activity and organisation. It is clear that in this process, Philadelphia's "club culture" was important and while there is nothing to compare with Peter Clark, *British Clubs and Societies, 1580–1800. The Origins of an Associational World* (Oxford, 2000), there have been a number of new and important studies on how these clubs contributed to the creation of a new public sphere in later- eighteenth-century Philadelphia. See especially David Waldstreicher, *In the Midst of Perpetual Fetes. The Making of American Nationalism, 1776–1820* (Chapel Hill & London, 1997); and John L. Brooke, "Ancient Lodges and Self-Created Societies: Voluntary Associations and the Public Sphere in the Early Republic" in Ronald Hoffman and Peter J. Albert eds., *Launching the "Extended Republic:" The Federalist Era* (Charlottesville, 1996), 273–377, as well as the two articles by Albrecht Koschnik, "Political Conflict and Public Contest: Rituals of National Celebration in Philadelphia, 1788–1815," *PMHB* cxviii (1994), 209–48, and "The Democratic Societies of Philadelphia and the Limits of the American Public Sphere, circa 1793–1795," *WMQ* lviii (2001), 615–36. For a more traditional interpretation of these clubs, see Eugene Perry Link, *Democratic-Republican Societies, 1790–1800* (New York, 1942).

In *Parades and the Politics of the Street: Festive Culture in the Early American Republic* (Philadelphia, 1997), Simon P. Newman discusses the ways in which foreign affairs influenced these developments. In *The Invention of George Washington* (Berkeley, 1988), Paul K. Longmore examines how images of one of the Founding Fathers was used to develop an "American" view of America. Gary Wills, *The Americanization of Benjamin Franklin* (New York, 2004), looks at another "American icon" through a similar lens while Simon Newman examines the controversies that such a process could cause in "Principles or Men? George

Washington and the Political Culture of National Leadership, 1776–1801," *Journal of the Early Republic* xii (1992), 479–95.

Central to the evolution of a new public sphere was the access to, and use of, information. For this, see Richard D. Brown, *The Strength of a People: The Idea of an Informed Citizenry in America, 1650–1870* (Chapel Hill, 1996). For a detailed survey of the role of the press in public life before 1800), see Donald H. Stewart, *The Opposition Press of the Federalist Period* (Albany, 1969). For more critical analysis, see Norman Victor Blantz, "Editors and Issues. The Party Press in Philadelphia, 1789–1801" (Ph.D. dissertation, Pennsylvania State University, 1974); Jeffrey L. Pasley, *"The Tyranny of Printers:" Newspaper Politics in the Early American Republic* (Charlottesville, 2001); James Tagg, *Benjamin Franklin Bache and the Philadelphia Aurora* (Philadelphia, 1991); and Richard N. Rosenfeld, *American Aurora. A Democratic-Republican Returns: The Suppressed History of Our Nation's Beginnings and the Heroic Newspaper that Tried to Report It* (New York, 1997).

It is clear that while newspapers informed public opinion, they also influenced the perception of the personalities, groups, and interests which also shaped contemporary politics. For the perception of the Irish in contemporary Philadelphia, see Edward C. Carter II, "A 'Wild Irishman' under every Federalist's Bed: Naturalization in Philadelphia, 1789–1806," *PMHB* xciv (1970), 331–46. Carter's dissertation also contains important observations on the city's politics during the 1790s and, in particular, on the role of the Irish, as well as on Carey's exchanges with William Cobbett. For the association of these events with the steady growth of "radicalism," see Margaret C. Jacob and James R. Jacob, eds., *The Origins of Anglo-American Radicalism* (Atlantic Highlands, NJ, and London, 1984); Gordon Wood, *The Radicalism of the American Revolution* (New York, 1992); and Alfred Young, ed., *Beyond the American Revolution: Explanations in the History of American Radicalism* (De Kalb, 1976).

Closure of these events and processes, in so far as this was signalled by the election of 1800, has been discussed most recently in James Horn, Jan Ellis, and Peter S. Onuf, eds., *The Revolution of 1800* (Charlottesville and London, 2002); Susan Dunn, *Jefferson's Second Revolution: The Election Crisis of 1800 and the Triumph of Republicanism* (Boston, 2004); and John Ferling, *Adams vs. Jefferson: The Tumultuous Election of 1800* (New York, 2004). For the challenges which Jefferson's election posed for "the character of America," see Stephen Howard Brown, *Jefferson's Call for Nationhood: The First Inaugural Address* (College Station, Tx., 2003), Peter S. Onuf, *Jefferson's Empire: The Language of American Nationhood* (Charlottesville and London, 2000). For contemporary Britain, see Linda Colley, *Britons: Forging the Nation, 1707–1837* (New Haven, 1992); and Colin Kidd, *British Identities before Nationalism: Ethnicity and Nationhood in the Atlantic World, 1699–1800* (Cambridge, 1999).

Index

Compiled by Helen Litton

343